Handbook of Personality and Health

Handbook of Personality and Health

Edited by

Margarete E. Vollrath
*Psychological Institute, University of Oslo,
Oslo, Norway*
and
*Division of Mental Health, Norwegian Institute of
Public Health, Oslo, Norway*

John Wiley & Sons, Ltd

Other Wiley Editorial Offices

John Wiley & Sons Inc., 111 River Street, Hoboken, NJ 07030, USA

Jossey-Bass, 989 Market Street, San Francisco, CA 94103-1741, USA

Wiley-VCH Verlag GmbH, Boschstr. 12, D-69469 Weinheim, Germany

John Wiley & Sons Australia Ltd, 42 McDougall Street, Milton, Queensland 4064, Australia

John Wiley & Sons (Asia) Pte Ltd, 2 Clementi Loop #02-01, Jin Xing Distripark, Singapore 129809

John Wiley & Sons Canada Ltd, 6045 Freemont Blvd, Mississauga, Ontario, Canada L5R 4J3

Wiley also publishes its books in a variety of electronic formats. Some content that appears
in print may not be available in electronic books.

Library of Congress Cataloging-in-Publication Data

Handbook of personality and health / Margarete E. Vollrath [editor].
    p. ; cm.
  Includes bibliographical references and index.
  ISBN-13: 978-0-470-02134-7 (cloth : alk. paper)
  ISBN-10: 0-470-02134-9 (cloth : alk. paper)
  ISBN-13: 978-0-470-02135-4 (pbk. : alk. paper)
  ISBN-10: 0-470-02135-7 (pbk. : alk. paper)
    1. Health behavior–Handbooks, manuals, etc.   2. Personality–Physiological aspects–Handbooks,
manuals, etc.   3. Neuropsychology–Handbooks, manuals, etc.   I. Vollrath, Margarete E.
   [DNLM: 1. Personality–physiology.   2. Psychophysiologic Disorders.   3. Emotions–physiology.
WM 90 H2377 2006]
  RA776.9.H36 2006
  362.196′89—dc22
                                      2006013279

British Library Cataloguing in Publication Data

A catalogue record for this book is available from the British Library

ISBN-13 978-0-470-02134-7 (ppc)   978-0-470-02135-4 (pbk)
ISBN-10 0-470-02134-9 (ppc)   0-470-02135-7 (pbk)

Typeset in 10/12pt Times by TechBooks, New Delhi, India
Printed and bound in Great Britain by Antony Rowe Ltd, Chippenham, Wiltshire
This book is printed on acid-free paper responsibly manufactured from sustainable forestry
in which at least two trees are planted for each one used for paper production.

Contents

About the Editor

Margarete E. Vollrath is Professor of Personality Psychology at the University of Oslo in Norway and affiliated with the Norwegian Institute of Public Health, Division of Mental Health. She has been a member of the Board of Directors of the European Association of Personality Psychology. She completed a PhD and obtained the *venia legendi* in psychology at the University of Zurich in Switzerland. Dr. Vollrath joined the Psychological Institute of the University of Oslo in Norway in 2001.

Dr Vollrath began her career with research on the epidemiology and course of mental disorders in young adults. She then turned to exploring the influence of personality and personality disorders on stress, coping, and risky health behaviors both in psychiatric patients and healthy young adults. In recent years, her interests have gradually shifted to child health. In a study conducted with University Children's Hospital in Zurich, she investigated how children with diabetes, cancer, and injuries adjust to their situation. In another project, a large cohort study in Norway, she is examining the impact of child personality traits on early appearing health behaviors, such as eating and physical activity.

The idea to edit this Handbook stems from her long experience in teaching health psychology at the Universities of Zurich and Oslo and the vivid discussions with her students during her seminars and lectures.

List of Contributors

Benjamin K. Barton, PhD
Postdoctoral Fellow,
Department of Psychology, University of Guelph, Guelph, Ontario, Canada

Lewis Donohew, PhD
Professor of Communication, post-retirement appointment,
Department of Communication, University of Kentucky, Lexington, Kentucky, USA

Katherine T. Fortenberry
Graduate Student of Psychology
Department of Psychology, University of Utah, Salt Lake City, Utah, USA

Derek R. Freres
Doctoral Student in Communication,
Annenberg School for Communication, University of Pennsylvania, Philadelphia,
    Pennsylvania, USA

David M. Frost
Doctoral Student of Psychology,
Doctoral Program in Social-personality Psychology,
The Graduate Center, The City University of New York, New York, USA

Jane E. Gillham, PhD
Assistant Professor of Psychology,
Psychology Department, Swarthmore College, Swarthmore, Pennsylvania.
Research Associate and Co-Director, The Penn Resiliency Program, Psychology
    Department, University of Pennsylvania, Philadelphia, Pennsylvania, USA

Amanda C. Jones
Graduate Student of Psychology,
Department of Psychology, The University of Texas, Austin, Texas, USA

Judith Lehnart, Dipl. Psych.
Doctoral Fellow of Psychology,
Institute of Psychology, Humboldt University Berlin, Berlin, Germany

Franz J. Neyer, Dr. phil.
Professor of Psychology,
Institute of Psychology, University of Vechta, Vechta, Germany

Suzanne C. Ouellette, PhD
Professor of Psychology,
Doctoral Program in Psychology, The Graduate School,
The City University of New York, New York, USA

James W. Pennebaker, PhD
Professor and Chair of Psychology,
Department of Psychology, The University of Texas, Austin, Texas, USA

Adelita V. Ranchor, PhD
Associate Professor of Health Psychology,
Department of Public Health and Health Psychology, Northern Center for Healthcare
    Research
University Medical Center Groningen, University of Groningen, Groningen, The
    Netherlands

Espen Røysamb, PhD
Professor of Psychology
Psychological Institute, University of Oslo
and Division of Mental Health, Norwegian Institute of Public Health, Oslo, Norway

Robbert Sanderman, PhD
Professor of Health Psychology,
Department of Public Health and Health Psychology,
Northern Center for Healthcare Research
University Medical Center Groningen, University of Groningen, Groningen, The
    Netherlands

David C. Schwebel, PhD
Associate Professor and Vice Chair of Psychology,
Department of Psychology,
University of Alabama at Birmingham, Birmingham, Alabama, USA

Suzanne C. Segerstrom, PhD
Associate Professor of Psychology
Department of Psychology,
University of Kentucky, Lexington, Kentucky, USA

Norbert K. Semmer, Dr. phil.
Professor of the Psychology of Work and Organizations
Department of Psychology, University of Bern, Bern, Switzerland

Timothy W. Smith, PhD
Professor of Psychology,
Department of Psychology, University of Utah, Salt Lake City, Utah, USA

Svenn Torgersen, Dr. philos.
Professor of Clinical Psychology,
Psychological Institute, University of Oslo,
and Regional Center for Child and Adolescent Mental Health, Oslo, Norway

Margarete E. Vollrath, PD Dr. phil.
Professor of Personality Psychology,
Psychological Institute, University of Oslo,
and Division of Mental Health, Norwegian Institute of Public Health, Oslo, Norway

Martha C. Whiteman, PhD
Senior Lecturer in Psychology,
Department of Psychology, University of Edinburgh, Edinburgh, Scotland

Deborah J. Wiebe, PhD
Associate Professor of Psychology,
Department of Psychology, University of Utah, Salt Lake City, Utah, USA

Paula G. Williams, PhD
Assistant Professor of Psychology,
Department of Psychology, University of Utah, Salt Lake City, Utah, USA

Redford B. Williams, MD
Professor of Psychiatry and Behavioral Sciences, Professor of Medicine, Professor of
    Psychology, Director,
Behavioral Medicine Research Center, Duke University Medical Center, Durham, North
    Carolina, USA

Virginia P. Williams, PhD
President,
Williams LifeSkills, Inc., Durham, North Carolina, USA

Introduction: Who Becomes Sick and Who Stays Healthy, How and Why, and What Can be Done About It

Margarete E. Vollrath
University of Oslo, Norway

WHY WE SHOULD STUDY PERSONALITY IN HEALTH PSYCHOLOGY

Since the beginning of the twentieth century, the leading causes of mortality and morbidity in the Western world are no longer infectious diseases but diseases of the heart, cerebrovascular diseases, cancer, chronic obstructive pulmonary diseases, and diabetes. The death of children, adolescents, and young adults is caused mainly by unintentional injuries (Kochane, Murphy, Anderson & Scott, 2004). Psychological factors, such as health-compromising behaviors as well as stress, are involved in all of these causes of death. Not surprisingly, health psychology, which is dedicated to explaining and preventing these behaviors, has been one of the fastest growing disciplines in psychology since the 1980s.

Among the psychological factors that impact health, personality—that is, stable individual differences in thinking, feeling, and behaving—plays a pivotal role. Indeed, the strength of the effects of personality on health can be similar to those of known biological risk factors, such as cholesterol (Hampson, Goldberg, Vogt & Dubanoski, 2006).

Why is this so? Most of the leading causes of death mentioned above are chronic diseases that develop slowly over an extended period. Even being involved in an accident tends to be the consequence of repeated exposure rather than of a single chance event. Consequently, the behaviors that precede and predict both good and ill health need to be enduring or repeated to achieve lasting effects on health. Lung cancer does not follow from smoking a few cigarettes in a lifetime; being overweight does not follow from eating fatty or sweet foods on a single occasion. The psychological characteristics necessary to achieve long-term effects on experiences and behavior, in turn, need to be stable across situations and over sufficient periods. Personality traits meet this requirement, as they develop early and show increasing continuity over the life span (Caspi, Roberts & Shiner, 2005).

Handbook of Personality and Health. Edited by Margarete E. Vollrath. © 2006 John Wiley & Sons, Ltd.

Indeed, personality traits identified in childhood predict *health outcomes* occurring many years later in life such as overweight and obesity, unintentional injuries, the metabolic syndrome, and even longevity. This has been demonstrated by impressive longitudinal studies tracking young children's lives for over 20 years into young adulthood (Caspi et al., 1997; Pulkkinen, 1995; Pulkki-Råback, Elovainio, Kivimäki, Raitakari & Keltikangas-Järvinen, 2005), for 40 years into middle adulthood (Hampson, Goldberg, Vogt & Dubanoski, 2006), and for 65 years into old age (H.S. Friedman et al., 1993; Martin et al., 2002). There is no other conceivable psychological predictor showing an impact that is comparable to that of personality.

Historically, research on the impact of personality on health has had a rich and long tradition both in psychology and medicine. One of the best known fields of investigation, widely popular also among the general public, is the research on the coronary prone personality (Dembroski & Costa, 1987) that is characterized by Type A behavior or Hostility (M. Friedman & Rosenman, 1959). These findings have become part of general knowledge today. A kindred topic is that of the distress-prone personality, which is characterized by vulnerability to stress and a proclivity to experience and report symptoms of distress. Because the distress-prone personality exhibits many bodily symptoms resembling those caused by coronary and other physical diseases, there has been a dispute about the delineation between these two personalities (H.S. Friedman, 1990; Stone & Costa, 1990). Another heated debate arose on the cancer-prone or Type C personality, which is characterized by depressed mood and the repression of feelings. This concept became quite popular, because many cancer patients do show signs of depression. To date, large prospective studies have proven that personality is not a risk factor for cancer (Nakaya et al., 2003), and the debate has quieted down, but the myth of a cancer-prone personality is still alive. Decidedly fewer studies have been conducted on the personality precursors of accidents or unintentional injuries—the accident-prone personality (Manheimer & Mellinger, 1967). Yet, consistent findings have been accumulating gradually, showing that childhood impulsivity predicts injuries both during childhood and later in life (Caspi, Begg, Dickson, Langley et al., 1995; Schwebel, 2004).

Stress and stress-related diseases are considered to be the health scourge of modern times. Personality researchers have been opening many parallel avenues of research on the contribution of personality to stress. One avenue explores which personality traits lead to increased exposure to stressful events and how this exposure is brought about (Headey & Wearing, 1989; Robins & Robertson, 1998). Another avenue is concerned with traits that increase the intensity and duration of physiological reactions, such as Hostility (Smith, Pope, Rhodewalt & Poulton, 1989), and the circumstances that trigger these reactions. A third avenue, stimulated by the influential theories of Richard S. Lazarus (Lazarus & Folkman, 1984), revolves around personality influences on cognitive appraisals and coping strategies (Vollrath, 2001).

A more recent pursuit is directed at positive health outcomes, such as happiness, self-fulfillment, and growth, animated by the emerging field of positive psychology (Snyder & Lopez, 2002). Here, two approaches to the study of personality can be distinguished. One of them is dedicated to the relation between personality traits and various measures of well-being and happiness and the mechanisms that mediate this relationship (DeNeve & Cooper, 1998). The other approach addresses the consequences of positive traits such as Positive Affectivity and Happiness for various health outcomes and longevity (Danner, Snowdon & Friesen, 2001; Lyubomirsky, King & Diener, 2005).

Parallel research efforts have been guided at more fine-grained analyses of *mechanisms* that act at the interface between personality and health. A major arena involves the study of *biological processes*, such as cardiovascular reactivity, cortical reactivity (Eysenck, 1967), neuroendocrine functioning (Cloninger, 2000), and lately also immune functioning (Miller, Cohen, Rabin, Skoner & Doyle, 1999). Another field is occupied with *illness behaviors*, i.e., the perception and reporting of symptoms of various diseases and the use and abuse of medical treatment. Illness behaviors are significantly affected by personality as well, particularly by Neuroticism or Negative Affectivity (Costa & McCrae, 1985; Larsen, 1992). This discovery emphasizes that objective measures of health are necessary if we are to study the relation between personality and stress or health (Costa & McCrae, 1990). Discovering the personality correlates of *risky health behaviors*, such as smoking, excessive drinking, and unprotected sex has fascinated personality researchers since the 1960s, not the least prompted by the confrontation with the hippie lifestyle. In this field, a major issue has been the biological foundation, delineation, and measurement of personality traits characterizing individuals with greater needs for stimulation and reward, such as Extraversion (Eysenck, 1973), Sensation Seeking (Zuckerman, 1979), and Novelty Seeking (Cloninger, 1987).

In the late 1970s, the tide changed back to family and friendship. Landmark prospective population studies disclosed remarkable effects of supportive *social relationships* and marriage on morbidity and health (Berkman & Syme, 1979; House, Landis & Umberson, 1988), adding a new domain to health psychological research. However, it took a long time before personality was put on to the map as a factor involved in the establishment, maintenance, and perception of social support (Sarason, Sarason & Shearon, 1986). In the last 15 years, a growing literature has shown that personality factors are implicated in a multitude of ways in the formation and transformation of social relationships (Asendorpf & Wilpers, 1998). To date, the notion that social support reflects personality differences just as much as differences of the social environment is still foreign to many researchers in the field.

LIMITATIONS AND PERSPECTIVES

There are several important research domains that are not represented by separate chapters in this book. One of them concerns the role of personality in coping with and adjustment to chronic diseases in children and adults (Eiser, 1993; Maes, Leventhal & DeRidder, 1996), where influences of personality on the physical as well as the psychosocial outcomes of diseases have been documented (Scheier et al., 1989; Sebregts, Falger & Bar, 2000). A separate field investigates cognitive belief systems, such as Hardiness (Kobasa, 1979), Optimism (Scheier & Carver, 1985), and life-goals (Little & Chambers, 2004), and their effects on health. An emerging field addresses pain-related disorders and their relation to personality, particularly Neuroticism and personality disorders (Ellertsen, 1992; Weisberg, 2000). Moreover, there is a growing awareness that temperament and personality is implicated in eating behavior and the development of overweight, which is one of the greatest threats to health today. These relations are already detectable from very early childhood (Agras, Hammer, McNicholas & Kraemer, 2004). Because the same temperamental and personality factors that are evident early on—Negative Emotionality, lack of Constraint, Hostility—determine a wide range of health outcomes from injuries to cardiovascular and endocrinological health, more studies ought to begin by early childhood and common genetic pathways leading to both personality and health outcomes should be explored.

Finally, the relation of various aspects of health with personality disorders, which are intimately related with normal personality traits (Saulsman & Page, 2004), would definitively deserve a large space in this Handbook as well. Future volumes on personality and health ought to include and explore these avenues both more broadly and in greater depth.

OVERVIEW OF THE CHAPTERS

This Handbook brings together state-of-the-art reviews on key domains of research addressing the complex relationship between personality and health, presented by outstanding researchers across Europe and the United States. The first part of the Handbook deals with the influence of personality on major health outcomes, in particular cardiovascular diseases, cancer, unintentional injuries, subjective well-being, and stress. The second part of the Handbook is dedicated to the mechanisms that mediate the relation between personality and health, including physiological and immunological pathways, illness behaviors, social relations, and risky health behaviors. This part is concluded by a call for an alternative approach, by taking the perspective of the persons, not their traits. The third part has an applied focus and looks at the possibilities of putting knowledge on personality into the service of specific and targeted strategies of prevention and intervention.

The following provides a brief sketch of the chapters.

Part I: Personality and Major Health Outcomes

Chapter 1 by Martha C. Whiteman focuses on the relationship between personality and cardiovascular disease. It includes a brief overview of the recent history of this research area, showing how results differ depending on how hostility and cardiovascular disease are assessed. The chapter discusses challenges for public health that arise from the research. In addition, it explores how life-course studies of interpersonal traits are helping to identify critical periods in which high hostility might develop and how it interacts with other risk factors. The chapter argues that these findings suggest new possibilities for interventions to prevent high hostility and reduce cardiovascular risk.

Chapter 2 by Adelita Ranchor and Robbert Sanderman discusses the role of personality in the onset of and survival from cancer. Studies with a sound methodological design were reviewed. A variety of operationalizations of the cancer prone personality (Type C personality) and of personality factors that supposedly influence survival were included in these studies. It is concluded that there was no evidence for a causal role of personality in relation to cancer. As to cancer survival, there seems to be a predictive role for helplessness/hopelessness in cancer survival. Other personality factors that were considered in relation to survival proved not to be predictive. Ranchor and Sanderman call for further research that can disentangle the pathways that are responsible for the relationship between helplessness/hopelessness and survival.

In Chapter 3, David C. Schwebel and Benjamin K. Barton address the relation between children's temperament and their risk for unintentional injuries. After presenting an extensive review of the literature in the field, which comprises large epidemiological studies, clinical studies, and laboratory studies, Schwebel and Barton conclude that the three key traits involved in children's greater injury risk are low Inhibitory Control, high Impulsivity, and high Activity Level. Mechanisms underlying this relation include increased exposure to risky environments, risky behavior when in unsafe environments, and reduced preventative behaviors. The authors also discuss methodological problems characterizing the field and point out potential implications of the findings for injury prevention.

In Chapter 4, Norbert K. Semmer extensively covers the complex relations between personality, stress, and coping. In a first section, Semmer discusses the mechanisms relating personality with the experience of stress, including exposure to, appraisal of, and dealing with stressful situations. The second section is devoted to the role of traits, goals, and motives for the experience of stress. In the third section, the concept of the vulnerable vs. resilient individual is discussed. The fourth section is dedicated to coping, with a special focus on the difficult concept of emotion focused coping. While the chapter clearly points to the important role of personality in the experience of stress, the contributor concludes with a note of caution, emphasizing that environments tend to reinforce and sustain vicious circles that reinforce stress.

In Chapter 5, Espen Røysamb puts the good life on the agenda. Subjective well-being is not only a valued positive health outcome in itself, but also a predictor of mental and physical good health. Røysamb discusses genetic and environmental influences on subjective well-being and proposes pathways through which these factors influence both stability and change in well-being. Røysamb demonstrates that subjective well-being is related to personality, chiefly Neuroticism, but also Extraversion, and – to a lesser degree – Agreeableness, Conscientiousness, and Openness. Finally, several avenues for future well-being research are suggested.

Part II: Mediators of the Personality Health Relationship

Chapter 6 by Deborah J. Wiebe and Katherine T. Fortenberry introduces this part of the book by providing an overview of mechanisms through which personality may predict physical health. The authors examine four broad models explaining personality-health associations: (1) transactional stress-moderation models; (2) health behavior models; (3) illness behavior and illness self-regulation models; and (4) biological models. The utility of these models is then selectively reviewed in the context of three personality variables documented to prospectively predict objective health outcomes (i.e., hostility, neuroticism/negative affectivity, and optimism). Although existing models are plausible, the authors conclude these models have not been fully tested, and provide suggestions for developing and testing more realistic and comprehensive models of personality-health associations.

In Chapter 7, Paula G. Williams discusses how personality influences illness behaviors such as symptom reporting, functional disability, treatment adherence, and health care utilization. Williams presents research showing that Neuroticism predicts greater frequency of reporting physical symptoms, being functionally disabled, and using health care. Optimism and Conscientiousness predict less disability and better treatment adherence, respectively. Williams points out that the literature is still small and that future research ought to include a broader range of personality traits and include mediators, such as emotional disorders, and moderators, such as gender and socioeconomic status. Moreover, curvilinear and interactive effects of personality traits ought to be considered.

In Chapter 8, Suzanne K. Segerstrom and Timothy W. Smith review evidence that personality is related to two organ systems, the cardiovascular and immune systems that are the basis of physiological pathways from personality to health and disease. One main pathway is cardiovascular reactivity, which is viewed either as an independent trait or as a mediating

mechanism between personality and cardiovascular disease. The other main pathway impli-
cates inflammatory and immunosuppressive processes, which in turn relate to a myriad of
pathologies. For each of these main pathways, the contributors discuss evidence for a link
to the personality traits of hostility, sociability, optimism, and repression. Segerstrom and
Smith conclude their contribution with a call for studies tying all three elements together:
personality, physiological and immunological mediators, and disease outcomes.

Chapter 9 by Franz Neyer and Judith Lehnart addresses the relation of personality, social
relationships, and health outcomes such as longevity, well-being, depression, and psychosocial stability. In contrast to a traditional perspective viewing relationships as a single
causal factor for physical and psychological health, the authors argue from a transactional
view that dynamic transactions between personality and relationships may affect health
outcomes. From this perspective, characteristics of the individual personality can lead to
relationship outcomes that either promote or impair health; yet, at the same time, relationship
experiences may induce personality change, which in turn can influence health. The chapter
gives an overview of the various kinds of personality-relationship transactions and discusses
the multiple pathways of how these may contribute to health outcomes.

Chapter 10 by Svenn Torgersen and Margarete E. Vollrath addresses the extent to which
personality, conceived of as both traits and types, is involved in a broad range of risky
health behaviors spanning from abuse of psychoactive substances to risky sex. The first
part of the chapter draws a line back to the Blocks' types, their modification by Caspi and
collaborators, and recent attempts at a validation of these types across different samples
and measures. Then, Torgersen's alternative typology is presented. In the second part of
the chapter, the authors sketch out the existing body of research on the link between the
Big Three personality factors (Neuroticism, Extraversion, and Constraint) and risky health
behaviors. By also providing analyses from their own body of work on Torgersen's types,
the contributors show how the study of types can explain inconsistencies in current research
findings and improve our understanding of how major personality traits act in combination.

In Chapter 11, Suzanne C. Ouellette and David M. Frost describe untapped resources
within basic personality research for the responsible depiction and understanding of personality and health – their changes and relationships. Ouellette and Frost demonstrate that the
majority of personality and health studies continue to rely on a limited conceptualization of
personality as simple traits. Drawing from the longstanding study of lives tradition and new
developments in narrative studies, using concepts such as self, identity, and discourse, they
argue that researchers can conceptualize personality as that which involves whole persons
as they live within complex interpersonal, social, and cultural settings. Ouellette and Frost
claim that researchers must do so if we are to understand and meaningfully do something
about health and illness. The contributors provide examples of narrative studies of health
and personality from their own research and the general field of social science and medicine.
These narrative and life studies reveal the person amongst health and illness phenomena,
address the person in context, recognize individual subjectivity and agency alongside the
power of social structures, and illustrate ethical research practice.

Part III: Targeting Personality: Prevention and Intervention

Personality researchers are often confronted with skeptical questions: if individuals are 'set
like plaster' (Costa & McCrae, 1994), then intervention and prevention will be of no value.

However, even if we might not be able to change the causes—the personality—we might be able to address the consequences—the behavior. This is what Part III of this book is about.

Chapter 12 by Redford W. Williams and Virginia Williams (1) addresses the adverse impact of hostility, along with other psychosocial risk factors, on the risk of developing cardiovascular disease and other medical disorders, (2) discusses biological and behavioral mechanisms that mediate this relationship, and (3) describes the cognitive behavioral approach, including Williams and Williams' own program that has strong potential to both prevent the development of hostility in healthy persons and to reduce it in persons whose health has already been affected.

Chapter 13 by Amanda C. Jones and James W. Pennebaker deals with the beneficial effects of writing. Writing about important personal experiences in an emotional way for as little as 15 minutes over the course of three days brings about improvements in both mental and physical health. Jones and Pennebaker discuss inhibition theory, cognitive processing theory, and affective processing theory, which are the most commonly proposed mechanisms for explaining how writing improves health. All three theories tie directly to personality and individual differences that may influence the effectiveness of expressive writing. In their contribution, Jones and Pennebaker explore who is most likely to benefit from expressive writing and under what conditions. Implications for personality theory are discussed.

In Chapter 14, Lewis Donohew describes a theoretical perspective on information exposure and processing that holds that, beyond verbal content, message characteristics such as intensity, movement, or novelty interact with biologically-based personality characteristics of the audiences to play a major role in attracting and holding attention. Donohew's central focus is on media messages, individual differences in how they are attended, and implications for media-based interventions designed to reach individuals most likely to engage in risk-taking behaviors such as drug abuse or risky sex.

In Chapter 15, Derek Freres and Jane E. Gillham discuss the potential linkages among optimism, depression, and physical health. Freres and Gillham describe a cognitive-behavioral intervention for young adolescents, The Penn Resiliency Program (PRP), which is designed to prevent depression by promoting more optimistic and accurate thinking styles. Consistent with cognitive-behavioral theories, increasing optimism (and accuracy) is hypothesized to prevent depression and through direct and indirect pathways may also promote better physical health. Studies evaluating the effects of the PRP on depression, optimism (often through explanatory style), and in some cases physical health are reviewed. The contributors also include a discussion of their work in progress and future research plans.

REFERENCES

Agras, W.S., Hammer, L.D., McNicholas, F. & Kraemer, H.C. (2004). Risk factors for childhood overweight: A prospective study from birth to 9.5 years. *Journal of Pediatrics, 145,* 20–25.

Asendorpf, J.B. & Wilpers, S. (1998). Personality effects on social relationships. *Journal of Personality and Social Psychology, 74(6),* 1531–1544.

Berkman, L.F. & Syme, S.L. (1979). Social networks, host resistance, and mortality: a nine-year follow-up study of Alameda County residents. *American Journal of Epidemiology, 109(2),* 186–204.

Caspi, A., Begg, D., Dickson, N., Harrington, H., Langley, J., Moffitt, T.E., et al. (1997). Personality differences predict health-risk behaviors in young adulthood: Evidence from a longitudinal study. *Journal of Personality and Social Psychology, 73(5),* 1052–1063.

Caspi, A., Begg, D., Dickson, N., Langley, J. et al. (1995). Identification of personality types at risk for poor health and injury in late adolescence. *Criminal Behaviour and Mental Health, 5(4)*, 330–350.

Caspi, A., Roberts, B.W. & Shiner, R.L. (2005). Personality development: Stability and change. *Annual Review of Psychology, 56*, 453–485.

Cloninger, C.R. (1987). A systematic method for clinical description and classification of personality variables. *Archives of General Psychiatry, 44*, 573–588.

Cloninger, C.R. (2000). Biology of personality dimensions. *Current Opinion in Psychiatry, 13(6)*, 611–616.

Costa, P.T. & McCrae, R.R. (1985). Hypochondriasis, neuroticism, and aging: when are somatic complaints unfounded? *American Psychologist, 40*, 19–28.

Costa, P.T. & McCrae, R.R. (1990). Personality: Another 'hidden factor' in stress research. *Psychological Inquiry, 1(1)*, 22–24.

Costa, P.T. & McCrae, R.R. (1994). Set like plaster? Evidence for the stability of adult personality. In T.F. Heatherton & J.L. Weinberger (eds), *Can personality change?* (pp. 21–40). Washington: American Psychological Press.

Danner, D.D., Snowdon, D.A. & Friesen, W.V. (2001). Positive emotions in early life and longevity: Findings from the Nun Study. *Journal of Personality and Social Psychology, 80(5)*, 804–813.

Dembroski, T.M. & Costa, P.T. (1987). Coronary prone behavior: Components of the Type A pattern and hostility. Special Issue: Personality and physical health. *Journal of Personality, 55(2)*, 211–235.

DeNeve, K.M. & Cooper, H. (1998). The happy personality: A meta-analysis of 137 personality traits and subjective well-being. *Psychological Bulletin, 124(2)*, 197–229.

Eiser, C. (1993). *Growing up with a chronic disease*. London: Jessica Kingsley Publishers.

Ellertsen, B. (1992). Personality factors in recurring and chronic pain. *Cephalgia, 12(3)*, 129–132.

Eysenck, H.J. (1967). *The biological basis of personality*. Springfield, IL: Thomas.

Eysenck, H.J. (1973). Personality and the maintenance of the smoking habit. In W. Dunn (ed.), *Smoking behavior: Motives and incentives* (pp. 113–146). Oxford, UK: V.H. Winston & Sons.

Friedman, H.S. (1990). Where is the disease-prone personality? Conclusion and future directions. In H. S. Friedman (ed.), *Personality and disease* (pp. 283–292). New York: John Wiley & Sons, Inc.

Friedman, H.S., Tucker, J.S., Tomlinson-Keasey, C., Schwartz, J.E., Wingard, D.L. & Criqui, M.H. (1993). Does childhood personality predict longevity? *Journal of Personality and Social Psychology, 65*, 176–185.

Friedman, M. & Rosenman, R.H. (1959). Association of a specific overt behavior pattern with increases in blood cholesterol, blood clotting time, incidence of arcus senilis and clinical coronary artery disease. *Journal of the American Medical Association, 2169*, 1286–1296.

Hampson, S., Goldberg, L.R., Vogt, T.M. & Dubanoski, J.P. (2006). Forty years on: Teachers' assessment of children's personality traits predict self-reported health behaviors and outcomes at midlife. *Health Psychology, 25(1)*, 57–64.

Headey, B. & Wearing, A. (1989). Personality, life events, and subjective well-being: toward a dynamic equilibrium model. *Journal of Personality and Social Psychology, 57*, 731–739.

House, J.S., Landis, K.R. & Umberson, D. (1988). Social relationships and health. *Science, 241(4865)*, 540–545.

Kobasa, S.C. (1979). Stressful life events, personality, and health: An inquiry into hardiness. *Journal of Personality and Social Psychology, 37*, 1–11.

Kochane, K.D., Murphy, S.L., Anderson, R.N. & Scott, C. (2004). Deaths: Final Data for 2002. *National Vital Statistics Report, 53(5)*, 1–116.

Larsen, R.J. (1992). Neuroticism and selective encoding and recall of symptoms: Evidence from a combined concurrent-retrospective study. *Journal of Personality and Social Psychology, 62(3)*, 480–488.

Lazarus, R.S. & Folkman, S. (1984). *Stress, appraisal, and coping*. New York: Springer.

Little, B.R. & Chambers, N.C. (2004). Personal project pursuit: On human doings and well-beings. In E. Klinger (ed.), *Handbook of motivational counseling: Concepts, approaches, and assessment* (pp. 65–82). New York, NY, US: John Wiley & Sons, Inc.

Lyubomirsky, S., King, L. & Diener, E. (2005). The benefits of frequent positive affect: does happiness lead to success? *Psychological Bulletin, 131(6)*, 803–855.

Maes, S., Leventhal, H. & DeRidder, D.T.D. (1996). Coping with chronic diseases. In M. Zeidner & N.S. Endler (eds), *Handbook of coping* (pp. 221–251). New York: John Wiley & Sons, Inc.

Manheimer, D.I. & Mellinger, G.D. (1967). Personality characteristics of the child accident repeater. *Child Development, 38(2)*, 491–513.

Martin, L.R., Friedman, H.S., Tucker, J.S., Tomlinson-Keasey, C., Criqui, M.H. & Schwartz, J.E. (2002). A life course perspective on childhood cheerfulness and its relation to mortality risk. *Personality and Social Psychology Bulletin, 28*, 1155–1165.

Miller, G.E., Cohen, S., Rabin, B.S., Skoner, D.P. & Doyle, W.J. (1999). Personality and tonic cardiovascular, neuroendocrine, and immune function. *Brain, Behavior, and Immunity, 13*, 109–123.

Nakaya, N., Tsubono, Y., Hosokawa, T., Nishino, Y., Ohkubo, T., Hozawa, A., et al. (2003). Personality and the risk of cancer. *Journal of the National Cancer Institute, 95(11)*, 799–805.

Pulkki-Råback, L., Elovainio, M., Kivimäki, M., Raitakari, O.T. & Keltikangas-Järvinen, L. (2005). Temperament in childhood predicts body mass in adulthood: the Cardiovascular Risk in Young Finns Study. *Health Psychology, 24(3)*, 307–315.

Pulkkinen, L. (1995). Behavioral precursors to accidents and resulting physical impairment. *Child Development, 66(6)*, 1660–1679.

Robins, L.N. & Robertson, J. (1998). Exposure to 'fateful' events: A confounder in assigning causal roles to life events. In B. P. Dohrenwend (ed.), *Adversity, stress, and psychopathology* (pp. 331–340). New York: Oxford University Press.

Sarason, I.G., Sarason, B.R. & Shearon, E.N. (1986). Social support as an individual difference variable: its stability, origins, and relational aspects. *Journal of Personality and Social Psychology, 50*, 845–855.

Saulsman, L.M. & Page, A.C. (2004). The five-factor model and personality disorders empirical literature: A meta-analytic review. *Clinical Psychology Review, 23*, 1055–1085.

Scheier, M.F. & Carver, C.S. (1985). Optimism, coping, and health: Assessment and implications of generalized outcome expectancies. *Health Psychology, 4*, 219–247.

Scheier, M.F., Matthews, K.A., Owens, J., Magovern, G.J., Sr., Lefebre, R.C., Abbott, R.A., et al. (1989). Dispositional optimism and recovery from coronary artery bypass surgery: The beneficial effects on physical and psychological well-being. *Journal of Personality and Social Psychology, 57*, 1024–1040.

Schwebel, D. (2004). Temperamental risk factors for children's unintentional injury: the role of impulsivity and inhibitory control. *Personality and Individual Differences, 37*, 567–578.

Sebregts, E.H.W.J., Falger, P.R.J. & Bar, F.W.H.M. (2000). Risk factor modification through non-pharmacological interventions in patients with coronary heart disease. *Journal of Psychosomatic Research, 48(4–5)*, 425–441.

Smith, T.W., Pope, M.K., Rhodewalt, F. & Poulton, J. (1989). Optimism, neuroticism, coping, and symptom reports: An alternative interpretation of the life orientation test. *Journal of Personality and Social Psychology, 56,* 640–648.

Snyder, C.R. & Lopez, S.J. (eds) (2002). *Handbook of positive psychology.* London: Oxford University Press.

Stone, S.V. & Costa, P.T., Jr. (1990). Disease-prone personality or distress-prone personality? The role of neuroticism in coronary heart disease. In H.S. Friedman (ed.), *Personality and disease* (pp. 178–200). New York: John Wiley & Sons, Inc.

Vollrath, M. (2001). Personality and stress. *Scandinavian Journal of Psychology, 42(3)*, 335–347.

Weisberg, J.N. (2000). Personality and personality disorders in chronic pain. *Current Pain and Headache Reports 4*, 60–70.

Zuckerman, M. (1979). *Sensation seeking: Beyond the optimal level of arousal.* Hillsdale, NJ: Erlbaum.

PART I

Personality and Major Health Outcomes

CHAPTER 1

Personality, Cardiovascular Disease and Public Health

Martha C. Whiteman
University of Edinburgh, Scotland

INTRODUCTION

People who have higher levels of hostility and anger are at greater risk for heart disease and atherosclerosis. This is the main pattern of findings from the many investigations into the relationship between personality and cardiovascular diseases over the past 50–60 years. However, that general conclusion is not as straightforward as it seems. This chapter discusses some of the history and progress of research into personality and cardiovascular diseases, covering measurement of disease and personality, pathways and networks of risk, and implications of the findings for public health. I will focus in this chapter on studies of the risk of the development of cardiovascular disease for the first time. The research into personality and recovery from and treatment for cardiovascular disease is rather different, and will be discussed by R.B. and V. Williams in Chapter 12 in this volume. Various aspects of personality have been investigated in relation to cardiovascular disease, such as depression (e.g., Frasure Smith & Lespérance, 2005; Joynt & O'Connor, 2005), but a large proportion of the research has concentrated on hostility. It is the association between hostility and cardiovascular disease that will be the focus of this chapter.

In section 1, I will briefly discuss the different types of cardiovascular disease and their assessment in research studies. Section 2 covers the definition and measurement of the personality traits of hostility and related concepts. Section 3 discusses the studies of personality and cardiovascular disease themselves, covering different study designs and different measurements. Section 4 discusses pathways of risk and challenges for public health that arise from this research, especially the complications that stem from hostility's close association with other major risk factors for cardiovascular disease such as socioeconomic status (SES) and smoking. I will also discuss new directions in research that may help public health psychologists understand these relationships better: life course studies of health and interpersonal risk that may help identify lifetime risk factors and critical periods for intervention. Section 5 summarises and concludes the chapter. But first, cardiovascular diseases.

Handbook of Personality and Health. Edited by Margarete E. Vollrath. © 2006 John Wiley & Sons, Ltd.

1. CARDIOVASCULAR DISEASES

There are several cardiovascular diseases. Some of them are heart-related (such as myocardial infarction, or 'heart attack') and some of them occur elsewhere in the body, such as stroke (in the brain). Narrowing of the arteries in the heart results in coronary heart disease (CHD), while narrowing of the arteries in the legs may result in leg pain. Investigations of personality and cardiovascular diseases may include any of these types of disease, and the results of the research may differ depending on the particular disease studied.

1.1 Coronary Heart Disease (CHD)

Coronary heart disease (CHD) results from a narrowing of the arteries that supply blood to the heart because fat deposits have built up on the arterial walls (these fat deposits are known as atherosclerosis). A person who has CHD may have one or more specific heart-related disorders such as angina pectoris (intermittent chest pain) or myocardial infarction (heart attack) (Henderson, 1996). The underlying cause of CHD is thought to be the coronary artery atherosclerosis, which reduces the amount of oxygen that can get to the heart muscle, which in turn causes the chest pain (angina) or, if the lack of oxygen is severe enough, muscle damage (myocardial infarction) (Maseri, 1995).

1.2 Myocardial Infarction (MI)

A myocardial infarction (MI) is said to have occurred when heart tissue dies because of severe, acute interruption of the heart's blood supply caused by a build-up, or 'rupture' of atherosclerotic deposits (Henderson, 1996; Julian & Cowan, 1992). Its main feature is severe chest pain that is extremely intense and that may radiate widely across the whole chest, into the jaw or the arms. In most cases the pain lasts for more than 20 minutes, and there are characteristic changes on the electrocardiogram (ECG) that can be traced during and after the MI (Julian & Cowan, 1992; Tunstall-Pedoe, 1997). The MI may be fatal, but if the person survives the first few minutes, the risk of death recedes over the hours and days following the MI. For research purposes, the MI is known as an 'objective' event, because it is verifiable by medical practitioners. That is, the electrocardiogram and other investigations confirm that the MI has taken place. With other types of cardiovascular disease, it is not always possible to verify that the disease is present, and the diagnosis may be made on the basis of the symptoms that a patient reports to the doctor. This can happen with angina pectoris, another of the CHD syndromes.

1.3 Angina Pectoris

Angina pectoris, often known simply as angina, is a pain or discomfort in the chest, and sometimes in the jaw or arm, caused by a temporary shortage of blood supply to the heart (Julian & Cowan, 1992). The term 'angina' refers to the symptoms, but the condition is usually only diagnosed if there is sufficient cause to believe the pain is caused by coronary atherosclerosis and reduced oxygen getting to the heart (Henderson, 1996). The pain is almost always brought on by physical effort (Tunstall-Pedoe, 1997). The diagnosis of angina is often based primarily on the patient's report of symptoms and the description of the onset and nature of the pain (Maseri, 1995). Further investigations can be carried out to verify the diagnosis, but these are expensive and carry some risk, so in most research studies, it is not warranted to follow up reported angina in this way. Therefore, the diagnosis of angina is more 'subjective' than the diagnosis of MI, because it depends so heavily on a person's report of their symptoms. The distinction between objective and subjective diagnosis is important, because some personality traits are associated with the perception of pain (e.g., Matthews, Deary & Whiteman, 2003). Therefore, the personality pattern of risk for objective versus subjective CHD diagnoses may be quite different.

1.4 Other Cardiovascular Diseases

A build-up of atherosclerosis can occur widely throughout the body. Strokes, for example, may occur because of a build-up of atherosclerosis in the arteries of the neck or brain that then causes an insufficient supply of blood flow and oxygen to one part of the brain. The arteries of the legs may also become partially blocked. If the atherosclerosis in the legs is severe enough to cause a shortage of oxygen to leg muscles then the affected person may experience pain when walking, particularly if walking quickly or uphill. Atherosclerosis in the legs can be measured using the ratio of leg blood pressure to arm blood pressure (ABI, or ankle-brachial index) (Fowkes et al., 1991). The extent of atherosclerosis in the arteries in the neck (carotid arteries) can also be assessed non-invasively, using special ultrasound scanners. The measurement is of the width of the artery (or 'intima'), so the shorthand is 'carotid IMT' (carotid intima-media thickness).

1.5 Risk Factors

Some people are at higher risk of developing CHD than others. Intensive research into the causes of CHD has identified several, now quite well known, risk factors. Three of the main risk factors for CHD are high blood pressure, high cholesterol levels in the blood, and smoking; additional factors are diet, obesity, diabetes, social class and family history of CHD (e.g., Pearson et al., 2003). In addition, men are at a higher risk than women up until the age of about 55, and the risk of CHD rises as a person gets older (e.g., Tunstall-Pedoe, 1997). Despite this improvement in our understanding of risk factors and preventive treatments, it has proved impossible to explain every case of CHD on the basis of these 'traditional' risk factors, and personality has been identified as another contributing factor (e.g., Miller, Smith, Turner, Guijarro & Hallet, 1996). However, because the evidence is so strong for the traditional factors, it is often necessary to use statistical techniques to take account of these factors before estimating the impact of personality that is 'independent' of the well known risk factors. All the studies I will describe in this chapter will have taken account of at least some of the traditional risk factors when examining the relationship between personality and CHD. Some of the complications of statistical adjustment in relation to socioeconomic status will be discussed in Section 4.

1.6 Section Summary

Cardiovascular diseases result from atherosclerosis in heart or other arteries in the body. The most widely known manifestation of coronary heart disease (CHD) is myocardial infarction, or heart attack. This is a diagnosis that is verifiable by medical practitioners; that is, it is an 'objective' diagnosis. Angina, or intermittent chest pain caused by atherosclerosis and insufficient oxygen to the heart muscle on exertion, is another common manifestation of CHD. For research purposes, this is sometimes referred to as a 'subjective' diagnosis, because it can be diagnosed on the basis of the symptoms alone, without further verification by medical practitioners. The extent of leg artery atherosclerosis can be verified objectively by using a simple index of blood pressure in the leg and arm (the ABI). The extent of disease in the carotid arteries can also be assessed non-invasively by measuring the intima-media thickness (IMT). These various types of cardiovascular diseases have all been examined in relation to personality, and the results suggest that hostility is another risk factor for CHD, in addition to well-established risk factors such as high blood pressure, high cholesterol levels and smoking. It is to the personality trait of hostility that I turn next.

2. PERSONALITY TRAITS: HOSTILITY

Personality, or 'an individual's characteristic patterns of thought, emotion, and behaviour' (Funder, 2001, p. 2), for the purposes of CHD research, can be thought of in terms of major, broad traits, such as the 'Big Five' of neuroticism, extraversion, openness, agreeableness and conscientiousness (e.g., Costa & McCrae, 1987), or in terms of narrower 'facets' or aspects of those broad traits, such as hostility or anger. There is broader agreement over the definition and measurement of the Big Five traits (Matthews et al., 2003) than on hostility and anger. The different ways of defining and measuring hostility and anger have made it somewhat difficult to make sense of the findings on the relationship between these traits and CHD (e.g., Miller et al., 1996), and some studies have begun to use the Big Five as an additional measure to try to overcome this (e.g., Smith & Williams, 1992; Whiteman, Deary & Fowkes, 2000). Nonetheless, careful analysis of the pattern of relationships across many studies has shown that outwardly expressed hostility is related to the risk of a first MI, while more inwardly focused 'neurotic' hostility is related to more subjective CHD diagnoses such as angina (Miller et al., 1996) as well as to other bodily symptom reporting (e.g., Stone & Costa, 1990; Matthews et al., 2003). The particular instrument used to measure hostility or anger makes a difference. Why?

2.1 Hostility and Related Concepts

Hostility has several components, which may include a negative attitude towards others, cynicism and mistrust of others' motives (a belief that they will be hurtful) and an evaluation of others as mean, non-social and dishonest (Barefoot, 1992; Eckhardt, Norlander & Deffenbacher, 2004; Whiteman, Fowkes & Deary, 1997). These attitudes and cognitions may then predispose a person to anger, an intense emotion that is coupled with physiological arousal, which may lead to verbal or physical aggression (Eckhardt et al., 2004). Since there are so many elements of both anger and hostility, and because the two are distinct, yet closely related, a large number of different measurements exist. While two instruments purport to measure 'hostility' or 'anger', they may in fact measure quite different concepts. For example, some measures may tap into the internal experience of hostility (e.g., thoughts and feelings), and some into the behavioural expression (e.g., insults or door-slamming). Examples of three of the most commonly used measures in CHD studies are discussed below; each has its own angle and focus.

2.1.1 Cook-Medley Hostility Inventory (Cook & Medley, 1954)

Cook and Medley (1954) developed a 50-item self-report scale that was part of a larger questionnaire (the Minnesota Multiphasic Personality Inventory). Higher scores on the scale indicated that the person disliked and mistrusted others. They described a high scorer as seeing people as 'dishonest, unsocial, immoral, ugly and mean...hostility amounts to chronic hate and anger' (Cook & Medley, 1954, pp. 417–418). Two items from the scale read: (1) 'When someone does me a wrong I feel I should pay him back if I can, just for the principle of the thing'; and (2) 'I have often met people who were supposed to be expert who were no better than I' (p. 417). The respondent answers 'true' or 'false' to each item. Many researchers agree that this scale mainly measures cynicism, with elements of social avoidance (Eckhardt et al., 2004; Miller et al., 1996; Smith & Frohm, 1985). Both cynicism and social avoidance overlap with the Big Five personality trait of neuroticism, which, as mentioned in Section 1, is associated with pain perception and symptom reporting (Matthews et al., 2003). The Cook-Medley scale has been widely used in CHD research, with a wide range of findings that vary according to the type of CHD studied and the study design (e.g., Miller et al., 1996).

2.1.2 Structured Interview: Potential for Hostility

The structured interview was developed for use in the Western Collaborative Group Study (Rosenman et al., 1964). The interview is scored in two ways: once for item content, and again for behavioural tendencies during the interview. For example, the interviewer asks about how the person feels if made to wait in line, and will also note the response when questions are deliberately asked slowly or fumblingly. Therefore, it taps reported as well as actual behaviour. The method was developed in order to assess The Type A Behaviour Pattern, which is a pattern of behaviour that was competitive, time urgent, achievement-driven and often hostile (Friedman & Rosenman, 1959). The original Type A interview scoring was revised during the 1980s, so that it was possible to obtain a score just for the 'Potential for Hostility' element as well as for the overall Type A pattern. This was because findings on Type A and CHD suggested that hostility was the 'toxic' element of the pattern (e.g., Johnston, 1993). The Structured Interview is more difficult and more expensive to administer than self-report questionnaires, since it requires special training and must be done in person. It is, therefore, often unfeasible to use it in large studies. However, it has a considerable advantage of tapping both internal and external aspects of hostility (Miller et al., 1996).

2.1.3 State-Trait Anger Expression Inventory (STAXI; Spielberger, 1988; 1999)

The STAXI assesses both the intensity of anger and differences in anger proneness (Spielberger et al., 1985; Spielberger, Jacobs, Russell & Crance, 1983). Trait anger reflects a person's tendency to feel anger, which is partially related to a person's frequency of episodes of 'state' anger (Spielberger et al., 1985). There are ten items for state anger (how the person feels at the time of filling in the questionnaire) and ten items for trait anger (how the person feels/acts more generally). Trait anger has two elements: angry temperament, or the tendency to express anger generally, and angry reaction, which addresses specific situations, such as how the person reacts when unfairly treated or frustrated. Two example items from the trait anger scale are: 'I am quick tempered' and 'When I get mad, I say nasty things'; the respondent answers on a scale from 'almost never' to 'almost always.' In addition, further items measure anger-out (e.g., 'I make sarcastic remarks to others'), anger-in (e.g., 'I boil inside, but I don't show it') and anger-control (e.g., 'I can stop myself from losing my temper') (Spielberger, 1988). The STAXI-2 (Spielberger, 1999) is a revised, shortened version of the STAXI that measures angry feelings and whether the person wants to express their anger either verbally or physically (Eckhardt et al., 2004). Because of their careful construction, both the STAXI and the STAXI-2 have been endorsed for use in research studies and in clinical settings (Eckhardt et al., 2004).

2.2 Section Summary

Hostility and anger share common features, and it is difficult to define and measure these concepts. Cognitive and emotional factors make up the experiential component of hostility, with outward behaviours and verbalisations making up the expressive component (Miller et al., 1996; Whiteman, Fowkes & Deary, 1997). The Cook-Medley Hostility Scale (Cook &Medley, 1954) mainly reflects cynical aspects of hostility, while the STAXI (Spielberger, 1988, 1999) assesses angry temperament and behaviours. The Structured Interview (Rosenman et al., 1964) method of assessing hostility allows an observational as well as a self-report component, but is more expensive and more difficult to use than standard questionnaire measures. These three instruments have been commonly used in studies of personality and CHD risk, and each of them measures something different. Moreover, there are many more measures of hostility than these, each of which may measure a slightly different concept. This has made conducting personality-CHD studies and interpreting their findings exciting, yet also challenging and frustrating. The next section reviews some of the personality-cardiovascular disease research that has been conducted over the last 50–60 years.

3. HOSTILITY AND CARDIOVASCULAR DISEASE

It was Friedman and Rosenman's (1959) research into the Type A Behaviour Pattern and CHD that generated a great deal of interest in studying the association between personality and cardiovascular disease. Although hostility and anger (and other negative emotions such as depression) have essentially replaced Type A as the main focus of personality-CHD research, Type A findings do continue to appear (e.g., Gallacher, Yarness, Sweetnam, Elwood & Stansfeld, 2003), and the Type A concept is quite widely understood beyond the research community. Nevertheless, the Type A findings are less consistent (Myrtek, 2001), so my focus in this chapter will be on the hostility research: the studies, the difficulties and the findings. Broadly, there are two types of study design (though there are variations on these) that can be used to study the associations between personality and CHD. One type of study design is prospective, in which personality is measured at the start, and then participants are followed-up over several years to see if there is a relationship between their initial levels of hostility and their risk of developing cardiovascular disease over time. The other design is cross-sectional, in which measures of disease and personality are taken at the same time, to see if there is an association between the presence of CHD and higher hostility, or a relationship between higher hostility and severity of atherosclerosis. It is more difficult to interpret cross-sectional findings because there is no way to tell whether a person with disease might have had personality changes as a result of their disease, rather than the reverse. Prospective studies remove some of that difficulty of temporal ordering of events, because they can often measure personality before a person develops CHD. Both types have helped build up the pattern of findings on personality and CHD.

3.1 Studies Using the Cook-Medley Hostility Scale

From the late 1950s onwards, several long-term studies were set up to study CHD risk, and many were able to include the MMPI and its Cook-Medley Hostility Scale (CMHS; Cook & Medley, 1954) in their package of measures. For example, the Western Electric Study (WES) began in 1957, and follow-ups have continued since then (e.g., Almada et al., 1991; Shekelle, Gale, Ostfeld & Paul, 1983). In the WES, 1,877 male employees of a Chicago Electric company were medically examined at the start of the study ('baseline') in 1957/58. The CMHS was administered at that time, and a follow-up of the men was reported by Shekelle et al. in 1983. The men had been seen annually for medical examinations, and they were assessed for MI each time, which was diagnosed on the basis of an ECG and reports of the symptoms the men experienced at the time of their MI. If a participant died during the follow-up, his case was investigated to see whether his death was caused by CHD. The pattern of results was puzzling: the CMHS scores were associated with CHD risk, but not in a linear fashion. Instead, the MI risk was lowest in the lowest scores on the CMHS, highest in the middle-scoring group, and intermediate in the high-scoring group. In a later analysis after a longer follow-up, Almada et al. (1991) reported that cynicism (separately from the overall hostility score on the CMHS) was associated with a 50 % increase in the risk of coronary death over 25 years. A similar magnitude of association, and another puzzling pattern of findings, was found in a Danish study of 436 men and 366 women followed up from 1954 until 1991 (Barefoot, Larsen, von der Leith & Schroll, 1995). A short version of the CMHS had been administered at baseline. The analysis showed that hostility was a significant predictor of MI, with higher hostility increasing the risk of MI by about 50 %, but the finding was not robust across all of their analyses. The relationship was different depending on the number of other risk factors that were included in the statistical model.

Other studies found no relationship between CMHS scores and cardiovascular disease. Four further studies illustrate this pattern. (1) In 478 physicians who had been followed up 25 years after their admission to medical school, there was no association found between baseline CMHS scores and risk of either non-fatal or fatal MI (McCranie, Watkins, Brandsma & Sisson, 1986); (2) In the Cardiovascular Disease Project of 280 men first recruited at the University of Minnesota in 1947, there was no evidence of a relationship between baseline CMHS scores and MI over the 30-year follow-up (Leon, Finn, Murray, & Bailey, 1988); (3) In a follow-up of 1,400 male alumni of the University of Minnesota, 33 years after their matriculation in 1953, no relationship between baseline CMHS scores and CHD risk was found (Hearn, Murray & Luepker, 1989); (4) In a study of 209 initially healthy women, there was no relationship between CMHS scores and progression of carotid artery atherosclerosis over 3 years (Räikkönen, Matthews, Sutton-Tyrell, & Kuller, 2004). These studies represent the types of findings that are very common with the CMHS and objectively-assessed cardiovascular disease: very weak, inconsistent or non-existent.

3.2 Studies Using the Potential for Hostility Scale (Structured Interview; SI)

The studies reporting findings on hostility scored from the SI were often later analyses of data that had originally been examined for the full Type A behaviour pattern and CHD. For example, Dembroski, MacDougall, Williams, Haney and Blumenthal (1985) selected a sub-group of 131 individuals from the 2,289 who had taken part in a study at Duke University (Williams et al., 1988). The 131 participants were at two extremes of disease severity. Approximately half had very minimal coronary artery disease and the other half had quite severe coronary artery disease. Dembroski et al. (1985) found that Potential for Hostility (PH) scores were higher in the group with more severe CHD – but only when the patients were also high on 'Anger-in' measures. In the Western Collaborative Group Study (WCGS) of 3,524 men, which was the seminal study of Type A behaviour and CHD (Rosenman et al., 1964), further analyses were reported on the relationships between PH and CHD. Hecker, Chesney, Black and Frautschi (1988) found that the hostility element of the SI was the only element of the Type A pattern that remained statistically significantly associated with the development of CHD over a follow-up of 8.5 years. There was about a 93 % increased risk of CHD (either MI or angina) associated with higher PH scores. In the Multiple Risk Factor Intervention Trial (MRFIT), Dembroski, MacDougall, Costa and Grandits (1989) found that high versus low PH scores were associated with an increased risk of CHD of about 50 % in the 192 participants with CHD compared to the 384 participants without CHD. Although the sample of studies presented here is small, and the analyses were cross-sectional, it is clear that the pattern of associations is different from that of the findings using the CMHS.

3.3 Studies Using the STAXI or Other Anger Measures

As the research on personality and CHD continued to develop, studies began that measured anger rather than, or in addition to, hostility. In the Normative Aging Study of 2,289 Boston-based, community-living male veterans, anger expression was assessed in 1986 using a new scale from the MMPI-2 (Kawachi, Sparrow, Spiro, Vokonas & Weiss, 1996). In the follow-up of the 1,305 men, it was found that the risk of CHD (combining MI and angina together) was increased by about 2.6 times in men with high versus low anger expression scores.

However, if the men were taking aspirin, there was no increased risk associated with high anger. This was an interesting finding, since it suggests that pharmacological treatment may provide a buffer against a behavioural risk factor, but a study specifically designed to test this has not yet been designed. In the Caerphilly study in the UK, anger-in, anger-out and suppressed anger were assessed (using the Framingham scales, a questionnaire-based measure of the Type A pattern) in 2,890 men aged 49–65 years, who were then followed up for CHD (Gallacher et al., 1999). This study's findings were different: low anger-out and suppressed anger were associated with an approximately 70 % greater risk of CHD. Here, keeping anger in seemed to be risky, rather than expressing it outwardly. Further research has reported mixed findings on expressed versus suppressed anger. As with hostility, it appears that the measurement instrument makes a difference, but this cannot fully explain the discrepancies. The lack of standardised measures continues to be a problem, and the Big Five trait framework has been suggested as a possible solution (e.g., Smith & Williams, 1992).

In the Edinburgh Artery Study (EAS) of 1,592 community-dwelling men and women (Fowkes et al., 1991; Leng et al., 1996), a study designed to gather information about cardiovascular disease and its risk factors, questionnaire measures of hostility, STAXI-assessed anger and the Big Five personality traits were administered. The study group was first recruited in 1987/88, and has been followed up since then. Participants had a medical examination at baseline, after 5 years of follow-up, and then after 12 years of follow-up. They received CHD health questionnaires annually, and hospital records were examined for CHD-related admissions and deaths. Full details on the study recruitment and methods have been published previously (Fowkes et al., 1991).

At the EAS baseline, participants completed the Bedford-Foulds Personality Deviance Scales-Revised (PDS-R), which measure the personality traits of dominance-submissiveness and hostility-friendliness (Deary, Bedford & Fowkes, 1995). It was found that higher levels of submissiveness were protective against MI over the first five years of follow-up (Whiteman, Deary, Lee & Fowkes, 1997): the risk of MI was reduced by about 41 % if the submissiveness score was higher – and the finding was statistically more robust in women (Table 1.1). Hostility was not related to the risk of MI. This was different from other patterns of findings on hostility. These results, however, were based on analysis of a personality scale that was not commonly used in CHD research. To help overcome this problem, at the 6-year annual follow-up participants were asked to complete two more personality questionnaires: the NEO-Five Factor Inventory (Costa & McCrae, 1992), which measures the 'Big Five' traits of personality, and the STAXI (Spielberger, 1988). In this way it was possible to examine the specific effects of anger on CHD, if any, as well as to examine whether

Table 1.1 Submissiveness scores and risk of non-fatal MI in men and women over a prospective 5-year follow-up in the Edinburgh Artery Study (Whiteman, Deary et al., 1997)

	MI	No MI	Percentage reduction in risk with higher Submissiveness[1]
Men	17.7 (n = 57)	18.9 (n = 618)	16 %
Women	18.2 (n = 28)	20.8 (n = 642)	41 %*

[1] Based on the relative risk of a one-standard deviation rise in Submissiveness, adjusted for age, extent of baseline disease, social class, blood pressure, cholesterol, body mass index and smoking.; *p < 0.01.

Table 1.2   Anger scores and risk of non-fatal MI in men and women in a cross-sectional analysis of the Edinburgh Artery Study

	MI	No MI	Percentage increase in risk with higher Anger Expression scores[1]
Men	21.3 (n = 57)	18.8 (n = 386)	54 %*
Women	20.7 (n = 31)	19.5 (n = 425)	8 %

[1] Based on the odds ratio of a one-standard deviation rise in Anger Expression, adjusted for age, social class, blood pressure, cholesterol, body mass index, smoking and Agreeableness; *p < 0.01.

the Big Five offered a good framework and measurement tool for personality-CHD investigations. That is, could measuring the Big Five alone be enough, thus removing the need for investigators to use widely varying measures of hostility across different study groups?

EAS participants filled in the NEO-FFI and STAXI in 1996, and were followed up for the next seven years to track their non-fatal and fatal CHD-related events. During that follow-up, 137 men (27.5 %) and 101 women (18.8 %) died (unpublished data). Although mean levels of Angry Temperament and Angry Reaction were slightly higher in men who later died from CHD, the statistical association was attenuated when other CHD risk factors were included in the model. The most consistent personality association with mortality was with conscientiousness. Men who were more conscientious were approximately 30 % less likely to die – from any cause – than men who were less conscientious. The Big Five trait of agreeableness, which is negatively related to hostility, showed no association with mortality risk once other factors were taken into account. Therefore, the hint of anger-CHD associations was there, but the finding was not robust when statistically adjusted for other risk factors. Moreover, (low) agreeableness was not a good substitute for STAXI Anger. On this basis, it seems important that both broader and narrower traits are measured in studies, since they predict quite different health outcomes. A similar pattern of findings was apparent in a cross-sectional analysis of CHD prevalence, STAXI Anger and the Big Five in the EAS. Whiteman et al. (unpublished) found that while the relationship between angry temperament and non-fatal MI was statistically significant, (low) agreeableness did not account for the relationship. It was anger specifically that related to the risk of CHD: the risk of MI was increased by approximately 54 % with higher Angry Temperament scores (Table 1.2).

3.4 Making Sense of the Findings: Review Papers

Review papers in the area of hostility-CHD research began to be published periodically from the mid-1980s. The purpose of a review is to look at a body of findings all together to discern the pattern of research. Quantitative reviews or meta-analyses statistically combine the results of many different studies together, thus creating one large data set – and statistical associations, particularly if they are small, are easier to detect in larger data sets. Therefore, a meta-analysis can bring coherence to a field that has produced quite mixed findings. Narrative reviews also look at the pattern of the evidence, but they do so without combining the results into one big data set. Instead, the reviewers carefully read published papers to see if patterns of results are different in different types of study design or with different types of measurements. Meta-analyses and quantitative reviews also group different types of studies together, but can sometimes be restricted in the studies that can be included, because the results have to be in a format that allows them to be numerically combined with others. Both quantitative and narrative reviews have helped to bring further understanding and coherence to the findings on hostility and CHD.

Booth-Kewley and Friedman published a meta-analysis of studies on the Type A behaviour pattern, hostility and CHD in 1987. Their paper included 83 studies, and when findings were collapsed across those studies, small but statistically significant correlations were found between anger ($r = 0.14$) and hostility ($r = 0.17$) and CHD. Combining all CHD outcomes together, only hostility was found to be significantly associated with CHD ($r = 0.19$). Booth-Kewley and Friedman noted that the relationships appeared to be stronger in cross-sectional rather than prospective studies, especially in those studies that used the SI to measure hostility. The overall, somewhat cautious, conclusion was that anger and hostility were predictive of CHD at a slightly smaller magnitude than other major risk factors such as smoking. A further review by Matthews (1988) reported similar results, and she also recommended caution in interpreting findings and called for more prospective studies in the area.

Smith's (1992) review focused on the problems about the definition of hostility and its measurement. He explained that the CMHS and SI-assessed hostility were not interchangeable. He also noted that some of the CMHS items overlapped with neuroticism, and that this could cause serious problems in interpretation of study findings unless the Big Five were simultaneously measured and used as a unifying framework for the personality measures. His further recommendations were to refine hostility measurements and to conduct prospective studies. He also suggested that hostility should be studied in social contexts, because it was possible that hostility could be more dangerous in some situations than others. (I will return to this idea, and further work by Smith, in Section 4, when discussing pathways of risk.)

A comprehensive meta-analysis was carried out by Miller et al. in 1996. Their paper included 45 studies, and the pattern of results they found was different depending on the way hostility and CHD were assessed. For example, in studies using experiential measures of hostility (such as the CMHS), they found that cross-sectional study designs tended to find a small to moderate ($r = 0.18$) relationship between hostility and CHD, whereas prospective studies using the CMHS did not. However, SI-assessed expressive hostility in prospective studies had a more consistent and stronger relationship with objectively-assessed CHD than did questionnaire-assessed experiential hostility. Miller et al. suggested that a battery of measures to assess hostility might be appropriate, or, in agreement with Smith (1992), that more comprehensive assessment of personality using the Big Five could provide a clear conceptual framework for examining associations between personality and CHD. Moreover, they noted that although the findings with prospective studies were smaller in magnitude than in cross-sectional studies, that only prospective studies could address the issue of cause-and-effect. The magnitude of the association was consistent, in that hostility, as an independent risk factor, generally accounted for around 2 % of the variance in CHD in the population (e.g., Booth-Kewley & Friedman, 1987; Miller et al., 1996). This seems small, except that a reduction in disease rates by 2 % in a disease as common as CHD would have a large impact on public health.

Reviews and meta-analyses published since 1996 drew together literature published between about 1990 and 2004 (e.g., Everson-Rose & Lewis, 2005; Hemingway & Marmot, 1999; Myrtek, 2001; Smith, Glazer, Ruiz, & Gallo, 2004; Smith & Ruiz, 2002; Steptoe,

1998; Strike & Steptoe, 2005; Suls & Bunde, 2005). Overall, the issues that were brought up in the earlier reviews were still arising in these later reviews. All of the reviews demonstrate the importance of hostility measurement and the separation of subjective and objective CHD diagnoses. They also raise the issue of the specificity of the association between hostility and CHD: it is important for public health issues of prevention and treatment to know if expressive hostility or anger rather than chronic cynicism is a risk factor for CHD; it is also important to know which type of CHD is related to which type of hostility. In addition, these reviews cover the possible biological routes by which hostility might influence CHD. For example, Strike & Steptoe (2005) reviewed papers that investigated whether a heart attack could be triggered by being angry, stressed, emotional or having engaged in extreme physical effort immediately before the MI; the results suggest that such factors can double or triple the risk. Other reviews (e.g., Everson-Rose & Lewis, 2005) outline the various hormonal and immune pathways that can be activated and disrupted by chronic or episodic hostility or other negative emotions, plausibly leading to build-up of atherosclerosis and therefore increasing CHD risk. Finally, although the balance of women to men in CHD research had improved since the earlier Type A and hostility studies, many reviews noted that the patterns of findings in men and women were different, and that future research must continue to include both men and women, and to analyse the results separately by sex.

3.5 Section Summary

Research into hostility and CHD grew from findings on the Type A behaviour pattern that suggested that hostility was the toxic element of the pattern. However, it became apparent that results differed according to the type of study that was conducted (cross-sectional versus prospective) and the way that hostility was measured (experiential versus expressive). As the different individual studies continued to increase in number, periodic reviews of the scientific literature helped to make sense of patterns that could only be seen when looking at several studies at once. Overall, these reviews suggested that expressive rather than cynical hostility was a risk factor for objectively-assessed CHD, and that the most informative studies were prospective rather than cross-sectional (because hostility could be measured first, before a person developed CHD, thus giving some insight into cause-and-effect). However, even expressive hostility can be measured in different ways, so reviews also called for studies to use a battery of measures or to try to fit hostility into the Big Five personality framework. Preliminary results using the Big Five, however, indicated that agreeableness could not replace anger/hostility measures; rather, the relationship with MI was quite specific to anger. Further studies will be required. The reviews recommended that the specificity of the association and the pathways through which personality might affect CHD, in both men and women, must be explored further.

   The findings regarding hostility and CHD are by turns exciting because they seem to enhance our understanding of CHD risk and offer glimpses of improvements in prevention research, frustrating because results of individual studies appear to be inconsistent, and predictable because the pattern across studies suggests that the association between expressive hostility and MI is consistently present, and that the strength of the association is consistently small to moderate. That is, hostility appears to act as an additional indicator of risk, alongside established risk factors such as high blood pressure, high blood cholesterol or smoking. However, the nature of the relationship is complicated, because personality could plausibly: act directly on biology; affect risk behaviours; or simply be inextricably linked to socioeconomic status, which itself is closely linked with CHD risk. I will explore these complications, challenges and implications next, in Section 4.

4. PUBLIC HEALTH IMPLICATIONS

The association between hostility and CHD is fairly well established. Cross-sectional and prospective studies that examine the risk factors for the first occurrence of MI in people in a given population find a small, reasonably consistent association between hostility levels and risk of CHD, with higher hostility accounting for around 2 % of the variance in CHD in the population. On a practical level, what does this mean? What can we do? One of the main aims of public health scientists is to gather information that will help us learn more about preventing ill health; this is what has happened with other CHD risk factors. Medications are prescribed to lower blood pressure and cholesterol levels, because the evidence tells us that these are risk factors for CHD; moreover, lowering them also reduces the risk of CHD. Giving up smoking reduces CHD risk. But can observational studies of personality and CHD give us similar insights into prevention? There is not a straightforward answer to the question, because the prevention strategy depends very heavily on the pathways and networks through which personality might act. If, for example, personality relates to risky behaviours such as smoking, then psychologists could help tailor smoking cessation advice to different personalities. If hostility raises blood pressure, then blood pressure may need to be monitored more closely in a person with higher hostility. If the association is direct, then this would suggest that hostility itself should be treated. In earlier sections of the chapter, I discussed studies of hostility and occurrence of CHD events, but there are many other studies that have investigated possible pathways of risk, including behavioural, social and biological mechanisms.

4.1 Pathways of Risk

There are several possible pathways through which hostility might affect risk of CHD. These are discussed in more detail in previous publications (e.g., Suls & Sanders, 1989; Houston, 1994; Williams, 2003) but I will summarise the main models here. Some of the proposed pathways involve the external environment that a person dwells within, and some of them involve the internal, bodily environment of the individual. Focusing on the internal environment, hostility might simply be a marker for an 'inborn structural weakness' of the cardiovascular system, and it is this weakness that predisposes to both CHD and hostility (Whiteman et al., 2000; Suls & Sanders, 1989). Hostility could also influence the bodily internal environment on a day-to-day basis, forming part of a pattern of intense responsiveness to physical or mental stressors, which in turn increases the rate of atherosclerosis (Houston, 1994; Smith & Christensen, 1992; Suls & Sanders, 1989; Whiteman et al., 2000; Williams, Barefoot & Shekelle, 1985). Turning to the external environment, hostility could have a negative impact on social interactions and relationships (Smith & Christensen, 1992), leading to isolation and increased stress from lack of social support. Higher hostility could be related to an increase in CHD-risk behaviours such as smoking or excessive alcohol consumption (Scherwitz et al., 1992; Siegler, 1994; Whiteman, Fowkes, Deary & Lee,

1997). Alternatively, hostility could act simultaneously externally and internally: this is the premise of the 'transactional model', which suggests that there are cycles of interactions between external behaviour and internal bodily effects, all of which increase the risk of atherosclerosis and CHD (Smith & Christensen, 1992). Finally, hostility could increase the likelihood of dangerous episodes of anger that in turn trigger physiological changes that result in a cardiovascular event (e.g., Strike & Steptoe, 2005).

4.2 Hostility and Socioeconomic Status (SES)

Discovering discrete CHD risk factors is a challenge, because risk factors, including hostility, tend to cluster together in individuals. For example, lower socioeconomic status (SES), increased smoking, higher cholesterol, high blood pressure, obesity, diabetes, high stress, low job control, inadequate social support and higher hostility – all of which are CHD risk factors – tend to go together (Christensen et al., 2004; Elovainio, Kivimäki, Kortteinen & Tuomikoski, 2001; Kubzansky, Kawachi & Sparrow, 1999; Niaura et al., 2002; Räikkönen et al., 2004; Steptoe & Marmot, 2003; Whiteman, Fowkes, Deary & Lee, 1997; Williams, 2003). Moreover, SES is consistently and strongly associated with CHD (and many other diseases) in the UK, USA and across the world (e.g, Marmot, 1992; Davey Smith, Dorling, Mitchell & Shaw, 2002); the relationship between SES and ill health is one of the best documented in public health research (e.g., Davey Smith, 2003; Whitehead, 1992). In the UK/USA, a middle-aged person in an unskilled occupation has about twice the risk of dying over a 20-year period than a person who works in a highly skilled occupation (Davey Smith & Hart, 1998). In the UK, a man in a professional occupation has a life expectancy 5.2 years longer than a man working in a semi-skilled or unskilled job (Davey Smith, Dorling, Gordon & Shaw, 1999).

Thus it is clear that SES and CHD are related, as are SES and hostility (e.g., Elovainio et al., 2001; Steptoe & Marmot, 2003; Whiteman, Fowkes, Deary & Lee, 1997; Williams, 2003). In Section 3, I described studies of hostility and CHD that tried to take SES into account and thus reported estimates of the 'independent' effect of hostility on CHD. However, it is likely that there is 'residual confounding' between hostility, SES and disease (Critchley & Capewell, 2003; Pulkki, Kivimäki, Elovainio, Viikari & Keltigangas-Järvinen, 2003). That is, it is nearly impossible using statistics to adjust completely for the effects of a lifelong risk such as SES, so the final estimates of risk of CHD associated with hostility is likely to remain 'contaminated' with the effects of SES. Moreover, the relationship between hostility and SES is lifelong (e.g., Harper et al., 2002; Lynch & Davey Smith, 2005), so studying the individual impact of either may be unproductive or misleading. Possible ways of thinking about the wider network of risks are discussed in the next section.

4.3 The Life-course Approach and the Interpersonal Perspective

The studies and reviews covered in Section 3 contain evidence that supports each of the various pathways of risk. Hostility has been shown to be independently associated with increased cardiovascular reactivity (e.g., Williams et al., 2001), smoking and alcohol consumption (e.g., Whiteman, Fowkes, Deary & Lee, 1997), social support (Vahtera, Kivimäki, Uutela & Pentti, 2000) and measures of stress (e.g., Vollrath, 2001). However, compelling evidence is building that hostility has a multiple role to play – that the transactional model of risk explains the data best. As shown above, there is a wide body of research showing that socioeconomic status (SES) is related to hostility. Therefore, it becomes very difficult to discern cause-and-effect with SES, physiology, social support and hostility, unless we begin to consider how disease risk develops over a lifetime, rather than just in adulthood. Looking at the various timings of risk factors (e.g., low SES in childhood versus low SES in adulthood; high hostility in early adulthood that declines with age versus low hostility throughout adulthood) offers a way to understand 'trajectories' of health risk (Friedman, 2000): this is sometimes known as the 'life-course approach' (Ben-Shlomo & Kuh, 2002; Lynch & Davey Smith, 2005).

The life-course approach to disease risk complements the 'interpersonal' perspective on the study of hostility and health (Smith et al., 2004). Researchers taking the interpersonal perspective note that an individual's personality traits, such as hostility, reflect that individual's early life treatment, their subsequent expectations of and interactions with others (Pincus & Ansell, 2003), their risk behaviours, their physiology, and ultimately, their risk of ill health (Smith et al., 2004). The interpersonal perspective is similar to the transactional model; both postulate that risk factors such as hostility, SES, or blood pressure will be a product of the person and their environment (Gallo & Smith, 1999; Smith et al., 2004). Research building on these ideas will necessarily be complex, yet rich, and may help us to unravel the web of relationships between hostility, SES, other cardiovascular risk factors, and CHD. As Williams (2003) states:

> the key issue is not whether it's hostility *or* low SES (or both) that leads to risky health behaviours that increase disease risk; instead, we need to determine the important *processes in the causal chain* leading from low SES to death and disease. (p. 743)

Given the SES gradient in health, it is also clear that public health workers, in addition to helping individuals, should (as many do) focus on helping to change policy and welfare systems that perpetuate rather than reduce SES disparities. But extra income alone may not be enough to help an individual who carries a cluster of social, psychological and biological risk factors, so pinpointing other elements in the causal chain is also necessary.

4.4 Research Applications and New Directions

The body of research taking the life course approach to hostility continues to grow, and research taking the interpersonal perspective for hostility and health is in its early stages (e.g., Smith et al., 2004; Smith & Spiro, 2002; Whiteman, Bedford, Grant & Deary, 2001), though there is overlap in the conceptualisation of both approaches. In life course studies, it has been shown that childhood and early adult SES relate to later hostility and cardiovascular risk (Pulkki et al., 2003), health behaviours (Friedman, 2000), immune functioning (Surtees et al., 2003), psychosocial functioning (Harper et al., 2002; Steptoe & Marmot, 2003) and health risk behaviours (Krueger, Caspi & Moffit, 2000). In addition, it has been shown in an observational study (the University of North Carolina Alumni Heart Study; UNCAHS) that changes in hostility from early adulthood to mid-life have an impact on cardiovascular risk factors (Siegler et al., 2003). The latter study is of high importance, because it is one of very few studies that has examined normal versus abnormal hostility change and its effects. An earlier study published by the same group also documented changes in hostility between the ages of 41 and 50 (Costa, Herbst, McCrae & Siegler, 2000). In the UNCAHS, participants were initially recruited to the study on their entry to higher education in 1964–65; and approximately 2,200 completed the CMHS at baseline and at a follow-up in 1988. During the follow-up, participants were sent questionnaires periodically that gathered data on factors such as SES, smoking, exercise, obesity and diet. The analyses revealed that a decline in hostility of about 4 points over 20 years was the norm (Siegler et al., 2003). Those participants who stayed stable rather than declined reported poorer social support and disappointing personal relationships. Consistent with interpersonal theory, participants who increased in hostility were at twice the risk of poor social support, depression, social isolation, self-reported underachievement, avoidance of exercise and obesity. Overall, the pattern of findings suggested that gaining in hostility increased risk of other risk factors substantially, although the health behaviours of smoking and alcohol consumption were not related to change in hostility.

The New Zealand based Dunedin Study of personality development has studied children from birth through to adulthood (Caspi et al., 1997). This study found that personality in adolescence was predictive of health behaviours at age 21 (Krueger et al., 2000). For example, 18-year-olds who had lower self-control, harm avoidance and social closeness together with higher aggression were more likely to have high-risk health patterns at age 21 (e.g., alcohol abuse, violent crime, unsafe sex and dangerous driving). The adolescents' personality profiles improved prediction of these unhealthy behaviour patterns beyond their SES background. This points towards a transactional – or interpersonal – explanation for the build-up of health risks. That is, neither SES nor personality explains risk well on its own; it is the individual's own interaction with their environment that is important. Moreover, such information has the potential to be used effectively in public health. As Krueger et al. (2000) explain:

> personality traits are styles of relating to the world; they represent tendencies to behave, think and feel in certain consistent ways, and personological information has the potential to contribute to more effective public-health campaigns by providing details about the characteristics of one's target audience. (p. 987)

Krueger et al. note that health promotion programmes that have targeted different groups such as 'high sensation seekers' have had good success. Similarly, Friedman (2000) reviewed evidence that different personality profiles lead to different pathways of risk across the life course, some towards better health (conscientious and stable personality), and some towards poorer health (unstable and impulsive personality). Furthermore, Smith et al. (2004) and Siegler et al. (2003) presented evidence that personality traits relevant to interpersonal interactions (dominance-submissiveness and friendliness-hostility) lead in different directions: either towards more satisfying and healthy relationships and behaviours (for example, more friendly and less hostile) or less satisfying ones (for example, less friendly and more hostile). These personality patterns may be a product of genetic inheritance, early parenting and childhood circumstances such as SES. Earlier studies also reported health associations with interpersonal traits: for example, higher self-reported submissiveness was related to an approximately 30 % lower risk of non-fatal MI in the Edinburgh Artery Study (with the effect stronger in women) (Whiteman, Deary et al., 1997), and behaviourally rated dominance was associated with higher risk of CHD and mortality (Houston, Babyak, Chesney, Black & Ragland, 1997; Siegman et al., 2000).

The evidence from life-course and interpersonal approaches to CHD risk suggests that a potentially rich (though difficult) area of research will incorporate prospective designs, long follow-ups and collection of comprehensive data on both the social environment and the person. Study measurements should include the known risk factors such as SES and hostility. However, studies can take a further step and analyse the 'trajectories' of risk arising from different combinations of interpersonal traits and the environment across the life course.

4.5 Section Summary

Public health practitioners and psychologists share a common interest in wishing to help reduce personality-related distress and disease. However, hostility-CHD research, although quite consistent, does not offer an obvious course of action, in part because of hostility's association with other major risk factors such as SES. The reciprocal nature of personality-environment interactions means that estimating the truly 'independent' effect of hostility on CHD is problematic. However, life-course and interpersonal research suggest that there are distinctive trajectories of risk and that improvements in prevention could be developed from our growing understanding of these.

5. CHAPTER SUMMARY AND CONCLUSIONS

Cardiovascular diseases such as myocardial infarction (MI) and angina have been studied in relation to hostility over the past 50–60 years. The study findings tend to differ depending on the type of CHD under study and the way that hostility is assessed. Expressive hostility is more consistently related to objective measures of CHD such as MI than to more subjective diagnoses such as angina. Experiential or cynical hostility overlap with the personality trait of neuroticism, which is known to be associated with pain perception and symptom reporting; this may be one reason why studies that combined objective and subjective CHD endpoints had mixed results for hostility. Review papers clarified that, overall, outwardly expressed hostility could account for around 2 % of the variance in CHD in the population. However, the reviews also suggested that using a standard personality framework such as the Big Five could bring coherence to the field, that further research was needed in women and that the pathways and networks of risk must be better understood.

Recent developments in life-course and interpersonal approaches to disease risk offer researchers the chance to help build a more comprehensive understanding of personality-environment transactions and patterns of risk over the life span. So far, we know that at the very least, hostility and anger are markers of risk, and that this risk is likely to be intensified by low SES or difficult life circumstances. Given the difficult interpersonal interactions that individuals higher in hostility are likely to generate/experience, and the challenging environment they may inhabit, outreach and treatment are likely to be more difficult, yet essential for public health improvement. Life-course studies and understanding of interpersonal traits may help pinpoint critical periods for intervention as well as improved strategies for prevention and treatment. The amassed research findings on hostility, SES and CHD risk were already compelling, but the course of action for researchers and practitioners was not always clear. Now, new ways of thinking about interpersonal interactions across the life course have opened up further opportunities to understand and help reduce personality-related distress and CHD risk, and public health psychologists must capitalize on them.

6 ACKNOWLEDGEMENTS

The Edinburgh Artery Study (EAS) is supported by the British Heart Foundation and the Chief Scientist's Office (Scotland). I thank my research mentors, Professor F.G.R. Fowkes (Director of the EAS) and Professor I.J.Deary, and the other members of the EAS research team: M. Apps, A. Bedford, E. Cawood, M. Carson, A. Clark, J.T. Dunbar, E. Kerracher, A.J. Lee, J. Price, K. Purves, A. Rattray, F. Smith, M. Stewart and N. Wright. I am grateful to Dr M.D. Taylor for carrying out analyses on personality and mortality in the EAS.

REFERENCES

Almada, S.J., Zonderman, A.B., Shekelle, R.B., Dyer, A.R., Daviglus, M.L., Costa, P.T. & Stamler, J. (1991). Neuroticism and cynicism and risk of death in middle-aged men: The Western Electric Study. *Psychosomatic Medicine, 53*, 165–175.

Barefoot, J.C. (1992). Developments in the measurement of hostility. In H.S. Friedman (ed.), *Hostility, coping and health*. Washington, DC: American Psychological Association.

Barefoot, J.C., Larsen, S., von der Lieth, L. & Schroll, M. (1995). Hostility, incidence of acute myocardial infarction, and mortality in a sample of older Danish men and women. *American Journal of Epidemiology, 142*, 477–484.

Ben-Shlomo, Y. & Kuh, D. (2002). A life course approach to chronic disease epidemiology: conceptual models, empirical challenges and interdisciplinary perspectives. *International Journal of Epidemiology, 31*, 285–293.

Booth-Kewley, S. & Friedman, H.S. (1987). Psychological predictors of heart disease: A quantitative review. *Psychological Bulletin, 101*, 343–362.

Caspi, A., Begg, D., Dickson, N., Harrington, H., Langley, J., Moffitt, R.E. & Silva, P.A. (1997). Personality differences predict health-risk behaviours in young adulthood: Evidence from a longitudinal study. *Journal of Personality and Social Psychology, 73*, 1052–1063.

Christensen, U., Lund, R., Damsgaard, M.T., Hostein, B.E., Ditlevsen, S., Diderichsen, F. et al. (2004). Cynical hostility, socioeconomic position, health behaviours, and symptom load: A cross-sectional analysis in a Danish population-based study. *Psychosomatic Medicine, 66*, 572–577.

Cook, W. & Medley, D. (1954). Proposed hostility and pharasaic-virtue scales for the MMPI. *Journal of Applied Psychology, 38*, 414–418.

Costa, P.T., Herbst, J.H., McCrae, R.R. & Siegler, I.C. (2000). Personality at midlife: stability, intrinsic maturation, and response to life events. *Assessment, 7*, 365–378.

Costa, P.T. & McCrae, R.R. (1992). *Revised NEO personality inventory (NEO-PI-R) and NEO five-factor inventory (NEO-FFI) professional manual*. Odessa, FL: Psychological Assessment Resources.

Costa, P.T. & McCrae, R.R. (1987). Neuroticism, somatic complaints and disease: Is the bark worse than the bite? *Journal of Personality, 55*, 299–316.

Critchley, J.A. & Capewell, S. (2003). Prospective cohort studies of coronary heart disease in the UK: a systematic review of past, present and planned studies. *Journal of Cardiovascular Risk, 10*, 111–119.

Davey Smith, G. (ed.) (2003). *Health inequalities: Life course approaches*. Bristol: The Policy Press.

Davey Smith, G., Dorling, D., Gordon, D. & Shaw, M. (1999). The widening health gap: what are the solutions? *Critical Public Health, 9*, 151–170.

Davey Smith, G., Dorling, D., Mitchell, R. & Shaw, M. (2002). Health inequalities in Britain: continuing increases up to the end of the 20th century. *Journal of Epidemiology & Community Health, 56*, 434–435.

Davey Smith, G. & Hart, C. (1998). Socioeconomic factors as determinants of mortality. *Journal of the American Medical Association, 280*, 1744–1745.

Deary, I.J., Bedford, A. & Fowkes, F.G.R. (1995). The Personality Deviance Scales: Their development, associations, factor structure and restructuring. *Personality and Individual Differences, 19*,
275–291.

Dembroski, T.M., MacDougall, J.M., Williams, R.B., Haney, T.L. & Blumenthal, J.A. (1985). Components of Type A, hostility and anger-in: relationship to angiographic findings. *Psychosomatic
Medicine, 47*, 219–233.

Dembroski, T.M., MacDougall, J.M., Costa, P.T. & Grandits, G.A. (1989). Components of hostility
as predictors of sudden death and myocardial infarction in the Multiple Risk Factor Intervention
Trial. *Psychosomatic Medicine, 51*, 514–522.

Eckhardt, C., Norlander, B. & Deffenbacher, J. (2004). The assessment of anger and hostility: a critical
review. *Aggression & Violent Behavior, 9*, 17–43.

Elovainio, M., Kivimäki, M., Kortteinen, M. & Tuomikoski, H. (2001). Socioeconomic status, hostility
and health. *Personality and Individual Differences, 31*, 303–315.

Everson-Rose, S.A. & Lewis, T.T. (2005). Psychosocial factors and cardiovascular diseases. *Annual
Review of Public Health, 26*, 469–500.

Fowkes, F.G.R, Housley, E., Cawood, E.H.H., Macintyre, C.C.A., Ruckley, C.V. & Prescott, R.J.
(1991). Edinburgh Artery Study: Prevalence of asymptomatic and symptomatic peripheral arterial
disease in the general population. *International Journal of Epidemiology, 20*, 384–392.

Frasure-Smith, N. & Lespérance, F. (2005). Reflections on depression as a cardiac risk factor.
Psychosomatic Medicine, 67 supplement 1, s19–s25.

Friedman, H.S. (2000). Long-term relations of personality and health: dynamisms, mechanisms,
tropisms. *Journal of Personality, 68*, 1089–1107.

Friedman, M. and Rosenman, R.H. (1959). Association of specific overt behaviour pattern with blood
and cardiovascular findings. *Journal of the American Medical Association, 169*, 1286–1296.

Funder, D.C. (2001). *The personality puzzle*, 2nd edn. London: Norton.

Gallacher, J.E.J., Sweetnam, P.M., Yarnell, J.W.G., Elwood, P.C. & Stansfeld, S.A. (2003). Is Type A
behavior really a trigger for coronary heart disease events? *Psychosomatic Medicine, 65*, 339–346.

Gallacher J.E.J., Yarness, J.W.G., Sweetnam, P.M., Elwood, P.C. & Stansfeld, S.A. (1999). Anger and
incident heart disease in the Caerphilly study. *Psychosomatic Medicine, 61*, 446–453.

Gallo, L.C. & Smith, T.W. (1999). Patterns of hostility and social support: Conceptualizing psychosocial risk factors as a characteristic of the person and the environment. *Journal of Research in
Personality, 33*, 281–310.

Harper, S., Lynch, J., Hsu, W.-L., Everson, S.A., Hillemeier, M.M., Raghunathan, T.E. et al. (2002).
Life course socioeconomic conditions and adult psychosocial functioning. *International Journal
of Epidemiology, 31*, 395–403.

Hecker, M.L., Chesney, M.A., Black, G.W. & Frautschi, N. (1988). Coronary-prone behaviours in the
Western Collaborative Group Study. *Psychosomatic Medicine, 50*, 153–164.

Hearn, M.D., Murray, D.M. & Luepker, R.V. (1989). Hostility, coronary heart disease, and total
mortality: A 33-year follow-up study of university students. *Journal of Behavioral Medicine, 12*,
105–121.

Hemingway, H. & Marmot, M. (1999). Evidence based cardiology: psychosocial factors in the aetiology and prognosis of coronary heart disease. Systematic review of cohort studies. *British Medical
Journal, 318*, 1460–1467.

Henderson, A. (1996). Coronary heart disease: overview. *Lancet, 348*, s1–s4.

Houston, B.K., (1994). Anger, hostility and physiological reactivity. In A.W. Siegman and T.W. Smith
(eds). *Anger, hostility and the heart*. London: Lawrence Erlbaum Associates.

Houston, B.K., Babyak, M.A., Chesney, M.A., Black, G. & Ragland, D.R. (1997). Social dominance
and 22-year all-cause mortality in men. *Psychosomatic Medicine, 59*, 5–12.

Johnston, D.W. (1993). The current status of the coronary-prone behaviour pattern. *Journal of the
Royal Society of Medicine, 86*, 406–409.

Joynt, K.E. & O'Connor, C.M. (2005). Lessons from SADHART, ENRICHD, and other trials.
Psychosomatic Medicine, 67 supplement 1, s63–s66.

Julian, D.G. & Cowan, J.C. (1992). *Cardiology*. London: Bailleire Tindall.

Kawachi, I., Sparrow, D., Spiro, A., Vokonas, P. & Weiss, S.T. (1996). A prospective study of anger
and coronary heart disease: The Normative Aging Study. *Circulation, 94*, 2090–2095.

Krueger, R.F., Caspi, A. & Moffitt, T.E. (2000). Epidemiological personology: The unifying role of personality in population-based research on problem behaviours. *Journal of Personality, 68,* 967–998.

Kubzansky, L. D., Kawachi, I. & Sparrow, D. (1999). Socioeconomic status, hostility, and risk factor clustering in the Normative Aging Study: Any help from the concept of allostatic load? *Annals of Behavioral Medicine, 21,* 330–338.

Leng, G.C., Lee, A.J., Fowkes, F.G.R., Whiteman, M., Dunbar, J., Housley, E. & Ruckley, C.V. (1996). Incidence, natural history and cardiovascular events in symptomatic and asymptomatic peripheral arterial disease in the general population. *International Journal of Epidemiology, 25,* 1172–1181.

Leon, G.R., Finn, S.E., Murray, D. & Bailey, J.M. (1988). Inability to predict cardiovascular disease from hostility scores or MMPI items related to Type A behaviour. *Journal of Consulting and Clinical Psychology, 56,* 597–600.

Lynch, J. & Davey Smith, G. (2005). A life course approach to chronic disease epidemiology. *Annual Review of Public Health, 26,* 1–35.

Marmot, M. (1992). Coronary heart disease: rise and fall of a modern epidemic. In: Marmot, M. & Elliott, P. (eds). *Coronary Heart Disease Epidemiology: From Aetiology to Public Health.* Oxford: Oxford Medical Publications.

Maseri, A. (1995). *Ischaemic heart disease: A rational basis for clinical practise and clinical research.* Edinburgh: Churchill Livingstone.

Matthews, G. Deary, I.J. & Whiteman, M.C. (2003). *Personality traits,* 2nd edn. Cambridge University Press.

Matthews, K.A. (1988). Coronary heart disease and Type A behaviors: Update on and alternative to the Booth-Kewley and Friedman (1987) quantitative review. *Psychological Bulletin, 104,* 373–380.

McCranie, E.W., Watkins, L.O., Brandsma, J.M. & Sisson, B.D. (1986). Hostility, coronary heart disease (CHD) incidence and total mortality: Lack of association in a 25-year follow-up of 478 physicians. *Journal of Behavioral Medicine, 9,* 119–125.

Miller, T.Q., Smith, T.W., Turner, C.W., Guijarro, M.L. & Hallet, A.J. (1996). A meta-analytic review of research on hostility and physical health. *Psychological Bulletin, 119,* 322–348.

Myrtek, M. (2001). Meta-analyses of prospective studies on coronary heart disease, type A personality, and hostility. *International Journal of Cardiology, 79,* 245–251.

Niaura, R., Todaro, J.F., Stroud, L., Spiro, A., Ward, K.D. & Weiss, S. (2002). Hostility, the metabolic syndrome, and incident coronary heart disease. *Health Psychology, 21,* 588–593.

Pearson, T.A., Bazzarre, T.L., Daniels, S.R., Fair, J.M., Fortmann, S.P., Franklin, B.A. et al. (2003). AHA guide for improving cardiovascular health at the community level. A statement for public health practitioners, healthcare providers, and health policy makers from the AHA Expert Panel on Population and Prevention Science. *Circulation, 107,* 645–651.

Pincus, A.L. & Ansell, E.B. (2003). Interpersonal theory of personality. In T. Millon & M.J. Lerner (eds) *Handbook of psychology.* New York: John Wiley & Sons, Inc.

Pulkki, L., Kivimäki, M., Elovainio, M., Viikari, J. & Keltikangas-Järvinen, L. (2003). Contribution of socioeconomic status to the association between hostility and cardiovascular risk behaviours: A prospective cohort study. *American Journal of Epidemiology, 158,* 736–742.

Räikkönen, K., Matthews, K.A., Sutton-Tyrell, K. & Kuller, L.H. (2004). Trait anger and the metabolic syndrome predict progression of carotid atherosclerosis in healthy middle-aged women. *Psychosomatic Medicine, 66,* 903–908.

Rosenman, R.H., Friedman, M., Straus, R., Wurm, M., Kositchek, R., Hahn, W. & Werthessen, N.T. (1964). A predictive study of coronary heart disease. *Journal of the American Medical Association, 189,* 103–110.

Scherwitz, L.W., Perkins, L.L., Chesney, M.A., Hughes, G.H., Sidney, S. & Manolio, T.A. (1992). Hostility and health behaviors in young adults: The CARDIA study. *American Journal of Epidemiology, 136,* 136–145.

Shekelle, R.B., Gale, M., Ostfeld, A. & Paul, O. (1983). Hostility, risk of coronary heart disease and mortality. *Psychosomatic Medicine, 45,* 109–114.

Siegler, I.C. (1994). Hostility and risk: Demographic and lifestyle variables. In A.W. Siegman & T.W. Smith (eds) *Anger, hostility and the heart.* London: Lawrence Erlbaum Associates.

Siegler, I.C., Costa, P.T., Brummet, B.H., Helms, M.J., Barefoot, J.C., Williams, R.B. et al. (2003). Patterns of change in hostility from college to midlife in the UNC Alumni Heart Study predict high-risk status. *Psychosomatic Medicine, 65*, 738–745.

Siegman, A.W., Kubzansky, L.D., Kawachi, I., Boyle, S., Vokonas, P.S. & Sparrow, D. (2000). A prospective study of dominance and coronary heart disease in the Normative Aging Study. *American Journal of Cardiology, 86*, 145–149.

Smith, T.W. (1992). Hostility and health: Current status of a psychosomatic hypothesis. *Health Psychology, 11*, 139–150.

Smith, T.W. & Frohm, K.D. (1985). What's so unhealthy about hostility? Construct validity and psychosocial correlates of the Cook and Medley Ho scale. *Health Psychology, 4*, 503–520.

Smith, T.W. & Christensen, A.J. (1992). Hostility, health and social contexts. In H.S. Friedman (ed.) *Hostility, coping and health.* Washington, D.C.: American Psychological Association.

Smith, T.W., Glazer, K., Ruiz, J.M. & Gallo, L.C. (2004). Hostility, anger, aggressiveness, and coronary heart disease: An interpersonal perspective on personality, emotion and health. *Journal of Personality, 72*, 1217–1270.

Smith, T.W. & Ruiz, J.M. (2002). Psychosocial influences on the development and course of coronary heart disease: current status and implications for research and practice. *Journal of Consulting and Clinical Psychology, 7*, 548–568.

Smith, T.W. & Spiro, A. (2002). Personality, health and aging: prolegomenon for the next generation. *Journal of Research in Personality, 36*, 363–394.

Smith, T.W. & Williams, P.G. (1992). Personality and health: advantages and limitations of the five-factor model. *Journal of Personality, 60*, 395–423.

Spielberger, C.D. (1988). *State-trait anger expression inventory (manual): Revised research edition.* Odessa, FL: Psychological Assessment Resources.

Spielberger, C.D. (1999). STAXI-2: *State-trait anger expression inventory-2: professional manual.* Odessa, FL: Psychological Assessment Resources.

Spielberger, C.D., Jacobs, G.A., Russell, S. & Crance, R.S. (1983). Assessment of anger: The State-Trait Anger Scale. In J.N. Butcher & C.D. Spielberger (eds). *Advances in personality assessment (vol 2).* Hillsdale, NJ: Lawrence Erlbaum Associates.

Spielberger, C.D., Johnson, E.H., Russell, S.R., Crane, R.J., Jacobs, G.A. & Worden, T.J. (1985). The experience and expression of anger: Construction and validation of an anger expression scale. In: Chesney, M.A. & Rosenman, R.H. (eds). *Anger and hostility in cardiovascular and behavioral disorders.* Washington, D.C.: Hemisphere.

Steptoe, A. (1998). Psychological factors and cardiovascular disease. *Current Opinion in Psychiatry, 11*, 655–660.

Steptoe, A. & Marmot, M. (2003). Burden of psychosocial adversity and vulnerability in middle age: Associations with biobehavioral risk factors and quality of life. *Psychosomatic Medicine, 65*, 1029–1037.

Stone, S.V. & Costa, P.T. (1990). Disease-prone personality or distress-prone personality? The role of neuroticism in coronary heart disease. In H.S. Friedman (ed.). *Personality and disease.* New York: John Wiley and Sons, Inc.

Strike, P.C. & Steptoe, A. (2005). Behavioral and emotional triggers of acute coronary syndromes: a systematic review and critique. *Psychosomatic Medicine, 67*, 179–186.

Suls, J. & Bunde, J. (2005). Anger, anxiety, and depression as risk factors for cardiovascular disease: the problems and implications of overlapping affective dispositions. *Psychological Bulletin, 131*, 260–300.

Suls, J. & Sanders, G.S. (1989). Why do some behavioral styles place people at coronary risk? In A.W. Siegman & T.M. Dembroski (eds). *In search of coronary prone behavior: Beyond Type A.* Hillsdale, NJ: Erlbaum.

Surtees, P., Wainwright, N., Day, N., Brayne, C., Luben, R. & Khaw, K.-T. (2003). Adverse experience in childhood as a developmental risk factor for altered immune status in adulthood. *International Journal of Behavioral Medicine, 10*, 251–268.

Tunstall-Pedoe, H. (1997). Cardiovascular diseases. In R. Detels, W.W. Holland, J. McEwen & G.S. Omenn (eds). *Oxford textbook of public health*, 3rd edn, vol. 3: *The practice of public health.* Oxford Medical Publications.

Vahtera, J., Kivimäki, M., Uutela, A. & Pentti, J. (2000). Hostility and ill health: role of psychosocial resources in two contexts of working life. *Journal of Psychosomatic Research, 48*, 89–98.

Vollrath, M. (2001). Personality and stress. *Scandinavian Journal of Psychology, 42*, 335–347.

Whitehead, M. (1992). *The health divide*. London: Penguin.

Whiteman, M.C., Bedford, A., Grant, E. & Deary, I.J. (2001). The Five Factor Model (NEO-FFI) and the Personality Deviance Scales-Revised (PDS-R): Going around in interpersonal circles. *Personality and Individual Differences, 31*, 259–267.

Whiteman, M.C., Deary, I.J & Fowkes, F.G.R. (2000). Personality and health: cardiovascular disease. In S.E. Hampson (ed.). *Advances in personality psychology, vol. 1*. Hove: Psychology Press.

Whiteman, M.C., Deary, I.J., Lee, A.J. & Fowkes, F.G.R. (1997). Submissiveness and protection from coronary heart disease in the general population: Edinburgh Artery Study. *Lancet, 350*, 541–545.

Whiteman, M.C., Fowkes, F.G.R. & Deary, I.J. (1997). Hostility and the heart: it's the hostility in Type A personality that matters, but which element of hostility? *British Medical Journal, 7105*, 379–380.

Whiteman, M.C., Fowkes, F.G.R., Deary, I.J. & Lee, A.J. (1997). Hostility, smoking and alcohol consumption in the general population. *Social Science and Medicine, 44*, 1089–1096.

Williams, R.B. (2003). Invited commentary: Socioeconomic status, hostility, and health behaviours– Does it matter which comes first? *American Journal of Epidemiology, 158*, 743–746.

Williams, R.B., Barefoot, J.C. & Shekelle, R.B. (1985). The health consequences of hostility. In M.A. Chesney, S.E. Goldston & R.M. Rosenman (eds). *Anger, hostility and behavioral medicine*. New York: Hemisphere.

Williams, R.B., Barefoot, J.C., Haney, T.L., Harrell, F.E., Blumenthal, J.A., Pryor, D.B. & Peterson, B. (1988). Type A behavior and angiographically documented atherosclerosis in a sample of 2,289 patients. *Psychosomatic Medicine, 50*, 139–152.

Williams, R.B., Marchuk, D.A., Gadde, K.M., Barefoot, J.C., Grichnik, K., Helms, M.J. et al. (2001). Central nervous system serotonin function and cardiovascular responses to stress. *Psychosomatic Medicine, 63*, 300–305.

CHAPTER 2

The Role of Personality in Cancer Onset and Survival

Adelita V. Ranchor and Robbert Sanderman

University of Groningen, The Netherlands

INTRODUCTION

This chapter deals with the role of personality in the onset of cancer and its medical course, including recurrence, and survival. We elaborate on our previous review of the role of personality in the onset of and survival from cancer (and coronary heart disease) (Sanderman & Ranchor, 1997). Before turning to the evidence for the role of personality in the onset of disease, we will discuss in general the rationale for studying personality in relation to disease, models linking personality to disease, methodological approaches and the cancer prone personality.

Why Study Personality and Disease?

The idea that personality is related to the onset of disease dates back to the time of the ancient Greeks. Since then, this proposed relationship continued to emerge in different guises, and became strongly rooted in lay theories in the 20th century. However, it was not until the 1950s that the notion of a link between personality and disease onset was empirically tested. Among other approaches, the work of Friedman and Rosenman (1959) on Type A Behavior Pattern (TABP) and coronary heart disease (CHD) initiated much research on the role of personality in the onset of disease, both in the cardiovascular field and in other medical fields. However, the idea behind a causal role of personality in the onset of cancer was also developed to a large extent independently from research on TABP and CHD. The results with respect to the role of personality in the onset of cancer were mixed and sometimes even conflicting.

Despite the mostly disappointing results, the idea that personality is related to the onset of disease and its medical outcomes is still rooted in lay theories about the onset of disease. Partly, these ideas are fed by the incapability of medical science to fully account for the onset of a variety of conditions, including cancer and coronary heart disease. For example, for coronary heart disease classical risk factors account for only 50 % of its onset. However, it is a misconception that the absence of convincing evidence from medical science implies

Handbook of Personality and Health. Edited by Margarete E. Vollrath. © 2006 John Wiley & Sons, Ltd.

a potential role for personality factors. Interestingly, the idea that personality is related to the onset of disease is rooted in spiritual movements such as New Age that emerged in the 1990s, which strongly propagate the belief that persons are predisposed to developing certain diseases on the basis of their personality.

Addressing the ideas that exist amongst the general public is one of the reasons for examining the role of personality in the onset of disease, although it should not be assumed that the researchers performing empirical testing necessarily believe in the idea under test. In addition, an important reason for taking into account personality as a potential risk factor for disease onset scientifically, is its stability. It has been shown repeatedly that personality is relatively stable over time (although gradually minor changes do take place; Terracciano, McCrae, Brant & Costa, 2005) and for this reason it has more potential for predicting the course of cancer over long periods of time than many other factors. Moreover, personality factors have been associated with a wide variety of biological, behavioural and cognitive factors and may therefore be involved in the development and outcome of disease, i.e. survival. In the context of cancer, personality seems to be related to hormonal factors and immune function, and through this mechanism may increase an individual's susceptibility for developing cancer (Garssen, 2004).

As previously mentioned, little supporting evidence exists for the etiological role of personality factors in the onset of disease in general, and for cancer in particular. Plausible doubts were raised as to the credibility of the studies of Grossarth-Maticek and colleagues (e.g. Grossarth-Maticek, Bastiaans & Kanazir, 1985) which provided strong support for a causal role of personality in the onset of cancer. These studies were severely criticized because of suspected manipulations and inconsistencies in the information concerning the realization of the study (see, e.g. Van der Ploeg, 1991). Thus, discarding these particular studies, at best the results are contradictory. For a large part, null and contradictory findings can be explained by weak research designs, the use of multifarious measures to assess a particular personality trait, and quite different operationalizations of the same concept. This holds true especially for the cancer prone personality, also known as the Type C personality (see the discussion of the cancer prone personality). In our previous review (Sanderman & Ranchor, 1997), we found that studies with a quasi-prospective design showed consistent evidence for a causal role of Type C personality in the onset of cancer. However, both the prospective and case-control studies showed conflicting findings. We concluded then that no definite answers could be given concerning the influence of personality on the onset of cancer.

Models for the Role of Personality in the Onset and Course of Disease (Including Survival)

Several models and approaches have been developed throughout the years to examine the role of personality in disease onset. Although these were mainly developed for the onset of disease, they are also applicable to the course of disease, including survival. These models do not refer to a specific disease, and therefore, they are discussed in a general way.

A first distinction is between the specificity and generality approach. The generality approach assumes that certain personality factors increase or decrease a person's susceptibility for ill health, regardless of specific diseases or personality traits. Alternatively, the specificity approach argues that specific personality traits (or combinations of traits) are indeed related to the onset of specific diseases. Typical examples are hostility, as part of the Type A Behaviour Pattern, which has been identified as a risk factor for coronary heart disease, and also Type C personality which includes a combination of personality traits that are suspected to increase risk of cancer. Research on personality and the onset of disease has often favoured the specificity approach, although there seems to be a recent trend towards revaluing the generality approach. This trend does not apply specifically to personality; but rather to risk factors for disease in general. It assumes that persons have a general susceptibility for illness, and that specific diseases are merely manifestations of this general susceptibility.

A second distinction concerns the role of personality in disease onset. Three different models have been identified, i.e. the etiologic trait approach, the illness behaviour approach and the stress moderator approach. In the *etiologic trait approach*, personality is viewed as an independent risk factor for the onset of disease. This means that having an unfavourable set of personality traits in itself increases the risk of developing a certain disease. This raises the question as to the mechanisms through which personality affects the onset of disease. This issue is partly addressed in the *illness behaviour approach*, which assumes that personality influences perception of illness and use of medical care, and that this in turn influences the onset of disease. In other words, the relation between personality and onset of disease is mediated by illness behaviour. Although not specified in this approach, other mediating variables are mentioned in the literature, including health behaviour and biological factors. Health behaviour concerns both healthy and unhealthy behaviours that are related to disease, such as smoking, alcohol use, exercise and diet, while in the context of cancer biological factors include immune function, which is a relevant biological factor in the progression of cancer. The underlying assumption is that personality traits are related to performance of particular behaviours. Personality traits are also thought to be related to biological factors. There is some evidence for a relation between the personality trait optimism and immune functioning (Segerstrom, Taylor, Kemeny & Fahey, 1998). Returning to the three approaches, the *stress moderator approach* assumes that personality in itself is not related to the onset of disease, rather, it moderates the relation between stress and disease, by either increasing or decreasing the effect of stress on disease.

It is difficult to assess the relative validity of these models since the different sets of relations specified in each approach have not been tested systematically or even explicitly. This highlights a general shortcoming in the research on personality and health, especially the older literature, that is characterized by a lack of theoretical guidance. This is also apparent in the lack of sound conceptualizations of personality traits that have supposed links to the onset of disease (see also the discussion of the cancer prone personality). Research in this area has often simply identified personality risk factors for disease, and has been less concerned with examining the underlying mechanisms.

Of relevance to the previous point, we must also consider the possibility that personality might be linked to a different factor, currently either known or unknown, which is causally determining survival, and that might be explained by a mechanism either unrelated to or independent of personality. In other words personality could be a statistically related factor (third variable) and therefore by definition conceptually of little interest for predicting survival. However, personality may be used for reasons of convenience if the relationship between personality and a particular factor is strong, although this approach would be very misleading.

Methodological Approaches to the Study of Personality and Disease

Research examining the causal role of personality in the onset of disease belongs to the field of (social) epidemiology. Social epidemiology refers to the scientific study of social factors (including psychological factors) in relation to the occurrence and distribution of diseases. Within social epidemiology, several research designs are available for studying the causal role of personality in the onset of disease. Here, we distinguish the case-control design and the (quasi-) prospective research design.

In case-control designs personality scores of patients with a particular disease are compared to those of persons without that disease. In these studies, personality is always measured *after* disease detection. This complicates drawing firm conclusions as to the causal role of personality, because the possibility cannot be excluded that personality has changed as a result of the diagnosis of the disease. Thus, cause (personality) and effect (disease) cannot be disentangled. The reason why researchers have applied this type of design has to do with feasibility (see the discussion of prospective studies). Another reason is that it is a suitable design for exploring possible relations that subsequently can be tested in a prospective design. To date, there is general agreement with respect to gradual changes of personality across life span (Terracciano, McCrae, Brant & Costa, 2005). Less is known, however, on the changeability of personality after confrontation with a stressful life event, such as the diagnosis of cancer. This may be different for specific personality traits. Hence, specific information on the changeability of personality traits is needed in order to evaluate the value of case-control designs in examining the role of personality in the onset of disease.

A prospective research design overcomes the shortcoming of entanglement of cause and effect, and is therefore considered to be the stronger design in this respect. In this design, personality is assessed before the onset of disease. It requires the inclusion of a large sample of persons from the general population who are free from the disease under study in order to subsequently obtain sufficient numbers of persons with that disease. In addition, a prospective research design often requires long follow-up periods, depending on the sample size and on the incidence (= number of new cases with a particular disease during one year) of the disease under study. High costs are involved in such a design. Moreover, study logistics are often quite complicated. Thus, although this type of design might be appropriate, in practice, it is not always feasible to undertake such studies.

Researchers, therefore, sometimes apply a quasi-prospective design, in which personality is measured shortly before diagnosis of disease, for instance, when persons are referred to further diagnostic tests. The cost-effectiveness of such a design is high, since there is a high chance of detecting the specific disease under study. However, this advantage is also a disadvantage, since this design generates data from a high risk group, which may yield only weak associations between personality and disease, because of restriction of range in the sample (Miller, Smith, Turner, Guijaroo & Hallet, 1996). In addition, similar to case-control studies, the possibility that personality has changed as a consequence of suspected disease cannot be excluded. For example, persons may be aware of the diagnosis, which might influence their scores on personality tests. Schwarz (1993) supported this notion in his finding that women who were referred for diagnostic tests upon suspicion of breast cancer could estimate their diagnosis fairly well.

A pitfall of social epidemiological research that also pertains to research in this area, is that a significant relation between personality and disease does not necessarily imply a causal role of personality. There are at least two reasons for this. First, one needs to adjust for all relevant confounding factors, including sociodemographic factors and medical factors in order to ascertain that the observed relation can be ascribed to personality. Not all studies take into account relevant confounders. Of course, in the case of a null finding (i.e. personality is *not* related to the onset of disease) this is less of a problem. Second, the pathways relating personality to disease need to be clarified before we can draw convincing conclusions; in other words, it needs to be clarified *how* personality affects the onset of disease. Supporting evidence, for example, for the mediating role of biological factors in the relation between personality and disease can be derived from laboratory studies, or other types of studies.

To conclude, the most appropriate design for the study of personality as a risk factor for disease is a truly prospective design. However, we can only draw causal conclusions when the pathways relating personality to disease have been clarified. Many recently published studies have utilized prospective designs, indicating that the research field is developing towards a higher scientific level.

Selection of Studies

The literature was systematically searched through Medline, Pubmed and PSYCinfo in order to detect studies on the role of personality in the onset and survival of cancer from 1996 onwards. We also searched the internet and used the reference lists of detected studies to identify additional studies that were not found through Medline, Pubmed or PSYCinfo.

Because of the interpretation difficulties that are attached to case-control studies, we decided only to include prospective and quasi-prospective studies. Although the latter study type may suffer from some of the same problems as case-control studies, we decided not to exclude them since they might provide important evidence; yet, the findings of these studies should be interpreted in light of the possible shortcomings.

PERSONALITY AND THE ONSET OF CANCER

Personality and Cancer: The Cancer Prone Personality

Compared to diseases such as coronary heart disease and pulmonary diseases, relatively little is known about biological and medical causes of the onset of cancer. This leaves even more space for speculations about the role of personality factors and other psychological and social factors, such as stress, in the onset of cancer. Strikingly, to the extent that there are clear-cut ideas about the role of personality in the onset of disease, these ideas pertain to all cancer types, while the etiological pathways for each cancer type might be different. The roles of behavioural factors are different for several cancer types; for example, smoking is related to the onset of lung cancer and head-neck tumours, while exposure to sunlight is responsible for skin cancers. These differences in onset of cancer types have generally been neglected in theories about the role of personality in the onset of cancer. Several studies have dealt with this issue by focusing on a specific type of cancer, most often breast cancer (Bleiker & Van der Ploeg, 1999).

The Type C personality was introduced by Morris and Greer (cf. Temoshok, 1987) as a conceptualization of the cancer prone personality, by analogy with the Type A Behaviour Pattern. Type C personality is characterized by repression of emotions, especially negative emotions such as anger, and the tendency to sacrifice oneself without the expression of personal demands (cf. Faller, Lang & Schilling, 1996). This concept is closely connected to alexithymia, which can be described as the extremely strong tendency to suppress anger and other negative feelings. However, in our previous review, we found that a broad and sometimes even contradictory set of personality factors were considered as potential risk factors for cancer onset. For example, both strict operationalizations of the cancer prone personality and Type A Behavior Pattern, which is the opposite of the Type C personality, were examined in relation to cancer onset. The lack of a sound conceptualization of the cancer prone personality gives room to ad hoc findings that are difficult to interpret.

Operationalization of the Cancer Prone Personality in the Reviewed Studies

In our previous review (Sanderman & Ranchor, 1997), there seemed to be a general congruence in the operationalization of the cancer prone personality when personality was considered as an etiologic risk factor for cancer. Most studies that we discussed focused on concepts that reflected the inability to express emotions, although some of them focused on the coronary prone personality (e.g. Fox, Ragland, Brand & Rosenman, 1987). In the literature from 1997 onwards, surprisingly, there seems to be more diversity in the operationalization of the cancer prone personality. Researchers seem to have drifted away from examining the inability to express emotions (which is most closely related to the original conceptualization of the cancer prone personality) in relation to cancer onset, towards a broader exploration of personality traits as risk factors for cancer. Traits considered were anger, rationality, anti-emotionality, pessimism, Neuroticism and Extraversion. Many studies seem to have included the Eysenck Personality Questionnaire, assessing Neuroticism and Extraversion, alongside Psychoticism and social desirability. We do not know if the reason for including the EPQ questionnaire was theoretically based or just an opportunistic addition of the questionnaire in order to test the relation between personality and the onset of cancer. Eysenck (1990) had provided a theoretical model in which the coronary prone personality was operationalized as *a combination* of high levels of Neuroticism (indicating the experiencing of negative feelings) and low levels of Extraversion (indicating the inability to express these feelings). Although this seems to be plausible, not all researchers examining Neuroticism and Extraversion as predictors of cancer onset have tested this combination model. As such, recent research on personality as a causal factor in the onset of cancer seems to be rather ad hoc in nature and less theory-based.

Empirical Findings on the Relation Between Personality and the Onset of Cancer

As previously mentioned, we have only selected prospective and quasi-prospective studies in our review. For the etiology part of our review, we found ten papers that met our criteria. All studies adjusted for relevant clinical variables. These studies will be discussed on the basis of the conceptualization of the cancer prone personality, and on the basis of the cancer type considered.

Three studies included measures of Neuroticism and Extraversion as a predictor of cancer onset. None of these studies could establish the predictive value of Neuroticism and Extraversion in the onset of specific cancer types, nor in the onset of cancer in general. One of these studies included an impressive large sample size (N = 30,277; Nakaya et al., 2003) and a follow-up period of seven years. Analyses were conducted for the total sample of incident cancer patients (N = 986) and for the four most common cancer sites, i.e., stomach, colorectum, lung and breast cancer (least N = 86 for breast cancer). None of these analyses yielded positive findings. Neuroticism and Extraversion were examined separately instead of using a combined score of high Neuroticism and low Extraversion. This was explicitly taken into account in the second study among Swedish twins and, again, with a large sample size (N = 29,595; Hansen, Floderus, Frederiksen & Johansen, 2005). The sample was followed over an extended period of 25 years (N = 1,989 incident cancer cases). Similar to the Nakaya et al. (2003) study, no effects were found for the separate scores of Neuroticism and Extraversion, nor for the joint effects. Again, this was examined in the total sample of cancer patients and for separate cancer sites separately. The results of the third study (Schapiro et al., 2001) with a smaller sample (N = 1,031) were consistent with the findings of the other two studies. Thus, neither Neuroticism and Extraversion nor their joint effects were predictive of cancer onset, regardless of specific cancer sites.

Three other studies examined a wide variety of personality factors in relation to the onset of breast cancer, two of them applying a prospective design (Bleiker, Van der Ploeg, Hendriks & Adèr, 1996; Lillberg, Verkasalo, Kaprio, Helenius & Koskenvuo, 2002) and one a quasi-prospective design (Price et al., 2001). The study of Lillberg, Verkasalo, Kaprio, Helenius and Koskenvuo (2002) included Extraversion, hostility and Type A behaviour in a study among 12,499 women. Again, no relation was found between Extraversion and the incidence of breast cancer; nor for Type A behaviour and hostility. Bleiker, van der Ploeg, Hendriks and Adèr (1996) examined various personality traits, including rationality, anti-emotionality, optimism, expression and control of emotions in a sample of 9,705 females, of whom 131 developed breast cancer in the follow-up of five years. Rationality, anti-emotionality and expression and control of emotions approached the operationalization of the Type C personality most closely in the studies reviewed here. With the exception of anti-emotionality, again, no relation between personality and the onset of cancer was found. Multivariate analyses, including all personality traits under study, family history and parity status, revealed that anti-emotionality showed a significant, independent but weak increased risk of breast cancer (odds ratio = 1.16). Clinically, this association is not of much relevance, hence, this study also suggests that personality may *not* be predictive of the onset of cancer. This was corroborated in the quasi-prospective study of Price et al. (2001) in a sample of N = 2,224 females who completed a questionnaire before medical examination at a breast cancer screening programme. The questionnaire included defense style, locus of control, emotional expression and control, self-esteem, and trait anxiety; none of which were related to the onset of breast cancer (N = 298).

Interestingly, in an unusual design, examining the predictive role of Type D (distressed) personality among 246 men diagnosed with coronary heart disease (CHD), Denollet (1998) found an increased risk of cancer for men with high scores on Type D personality. The interest of this study lies in the concept of Type D personality which closely resembles the Type C personality, in that Type D is defined as the experiencing of negative emotions and simultaneously suppressing the expression of these emotions. However, the number of diagnosed patients was low (N = 12) and 9 of them died. In earlier research, Denollet et al. (1996) had shown that Type D personality was related to survival after CHD onset but it is unclear in this study if Type D was predictive of mortality after CHD or of cancer onset as such.

To conclude, there is no clear evidence of a relationship between personality and the onset of cancer. The evidence provided here was derived from high quality studies.

PERSONALITY AND SURVIVAL OF CANCER

Conceptual Issues

Given the intertwining of coping styles and personality it is hard to draw a sharp line between these constructs. Coping can be described by the cognitive and behavioural actions used to adapt to a stressful situation, whereas personality traits are typified by cognitions and behavioural characteristics which are stable over time but which are also of influence when handling stressful situations. Evidence concerning coping (styles) and survival might be considered for reasons apart from the fact that outcomes of studies on coping may be partially dependent on the influence of personality. Quite often coping is operationalized in a way resembling personality. Moreover, if coping (styles) are related to endpoints over time such as survival and recurrence, they must logically be quite stable factors which resemble personality traits. In contrast, a variable highly dependent on context or state is not expected to be able to predict outcomes like the one we discuss here. Furthermore, coping variables are sometimes a better conceptualization of theoretical and common sense notions about personality, and consequently, they are much better studied in relation to cancer survival. Excluding these variables would give a much too limited view on the role of personality in cancer survival. Indeed, there are some interesting findings with coping which may shed light on how the trait-like resources of subjects are of influence on outcomes. Hence, for the reasons given we take a broad-minded view on personality including coping (styles).

However, the role of personality and coping style in predicting survival might be different. For example, cancer survival may be related to coping with stress, which in turn may be dependent upon personality. Coping with stress may again undermine the biological suppression of the disease process (e.g. through immunological and neuroendocrine mechanisms). Given the notions concerning the influence of coping and stress and outcome of disease, and given what has been stated above regarding personality and coping, it is of interest to consider the concept of coping at least for its contribution to our understanding of personality and disease outcome.

Empirical Findings on the Relation Between Personality and Survival of Cancer

In this section we focus on the associations between personality and survival. The well-known study of Greer, Morris and Pettingale (1979) gave an impetus to the idea that coping or traits may have an influence on survival and clearly stimulated research in the area. They found that 'fighting spirit' was associated with increased survival among women with breast cancer. Petticrew, Bell and Hunter (2002) conscientiously reviewed the evidence available concerning several indicators of coping or coping styles and both survival and recurrence of cancer. They ended up with 26 studies which were for the main part small scale studies; i.e. only four studies included more than 200 patients. They clustered their results around the following coping styles: (1) fighting spirit, (2) helplessness/hopelessness, (3) denial or avoidance, (4) stoic acceptance and fatalism, (5) anxious coping/anxious preoccupation, depressive coping, (6) active or problem focused coping, and (7) suppression of emotions/emotion focused coping.

In their summary they stated that, taking the results of their review together, there is hardly any evidence supporting an association with survival with respect to the concepts mentioned. There are however some exceptions to this trend. Remarkably these are most often small scaled studies. However, one may question Petticrew et al.'s (2002) summary since, for example, Watson and Davidson-Homewood (2003) suggest a somewhat different conclusion (cf. Garssen, 2004). In addition, some recent studies add new evidence to that available in 2002. Moreover, we think that it is also important to include evidence on studies with personality measures.

Another issue which has been discussed by Petticrew et al. (2002) has to do with predicting recurrence. The overall trend seems to be slightly ambiguous; there seem to be at least some indications that avoidance and helplessness/hopelessness is related to a higher chance of recurrence as summarized in 2002. Turning back to the issue of (length) of survival it is interesting to note that Watson, Homewood, Haviland and Bliss (2005) published a study including the Mental Adjustment to Cancer (MAC) scale (which assesses for example 'fighting spirit' and 'helplessness/hopelessness') and a depression scale (HADS) in a 10-year follow-up study (initial sample 578 patients) as an extention to their study on a five-year follow-up (Watson, Haviland, Greer, Davidson & Bliss, 1999),which produced similar findings. The outcome of this study, given the sound methodology, is very important. It shows that specifically a low *helplessness/hopelessness* is associated with a shorter disease free survival. The authors call for research to clarify the mechanisms and to develop therapies to influence disease outcome. The Reynolds et al. study (2000), which included 847 patients with a number of negative findings, also reported an association between expressing emotions and increased survival.

Cassileth, Lusk, Miller, Brown and Miller (1985), however, did not find a relationship between psychosocial variables like hopelessness and survival. They stated that 'the biology of the disease appears to predominate and override the potential influence of life-style and psychosocial variables'. Their later paper on this study presenting data up to eight years after diagnosis (Cassileth, Walsh & Lusk, 1988) offered the same conclusion.

If we take a closer look at some studies with *'traditional' personality factors* there are some interesting findings to mention. Several studies used the Eysenck Personality Questionnaire (EPQ or a earlier version – the EPI) or similar instruments and produced interesting results which set the stage for a clear summary.

A quite provocative population-based prospective study was carried out by Nakaya et al. (2005) and focused on personality and survival. Over 41,000 persons filled out the EPQ and a questionnaire about health habits in 1990. Subsequently cancer incident cases were identified and monitored (from 1993 up to 2001). The pre-morbid personality scores were analysed taking into account health habits and medical parameters. The results are clear and of great importance to this area of research. As expected, metastases increase the risk of dying considerably. Personality factors, however, do not add explanatory power to the prediction of survival. This is a study with a high number of subjects and with impressive methodological rigor. Of importance is the fact that personality is assessed long before the onset of cancer and the design includes various confounding variables. One interesting finding in this study was the difference in the percentage of in situ or localized tumours in patients with low Neuroticism scores (35.4 %) compared to patients with high Neuroticism scores (44.8 %). It might well be the case that persons higher in Neuroticism are referred earlier.

Although Aarstad, Heimdal, Aarstad and Oloffson (2002) were unable to find a relationship between Neuroticism and Extraversion and survival, they did find such a relationship for the Lie scale, indicating social desirability. The results indicated that persons with a lower Lie score had a higher risk of dying early. In direct contrast to this, Ratcliff, Dawson and Walker (1995) reported exactly the opposite. Adding to the confusion, Canada, Fawzy and Fawzy (2005) reported a null result for a similar comparison.

In the 10-year follow-up study of Canada, Fawzy and Fawzy (2005) the relationship between the EPQ (long version) and recurrence and survival among patients with melanoma is reported. Gender (worse outcome for males) and biological markers were reported as important for both recurrence and survival. Personality factors, however, did not add to the prediction of either outcome. A limitation here, as with many other studies, was the low number of patients involved and the resultant low numbers of patients with a recurrence or death. Many more studies were unable to find evidence for a link between personality and survival, all of which suffered from low patient numbers, i.e. Kukull et al. (1986), Ratcliff et al. (1995) and the classical study of Greer et al. (1979) who also included the EPI.

It is important to be aware of the often vast array of control variables included in these studies, such as disease specific biological markers. A closer look at these data provides quite strong evidence that Neuroticism and Extraversion are not related to (length) of survival.

There are some additional research findings with respect to *other personality traits*. Neuser (1988) used the Personality Research Form (PRF) and found that 'Strive for recognition and help' was related to a higher survival probability among patients with acute leukaemia. Broers et al. (1998) reported a relationship between low self-esteem and shorter survival among 123 patients who underwent a Bone Marrow Transplantation, but this was only observed after dividing the group based on the 25th, 50th and 75th percentiles, and could not be found in multivariate analyses. Interestingly, a 27-year follow-up analysis of the renowned Western Collaborative study (Carmelli et al., 1991) showed that specifically subjects of younger age (<49) who scored higher on Type A hostility proved to have a shorter survival compared to low scoring individuals. Interestingly Ragland, Brand and Fox (1992) published a study on the same data (without referring to the Carmelli study) stating that the association is confounded or mediated by life-style factors. Schulz, Bookwala, Knapp, Scheier and Williamson (1996) measured pessimism in their eight-month follow-up study among patients with recurrent or metastasized cancer (N = 268). Results indicate that 'the endorsement of a pessimistic life orientation may function as an important risk factor for mortality among younger (age 30–59) cancer patients'. The authors suggest that this 'pessimistic life orientation' is not the simple opposite of optimism and can be distinguished from depression.

To conclude, there are some mixed findings as indicated by others who have reviewed research on the relationship between personality and survival of cancer (e.g. Petticrew et al., 2002; Garssen, 2004). On the whole there is as yet no strong evidence to support the proposed influence of personality on survival, the only notable exception being the effect of helplessness/hopelessness.

DISCUSSION

Onset of Cancer

The studies reviewed in this chapter could not provide evidence for a predictive role of personality in the onset of cancer. The studies applied a sound research design, i.e. prospective in nature and with large sample sizes, and took into account relevant clinical variables. Compared to our previous review (Sanderman & Ranchor, 1997), the number of truly prospective studies has increased considerably. Simultaneously, the number of studies with a weaker design, such as the case-control, have diminished due to changes within this research area. The research field has now developed beyond the explorative stage, so that stronger research designs are replacing weaker designs with the result that weaker research is less likely to be published.

Personality factors have been examined both in relation to cancer onset in general and the onset of specific cancer types. Although studies have used various conceptualizations of the cancer prone personality, some of them explicitly took into account personality factors that closely approached the concept of Type C personality. These factors included non-expression of emotions, rationality, anti-emotionality and combined scores of Neuroticism and Extraversion. None of these factors were related to the onset of cancer, with the exception of a weak significant relation between anti-emotionality and the onset of breast cancer. Other, more diverse personality factors that were examined in relation to cancer onset also yielded only null findings.

Of course, we cannot exclude the possibility that other personality factors might be related to cancer onset. This could be tested through the use of an explorative approach with an accompanying theoretical foundation. Of course, if there are possibilities to exploratively study the role of other personality characteristics in the onset of disease in a truly prospective design, we should not discard that possibility. However, a more systematic approach would be to continue to test those models already in existence, thus, exploring the possible pathways relating personality to onset of disease. In that respect it would be wise to take into account the various etiological pathways to the onset of cancer, and to focus on those cancer types for which the etiological pathways are known, and which might have a potential link to personality factors. In fact, this line of reasoning points to the need for examining the role of personality in the onset of specific cancer types. For example, smoking is the most important predictor for onset of lung cancer. Hence, personality factors that are linked to smoking behaviour are potential predictors for the onset of lung cancer. Van Loon, Tijhuis, Surtees and Ormel (2001) found that Neuroticism and Extraversion were positively related to smoking initiation.

However, this possibility does not alter the fact that personality factors that have been considered up till now to be potential causal factors in the onset of cancer, have shown no evidence for such a causal role. Hence, we can only conclude that with the present evidence personality is not related to the onset of disease.

Survival

Clearly basic personality traits like Neuroticism and Extraversion do not seem to be linked to survival. The same holds true for most other personality and coping variables. The outcomes have been too inconsistent to provide a trend that might stimulate more research. The only exception is that of helplessness/hopelessness which shows some influence on survival. It seems justifiable to attempt to disentangle the processes underlying this effect, since this knowledge may ultimately be of use for targeting patients in clinical practice who score high on this concept.

The studies which are most often published in this field also include biological markers (which indeed show clear relationships with survival). The added value of personality-like variables is minimal, with the exception of helplessness/hopelessness. In general studies with a sound methodology outweigh the evidence of smaller studies with positive or in-clusive results. Ideally, however, a true meta-analysis (as with the Cochrane system) could provide more conclusive results whilst maximally utilizing existing evidence through the synthesis of current research.

The very fact that coping styles are not convincingly reported to be related to survival, indicates that, as it stands now, we should also be very cautious about the possibility that per-sonality has an influence on stress via the mechanism of coping. In addition well designed prospective studies show no strong evidence for a direct association between personality and survival and this holds also for coping styles which might be sometimes considered as 'personality-like' factors. The claim that personality could serve as an important factor in the stress-coping process does not hold, because for this to be sufficiently supported a clear pattern of associations should have been found between coping styles and survival. The review of Petticrew et al. (2002) is quite convincing in claiming that coping does not have an important effect on survival – with the very important exception of helpless-ness/hopelessness. Watson et al. (2005) in fact gave additional support to the idea that this type of coping is of influence on (disease free) survival and they argue for research that focuses on the mechanism of helplessness/hopelessness. In that context it may be of interest to study the relationship between this seemingly important coping style and Big Five traits, to see what may contribute to patient vulnerability.

In our view the implication of summarized findings concerning the link between person-ality and survival is that any proposed influence or effect of personality should be treated with caution. This is especially important with respect to clinical work and the way in which patients are treated or approached. There is as yet no evidence to suggest that patients have any control over cancer outcome in terms of their psychological make-up. Alluding to such a mechanism may even be harmful since it 'blames the victim'.

It seems improvident to put further effort into personality in research using a simple predictive model. It is believed however, at least from a theoretical point of view, that it may be of interest to study personality as a variable that may interact with other variables or mechanisms leading to an unfavourable outcome, perhaps in conjunction with helpless-ness/hopelessness. In such a case, it is important to propose a theoretical mechanism prior to testing. Further, if certain factors are found to be related to survival and to personality, what might be the ultimate implication of such a relationship for theory and for clinical practice? We strongly stress that if studies focusing on personality and outcome of the cancer process are undertaken, several issues should be taken into account. It is impor-tant to have adequate biological markers included to control for disease severity to include treatment variables, to include enough patients to reach the appropriate power to provide robust analyses and to include adequate personality factors as well as other variables on the basis of a theoretical model. It may also be inappropriate to generalize too easily across different forms of cancer and across different disease stages, which is unfortunately rather common in this research field. In addition, we strongly warn researchers against focusing only on oncological markers and advise a broader view, for example by including issues like co-morbidity since pre-existing diseases may be of influence on coping with cancer or may have impact on the biological system.

General Conclusion

Personality is clearly unrelated to the onset of and survival from cancer. However, there seems to be a predictive role for helplessness/hopelessness in cancer survival. Further research is needed to disentangle the pathways that are responsible for this relationship. In addition, as far as the research on survival of cancer is concerned, a meta-analysis would provide concluding evidence on the role of personality. Concerning the onset of cancer, such a meta-analysis would not be necessary since the results of good quality studies with extremely large samples already provide strong evidence for the lack of a causal role of personality.

REFERENCES

Aarstad, H.J., Heimdal, J.H., Aarstad, A.K.H. & Olofsson, J. (2002). Personality traits in HNSCC patients in relation to the disease state, disease extent and prognosis. *Acta Otolaryngol, 122*, 892–899.

Bleiker, M.E.H. & Van der Ploeg, H.M. (1999). Psychosocial factors in the etiology of breast cancer: Review of a popular link. *Patient Education & Counseling, 37*, 201–214.

Bleiker, E.M., van der Ploeg, H.M., Hendriks, J.H. & Ader, H.J. (1996). Personality factors and breast cancer development: a prospective longitudinal study. *Journal of the National Cancer Institute, 88*, 1478–1482.

Broers, S., Hengeveld, M.W., Kaptein, A.A., Le Cessie, S., Van de Loo, F. & De Vries, Th. (1998). Are pretransplant psychological variables related to survival after bone marrow transplantation? A prospective study of 123 consecutive patients. *Journal of Psychosomatic Research, 45*, 341–351.

Canada, A., Fawzy, N. & Fawzy, F. (2005). Personality and disease outcome in malignant melanoma. *Journal of Psychosomatic Research, 58*, 19–27.

Carmelli, D., Halpern, J., Swan, G.E., Dame, A., McElroy, M., Gelb, A.B. & Rosenman R.H. (1991). 27-year mortality in the Western collaborative group study: construction of risk groups by recursive partitioning. *Journal of Clinical Epidemiology, 44*, 1341–1351.

Cassileth, B.R., Lusk, E.J., Miller, D.S., Brown, L.L. & Miller, C. (1985). Psychosocial correlates of survival in advanced malignant disease? *New England Journal of Medicine, 312*, 1551–1555.

Cassileth, B.R., Walsh, W.P. & Lusk, E.J. (1988). Psychosocial correlates of cancer survival: a subsequent report 3 to 8 years after cancer diagnosis. *Journal of Clinical Oncology, 6*, 1753–1759.

Denollet, J. (1998). Personality and risk of cancer in men with coronary heart disease. *Psychological Medicine, 28*, 991–995.

Denollet, J., Sys, S.U., Stroobant, N., Rombouts, H., Gillebert, T.C. & Brutsaert, D.L. (1996). Personality as independent predictor of long-term mortality in patients with coronary heart disease. *Lancet, 347*, 417–421.

Eysenck, H.J. (1990). Type A behavior and coronary heart disease: The third stage. *Journal of Social Behavior and Personality, 5*, 25–44.

Faller, H., Lang, H. & Schilling, S. (1996). Causal 'cancer personality' attribution – an expression of maladaptive coping with illness? *Zeitschrift für Klinische Psychologie, Psychopathologie und Psychotherapie, 44*, 104–116.

Fox, B.H., Ragland, D.R., Brand, R.J. & Rosenman, R.H. (1987). Type A behaviour and cancer mortality. Theoretical considerations and preliminary data. *Annals of the New York Academy of Sciences, 496*, 620–627.

Friedman, M. & Rosenman, R.M. (1959). Association of a specific overt behavior pattern with increases in blood cholesterol, blood clotting time, incidence of arcus senilis and clinical coronary artery disease. *Journal of the American Medical Association, 169*, 1296.

Garssen, B. (2004). Psychological factors and cancer development: Evidence after 30 years of research. *Clinical Psychology Review, 24*, 315–338.

Greer, S., Morris, T. & Pettingale, K.W. (1979). Psychological response to breast cancer: effect on outcome. *Lancet, 13*, 758–787.

Grossarth-Maticek, R., Bastiaans, J. & Kanazir, D.T. (1985). Psychosocial factors as strong predictors of mortality from cancer, ischaemic heart disease and stroke: the Yugoslav prospective study. *Journal of Psychosomatic Research, 29*, 167–176.

Hansen, P.E., Floderus, B., Frederiksen, K. & Johansen, C. (2005). Personality traits, health behavior, and risk for cancer: a prospective study of Swedish twin court. *Cancer, 103*, 1082–1091.

Kukull, W.A., Koepsell, T.D., Inui, T.S., Borson, S., Okimoto, J.T., Raskind, M.A. & Gale, J.L. (1986). Depression and physical illness among elderly general medical clinic patients. *Journal of Affective Disorders, 10*, 153–162.

Lillberg, K., Verkasalo, P.K., Kaprio, J., Helenius, H. & Koskenvuo, M. (2002). Personality characteristics and the risk of breast cancer: a prospective cohort study. *International Journal of Cancer, 100*, 361–366.

Miller, T.Q., Smith, T.W., Turner, C.W., Guijaroo, M. L. & Hallet, A.J. (1996). A meta-analytic review of research on hostility and physical health. *Psychological Bulletin, 119*, 322–348.

Nakaya, N., Tsubono, Y., Hosokawa, T., Nishino, Y., Ohkubo, T., Hozawa, A., Shibuya, D., Fukudo, S., Fukao, A., Tsuji, I. & Hisamichi, S. (2003). Personality and the risk of cancer. *Journal of the National Cancer Institute, 95*, 799–805.

Nakaya, N., Tsubono, Y., Nishino, Y., Hosokawa, T., Fukudo, S., Shibuya, D., Akizuki, N., Yoshikawa, E., Kobayakawa, M., Fujimori, M., Saito-Nakaya, K., Uchitomi, Y. & Tsuji, I. (2005). Personality and cancer survival: the Miyagi cohort study. *British Journal of Cancer, 92*, 2089–2094.

Neuser, J. (1988). Personality and survival time after bone marrow transplantation. *Journal of Psychosomatic Research, 32*, 451–455.

Petticrew, M., Bell, R. & Hunter, H. (2002). Influence of psychological coping on survival and recurrence in people with cancer: systematic review. *British Medical Journal, 325*, 1066–1075.

Price, M.A., Tennant, C.C., Smith, R.C., Butow, P.N., Kennedy, S.J., Kossoff, M.B. & Dunn, S.M. (2001). The role of psychosocial factors in the development of breast carcinoma: Part I. The cancer prone personality. *Cancer, 91*, 679–685.

Ragland, D.R., Brand, R. J. & Fox, B.H. (1992). Type A/B behavior and cancer mortality: the confounding/mediating effect of covariates. *Psycho-oncology, 1*, 25–33.

Ratcliffe, M.A., Dawson, A.A. & Walker, L.G. (1995). Eysenck Personality Inventory L-Scores in patients with Hodgkin's Disease and Non-Hodgkin's Lymphoma. *Psycho-oncology, 4*, 39–45.

Reynolds, P., Huley, S., Torres, M., Jackson, J., Boyd, P. & Chen, V. W. (2000). Use of coping strategies and breast cancer survival: Results from the Black/White Cancer Survival Study. *American Journal of Epidemiology, 152*, 940–949.

Sanderman, R. & Ranchor, A.V. (1997). The predictor status of personality variables: Etiological significance and their role in the course of disease. *European Journal of Personality, 11*, 359–382.

Shapiro, I.R., Ross-Petersen, L., Saelan, H., Garde, K., Olsen, J.H. & Johansen, C. (2001). Extraversion and neuroticism and the associated risk of cancer: A Danish cohort study. *American Journal of Epidemiology, 153*, 757–63.

Schwarz, R. (1993). Psychosoziale Faktoren in der Karzinogenese: zur Problematik der sogenannten Krebspersonlichkeit. *Psychotherapy and Psychosomatic Medische Psychologie, 43*, 1–9.

Schulz, R., Bookwala, J., Knapp, J.E., Scheier, M. & Williamson, G.M. (1996). Pessimism, age, and cancer mortality. *Psychology and Aging, 11*, 304–309.

Segerstrom, S.C., Taylor, S.E., Kemeny, M.E. & Fahey, J.L. (1998). Optimism is associated with mood, coping, and immune change in response to stress. *Journal of Personality and Social Psychology, 74*, 1646–1655.

Temoshok, L. (1987). Personality, coping style, emotion and cancer: towards an integrative model. *Cancer Survival, 6*, 545–567.

Terracciano, A., McCrae, R.R., Brant, L.J. & Costa, P.T. (2005). Hierarchical Linear Modeling analyses of the NEO-PI-R scales in the Baltimore Longitudinal Study of Aging. *Psychology and Aging*, *20*, 493–506.

Van der Ploeg, H.M. (1991). What a wonderful world it would be: a reanalysis of some of the work of Grossarth-Maticek. *Psychological Inquiry*, *2*, 280–285.

Van Loon, A.J., Tijhuis, M., Surtees, P. & Ormel, J. (2001). Personality and coping: Their relationship with lifestyle risk factors for cancer. *Personality & Individual Differences*, *31*, 541–553.

Watson, M., Haviland, J.S., Greer, S., Davidson, J. & Bliss, J.M. (1999). Influence of psychological response on survival in breast cancer: a population-based cohort study. *Lancet*, *354*, 1331–1336.

Watson, M., Homewood, J., Haviland, J. & Bliss, J.M. (2005). Influence of psychological response on breast cancer survival: 10-year follow-up of a population-based cohort. *European Journal of Cancer*, *41*, 1710–1714.

Watson, M. & Davidson-Homewood, J. (2003). The review by Petticrew et al. is flawed. *British Medical Journal*, *326*, 598.

CHAPTER 3

Temperament and Children's Unintentional Injuries

David C. Schwebel
University of Alabama at Birmingham, USA
and
Benjamin K. Barton
University of Guelph, Canada

INTRODUCTION

Unintentional injury is the leading cause of pediatric mortality among children in the United States and the developed world, killing more children than the next 10 leading causes of death combined (National Safety Council, 2004). Among children in middle childhood (ages 5–14), the annual mortality rate from unintentional injury is 6.9 individuals per 100,000 in the population, about 5,100 children (National Safety Council, 2004). The morbidity rate is much higher, of course, with over 15 million American children (about 3 of every 10 children) requiring professional medical attention annually following an injury (Miller, Romano & Spicer, 2000). In addition to the tremendous number of injuries and loss of life, long-term psychosocial and economic consequences are tremendous. Epidemiological data indicate roughly 150,000 children and adolescents are permanently disabled from injuries annually—most of them needing lifelong medical care for their injuries (Miller et al., 2000). Others estimate a loss of 14 million school days annually (National Safety Council, 1991) and a societal financial cost of over 80 billion US dollars annually (Miller et al., 2000). Due to the scope of unintentional injuries as a threat to children's health, a sense of urgency to identify risk factors for child injury has emerged among public health professionals and policymakers (e.g., National Center for Injury Prevention and Control, 2002; Sleet & Bryn, 2003).

Over the previous several decades, behavioral scientists have identified a wide range of intrapersonal and interpersonal factors that increase children's risk of unintentional injury (see Matheny, 1987; Wazana, 1997, for reviews). Among the factors that consistently predict children's risk for unintentional injury is their behavioral style, or temperament. Children who behave in more active, impulsive, undercontrolled, and aggressive ways tend to experience more unintentional injuries than those who behave in more controlled, cautious, and passive ways. This chapter examines that trend. We have two primary objectives.

Handbook of Personality and Health. Edited by Margarete E. Vollrath. © 2006 John Wiley & Sons, Ltd.

First, the literature on links between children's temperament and unintentional injury risk is reviewed. Second, significant challenges facing the field are offered and discussed.

Before proceeding, we define the critical constructs of interest. We characterize temperament as a biologically-based but environmentally-influenced set of traits that influence an individual's reactivity to the external environment as well as his or her internal regulation (e.g., Rothbart & Bates, 1998; Wachs & Kohnstamm, 2001). Because temperament is driven largely by genetic and biological predispositions, it is moderately stable both cross-situationally and cross-temporally, including throughout development, but can be altered through environmental modification and influences (Rothbart & Bates, 1998).

We characterize unintentional injury as any damage to bodily tissues incurred through non-intentional (that is, not abusive or purposefully self-inflicted) channels. We admit the boundary between unintentional and intentional injury is fuzzy, but refer the interested reader to other sources for discussion of the matter (e.g., Peterson & Brown, 1994).

A REVIEW OF THE LITERATURE: WHAT DO WE KNOW?

Behavioral scientists have long recognized links between children's behavior and risk for injury. Psychoanalytic thinkers were among the first to discuss such links in the published literature, identifying an 'accident-prone' personality trait in their psychoanalysis patients (Dunbar, Wolfe & Rioch, 1939). Later, child clinicians identified aggression and disinhibition in the doll play of 'accident-prone' children and interpreted it as an indication that such children somehow differed from others (Krall, 1953). Contemporary research on the topic can arguably be traced to the groundbreaking article by Manheimer and Mellinger (1967). In that study, over 600 children and adolescents ages 4–18 were divided into high, medium, and low injury liability groups, as coded through review of insurance and medical records. A wide range of links between individual differences and injury risk were found. Among the findings was a link between behavioral control and injury liability: Children in the low injury liability group tended to have greater behavioral control than those in the high injury group.

Since the landmark study by Manheimer and Mellinger, researchers have generally adopted a two-pronged approach to understanding links between children's temperament and risk for injury: (a) epidemiologists have addressed the question using large samples and questionnaire methods, and (b) developmental and child clinical psychologists have examined links using smaller-scale laboratory studies with somewhat more precise measures of temperament. Below, each of those two literatures is reviewed, followed by brief discussion of four other related literatures: (a) studies linking psychopathology to risk of injury, (b) research studying cognitive processes related to expression of temperament and their role in injury risk, (c) the personality literature examining sensation-seeking and risk-taking personality and its role in risk for injury, and (d) the role of gender in the link between temperament and injury risk. We conclude with a discussion of challenges and issues remaining in the field.

Epidemiological Findings

At least four large-scale longitudinal epidemiological studies have considered temperament or temperament-like measures and their relations to unintentional injuries. Chronologically, the first influential study was conducted by Langley and colleagues in the late 1970s and early 1980s in New Zealand. Nine hundred and fifty-four children were assessed at ages 3, 5, and 7 (Langley et al., 1983). Data on problem behaviors were collected via parent- and teacher-reports using the Rutter Child Behavior Questionnaire and through behavioral observations during laboratory assessments. The number of injuries requiring professional medical attention was reported biannually by parents. Higher ratings of motor activity and aggression were associated with greater numbers of injuries.

Bijur and her colleagues assessed links between behavioral characteristics and unintentional injuries among a large sample of youth in the United Kingdom. In the initial wave of data collection, aggression and overactivity were measured by parent report in a sample of almost 12,000 five-year-olds, and both were significantly correlated to mother-reported injury history (Bijur, Stewart-Brown & Butler, 1986). Follow-up papers published a few years later examined the sample as it developed from age 5 to age 10. Over 10,000 children were tested at age 5 using the parent-report Rutter Child Behavior Questionnaire; aggressive behavior at age 5 was associated with greater frequency of injury at age 10 (Bijur, Golding & Haslum, 1988; Bijur, Golding, Haslum & Kurzon, 1988).

Simultaneous to the Bijur study, Nyman studied relations between temperament and injury risk among a sample of 1,855 Finnish infants (Nyman, 1987). Temperament was assessed through parent report of the 6- through 8-month-old infants' typical behaviors during everyday situations such as sleeping, playing, and feeding. Infants were then followed for 5 years to track hospitalizations due to injury or illness. Of the initial sample of 1,855, thirty-five were hospitalized due to unintentional injury and 235 children were hospitalized due to illness. Children hospitalized due to injury were more likely to be characterized as having a negative mood, having more intense responses to stimuli, being more active and more persistent, and reacting more negatively to new situations than other children in the sample. When compared only to children hospitalized due to illness, fewer differences emerged, but children hospitalized due to injury did have higher scores on temperament measures of activity, persistence, and negative reactions to new situations.

The most recent large epidemiological study linking behavioral style with temperament was also conducted in Finland. Pulkkinen (1995) reported findings from a sample of 289 individuals followed from age 8 until age 27. Data on behavioral and personality characteristics were obtained through peer and teacher reports at ages 8 and 14. History of frequency and types of injuries were measured with interviews at age 27. Males rated higher on measures of aggression and disobedience, and lower on self-control, at ages 8 and 14, tended to have a greater reported history and severity of injuries by adulthood. Results for females were similar, but were somewhat less consistent and generally had lower effect sizes.

Psychological Findings

Others have approached the question of links between temperament and unintentional injury from a psychological rather than an epidemiological perspective. These studies, conducted mostly in North America, typically use smaller samples but more behaviorally-focused methodology. In particular, the methodology used to assess temperament often includes laboratory-based behavioral assessments as well as or in place of parent-report measures. Some studies utilized longitudinal designs.

Although a few published studies report no relation between psychological measures of temperament and children's injury history (e.g., Matheny, 1986; Mayes, Roberts, Boles & Brown, 2005; Morrongiello, Ondejko & Littlejohn, 2004; Schwebel & Brezausek, 2004), most find modest but statistically significant findings with small to medium effect sizes. Below, we review the more influential of those studies.

Using data from the Louisville Twin Study, Adam Matheny conducted the first major studies that assessed temperament through structured observational and behavioral measures and then correlated those measurements to children's injury histories (Matheny, 1986, 1987). Matheny's first report included about 100 toddler-aged twins. 'Tractable' temperament was assessed through an aggregate of ratings of videotaped laboratory batteries conducted when children were ages 12, 18, 24, and 30 months; aspects of the ratings examined children's emotional tone, attentiveness, activity, social orientation, and resistance to restraint. Injuries were assessed through semi-annual mother report of all injuries the toddlers experienced, whether or not they were medically attended. Tractable toddlers had fewer injuries (Matheny, 1986).

In Matheny's second report, a cohort of children ages 6–9 was included along with the cohort of younger children (Matheny, 1987). Temperament was assessed via mother-report. Results from the younger cohort suggested children with low levels of rhythmicity, adaptability, mood, and persistence were more susceptible to injury. In the older cohort, activity, rhythmicity, adaptability, and distractibility were related to injury risk.

Matheny's papers laid the groundwork for a burgeoning of research on the topic of temperament and unintentional injury risk in the late 1990s and early 2000s. This body of research extends beyond simple correlations between temperament and unintentional injury history to instead consider mechanisms through which temperament—and the behavior patterns associated with temperament—might influence children's risk for injury. Plumert and Schwebel (1997), for example, considered not just how temperament related to children's injury histories but also how temperament was related to a hypothesized mechanism for unintentional injury occurrence: children's tendency to overestimate their ability to complete basic physical tasks such as reaching and stepping. Temperament was assessed via two parent-report measures, the Child Behavior Questionnaire (CBQ; Rothbart, Ahadi & Hershey, 1994) and the Matthews Youth Test for Health (Matthews & Angulo, 1980). Relevant subscales were aggregated from each measure into a single measure of temperamental Surgency/Undercontrol. High scores on the aggregated temperament measure were related to a tendency to overestimate physical abilities among the 6-year-olds in the study and to reduced latency to make judgments among the 8-year-olds. Temperament was also related to severity of injuries reported in the child's history among 8-year-olds.

A second study by Schwebel and Plumert (1999) extended those findings using a longitudinal design. In that report, 59 children were followed from age 32 months until age 6. Temperament was assessed at 32 and 46 months using both the parent-report CBQ and a structured behavioral battery. The age 6 battery included three measures: temperament via parent-report, lifetime history of injuries requiring professional medical attention by parent report, and children's estimation of physical abilities. Results varied somewhat across measurement times, but overall suggested that extraverted and undercontrolled children had more injuries in their history. Children scoring high on extraversion and undercontrol also showed different patterns in their estimation of physical abilities. Compared to less extraverted and more controlled children, extraverted, undercontrolled children tended to overestimate their physical abilities more often – that is, they claimed they could complete physical tasks that were actually beyond their ability – and they tended not to underestimate their physical abilities – that is, they accurately perceived when tasks were within their physical abilities.

Subsequent work by Schwebel and his colleagues confirmed earlier findings. In one paper, temperament was related not just to children's judgment of abilities, but also to the influence of supervision on those judgments (Schwebel & Bounds, 2003). Temperamentally impulsive and undercontrolled children were more cautious in their judgments of ability when supervised by a parent; temperamentally nonimpulsive and controlled children were not affected much by parental supervision. A second report used data from a sample of over 1,200 children in the National Institute of Child Health and Human Development (NICHD) Study of Early Child Care and found statistically significant correlations between children's activity level and children's positive mood, both assessed through a behavioral battery when children were 6 months old, and injuries requiring professional medical treatment between the ages of 6 and 60 months (Schwebel, Brezausek & Belsky, 2006). In a third study, a sample of 57 six-year-olds was recruited for a detailed examination of the links between temperament and unintentional injury risk (Schwebel, 2004a). Temperament was assessed through three techniques: parent-report using the CBQ, child-report using a modified version of the CBQ, and a structured behavioral battery. Parent-reported effortful control emerged as the best correlate to children's lifetime history of injuries requiring professional medical treatment.

Recent work also considered relations between temperament and pediatric injury risk in one specific context, pedestrian settings (Barton & Schwebel, 2006b). Data were gathered from a sample of 122 children ages 6, 8, and 10. Temperamental impulsivity and inhibitory control were measured with parent reports, child reports, and a structured behavioral battery. Pedestrian injury risk behaviors were assessed through vignettes and tabletop models of street crossing. Results revealed children with less behavioral control engaged in riskier street crossing behaviors on both pedestrian tasks. For example, children with low behavioral control more often chose to cross outside a crosswalk, instead crossing model streets diagonally across intersections.

Other laboratories report results that largely match those described by Schwebel and his colleagues. Bagley (1992) reported correlational links between aggression and overactivity scores on the Rutter Temperament scale and pedestrian injury history. Boles and colleagues (Boles, Roberts, Brown & Mayes, 2005) found links between temperamental activity level and risky behavior in a simulated home environment. In a large recent study, Vollrath and her colleagues (Vollrath, Landolt & Ribi, 2003) asked mothers of over 300 Swiss children to complete the Hierarchical Personality Inventory for Children (HiPIC; Mervielde & De Fruyt, 1999), a measure that assesses the Big Five personality traits in children. About 40 % of the sample had recently been treated for an unintentional injury that led to hospitalization; the remainder of the sample had not been injured. Case vs. control effects emerged for several personality traits. Most prominently, from the broad personality factor of extraversion, cases scored higher on measures of energy and optimism, and lower on shyness. From the conscientiousness factor, cases scored lower than controls on measures of concentration and achievement striving.

RELATED LITERATURES: WHAT DO THEY CONTRIBUTE?

Along with research designed specifically to examine links between temperament and pediatric unintentional injury, a number of related literatures contribute to our thinking about links between temperament and child injury. Below, we briefly review four such literatures: links between psychopathology and injury, how cognitive deficits in attention and visual tracking might relate to injury risk, links between risk-taking/sensation-seeking personality and injury, and how gender might interact with temperament to create risk for injury.

Psychopathology and Injury Risk

Clinicians continue to debate whether psychopathological traits such as depression should be viewed on a continuum, with psychopathological disorders falling at the extreme end of a continuum that includes normality, or whether psychopathological disorders should instead be considered as distinct and separate categories from mental health (e.g., Flett, Vredenburg & Krames, 1997; Santor & Coyne, 2001). Those who endorse the continuum hypothesis might argue, for example, that a child with ADHD should be viewed not as an individual with a cluster of pathological behavior patterns but instead as an individual whose impulsive, hyperactive, and attentive patterns fall at one end of a continuum in temperament-driven behavioral style. The more conservative perspective might suggest psychopathology is distinct from measures of behavioral style such as temperament, but that the literature examining links between psychopathology and injury still educates the literature on links between temperament and injury because there is overlap in their inquiries and findings.

Either way, the rapidly-growing literature on the links between psychopathology and child injury (e.g., Brehaut, Miller, Raina & McGrail, 2003; Byrne, Bawden, Beattie & DeWolfe, 2003; Rowe, Maughan & Goodman, 2004; Schwebel, Speltz, Jones & Bardina, 2002) is relevant to a discussion of how temperament might influence children's risk for unintentional injury. Two disorders in particular are implicated as correlates to increased unintentional injury risk: Oppositional Defiant Disorder (ODD), which is hallmarked by negativistic, hostile, and defiant behavior patterns, and Attention-Deficit/Hyperactivity Disorder (ADHD), which is hallmarked by impulsive, inattentive, and hyperactive behavior patterns.

Links between ODD and injury are the more firmly established (e.g., Davidson, 1987; Davidson, Hughes & O'Connor, 1988; Schwebel et al., 2002). It has been proposed that this link may be driven, at least in part, by the fact that children with ODD are likely to be defiant toward following safety rules and directions from supervisors when danger is present (Schwebel, Hodgens & Sterling, in press).

Links between ADHD and injury are inconsistent, with some studies finding statistically significant correlations (Brehaut et al., 2003; DiScala, Lescohier, Barthel & Li, 1998) and others reporting either mixed results (Rowe et al., 2004; Schwebel et al., 2002) or no relation at all (Byrne et al., 2003; Davidson, Taylor, Sandberg & Thorley, 1992). Those studies that do find links between ADHD and injury suggest it is a combination of hyperactive, impulsive, and inattentive patterns of behavior that lead children with ADHD to experience injuries more often. Those who do not find links suggest children with ADHD, although prone to act quickly and without attention or thought because of their behavior patterns, are able to restrain themselves either through external instruction or perhaps through internal regulation, when serious danger emerges.

The relation between behavior disorders and unintentional injury risk remains poorly understood and further inquiries are needed. Even the presence or absence of links remains contentious in the literature; mechanisms for such links remain very poorly understood.

Cognitive Functioning and Injury Risk

Some aspects of cognitive functioning are closely tied to temperament. Children who score poorly on cognitive tasks assessing visual tracking and attention, for example, are often described as temperamentally impulsive or inattentive. Below, we consider two aspects of cognitive functioning as predictors of unintentional injury risk, cognitive control and selective attention skills.

Studies investigating cognitive control in relation to children's risk for unintentional injury generally focus on pedestrian safety. Using a case-control design, for example, Pless and colleagues compared children ages 5–15 involved in pedestrian injuries to a set of matched controls (Pless, Taylor & Arsenault, 1995). Participants completed a delayed response task in which they were given instructions and then asked to wait several seconds before responding. Children previously injured as pedestrians were less able than non-injured matched controls to inhibit their behavior. A second study used a correlational design with a sample of children ages 3–6 (Briem & Bengtsson, 2000). Cognitive functioning was assessed with the NEPSY neuropsychological battery, which includes tests of activity, distraction, and impulse control. Pedestrian behaviors were assessed through a laboratory model of a pedestrian environment and in real street crossings with the child accompanied by a researcher. Children with greater impulse control on the neuropsychological tasks engaged in safer pedestrian behaviors.

A second body of research considers children's selective attention skills in relation to risky pedestrian behaviors (e.g., Foot, Tolmie, Thomson, McLaren & Whelan, 1999; Whitebread & Nielson, 1999). These studies are largely concerned with children's ability to attend to relevant stimuli and filter out irrelevant stimuli. For example, a young child may consider the mere presence of a vehicle to indicate danger, without considering the vehicle's speed, its distance from the crossing, or the traffic density (Connelly et al., 1998). An impulsive or undercontrolled temperament style may interact with poor selective attention skills to hinder a child's ability to carefully attend to relevant safety cues in pedestrian settings.

Risk-taking, Sensation-seeking, and Injury Risk

There is a great amount of overlap between temperament and personality; in fact, one pair of prominent personality researchers labeled the constructs 'essentially isomorphic' (Costa & McCrae, 2001: p. 2). Attempting to separate personality traits from temperament traits, particularly in children, is challenging. However, two highly overlapping individual difference constructs often described as personality traits rather than as temperament – sensation-seeking and risk-taking – are implicated as risk factors for children's unintentional injury (e.g., Bijttebier, Vertommen & Florentie, 2003; Hoffrage, Weber, Herwig & Chase, 2003; Morrongiello, Ondejko & Littlejohn, 2004) and merit mention.

Studies reporting development and validation of the Injury Behavior Checklist (IBC) offered early evidence that risk taking behaviors were linked to risk for injury. In one, the predictive ability of the IBC was tested in a sample of 254 children ages 2–5 (Speltz, Gonzales, Sulzbacher & Quan, 1990). Parents reported on children's recent injuries and the IBC significantly and strongly predicted recent injury history. In a second study (Potts,

Martinez & Dedmon, 1995), relations between risk taking, sensation-seeking, and injury history were examined in a sample of 83 children age 6–9. Sensation seeking was measured using the self-report Zuckerman Sensation Seeking Scale (Zuckerman, Eysenck & Eysenck, 1978) and risk taking through peer-, teacher-, and self-ratings. Results indicated that parent-reported recent injury history was related to measures of risk taking but not sensation-seeking.

More recently, Morrongiello and her colleagues recruited a sample of 62 children age 2–2.5 years and their parents to assess risk taking, sensation seeking, and in-home injury history (Morrongiello et al., 2004). Among the measures included were the Toddler Temperament Scale (Fullard, McDevitt & Carey, 1984), a parent-report measure that categorizes toddlers as easy, difficult, slow to warm up, or intermediate; the Toddler Sensation Seeking Scale, a measure developed for the study based on existing instruments to assess boredom susceptibility, intensity of behavior, and thrill seeking; the IBC; and an injury history questionnaire concerning frequency of various moderate and severe injuries over the past 6 months. Mothers also completed an injury diary over the course of 12 weeks to report all injuries occurring at home that involved damage to bodily tissue that lasted longer than 30 minutes. Results suggested that risk taking and sensation-seeking each independently predicted risk for children's in-home injuries.

One final recent study examined the relation between risk-taking personality and dangerous street crossing decisions among 44 five- and six-year-old children (Hoffrage et al., 2003). Risk-takers were identified through a child-oriented gambling game in which increasing risk garnished more reward, but greater risk of losing all the rewards. Street crossing behavior was assessed in two ways: (a) through a task that required children to stand beside a real road and indicate when they believed it safe to cross by taking two steps toward the curb and (b) via a computer game in which children pushed a button to send a figure across a simulated street. Children classified as risk-takers in the gambling game engaged in riskier pedestrian crossing behaviors on both tasks.

Gender, Temperament, and Injury Risk

Temperament differs somewhat across the genders; boys tend to be more active and under-controlled while girls tend to be more cautious and controlled (Rothbart & Bates, 1998). The genders also differ in injury risk, with boys experiencing more injuries than girls (National Safety Council, 2004).

Given these facts, it is worth positing whether the links between temperament and injury risk might vary across the genders. Evidence on the topic is mixed. At least three studies report stronger links between temperament and injury risk among boys than among girls (Bijur, Golding, Haslum & Kurzon, 1988; Manheimer & Mellinger, 1967; Pulkkinen, 1995); most other studies fail to report data specifically addressing the topic, but our own analyses suggest there are not strong differences in correlations between temperament and unintentional injury across the genders (Schwebel, unpublished data). One explanation for the stronger correlations among boys may be that the findings are an artifact of reduced variance in injury and temperament measures for girls rather than actual differences. Another explanation is that temperament may play a stronger role in boys' behaviors, whereas girls are influenced more by environmental, cognitive, or social risks for injury. Future research is needed.

SO WHICH TEMPERAMENT TRAITS REALLY MATTER? AND WHY?

Identification of a finite number of temperamental traits that predict children's risk for unintentional injury is a challenging pursuit. Partly this is due to semantics. Different researchers label the same temperamental constructs with different descriptors, creating a situation whereby two laboratories are studying the same construct but labeling it differently. The opposite problem also arises: a single label, such as 'impulsivity', is used by different researchers to signify different constructs. To cope with both problems, we have chosen to use the construct labels coined by Mary Rothbart and her colleagues (e.g., Rothbart et al., 1994; Rothbart, Ahadi, Hershey & Fisher, 2001). These labels have emerged as among the most-accepted and often-used terms in the temperament literature over the past decade.

A second challenge to identifying just a few temperament traits linked to injury risk is the fact that researchers have approached the problem from varying disciplinary and methodological perspectives. Part of the richness of the child injury field is the fact that epidemiologists, pediatricians, nurses, educators, and psychologists, among others, actively conduct research on the topic. But this richness also creates barriers. Our literature review seeks to tie together the epidemiological, medical, and psychological literatures.

The Three Key Traits: Inhibitory Control, Impulsivity, and Activity Level

With semantic and methodological barriers overcome, we offer three temperamental traits that we consider the strongest and most consistently reported predictors of pediatric unintentional injury risk: inhibitory control, impulsivity, and activity level. We caution that these are not necessarily the only temperament traits that contribute to children's injury risk, nor are they definitely proven as causal risk factors, but we feel the existing literature supports them as the strongest and most often-replicated correlates to pediatric unintentional injury.

Inhibitory Control

Inhibitory control is conceptualized as the child's ability to inhibit impulses when faced with novel or desirable stimuli, or when instructed to do so by a superior. It encompasses planning and processing, and is driven through internal regulation rather than external motivation (e.g., Cole, Martin & Dennis, 2004; Eisenberg & Spinrad, 2004; Rothbart et al., 1994, 2001). Although tendencies toward good or poor control are relatively stable throughout the lifespan (Rothbart & Bates, 1998), the ability to control one's impulses also develops somewhat through childhood and into adulthood with increasing cognitive and intellectual maturity (Eisenberg & Spinrad, 2004). Across the literature, inhibitory control appears to be among the most consistent and strongest temperamental predictors of injury (Matheny, 1986; Schwebel, 2004a; Schwebel & Plumert, 1999).

Children with poor inhibitory control are likely to increase their risk for unintentional injury because they fail to restrain themselves when told an activity might be dangerous. They also fail to plan ways to avoid danger. For example, an uninhibited toddler will touch a hot pan even when told not to. An uninhibited 7-year-old will run across the street despite knowing he should look both ways. An uninhibited 17-year-old will drink four beers without planning for a safe way to drive home, and then will complete the drive despite the fact that she knows it is dangerous. This conceptualization of inhibitory control overlaps somewhat with descriptions of oppositionality and antisocial behavior in clinical psychology. It also overlaps with some conceptualizations of aggression and disobedience.

Impulsivity

Impulsivity is defined as the speed of a child's initiation of a stimulus and is another trait commonly reported as linked to risk or history of unintentional injury (e.g., Schwebel, 2004a; Vollrath et al., 2003). Impulsivity is externally driven; that is, it reflects how the child responds to external stimulation rather than how the child regulates his or her own responses internally (e.g., Eisenberg & Spinrad, 2004; Rothbart et al., 1994, 2001). Impulsive children are likely to increase their risk for unintentional injury because they respond quickly and without thought to potentially dangerous situations. When the impulsive 12-year-old accidentally throws his ball into the street, he will run to get it without inspecting the street for traffic. When the impulsive 8-year-old discovers a cigarette lighter, she will play with it before considering the dangers involved. When an impulsive 3-year-old finds a cleaning fluid bottle, he will drink it. In each of these cases, a less impulsive child might display different temperamental tendencies that would protect him or her from injury.

Some theorists argue that impulsivity and inhibitory control are the same construct. The two traits are related both conceptually and quantitatively, but they also have important differences that make them orthogonal constructs. From a quantitative viewpoint, the two traits correlate modestly but fall into different factors in analyses of parent-report temperament (Ahadi, Rothbart & Ye, 1993; Rothbart et al., 2001). From a theoretical viewpoint, one key to distinguishing impulsivity from inhibitory control is an evaluation of whether the behavior is internally motivated or externally driven. Inhibitory control is viewed to be driven from within; in some circles, it is considered one aspect of emotion regulation (Cole et al., 2004; Eisenberg & Spinrad, 2004). A child with good inhibitory control can control his or her emotions effectively, and under varying contextual situations, including potentially dangerous ones. Impulsivity is viewed instead to be driven externally, by outside stimuli such as social interactions and environmental changes (Eisenberg & Spinrad, 2004). A child with low impulsivity is able to respond appropriately and safely to a variety of external stimuli, including potentially dangerous ones.

Neurobiologically, impulsivity is likely driven by the Behavioral Activation System (BAS) proposed by Jeffrey Gray (1975, 1982, 1987). The BAS, which is activated in response to reward or active avoidance of punishment, elicits behaviors including motoric activity toward desirable stimuli and sensation-seeking actions. Inhibitory control, contrarily, is likely driven by Gray's Behavioral Inhibition System (BIS; Gray, 1975, 1982, 1987), which affects the sensitivity with which an individual responds to stimuli. Activation of the BIS system results in internal regulation and passive avoidance of external stimuli rather than external activity or active avoidance.

Activity Level

A third trait consistently linked to risk for unintentional injury is activity level (e.g., Bijur et al., 1986; Langley et al., 1983; Nyman, 1987; Schwebel et al., in press). Conceptualized as the rate and amount of gross motor activity, children who are restless and hyperactive and who move quickly will score high on scales that assess this construct. Many researchers linking activity with injury risk study young children, suggesting that this may be a more significant risk factor for injury in early to middle childhood than it is during late childhood or adolescence.

Putting the Three Traits Together: Some Proposed Models of the Mechanisms at Work

In most cases, individual pediatric injury events are the result of an unfortunate confluence of child behaviors, adult behaviors, and environmental factors. Within each domain, multiple factors contribute to injury risk. Thus, temperament is just one of many, many factors that contribute to child injury risk. Many unintentional injuries might have occurred no matter what the child's temperament – and, of course, non-impulsive, inhibited, and inactive children are not immune from injury. The statistical strength of temperament as a predictor of unintentional injury risk is small, and effect sizes in most published studies typically fall in the small to medium range (Cohen, 1988).

With this caveat in mind, what role might the three temperamental traits identified – inhibitory control, impulsivity, and activity level – play in children's behavior to influence their risk for unintentional injury? How might temperament create child-environment inter-actions that ultimately increase or decrease risk for unintentional injury (Lerner, Theokas & Jelicic, 2005; Scarr & McCartney, 1983; Wachs & Kohnstamm, 2001)? Although almost all existing literature relies on correlational designs and therefore does not permit inference of causality, temperament – and the behaviors associated with particular temperamental styles – likely causally influences child injury risk in a multitude of ways (Peterson, Brown, Bartelstone & Kern, 1996; Peterson, Farmer, & Mori, 1987; Manheimer & Mellinger, 1967).

Two decades ago, Lizette Peterson coined the term *process analysis* (Peterson et al., 1987, 1996) to refer to a behavioral analysis of the antecedents and consequences of individual injury events. In particular, she was interested in considering the process through which behaviors and decisions precede an injury event, how those behaviors and decisions interact with the environment to influence injury risk in particular situations, and what factors following an injury influence its likelihood of re-occurring. In other words, through a careful analytic perspective, Peterson argued, researchers can parse out the decisions, behaviors, and environmental factors that influence whether an unintentional injury occurs or is averted.

Behavioral patterns related to the expression of temperament are undeniably involved in a process analysis evaluation of injuries (Scarr & McCartney, 1983). Temperament theorists have long considered such theoretical issues, as evidenced by the classic goodness-of-fit paradigm described by Thomas and Chess (1977) and, more recently, by the notion of temperament by environment interactions that occur within particular contextual environments (Wachs & Kohnstamm, 2001). The principle is rather simple: the way a child behaves, as motivated by temperament, interacts with environmental context to create decisions, actions, and behaviors. When the child's temperament includes high impulsivity and the contextual environment includes risk factors such as poor supervision, injuries are more likely to occur. When the child's temperament includes high inhibitory control and the contextual environment includes influences such as close adult supervision, injuries are less likely.

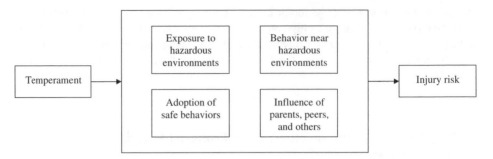

Figure 3.1   How temperament might interact with environmental influences to increase risk for child unintentional injury

Below, we outline four processes through which temperament might interact with the environment to create a situation ripe for an injury event (see also Figure 3.1).

1. *Temperamental behavior patterns increase children's exposure to hazardous environments.* Due to the expression of temperament, a child with temperamental traits such as high activity will encounter more varied environments than a temperamentally inactive peer. By chance, some portion of environments includes danger – the more temperamentally active a child is, the more likely he or she might eventually encounter a dangerous environment.
2. *Temperamental behavior patterns influence how children behave once they encounter a hazardous environment.* When faced with a potential hazard, a wide range of variables influences how a particular child might behave. There is some evidence that children with varying temperamental patterns have similar knowledge about injury risk (Mori & Peterson, 1995), but knowledge does not necessarily translate to behavior when faced with a hazard (Barton & Schwebel, 2006a; Schwebel & Plumert, 1999). Temperamentally impulsive and undercontrolled children apparently take more risks around hazards than do temperamentally non-impulsive and controlled children (e.g., Barton & Schwebel, 2006a; Schwebel & Plumert, 1999).
3. *Temperamental behavior patterns influence children's adoption of safe behaviors.* The expression of temperament affects not just behavior when faced with hazards, but also preventative behavior before exposure to hazards. Thuen (1994) found adolescents' use of bicycle helmets is non-random. Among a sample of Norwegian teens, those scoring higher in sensation-seeking were less likely to engage in safety behaviors such as wearing a bicycle helmet or wearing reflectors on clothing when outside after dark than those lower in sensation-seeking.
4. *Temperamental behavior patterns influence how others react when children are exposed to potential hazards.* Each of the above three aspects of the injury process considers how the expression of temperament might influence intrapsychic behaviors and decisions – that is, how temperament affects the child's own behaviors and decisions. The expression of temperament also affects how others interact with the target child. Parents and teachers are likely to supervise children differently based on children's temperament-driven behavior patterns, for example. A skilled parent of an impulsive and undercontrolled child will likely monitor that child's behavior more carefully than a skilled parent of a cautious and controlled youngster (Morrongiello & Dawber, 2000; Schwebel & Bounds,

2003). Further, impulsive children appear to be more responsive to adult supervision than less impulsive children: in our laboratory, we have found that impulsive children become much more cautious when monitored by parents whereas the behavior of non-impulsive children does not change much when supervised (Schwebel & Barton, 2005; Schwebel & Bounds, 2003).

Together, therefore, we hypothesize that the temperamental traits of inhibitory control, impulsivity, and activity level interact with children's environments to influence risk for pediatric unintentional injury through several different mechanisms. Understanding those mechanisms is an important endeavor for researchers in the field, but it represents only part of the battle.

A second significant hurdle concerning the role of temperament in children's risk for unintentional injury is understanding how temperamental traits work together to create risk. That is, do temperamental traits predict injury additively, with each contributing independently to risk for injury? Or do temperamental traits predict injury multiplicatively, with children having multiple risk factors suffering far greater risk than a child with just one temperamental trait of interest? Figure 3.2 illustrates the potential impact of additive versus multiplicative influences. As shown in Part 1 of the figure, a child with theoretical temperament contributions of very low activity level (level = 1), low control (reversed, level = 2), and high impulsivity (level = 5) will have a theoretical risk level of 8 if the three temperament traits are added together $(1 + 2 + 5 = 8)$. If a multiplicative model is instead invoked, the child's risk will be just a bit higher $(1 \times 2 \times 5 = 10)$.

The situation changes dramatically in Part 2 of Figure 3.2, which illustrates a child who also scores high on impulsivity (level = 5) and low in inhibitory control (reversed, level = 2), but who also has a high score on activity level (level = 5). In this case, the additive effect

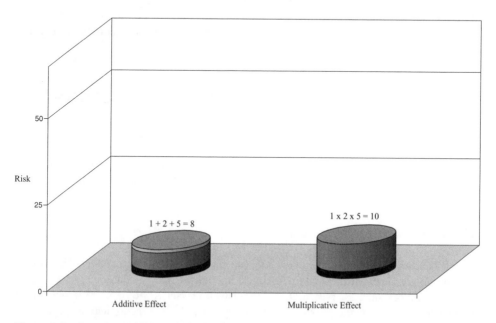

Figure 3.2 Part 1. Additive vs. Multiplicative Effect, where Activity Level = 1, Inhibitory Control = 2, and Impulsivity = 5.

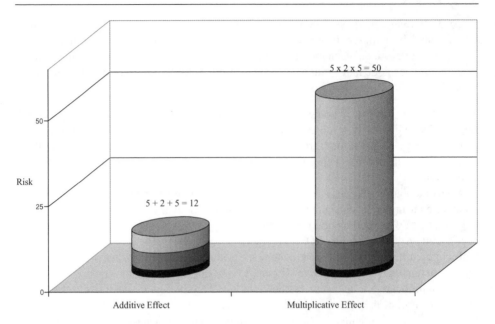

Figure 3.2 Part 2. Additive vs. Multiplicative Effect, where Activity Level = 5, Inhibitory Control = 2, and Impulsivity = 5.

equals a theoretical risk of 12 (5 + 2 + 5) but the multiplicative effect is much higher, at 50 (5 × 2 × 5). The multiplicative effect would be even more dramatic in the case of a child scoring high on all three risk factors (e.g., scores of 5 on all three traits, 5 × 5 × 5 = 125). We are unaware of any empirical work examining the additive vs. multiplicative issue in regards to how temperament might influence children's risk for unintentional injury, but view it as a research priority for the field.

CONCLUDING ISSUES: MEASUREMENT AND TRANSLATION

Measurement Issues

Both temperament and unintentional injury are complex constructs to assess. Below, we consider measurement issues for each construct as it pertains to research in the area.

Measurement of Temperament

One obstacle to measuring temperament is proper identification of the construct of interest. A large portion of the existing literature linking temperament and unintentional injury utilizes vague descriptors such as 'risk-taking', 'impulsive', or 'active' to describe temperament without specifying how the constructs are conceptualized, what theoretical underpinnings they might possess, or what a child with those sets of behavior patterns might look like. Frequently, temperamental constructs are viewed as synonymous with personality traits or psychopathological behavior patterns.

A second obstacle to measurement of a temperamental construct is determining what techniques that construct might be measured through. Agreement between independent reporters of children's temperament is typically modest, as is agreement between structured or unstructured behavioral batteries and reports from parents, teachers, or the children themselves (Rothbart & Bates, 1998). The most parsimonious solution to this problem, rarely utilized in the literature, is to measure the construct of interest through multiple techniques and over multiple time points, and then to aggregate multiple assessments to obtain the most valid assessment possible of the construct (Rothbart & Bates, 1998).

A third measurement obstacle is reporting bias. When parents are asked to complete a personality inventory as part of an assessment of their child's injury risk, the assessment of the child's behavior patterns is likely to be influenced by the parent's knowledge of the research objectives, among other factors (Rothbart & Bates, 1998). Longitudinal designs that do not mention injury as a primary research objective at the outset are desirable but rare (Matheny, 1986, 1987; Schwebel, Brezausek, Ramey & Ramey, 2004; Schwebel & Plumert, 1999); retrospective or concurrent reports are more common but less precise.

Measurement of Unintentional Injury

One challenge to measuring unintentional injury is identification of a reliable means to assess children's injury history. Perhaps the most accurate assessment tool is gathering information from hospital or medical records. This tactic, which requires surmounting of substantial legal and ethical hurdles, offers relatively reliable records collected by impartial third parties (medical staff), but also has disadvantages. Due to a combination of individual and cultural differences, as well as insurance and health care accessibility issues, parents have widely varying thresholds in deciding when professional medical treatment is needed to treat a child's injuries. Some parents might seek professional medical attention for an injury other parents treat at home. A second limitation to gathering injury history information from local medical records is the fact that some children might be injured while traveling outside of the area, and evidence of such incidents might be absent from local records.

A second option to gather children's injury history is through questionnaires or interviews with the child's parents. This technique, typically cheaper and quicker than gathering of medical records, offers good reliability when the recall period is relatively short (Cummings, Rivara, Thompson & Reid, 2005; Harel et al., 1994; Moshiro, Heuch, Åstrøm, Setel & Kvåle, 2005; Peterson, Harbeck & Moreno, 1993; Pless & Pless, 1995). However, when recall periods are long (greater than a year, and perhaps greater than 3–6 months), accuracy of recall declines sharply and measures become less valid.

A second significant challenge to measurement of unintentional injury is the fact that injuries are infrequent but serious events, and therefore cause analytical obstacles because of their low base rate frequencies. One solution to prediction of low base rate events is to recruit large sample sizes. A large sample size increases statistical power and aids in identification of effects despite the poor variance of an outcome measure such as injury. Of course, recruitment of large sample sizes is expensive and limits the researcher's ability to administer behavioral observations or lengthy questionnaires to assess other constructs of interest. A second solution is collection of data concerning minor daily injuries (Morrongiello & Hogg, 2004; Peterson et al., 1993; Schwebel, Binder, Sales & Plumert, 2003). Recent evidence suggests the correlation between major injuries requiring professional medical attention and more minor daily injuries is around $r = .45$ (Morrongiello & Hogg, 2004), and most injury scientists agree the risk factors for minor injuries are similar to those for major injuries (e.g., Morrongiello & Hogg, 2004; Peterson, et al., 1993; Schwebel et al., 2003).

Translation to Prevention and Intervention

Although temperament is viewed to be relatively stable, most theorists agree that temperament does change somewhat over development in response both to direct stimuli and to interactions with the environment (Rothbart & Bates, 1998). The fact that temperamentally-driven behavior patterns might change in response to external stimuli opens the possibility that successful injury prevention techniques could be developed that target behavior patterns associated with temperament.

Empirical tests of interventions designed to alter temperamental expression of behavior in potentially dangerous environments are sparse. In one study, Schwebel (2004b) asked children to judge their ability to complete basic physical tasks such as reaching and stepping. Using a between-subjects design, a sample of 57 six-year-olds was divided into one group who was permitted to make judgments and then attempt the tasks immediately and a second group who was forced to 'think about' their judgments for 7 seconds before deciding and then attempting the tasks. No differences emerged in accuracy of judgment between the two groups, suggesting the intervention was unsuccessful in forcing temperamentally impulsive children to slow their decision-making process enough to increase accuracy of physical ability judgments.

A second attempt to change children's behavior patterns was more successful in altering children's decisions (Schwebel & Bounds, 2003). That study, which used the same apparatus for children to judge their physical abilities, implemented a within-subjects design where 6- and 8-year-olds made judgments both in the presence of a parent and without a parent present. All children – but in particular those who scored high on an aggregated temperament measure of impulsivity, activity level, high intensity pleasure, and undercontrol – judged their ability more cautiously when a parent was present. These results were replicated in a second study, where children were asked to judge their ability to cross busy streets under varying intensities of parental supervision (Barton & Schwebel, 2006b).

From the perspective of temperament theory, the results of these studies are consistent with the proposition that it might be hard to change behavior resulting from poor inhibitory control. Inhibitory control is theorized to be driven by internal regulation, and therefore is recalcitrant to alteration through environmental manipulations. Changing the external stimuli that a child faces may be easier – and thus the expression of high impulsivity and high activity level – might be more amenable to injury prevention efforts than changing the expression of poor inhibitory control. For example, a change in adult supervision may alter how an impulsive, active child engages in a dangerous environment. When supervised, a child with high impulsivity and high activity might heed warnings about danger in the environment. However, a child with particularly poor inhibitory control will not have the internal restraint to listen to warnings from an adult supervisor. Clinically, the child with ADHD might be very active and very impulsive, but when instructed to stop doing something dangerous, he will do so. When Oppositional Defiant Disorder is comorbidly present, the child no longer heeds warnings from adults reliably and may place him or herself at danger.

Controlling externally-driven behaviors such as impulsivity and activity level is likely to be achieved best through increased quantity and intensity of adult supervision when children engage in potentially dangerous environments. Laboratory and field studies support the possibility that parental supervision might help restrain impulsive children from risky decision-making (Barton & Schwebel, 2006b; Schwebel & Bounds, 2003). Further work is needed to understand the process through which supervision might help restrain impulsive or active behavior patterns when children face dangerous environments. Simultaneously, interventions that might prevent children's impulsive or active behaviors when danger is present should be developed and tested (e.g., Schwebel, Summerlin, Bounds & Morrongiello, 2006).

Another unexplored injury prevention approach that holds promise is cognitive intervention. Older children display more inhibitory control and less impulsivity and activity than younger children. Temperament theorists cite inhibitory control as a temperament trait that matures somewhat with development (Eisenberg & Spinrad, 2004). In other domains, behavioral deficits have been improved through cognitive intervention methods. For example, impulsive behaviors of children with ADHD can be reduced through cognitive training (Hall & Kataria, 1992) and cognitive training using virtual reality methods improves the attention span of children with behavior problems (Cho et al., 2002). Similar applications of cognitive training might be used to train uninhibited children to express necessary control when exposed to potentially dangerous environments.

Conclusion

Repeated empirical studies have demonstrated that children's behavioral style, conceptualized in this chapter as temperament, is related to their risk for unintentional injury. In reviewing the literature with an eye toward overcoming semantic, measurement, and methodological variation, we identified three temperament constructs as particularly pertinent to understanding pediatric injury risk: inhibitory control, impulsivity, and activity level. High scores on these temperamental traits are theorized to increase risk for injury through various mechanisms, including increased exposure to risky environments, increased risky behavior when in potentially dangerous environments, reduced preventative behavior, and influences on the behavior of adults and others. It is unclear whether multiple temperamental traits might contribute to children's injury risk in an additive or multiplicative manner.

Despite holes in current knowledge, we feel the literature has much to offer to the development of injury prevention programs. Broadly, interventions that target particular populations might focus on children scoring high in impulsivity and activity level, and scoring low in inhibitory control. Children diagnosed with ADHD and especially ODD fall within potential target populations. Increased adult supervision and cognitive interventions targeting poor self-control are among the intervention options that might prove most fruitful.

REFERENCES

Ahadi, S.A., Rothbart, M.K. & Ye, R. (1993). Children's temperament in the US and China: Similarities and differences. *European Journal of Personality, 7*, 359–377.

Bagley, C. (1992). The urban environment and child pedestrian and bicycle injuries: Interaction of ecological and personality characteristics. *Journal of Community and Applied Social Psychology, 2*, 281–289.

Barton, B.K. & Schwebel, D.C. (2006a). *The influences of age, gender, and temperament on children's selection of risky pedestrian routes.* Manuscript submitted for publication.

Barton, B.K. & Schwebel, D.C. (2006b). *The roles of age, gender, temperament, and parental supervision in children's pedestrian safety.* Manuscript submitted for publication.

Bijttebier, P., Vertommen, H. & Florentie, K. (2003). Risk-taking behavior as a mediator of the relationship between children's temperament and injury liability. *Psychology and Health, 18,* 645–653.

Bijur, P., Golding, J. & Haslum, M. (1988). Persistence of occurrence of injury: Can injuries of preschool children predict injuries of school-aged children? *Pediatrics, 82,* 707–712.

Bijur, P., Golding, J., Haslum, M. & Kurzon, M. (1988). Behavioral predictors of injury in school-age children. *American Journal of Diseases of Children, 142,* 1307–1312.

Bijur, P., Stewart-Brown, S. & Butler, N. (1986). Child behavior and accidental injury in 11,966 preschool children. *American Journal of Diseases of Children, 140,* 487–492.

Boles, R.E., Roberts, M.C., Brown, K. J. & Mayes, S. (2005). Children's risk-taking behaviors: The role of child-based perceptions of vulnerability and temperament. *Journal of Pediatric Psychology, 30,* 562–570.

Brehaut, J.C., Miller, A., Raina, P. & McGrail, K.M. (2002). Childhood behavior disorders and injuries among children and youth: A population-based study. *Pediatrics, 111,* 262–269.

Briem, V. & Bengtsson, H. (2000). Cognition and character traits as determinants of young children's behaviour in traffic situations. *International Journal of Behavioral Development, 24,* 492–505.

Byrne, J.M., Bawden, H.N., Beattie, T. & DeWolfe, N.A. (2003). Risk for injury in preschoolers: Relationship to attention deficit hyperactivity disorder. *Child Neuropsychology, 9,* 142–151.

Cho, B.H., Ku, J., Jang, D.P., Kim, S., Lee, Y.H., Kim, Y.I., Lee, J.H. & Kim, S.I. (2002). The effect of virtual reality cognitive training for attention enhancement. *Cyber Psychology and Behavior, 5,* 129–137.

Cohen, J. (1988). *Statistical power analysis for the behavioral sciences* (2nd edn). Hillsdale, NJ: Erlbaum.

Cole, P.M., Martin, S.E. & Dennis, T.A. (2004). Emotion regulation as a scientific construct: Methodological challenges and directions for child development research. *Child Development, 75,* 317–333.

Connelly, M.L., Conaglen, H.M., Parsonson, B.S. & Isler, R.B. (1998). Child pedestrians' crossing gap thresholds. *Accident Analysis and Prevention, 30,* 443–453.

Costa, Jr., P.T. & McCrae, R.R. (2001). A theoretical context for adult temperament. In T.D. Wachs & G.A. Kohnstamm (eds), *Temperament in context* (pp. 1–21), Mahwah, NJ: Erlbaum.

Cummings, P., Rivara, F.P., Thompson, R.S. & Reid, R.J. (2005). Ability of parents to recall the injuries of their young children. *Injury Prevention, 11,* 43–47.

Davidson, L.L. (1987). Hyperactivity, antisocial behavior, and childhood injury: A critical analysis of the literature. *Developmental and Behavioral Pediatrics, 8,* 335–340.

Davidson, L.L., Hughes, S.J. & O'Connor, P.A. (1988). Preschool behavior problems and subsequent risk of injury. *Pediatrics, 82,* 644–651.

Davidson, L.L., Taylor, E. A., Sandberg, S. T. & Thorley, G. (1992). Hyperactivity in school-age boys and subsequent risk of injury. *Pediatrics, 90,* 697–702.

DiScala, C., Lescohier, I., Barthel, M. & Li, G. (1998). Injuries to children with Attention Deficit Hyperactivity Disorder. *Pediatrics, 102,* 1415–1421.

Dunbar, H.R., Wolfe, T. & Rioch, J. (1939). Psychic component in fracture. *American Journal of Psychiatry, 95,* 1319–1342.

Eisenberg, N. & Spinrad, T.L. (2004). Emotion-related regulation: Sharpening the definition. *Child Development, 75,* 334–339.

Flett, G.L., Vredenburg, K. & Krames, L. (1997). The continuity of depression in clinical and non-clinical samples. *Psychological Bulletin, 121,* 395–416.

Foot, H., Tolmie, A., Thomson, J., McLaren, B. & Whelan, K. (1999). Recognising the hazards. *The Psychologist, 12,* 400–402.

Fullard, W., McDevitt, S. & Carey, W. (1984). Assessing temperament in one- to three-year-old children. *Journal of Pediatric Psychology, 9,* 205–217.

Gray, J. (1975). *Elements of a two-process theory of learning.* New York: Academic.

Gray, J. (1982). *The neuropsychology of anxiety*. Oxford: Oxford University Press.

Gray, J. (1987). The neuropsychology of emotion and personality. In S.M. Stahl, S. Iverson & E. Goodman (eds), *Cognitive neurochemistry* (pp. 171–190). Oxford: Oxford University Press.

Hall, C.W. & Kataria, S. (1992). Effects of two treatment techniques on delay and vigilance tasks with attention deficit hyperactive disorder (ADHD) children. *The Journal of Psychology, 126,* 17–25.

Harel, Y., Overpeck, M.D., Jones, D.H., Scheidt, P.C., Bijur, P.E., Trumble, A.C. & Anderson, J. (1994). The effects of recall on estimating annual nonfatal injury rates for children and adolescents. *American Journal of Public Health, 84,* 599–605.

Hoffrage, U., Weber, A., Hertwig, R. & Chase, V.M. (2003). How to keep children safe in traffic: Find the daredevils early. *Journal of Experimental Psychology: Applied, 9,* 249–260.

Krall, V. (1953). Personality characteristics of accident repeating children. *Journal of Abnormal and Social Psychology, 48,* 99–107.

Langley, J., McGee, R., Silva, P. & Williams, S. (1983). Child behavior and accidents. *Journal of Pediatric Psychology, 8,* 181–189.

Lerner, R.M., Theokas, C. & Jelicic, H. (2005). Youth as active agents in their own positive development: A developmental systems perspective. In W. Gerner, K. Rothermund & D. Wentura (eds), *Adaptive self: Personal continuity and intentional self-development* (pp. 31–47). Ashland, OH: Hogrefe & Huber.

Manheimer, D.I. & Mellinger, G.D. (1967). Personality characteristics of the child accident repeater. *Child Development, 38,* 491–514.

Matheny, A.P. (1986). Injuries among toddlers: Contributions from child, mother, and family. *Journal of Pediatric Psychology, 11,* 163–176.

Matheny, A.P. (1987). Psychological characteristics of child accidents. *Journal of Social Issues, 43,* 45–60.

Matthews, K.A. & Angulo, J. (1980). Measurement of the Type A behavior pattern in children: Assessment of children's competitiveness, impatience-anger, and aggression. *Child Development, 51,* 466–475.

Mayes, S., Roberts, M.C., Boles, R.E. & Brown, K.J. (2005). *Children's knowledge of household safety rules*. Manuscript submitted for publication.

Mervielde, I. & De Fruyt, F. (1999). Construction of the hierarchical personality inventory for children (HiPIC). In I. J. Deary, F. De Fruyt & F. Ostendorf (eds), *Personality psychology in Europe* (Vol. 7, pp. 107–127). Tilburg: Tilburg University Press.

Miller, T.R., Romano, E.O. & Spicer, R.S. (2000). The cost of childhood unintentional injuries and the value of prevention. *The Future of Children, 10,* 137–163.

Mori, L. & Peterson, L. (1995). Knowledge of safety of high and low active-impulsive boys: Implications for child injury prevention. *Journal of Clinical Child Psychology, 24,* 370–376.

Morrongiello, B.A. & Dawber, T. (2000). Mothers' responses to sons and daughters engaging in injury-risk behaviors on a playground: Implications for sex differences in injury rates. *Journal of Experimental Child Psychology, 76,* 89–103.

Morrongiello, B.A. & Hogg, K. (2004). Mothers' reactions to children misbehaving in ways that can lead to injury: Implications for gender differences in children's risk taking and injuries. *Sex Roles, 50,* 103–118.

Morrongiello, B.A., Ondejko, L. & Littlejohn, A. (2004). Understanding toddlers' in-home injuries: I. Context, correlates, and determinants. *Journal of Pediatric Psychology, 29,* 415–431.

Moshiro, C., Heuch, I., Åstrøm, A.N., Setel, P. & Kvåle, G. (2005). Effect of recall on estimation of non-fatal injury rates: A community based study in Tanzania. *Injury Prevention, 11,* 48–52.

National Center for Injury Prevention and Control (2002). *CDC Injury Research Agenda*. Atlanta, GA: Centers for Disease Control and Prevention.

National Safety Council (2004). *Injury facts: 2004 edition*. Itasca, IL: Author.

Nyman, G.T. (1987). Infant temperament, childhood accidents, and hospitalization. *Clinical Pediatrics, 26,* 398–404.

Peterson, L., Bartelstone, J., Kern, T. & Gillies, R. (1995). Parents' socialization of children's injury prevention: Description and some initial parameters. *Child Development, 66,* 224–235.

Peterson, L. & Brown, D. (1994). Integrating child injury and abuse-neglect research: Common histories, etiologies, and solutions. *Psychological Bulletin, 116,* 293–315.

Peterson, L., Brown, D., Bartelstone, J. & Kern, T. (1996). Methodological considerations in participant event monitoring of low-base-rate events in health psychology: Children's injuries as a model. *Health Psychology, 15*, 124–130.

Peterson, L., Farmer, J. & Mori, L. (1987). Process analysis of injury situations: A complement to epidemiological methods. *Journal of Social Issues, 43*, 33–44.

Peterson, L., Harbeck, C. & Moreno, A. (1993). Measures of children's injuries: Self-reported versus maternal-reported events with temporally proximal versus delayed reporting. *Journal of Pediatric Psychology, 18*, 133–147.

Pless, C.E. & Pless, I.B. (1995). How well they remember: The accuracy of parent reports. *Archives of Pediatric Adolescent Medicine, 149*, 553–558.

Pless, I.B., Taylor, H.G. & Arsenault, L. (1995). The relationship between vigilance deficits and traffic injuries involving children. *Pediatrics, 95*, 219–224.

Plumert, J.M. & Schwebel, D.C. (1997). Social and temperamental influences on children's overestimation of their physical abilities: Links to accidental injuries. *Journal of Experimental Child Psychology, 67*, 317–337.

Potts, R., Martinez, I.G. & Dedmon, A. (1995). Childhood risk taking and injury: Self-report and informant measures. *Journal of Pediatric Psychology, 20*, 5–12.

Pulkkinen, L. (1995). Behavioral precursors to accidents and resulting physical impairment. *Child Development, 66*, 1660–1679.

Rothbart, M.K., Ahadi, S. & Hershey, K.L. (1994). Temperament and social behavior in children. *Merrill-Palmer Quarterly, 40*, 21–39.

Rothbart, M.K., Ahadi, S.A., Hershey, K.L. & Fisher, P. (2001). Investigations of temperament at three to seven years: The Children's Behavior Questionnaire. *Child Development, 72*, 1394–1408.

Rothbart, M.K. & Bates, J.E. (1998). Temperament. In W. Damon (Series ed.) & N. Eisenberg (Vol. ed.), *Handbook of child psychology: Vol. 3. Social, emotional and personality development* (5th edn, pp. 105–176). New York: John Wiley & Sons, Inc.

Rowe, R., Maughan, B. & Goodman, R. (2004). Childhood psychiatric disorder and unintentional injury: Findings from a national cohort study. *Journal of Pediatric Psychology, 29*, 119–130.

Santor, D.A. & Coyne, J.C. (2001). Evaluating the continuity of symptomatology between depressed and nondepressed individuals. *Journal of Abnormal Psychology, 110*, 215–225.

Scarr, S. & McCartney, K. (1983). How people make their own environments: A theory of genotype environment effects. *Child Development, 54*, 424–435.

Schwebel, D.C. (2004a). Temperamental risk factors for children's unintentional injury: The role of impulsivity and inhibitory control. *Personality and Individual Differences, 37*, 567–578.

Schwebel, D.C. (2004b). The role of impulsivity in children's estimation of physical ability: Implications for children's unintentional injury risk. *American Journal of Orthopsychiatry, 74*, 584–588.

Schwebel, D.C. (2005). [Research on temperament and child injury]. Unpublished raw data.

Schwebel, D.C. & Barton, B.K. (2005, May). *Parental supervision and child pedestrian traffic gap selection*. Poster presented at the annual National Injury Prevention and Control Conference, Denver, CO.

Schwebel, D.C., Binder, S.C., Sales, J.M. & Plumert, J.M. (2003). Is there a link between children's motor coordination and unintentional injuries? *Journal of Safety Research, 34*, 135–141.

Schwebel, D.C. & Bounds, M.L. (2003). The role of parents and temperament on children's estimation of physical ability: Links to unintentional injury prevention. *Journal of Pediatric Psychology, 28*, 505–516.

Schwebel, D.C. & Brezausek, C.M. (2004). The role of fathers in toddlers' unintentional injury risk. *Journal of Pediatric Psychology, 29*, 19–28.

Schwebel, D.C., Brezausek, C.M. & Belsky, J. (2006). Does time spent in child care influence risk for unintentional injury? *Journal of Pediatric Psychology, 31*, 184–193.

Schwebel, D.C., Brezausek, C.M., Ramey, S.L. & Ramey, C. (2004). Interactions between child behavior patterns and parenting: Implications for children's unintentional injury risk. *Journal of Pediatric Psychology, 29*, 93–104.

Schwebel, D.C., Hodgens, J.B. & Sterling, S. (in press). How mothers parent their children with behavior disorders: Implications for unintentional injury risk. *Journal of Safety Research*.

Schwebel, D.C. & Plumert, J.M. (1999). Longitudinal and concurrent relations among temperament, ability estimation, and injury proneness. *Child Development, 70*, 700–712.

Schwebel, D.C., Speltz, M.L., Jones, K. & Bardina, P. (2002). Unintentional injury in preschool boys with and without early onset of disruptive behavior. *Journal of Pediatric Psychology, 27*, 727–737.

Schwebel, D.C., Summerlin, A.L., Bounds, M.L. & Morrongiello, B.A. (2006). The Stamp-in-Safety program: A behavioral intervention to reduce behaviors that can lead to unintentional playground injury in a preschool setting. *Journal of Pediatric Psychology, 31*, 152–162.

Sleet, D.A. & Bryn, S. (eds). (2003). Injury prevention for children and youth. *American Journal of Health Education (Supplement), 34(5)*, S5–S66.

Speltz, M.L., Gonzales, N., Sulzbacher, S. & Quan, L. (1990). Assessment of injury risk in young children: A preliminary study of the Injury Behavior Checklist. *Journal of Pediatric Psychology, 15*, 373–383.

Thomas, A. & Chess, S. (1977). *Temperament and development*. New York: Brunner/Mazel.

Thuen, F. (1994). Injury-related behaviours and sensation seeking: An empirical study of a group of 14-year-old Norwegian school children. *Health Education Research, 9*, 465–472.

Vollrath, M., Landolt, M.A. & Ribi, K. (2003). Personality of children with accident-related injuries. *European Journal of Personality, 17*, 299–307.

Wachs, T.D. & Kohnstamm, G.A. (2001). *Temperament in context*. Mahwah, NJ: Erlbaum.

Wazana, A. (1997). Are there injury-prone children? A critical review of the literature. *Canadian Journal of Psychiatry, 42*, 602–610.

Whitebread, D. & Neilson, K. (2000). The contribution of visual search strategies to the development of pedestrian skill by 4–11-year-old children. *British Journal of Educational Psychology, 70*, 539–557.

Zuckerman, M., Eysenck, S.B. & Eysenck, H.J. (1978). Sensation seeking in England and America: Cross-cultural, age, and sex comparisons. *Journal of Consulting and Clinical Psychology, 46*, 139–146.

CHAPTER 4

Personality, Stress, and Coping

Norbert K. Semmer
University of Bern, Switzerland

INTRODUCTION

There can be no doubt that personality plays an important role in the experience of stress and in the way people deal with stress. Although there are several mechanisms involved, the most obvious indicator of the importance of personality (in a broad sense – see below) probably can be seen in the large interindividual differences in coping with stress (e.g., Kiecolt-Glaser, McGuire, Tobles & Glaser, 2002).

The way the term personality is used in this chapter is a broad one, referring to tendencies in perceiving, thinking, feeling, and acting that have some stability. Thus, the discussion does not restrict itself to very general traits, such as the Big Five and its sub facets (Costa & McCrae, 1998) but also to more specific concepts such as motives, or belief systems.

In this chapter, I will first discuss various mechanisms by which personality may play a role in the stress process. This will be followed by a section that deals with the question of what is stressful for whom, depending on 'classic' personality traits but also on motives and goals. The third part will deal with characteristics of resilient vs. vulnerable people, and the fourth part will discuss the issue of coping.

However, one important caveat seems necessary: One sometimes encounters a tendency to emphasize individual differences to the point where stress is reduced to nothing but a problem of idiosyncratic appraisals and coping styles, rendering such concepts as 'environmentally induced stress' useless, as Lazarus and Folkman (1986, p. 75) assert (see also Perrewé & Zellar, 1999). This view tends to equate 'interpretation' with 'confined to the individual', and 'environment' with 'physical environment', and to neglect that the social environment is a powerful reality, where people in the same culture share 'rules of appraisal' (Averill, 1986) and ways of dealing with the world (cf. Semmer, McGrath & Beehr, 2005; see Hobfoll, 2001 or Kahn & Byosiere, 1992, for a similar argument, and cf. the analysis of Cooper & Payne, 1992, of cultural differences in stress appraisal and coping). Thus, it should be kept in mind that not all individual differences found are only differences between individuals, but often differences between the (sub-) cultures they belong to (Diener, Oishi & Lucas, 2003; Semmer et al., 2005). As this chapter deals with individual differences, and thus tends to support the tendency to lose sight of this fact, it is emphasized here and should be kept in mind.

A final personal note is important with regard to this chapter. My background is in the psychology of work and organizations. This contribution is on personality, stress, and coping *in general*. Accordingly, I have tried to incorporate literature independent of any relationship to the world of work. Nevertheless, I cannot hide a certain 'bias' in that direction. The chapter is based on Semmer (2003a) to a considerable degree, and many research examples come from the occupational health field. I do hope that readers will see this as an interesting 'accent' rather than a serious bias.

PERSONALITY AND THE STRESS EXPERIENCE: MECHANISMS

If personality plays a role in the stress experience, it somehow must 'translate' into stressful experiences, that is, the perception of threat or loss and the concomitant emotional and physiological reactions (Lazarus & Folkman, 1984). Dispositions must, therefore, relate to dynamics of appraisal, coping, etc. (Mischel & Shoda, 1998; Smith & Spiro, 2002). Specifically, four mechanisms will be discussed by which personality may influence how people experience stress and how they deal with it (Suls & Martin, 2005; Vollrath, 2001; cf. Watson, David & Suls, 1999): Depending on their personal characteristics, people (1) have different probabilities of encountering certain stressors, (2) will perceive specific aspects of a given situation as more or less stressful, (3) will react differently to situations, even when severity of stress-appraisal is held constant, and (4) will show different coping tendencies.

Often, however, it is not easy to differentiate between these processes. If a study relies on self-report only, it is difficult to ascertain whether more frequent reports of negative events by people with high levels in a given trait, such as Neuroticism, may be due to differential exposure but also to a lower threshold for appraising relatively trivial, or ambiguous, events as negative (Suls & Martin, 2005). And if the same participants show greater negative affect after experiencing negative events, this may be due (a) to a more negative appraisal or (b) to higher reactivity. Only if a number of events, appraisals, and affective reactions are assessed, can these processes be differentiated. Nevertheless, these aspects provide a useful way of conceptualizing the mechanisms involved in the translation of personality into affective reactions.

Encountering Stressful Situations

One important way by which personality may influence the experience of stress is by changing the probability of encountering stressful situations. Getting into stressful situations has mostly been studied from the perspective of socio-economic status, where it has clearly been established that low social status increases the risk of being exposed to a number of adverse conditions, both physical and psychological (Adler, Marmot, McEwen & Stewart, 1999; Adler & Matthews, 1994). Studying exposure from a personality perspective is less common, although many theorists now agree that one important manifestation of stable interindividual differences can be seen in what situations people prefer and select – or shy away from (cf. Krahé, 1992; Mischel & Shoda, 1998).

Thus, people high in avoidance motivation (McClelland, 1987), or prevention orienta-tion (Brockner & Higgins, 2001) may shy away from challenges, thus avoiding stress in the short term but also forgoing chances for success and development. People who are high in competitiveness may seek jobs in highly competitive environments (cf. the 'Attraction-Selection-Attrition' framework by Schneider—e.g., Schneider, Goldstein & Smith, 1995), which then will expose them to the typical stressors (e.g., low cohesiveness, low cooperativeness, low trust) but, if successful, also to the typical benefits (e.g., a sense of mastery) of such an environment.

While this type of mechanism involves active choices (Zautra, Affleck, Tennen, Reich & Davis, 2005, therefore speak of 'engagement in . . . ', rather than of 'exposure to . . . '), there is another mechanism that is characterized by a more involuntary inducement of reactions by others that may increase one's level of stress. Thus, there is evidence that depressed people are less attractive to others, and this may alienate potential supporters and increase social isolation (Sacco, Dumont & Dow, 1993; cf. Winnubst, Buunk & Marcelissen, 1988). In a similar vein, people who are low in emotional stability, high in hostility, or low in social competence may provoke social conflict, and thus create social stress, which affects others as well as themselves (cf. Depue & Monroe, 1986; Dohrenwend, Dohrenwend, Dodson & Shrout, 1984; Smith, Glazer, Ruiz & Gallo, 2004; Smith & Spiro, 2002; Suls & Martin, 2005). Conversely, people high in Agreeableness report fewer social conflicts (Asendorpf & Wilpers, 1998), and they both give and received more social support (as do people high in Extraversion; Bowling, Beehr & Swader, 2005; Zellars & Perrewé, 2001). Bolger and Zuckerman (1995), in a diary study with a longitudinal design, demonstrated that people high in Neuroticism not only display greater reactivity to social conflict (in terms of anger and depression) but also tend to report more social conflict (cf. also Gunthert, Cohen & Armeli, 1999). In a similar vein, Zautra et al. (2005) report that Neuroticism predicts a greater number of negative events, whereas Extraversion predicts a greater number of positive events. Suls and Martin (2005) summarize a number of studies showing greater exposure to a great variety of problems by people high in Neuroticism (although, due to the self-report character of most studies, exposure cannot be clearly separated from appraisal). Conversely, people high in Conscientiousness, who are known to perform better than those low in Conscientiousness, may receive more positive feedback as a result of their superior performance, compared to people low in Conscientiousness (Weiss & Kurek, 2003). In work psychology, there are some indications that people's well-being influences future working conditions (or the perception of these conditions), although these effects tend to be weaker than the effect of stressors on well-being (cf. de Lange, Tairs, Kompier, Houtman & Bongers, 2005; Zapf, Dormann & Frese, 1996).

While these are rather direct sources of 'self-produced social stress' (or resources, as in the case of conscientiousness), other paths may be more indirect, as when people high in sensation seeking may drive in a more risky way, or be more inclined to engage in unsafe sex practices (Greene, Krcmar, Walters, Rubin & Hale, 2000; Hoyle, Feifar & Miller, 2000). Vollrath and Torgersen (2002) report the combination of low Conscientiousness with either high Neuroticism or high Extraversion as especially 'risk-prone'.

Appraising Different Situations as Stressful

A second way in which personality may be tied to stress is appraisal, a key component in the stress process (Lazarus, 1999). That people high in Resilience appraise similar events as less threatening is theoretically plausible. After all, many personality variables are conceived of, and, at least partly, measured in terms of tendencies to perceive and interpret events in a given way. Thus, Neuroticism relates to perceiving many things as problems, self-esteem and self-efficacy to perceiving problems as manageable, Agreeableness to perceiving people as trustworthy, etc. Although there is some debate about micro-processes involved in this (e.g., do people attend to different cues, and/or interpret cues differently), there is substantial evidence that traits influence how people appraise what is going on (Rusting, 1998).

Thus, people high in Trait Anxiety (a core component of Neuroticism, or Negative Affect) attend selectively to potentially threatening stimuli and show a tendency to give threatening interpretations to ambiguous situations (Eysenck, 1988; Gunthert et al., 1999; Suls & Martin, 2005). Hostile people tend to focus more strongly on cues that signal hostility in others, and they are prone to interpret ambiguous cues as indicating hostility (Berkowitz, 1998). People low in self-esteem tend to interpret failure as 'self-diagnostic', and thus more stressful (Brockner, 1988). Conversely, people high in resources, such as self-esteem, or optimism, tend to interpret stressful events in a less extreme way than people low in these resources (Major, Richards, Cooper, Cozzarelli & Zubek, 1998). Indeed, many concepts of resourceful people are defined in ways that relate to tendencies in interpreting events (e.g., hardiness, sense of coherence—see below).

Of course, besides the relatively global, and rather stable, traits discussed here, many other person variables that also display quite some stability, may influence stress appraisals. This will be discussed below, with regard to goals and motives.

Reacting Differently to Stressful Situations

Reacting strongly to negative events that are appraised in a similar way constitutes another mechanism for the translation of personality variables into stress experiences. In fact, an important component of the very general traits of Negative and Positive Affectivity (Neuroticism, Extraversion) can be seen in physiologically routed differential responsivity to negative and positive stimuli, respectively (Eysenck, 1988; Gray, 1987; Larsen & Ketelaar, 1991).

Thus, anxiety is associated with higher reactivity to stressors (Eysenck, 1988; Suls & Martin, 2005), Neuroticism can 'magnify' the impact of negative events (Zautra et al., 2005). Extraverts are characterized by a higher responsivity to positive events (Weiss & Kurek, 2003; see, however, the disconfirming finding by Zautra et al., 2005), hostile people tend to react especially strongly to social stressors (Smith et al., 2004), and so do people high in Agreeableness (Suls & Martin, 2005).

Outside of the laboratory, it is often not easy to attribute reactions to reactivity in an unambiguous way, as differences in appraisal may be responsible for the differences in reactivity (Suls & Martin, 2005). Nevertheless, differential reactivity has been demonstrated in studies dealing with daily experiences. Thus, Kamarck, Schwartz, Shiffman, Muldoon, Sutton-Tyrrell and Janicki (2005) show that high physiological responders, as determined by a laboratory task, also showed stronger reactivity during periods of the day that they rated as demanding. Gunthert et al. (1999) show that, over and above a more negative appraisal by participants higher in Neuroticism, Neuroticism moderated the relationship between an appraisal of a situation as 'undesirable' and the negative affect experienced. The association between secondary appraisal (expected coping efficiency) and negative affect also was stronger for participants high in N. Grebner, Elfering, Semmer, Kaiser-Probst and Schlapbach (2004) demonstrated that Neuroticism was related to situational well-being during stressful events, controlling for the appraisal of the stressfulness of the situation.

Dealing with Stressful Situations

There has been some debate about whether or not people display consistency—temporal as well as cross-situational—in coping, with some authors emphasizing the situational approach and expressing skepticism about a more trait-oriented approach (Aldwin, 2000; Lazarus, 1999). Putting aside for the moment the fact that much of the stability may lie in consistent situation-behavior combinations (Mischel & Shoda, 1998), there is now ample evidence that there are coping tendencies that are characteristic of people, in that they tend to show specific ways of coping more often than other people (cf. Carver, Scheier & Weintraub, 1989; Ferring & Filipp, 1994; McCrae & Costa, 1986; Miller, 1990; Watson et al., 1999). Such tendencies are not at all incompatible with findings that, overall, people seem to take situational variables into account and adjust their ways of coping to them (Reicherts & Pihet, 2000). In addition, stable individual differences in coping do not require that certain people will always employ strategy A and others strategy B. There may also be differences on a 'meta-level', in that some people are habitually more flexible in their strategies. Thus, Scheier, Weintraub and Carver (1986) have shown that optimists are more likely to accept uncontrollable situations and more likely to use active coping strategies in controllable situations than are pessimists. In other words: optimists show a tendency towards coping strategies that are adequate for the situation (Carver & Scheier, 1999). Similar results are reported by Perrez and Reicherts (1992c) and by Reicherts, Kaeslin, Scheurer, Fleischhauer and Perrez (1992) who find that depressives tend to be more rigid, to adjust their coping strategies less in the course of events.

Watson et al. (1999) summarize literature showing that especially Neuroticism and Extraversion (or Negative vs. Positive Emotionality) are associated with adaptive vs. maladaptive ways of coping (Costa, Somerfield & McCrae, 1996; McCrae & Costa, 1986); the other facets of the Big Five—Conscientiousness, Openness to Experience, and Agreeableness—also show characteristic associations with coping tendencies, but with less consistency (Lee-Baggley, Preece & DeLongis, 2005). Many studies that investigate coping, however, have concentrated on more 'mid-level' constructs, such as self-esteem, optimism, etc. These will be discussed later.

As with the other mechanisms, it is especially studies that investigate daily coping in natural environments that have increased our understanding of the processes involved. For example, Gunthert et al. (1999) found that people high in Neuroticism used more maladaptive coping strategies than those low in N. Similar findings are reported by Bolger and Zuckerman (1995), and by David and Suls (1999). The latter report, furthermore, that emotion-focused strategies were used by people with higher scores on Neuroticism in response to less severe problems. Furthermore, high N participants in the Gunthert et al. study were not very successful with any type of coping, and they even profited less from the resolution of the stressful situation than low N participants, the interaction being marginally significant. Similarly, Suls and Martin (2005) report that people high in N used more strategies overall, which may indicate that they 'had difficulty finding a strategy that helped' (p. 16). Suls and Martin further report evidence that spillover of negative mood from one day to the next was greater for people high in N, and that N also correlated with difficulties encountered in 'old' problems, indicating a lack of habituation (McEwen, 1999). Taken together, these findings point to a lack of efficient coping.

In line with the 'differential choice-effectiveness model' advanced by Bolger and Zuckerman (1995), implying that personality may influence both the choice and the effectiveness of a given coping strategy, there is evidence indicating that people high in N do not profit equally from the same coping strategies as people low in N do. Thus, Bolger and Zuckerman report that people high in N show more depression on the next day when using 'self-control' as a coping mechanism, whereas people low in N profited from this strategy in terms of depression. Such effects were not very consistent, however, as high N's were *not* negatively affected by escape-avoidance, whereas low N's were. Confirming the negative impact of N, however, Guntert et al. (1999) found that people high in N not only used more maladaptive coping strategies but also showed a stronger increase in negative affect when employing these strategies. The 'differential choice-effectiveness model' certainly deserves further attention.

Mechanisms: Conclusions

Thus, although the picture is far from being unambiguous in detail, there is substantial evidence that personality has an impact on the experience of stress via exposure, appraisal, reactivity, and coping.

These mechanisms are, of course, not independent from one another, and they may well combine into a 'cascade' (Suls & Martin, 2005). For instance, optimistic people may, due to their displaying positive attitudes, encounter more positive behavior of interaction partners (mechanism 1), tend to perceive the strange behavior of others as a sign of clumsiness rather than hostile intentions (mechanism 2), be less bothered if the other's behavior does, indeed, turn out to be unfriendly (mechanism 3), and have better coping strategies available to deal with unfriendly behavior (mechanism 4). The various aspects therefore converge in suggesting a number of characteristics that make people vulnerable vs. resilient with regard to stress, and these characteristics seem to play a role in each of the four mechanisms.

TRAITS, GOALS, AND MOTIVES: WHAT IS STRESSFUL FOR WHOM?

As we have seen, Neuroticism seems to dispose people towards a very general reactivity. People high in N have a higher tonic negative affect, they tend to perceive a great variety of events as stressful, and react correspondingly. On the positive side, Extraversion has similar implications, although the picture is not as pervasive (Zautra et al., 2005, for instance, report extraverts to have higher trait positive affect but not greater reactivity to positive events; rather, it was introverts who responded more strongly to positive events).

Other general traits tend to have more specific implications. Thus, Agreeableness seems to predispose towards reactivity especially to social events, which is plausible, as people high in this trait value good relationships with others especially highly (Suls & Martin, 2005). Conscientiousness goes along with higher attentiveness (as part of Positive Affectivity; Watson et al., 1999), and with more problem-oriented coping (Costa et al., 1996; Vollrath, 2001).

What has seldom been considered are unique profiles of personality traits. Vollrath has investigated the effect of certain combinations of the Big Five, and she finds the combination of high N and low C especially problematic (and the combination of low N and high C especially resilient) in terms of stress and coping (Vollrath & Torgersen, 2000). Risk behaviors were also associated with this combination and, in addition, with the combination of low C and high E (Vollrath & Torgersen, 2002).

As one looks into more specific relationships, *goals* have to be taken into account (Smith & Spiro, 2002). Basically, stress has to do with appraisals of threat and/or loss (Lazarus & Folkman, 1984). Challenge, which is mentioned as the third category belonging to stressful appraisals, is not considered as stressful per se, as it involves positive appraisals and emotions, and the re-appraisal of a threatening demand as challenge actually has the potential of terminating the state of stress (cf. the concept of hardiness, as discussed below).[1]

This implies that stress has to do with the—anticipated or experienced—thwarting of goals. This term is used in a broad sense here, referring to all kinds of desired states at different levels of abstraction—cf. Carver and Scheier (1990); Cropanzano, James and Citera (1993); Schönpflug (1985).

As Cropanzano et al. (1993) point out, personality may be described as a hierarchy of goals, ranging from very general dispositions (such as approach positive or avoid negative states) over values, self-identities, personal projects, to task goals. Emmons (1989) presents a similar hierarchical approach (see also Emmons, 1996).

Values are rather abstract guiding principles, such as achievement, comfort, power, good relations to others, justice, or maintaining a positive self-image. Self-identities are roles one identifies with, such as 'citizen', 'parent', 'spouse', 'executive', 'lathe operator', etc. Personal projects is a term introduced by Little (1983). As used by Cropanzano et al. (1993) it is an umbrella term encompassing a variety of similar terms such as 'personal strivings' (Emmons, 1989), 'current concerns' (Klinger, 1987), life tasks (Cantor & Langston, 1989), which have in common that they 'are all explicitly goal-directed and situated in a hierarchy just below relatively abstract self-identities and just above more specific action plans' (Cropanzano et al., 1993, p. 289). They may include such things as 'trying to build or maintain a good relationship with colleagues', 'trying to always beat the deadlines', 'avoiding being made responsible for things outside one's control', etc.

More specific goals at lower levels, that is, goals that refer to specific actions, are not at the center of these conceptions, as such goals do not refer to motivation and personality in a more general sense but refer to momentary actions. It may be noted in passing, however, that the thwarting of such goals by 'barriers to task-fulfilment' (e.g., having to work with poor tools or materials, encountering frequent interruptions, and the like) has been shown to be an important stressor at work, which is related to stress symptoms (e.g., Greiner, Ragland, Krause, Syme & Fisher, 1997; Leitner & Resch, 2005; Semmer, Zapf & Greif, 1996; Spector & Jex, 1998).

Stress and Commitment to Goals

If the reasoning is correct that stress has to do with thwarted goals, then people with high goals should experience more stress under the same threat to these goals – all other things being equal. However, this is only part of the picture. The other side of the coin is that having goals one is trying to achieve gives a sense of purpose to life, and offers opportunities for goal fulfillment (e.g., Emmons, 2005; Locke, 2005).

---

[1] Of course, the appraisal of challenge may be ambivalent, oscillating between the concentration on the potential gains and the reflection of the potential dangers. To the extent that the dangers are salient, there is appraisal of threat, and thus, stress (cf. Semmer et al., 2005).

In line with this reasoning, Reilly (1994) reports for a sample of nurses that participants that were more committed to their profession showed *lower mean levels* of emotional exhaustion (the core component of burnout), as one would expect. At the same time, however, the *relationship* between the frequency of experienced stressors and emotional exhaustion was *stronger* for the more committed, as one would expect from the perspective of identity theory (Burke, 1991; Thoits, 1991). Brown (2002) also reports how the effect of loss on depression is aggravated by strong commitment, and Frone, Russel and Cooper (1995) find moderate support for the stress-exaggerating influence of job involvement. Brockner, Tyler and Cooper-Schneider (1992) show that 'people reacted particularly negatively when they were highly committed to the institution beforehand, but felt that they had been treated unfairly in some recent encounter with the institution' (Brockner, Wiesenfeld & Raskas, 1993, p. 237). There is non-supportive evidence as well, however (Thoits, 1995). One reason for this may be that commitment may exert such an exaggerating influence only in conjunction with other factors (e.g., humiliation, entrapment, in Brown's research). Also, role-identities may be both positive and negative, and the balance between positive and negative meanings seems to be an important factor with regard to their relationships with well-being (Simon, 1997).

This becomes especially apparent when looking at *multiple roles* of women, especially the combination of work and family roles. The bulk of the evidence indicates that multiple roles do, in general, not have detrimental, and often positive effects on women's well-being (e.g., Barnett & Hyde, 2001; Repetti, Matthews & Waldron, 1989; Ross & Mirowsky, 1995), although having multiple roles also is associated with specific vulnerabilities and symptoms (Bekker, Gjerdingen, McGovern & Lundberg, 1999). Again, commitment to goals seems to play an important role, since positive effects of labor force participation seem to depend, at least in part, on the women's positive attitude towards, and thus acceptance of, this working role (Repetti et al., 1989). At the same time, there are also indications that participation in the work force makes women (who still carry the bulk of the duties involving home and children; Bekker et al., 1999) more vulnerable with regard to parental stress (Cleary & Mechanic, 1983; Emmons, Biernat, Tiedje, Lang & Wortmann, 1991; Frankenhaeuser, 1991; Simon, 1992). While the picture is much less clear with regard to marital stress, there are indications that the impact of marital stress on well-being may be reduced for working women (Cleary & Mechanic, 1983; Kandel, Davies & Raveis, 1985). It is tempting to speculate that it is easier to put marital stress 'into perspective' if one is involved in a working role outside the house, whereas the obligations towards children who, after all, are dependent on their parents, do not allow for such a philosophical attitude towards problems connected with their upbringing. A study by Simon (1992) shows that the identification with the parental role is important in this respect. Women in this study showed higher symptoms of distress, and they were more strongly committed to their parental role. Controlling for parental stress rendered the coefficient for gender insignificant, and for both men and women there was a stronger relationship between parental stress and distress when commitment to the parental role was high. Thus, for multiple roles, there may also be a picture of better well-being in general but at the same time high vulnerability to specific stressors.

Another approach is concerned with motives, which, by definition, refer to the kind of things that one considers important and valuable. Research by McClelland and associates (McClelland, 1989) indicates that people with a high, but inhibited, power motive (n Pow) are likely to report more physical illness and to show lower immune function when experiencing 'power stress', that is, stressful life events the content of which has to do with power. People with a high power motive but without stress, however, show signs of better health. The impact of the power motive extends, however, beyond stressors that are related to the power theme. People high in n Pow also show the strongest association between *affiliative* stress (losing a loved one) and illness, thus implying that this group may be particularly prone to react strongly to *all* kinds of stressful events (Jemmott, 1987; see also Furnham, 1992).

The role of the affiliation motive is somewhat less clear. McClelland (1987, p. 366) speaks of a 'relaxed affiliative syndrome' (high N Aff combined with low inhibition), which is associated with better health and superior immune function. In 1989, he refers to 'affiliative trust', a subcategory of the Affiliation motive, as being associated with better health. By contrast, he refers to the combination of high need for achievement, high need for power but low need for affiliation as 'agency' and presents data showing that high agency is related to better health, but only if combined with low stress—the same picture we saw above for commitment.

There has been less research on the need for achievement and its relationship to stress. There is some evidence that people high in n Ach tend to be rather healthy in general (Veroff, 1982), and this would correspond to the more positive tendency found for people high in Conscientiousness, especially with regard to problem-focused coping (Vollrath, 2001; Watson et al., 1999). However, Roger and colleagues have suggested that n Ach may be separated into a 'toxic' (TA) and a 'non-toxic' (NTA) component (cf. the separation of the affiliation motive into a trustful and a cynical component reported by McClelland, 1989). The first 'is characterized by impatience, a hostile need to win at all costs, and anger if that goal is thwarted', the latter is characterized by items such as 'I play to win but if I lose I don't hold a grudge' (Birks & Roger, 2000, p. 1095). They report data suggesting that TA is a risk factor for males, while NTA is a protective factor for females.

This toxic achievement is reminiscent of the high need for control attributed to *Type A* people (see below). Type As show a tendency to maintain control under all conditions (even conditions where control cannot be attained), and they react strongly—both behaviorally and in terms of cardiovascular reactivity—to threats to control (Contrada & Krantz, 1988; Edwards, 1991; Glass, 1977). Siegrist and associates have shown that a high need for control was associated with an elevated risk for cardiovascular disease both in cross-sectional and in longitudinal studies, beyond job-related measures (high quantitative demands, working in a job which does not match one's training level ['status inconsistency'], and job insecurity), and medical variables (systolic blood pressure and LDL-cholesterol; Marmot, Siegrist, Theorell & Feeney, 1999; Siegrist, 2002). Thus, the threat to a highly valued attribute (in this case, control) contributes to the experience of stress and, in the long run, disease. In addition to the more generic goal of keeping control, there is also evidence that, compared to Type Bs, Type As tend to set task goals for themselves that are too high with regard to their capabilities. This leads to a higher percentage of failures to reach the goal which, in turn, leads to dissatisfaction and distress (Ward & Eisler, 1987).

The conclusion from these considerations is that one of the most important differences in vulnerability to stressful experiences should be sought in people's goals—be they connected with specific tasks, concrete projects, more or less permanent roles, more global identities, or even more general motive structures. Hobfoll's (1989, 2001) concept of stress as an experienced or anticipated loss of resources emphasizes this aspect, as does the approach by Schönpflug (1985). At the same time, it should be emphasized once again, that being committed to goals may increase vulnerability but at the same time be associated with better health and well-being in general.

Reducing Goals (or Goal Commitment) as a Way of Reducing Stress

If goal commitment makes one more vulnerable, it follows that an efficient way of dealing with stress might be to alter one's goals. And, indeed, one of the recommendations given by Jackson (1984) for preventing burnout is to foster realistic expectations of what can and cannot be achieved. Krenauer & Schönpflug (1980; Schönpflug, 1985) have shown experimentally that the reduction of goals can alleviate stress. Avoiding unrealistically high goals and expectations also lies at the heart of Ellis' 'rational-emotive therapy' with its emphasis on correcting 'irrational beliefs' such as being liked by everybody (Ellis & Bernard, 1985), as well as of Wanous' concept of 'realistic job preview' (Wanous, 1992). Perrez & Reicherts (1992b) propose a coping category which they call 'evaluation-oriented' and which contains the change of intention or goals, and Siegrist, who emphasizes an exaggerated need for control as a risk factor, incorporates its reduction in stress management courses (Aust, Peter & Siegrist, 1997). Regarding old age, reducing one's goals seems to be a recommendable strategy to the extent that one's resources have diminished to a point where compensatory effort does not yield a good return (Rothermund & Brandtstädter, 2003). Thus, there are many instances where giving up is important, useful, and conducive to well-being (Wrosch, Scheier, Carver & Schulz, 2003).

Yet, reducing one's aspirations is a double-edged sword (Hobfoll, 2001). It may be helpful and recommendable in many cases, but it may have high costs in others. Recall that goal commitment, while possibly increasing vulnerability, is often associated with better well-being in general. Reducing, or renouncing, one's goals may therefore be disadvantageous.

This is shown, for instance, in the work domain by the analyses of Edwards and Van Harrison (1993) with regard to Person-Environment (P-E) Fit. One would expect that people are better off if what they have corresponds to what they aspire to. And, indeed, there are some cases in these analyses where perfect fit is associated with least strain. There are cases, however, where 'fit' at low levels is different from 'fit' at high levels: Distress symptoms were higher for people who wanted, and had, little complexity than for those who aspired to, and had, high complexity. Thus, aspiring to only little complexity might indicate a problem. In the same vein, Menaghan & Merves (1984) report that restriction of expectations as a coping strategy was associated with higher symptoms of distress. Similarly, 'control rejection', that is, a preference for being told what to do, not taking responsibility, etc. does not protect against the impact of stressors (Frese, 1992), but rather is associated with a number of indicators of strain and well-being, such as depression, psychosomatic complaints, job satisfaction, self-esteem, and self-efficacy—always in the direction of more control rejection being related to lower well-being (Frese, Erbe-Heinbokel, Grefe, Rybowiak & Weike, 1994). Bruggemann (1974; see Büssing, Bissels, Fuchs & Perrar, 1999) has proposed the concept of 'resigned job satisfaction', which is based on a reduction in aspirations. Studies in our group (Semmer & Elfering, 2002) show that this type of 'satisfaction' is associated with lower values in well-being.

Evidently, the reduction of aspiration levels can be both beneficial or problematic. What would distinguish the two?

One possibility is that the reduction does not really succeed. The original standards are not really given up, rather, a 'double standard' is established: One that one would desire, and one that one *feels forced to settle for*. Items from the 'resignation' aspect of job satisfaction show this quite clearly, including phrases such as 'My job is not ideal but, after all, it could be worse' or 'in my position, one can really not expect too much'. This is a sort of defensive adaptation, aiming at avoiding further disappointment rather than a positive reappraisal of the situation. This applies also for Frese's control rejection: If I reject responsibility, I cannot be blamed . . . Hallsten (1993) speaks of a 'strenuous non-commitment'. Wrosch et al. (2003) characterize this mechanism as 'giving up effort, but remaining committed to the goal' (cf. also Schönpflug, 1985).

But even if a goal is truly given up or lowered, the issue arises as to what goals remain. If giving up or lowering a goal is to have positive consequences, the goal in question should be replaced by something else to strive for. This might be accomplished by finding new ways to reach the higher order goal that is served by the abandoned one, or by forming, or emphasizing, other goals instead (Wrosch et al., 2003).

This points to the necessity to consider individual processes of adaptation in relation to reality, and not only as an intrapsychic problem, a tendency often found in stress research where things tend to be regarded as idiosyncratic as soon as interpretations are involved (e.g. Vossel, 1987). This reality is, for the most part, a *social* reality, a cultural environment that provides 'rules of appraisal' (Averill, 1986) as well as norms and standards (Semmer et al., 2005, see Hobfoll, 2001, for a similar point). The implication is that standards and goals often cannot be given up *ad lib*, simply by the individual 'deciding' to do so. People cannot easily choose to ignore standards set by society at large, or by their more proximal reference group (Wrosch et al., 2003).

As Harter (1993) argues for the case of the relation of self-esteem to certain goals, such as scholastic achievement or social acceptance, such standards are upheld by many people in the mainstream culture, 'making it difficult for those feeling inadequate to discount their importance' (p. 93). (She adds that this applies only to those who choose to remain within the cultural mainstream—however, leaving this mainstream may in itself be associated with high costs.) In a similar vein, giving up the goal of having work that is interesting may be difficult in an environment where interesting work is highly valued, resulting in the 'resentful' lowering of aspirations mentioned above. Furthermore, sometimes it is part of one's role obligations to set high standards. Managers, for instance, will be expected to have ambitious goals for themselves as well as for their subordinates. Reducing them would certainly be associated with quite high costs (Semmer & Schallberger, 1996), and 'reappraisal of more basic aspects of the self and the environment are more likely to backfire against the individual—resulting in a sense of insecurity and despair—than they are to have stress-moderating effects' (Hobfoll, 1989, p. 520). Thus, in many cases it is prohibitive to distance oneself from standards for ethical (parent role) or social (norms defined by one's (sub) culture) reasons, or because these goals are integral to one's self-integrity (Hobfoll, 2001).

The problem, therefore, arises that sometimes it is helpful to give up, or reduce, goals, and sometimes it is dysfunctional. To determine when exactly it is appropriate is not easy (Wrosch et al., 2003). To what extent the ability to diagnose situations accurately with regard to this issue is in itself tied to personality is an interesting question. It may well be associated with secure self-esteem. There is some evidence that high self-esteem is related to setting appropriate aspirations. If their self-esteem is high but fragile (e.g. unstable or contingent; Kernis, 2003), however, people may adopt too high standards and miss the right time to reduce them (Baumeister, Heatherton & Tice, 1993; Kernis, 2003).

VULNERABLE VS. RESILIENT PERSONS

As we have seen, broad traits such as Neuroticism, motives such as need for achievement, or commitment to goals all are related to stress and health. This section deals with constructs that have specifically been proposed with reference to vulnerability vs. resilience.

They tend to be more specific than the broad traits of the Big Five, but they often can be considered facets of these broad traits. Most of them refer to belief-systems and emphasize appraisal, and the related coping tendencies, rather than reactivity *per se*, which is more strongly related to physiological mechanisms. Concepts range from very broad ones such as hardiness (e.g. Maddi, 1999; Maddi, Khoshaba, Persico, Lu, Harvey & Bleecker, 2002) or sense of coherence (Antonovsky, 1991, 1993) to more specific ones such as explanatory style (Peterson & Seligman, 1984), locus of control (Rotter, 1966), self-efficacy (Bandura, 1989; 1992), optimism (Carver & Scheier, 2005), or self-esteem (Brockner, 1988; Mossholder, Bedeian & Armenakis, 1981—see also Hobfoll, 2001, Jerusalem & Schwarzer, 1992; Lazarus & Folkman, 1984). Finally, hostility is a central concept here (cf. Siegman, 1994a). In the following part, these concepts will be discussed briefly.

Beliefs About the World and One's Relationship to it: Popular Concepts

Hardiness is conceived of as being composed of the three components: commitment, challenge, and control (Maddi, 1997; Maddi, 1999; Maddi et al., 2002). '*Commitment* is the ability to believe in the truth, importance, and interest value of who one is and what one is doing; and thereby, the tendency to involve oneself fully in the many situations of life . . . *Control* refers to the tendency to believe and act as if one can influence the course of events . . . *Challenge* is based on the belief that change, rather than stability, is the normative mode of life . . . ' (Kobasa, 1988, p. 101). Especially for the components of control and challenge there is some overlap with Rosenbaum's (1990) concept of '*learned resourcefulness*', which refers to 'a general belief in one's ability to self-regulate internal events'—p. 15), and the use of corresponding coping strategies (problem-solving and planning).

Conceptually, the hardiness construct implies that people should be able to deal with stressful aspects of life better the more hardy they are (Beehr & Bowling, 2005). Research often shows the main effects of hardiness on physical and psychological health (Bartone, 2000; Cohen & Edwards, 1989; Contrada, 1989; Greene & Nowack, 1995; King, King, Fairbank, Keane & Adams, 1998; Maddi, 1999; Okun, Zautra & Robinson, 1988; Orr & Westman, 1990). Both stress appraisal and coping seem to be mediators of this relationship (Florian, Mikulincer & Taubman, 1995), as implied by the concept. Evidence on moderator effects is mixed (Cohen & Edwards, 1989; Orr & Westman, 1990; see also Steptoe, 1991), with some studies finding interactions (e.g., Maddi, 1999), and others not (e.g., Greene & Nowack, 1995; cf. Beehr & Bowling, 2005).

The measurement of hardiness has been a concern for many authors (cf. Beehr & Bowling, 2005; Funk, 1992; Maddi, 1997). It was originally measured by several existing scales (Ouellette, 1993). Since then, several hardiness scales have been produced, most notably the 'Personal Views Survey' (Maddi, 1997), the—related—'Dispositional Resilience Scale' (cf. Bartone, 2000), and the 'Cognitive Hardiness Scale' (cf. Greene & Nowack, 1995), which avoid the highly negative formulations of the original Alienation scales. This is important, as many studies find a strong overlap between hardiness and Neuroticism, which seems mainly to be due to negatively formulated items. Controlling for Neuroticism sometimes eliminates the effects of hardiness (cf. Allred & Smith, 1989; Williams, Wiebe & Smith, 1992; cf. Funk, 1992; Orr & Westman, 1990). Results by Kravetz, Drory and Florian (1993) suggest, however, that hardiness scales may be important indicators for a 'health proneness' factor which is strongly related to, but not identical with, a 'negative affect' factor. Also, Sinclair and Tetrick (2000) found that hardiness was confounded with, yet distinct from Neuroticism; the overlap was due to the negatively worded items. Controlling for Negative Affect, the positively worded items were related to academic problems, anxiety, and depression, and with regard to the negatively worded items the three-way interaction between the components was significant in predicting anxiety and depression. The authors suggest that positive items reflect stress resilience, whereas negative items (which are largely redundant with Neuroticism) reflect stress sensitivity. This notion is somewhat similar to that of Kravetz et al. (1993). Maddi and Khoshaba (1994) show that a number of relationships between hardiness and MMPI scales remain significant when controlling for Negative Affectivity. Maddi et al. (2002) also show that the Personal Views Survey II is related to scales of the MMPI as expected. It also is related to the Big Five, notably with Neuroticism ($r = -0.46$) and Extraversion ($r = 0.47$). Although these latter associations do not speak for complete redundancy with broader constructs (notable N and E), the multiple R with the Neo-FFI is substantial (0.68). Unfortunately, the studies by Maddi et al. do not report associations with third variables when controlling for N or E. Altogether, relations with broader personality constructs are substantial, and associations with third variables usually drop considerably when controlling for these broader constructs. In a number of studies, however, associations do remain even with these controls.

Sense of Coherence (SOC) also is quite a broad construct. Its three main features are (1) that the environment is perceived as structured, predictable, and explicable, and thus as *comprehensible*, (2) that one perceives oneself as having the resources necessary to deal with one's environment, thus perceiving *manageability*, and (3) that the demands posed by one's environment are interpreted as challenges that are worthy to be taken up, leading to the perception of *meaningfulness* (Antonovsky, 1991). The overlap with hardiness is obvious (Antonovsky, 1993; Geyer, 1997; Maddi, 1997), and in the analyses of Kravetz et al. (1993) both load on the same factor of health proneness. As summarized by Eriksson and Lindström (2005), measurement is usually based on a 29-item version or a 13-item version, both of which seem to have adequate psychometric properties. However, a large number of more idiosyncratic versions are also in use. The factor structure is not completely clear, with many studies finding one factor (as proposed by Antonovsky, 1993) while others find sub-factors, which are not always identical with the three concepts of comprehensibility, manageability, and meaningfulness. Some research using the 13-item version has produced evidence that a reduction to 11 items yields a clearer structure, with three correlated sub-factors that correspond to the three theoretical dimensions that can be combined into one general second-order factor (Feldt, Leskinen & Kinnunen, 2005).

Research on SOC shows relationships with a number of indicators of well-being and health (Antonovsky, 1993; Feldt, 1997; Johansson Hanse & Engström, 1999; Söderfeldt, Söderfeldt, Ohlson, Theorell & Jones, 2000). Main effects are predominant, but interactions with working conditions also are sometimes found (e.g. Feldt, 1997; Johansson Hanse & Engström, 1999; Söderfeldt et al., 2000). Effects of SOC have also been demonstrated longitudinally. Thus, Feldt, Kinnunen and Mauno (2000) find that some of the effects of adverse working conditions on well-being over time are mediated by SOC. Suominen, Helenius, Blomberg, Uutela and Koskenvuo (2001) demonstrate that SOC predicts subjective health ratings over four years, controlling for initial health status. Eriksson and Lindström (2005) provide a short synthesis of empirical work with the SOC concept.

As with hardiness, rather strong relationships with anxiety (Antonovsky, 1993), depression (Geyer, 1997), and other indicators of well-being (Eriksson & Lindström, 2005; Ryland & Greenfeld, 1991; Udris & Rimann, 2000) have raised doubts about SOCs distinctiveness from Neuroticism, or Negative Affectivity (see Geyer, 1997). This is supported by the finding by Kravetz et al. (1993) that their model could be improved substantially by allowing SOC to load on both the 'health proneness' and the 'negative affect' factor. Thus, although effects of SOC have clearly been demonstrated, the overlap with NA is considerable, although a number of studies have found effects of SOC when controlling for NA (e.g., Höge & Büssing, 2004).

Locus of Control is one of the variables that has very often been shown to be related to well-being (Cvetanovski & Jex, 1994; Spector, 2003). (Remember also that many measures of hardiness include locus of control). It is the only variable where even the very cautious reviews by Cohen and Edwards (1989) conclude that it is likely to act as a buffer between stress and health (see also Kahn & Byosiere, 1992), which is confirmed in a study by May, Schwoerer, Reed and Potter (1997). Locus of control may also be a moderator of the interaction proposed by Karasek (Karasek & Theorell, 1990). Thus, Parkes (1991), finds such an interaction between demands and control only for those high in external locus of control. Her findings refer to both cross-sectional and longitudinal data. Nevertheless, in general the evidence for moderator effects is less conclusive in longitudinal studies (Sonnentag & Frese, 2003). Pruessner, Gaab, Hellhammer, Lintz, Schommer and Kirschbaum (1997) have shown that external LOC in terms of chance, although not significantly correlated with cortisol reactions to a single stress situation, does show an association to aggregated cortisol responses over several sessions. The same applied to self-esteem, which is discussed next.

Like locus of control, *self-efficacy* and *self-esteem* have very consistently been shown to be related to well-being (cf. Bandura, 1992). In its generalized form (Jerusalem & Schwarzer, 1992) self-efficacy seems quite indistinguishable from *self-esteem*, at least from those parts of self-esteem that are related to one's perceived competences (cf. Judge & Bono, 2001). Self-efficacy and self-esteem seem especially important for dealing with negative feedback and failure in terms of distress as well as persistence (Bandura, 1989; Brockner, 1988; Jerusalem & Schwarzer, 1992; Kernis, Brockner & Frankel, 1989). A number of studies indicate that it is not simply the level of self-esteem that is important but also its stability. High but unstable self-esteem is associated with more hostility and anger (Kernis, Grannemann & Barclay, 1989). More recently, Kernis and associates (e.g., Kernis, 2003) have suggested that unstable high self-esteem is only one of several forms of 'fragile self-esteem', with other forms relating to discrepancies between explicit and implicit self-esteem, contingent self-esteem, or defensive self-esteem (i.e. driven by self-presentation concerns). According to Kernis, fragile self-esteem is related to poorer well-being (e.g., the experience of anger). Furthermore, fragile self-esteem may be related to efforts to protect one's self-esteem in a way that is, at least in the long run, dysfunctional (Crocker & Park, 2004; cf. Morf & Rhodewalt, 2001).

That (genuine) self-esteem is related to well-being is rather obvious, as it can legitimately be regarded as an indicator of well-being (Judge, Bono & Locke, 2000; Schaubroeck & Ganster, 1991; Wofford & Daly, 1997). Interactions are therefore more interesting, since it is plausible to assume that self-esteem might buffer the influence of stressors. Cohen & Edward (1989) are very skeptical about this; some more recent studies do, however, show such interactions (Ganster & Schaubroeck, 1991; Jex & Elaqua, 1999; Pierce, Gardner, Dunham & Cummings, 1993). Similarly, a number of studies have found self-efficacy to buffer the effects of stressors (Jex & Bliese, 1999; Jex, Bliese, Buzzell & Primeau, 2001; May et al., 1997; van Yperen & Snijders, 2000) or of resources like control (Jimmieson, 2000). Schaubroeck, Lam and Xie (2000) report such interactive effects for individual self-efficacy in the US but for collective self-efficacy in Hong Kong. It also seems noteworthy that some recent findings suggest that the interaction between demands and control as specified in the Karasek model (Karasek & Theorell, 1990) might be valid only for people high in self-efficacy or related personal resources (Jimmieson, 2000; Schaubroeck, Jones & Xie, 2001; Schaubroeck & Merritt, 1997).

Optimism is distinct from control-related concepts because it does not require that the course of events is influenced by one's own actions (even though it may instigate active attempts to exert influence). Rather, it includes the belief that things are likely to turn out reasonably well anyway (thus being related to a belief in a basically benign world). It has been shown to influence stress appraisals, well-being and health, and coping strategies (Carver & Scheier, 1999; 2005; Scheier & Carver, 1992; see Smith & Ruiz, 2002, for protective effects with regard to CHD). Optimists tend to employ more problem-solving strategies under controllable conditions, and more reinterpretation and acceptance under less controllable conditions. Pessimists, in contrast, tend to use more denial oriented strategies. Of special importance is the finding, already mentioned above, that optimists tend to accept failures better, which relates to the 'circumscribed' frustration as described by Hallsten (1993) and is indicative of the capability of putting things into perspective. Optimists show more acceptance, but not in a resignative, fatalistic way but rather in the sense of a realistic appraisal upon which proactive behavior can be based (Carver & Scheier, 2005). There seems to be an interesting parallel to the concept of 'self-compassion'. It indicates a tendency not to put oneself down in the face of failures and shortcomings—and thus a kind of acceptance of oneself with one's strong *and* weak points—and it is positively related to well-being (Neff, 2003).

Finally, *optimistic explanatory style* (Peterson & Seligman, 1984; Peterson & Steen, 2005) contains elements of optimism as well as control, in that it implies the belief that events are due to stable, global, and internal causes. Stability implies the conviction that things are going to stay that way, globality concerns the question of whether success or failure have circumscribed reasons or are indicative of one's (lack of) capabilities in general (cf. the notion of negative feedback being interpreted as more 'self-diagnostic'—Brockner, 1988). Internality concerns the aspect of locus. Note, however, that the internal attribution of negative events here implies negative consequences, whereas internality in general is associated with positive consequences. Internality may, therefore, be related both to self-blame and to self-esteem (or self-efficacy), which is probably the reason why empirical results concerning the internality dimension have been less consistent, leading to a concentration on the aspects of stability and globality (Peterson & Steen, 2005). Optimistic explanatory style has been shown to be related to psychological well-being, especially depression (Peterson & Seligman, 1984) but also to physical health (Buchanan, 1995; Peterson, Seligman & Vaillant, 1988) and to immune functioning (Kamen-Siegel, Rodin, Seligman & Dwyer, 1991).

Hostility is regarded as the major 'toxic' component of the Type A Behavior Pattern (Adler & Matthews, 1994; Ganster, Schaubroeck, Sime & Mayes, 1991; Siegman, 1994a). The accumulated evidence suggests 'that hostility is associated with and predictive of ill health, CHD, and all-cause mortality' (Miller, Smith, Turner, Guijarro & Hallet, 1996; see also Williams, 1996). Recent studies show it to be associated with vascular resistance during interpersonal stress (Davis, Matthews & McGrath, 2000), stronger neuroendocrine, cardiovascular and emotional responses to interpersonal harassment (Suarez, Kuhn, Schanberg,

Williams & Zimmermann, 1998), coronary artery calcification (Iribarren et al., 2000), and higher peak blood pressure at work in people in low prestige jobs (Flory, Matthews & Owens, 1998). Hostility shows an inverse relationship with socio-economic status, and might be one of the factors that mediate the relationship between SES and mortality (Flory et al., 1998; Kubzansky, Kawachi & Sparrow, 1999; Siegler, 1994). The evidence for the role of hostility is stronger for initially healthy persons than for people with established CHD (Smith & Ruiz, 2002).

Conceptually, one can distinguish between (1) a cognitive component, involving hostile beliefs and attitudes about others (cynicism, mistrust, hostile attributions of others' undesired behaviors), (2) an emotional component, involving anger, and (3) a behavioral component, involving physical or verbal assault (Buss & Perry, 1992). Smith et al. (2004) reserve the term hostility to the first, that is, the cognitive, component and talk about the triad of hostility, anger, and aggressiveness as related but distinct constructs. This is in line with the results of a factor analysis with a large number of scales reported by Martin, Watson and Wan (2000). They show that anger (the affective, experiential component) is most strongly related to Neuroticism, and aggression (the behavioral component) to Agreeableness. Cynicism (the cognitive component) represents a blend of high Neuroticism and low Agreeableness. Given the cultural constraints on physical assault, aggressiveness typically contains the expression of hostility and anger through verbal or nonverbal and paraverbal, rather than physical means (Barefoot, 1992; Siegman, 1994b). Many of the findings cited above are based on the (MMPI-derived) Cook-Medley Ho Scale (Cook & Medley, 1954), which is heterogeneous but predominantly seems to measure the cognitive component of cynicism, distrust, and hostile attributions (Barefoot, 1992; Martin et al., 2000; Smith et al. 2004).

The *expression* of anger and hostility has received special attention, as it shows the clearest association with coronary heart disease (Miller et al., 1996). This expressive component seems to be revealed best in overt behavior. Thus, the potential for hostility that is derived from the Structured Interview measure of Type A, or related measures, which code not only for hostile content but emphasize expressive style, quite consistently emerge as predictors of cardiovascular reactivity, CAD or CHD. A hostile expressive style is characterized by such behaviors as talking in a loud and explosive voice, having a short response latency, interrupting the interviewer, classifying questions as pointless, and showing a demeaning attitude towards the interviewer. For instance, the 'Interpersonal Hostility Assessment Technique' (IHAT—Brummett, Maynard, Haney, Siegler & Barefoot, 2000; Haney, Maynard, Houseworth, Scherwitz, Williams & Barefoot, 1996) yields four subscores, relating to 'direct challenges', 'hostile withhold-evade', 'indirect challenges', and 'irritation'.

Results based on self-report measures typically are somewhat weaker (Barefoot, 1992; Helmers, Posluszny & Krantz, 1994; Siegman, 1994b), although more recent accounts tend to be more positive (Smith & Ruiz, 2002; Smith et al., 2004). Many of the self-report instruments contain both the expressive component (often labeled as 'antagonistic hostility'—Dembroski & Costa, 1987) and contained, for instance, in the State-Trait Anger Expression Inventory (STAXI—Spielberger, Reheiser & Sydeman, 1995, and in the Buss-Durkee Hostility Inventory (BDHI—Buss & Durkee, 1957), where it typically yields one of two factors) and the experiencing component (often called 'neurotic' hostility—Dembroski & Costa, 1987), which is more characterized by the *experience* of anger and is contained in the other factor of the BDHI, and in the Trait Anger as measured by the STAXI. The Ho Scale loads on both components, but higher on neurotic than antagonistic hostility (Siegman, 1994a). The revised Buss-Durkee Hostility Inventory, called the Aggression Questionnaire

(Buss & Perry, 1992), contains the three components mentioned above, that is, hostility, anger, and aggressiveness, but the latter is separated into verbal and physical aggressiveness.

There has been some debate on the role of anger-in vs. anger-out as predictors of disease. Recent evidence seems to be more supportive for anger-out as predictor of CHD (Miller et al., 1996), but there is evidence for both components, which Smith et al. (2004) attribute to the fact that both are associated with cold and unfriendly hostility in the Interpersonal Circumplex. Anger-out has also been predictive of stroke in participants with a history of ischemic heart disease (Everson, Kaplan, Goldberg, Lakka, Sivenius & Salonen, 1999), and of early morning elevations in Cortisol among people with high job strain (Steptoe, Cropley, Griffith & Kirschbaum, 2000). Instructing people to describe anger-arousing events in a loud and rapid voice results in stronger elevations of blood pressure and heart rate than asking them to describe them in a low and soft voice (Siegman, 1994b).

Note, however, that the implication is not that components of hostility other than anger-out are irrelevant. They are weaker predictors only with regard to CHD, but they are good predictors of mortality from all causes (Miller et al., 1996). Anger-in may be especially important for the development of cancer (Siegman, 1994b), and being low in anger expression may be involved in the development of high blood pressure (Steptoe, 2001). Nevertheless, the expression of anger may be especially important not only because the feedback of one's own behavior may 'feed' the anger, but also because it may imply offenses to others, leading to prolonged aversive interactions and the undermining of social relationships (Flory et al., 1998; Siegman, 1994b).

What is especially intriguing with regard to anger-in vs. anger-out is the question of what expressing, or not expressing, one's anger does to the person in terms of ending vs. prolonging the anger (Davidson, MacGregor, Stuhr, Dixon & MacLean, 2000). This issue will be taken up later, when 'expressing emotions' is discussed in the context of coping.

Convergences

Judging from one perspective, the different concepts and the findings related to them are rather confusing. There is quite some overlap between different concepts, and it is quite unclear how many different constructs are involved. Some authors work only with a single construct, such as hardiness, or SOC, ignoring overlap with other concepts or being satisfied if it can be shown that their construct explains variance over and above Negative Affectivity. Those who compare several constructs sometimes find two—distinct but highly related— factors (e.g. Kravetz et al., 1993; Sinclair & Tetrick, 2000), sometimes one very general construct (e.g., Judge et al., 2000, Judge & Bono, 2001, who propose to combine self-esteem, generalized self-efficacy, locus of control, and emotional stability into one construct called 'core self-evaluations'), sometimes a hierarchical structure with one very general construct at the top but lower-order factors as well (Bernard, Hutchison, Lavin & Penningston, 1996).

Nevertheless, there clearly are common elements in these approaches. So, if one looks at the 'great lines', one might come to a conclusion like the following:

People who are resilient:

- Tend to interpret their environment basically as benign, that is, they expect that things are likely to go well (optimism) and that people do not intend harm (trust, agreeableness). All this does not apply unconditionally—which would be a sign of naiveté—but it is the 'default' interpretation as long as there are no reasons to believe otherwise.

- Tend to accept setbacks and failures (and, thus, stressful experiences) as normal, not necessarily indicative of their own incompetence nor indicative of a basically hostile world. Negative experiences are, therefore, put into perspective, interpreted as part of a larger picture, as having meaning beyond the present situation—for instance, as aversive but necessary and legitimate experiences on one's way to a larger, more overarching goal, as corresponding to the will of God, etc. Optimism is relevant here, as is optimistic attributional style, as it implies negative experiences to be not indicative of a global negative picture (globality), of a general failure which will go on (stability) and of one's general incompetence (internality). Sense of coherence is also relevant here, especially with regard to the dimensions of comprehensibility and meaningfulness, as is the hardiness dimension of commitment which includes 'an overall sense of purpose' (cf. Antonovsky, 1991; Kobasa, 1988; Thompson, 1981).
- Tend to see life as something that can be influenced and acted upon (internal locus of control), and to see themselves as capable of doing so (self-efficacy, manageability dimension of sense of coherence, competence-elements of self-esteem). Related to this is the tendency to see stressful events as a challenge (challenge dimension of hardiness; challenge aspect of the meaningfulness dimension of sense of coherence).
- All this implies also that people who are resilient do show emotional stability and do not have a tendency to experience negative emotions of all kinds and to overreact to negative experiences (Neuroticism, Negative Affectivity).

Is it only Negative Affectivity?

As the seemingly endless diversity of concepts in the end fits into a rather coherent picture, the question arises of whether they are really distinguishable. One might argue, for instance, that in the end it all boils down to a few traits, such as Neuroticism, or perhaps to the combination of a few traits, such as Neuroticism, Extraversion, and Agreeableness. This raises the suspicion that old traits are re-invented under new labels (Vollrath, 2001).

Negative Affectivity (Watson, Pennebaker & Folger, 1987), or Neuroticism (Dembroski & Costa, 1987) certainly is the most obvious candidate that many of the concepts might be reduced to. Indeed, the measures discussed here are often found to correlate with one another, some have been shown to be part of a larger construct, as discussed above (see, for instance, Bernard et al., 1996; Judge & Bono, 2001; Kravetz et al., 1993; Wofford & Daly, 1997). In many cases controlling for NA significantly reduces associations between belief systems and symptoms (e.g. Orr & Westman, 1990; Schaubroeck & Ganster, 1991; Sinclair & Tetrick, 2000; Smith, Pope, Rhodewalt & Poulton, 1989).

Indeed, it would be quite strange if belief systems that have to do with an environment that is meaningful, basically benign, and can be influenced, and with a self-concept that involves the capability to actually influence this environment in accordance with one's goals, did *not* show strong relationships with such a broad construct as NA. Also, the etiology being proposed for constructs like hardiness, locus of control, sense of coherence, or self-esteem involves experiences of mastery, of failure that can be dealt with and thus stays circumscribed, etc. (cf. Antonovsky, 1991; Bandura, 1992; Brockner, 1988), and, of course, these are conditions that one would also assume to influence the development of NA.

The most plausible relationship, it seems to me, would be a model that assumes a very high level construct of health (or disease) proneness (e.g., Bernard et al., 1996; Judge & Bono,

2001; Wofford & Daly, 1997) but would follow a hierarchical approach, with subconstructs that contain a more belief-oriented factor (as, for instance, in Kravetz et al.: hardiness and locus of control) on the one hand and a more affectively oriented factor (e.g., Neuroticism, negative affect, anger, anxiety) on the other. Interestingly, this would not be too far from concepts in research on subjective well-being, where the basic distinction seems to be similarly between more cognitive (satisfaction) and affective aspects (Diener, Suh, Lucas & Smith, 1999). Further down, finer and finer distinctions can be made.

Such hierarchical concepts seem to be widely accepted, and they have some very important implications. One important aspect is that lower-level constructs are especially important for understanding the mechanisms by which higher-level traits 'translate' into experience and behavior. Also, the hierarchy is not perfect: lower-level constructs are influenced, but not completely determined, by higher level traits. This is reflected in findings that controlling for NA does not always render the impact of lower-level constructs insignificant, although it does tend to reduce it. Furthermore, and related to this aspect, very high-level traits show substantial stability in adulthood (McCrae & Costa, 1990). This does not imply that they cannot be changed at all (see Diener et al., 1999; Spector, Zapf, Chen & Frese, 2000), but it does imply that they are not changed easily. Lower-level characteristics, such as belief systems, or coping tendencies, are likely to change, and be changed, more easily (Semmer & Schallberger, 1996). This is encouraging with regard to interventions, as it may be difficult to induce strong changes in Neuroticism, but much easier to change more specific tendencies of appraisal, reactivity, and coping that are important for the individual in question. The usefulness of such an approach is reflected in the success of stress management training, where effects can be achieved with a surprisingly small number of sessions, often between 10 and 15 (Kaluza, 1997; van der Klink, Blonk, Schene & van Dijk, 2001; cf. Semmer & Zapf, 2004). Another example is the success of a hostility intervention on the constructive expression of anger and the concomitant change in diastolic blood pressure (Davidson, McGregor, Stuhr & Gidron, 1999). More specific constructs, therefore, are important despite their relationships with high level traits, such as Neuroticism, Extraversion, and Agreeableness.

Beliefs and Reality

One final word of caution seems in order: No matter how they are conceived of in detail, the conclusion might seem plausible that resourceful belief systems as depicted here will always be positive, helping to interpret things in a positive way, dealing with them in an efficient way, etc. While this is true in general, it should be pointed out that there must be a minimum amount of correspondence between one's beliefs and reality. Positive illusions seem to be healthy, but only if they are moderate, that is, not completely illusory (Taylor & Brown, 1988), and if they are amenable to clear feedback (Colvin & Block, 1994). High self-esteem may induce poor strategies such as overconfidence in seemingly plausible, but premature solutions to a problem where further information should be sought (Weiss & Knight, 1980); too high hopes may lead to equally high disappointment, as shown by Frese & Mohr (1987; see also Frese, 1992) with regard to unemployed people; and the belief in a benign world, if fostered too strongly, may lead to a threatening challenge to one's total world view by single experiences to the contrary (Brown, 2002; Wortman & Silver, 1992). An optimistic outlook, a positive evaluation of one's own competencies, and a view of the world as controllable are healthy, but 'Illusions destroyed are worse than realistic pessimism' (Frese, 1992, p. 82).

COPING

Coping is one of the most important concepts in research on stress. It refers to all attempts (regardless of their success) to manage a stressful transaction, to make it less stressful (cf. Lazarus & Folkman, 1984). These attempts are based on an appraisal of the situation (primary appraisal) and one's possibilities to deal with it (secondary appraisal). They are, therefore, specific to the characteristics of the situation (e.g. a controllable situation tends to elicit more active coping strategies than an uncontrollable one; Elfering et al. 2005; Grebner et al., 2004). Although there is no doubt that coping is highly situation-specific, and that people do adjust their way of coping to the characteristics of the situation (e.g., Reicherts & Pihet, 2000), there also is no doubt that people also have certain tendencies to cope in a given way (Costa et al., 1996).

Classifications of Coping

There are many classifications of coping, the most basic one being the dichotomy between problem-focused vs. emotion-focused coping, as suggested by Lazarus and his group (Lazarus & Folkman, 1984). Others expand this by adding a category like 'appraisal-focused' (Billings & Moos, 1984) or 'perception-focused' (Pearlin & Schooler, 1978) coping.

A somewhat different approach concentrates on the tendency to seek or avoid information concerning the stressful aspects of the situation. This is most clearly expressed in the coping styles called 'monitoring' and 'blunting' by Miller (e.g. 1990). Somewhat similarly, Cronkite and Moos (1984) distinguish between 'approach and avoidance'. Stanton, Parsa and Austenfeld, (2005) regard this as the most important distinction. A special variant of this is the concept of 'repression-sensitization', which distinguishes between people who are 'truly' non-anxious and people who report low anxiety but at the same time high social desirability. These latter are called 'repressors', and they tend to show physiological reactions to stressful situations that are higher than those of the 'truly non-anxious', thus being more similar to those that do report high anxiety (the sensitizers) in terms of physiology but more similar to the low-anxious in terms of self-report (Weinberger & Schwartz, 1990; Weinberger, Schwartz & Davidson, 1979; cf. Krohne, 1996).

There are many expansions and blends of these approaches. Thus, Endler and Parker (1990) distinguish between problem-focused, emotion-focused and avoidance coping. Carver et al. (1989) have four (second order) factors which involve active coping, denial and disengagement, acceptance, and a combination of seeking social support and concentration on, as well as venting of, emotions. McCrae and Costa (1986) distinguish only two main factors which they call 'mature' vs. 'neurotic' coping; a similar dichotomy is suggested by Koeske, Kirk and Koeske (1993) who distinguish between 'control coping' and 'avoidance coping'. Finally, Thoits (1986) proposes a two-by-two matrix involving problem-focused vs. emotion-focused coping as one dimension and behavioral vs. cognitive strategies as the second. A similar distinction is made by Steptoe (1991) who further adds the possibility of an approach vs. avoidance strategy in each of the four cells.

This short (and not exhaustive) enumeration shows that there is by no means consensus over number and kind of the dimensions to be employed. This problem is further aggravated by the fact that the same labels do not necessarily imply the same concept.

Thus, items like 'consuming alcohol', 'eating', and 'smoking' are sometimes part of an avoidance or denial factor (e.g. Carver et al., 1989; Endler & Parker, 1990; Koeske et al. 1993), but sometimes they belong to an emotion-focused factor (e.g. Billings & Moos, 1984; Latak, 1986); this is especially interesting as Endler and Parker also have an emotion factor, and Latak also has an avoidance factor. 'Distraction' is part of 'cognitive problem-focused coping' in Thoits' classification but belongs to denial and disengagement in the analysis of Carver et al. (1989). These examples could easily be continued.

In light of this confusion it is surprising that nevertheless there are some tendencies where research is converging. Thus, in general (and with many exceptions), the tendency to employ problem-focused coping (including problem-focused cognitive coping as defined by Steptoe, 1991, that is, a positive reinterpretation) is associated with better mental (and sometimes, physical) health while emotion-focused coping tends to show the opposite relationship (cf. Aldwin & Revenson, 1987; Billings & Moos, 1984; Carver et al., 1989; Elfering et al., 2005; Grebner et al, 2004; Kälin, 2004; Koeske et al., 1993; Latak, 1986; McCrae & Costa, 1986; Scheier & Carver, 1992; Lee-Baggley et al., 2005). This applies also to self-rated coping-efficiency which is higher in the study by McCrae & Costa (1986) for what they call 'mature' coping and lower for what they label 'neurotic' coping. Problem-focused coping has also been found to moderate the relationship between control and demands according to the Karasek model of job stress (Karasek & Theorell, 1990), in that people who show 'active coping' profit from control under conditions of high stress (de Rijk, Le Blanc, Schaufeli & de Jonge, 1998); this is confirmed in multilevel-analyses of situational data by Elfering et al. (2005) and Grebner et al. (2004). Avoidance-oriented coping is often found to be beneficial in the short run but detrimental in the long run (Suls & Fletcher, 1985; cf. Ayduk, Mischel & Downey, 2002; Thayer, Newman & McClain, 1994). Also, not surprisingly, avoidance is more beneficial if the problem is uncontrollable whereas approach is more instrumental when something can be done about the situation (Miller, 1990). Finally, Miller (1990) finds that a discrepancy between one's preferred style and aspects of the situation (e.g. being a monitor but not getting enough information, and being a 'blunter' but getting a lot of information) may be more detrimental in many situations than coping style per se. Stanton et al. (2005) report similar results for 'emotional approach' coping (see below).

The Difficult Role of 'Emotion-focused Coping'

Instrumental and Detrimental Aspects of Emotion-focused Coping

One of the aspects of coping research that are somewhat difficult to interpret is the often-reported finding that 'emotional coping' tends to be associated with poorer mental health and poorer outcomes (Edwards, 1998; Lee-Baggley et al., 2005). The reason why this is puzzling is that many authors postulate that emotional coping should not be detrimental per se. Rather, highly stressful experiences may require some management of one's intensive emotions before one is able to deal with the problem in a more active and direct way, thus making strategies like symptom management, denial, avoidance, etc. potentially instrumental in regaining the resources needed for active, problem-oriented coping (Lazarus, 1999; Lazarus & Folkman, 1984; Reicherts & Perrez, 1992).

When used alone, or as the dominant mode of coping, however, it does make sense theoretically that emotional coping should not be very helpful, unless the problem is uncontrollable to a large extent, since the problem as such will persist. From this point of view, emotion-focused coping is often not very adaptive, and it is, therefore, not surprising that these forms of coping tend to correlate with personality traits such as Neuroticism (e.g. Carver et al. 1989; Frese, 1986; Lee-Baggley et al. 2005; McCrae & Costa, 1986), in some cases with hostility (Dembroski & Costa, 1987), or with a low standing in resourceful belief systems such as optimism, internal locus of control, self-esteem, or hardiness (Carver et al., 1989). Conversely, problem-oriented forms of coping (including cognitive ones like positive reappraisal) tend to show the opposite pattern of associations.

One should expect, however, that these associations would be different if people applied emotion-focused coping first, followed by problem-focused coping. The emotion-focused phase would then be functional by enabling the person to concentrate on means of solving the problem, because strong emotions that otherwise might interfere with this process have calmed down. As long, however, as we do not have more studies on the combination of different coping modes and their change over time, it will be quite difficult to detect positive effects of emotional coping. The results on positive short-term effects of avoidance-strategies do point in this direction (Ayduk et al., 2002; Thayer et al., 1994), but there is surprisingly little research on the instrumentality of emotional coping for (re-) gaining the resources needed to deal with the problem effectively.

Some support for this reasoning can be found in a study by Koeske et al. (1993) who conclude that 'avoidance coping' tends to be detrimental only when it is used alone, but may even be beneficial if used in conjunction with 'control'-coping. It is also interesting to note that the concept of 'learned resourcefulness' mentioned above (Rosenbaum, 1990) contains items on the effective regulation of emotions. Also, Billings and Moos (1984) have two scales on emotion-focused coping which seem especially interesting. One is called 'affective regulation', and it contains items such as 'got away from things for a while', 'told myself things that helped me to feel better', 'exercised more to reduce tension', 'got busy with other things to keep my mind off the problems'. This scale has some connotation of using palliative strategies in the instrumental way discussed here. Theoretically, therefore, it should be more beneficial than the other emotion-focused scale, which is called 'emotional discharge' and contains items like 'took it out on other people' or 'tried to reduce tension by drinking more'. And, indeed, the 'affective regulation' scale correlates positively with self-confidence and negatively (albeit significantly only for women) with depression severity, while the 'emotional discharge' scale correlates positively with depression and physical symptoms, and negatively with self-confidence.

An especially interesting approach to this problem is presented by Perrez and Reicherts (1992b; Reicherts & Perrez, 1992; Reicherts & Pihet, 2000). They formulate a 'behavior rules approach' that specifies which coping strategies should work best under what conditions. Thus, in line with many others, they postulate that under conditions of greater controllability there should be more active and less avoidance coping. With regard to 'self-directed' coping, they 'prescribe' more palliative coping under high stressfulness (high negative valence) and more re-evaluation of standards when the probability of re-occurrence of the situation is judged to be high. In their studies, they used a computer-assisted self-observation system where subjects record events in a pocket computer and are then guided through a number of questions concerning their appraisal of the situation, their coping behavior, etc. Their results show that conforming to these rules is associated with greater coping effectiveness (measured as reports about to what extent the problem was solved and to what extent people coped in a way they would like to cope). Also, depressives and schizophrenics conform less to these rules. Especially interesting in the present context is the finding that conformity to the rules regarding 'self-directed coping', i.e. palliation and re-evaluation, is related to indicators of psychological health. In our own studies, however, using a variant of their instrument, we could find support only for the 'active coping rule' (prescribing problem-solving under high controllability) but not for the 'palliative coping rule' (prescribing palliative coping in highly stressful situations) in multilevel analyses (Elfering et al., 2005; Grebnet et al. 2004).

A further attempt to combine individual differences and situational aspects can be seen in research that assesses how people with different characteristics deal with specific stress situations.

Thus, DeLongis and associates (e.g., DeLongis & Holtzman, 2005; Lee-Baggley et al., 2005) report that people high in N in general tend to cope in ways that are likely not to be very adaptive (e.g., low problem solving, high avoidance). However, they do not necessarily cope in a rigid and unchanging way. Rather, they do change their coping behavior—but evidently not in a way that is appropriate for the situation. For instance, they tend to react with confrontative coping in stress situations involving people close to them, but to respond more empathically when someone distant is involved. People high in extraversion, being 'good copers' in general, showed more empathy with their children but more confrontation towards their spouses. People high in A, on the other hand, had the opposite pattern, responding with more empathy towards spouses and more confrontation with their children. People high in Conscientiousness showed more problem solving vis-à-vis noninterpersonal than interpersonal stress situations.

This type of research seems very promising, making it possible to throw more light on typical behavior-situation combinations that characterize individuals (Mischel & Shoda, 1998).

Emotion-focused Coping as 'Inability to Cope'

There is an additional problem, however, with the conceptualization and, especially, the operationalization of 'emotion-focused' coping. For a number of items typically contained in scales with this label it is doubtful whether they actually measure coping, that is, an attempt to deal with the problem and/or with one's reaction to it.

Consider a few examples: Carver et al. (1989) report a scale they call 'focus on and venting of emotions', with items such as 'I get upset and let my emotions out', or 'I get upset, and am really aware of it'. This scale correlates with anxiety. Aldwin and Revenson (1987) report an emotion-focused scale that taps 'self-blame' and is positively related to symptoms and negatively related to perceived coping efficiency. McCrae and Costa (1986) also have a self-blame scale and also report items such as 'thought about the problem over and over without reaching a decision'. Both are related to neuroticism (see also Costa et al., 1996). Endler & Parker (1990) report an 'emotion-oriented subscale' containing, again, self-blame but also items like 'I became very tense'. The scale correlates with several scales indicative of NA, such as anxiety, depression, or neuroticism. Frese (1986) reports a 'brooding' scale (e.g. 'I think about it for some days'), which correlates with psychosomatic complaints. Nowack (1989) reports a scale on 'intrusive negative thoughts' (e.g. 'blame and criticize myself...'), which correlates with distress.

There are many more examples of this, but the point should be clear: If one defines coping as cognitions and behaviors designed to deal with the stressful transaction (Cox & Ferguson, 1991, p. 19) or as 'efforts to manage specific external and/or internal demands' (Lazarus & Folkman, 1984, p. 141)—in other words, as an *attempt to do something about the stress experienced,* be that changing of the situation or changing one's feelings about it—then it is doubtful whether what is being measured here can really be called *coping.* Rather, items like these seem to measure how strongly one feels distressed (e.g. 'I become very tense') and the inability to concentrate on anything other than the distressing thoughts (brooding, blaming). Nothing in these items indicates that one is trying to *regulate* one's emotions, rather, they seem to measure the inability to do so!

Not surprisingly, there are scales that intend to measure the *impact* of events, and which contain items that overlap with 'coping items'of this sort—for instance, by measuring 'intrusion', that is, the tendency to ruminate about stressful events and, in doing so, to keep experiencing the feelings associated with them (Ferring & Filipp, 1994; Horowitz, Wilner & Alvarez, 1979). In a similar vein, Keenan and Newton (1984) describe 'emotional reactions' to frustration in organizations, consisting of items such as 'I sometimes feel quite frustrated over things that happen at work' or 'On occasion I have found it difficult to keep my temper at work'.

In other words, the suspicion arises that scales like these, rather than being measures of coping, really come close to being measures of emotional reactivity in response to potentially stressful events or circumstances—or, to put it differently, measures of stress reactions as far as they ask about circumscribed events, and measures of the tendency to experience stress in the case of generalized 'coping' styles. If Neuroticism is regarded as 'a chronic condition of irritability and distress-proneness which is relatively independent of objective conditions' (Costa & McCrae, 1987, p. 302), then 'coping' measures of this type may well be regarded as 'distress-proneness' vis-à-vis potentially stressful conditions—which corresponds to Costa and McCrae's (1987, p. 302) definition of Neuroticism. See David and Suls (1999), and Stanton et al. (2005) for similar arguments.

It therefore seems necessary to develop instruments that assess 'true' palliative coping. Two attempts to do so will briefly be considered.

In our research group, Kälin (2004) compared the effects of a 'classical' emotion-oriented coping measure (CISS—Endler & Parker, 1990; see Endler, 1998) with an item from the instrument by Perrez and Reicherts (1992a) that measures successful palliative coping ('normally, I succeed in calming down'). This item correlates negatively with 'emotional coping' as measured by the CISS, and it is associated with better well-being, or less strain, as assessed by a variety of measures. As this item measures *successful* palliative coping, it does not permit clear conclusions about *attempts* to cope in a palliative way. We therefore investigated such attempts at calming down in an event-sampling assessment of stressful situations (Elfering et al., 2005; Grebner et al., 2004). And, indeed, in multilevel analyses, palliative coping was associated with increased chances of calming down in stressful situations, controlling for variables like 'stressfulness' and 'controllability' of the situation as well as for problem-focused coping attempts (Elfering et al., 2005; Grebner et al., 2004). Interestingly, palliative coping had very specific effects. Whereas problem-focused coping was associated with both perceived problem solving and calming down, palliative coping was associated with calming down only.

Another approach along these lines has been developed by Stanton and colleagues (Stanton & Franz, 1999; Stanton, Kirk, Cameron & Danoff-Burg, 2000; Stanton et al., 2005). They developed a scale that measures approach-oriented aspects of emotional coping, namely 'emotional processing' and 'emotional expression'. At least for women, emotional approach coping seems to be beneficial, whereas for men, associations with rumination were found. However, coping through emotional expression was found to be associated with higher life satisfaction in both sexes, and a receptive context seems to render emotional approach coping adaptive for men as well. Certainly more work on the adaptiveness of emotional processing and expression is needed, investigating its relationship to gender and to context, and analysing the effect of the combination of different strategies (for instance, in one of the studies by Stanton et al. the joint use of emotional processing and emotional expression turned out to be maladaptive). Thus, there is still no consistent picture on this scale. Nevertheless, the concept of 'coping through emotional approach' is a major breakthrough that deserves attention in future research.

More work certainly is warranted on what emotional coping really means, how it can be distinguished from receptivity to stress, and which aspects of what has been measured under the heading of 'emotional coping' tend to be adaptive, and which do not (cf. Semmer et al., 2005).

Expressing Emotions: Coping or Intensifying of Distress?

Another important issue with regard to emotional coping concerns the role of expressing emotions. 'Venting' of emotions, that is, showing them, letting them out on other people etc., are part of some scales on emotional coping (e.g., Carver et al., 1989), and expressing, or not expressing, anger has been hotly debated in the literature on hostility for many years (see above).

In many cases, the expression of an emotion does not lead to a positive 'cathartic' effect; rather, it tends to make the emotion stronger (cf. Baumeister, Heatherton & Tice, 1994; Schwenkmezger & Hank, 1996; Siegman 1994b). Venting the emotion often feeds back into the experience of the emotion; it keeps the attention on the emotion and on the circumstances that elicited it, thus 'nourishing' the emotional experience. In addition, in many cases it elicits negative or avoidance reactions in others.

Thus, the expression of anger may antagonize others and undermine their willingness to give social support (Weber, 1993); 'dysphoric interactions' may elicit negative reactions (Strack & Coyne, 1983), and distress in general may lead to feelings of helplessness, rejection, and unwillingness to give social support in interaction partners. Such reactions are especially likely if the 'victim' does not 'behave like a "good" victim', that is, show signs of efforts to deal effectively with his or her situation (Silver, Wortman & Crofton, 1990). Fenlason and Beehr (1994) and Zellars and Perrewé (2001) report negative associations between well-being and social support when the content of what people talk about is negative, thus representing something like 'collective rumination'.

That the expression of emotions keeps them alive is, of course, a somewhat controversial statement (and, as we shall see shortly, it is not true unconditionally). Especially in the case of anger and its association with coronary heart disease it has often been found that *not* expressing one's anger (anger-in) might be risky (see above). In line with this argument, Gross and associates (e.g., John & Gross, 2004) show that suppressing negative emotions tends to suppress only the expression of an emotion but not its experience, and it tends to have negative consequences in terms of memory for socially relevant information and in terms of reduced social closeness.

However, surprisingly little research deals with the crucial question of whether the (non) expression of anger is effective in ending one's state of anger. As Baumeister et al. (1994) state, 'the decisive issue is whether the person stays angry or not' (p. 108). And this may not depend simply on whether the anger is expressed or not. Expressing it may give relief, but it also may keep the focus on the emotion and the circumstances that caused it (Roger & Jamieson, 1998; Rusting & Nolen-Hoeksema, 1998). Part of the problem may be the fit with personality. Thus, Engebretson, Matthews and Scheier (1989) found that it was more effective for people high in anger-out to express their anger than not to express it. Note, however, that this effect was relative: Although people high in anger-out fared better when they expressed their anger, they nevertheless showed higher blood-pressure during and after the provoking situation than those high in anger-in.

The crucial variable may well be the *style* of expressing one's emotions. Results by Weber (1993) show that both strategies have helpful and hindering aspects, the most crucial variable being what Weber terms 'antagonism': Expression of anger can be constructive (e.g. explaining one's feelings to a partner) or antagonistic (offending, blaming the partner). Likewise, not expressing the anger may be antagonistic if associated with ruminating, self-pity, dreaming about revenge, etc. ('silent seething'—Baumeister et al., 1994; see also Roger & Jamieson, 1998) but it may be non-antagonistic by putting things into perspective, trying to see them from a humorous side, trying to understand the other's perspective, etc. This would actually imply a form of re-appraisal, which has been shown to have positive affective consequences (John & Gross, 2004). The non-antagonistic mode will tend to end the state of anger while the antagonistic one will tend to sustain or even increase it (Davidson et al. 2000). This reasoning is supported by the work of Pennebaker and colleagues on the health effects of talking or writing about traumatic experience (e.g., Niederhoffer & Pennebaker, 2005; Smyth & Pennebaker, 1999). They conclude that the positive effects are attained only if the experience is translated into a coherent narrative that has meaning. Increased used of terms implying causality or insight is associated with gaining from sharing the experience. Using very few negative emotion words (repression) hinders this constructive process, but so does overuse of negative emotion words, which may indicate 'a recursive loop of complaining without attaining closure' (Smyth & Pennebaker, 1999, p. 81). Thus, the real question may not necessarily be whether people express their emotions or not, but whether not expressing them results in unprocessed, and recurring, negative emotions or in getting over things, and whether expressing them creates a positive feedback loop or a constructive process of coming to terms with one's emotions. These distinctions have to be taken up in measures of emotional coping in order to gain insight in its effectiveness (cf. Davidson et al. 2000).

Summary

Thus, in general, people who have the tendency to cope by dealing actively with the problem tend to be better off. However, where the situation is taken into account, it becomes clear that a palliative mode of coping may be beneficial (a) if it is used to build up resources needed for other forms of coping, and (b) in situations that cannot be controlled. The latter also call for a re-evaluation of one's goals. These benefits are likely not to apply to all kinds of 'emotional coping'. Rather, specific ways of expressing one's emotions (e.g., in a way that communicates *about* one's emotions rather than in an 'unfiltered' expression), and specific efforts to calm oneself down (what I referred to as palliative coping) are candidates for such beneficial ways of emotional coping. Furthermore, assessment of emotional coping should focus more on coping proper, in the sense of trying to manage one's emotions and try to avoid items that tap Neuroticism more than coping.

Given the diversity of what has been 'lumped' into the category of 'emotional coping', including strategies that are rather promising (e.g., 'true' palliative coping, emotional approach coping, finding meaning) and others that are likely to be dysfunctional in many contexts, it may well be that this dichotomy will turn out not to be satisfying and that dimensions such as approach-avoidance are more important (Aldwin & Yancura, 2003; Stanton et al. 2005; cf. also Krohne's, 1996 concept of two-dimensional avoidance, developed in the context of the repression-sensitization construct).

FINAL COMMENTS

While there are many qualifications and differentiations to this, the picture seems to be emerging of a person that is low on Neuroticism and Antagonism, has resources such as resourceful belief systems and a tendency to treat people in a way that elicits sympathy and social support, as well as the tendency to use active, problem oriented coping strategies wherever possible, but also the capability to realistically (and not resentfully) adjust to reality where it cannot be altered, and the capability of dealing with one's negative emotions in a constructive way.

Three final comments are in order with regard to this picture:

1. As already emphasized above, resilient people have a certain way of dealing with *reality*. Coping actively under all circumstances, nourishing illusions over one's capabilities that are far from reality, or having a naive optimism, are not characteristics of this effectiveness. While individual differences with regard to coping with, and suffering from, stressors are pervasive, they should not seduce us to reduce everything to idiosyncratic, exclusively subjective, phenomena (see Hobfoll, 2001; Sapolsky, 1999; Semmer et al., 2005).
2. Reality also is important in yet another way. Although stressful experiences of vulnerable people are, to some degree, 'self-produced', and although vulnerable people tend to show exaggerated appraisals and reactions to such stress experiences, the environment still plays an important role. It may trigger such reactions to a greater or lesser degree, and it may provide external resources (e.g., in terms of social networks and social support, but also in terms of money, available services, etc.). Thus, more vulnerable people may show stronger reactions to task demands and control at work, or to social conflict. Yet, there still must be incidents of very demanding activities, etc. to elicit cardiovascular reactions (Kamarck et al., 2005). Or, to take another example, it evidently is the combination of high anger/hostility and low social support that is associated with atherosclerosis or CHD (Smith et al., 2004). And although the amount of task demands, control, social conflict, and social support may well depend in part on these vulnerable people themselves, these environmental characteristics are likely to exist independent of them to a considerable

degree (cf. Semmer, Zapf & Greif, 1996; Semmer, Grebner & Elfering, 2004; cf. the research on the impact of SES on health, e.g. Adler & Matthews, 1994; Adler et al., 1999). The role of the external environment should, therefore, not be lost sight of, and intervention efforts should focus on both the environment and the person (see Semmer, 2003b).

3. While, in many cases, it is not the objective situation per se but the way people appraise it and deal with it that decides about outcomes, it should be kept in mind that resiliency itself is, albeit only partly, a product of such circumstances. If one examines the effects of stress on (physical or psychological) health on the one hand and on the development of resiliency vs. vulnerability on the other, the parallels are striking. Apart from overwhelming, traumatic single experiences, it is *chronically stressful conditions* that overtax people's resources, which impair their health and well-being— and it is the same conditions that undermine their coping resources. The same applies to a lack of challenge, because the experience of mastering difficult situations also seems necessary for the development of both well-being and coping resources. Thus, a vicious circle may develop in which the most damaging long-term effect of stress may be its capacity to undermine the very resources needed to deal with it effectively (Demerouti, Bakker & Bulters, 2004; Hobfoll, Johnson, Ennis & Jackson, 2003; cf. Semmer et al. 2005; Smith & Spiro, 2002).

All this may well lead to the perception of the person being 'the cause' of the problems, because he or she seems unable to deal with problems that other people deal with effectively. This supports an attribution error—for lay people and scientists alike—that induces people to overemphasize individual differences and to underemphasize reality and not to see the vicious circle in which one is reinforcing the other. The picture worsens when some of these cumulative effects refer to characteristics of the person which, by themselves, tend to irritate others (e.g. excessive complaints—Silver et al., 1990) or even antagonize them (e.g. aggressive behavior, lack of dependability in cooperative work, etc.). In such a case, the person does, indeed, create new stressors for him- or herself as well as for others, and it becomes very difficult for others to see how much this 'actor' is also a 'victim' of stressful life circumstances during his or her life.

REFERENCES

Adler, N.E., Marmot, M., McEwen, B.S. & Stewart, J. (1999). Socioeconomic status and health in industrial nations: Social, psychological, and biological pathways [Entire issue]. *Annals of the New York Academy of Sciences, 896.*

Adler, N. & Matthews, K. (1994). Health psychology: Why do some people get sick and some stay well? *Annual Review of Psychology, 45,* 229–259.

Aldwin, C.M. (2000). *Stress, coping, and development: An integrative perspective.* New York: Guilford Press.

Aldwin, C.M. & Revenson, G.A. (1987). Does coping help? A reexamination of the relation between coping and mental heatlh. *Journal of Personality and Social Psychology, 53,* 337–348.

Aldwin, C.M. & Yancura, L.A. (2003). Coping and health: A comparison of the stress and trauma literatures. In P.P. Schnurr & B.L. Green (eds), *Trauma and health: Physical health consequences of exposure to extreme stress* (pp. 99–125). Washington, DC: American Psychological Association.

Allred, K.D. & Smith, T.W. (1989). The hardy personality: Cognitive and physiological responses to evaluative threat. *Journal of Personality and Social Psychology, 56,* 257–266.

Antonovsky, A. (1991). The structural sources of salutogenic strengths. In C.L. Cooper & R. Payne, (eds), *Personality and stress: Individual differences in the stress process* (pp. 67–104). Chichester: John Wiley & Sons, Ltd.

Antonovsky, A. (1993). The structure and properties of the Sense of Coherence Scale. *Social Science and Medicine, 36,* 725–733.

Asendorpf, J.B. & Wilpers, S. (1998). Personality effects on social relationships. *Journal of Personality and Social Psychology, 74,* 1531–1544.

Aust, B., Peter, R. & Siegrist, J. (1997). Stress management in bus drivers: A pilot study based on the model of effort-reward imbalance. *International Journal of Stress Management, 4,* 297–305.

Averill, J.R. (1986). The acquisition of emotions during adulthood. In R. Harré (ed.), *The social construction of emotions* (pp. 98–118). Oxford: Basil Blackwell.

Ayduk, O., Mischel, W. & Downey, G. (2002). Attentional mechanisms linking rejection to hostile reactivity: The role of 'hot' versus 'cool' focus. *Psychological Science, 13,* 443–448.

Bandura, A. (1989). Self-regulation of motivation and action through internal standards and goal systems. In L.A. Pervin (ed.), *Goal concepts in personality and social psychology* (pp. 19–85). Hillsdale, NJ: Lawrence Erlbaum.

Bandura, A. (1992). Exercise of personal agency through the self-efficacy mechanism. In R. Schwarzer (ed.), *Self-efficacy: Thought control of action* (pp. 3–38). Washington DC: Hemisphere.

Barefoot, J.C. (1992). Developments in the measurement of hostility. In H.S. Friedman (ed.), *Hostility, coping and health* (pp. 13–31). Washington, DC: APA.

Barnett, R.S. & Hyde, J.S. (2001). Women, men, work, and family. *American Psychologist, 56,* 781–796.

Bartone, P.T. (2000). Hardiness as a resilience factor for United States forces in the Gulf War. In J.M. Violanti, D. Paton & C. Dunning (eds), *Posttraumatic stress intervention: Challenges, issues, and perspectives.* Springfield, IL: Charles C. Thomas.

Baumeister, R.F., Heatherton, T.F. & Tice, D.M. (1993). When ego threat leads to self-regulation failure: Negative consequences of high self-esteem. *Journal of Personality and Social Psychology, 64,* 141–156.

Baumeister, R.F., Heatherton, T.F. & Tice, D.M. (1994). *Losing control. How and why people fail at self-regulation.* San Diego: Academic Press.

Beehr, T.A. & Bowling, N.A. (2005). Hardy personality, stress, and health. In C.L. Cooper (ed.), *Handbook of Stress and Health* (2nd edn, pp. 193–211). New York: CRC Press.

Bekker, M., Gjerdingen, D., McGovern, P. & Lundberg, U. (1999). Multiple roles: Health protection and health risk? In A. Kolk, M. Bekker & K. van Vliet (eds), *Advances in women and health research: towards gender-sensitive strategies.* Tilburg, NL: Tilburg University Press.

Berkowitz, L. (1998). Aggressive personalities. In D.F. Barone, M. Hersen & V.B. van Hasselt (eds), *Advanced personality* (pp. 263–285). New York: Plenum.

Bernard, L.C., Hutchison, S., Lavin, A. & Pennington, P. (1996). Ego-strength, hardiness, self-esteem, self-efficacy, optimism, and maladjustment: Health-related personality constructs and the 'Big Five' model of personality. *Assessment, 3,* 115–131.

Billings, A.G. & Moos, R.H. (1984). Coping, stress, and social resources among adults with unipolar depression. *Journal of Personality and Social Psychology, 46,* 877–891.

Birks, Y. & Roger, D. (2000). Identifying components of type-A behaviour: 'toxic' and 'non-toxic' achieving. *Personality and Individual Differences, 28,* 1093–1105.

Bolger, N. & Zuckerman, A. (1995). A framework for studying personality in the stress process. *Journal of Personality and Social Psychology, 69,* 890–902.

Bowling, N.A., Beehr, T.A. & Swader, W.M. (2005). Giving and receiving social support at work: the roles of personality and reciprocity. *Journal of Vocational Behavior, 67,* 476–489.

Brockner, J. (1988). *Self-esteem at work.* Lexington MA: Lexington Books.

Brockner, J. & Higgins, E.T. (2001). Regulatory focus theory: Implications for the study of emotions at work. *Organizational Behavior and Human Decision Processes, 86,* 35–66.

Brockner, J., Tyler, T.R. & Cooper-Schneider, R. (1992). The influence of prior commitment to an institution on reactions to perceived unfairness: The higher they are, the harder they fall. *Administrative Science Quarterly, 37,* 241–261.

Brockner, J., Wiesenfeld, B.A. & Raskas, D.F. (1993). Self-esteem and expectancy-value discrepancy. The effects of believing that you can (or can't) get what you want. In R.F. Baumeister (ed.), *Self-esteem: The puzzle of low self-regard* (pp. 219–240). New York: Plenum.

Brown, G.W. (2002). Social roles, context and evolution in the origins of depression. *Journal of Health and Social Behavior, 43*, 255–276.

Bruggemann, A. (1974). Zur Unterscheidung verschiedener Formen von 'Arbeitszufriedenheit' (The distinction of different forms of job satisfaction). *Arbeit und Leistung, 28*, 281–284.

Brummet, B.H., Maynard, K.E., Haney, T.L., Siegler, I.C. & Barefoot, J.C. (2000). Reliability of interview-assessed hostility ratings across mode of assessment and time. *Journal of Personality Assessment, 75*, 225–236.

Buchanan, G.M. (1995). Explanatory style and coronary heart disease. In G.M. Buchanan & M.E.P. Seligman (eds), *Explanatory style*. Hillsdale, NJ: Erlbaum.

Burke, P.J. (1991). Identity processes and social stress. *American Sociological Review, 56*, 835–849.

Buss, A.H. & Durkee, A. (1957). An inventory for assessing different kinds of hostility. *Journal of Consulting Psychology, 21*, 343–349.

Buss, A.H. & Perry, M. (1992). The aggression questionnaire. *Journal of Personality and Social Psychology, 63*, 452–459.

Büssing, A., Bissels, T., Fuchs, V. & Perrar, K.-M. (1999). A dynamic model of work satisfaction: Qualitative approaches. *Human Relations, 52*, 999–1028.

Cantor, N. & Langston, C.A. (1989). Ups and downs of life tasks in a life transition. In L.A. Pervin (ed.), *Goal concepts in personality and social psychology* (pp. 127–167). Hillsdale, NJ: Lawrence Erlbaum.

Carver, C.S. & Scheier, M.F. (1990). Principles of self-regulation: Action and emotion. In E.T. Higgins & R.M. Sorrentino (eds), *Handbook of motivation and cognition, Vol. 2* (pp. 3–52). New York: The Guilford Press.

Carver, C.S. & Scheier, M.F. (1999). Optimism. In C.R. Snyder (ed.), *Coping: The psychology of what works* (pp. 182–204). New York: Oxford University Press.

Carver, C.S. & Scheier, M.F. (2005). Optimism. In C.R. Snyder & S.J. Lopez (eds), *Handbook of positive psychology* (pp. 231–243). Oxford: Oxford University Press.

Carver, C.S., Scheier, M.F. & Weintraub, J.K. (1989). Assessing coping strategies: A theoretically based approach. *Journal of Personality and Social Psychology, 56*, 267–283.

Cleary, P.D. & Mechanic, D. (1983). Sex differences in psychological distress among married people. *Journal of Health and Social Behavior, 24*, 111–121.

Cohen, S. & Edwards, J.R. (1989). Personality characteristics as moderators of the relationship between stress and disorder. In R.W.J. Neufeld (ed.), *Advances in the investigation of psychological stress* (pp. 235–283). New York: John Wiley & Sons, Inc.

Colvin, C.R. & Block, J. (1994). Do positive illusions foster mental health? An examination of the Taylor and Brown formulation. *Psychological Bulletin, 116*, 3–20.

Contrada, R.J. (1989). Type A behavior, personality hardiness, and cardiovascular responses to stress. *Journal of Personality and Social Psychology, 57*, 895–903.

Contrada, R.J. & Krantz, D.S. (1988). Stress, reactivity, and type A behavior: current status and future directions. *Annals of Behavioral Medicine, 10*, 64–70.

Cook, W.W. & Medley, D.M. (1954). Proposed hostility and pharasaic-virtue scales for the MMPI. *Journal of Applied Psychology, 38*, 414–418.

Cooper, C.L. & Payne, R.L. (1992). International perspectives on research into work, well-being and stress management. In J. Campbell Quick, L.R. Murphy & J.J. Hurrell, Jr. (eds), *Stress and well-being at work. Assessments and interventions for occupational mental health* (pp. 348–368). Washington, DC: American Psychological Association.

Costa, P.T. & McCrae, R.R. (1987). Neuroticism, somatic complaints, and disease: Is the bark worse than the bite? *Journal of Personality, 55*, 299–316.

Costa, P.T. & McCrae, R.R. (1998). Trait theories of personality. In D.F. Barone, M. Hersen & V.B. van Hasselt (eds), *Advanced personality* (pp. 103–121). New York: Plenum.

Costa, P.T., Somerfield, M.R. & McCrae, R.R. (1996). Personality and coping: A reconceptualization. In M. Zeidner & N.S. Endler (eds), *Handbook of coping: Theory, research, applications* (pp. 44–61). New York: John Wiley & Sons, Inc.

Cox, T. & Ferguson, E. (1991). Individual differences, stress and coping. In C.L. Cooper & R. Payne (eds), *Personality and stress: Individual differences in the stress process* (pp. 7–30). Chichester: John Wiley & Sons, Ltd.

Crocker, J. & Park, L.E. (2004). The costly pursuit of self-esteem. *Psychological Bulletin, 130*, 392–414.

Cronkite, R.C. & Moos, R.H. (1984). The role of predisposing and moderating factors in the stress-illness relationship. *Journal of Health and Social Behavior, 25*, 372–393.

Cropanzano, R., James, K. & Citera, M. (1993). A goal hierarchy model of personality, motivation, and leadership. *Research in Organizational Behavior, 15*, 267–322.

Cvetanovski, J. & Jex, S.M. (1994). Locus of control of unemployed people and its relationship to psychological and physical well-being. *Work & Stress, 8*, 60–67.

David, J.P. & Suls, J. (1999). Coping efforts in daily life: Role of Big Five traits and problem appraisals. *Journal of Personality, 67*, 254–294.

Davidson, K., MacGregor, M.W., Stuhr, J. & Gidron, Y. (1999). Increasing constructive anger verbal behavior decreases resting blood pressure: A secondary analysis of a randomized controlled hostility intervention. *International Journal of Behavioral Medicine, 6*, 268–278.

Davidson, K., MacGregor, M.W., Stuhr, J., Dixon, K. & MacLean, D. (2000). Constructive anger verbal behavior predicts blood pressure in a population-based sample. *Health Psychology, 19*, 55–64.

Davis, M.C., Matthews, K.A. & McGrath, C.E. (2000). Hostile attitudes predict vascular resistance during interpersonal stress in men and women. *Psychosomatic Medicine, Vol. 62(1)*, 17–25.

De Rijk, A.E., Le Blanc, P.M., Schaufeli, W.B. & de Jonge, J. (1998). Active coping and need for control as moderators of the job demand-control model: Effects on burnout. *Journal of Occupational and Organizational Psychology, 71*, 1–18.

DeLongis, A. & Holtzman, S. (2005). Coping in context: The role of stress, social support, and personality in coping. *Journal of Personality, 73*, 1–24.

Dembroski, T.M. & Costa, P. (1987). Coronary prone behavior: Components of the Type A pattern and hostility. *Journal of Personality, 55*, 211–235.

Dembroski, T.M. & Costa, P.T. (1988). Assessment of coronary prone behavior: A current overview. *Annals of Behavioral Medicine, 10*, 60–63.

Demerouti, E., Bakker, A.B. & Bulters, A.J. (2004). The loss spiral of work pressure, work-home interference and exhaustion: Reciprocal relations in a three-wave study. *Journal of Vocational Behavior, 64*, 131–149.

Depue, R.A. & Monroe, S.M. (1986). Conceptualization and measurement of human disorder in life stress research: The problem of chronic disturbance. *Psychological Bulletin, 99*, 36–51.

Diener, E., Oishi, S. & Lucs, R.E. (2003). Personality, culture, and subjective well-being: Emotional and cognitive evaluations of life. *Annual Review of Psychology, 54*, 403–425.

Diener, E., Suh, E.M., Lucas, R.E. & Smith, H. (1999). Subjective well-being: Three decades of progress. *Psychological Bulletin, 125*, 276–302.

Dohrenwend, B.S., Dohrenwend, B.P., Dodson, M. & Shrout, P.E. (1984). Symptoms, hassles, social supports, and life events: Problem of confounded measures. *Journal of Abnormal Psychology, 93(2)*, 222–230.

Edwards, J.E. (1991). The measurement of Type A Behavior Pattern: An assessment of criterion-oriented validity, content validity, and construct validity. In C.L. Cooper & R. Payne (eds), *Personality and stress: Individual differences in the stress process* (pp. 151–180). Chichester: John Wiley Sons, Ltd.

Edwards, J.R. & van Harrison, R. (1993). Job demands and worker health: Three-dimensional re-examination of the relationship between person-environment fit and strain. *Journal of Applied Psychology, 78*, 628–648.

Edwards, J.R. (1998). A cybernetic theory of organizational stress. In C.L. Cooper (ed.), *Theories of organizational stress* (pp. 122–152). Oxford: Oxford University Press.

Elfering, A., Grebner, S., Semmer, N.K., Kaiser-Freiburghaus, D., Lauper-Del Ponte, S. & Witschi, I. (2005). Chronic job stressors and job control: Effects on event-related coping success and well-being. *Journal of Occupational and Organizational Psychology, 78*, 237–252.

Ellis, A. & Bernard, M.E. (1985). What is rational-emotive therapy (RET)? In A. Ellis & M.E. Bernard (eds), *Clinical applications of rational-emotive therapy* (pp. 1–30). New York: Plenum.

Emmons, R.A. (1989). The personal striving approach to personality. In L.A. Pervin (ed.), *Goal concepts in personality and social psychology* (pp. 87–126). Hillsdale, NJ: Lawrence Erlbaum.

Emmons, R.A. (1996). Striving and feeling: Personal goals and subjective well-being. In J. Bargh & P. Gollwitzer (eds), *The psychology of action: Linking motivation and cognition to behavior* (pp. 314–337). New York: Guilford.

Emmons, R.A. (2005). Striving for the sacred: Personal goal, life meaning, and religion. *Journal of Social Issues, 61*, 731–745.

Emmons, C.-A., Biernat, M., Tiedje, L.B., Lang, E.L. & Wortman, C.B. (1991). Stress, support, and coping among women professionals with preschool children. In J. Eckenrode & S. Gore (eds), *Stress between work and family* (pp. 61–93). New York: Plenum.

Endler, N.S. (1998). Stress, anxiety and coping: The multidimensional interaction model. *Canadian Psychology, 38*, 136–153.

Endler, N.S. & Parker, J.D.A. (1990). Multidimensional assessment of coping: A critical evaluation. *Journal of Personality and Social Psychology, 58*, 844–854.

Engebretson, T.O., Matthews, K.A. & Scheier, M.F. (1989). Relations between anger expression and cardiovascular reactivity: Reconciling inconsistent findings through a matching hypothesis. *Journal of Personality and Social Psychology, 57*, 513–521.

Eriksson, M. & Lindström, B. (2005). Validity of Antonovsky's sense of coherence scale: A systematic review. *Journal of Epidemiology and Community Health, 59*, 460–466.

Everson, S.A., Kaplan, G.A., Goldberg, D.E., Lakka, T.A., Sivenius, J. & Salonen, J.T. (1999). Anger expression and incident stroke: Prospective evidence from the Kuopio Ischemic Heart Disease Study. *Stroke, 30*, 523–528.

Eysenck, M. (1988). Trait anxiety and stress. In S. Fisher & J. Reason (eds), *Handbook of life stress, cognition and health* (pp. 476–482). Chichester: John Wiley Sons, Ltd.

Feldt, T. (1997). The role of sense of coherence in well-being at work: Analysis of main and moderator effects. *Work & Stress, 11*, 134–147.

Feldt, T., Kinnunen, U. & Mauno, S. (2000). A mediational model of sense of coherence in the work context: A one-year follow-up study. *Journal of Organizational Behavior, 21*, 461–476.

Feldt, T., Leskinen, E. & Kinnunen, U. (2005). Structural invariance and stability of sense of coherence. A longitudinal analysis of two groups with different employment experiences. *Work & Stress, 19*, 68–83.

Fenlason, K.J. & Beehr, T.A. (1994). Social support and occupational stress: Effects of talking to others. *Journal of Organizational Behavior, 15*, 157–175.

Ferring, D. & Filipp, S.-H. (1994). Teststatistische Ueberprüfung der Impact of Event-Skala: Befunde zu Reliabilität und Stabilität [Statistical testing of the Impact of Event Scale: Reliability and stability]. *Diagnostica, 40*, 344–362.

Florian, V., Mikulincer, M. & Taubman, O. (1995). Does hardiness contribute to mental health during a stressful real-life situation? The roles of appraisal and coping. *Journal of Personality and Social Psychology, 68*, 687–695.

Flory, J.D., Matthews, K. & Owens, J.F. (1998). A social information processing approach to dispositional hostility: Relationships with negative mood and blood pressure elevations at work. *Journal of Social and Clinical Psychology, vol 17(4)*, 491–504.

Frankenhaeuser, M. (1991). The psychophysiology of workload, stress, and health: Comparison between the sexes. *Annals of Behavioral Medicine, 13*, 197–204.

Frese, M. (1986). Coping as a moderator and mediator between stress at work and psychosomatic complaints. In M.H. Appley and R. Trumbull (eds) *Dynamics of Stress* (pp. 183–206). New York: Plenum Press.

Frese, M. (1992). A plea for realistic pessimism: On objective reality, coping with stress, and psychological dysfunction. In L. Montada, S.-H. Filipp & M.J. Lerner (eds), *Life crises and experiences of loss in adulthood* (pp. 81–94). Hillsdale, NJ: Lawrence Erlbaum.

Frese, M., Erbe-Heinbokel, M., Grefe, J., Rybowiak, V. & Weike, A. (1994). 'Mir ist es lieber, wenn ich genau gesagt bekomme, war ich tun muß': Probleme der Akzeptanz von Verantwortung und

Handlungsspielraum in Ost und West ('I prefer to be told exactly what to do': Problems with accepting responsibility and control in East and West). *Zeitschrift für Arbeits- und Organisationspsychologie, 38*, 22–33.

Frese, M. & Mohr, G. (1987). Prolonged unemployment and depression in older workers: A longitudinal study of intervening variables. *Social Science and Medicine, 25*, 173–178.

Frone, M.R., Russell, M. & Cooper, M.L. (1995). Job stressors, job involvement and employee health: A test of identity theory. *Journal of Occupational and Organizational Psychology, 68*, 1–11.

Funk, S.C. (1992). Hardiness: A review of theory and research. *Health Psychology, 11*, 335–345.

Furnham, A. (1992). *Personality at work. The role of individual differences in the workplace.* London: Routledge.

Ganster, D.C. & Schaubroeck, J. (1991). Role stress and worker health: An extension of the plasticity hypothesis of self-esteem. *Journal of Social Behavior and Personality, 6*, 349–360.

Ganster, D.C., Schaubroeck, J., Sime, W.E. & Mayes, B.T. (1991). The nomological validity of the Type A Personality among employed adults. *Journal of Applied Psychology, 76*, 143–168.

Geyer, S. (1997) Some conceptual considerations on the sense of coherence. *Social Science and Medicine, 44*, 1771–1780.

Glass, D.C. (1977). *Behavior patterns, stress, and coronary disease.* Hillsdale, NJ: Lawrence Erlbaum.

Gray, J.A. (1987). *The psychology of fear and stress* (2nd edn). Cambridge: Cambridge University Press.

Grebner, S., Elfering, A., Semmer, N.K., Kaiser-Probst, C. & Schlapbach, M.-L. (2004). Stressful situations at work and in private life among young workers: An event sampling approach. *Social Indicators Research, 67*, 11–49.

Greene, K., Krcmar, M., Walters, L.H., Rubin, D.L. & Hale, J.L. (2000). Targeting adolescent risk-taking behaviors: The contributions of egocentrism and sensation-seeking. *Journal of Adolescence, 23*, 439–461.

Greene, R.L. & Nowack, K.M. (1995). Hassles, hardiness and absenteeism: Results of a 3-year longitudinal study. *Work & Stress, 9*, 448–462.

Greiner, B.A., Ragland, D.R., Krause, N., Syme, S.L. & Fisher, J.M. (1997). Objective measurement of occupational stress factors: An example with San Francisco urban transit operators. *Journal-of-Occupational-Health-Psychology, Vol 2(4)*, 325–342.

Gunthert, K.C., Cohen, L.H. & Armeli, S. (1999). The role of neuroticism in daily stress and coping. *Journal of Personality and Social Psychology, 77*, 1087–1100.

Hallsten, L. (1993). Burning out: A framework. In W.B. Schaufeli, C. Maslach, & T. Marek (eds), *Professional burnout. Recent developments in theory and research* (pp. 95–113). London: Taylor & Francis.

Haney, T.L., Maynard, K.E., Houseworth, K.E., Scherwitz, L.W., Williams, R.B. & Barefoot, J.C. (1996). Interpersonal hostility assessment technique: Description and validation against the criterion of coronary artery disease. *Journal of Personality Assessment, 66*, 386–401.

Harter, S. (1993). Causes and consequences of low self-esteem in children and adolescents. In R.F. Baumeister (ed.), *Self-esteem: The puzzle of low self-regard.* New York: Plenum.

Helmers, K.F., Posluszny, D.M. & Krantz, D.S. (1994). Associations of hostility and coronary artery disease: A review of studies. In A.W. Siegman & T.W. Smith (eds), *Anger, hostility, and the heart* (pp. 67–96). Hillsdale, NJ: Erlbaum.

Hobfoll, S.E. (1989). Conservation of resources: A new attempt at conceptualizing stress. *American Psychologist, 44*, 513–524.

Hobfoll, S.E. (2001). The influence of culture, community, and the nested-self in the stress process: Advancing conservation of resources theory. *Applied Psychology: An International Review, 50*, 337–421.

Hobfoll, S.E., Johnson, R.J., Ennis, N. & Jackson, A.P. (2003). Resource loss, resource gain, and emotional outcomes among inner city women. *Journal of Personality and Social Psychology, 84*, 632–643.

Höge, T. & Büssing, A. (2004). The impact of sense of coherence and negative affectivity on the work stressor-strain relationship. *Journal of Occupational Health Psychology, 9*, 195–205.

Horowitz, M.J., Wilner, N. & Alvarez, W. (1979). Impact of event scale: A measure of subjective stress. *Psychosomatic Medicine, 41*, 209–218.

Hoyle, R.H., Feifar, M.C. & Miller, J.D. (2000). Personality and sexual risk taking: A quantitative review. *Journal of Personality*, *68*, 1203–1231.

Iribarren, C., Sidney, S., Bild, D.E., Kiang, L., Markovitz, J.H., Roseman, J.M. & Matthews, K. (2000). Association of hostility with coronary artery calcification in young adults: The CARDIA study. *Journal of the American Medical Association*, *283(19)*, 2546–2551.

Jackson, S.E. (1984). Organizational practices for preventing burnout. In A.S. Sethi & R.S. Schuler (eds), *Handbook of organizational stress coping strategies* (pp. 89–111). Cambridge MA: Ballinger.

Jemmott, J.B. III (1987). Social motives and susceptibility to disease: Stalking individual differences in health risks. *Journal of Personality*, *55*, 267–298.

Jerusalem, M. & Schwarzer, R. (1992). Self-efficacy as a resource factor in stress appraisal. In R. Schwarzer (ed.), *Self-efficacy: Thought control of action* (pp. 195–213). Washington DC: Hemisphere.

Jex, S.M. and Bliese, P.D. (1999) Efficacy beliefs as a moderator of the impact of work-related stressors: A multilevel study. *Journal of Applied Psychology, Vol. 84(3)*, 349–361.

Jex, S.M., Bliese, P.D., Buzzell, S. & Primeau, J. (2001). The impact of self-efficacy on stressor-strain relations: Coping style as an explanatory mechanism. *Journal of Applied Psychology*, *86*, 401–409.

Jex, S.M. & Elaqua, T.C. (1999). Self-esteem as a moderator: A comparison of global and organization-based measures. *Journal of Occupational and Organizational Psychology*, *72*, 71–81.

Jimmieson, N.L. (2000). Employee reactions to behavioural control under conditions of stress: The moderating role of self-efficacy. *Work & Stress*, *14*, 262–280.

Johansson Hanse, J. & Engström, T. (1999). Sense of coherence and ill health among the unemployed and re-employed after closure of an assembly plant. *Work & Stress*, *13*, 204–222.

John, O.P. & Gross, J.J. (2004). Healthy and unhealthy emotion regulation: Personality processes, individual differences, and life span development. *Journal of Personality*, *72*, 1301–1333.

Judge, T.A. & Bono, J.E. (2001). Relationship of core self-evaluations traits—self-esteem, generalized self efficacy, locus of control, and emotional stability—with job satisfaction and job performance: A meta-analysis. *Journal of Applied Psychology*, *86*, 80–92.

Judge, T.A., Bono, J.E. & Locke, E.A. (2000). Personality and job satisfaction: The mediating role of job characteristics. *Journal of Applied Psychology, Vol. 8(2)*, 237–249.

Kahn, R.L. & Byosiere, P. (1992). Stress in organizations. In M.D. Dunnette & L.M. Hough (eds), *Handbook of industrial and organizational psychology, vol. 3* (pp. 571–650). Palo Alto CA: Consulting Psychologists Press.

Kälin, W. (2004). *Coping—Moderator oder Mediator zwischen Stressoren und Befinden?* [Coping—Moderator or mediator of the association between stressors and well-being?]. Unpublished dissertation, Bern: University of Bern.

Kaluza, G. (1997). Evaluation von Stressbewältigungstrainings in der primären Prävention—eine Metaanalyse (quasi-)experimenteller Feldstudien [Evaluation of stress management training in primary prevention—a meta-analysis of (quasi-)experimental field studies]. *Zeitschrift für Gesundheitspsychologie*, *5*, 149–169.

Kamarck, T.W., Schwartz, J.E., Shiffman, S., Muldoon, M.F., Sutton-Tyrrell, K. & Janicki, D.L. (2005). Psychosocial stress and cardiovascular risk: What is the role of daily experience? *Journal of Personality*, *73*, 1749–1774.

Kamen-Siegel, L., Rodin, J., Seligman, M.E.P. & Dwyer, J. (1991). Explanatory style and cell-mediated immunity in elderly men and women. *Health Psychology*, *10*, 229–235.

Kandel, D.B., Davies, M. & Raveis, V.H. (1985). The stressfulness of daily social roles for women: Marital, occupational, and household roles. *Journal of Health and Social Behavior*, *26*, 64–78.

Karasek, R.A. & Theorell, T. (1990). *Healthy Work: Stress, Productivity and the Reconstruction of Working Life*. Basic Books, New York.

Keenan, A. & Newton, T.J. (1984). Frustration in organizations: Relationships to role stress, climate, and psychological strain. *Journal of Occupational Psychology*, *57*, 57–65.

Kernis, M.H. (2003). Toward a conceptualization of optimal self-esteem. *Psychological Inquiry*, *14*, 1–26.

Kernis, M.H., Brockner, J. & Frankel, B.S. (1989). Self-esteem and reactions to failure: The mediating role of overgeneralization. *Journal of Personality and Social Psychology*, *57*, 707–714.

Kernis, M.H., Grannemann, B.D. & Barclay, L.C. (1989). Stability and level of self-esteem as predictors of anger arousal and hostility. *Journal of Personality and Social Psychology, 56,* 1013–1022.

Kiecolt-Glaser, J.K., McGuire, L., Tobles, T.F. & Glaser, R. (2002). Emotions, morbidity, and mortality: New perspectives from psychoneuroimmunology. *Annual Review of Psychology, 53,* 83–107.

King, L.A., King, D.W., Fairbank, J.A., Keane, T.M. & Adams, G.A. (1998). Resilience-recovery factors in post-traumatic stress disorder among female and male Vietnam veterans: Hardiness, postwar social support, and additional stressful life events. *Journal of Personality and Social Psychology, 74,* 420–434.

Klinger, E. (1987). Current concerns and disengagement from incentives. In F. Halisch & J. Kuhl (eds), *Motivation, intention, and volition* (pp. 337–347). New York: Springer.

Kobasa, S.C.Q. (1988). Conceptualization and measurement of personality in job stress research. In J.J. Hurrell, Jr., Lawrence R. Murphy, S.L. Sauter & C.L. Cooper (eds), *Occupational Stress: Issues and developments in research* (pp. 100–109). New York: Taylor & Francis.

Koeske, G.F., Kirk, S.A. & Koeske, R.D. (1993). Coping with job stress: Which strategies work best? *Journal of Occupational and Organizational Psychology, 66,* 319–335.

Krahé, B. (1992). *Personality and social psychology: Towards a synthesis.* London: Sage.

Kravetz, S., Drory, Y. & Florian, V. (1993). Hardiness and sense of coherence and their relation to negative affect. *European Journal of Personality, 7,* 233–244.

Krenauer, M. & Schönpflug, W. (1980). Regulation und Fehlregulation im Verhalten. III. Zielsetzung und Ursachenbeschreibung unter Belastung [Regulation and misregulation of behavior. III. Goal setting and causal attribution under stress]. *Psychologische Beiträge, 22,* 414–431.

Krohne, H.W. (1996). Individual differences in coping. In M. Zeidner & N.S. Endler (eds), *Handbook of coping: Theory, research, applications* (pp. 381–409). New York: John Wiley & Sons, Inc.

Kubzansky, L.D., Kawachi, I. & Sparrow, D. (1999). Socioeconomic status, hostility, and risk factor clustering in the normative aging study: Any help from the concept of allostatic load? *Annals of Behavioral Medicine, 21,* 330–338.

Lange, A.H., Taris, T.W., Kompier, M.A.J., Houtman I.L.D. & Bongers, P.M. (2005). Different mechanisms to explain the reversed effects of mental health on work characteristics. *Scandinavian Journal of Work, Environment and Health, 31,* 3–14.

Larsen, R.J. & Ketelaar, T. (1991). Personality and susceptibility to positive and negative emotional states. *Journal of Personality and Social Psychology, 61,* 132–140.

Latak, J.C. (1986). Coping with job stress: Measures and future directions for scale development. *Journal of Applied Psychology, 71,* 377–385.

Lazarus, R.S. (1999). *Stress and emotion.* London: Free Association Books.

Lazarus, R.S. & Folkman, S. (1984). *Stress, appraisal, and coping.* New York: Springer.

Lazarus, R.S. & Folkman, S. (1986). Cognitive theories of stress and the issue of circularity. In M. Appley & R. Trumbull (eds), *Dynamics of stress* (pp. 63–80). New York: Plenum.

Lee-Baggley, D., Preece, M. & DeLongis, A. (2005). Coping with interpersonal stress: Role of Big Five traits. *Journal of Personality, 73,* 1141–1180.

Leitner, K. & Resch, M.G. (2005). Do the effects of job stressors on health persist over time? A longitudinal study with observational stressor measures. *Journal of Occupational Health Psychology, 10,* 18–30.

Little, B.R. (1983). Personal projects: A rationale and method for investigation. *Environment and Behavior, 15,* 273–309.

Locke, E.A. (2005). Setting goals for life and happiness. In C.R. Snyder & S.J. Lopez (eds), *Handbook of positive psychology* (pp. 299–312). Oxford: Oxford University Press.

Maddi, S.R. (1999). The personality construct of hardiness: I. Effects on experiencing, coping, and strain. *Consulting Psychology Journal: Practice and Research, 51,* 83–94.

Maddi, S.R. (1997). Personal Views Survey II: A measure of dispositional hardiness. In C.P. Zalaquett & R.J. Wood (eds), *Evaluating stress: A book of resources* (pp. 292–309). Lanham, MD: The Scarecrow Press.

Maddi, S.R. & Khoshaba, D.M. (1994). Hardiness and mental health. *Journal of Personality Assessment, 63,* 265–274.

Maddi, S.R., Khoshaba, D.M., Persciso, M., Lu, J., Harvey, R. & Bleecker, F. (2002). The personality construct of hardiness: II. Relationships with comprehensive tests of personality and psychopathology. *Journal of Research in Personality, 36*, 72–85.

Major, B., Richards, C., Cooper, M.L., Cozzarelli, C. & Zubek, J. (1998). Personal resilience, cognitive appraisals, and coping: An integrative model of adjustment to abortion. *Journal of Personality and Social Psychology, 74*, 734–752.

Marmot, M., Siegrist, J., Theorell, T. & Feeney, A. (1999). Health and the psychosocial environment at work. In M. Marmot & R.G. Wilkinson (eds), *Social determinants of health* (pp. 105–131). Oxford: Oxford University Press.

Martin, R., Watson, D. & Wan, C.K. (2000). A three-factor model of trait anger: Dimensions of affect, behavior, and cognition. *Journal of Personality, 68*, 869–897.

May, D.R., Schwoerer, C.E., Reed, K. & Potter, P. (1997). Employee reactions to ergonomic job design: The moderating effects of health locus of control and self-efficacy. *Journal of Occupational Health Psychology, 2*, 11–24.

McClelland, D.C. (1987). *Human motivation*. Cambridge: Cambridge University Press.

McClelland, D.C. (1989). Motivational factors in health and disease. *American Psychologist, 44*, 675–683.

McCrae, R.R. & Costa, P.T. (1986). Personality, coping, and coping effectiveness in an adult sample. *Journal of Personality, 54*, 385–405.

McCrae, R.R. & Costa, P.T. (1990). *Personality in adulthood*. New York: Guilford Press.

Menaghan, E.G. & Merves, E.S. (1984). Coping with occupational problems: The limits of individual efforts. *Journal of Health and Social Behavior, 25*, 406–423.

Miller, S.M. (1990). To see or not to see: Cognitive informational styles in the coping process. In M. Rosenbaum (ed.), *Learned resourcefulness: On coping skills, self-control, and adaptive behavior* (pp. 95–126). New York: Springer.

Miller, T.Q., Smith, T.W., Turner, C.W., Guijarro, M.L. & Hallet, A.J. (1996). A meta-analytic review of research on hostility and physical health. *Psychological Bulletin, 119*, 322–348.

Mischel, W. & Shoda, Y. (1998). Reconciling processing dynamics and personality dispositions. *Annual Review of Psychology, 49*, 229–258.

Morf, C.C. & Rhodewalt, F. (2002). Unraveling the paradoxes of narcissism: A dynamic self-regulatory processing model. *Psychological Inquiry, 12*, 177–196.

Mossholder, K.W., Bedeian, A.G. & Armenakis, A.A. (1981). Role perceptions, satisfaction, and performance: Moderating effects of self-esteem and organizational level. *Organizational Behavior and Human Performance, 28*, 224–234.

Neff, K.D. (2003). The development and validation of a scale to measure self-compassion. *Self and Identity, 2*, 223–250.

Niederhoffer, K.G. & Pennebaker, J.W. (2005). Sharing one's story: On the benefits of writing or talking about emotional experience. In C.R. Snyder & S.J. Lopez (eds), *Handbook of positive psychology* (pp. 573–583). Oxford: Oxford University Press.

Nowack, K.M. (1989). Coping style, cognitive hardiness, and health status. *Journal of Behavioral Medicine, 12*, 145–158.

Okun, M.A., Zautra, A.J. & Robinson, S.E. (1988). Hardiness and health among women with rheumatoid arthritis. *Personality and Individual Differences, 9*, 101–107.

Orr, E. & Westman, M. (1990). Does hardiness moderate stress, and how?: A review. In M. Rosenbaum (ed.), *Learned resourcefulness: On coping skills, self-control, and adaptive behavior* (pp. 64–94). New York: Springer.

Ouellette, S.C. (1993). Inquiries into hardiness. In L. Goldberger & S. Breznitz (eds), *Handbook of stress: Theoretical and clinical aspects* (2nd edn, pp. 77–100). New York: The Free Press.

Parkes, K.S. (1991). Locus of control as moderator: An explanation for additive versus interactive findings in the demand-discretion model of work stress? *British Journal of Psychology, 82*, 291–312.

Pearlin, L.I. & Schooler, C. (1978). The structure of coping. *Journal of Health and Social Behavior, 22*, 337–356.

Perrewé, P.L. & Zellars, K.L. (1999). An examination of attributions and emotions in the transactional approach to the organizational stress process. *Journal of Organizational Behavior, 20*, 739–752.

Perrez, M. & Reicherts, M. (1992a). *Stress, coping, and health*. Seattle: Hogrefe & Huber.

Perrez, M. & Reicherts, M. (1992b). A situation-behavior approach to stress and coping. In M. Perrez & M. Reicherts, *Stress, coping, and health* (pp. 17–38). Seattle: Hogrefe & Huber.

Perrez, M. & Reicherts, M. (1992c). Depressed people coping with aversive situations. In M. Perrez & M. Reicherts, *Stress, coping, and health* (pp. 103–111). Seattle: Hogrefe & Huber.

Peterson, C. & Seligman, M.E.P. (1984). Causal explanations as a risk for depression: Theory and evidence. *Psychological Review, 91*, 347–374.

Peterson, C., Seligman, M.E.P. & Vaillant, G.E. (1988). Pessimistic explanatory style is a risk factor for physical illness: A thirty-five-year longitudinal study. *Journal of Personality and Social Psychology, 55*, 23–27.

Peterson, C. & Steen, T.A. (2005). Optimistic explanatory style. In C.R. Snyder & S.J. Lopez (eds), *Handbook of positive psychology* (pp. 244–256). New York, NY: Oxford University Press.

Pierce, J.L., Gardner, D.C., Dunham, R.B. & Cummings, L.L. (1993). Moderation by organization-based self-esteem on role condition-employee response relationships. *Academy of Management Journal, 36*, 271–288.

Pruessner, J.C., Gaab, J., Hellhammer, D.H., Lintz, D., Schommer, N. & Kirschbaum, C. (1997). Increasing correlations between personality traits and cortisol stress responses obtained by data aggregation.

Reicherts, M., & Perrez, M. (1992). Adequate coping behavior: The behavior rules approach. In M. Perrez & M. Reicherts, *Stress, coping, and health* (pp. 161–182). Seattle: Hogrefe & Huber.

Reicherts, M. & Pihet, S. (2000). Job newcomers coping with stressful situations: A micro-analysis of adequate coping and well-being. *Swiss Journal of Psychology, 59*, 303–316.

Reicherts, M., Kaeslin, S., Scheurer, F., Fleischhauer, J. & Perrez, M. (1992). Depressed people coping with loss and failure. In M. Perrez & M. Reicherts, *Stress, coping, and health* (pp. 113–123). Seattle: Hogrefe & Huber.

Reilly, N.P. (1994). Exploring a paradox: Commitment as a moderator of the stressor-burnout relationship. *Journal of Applied Social Psychology, 24*, 397–414.

Repetti, R.L., Matthews, K.A. & Waldron, I. (1989). Employment and women's health: Effects of paid employment on women's mental and physical health. *American Psychologist, 44*, 1394–1401.

Roger, D. & Jamieson, J. (1998). Individual differences in delayed heart-rate recovery following stress: The role of extraversion, neuroticism and emotional control. *Personality and Individual Differences, 9*, 721–726.

Rosenbaum, M. (1990). The role of learned resourcefulness in the self-control of health behavior. In M. Rosenbaum (ed.), *Learned resourcefulness: On coping skills, self-control, and adaptive behavior* (pp. 3–30). New York: Springer-Verlag.

Ross, C.E. & Mirowsky, J. (1995). Does employment affect health? *Journal of Health and Social Behavior, 36*, 230–243.

Rothermund, K. & Brandstädter, J. (2003). Coping with deficits and losses in later life: From compensatory action to accommodation. *Psychology and Aging, 19*, 896–905.

Rotter, J.B. (1966). Generalized expectancies for internal versus external control of reinforcement. *Psychological Monographs: General and Applied, 80*, 1 (Whole No. 609).

Rusting, C.L. (1998). Personality, mood, and cognitive processing of emotional information: Three conceptual frameworks. *Psychological Bulletin, 124*, 165–196.

Rusting, C.L. & Nolen-Hoeksema, S. (1998). Regulating responses to anger: Effects of rumination and distraction on angry mood. *Journal of Personality and Social Psychology, 74*, 790–803.

Ryland, E. & Greenfeld, S. (1991). Work stress and well being: An investigation of Antonovsky's Sense of Coherence model. In P.L. Perrewé (ed.), Handbook on Job Stress (Special Issue), *Journal of Social Behavior and Personality, 6*, 39–54.

Sacco, W.P., Dumont, C.P. & Dow, M.G. (1993). Attributional, perceptual, and affective responses to depressed and nondepressed marital partners. *Journal of Consulting and Clinical Psychology, 61*, 1076–1082.

Sapolsky, R.M. (1999). The psychophysiology and pathophysiology of unhappiness. In D. Kahneman, E. Diener & N. Schwarz (eds), *Well-being: The foundations of hedonic psychology* (pp. 453–469). New York: Russel Sage Foundation.

Schaubroeck, J. & Ganster, D.C. (1991). Associations among stress-related individual differences. In C.L. Cooper & R. Payne (eds.), *Personality and stress: Individual differences in the stress process* (pp. 33–66). Chichester: John Wiley & Sons, Ltd.

Schaubroeck, J., Jones, J.R. & Xie, J.L. (2001). Individual differences in utilizing control to cope with job demands: Effects on susceptibility to infectious disease. *Journal of Applied Psychology, 86,* 265–278.

Schaubroeck, J., Lam, S.S.K. & Xie, J.L. (2000). Collective efficacy versus self-efficacy in coping responses to stressors and control: A cross-cultural study. *Journal of Applied Psychology, 85,* 512–525.

Schaubroeck, J. & Merritt, D.E. (1997). Divergent effects of job control on coping with work stressors: The key role of self-efficacy. *Academy of Management Journal, 40,* 738–754.

Scheier, M.F. & Carver, C.S. (1992). Effects of optimism on psychological and physical well-being: Theoretical overview and empirical update. *Cognitive Therapy and Research, 16,* 201–228.

Scheier, M.F., Weintraub, J.K. & Carver, C.S. (1986). Coping with stress: Divergent strategies of optimists and pessimists. *Journal of Personality and Social Psychology, 51,* 1257–1264.

Schneider, B., Goldstein, H.W. & Smith, D.B. (1995). The ASA framework: An update. *Personnel Psychology, 48,* 747–773.

Schönpflug, W. (1985). Goal directed behavior as a source of stress: Psychological origins and consequences of inefficiency. In M. Frese & J. Sabini (Hrsg.), *Goal directed behavior: The concept of action in psychology* (pp. 172–88). Hillsdale, NJ: Lawrence Erlbaum.

Schwenkmezger, P. & Hank, P. (1996). Anger expression and blood pressure. In J.M.T. Brebner, E. Greenglass, P. Laungani & A.M. O'Roark (eds), *Stress and emotion: Anxiety, anger and curiosity, Vol. 16* (pp. 241–259). London: Taylor & Francis.

Semmer, N.K. (2003a). Individual differences, work stress and health. In M.J. Schabracq, J.A. Winnubst & C.L. Cooper (eds), *Handbook of work and health psychology* (2nd edn, pp. 83–120). Chichester: John Wiley & Sons, Ltd.

Semmer, N.K. (2003b). Job stress interventions and organization of work. In L.E. Tetrick & J.C. Quick (eds), *Handbook of occupational health psychology* (pp. 325–353). Washington, DC: American Psychological Association.

Semmer, N.K. & Elfering, A. (2002). *Job satisfaction: A central but underestimated concept in the psychology of work.* Paper given at the Work Psychology Colloquium of the University of Giessen, Germany, 8 January 2002.

Semmer, N.K., Grebner, S. & Elfering, A. (2004). Beyond self-report: Using observational, physiological, and situation-based measures in research on occupational stress. In P.L. Perrewé & D.C. Ganster (eds), *Emotional and physiological processes and positive intervention strategies (Research in Occupational Stress and Well-being, Vol. 3,* pp. 207–263). Amsterdam: JAI.

Semmer, N.K., McGrath, J.E. & Beehr, T.A. (2005). Conceptual issues in research on stress and health. In C.L. Cooper (ed.), *Handbook of stress and health* (2nd edn, pp. 1–43). New York: CRC Press.

Semmer, N. & Schallberger, U. (1996). Selection, socialization, and mutual adaptation: Resolving discrepancies between people and their work. *Applied Psychology: An International Review, 45,* 263–288.

Semmer, N.K. & Zapf, D. (2004). Gesundheits- und verhaltensbezogene Interventionen in Organisationen [Health- and behavior-related interventions at the worksite]. In H. Schuler (Hrsg.), *Organisationspsychologie—Gruppe und Organisation* (Enzyklopädie der Psychologie, D III, Vol. 4, pp. 773–843). Göttingen: Hogrefe.

Semmer, N., Zapf, D. & Greif, S. (1996). 'Shared job strain'. A new approach for assessing the validity of job stress measurements. *Journal of Occupational and Organizational Psychology, 69,* 293–310.

Siegler, I.C. (1994). Hostility and risk: Demographic and lifestyle variables. In A.W. Siegman & T.W. Smith (eds), *Anger, hostility, and the heart* (pp. 199–214). Hillsdale, NJ: Erlbaum.

Siegman, A.W. (1994a). From Type A to hostility to anger: Reflections on the history of coronary-prone behavior. In A.W. Siegman & T.W. Smith (eds), *Anger, hostility, and the heart* (pp. 1–21). Hillsdale, NJ: Erlbaum.

Siegman, A.W. (1994b). Cardiovascular consequences of expressing and repressing anger. In A.W. Siegman & T.W. Smith (eds), *Anger, hostility, and the heart* (pp. 173–197). Hillsdale, NJ: Erlbaum.

Siegrist, J. (2002). Effort-reward imbalance at work and health. In P.L. Perrewé & D.C. Ganster (eds), *Historical and current perspectives on stress and health* (Research in occupational stress and well being, vol. 2, pp. 261–291). Amsterdam: JAI.

Silver, R.C., Wortman, C.B. & Crofton, C. (1990). The role of coping in support provision: The self-presentational dilemma of victims of life crises. In B.R. Sarason, I.G. Sarason & G.R. Pierce (eds), *Social support: An interactional view* (pp. 397–426). New York: John Wiley & Sons, Inc.

Simon, R.S. (1992). Parental role strains, salience of parental identity and gender differences in psychological distress. *Journal of Health and Social Behavior, 33*, 25–35.

Simon, R.W. (1997). The meanings individuals attach to role identities and their implications for mental health. *Journal of Health and Social Behavior, 38*, 256–274.

Sinclair, R.R. & Tetrick, L.E. (2000). Implications of item wording for hardiness structure, relation with neuroticism, and stress buffering. *Journal of Research in Personality, 34*, 1–25.

Smith, T.W., Glazer, K., Ruiz, J.M. & Gallo, L.C. (2004). Hostility, anger, aggressiveness, and coronary heart disease: An interpersonal perspective on personality, emotion, and health. *Journal of Personality, 72*, 1217–1270.

Smith, T.W., Pope, M.K., Rhodewalt, F. & Poulton, J.L. (1989). Optimism, neuroticism, coping, and symptom reports: An alternative interpretation of the Life Orientation Test. *Journal of Personality and Social Psychology, 56*, 640–648.

Smith, T.W. & Ruiz, J.M. (2002). Psychosocial influences on the development and course of coronary heart disease: Current status and implications for research and practice. *Journal of Consulting and Clinical Psychology, 7*, 548–568.

Smith, T.W. & Spiro, A. (2002). Personality, health, and aging: Prolegomenon for the next generation. *Journal of Research in Personality, 36*, 363–394.

Smyth, J.M. & Pennebaker, J.W. (1999). Sharing one's story: Translating emotional experiences into words as a coping tool. In C.R. Snyder (ed.), *Coping: The psychology of what works* (pp. 70–89). New York: Oxford University Press.

Söderfeldt, M., Söderfeldt, B., Ohlson, C.-G., Theorell, T. & Jones, J. (2000). The impact of sense of coherence and high demand/low-control job environment on self-reported health, burnout and psychophysiological stress indicators. *Work & Stress, 14*, 1–15.

Sonnentag, S. & Frese, M. (2003). Stress in organizations. In W.C. Borman, D.R. Ilgen & R.J. Klimoski (eds), *Handbook of psychology, Vol. 12: Industrial and organizational psychology* (pp. 453–491). Hoboken, NJ: John Wiley & Sons, Inc.

Spector, P.E. (2003). Individual differences in health and well-being in organizations. In D.A. Hofmann & L.E. Tetrick (eds). *Health and safety in organizations: A multilevel perspective* (pp. 29–55). San Francisco: Jossey-Bass.

Spector, P.E. & Jex, S.M. (1998) Development of four self-report measures of job stressors and strain: Interpersonal Conflict at Work Scale, Organizational Constraints Scale, Quantitative Workload Inventory, and Physical Symptoms Inventory. *Journal of Occupational Health Psychology, Vol. 3* (4), 356–367.

Spector, P.E., Zapf, D., Chen, P.Y. & Frese, M. (2000). Why negative affectivity should not be controlled in job stress research: Don't throw out the baby with the bath water. *Journal of Organizational Behavior, 21*, 79–95.

Spielberger, C.D., Reheiser, E.C. & Sydeman, S.J. (1995). Measuring the experience, expression, and control of anger. In H. Kassinove (ed.), *Anger disorders: Definitions, diagnosis, and treatment* (pp. 49–76). Washington, DC: Taylor & Francis.

Stanton, A.L. & Franz, R. (1999). Focusing on emotion: An adaptive coping strategy? In C.R. Snyder (ed.), *Coping: The psychology of what works* (pp. 90–118). New York: Oxford University Press.

Stanton, A.L., Kirk, S.B., Cameron, C.L. & Danoff-Burg, S. (2000). Coping through emotional approach: Scale construction and validation. *Journal of Personality and Social Psychology, 78*, 1150–1169.

Stanton, A., Parsa, A. & Austenfeld, J.L. (2005). The adaptive potential of coping through emotional approach. In C.R. Snyder & S.J. Lopez (eds), *Handbook of positive psychology* (pp. 148–158). Oxford: Oxford University Press.

Steptoe, A. (1991). Psychological coping, individual differences and physiological stress responses. In C.L. Cooper & R. Payne (eds), *Personality and stress: Individual differences in the stress process* (pp. 205–233). Chichester: John Wiley & Sons, Ltd.

Steptoe, A. (2001). Psychophysiological bases of disease. In D.W. Johnston & M. Johnston (eds), *Health psychology. Vol. 8: Comprehensive clinical psychology* (pp. 39–78). Amsterdam: Elsevier.

Steptoe, A., Cropley, M., Griffith, J. & Kirschbaum, C. (2000). Job strain and anger expression predict early morning elevations in salivary Cortisol. *Psychosomatic Medicine, 62*, 286–292.

Strack, S. & Coyne, J.C. (1983). Social confirmation of dysphoria: Shared and private reactions to depression. *Journal of Personality and Social Psychology, 44*, 798–806.

Suarez, E.D., Kuhn, C.M., Schanberg, S.M., Williams, R.B. & Zimmermann, E.A. (1998). Neuroendocrine, cardiovascular, and emotional responses of hostile men: the role of interpersonal challenge. *Psychosomatic Medicine, 60*, 78–88.

Suls, J. & Fletcher, B. (1985). The relative efficacy of avoidant and non-avoidant coping strategies: A meta-analysis. *Health Psychology, 4*, 247–288.

Suls, J. & Martin, R. (2005). The daily life of the garden-variety neurotic: Reactivity, stressors exposure, mood spillover, and maladaptive coping. *Journal of Personality, 73*, 1–25.

Suominen, S., Helenius, H., Blomberg, H., Uutela, A. & Koskenvuo, M. (2001). Sense of coherence as a predictor of subjective state of health: Results of 4 years of follow-up of adults. *Journal of Psychosomatic Research, 50*, 77–86.

Taylor, S.E. & Brown, J.D. (1988). Illusion and well-being: A social psychological perspective on mental health. *Psychological Bulletin, 103*, 193–210.

Thayer, R.E., Newman, J.R. & McClain, T.M. (1994). Self-regulation of mood: Strategies for changing a bad mood, raising energy, and reducing tension. *Journal of Personality and Social Psychology, 67*, 910–925.

Thoits, P.A. (1986). Social support as coping assistance. *Journal of Consulting and Clinical Psychology, 54*, 416–423.

Thoits, P.A. (1991). On merging identity theory and stress research. *Social Psychology Quarterly, 54*, 101–112.

Thoits, P.A. (1995). Identity-relevant events and psychological symptoms: A cautionary tale. *Journal of Health and Social Behavior, 36*, 72–82.

Thompson, S.C. (1981). Will it hurt less if I can control it? A complex answer to a simple question. *Psychological Bulletin, 90*, 89–101.

Udris, I. & Rimann, M. (2000). Das Kohärenzgefühl: Gesundheitsressource oder Gesundheit selbst? [Sense of Coherence: Health resource or health itself?] In H. Wydler, P. Kolip & T. Abel (Hrsg.), *Salutogenese und Kohärenzgefühl* (S. 129–147). Weinheim: Juventa.

Van der Klink, J.J.L., Blonk, R.W.B., Schene, A.H. & van Dijk, F.J.H. (2001). The benefits of interventions for work-related stress. *American Journal of Public Health, 91*, 270–276.

Van Yperen, N.W. & Snijders, T.A. (2000). A multilevel analysis of the demands-control model: Is stress at work determined by factors at the group level or the individual level? *Journal of Occupational Health Psychology, 5*, 182–190.

Veroff, J.B. (1982). Assertive motivations: Achievement vs. power. In D.G. Winter & A.J. Stewart (eds), *Motivation and society*. San Francisco: Jossey-Bass.

Vollrath, M. (2001). Personality and stress. *Scandinavian Journal of Personality, 42*, 355–347.

Vollrath, M. & Torgersen, S. (2000). Personality types and coping. *Personality and Individual Differences, 29*, 367–378.

Vollrath, M. & Torgersen, S. (2002). Who takes health risks? A probe into eight personality types. *Personality and Individual Differences, 32*, 1185–1197.

Vossel, G. (1987). Stress conceptions in live event research: Towards a person-centred perspective. *European Journal of Personality, 1*, 123–140.

Wanous, J.P. (1992). *Organizational Entry*, 2nd edn. Reading, MA: Addison-Wesley.

Ward, C.H. & Eisler, R.M. (1987). Type A behavior, achievement striving, and a dysfunctional self-evaluation system. *Journal of Personality and Social Psychology, 53*, 318–326.

Watson, D., David, J.P. & Suls, J. (1999). Personality, affectivity, and coping. In C.R. Snyder (ed.), *Coping: The psychology of what works* (pp. 119–140). Oxford: Oxford University Press.

Watson, D., Pennebaker, J.W. & Folger, R. (1987). Beyond negative affectivity: Measuring stress and satisfaction in the work place. In J.M. Ivancevich & D.C. Ganster (eds), *Job stress: From theory to suggestion* (pp. 141–157). New York: Haworth Press.

Weber, H. (1993). Ärgerausdruck, Ärgerbewältigung und subjektives Wohlbefinden [Expression of anger, coping with anger, and subjective well-being]. In V. Hodapp & P. Schwenkmezger (eds), *Ärger und Ärgerausdruck* (pp. 253–275). Bern: Huber.

Weinberger, D.A. & Schwartz, G.E. (1990). Distress and restraint as superordinate dimensions of self-reported adjustment: A typological perspective. *Journal of Personality*, *58*, 381–417.

Weinberger, D.A., Schwartz, G.E. & Davidson, R.J. (1979). Low-anxious, high-anxious, and repressive coping-styles: Psychometric patterns and behavioral and physiological responses to stress. *Journal of Abnormal Psychology*, *88*, 369–380.

Weiss, H.B. & Knight, P.A. (1980). The utility of humility: Self-esteem, information search, and problem solving efficiency. *Organizational Behavior and Human Performance*, *25*, 216–223.

Weiss, H.M. & Kurek, K.E. (2003). Dispositional influences on affective experiences at work. In M. R. Barrick & A.M. Ryan (eds), *Personality and work: Reconsidering the role of personality in organizations* (pp. 121–149). San Francisco, CA: Jossey-Bass.

Williams, P.G., Wiebe, D.J. & Smith, T.W. (1992). Coping processes as mediators of the relationship between hardiness and health. *Journal of Behavioral Medicine*, *15*, 237-255.

Williams, R.B. (1996). Coronary-prone behaviors, hostility, and cardiovascular health: Implications for behavioral and pharmacological interventions. In K. Orth-Gomér & N. Schneiderman (eds), *Behavioral medicine approaches to cardiovascular disease prevention* (pp. 161–168). Mahwah, NJ: Erlbaum.

Winnubst, J.A.M., Buunk, B.P. & Marcelissen, F.H.G. (1988). Social support and stress: Perspectives and processes. In S. Fisher & J. Reason (eds), *Handbook of life stress, cognition and health* (pp. 511–528). Chichester: John Wiley & Sons, Ltd.

Wofford, J.C. & Daly, P.S. (1997). A cognitive-affective approach to understanding individual differences in stress propensity and resultant strain. *Journal of Occupational Health Psychology*, *2*, 134–147.

Wortman, C.B. & Silver, R.C. (1992). Reconsidering assumptions about coping with loss: An overview of current research. In L. Montada, S.-H. Filipp & M.J. Lerner (eds), *Life crises and experiences of loss in adulthood* (pp. 341–365). Hillsdale, NJ: Lawrence Erlbaum.

Wrosch, C., Scheider, M.F., Carver, C.S. & Schulz, R. (2003). The importance of goal disengagement in adaptive self-regulation: When giving up is beneficial. *Self and Identity*, *2*, 1–20.

Zapf, D., Dormann, C. & Frese, M. (1996). Longitudinal studies in organizational stress research: A review of the literature with reference to methodological issues. *Journal of Occupational Health Psychology*, *1*, 145–169.

Zautra, A.J., Affleck, G.G., Tennen, H., Reich, J.W. & Davis, M.C. (2005). Dynamic approaches to emotion and stress in everyday life: Bolger and Zuckerman reloaded with positive as well as negative affects. *Journal of Personality*, *73*, 1511–1538.

Zellars, K.L. & Perrewé, P.L. (2001). Affective personality and the content of emotional social support: Coping in organizations. *Journal of Applied Psychology*, *86*, 459–467.

CHAPTER 5

Personality and Well-being

Espen Røysamb
University of Oslo, Norway

INTRODUCTION

What is happiness? Why are some people happy and others not? To what extent and in what ways is happiness related to personality? Questions like these reflect core issues in the field of well-being research. The Greek philosopher Aristotle proposed happiness to be the ultimate goal of human life. However, despite this early focus on happiness, psychological research on the issue has flourished only recently. Today, knowledge about the nature, sources and consequences of human well-being is increasing rapidly (Diener & Lucas, 1999; Kahneman, Diener & Schwarz, 1999; Seligman & Csikszentmihalyi, 2000).

The aims of this chapter are, first, to outline and contextualise the field of subjective well-being research. The issues to be addressed are basic reasons for studying well-being, the place of well-being in a framework of positive psychology, and the relation of the well-being construct to mental and physical health. Second, I want to elaborate on the notion of stability and change and to review the research on genetic and environmental factors in well-being. Finally, the relationships between personality and well-being will be addressed. The review will summarise central empirical findings with regard to several different personality factors and discuss issues of causality and mechanisms.

WHY STUDY WELL-BEING?

Is the scientific study of human happiness and satisfaction warranted? Throughout this chapter, theoretical and empirical evidence supporting the endeavour of well-being research will be presented and discussed. Yet, it might be fruitful to explicitly outline a few of the arguments for diving into human happiness.

First, throughout its history, psychology has paid more attention to disorders and problems than to strengths and pleasant experiences. A literature review yielded a 17:1 ratio of scientific publications with a focus on negative versus positive states and conditions (Myers & Diener, 1995). Yet, human lives are as much filled with joy, interest, love, satisfaction, excitement and engagement as they are with sadness, anxiety, distress, confusion and anger. Given that psychology seeks to understand human nature, the study of well-being should

Handbook of Personality and Health. Edited by Margarete E. Vollrath. © 2006 John Wiley & Sons, Ltd.

be no less important than other topics covered. Second, in view of the bias towards focus on disorders and problems, it can easily be argued that the well-being approach contributes to complementing and balancing the mental health field. Third, well-being has repeatedly been found to represent a central human value. When asked about the value or importance of life aspects such as money, health, education, happiness and life satisfaction, across nations respondents typically value different aspects of well-being highly (Diener, 2000; Seligman, Park & Peterson, 2004; Suh, Diener, Oishi & Triandis, 1998). Last but not least, well-being is important not only as a valued end-state, but also through its consequences. Recent studies have shown long term effects of well-being on, for example, work-related functioning (Diener, Nickerson, Lucas & Sandvik, 2002), marriage (Harker & Keltner, 2001) and longevity (Danner, Snowdon & Friesen, 2001).

CONTEXTUALISING SUBJECTIVE WELL-BEING

Subjective well-being (SWB) should be seen in a context of the general perspective of positive psychology. Constructs such as optimism, hope, engagement, growth, capabilities and life satisfaction have received increased attention recently (Ryff & Singer, 1998; Seligman, 2000). Although representing distinct constructs referring to assumedly unique phenomena, they share a common denominator in the focus on positive aspects of human lives and functioning. This focus involves not only turning negative constructs such as depression and pessimism upside down but also shifting the focus from weaknesses to strengths. The good life is characterised not only by the absence of problems but, and equally importantly, by the presence of positive conditions.

The launching of the *Journal of Happiness Studies* and *Journal of Positive Psychology*, for example, is an expression of the recent flourishing of positive psychology. The *American Psychologist* devoted its entire first issue in the new millennium (January, 2000) to positive psychology. Leading international researchers, such as Nobel laureate Daniel Kahneman, Ed Diener, Martin Seligman and Robert Cummins, have in different ways contributed strongly to putting the field on the map.

Within the field of positive psychology, SWB is one of the core constructs. More specifically, SWB is typically defined as constituted by three main components: a cognitive evaluation of *life satisfaction*, the presence of *positive affect* and the relative absence of *negative affect* (Diener & Lucas, 1999). The three components are related, yet separable, both theoretically and empirically. Together they constitute what is currently conceived of as SWB. Further, in addition to global conceptualisations (e.g., general life satisfaction), domain-specific well-being—such as satisfaction with work, health or family-life—is a part of the SWB field.

With regard to the relations between SWB, its sub-components and other conditions, such as optimism, interest, virtues, engagement, love and flow, future research with advanced designs will have to try and disentangle the causality and mechanisms involved. However, at present one important distinction between classes of constructs is that of *hedonism* versus *eudaimonism* (Bauer, McAdams & Sakaeda, 2005; Ryan & Deci, 2000; Vitterso, 2003, 2004). The hedonistic perspective focuses on experiences of life as good—or not so good—with enjoyment, pleasure, happiness and satisfaction as typical exemplars. Eudaimonism, on the other hand, is more concerned with human growth, self-actualisation and engagement. This distinction corresponds highly with the notion of subjective versus psychological well-being (PWB), as proposed by Carroll Ryff and colleagues (Keyes, Shmotkin & Ryff,

2002; Ryff, Keyes & Hughes, 2003). Although common sense might suggest that these two categories are highly intertwined, empirical studies have shown that two different factors are involved and that interrelations between constructs in the two categories are limited (Keyes et al., 2002; van Dierendonck, 2004). Thus, it is possible to live a life with a high level of satisfaction and pleasant affect without necessarily having a high level of engagement and without fulfilling personal potentials, and vice versa. It should be noted, however, that this typical finding does not imply a rejection of either the *hedonic* or *eudaimonic* perspective as irrelevant. Rather, the identification of two different aspects of life quality, mutually complementing each other, only contributes to painting the full picture of human nature. Note also that whereas there is reason to believe that the eudaimonic perspective will receive increased attention in the coming years, the present review will focus primarily on the hedonic perspective and the research on subjective well-being.

SUBJECTIVE WELL-BEING AND HEALTH

When asked what it is that we would want for our own lives and for our loved ones' lives, a typical answer is 'a long life and a good life'—that is, life quantity and life quality.

In 1948 the World Health Organization (WHO, 1948) defined health as '... a state of complete physical, mental and social well-being and not merely the absence of disease or infirmity'. This definition, with its inclusion of 'complete ... well-being' should be seen as more of a politically based vision than a scientific definition. Yet, the formulation is important both with regard to the tri-component model implied in 'physical, mental and social ...' and to the focus on the presence of well-being rather than on only the absence of problems.

To start with the mental aspects of health, although well-being research can be seen as an alternative or even contrast to the long lasting focus on mental illness in psychology and psychiatry, both approaches should be seen as addressing issues concerning mental health. Well-being research and mental illness research differ in the focus on positive versus negative states and conditions and to some extent in the assumptions concerning the underlying nature of the phenomena of interest. That is, whereas well-being research typically conceives of the conditions examined as continuous phenomena, the mental illness tradition has operated with categories of ill-health and disorders, as indicated, for example, by the categorical DSM-IV (Widiger & Clark, 2000; Widiger & Sankis, 2000). Nevertheless, the two approaches complement each other within the mental health field.

It should also be noted that although well-being and mental disorders are not conceptualised as polar opposites, a number of studies have provided empirical evidence of negative associations between SWB and disorders like depression, anxiety, schizophrenia, social phobia, PTSD and substance abuse (Cramer, Torgersen & Kringlen, 2005; Headey, Kelley & Wearing, 1993; Rapaport, Clary, Fayyad & Endicott, 2005; Rush et al., 2005; Xie, McHugo, Helmstetter & Drake, 2005). Thus, mental disorders are in general not compatible with high levels of well-being, yet the absence of disorders is not a sufficient requirement for high SWB. Moreover, persons low on SWB, but still not qualifying for a disorder diagnosis, are probably more vulnerable for developing disorders than are people high on SWB. In this sense, high SWB might act as a protective factor for mental disorders. One important, yet largely unanswered, question is that of potentially different sources of change in the illness range versus the normal SWB range. For example, continued work-stress might contribute to burnout and depression, and successful treatment might depend on reduction of stress. Yet, the total removal of stress is no guarantee of change from moderate to high SWB.

Given that subjective well-being can be conceived of as falling under the term mental health, which together with physical health falls under the general term health, one obvious question is what the relations are between well-being and physical health. To what extent and in what ways does physical health influence well-being, and vice versa? Theoretically, physical health represents one possible source of well-being. Given that well-being involves an evaluation of life with reference to personal and societal standards and values (Diener & Lucas, 1999) and that physical health is highly valued by most people, it seems reasonable to assume that physical health is a predictor of and causal factor in well-being. However, the empirical findings in this field yield a rather complex picture.

Self-reported or perceived health has repeatedly been found to be moderately to strongly associated with subjective well-being (Harris et al., 1992; Okun & George, 1984; Roysamb, Tambs, Reichborn Kjennerud, Neale & Harris, 2003; Watten, Vassend, Myhrer & Syversen, 1997). In contrast, studies of the effects of 'objective' measures of physical health on well-being have provided mixed results. Several studies have reported evidence that people with chronic and even severe disorders have well-being levels comparable to those of healthy individuals (Brief, Butcher, George & Link, 1993; Diener, Suh, Lucas & Smith, 1999; Okun & George, 1984; Roysamb et al., 2003; Watten et al., 1997). This apparently paradoxical finding can probably best be understood in a theoretical framework of adaptation and homeostasis (Headey & Wearing, 1989; Lucas, Clark, Georgellis & Diener, 2003; Suh, Diener & Fujita, 1996). That is, one central virtue of human beings seems to be the ability to adapt to changing life circumstances, including somatic illness. This does not imply that dramatic negative life events and severe illness are totally without effects on well-being, but in many cases people are able to regain their previous level of well-being after periods of hardship and change (Suh et al., 1996).

So, what about the possible effects of well-being on physical health? In fact, some studies have provided evidence for important consequences of well-being in the health domain. In the 'nun study' (Danner et al., 2001), positive affective content in autobiographies written during young adulthood predicted longevity six decades later, with the lower and upper quartile in affective content showing differences in longevity up to ten life years. Other studies have found associations between positive mood and responses in the immune system, such as natural killer cell activity (Fortes et al., 2003; Lutgendorf et al., 1999; Segerstrom, Castaneda & Spencer, 2003; Stone et al., 1987).

In summary, the interrelations between SWB and physical health are complex. Perceived health and SWB are rather strongly related, possibly due to a general tendency to both perceive life as good and different sub-domains—health, work and marriage—as correspondingly good, or not so good. Whereas the effects of actual physical health problems on SWB appear to be modest and mostly only temporary, there is some evidence of important effects of well-being on physical health.

MEASURING SUBJECTIVE WELL-BEING

Is happiness truly measurable, and if so, how? A number of studies have addressed measurement issues in well-being (Cummins, 2003; Diener, Sandvik, Pavot & Gallagher, 1991; Larsen & Fredrickson, 1999; Robbins & Kliewer, 2000; Schwarz & Strack, 1999; Watson & Clark, 1997). Suffice it here to outline a few of the central topics and approaches in the field.

The majority of recent studies of SWB have used questionnaire scales. This is a rather obvious approach, given both the cost-effectiveness of such scales and the inherent subjective nature of the phenomenon of interest.

To take an example, one of the most widely used scales measuring the cognitive component of SWB is the Satisfaction With Life Scale (SWLS) (Pavot & Diener, 1993; Pavot, Diener, Colvin & Sandvik, 1991). The SWLS includes five items, such as 'I am satisfied with my life'; respondents indicate their degree of agreement or disagreement with the items on a 7-point Likert-type scale. A central line of reasoning behind this scale is the notion of neutral content that allows each respondent to evaluate his or her life according to personal standards and goals, whether that may be owning a Lamborghini, having children, passing an exam, enjoying good health or helping other people.

Self-report scales have been developed that measure the affective components of SWB and various sub-domains such as health, wealth, family and work. Experience sampling methods (ESM), in which participants are paged at random times of the day, have been used to measure in-situation experiences (Larsen & Fredrickson, 1999; Schimmack, 2003). Recently, the Day Reconstruction Method, using a daily diary approach to moods-in-activities, was developed (Kahneman, Krueger, Schkade, Schwarz & Stone, 2004).

In addition to self-report questionnaires, different forms of other-report and peer report have been used, partly to validate self-report data. Also, interview data have been collected, based partly on questionnaire scales and partly by using more qualitative approaches. Interestingly, special methods for children and illiterate participants have been developed and validated, such as, for example, visual analogue scales (Diener et al., 1999; Larsen & Fredrickson, 1999).

Finally, it should be mentioned that recent developments in brain scanning using fMRI techniques are yielding promising results for SWB research. For example, studies showing brain lateralisation of negative and positive affect and correlates with self-reported affect and personality do indeed have a potential for shedding new light upon the biological aspects of SWB (Davidson, 2004; Ekman, Davidson, Ricard & Wallace, 2005; Pizzagalli, Shackman & Davidson, 2003; Urry et al., 2004).

SOURCES OF WELL-BEING

On average, people tend to be satisfied with their lives. Cross-national data show that most people score above neutral; typically, population based samples yield mean scores of around seven on a scale from 0 to 10 (Cummins, 2003; Diener & Diener, 1996). Even respondents living in poverty and harsh life-conditions, such as in the slums of Calcutta, tend to be more satisfied than would be expected from a wealth perspective (Biswas-Diener & Diener, 2001). Recent findings also confirm that indigenous groups, such as the Inuit of Greenland and the Maasai of Kenya, are satisfied with life (Biswas-Diener, Vitterso & Diener, 2005). Moreover, mean levels do not seem to differ much across age-groups, even though there is some divergence in the findings on age effects (Mroczek & Spiro, 2005).

Yet, there are substantial individual differences in SWB. A major aim of current SWB research is to delineate the factors and mechanisms involved in generating these differences. In brief, demographic factors such as gender, education, occupation, ethnicity, wealth and living conditions account for only a small portion of the variance in well-being (Campbell, Converse & Rodgers, 1976; Diener et al., 1999). In contrast, genetic factors and personality appear to predict SWB to a fairly high extent (DeNeve & Cooper, 1998; Lucas & Diener,

2000; Roysamb, Harris, Magnus, Vitterso & Tambs, 2002; Vitterso, 2001). Central findings will be outlined below. Here, however, two main issues concerning sources of SWB will be discussed briefly, namely, the issue of bottom-up versus top-down processes and the issue of stability versus change.

According to a bottom-up perspective, SWB is the result of a summarised evaluation of events and sub-domains of well-being. That is, with good events occurring and positive evaluations of domains such as health, wealth, housing and work, global SWB should be high. The top-down approach posits that people tend generally to have a positive—or not so positive—view of life and that global evaluations of life colour their evaluations of different sub-domains. There is empirical evidence for both processes, yet for global SWB, top-down processes seem to be at least as important as bottom-up processes are (Brief et al., 1993; Feist et al., 1995; Headey, Veenhoven & Wearing, 1991).

STABILITY AND CHANGE

Further, the general question of sources of SWB needs to be addressed in a framework of stability versus change. The relative stability of SWB (i.e., the degree to which individuals retain their original score relative to others) is fairly high, with typical cross-time correlations ranging from 0.2 to 0.8 and with highest correlations across short time spans (Diener & Lucas, 1999; Fujita & Diener, 2005; Suh et al., 1996). Given a typical correlation of around 0.5 across several years (Lucas, Diener & Suh, 1996; Nes, Røysamb, Tambs, Harris & Reichborn-Kjennerud, 2005) and assuming underlying factors contributing to stability, this means that roughly 50% of the variance at any time-point is due to long-term stability factors and that the remaining 50% is due to changes or time-specific variance (including random measurement error). In principle, the factors influencing stability and change might be only partially overlapping. It is reasonable to hypothesise that the stability of SWB is closely related to top-down mechanisms, whereas changes in SWB are more closely related to bottom-up processes. However, future studies with advanced designs will be required to disentangle the specific mechanisms involved.

So far there is evidence that life events have important effects on SWB, but the effects are generally only temporary. For example, it was found that events like having an operation, being assaulted, experiencing illness, accident, death of a close family member, break-up of a relationship and economic problems were related to SWB scores, but the effects faded after three to six months (Suh et al., 1996). Findings like these fit with notions of adaptability and with the dynamic equilibrium model and support the idea of a base-line or set-point around which people fluctuate (Headey & Wearing, 1989; McCrae & Costa, 1988; Suh et al., 1996). It should be noted, however, that some life-changing or traumatic events (such as unemployment or widowhood) appear to have possible long-term adverse effects (Lichtenstein et al., 1996; Lucas, Clark, Georgellis & Diener, 2004).

GENETIC AND ENVIRONMENTAL FACTORS IN WELL-BEING

To what extent is subjective well-being influenced by genetic factors? Only a small handful of studies have ventured into the SWB field from a behaviour genetics perspective. Using data on twins and/or families, behaviour genetic studies in general aim to estimate the magnitude of genetic and environmental effects on various phenotypes. Moreover, rather than only estimating heritabilities, current aims in this field include investigating factors accounting for associations between different phenotypes, delineating the mechanism through which these factors operate, and also identifying the specific genes involved (Kendler, 2001; Moffitt, 2005; Neale & Cardon, 1992; Plomin, DeFries, McClearn & Rutter, 1997).

Four major sources of variance and covariance can be estimated based on twin-data: additive genetic factors, non-additive genetic factors, common environment and non-shared environment (Neale & Cardon, 1992). Whereas the non-shared environment contributes to twin dissimilarity, genetic factors and common environment contribute to familial aggregation (e.g., twin similarity), but they do so in different ways. Based on observed twin correlations and the fact that monozygotic (MZ) twins share 100 % of their genes and dizygotic (DZ) twins share on average 50 % of the segregating genes, the effects of genetic and environmental factors can be estimated. Additive genetic factors contribute to twin similarity for both zygosity groups, but contribute twice as much to MZ correlations as to DZ correlations. A crude measure of heritability is given by twice the difference between the MZ and DZ correlations. Common environment contributes equally to correlations among MZ and DZ twins. For example, an observed MZ correlation of 0.5 and a DZ correlation of 0.3 would suggest the presence of both additive genetic factors and common environment as sources of twin similarity (i.e., in this example 40 % variance is accounted for by genetic factors, 10 % is accounted for by common environment, and the remaining 50 % is due to non-shared environment). It should be noted that common environment is defined in terms of its consequences on similarity rather than as a set of common events experienced by both twins in a pair. That is, a certain event to which both twins are exposed may contribute to twin similarity and thereby represents common environment, or it may affect the twins differently (e.g., through differences in perception, interpretation, responding) and will as such represent non-shared environment.

So, what is known about genetic effects on well-being? In the studies currently published, findings converge in finding heritabilities in the 0.30 to 0.55 range, and the remaining variance is in general accounted for by non-shared environmental factors (Lykken, 1999; Lykken & Tellegen, 1996; Roysamb et al., 2003; Stubbe, Posthuma, Boomsma & De Geus, 2005). Despite the relatively few studies available, it should be noted that these studies include thousands of twins, have been conducted in different countries and include twins reared together and apart. Thus, the findings should be seen as solid evidence for genetic factors in SWB. Moreover, the estimates are comparable to those typically found for personality traits (Loehlin, McCrae, Costa & John, 1998) and for mental health problems and disorders such as depression and anxiety (Kendler, 1993, 2001).

MECHANISMS IN GENETIC AND ENVIRONMENTAL INFLUENCES

Heritability estimates are just the beginning of the story of how genes and environments operate in affecting SWB. With regard to the issue of stability and change of SWB, and given that genes are stable throughout the life course whereas environments change, theoretically it would be reasonable to expect a differentiated pattern of effects. The empirical evidence in fact suggests that genetic factors account for around 80 % of the stable variance in

SWB (Lykken & Tellegen, 1996; Nes et al., 2006). However, focusing on change, or the time-specific variance, roughly 80 % is accounted for by environmental factors (Nes et al., 2005). This means that researchers investigating stability in SWB will definitely have to take genetic factors into account, and, as will be discussed below, the role of personality might partly be understood in this perspective. On the other hand, and equally important, life also consists of change, whether involving long-term trajectories or fluctuations around certain set-points, and environmental factors are the main source of such change.

Interestingly, a certain amount of stable variance is environmental, and likewise, a certain amount of change variance is genetic (Nes et al., 2006). The stability effects of environmental factors might be due to past events with long term effects, or stable factors in the environment, which operate as continuous psychological nutrition—or malnutrition. The genetic effects on change in SWB are a reminder that although the DNA does not change, different life situations at different ages might make different genetic factors salient. Depending on age-specific life circumstances and challenges, different psychological characteristics and abilities—which are partly genetic—might be required to generate fruitful outcomes and well-being. Thus, the genes that contribute to happiness in adolescents are not necessarily the same as those that contribute to happiness in their grandparents.

The notion of differentiated genetic effects also pertains to gender differences. Typically, men and women are found to score equally high on SWB measures (Diener et al., 1999). Yet, there are some indications that partly different genetic factors operate to generate individual differences in SWB (Roysamb et al., 2002). Although perhaps counterintuitive, this finding might shed light upon the ways in which SWB is developed and sustained. Given that well-being is about evaluating life in light of personal and societal standards and ideals (Diener & Lucas, 2000) and that different values and ideals prevail for men and women in many societies, it makes sense that different factors (genetic as well as environmental) might influence well-being for men and women. For example, if some physical (e.g., body shape, facial hair) or personality characteristics (e.g., competitiveness, caring) tend to be more highly valued for either sex in a given culture, the genetic factors contributing to these characteristics might indirectly affect well-being differently for men and women. The important point is that genetic effects on well-being do not only operate in a direct fashion. Instead, the effects might be moderated by life situations and cultural value systems.

The possible mechanisms described above can be conceived of as gene-environment interaction, that is, the effects of certain genetic factors depend on the environmental factors present. Another type of interplay is that of gene-environment correlation. For example, a child with a genetic disposition to be happy might also be exposed to happy parents, implying correlated genes and environments. Further, if a high SWB disposition contributes to seeking environments and activating responses that are conducive to happiness, the original genetic factor might operate by mediation through the environment.

Figure 5.1 shows several of the general mechanisms that might be operating in influencing SWB. G1-G4 represent genetic factors, E1-E4 are environmental factors, and P1 is a particular phenotype (e.g., personality). G1 affects SWB in a direct manner and might be exemplified by a neurobiological propensity involving the dopamine and serotonin systems of the brain. G2 also affects SWB directly, but the effect is moderated by an environmental factor, E3. For example, genetically based characteristics that are differentially valued for different groups might operate in this manner. Likewise, as recently shown, a certain variant of the 5HTT genotype contributes to depression, but only in combination with exposure to maltreatment during childhood (Caspi et al., 2003). G3 and E1 contribute together to a

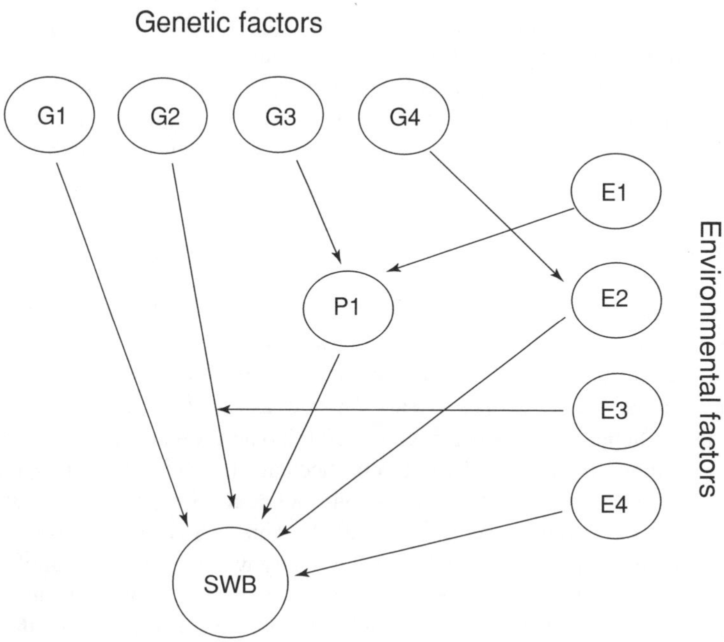

Genetic factors

Figure 5.1 Theoretical model of genetic and environmental factors influencing well-being

certain phenotype, P1 (for example, a personality trait) that mediates the effects on SWB. The factor G4 contributes to environmental exposure, E2, which also operates as a mediator on the pathway to SWB. G4 can be exemplified by a tendency to choose certain environments or activate social responses. Although perhaps counterintuitive, several studies have shown that genetic factors affect life events to a certain extent (Bolinskey, Neale, Jacobson, Prescott & Kendler, 2004; Kendler et al., 1993). Finally, the model shows an effect from E4, exemplified by positive or negative life events, which in this case are additive and independent of the other factors. Note that despite the complexity of the model presented, in reality several more complex mechanisms assumedly operate, including GxG and ExE interactions as well as chains of mediation and moderation.

Does the finding of substantial heritability for SWB imply that we are all stuck with a genetically based set-point and that there is little room for change? No, and there are several points to be made in this regard. First, the twin studies published to date have used global measures of well-being and life satisfaction. Only future research will be able to address the issue of genetic effects on domain-specific well-being (e.g., work, family, economy, health) and on current in-situation experiences of satisfaction and affect. Secondly, all heritability estimates are relative, that is, they represent the amount of total variance accounted for by genetic variance in a given population at a given time. Increases in environmental variance will increase total variance, thereby reducing the relative effect of genetic factors. In the same vein, environmental variance typically comprises the naturally occurring events and factors that influence us, implying that potential interventions are not included in the heritability equation. Thus, there is no need for pessimism regarding the potential for change. Furthermore, the fact that changes occur, that change is predominantly environmentally caused, and that changes can be nurtured and sustained again is a reminder that enhancement of well-being is always an option. Nevertheless, a neglect of the genetic factors involved in well-being is not very fruitful, neither for researchers nor laypersons. To some extent, well-being is more about becoming oneself than becoming someone else, and acceptance of our own inherited constitutions in combination with a willingness to take on new challenges might represent an important road to increased well-being by itself.

PERSONALITY TRAITS

Turning now explicitly to the issue of relations between personality and SWB, in general personality appears to be able to account for substantial amounts of variance in SWB. Empirical evidence for personality-SWB relations has been reviewed recently in several publications (Diener & Lucas, 1999; Diener, Oishi & Lucas, 2003; Lucas & Diener, 2000; Pavot, Fujita & Diener, 1997; Steel & Ones, 2002). The present outline will summarise some central findings and discuss the issues of mechanisms, causality and measurement.

The Five-Factor Model has obtained a strong position within personality psychology in recent years (Costa, McCrae & Jonsson, 2002; John & Srivastava, 1999). The model comprises the notion of five universal dimensions along which people vary and that capture important aspects of individual differences in personality. The dimensions have been denoted by partly different labels, yet there is fairly broad consensus regarding their content. For the present review, the following terms will be used: extraversion, neuroticism, agreeableness, conscientiousness, and openness to experience (McCrae & Costa, 2003; McCrae, Costa & Martin, 2005).

A number of studies have confirmed that extraversion is positively related to SWB and that neuroticism is negatively associated with SWB (DeNeve & Cooper, 1998; Diener & Lucas, 1999; Emmons & Diener, 1985; King & Miner, 2000). In a meta-analysis of earlier studies, correlations were in the range around 0.20 (DeNeve & Cooper, 1998). However, recent studies applying advanced methods to control for measurement error have yielded correlations around 0.70 to 0.80 (Diener & Lucas, 1999). Divergence of opinions has prevailed regarding whether extraversion or neuroticism is the most important trait for SWB, yet recent evidence appears to point to neuroticism as the most potent (negative) source and predictor (DeNeve & Cooper, 1998; Vitterso, 2001). Furthermore, the different aspects of SWB (i.e., life satisfaction, positive affect and absence of negative affect) yield different associations with these two personality traits. Typically, whereas extraversion is most highly related to positive affect, neuroticism is most highly associated with negative affect (Diener & Lucas, 1999). With regard to the traits of agreeableness, conscientiousness and openness to experience, relations with SWB are generally weaker, but findings show that all three traits are positively related to SWB (DeNeve & Cooper, 1998; Watson & Clark, 1992).

TRAITS AND MECHANISMS

Several theories attempt to explain the ways in which personality traits in general, and neuroticism and extraversion in particular, are related to SWB. Watson and Clark proposed that neuroticism and extraversion involve temperamental dispositions to experience negative and positive affect, respectively (Watson & Clark, 1984; 1997). Thus, the links between neuroticism and negative affect, and between extraversion and positive affect, may partly be biological and temperamental. Gray proposed a model involving two neurobio-logical systems: the behaviour activation system (BAS) and the behaviour inhibition system (BIS) (Pickering & Gray, 1999). Dispositional differences in the BAS involve differences in sensitivity to reward stimuli, whereas the BIS is based on punishment sensitivity. These differences contribute to generating negative and positive experiences and thereby influ-ence SWB. According to the dynamic equilibrium perspective (Headey & Wearing, 1989), personality contributes to SWB both directly and indirectly by generating life events. Thus, not only the perception and interpretation of events differ according to personality; life events as such are influenced by traits, and people fluctuate around an equilibrium of both events and SWB. Related perspectives include the notion of extraversion and neuroticism contributing to differences in lifestyles and social relations and thereby to SWB (Larsen & Buss, 2005). For example, given that high extraversion might promote social relations, whereas high neuroticism might make relations complicated, and given that high quality social networks contribute to SWB, it is obvious that there are several possible pathways linking traits and SWB. In a similar vein, the effect of agreeableness on SWB might operate through contributing to social relations, and the effect of conscientiousness might involve a tendency to manage one's life well, to perform fruitful decision making, and to follow and reach goals. In addition to potentially influencing SWB through different mechanisms, personality traits have also been proposed as underlying factors in associations involving SWB. For example, there is evidence that the relatively strong relation between SWB and self-rated health is partly accounted for by neuroticism (Okun & George, 1984).

Based on findings on stability and change, heritability and personality traits, the emerging picture of mechanisms in SWB is rather complex. Yet, the main features of the picture are a global disposition to long term stable SWB involving genetic factors, personality traits such as neuroticism and extraversion, and top-down processes that colour sub-domains of SWB. Given the stabilities and heritabilities of both traits and SWB, it is reasonable to hypothesise that to a high extent, the interrelations between traits and SWB are due to common genetic factors, in the same way that, for example, low self-esteem and anxious-depressive symptoms are influenced by the same genetic factors (Kendler, Myers & Neale, 2000). Future multivariate twin studies will be able to test this hypothesis with regard to SWB.

On the other hand, the complex picture of SWB also includes change, fluctuations and development. Environmental factors are important in change processes; personality might play a role through a match or discrepancy between traits and new circumstances or events, through coping mechanisms and through generating life events. Although most changes are only temporary, new changes are continuously occurring, thus we are always somewhere along a change curve. The ways in which traits contribute to change processes should be a topic for future research.

CRITICAL ISSUES IN TRAIT-SWB RELATIONS

Despite the large number of replications of SWB relations with neuroticism and extraversion and the several important theoretical approaches proposed to explain the relations, some conceptual and methodological caveats need to be addressed. First, it is common practice to think of personality traits as causes and SWB as an effect. However, given that global SWB shows cross-time stability and heritability comparable to personality traits (Diener & Lucas,

1999; Eid & Diener, 2004; Roysamb et al., 2003), it can be argued that SWB operates in a trait-like fashion (Costa & McCrae, 1980; Diener et al., 1999; Watson & Clark, 1997). Why not then refer to SWB as a personality trait, either as subsumed within the Five-Factor Model or as a separate factor beyond the Big Five? One representative answer is that inasmuch as SWB is also influenced by life-events and life circumstances, subjectively experienced well-being is more than only an internal disposition (Veenhoven, 1994).

Another, and partly related, intricate issue regarding the trait-SWB relation concerns the conceptual and measurement-related overlap (Schmutte & Ryff, 1997). For example, in one of the most widely used measures of the Big Five, the NEO-PI (Costa & McCrae, 1997; Costa et al., 2002), the Extraversion factor comprises six facets, or sub-factors, including 'Activity' and 'Positive Emotions'. Likewise, in the shorter Big Five Inventory (BFI) (John & Srivastava, 1999), which measures only the main factors, the Extraversion factor is represented by items containing terms such as 'full of energy' and 'generates enthusiasm'. The potential problem lies in the obvious overlap with terms typically used to measure the positive affect component in SWB. For example, in the PANAS (Watson, Clark & Tellegen, 1988), which is frequently used as a measure of emotional well-being (Kercher, 1992; Kim & Hatfield, 2004), positive affect is measured by items such as 'enthusiastic', 'active' and 'excited'. Correspondingly, the Neuroticism factor of the NEO-PI-R comprises facets such as Anxiety, Hostility and Depression, and the BFI uses item terms such as 'upset', 'nervous', 'depressed', 'tense', 'moody'. The PANAS measures negative affect by items such as 'upset', 'nervous', 'irritable', 'distressed'.

The overlap in measurement and concepts represents a problem if high correlations between the overlapping measures are used to conclude that one is a strong predictor or cause of the other. 'A disposition to experience positive emotions predicts experiences of positive emotions' becomes rather nonsensical. It could be argued that it is meaningful to investigate how emotion traits influence emotion states. Yet, inasmuch as emotional well-being often is measured with reference to 'how you feel in general', it is the underlying emotion trait that is being indicated. This issue represents a challenge for the personality-SWB field, and remedies should be sought along several levels. First, there is a need for more stringent definitions as to what belongs to the personality domain versus the SWB domain. Based on this conceptual cleaning, measures with both convergent and divergent validity should be further developed. Moreover, at the theoretical level the traditional cause-effect perspective might benefit from a more integrative approach. For example, a partly inherited disposition to experience positive emotions might both represent a core aspect of the extraversion trait and the positive affect component of SWB. Thus, given that we are currently moving towards a more nuanced picture of personality traits, including a number of sub-factors or facets, we should probably ask what affective and cognitive dispositions *constitute* core elements of both personality traits and SWB.

BEYOND THE BIG FIVE TRAITS

Although the Five-Factor Model has a strong standing today, personality is more than the Big Five traits. Optimism and self-esteem represent more narrow traits that are only partly covered by the Five-Factor Model and have important relations to SWB. In fact, self-esteem has been found to be among the characteristics most strongly associated with several measures of SWB, yielding correlations up to 0.60 to 0.70 (Lucas et al., 1996).

Interestingly, however, the self-esteem-SWB relation appears to be moderated by culture. Whereas strong correlations are found in individualistic cultures, such as North American and Western European countries, the corresponding correlation is low or negligible in some collectivistic cultures, such as Japan, India, and China and other Asian cultures (Diener & Diener, 1995).

Dispositional optimism also correlates highly with SWB (Lucas et al., 1996; Roysamb & Strype, 2002). Although perhaps rather intuitive, the empirical evidence is important, in that optimism refers to expectations about the future, whereas SWB typically refers to evaluations of the past and current life. Thus, SWB and optimism differ in time orientation, but appear to some extent to go hand in hand. One way to put it is that SWB, as it is typically operationalised, is about construals of life as it is and has been, and these construals are closely related to construals of life to come. The problems of causality and mechanisms as discussed with regard to the Big Five traits clearly also pertain to self-esteem and optimism. Nevertheless, the two constructs contribute to a nuanced picture of what SWB is about.

At another level, social-cognitive perspectives of personality have contributed theories and findings on how aspects of personality such as motivation, goals, congruency and discrepancy, and social comparison relates to SWB. Happy and unhappy people have been shown to differ systematically in the motivational and cognitive strategies that they utilise. For example, happy people appear to avoid negative self-reflection after experiencing failures, and they focus on 'satisficing' rather than maximising decision-making. That is, rather than always aiming for the maximum of an outcome, people tend to construe conditions (like the weather, health or income) as more-than-good-enough. Furthermore, happy people tend to construe and respond to negative life events in positive and affirming ways, and they are relatively insensitive to social comparison (Abbe, Tkach & Lyubomirsky, 2003; Lyubomirsky, 2001).

Within a goal-perspective, several studies have found substantial relations between people's SWB and various aspects of their goals (Cantor & Sanderson, 1999; Emmons, 1991, 1992; McGregor & Little, 1998). More specifically, Cantor and Sanderson propose that SWB is influenced by sustained participation in individually and culturally valued tasks. Commitment to goals and activities and pursuit of and progression towards valued and chosen goals are conducive to happiness (Cantor & Sanderson, 1999). In the same vein, high SWB is related to being engaged in pursuit of core projects and to the projects being experienced as meaningful, high on structure and efficacy, and relatively non-stressful (Little & Chambers, 2004). Based on the personal strivings perspective, and addressing issues of person-event interaction, Emmons (1991) found that individuals striving for achievement tended to be affected by good achievement events, whereas respondents striving more for affiliation/intimacy to a higher extent were affected by interpersonal events. Thus, not only the type and content of goals—whether being conceived of as projects or strivings—but the match between goals and events seems to be related to SWB.

FUTURE CHALLENGES

Where should future research focus? One challenge is to use improved measures, advanced designs and analyses in order to produce stronger evidence and contribute towards a deeper understanding of the mechanisms and causal processes involved both in generating SWB and in the consequences of SWB. With longitudinal data, for example, the testing of different theory-based models of mechanisms will become feasible. Moreover, such designs will provide unique opportunities for separating effects on stability and change in SWB. Equally important, genetically informative designs (e.g., twin data) will further our understanding of the complex interplay between genetic and environmental factors. Genetic expression might depend on life circumstances, genetic factors might influence life events that affect SWB, and genetic factors might be correlated with environmental factors. We are only at the beginning of theorising and testing models that include such mechanisms in the SWB field.

In addition to providing better answers to current questions, future research should also try to raise new questions. One suggestion concerns the interpersonal relation between personality and SWB, that is, the cross-trait cross-person relationship. As reviewed above, and as seen clearly in the available literature, the general implicit question being asked is: 'To what extent and in what ways do my traits, goals, behaviours and construals affect my SWB?' An additional, and perhaps equally important, question is: '*To what extent and in what ways do my traits, goals, behaviours and construals affect other people's SWB?*' That is, given that we all play important roles in the lives of other people and others play important roles in our lives, there is reason to believe that our understanding of SWB would benefit from a cross-person perspective. Theoretically, our family, friends and colleagues do indeed have an impact on our SWB, but these influences have not received much attention in personality psychology.

As stated earlier on in this chapter, satisfaction and well-being appear to be highly valued by most people, with national averages of importance ratings ranging between 5.06 and 6.78 (on a scale from 1 to 7, with 7 representing 'extraordinarily important and valuable') (Diener, 2000). Especially in individualistic cultures, our own happiness is considered highly important. In the United States, the '... pursuit of happiness ... ' is even written into the nation's Constitution. Yet, it seems warranted to ask: 'Do we value the happiness of other people as highly as our own happiness?' In a recent study conducted by Joar Vittersø and the present author, a random sample ($N = 443$) of the Norwegian population was asked about the importance of different life domains, including personal life satisfaction and the life satisfaction of significant others. On a scale from 1 to 7, with seven representing 'very important', the mean score for agreement with 'That I am satisfied with life' was 6.11. The corresponding score for 'That people close to me are satisfied with life' was 6.44 and significantly ($p < 0.01$) higher. Thus, we do indeed care about the happiness of others, yet the ways in which we contribute to the happiness—or unhappiness—of others have mostly been disregarded in current research. Only a few studies have investigated such issues explicitly or implicitly. For example, adult children's expressed affection and emotional support, but not informative support, have been found to predict elderly parents' SWB longitudinally (Lang & Schutze, 2002). Other studies showing effects of personality traits on spouse marital satisfaction (Arrindell & Luteijn, 2000; Caughlin, Huston & Houts, 2000; Donnellan, Conger & Bryant, 2004) contribute to our understanding of cross-person effects of personality. For future research agendas, the question of personality effects across persons, including also the issue of interactions between self and other's personality, should be promoted.

A third suggestion with regard to future challenges concerns the development and validation of interventions designed to promote well-being. Now that a decent amount of knowledge is available on correlates and predictors of SWB, the practical applicability of this information is on the agenda. Recently, several research groups have undertaken the task of testing interventions developed to increase SWB-related phenomena, and the results are promising (Lyubomirsky, Sheldon & Schkade, 2005; Seligman, Steen, Park & Peterson, 2005; Sheldon & Lyubomirsky, 2004). One avenue for further developments in this field might be based on current knowledge concerning genetic factors and personality traits integrated with knowledge on goals, coping mechanisms, cognitive strategies, emotional reactions and social relations. Optimal interventions might have to take into account the different dispositions of individuals and develop flexible strategies with individually-focused targets.

CONCLUSIONS

The SWB field has definitely moved beyond its infancy and is attracting an increasing number of researchers. From being a rather narrow field, well-being has become a topic for cross-cultural research, epidemiological studies, experimental studies and twin research across sub-disciplines such as personality, social, developmental and abnormal psychology.

Subjective well-being is highly valued by most people, is negatively related to a number of mental disorders, and appears to have important consequences in life areas such as work, marriage and health. Further, well-being is relatively stable across time, yet there are also continuous change processes operating. Global well-being is moderately heritable, and genetic factors play important roles in the stability of well-being. Life events and other environmental factors are the main sources of change, and although most effects are only temporary, the continuous stream of occurring life events implies incessant change and fluctuation in well-being.

Personality factors show relatively strong associations with well-being. Traits such as neuroticism and extraversion appear to account for a substantial amount of individual differences in well-being. Other aspects of personality, such as self-esteem, affective dispositions, and personal projects and goals also seem to play important roles in generating and sustaining well-being. Current research efforts are attempting to disentangle the mechanisms and processes by which personality and well-being are interrelated.

Regarding suggestions for future research topics, a number of different paths might prove fruitful. Three specific directions are proposed here. First, SWB research should continue its development of advanced designs, conceptual clarification and measurement. Secondly, issues of across-individual relations between personality and well-being should be addressed. That is, what are the effects of my personality upon your well-being? Thirdly, based on current knowledge about correlates and sources of well-being, intervention studies should continue to investigate ways in which well-being can be promoted.

REFERENCES

Abbe, A., Tkach, C. & Lyubomirsky, S. (2003). The art of living by dispositionally happy people. *Journal of Happiness Studies, 4(4)*, 385–404.

Arrindell, W.A. & Luteijn, F. (2000). Similarity between intimate partners for personality traits as related to individual levels of satisfaction with life. *Personality and Individual Differences, 28(4)*, 629–637.

Bauer, J.J., McAdams, D.P. & Sakaeda, A.R. (2005). Interpreting the good life: Growth memories in the lives of mature, happy people. *Journal of Personality and Social Psychology, 88(1)*, 203–217.

Biswas-Diener, R., Vitterso, J. & Diener, E. (2005). Most people are pretty happy, but there is cultural variation: The Inughuit, the Amish, and the Maasai. *Journal of Happiness Studies, 6*, 205–226.

Biswas-Diener, R. & Diener, E. (2001). Making the best of a bad situation: Satisfaction in the slums of Calcutta. *Social Indicators Research, 55(3)*, 329–352.

Bolinskey, P., Neale, M.C., Jacobson, K.C., Prescott, C.A. & Kendler, K.S. (2004). Sources of individual differences in stressful life event exposure in male and female twins. *Twin Research, 7(1)*, 33–38.

Brief, A.P., Butcher, A.H., George, J.M. & Link, K.E. (1993). Integrating bottom-up and top-down theories of subjective well-being: The case of health. *Journal of Personality and Social Psychology, 64(4)*, 646–653.

Campbell, A., Converse, P.E. & Rodgers, W.L. (1976). *The quality of American life: Perceptions, evaluations, and satisfactions.* New York: Russel Sage Foundation.

Cantor, N. & Sanderson, C.A. (1999). Life task participation and well-being: The importance of taking part in daily life. In D. Kahneman, E. Diener & N. Schwarz (eds), *Well being: The foundations of hedonic psychology* (pp. 230–243). New York: Russell Sage Foundation.

Caspi, A., Sugden, K., Moffitt, T.E., Taylor, A., Craig, I.W., Harrington, H., et al. (2003). Influence of life stress on depression: Moderation by a polymorphism in the 5-HTT gene. *Science, 301(5631)*, 386–389.

Caughlin, J.P., Huston, T.L. & Houts, R.M. (2000). How does personality matter in marriage? An examination of trait anxiety, interpersonal negativity, and marital satisfaction. *Journal of Personality and Social Psychology, 78(2)*, 326–336.

Costa, P.T., Jr. & McCrae, R.R. (1997). Stability and change in personality assessment: The Revised NEO Personality Inventory in the Year 2000. *Journal of Personality Assessment, 68(1)*, 86–94.

Costa, P.T., Jr., McCrae, R.R. & Jonsson, F.H. (2002). Validity and utility of the revised NEO personality inventory: Examples from Europe. In B. de Raad (ed.), *Big five assessment* (pp. 61–72). Ashland, OH, US: Hogrefe & Huber Publishers.

Costa, P.T. & McCrae, R.R. (1980). Influence of extraversion and neuroticism on subjective well-being: Happy and unhappy people. *Journal of Personality and Social Psychology, 38(4)*, 668–678.

Cramer, V., Torgersen, S. & Kringlen, E. (2005). Quality of life and anxiety disorders: A population study. *Journal of Nervous and Mental Disease, 193(3)*, 196–202.

Cummins, R.A. (2003). Normative life satisfaction: Measurement issues and a homeostatic model. *Social Indicators Research, 64(2)*, 225–256.

Danner, D.D., Snowdon, D.A. & Friesen, W.V. (2001). Positive emotions in early life and longevity: Findings from the nun study. *Journal of Personality and Social Psychology, 80(5)*, 804–813.

Davidson, R.J. (2004). Affective style: Causes and consequences. In G.G. Berntson & J.T. Cacioppo (eds), *Essays in social neuroscience* (pp. 77–91). Cambridge, MA, US: MIT Press.

DeNeve, K.M. & Cooper, H. (1998). The happy personality: A meta-analysis of 137 personality traits and subjective well-being. *Psychological Bulletin, 124(2)*, 197–229.

Diener, E. (2000). Subjective well-being: The science of happiness and a proposal for a national index. *American Psychologist, 55(1)*, 34–43.

Diener, E. & Diener, C. (1996). Most people are happy. *Psychological Science, 7(3)*, 181–185.

Diener, E. & Diener, M. (1995). Cross-cultural correlates of life satisfaction and self-esteem. *Journal of Personality and Social Psychology, 68(4)*, 653–663.

Diener, E. & Lucas, R.E. (1999). Personality and subjective well-being. In D. Kahneman, E. Diener & N. Schwarz (eds), *Well being: The foundations of hedonic psychology* (pp. 213–229). New York, NY, US: Russell Sage Foundation.

Diener, E. & Lucas, R.E. (2000). Explaining differences in societal levels of happiness: Relative standards, need fulfillment, culture and evaluation theory. *Journal of Happiness Studies, 1(1)*, 41–78.

Diener, E., Nickerson, C., Lucas, R.E. & Sandvik, E. (2002). Dispositional affect and job outcomes. *Social Indicators Research, 59(3)*, 229–259.

Diener, E., Oishi, S. & Lucas, R.E. (2003). Personality, culture, and subjective well-being: Emotional and cognitive evaluations of life. *Annual Review of Psychology, 54*, 403–425.

Diener, E., Sandvik, E., Pavot, W. & Gallagher, D. (1991). Response artifacts in the measurement of subjective well-being. *Social Indicators Research, 24(1)*, 35–56.

Diener, E., Suh, E.M., Lucas, R.E. & Smith, H.L. (1999). Subjective well-being: Three decades of progress. *Psychological Bulletin, 125(2)*, 276–302.

Donnellan, M., Conger, R.D. & Bryant, C.M. (2004). The Big Five and enduring marriages. *Journal of Research in Personality, 38(5)*, 481–504.

Eid, M. & Diener, E. (2004). Global judgments of subjective well-being: Situational variability and long-term stability. *Social Indicators Research, 65(3)*, 245–277.

Ekman, P., Davidson, R.J., Ricard, M. & Wallace, B.A. (2005). Buddhist and psychological perspectives on emotions and well-being. *Current Directions in Psychological Science, 14(2)*, 59–63.

Emmons, R.A. (1991). Personal strivings, daily life events, and psychological and physical well-being. *Journal of Personality, 59(3)*, 453–472.

Emmons, R.A. (1992). Abstract versus concrete goals: Personal striving level, physical illness, and psychological well-being. *Journal of Personality and Social Psychology, 62(2)*, 292–300.

Emmons, R.A. & Diener, E. (1985). Personality correlates of subjective well-being. *Personality and Social Psychology Bulletin, 11(1)*, 89–97.

Feist, G.J., Bodner, T.E., Jacobs, J.F., Miles, M. et al. (1995). Integrating top-down and bottom-up structural models of subjective well-being: A longitudinal investigation. *Journal of Personality and Social Psychology, 68(1)*, 138–150.

Fortes, C., Farchi, S., Forastiere, F., Agabiti, N., Pacifici, R., Zuccaro, P., et al. (2003). Depressive symptoms lead to impaired cellular immune response. *Psychotherapy and Psychosomatics, 72(5)*, 253–260.

Fujita, F. & Diener, E. (2005). Life satisfaction set point: Stability and change. *Journal of Personality and Social Psychology, 88(1)*, 158–164.

Harker, L. & Keltner, D. (2001). Expressions of positive emotion in women's college yearbook pictures and their relationship to personality and life outcomes across adulthood. *Journal of Personality and Social Psychology, 80(1)*, 112–124.

Harris, J.R., Pedersen, N.L., Stacey, C., McClearn, G.E. et al. (1992). Age differences in the etiology of the relationship between life satisfaction and self-rated health. *Journal of Aging and Health, 4(3)*, 349–368.

Headey, B., Veenhoven, R. & Wearing, A. (1991). Top-down versus bottom-up theories of subjective well-being. *Social Indicators Research, 24(1)*, 81–100.

Headey, B. & Wearing, A. (1989). Personality, life events, and subjective well-being: Toward a dynamic equilibrium model. *Journal of Personality and Social Psychology, 57(4)*, 731–739.

Headey, B.W., Kelley, J. & Wearing, A.J. (1993). Dimensions of mental health: Life satisfaction, positive affect, anxiety and depression. *Social Indicators Research, 29(1)*, 63–82.

John, O.P. & Srivastava, S. (1999). The Big Five Trait taxonomy: History, measurement, and theoretical perspectives. In O.P. John & L. Pervin (eds), *Handbook of personality: Theory and research*. New York: Guilford Press.

Kahneman, D., Diener, E. & Schwarz, N. (eds). (1999). *Well-being: The foundations of hedonic psychology*. New York: Russell Sage Foundation.

Kahneman, D., Krueger, A.B., Schkade, D.A., Schwarz, N. & Stone, A.A. (2004). A survey method for characterizing daily life experience: The day reconstruction method. *Science, 306(5702)*, 1776–1780.

Kendler, K.S. (1993). Twin studies of psychiatric illness: Current status and future directions. *Archives of General Psychiatry, 50(11)*, 905–915.

Kendler, K.S. (2001). Twin studies of psychiatric illness: An update. *Archives of General Psychiatry, 58(11)*, 1005–1014.

Kendler, K.S., Myers, J.M. & Neale, M.C. (2000). A multidimensional twin study of mental health in women. *American Journal of Psychiatry, 157(4)*, 506–513.

Kendler, K.S., Neale, M.C., Kessler, R., Heath, A.C. et al. (1993). A twin study of recent life events and difficulties. *Archives of General Psychiatry, 50(10)*, 789–796.

Kercher, K. (1992). Assessing subjective well-being in the old-old: The PANAS as a measure of orthogonal dimensions of positive and negative affect. *Research on Aging, 14(2)*, 131–168.

Keyes, C.L.M., Shmotkin, D. & Ryff, C.D. (2002). Optimizing well-being: The empirical encounter of two traditions. *Journal of Personality and Social Psychology, 82(6)*, 1007–1022.

Kim, J. & Hatfield, E. (2004). Love types and subjective well-being: A cross-cultural study. *Social Behavior and Personality, 32(2)*, 173–182.

King, L.A. & Miner, K.N. (2000). Writing about the perceived benefits of traumatic events: Implications for physical health. *Personality and Social Psychology Bulletin, 26(2)*, 220–230.

Lang, F.R. & Schutze, Y. (2002). Adult children's supportive behaviors and older parents' subjective well-being: A developmental perspective on intergenerational relationships. *Journal of Social Issues, 58(4)*, 661–680.

Larsen, R.J. & Buss, D.M. (2005). *Personality psychology. Domains of knowledge about human nature* (2nd edn). Boston: McGraw Hill.

Larsen, R.J. & Fredrickson, B.L. (1999). Measurement issues in emotion research. In D. Kahneman, E. Diener & N. Schwarz (eds), *Well being: The foundations of hedonic psychology* (pp. 40–60). New York, NY: Russell Sage Foundation.

Lichtenstein, P., Gatz, M., Pedersen, N.L., Berg, S. et al. (1996). A co-twin-control study of response to widowhood. *Journals of Gerontology: Series B: Psychological Sciences and Social Sciences, 51B(5)*, P279–P289.

Little, B.R. & Chambers, N.C. (2004). Personal project pursuit: On human doings and well beings. In E. Klinger & W.M. Cox (eds), *Handbook of motivational counseling: Concepts, approaches, and assessment* (pp. 65–82). New York: John Wiley & Sons, Inc.

Loehlin, J.C., McCrae, R.R., Costa, P.T., Jr. & John, O.P. (1998). Heritabilities of common and measure-specific components of the Big Five personality factors. *Journal of Research in Personality, 32(4)*, 431–453.

Lucas, R.E., Clark, A.E., Georgellis, Y. & Diener, E. (2003). Reexamining adaptation and the set point model of happiness: Reactions to changes in marital status. *Journal of Personality and Social Psychology, 84(3)*, 527–539.

Lucas, R.E., Clark, A.E., Georgellis, Y. & Diener, E. (2004). Unemployment alters the set point for life satisfaction. *Psychological Science, 15(1)*, 8–13.

Lucas, R.E. & Diener, E. (2000). Personality and subjective well-being across the life span. In D.L. Molfese & V.J. Molfese (eds), *Temperament and personality development across the life span* (pp. 211–234). Mahwah: Lawrence Erlbaum Associates.

Lucas, R.E., Diener, E. & Suh, E. (1996). Discriminant validity of well-being measures. *Journal of Personality and Social Psychology, 71(3)*, 616–628.

Lutgendorf, S.K., Vitaliano, P.P., Tripp Reimer, T., Harvey, J.H. & Lubaroff, D.M. (1999). Sense of coherence moderates the relationship between life stress and natural killer cell activity in healthy older adults. *Psychology and Aging, 14(4)*, 552–563.

Lykken, D. (1999). *Happiness: What studies on twins show us about nature, nurture, and the happiness set-point.* New York: Golden Books.

Lykken, D. & Tellegen, A. (1996). Happiness is a stochastic phenomenon. *Psychological Science, 7(3)*, 186–189.

Lyubomirsky, S. (2001). Why are some people happier than others? The role of cognitive and motivational processes in well-being. *American Psychologist, 56(3)*, 239–249.

Lyubomirsky, S., Sheldon, K.M. & Schkade, D. (2005). Pursuing happiness: The architecture of sustainable change. *Review of General Psychology, 9(2)*, 111–131.

McCrae, R.R. & Costa, P.T. (1988). Psychological resilience among widowed men and women: A 10-year follow-up of a national sample. *Journal of Social Issues, 44(3)*, 129–142.

McCrae, R.R. & Costa, P.T., Jr. (2003). *Personality in adulthood: A five-factor theory perspective* (2nd edn) New York: Guilford Press.

McCrae, R.R., Costa, P.T. Jr. & Martin, T.A. (2005). The NEO-PI-3: A more readable revised NEO personality inventory. *Journal of Personality Assessment, 84(3)*, 261–270.

McGregor, I. & Little, B.R. (1998). Personal projects, happiness, and meaning: On doing well and being yourself. *Journal of Personality and Social Psychology, 74(2)*, 494–512.

Moffitt, T.E. (2005). The new look of behavioral genetics in developmental psychopathology: Gene-environment interplay in antisocial behaviors. *Psychological Bulletin, 131(4)*, 533–554.

Mroczek, D.K. & Spiro, A., III. (2005). Change in life satisfaction during adulthood: Findings from the veterans affairs normative aging study. *Journal of Personality and Social Psychology, 88(1)*, 189–202.

Myers, D.G. & Diener, E. (1995). Who is happy? *Psychological Science, 6(1)*, 10–19.

Neale, M.C. & Cardon, L.R. (1992). *Methodology for genetic studies of twins and families.* Dordrecht: Kluwer Academic Press.

Nes, R.B., Røysamb, E., Tambs, K., Harris, J.R. & Reichborn-Kjennerud, T. (2006). Subjective well-being: Genetic and environmental contributions to stability and change. *Psychological Medicine* (in press).

Okun, M.A. & George, L.K. (1984). Physician- and self-ratings of health, neuroticism and subjective well-being among men and women. *Personality and Individual Differences, 5(5)*, 533–539.

Pavot, W. & Diener, E. (1993). Review of the Satisfaction With Life Scale. *Psychological Assessment, 5(2)*, 164–172.

Pavot, W., Fujita, F. & Diener, E. (1997). The relation between self-aspect congruence, personality and subjective well-being. *Personality and Individual Differences, 22(2)*, 183–191.

Pavot, W.G., Diener, E., Colvin, C. & Sandvik, E. (1991). Further validation of the Satisfaction With Life Scale: Evidence for the cross-method convergence of well-being measures. *Journal of Personality Assessment, 57(1)*, 149–161.

Pickering, A.D. & Gray, J.A. (1999). The neuroscience of personality. In O.P. John & L. Pervin (eds), *Handbook of personality: Theory and research* (pp. 277–299), New York: Guilford Press.

Pizzagalli, D., Shackman, A.J. & Davidson, R.J. (2003). The functional neuroimaging of human emotion: Asymmetric contributions of cortical and subcortical circuitry. In R.J. Davidson & K. Hugdahl (eds), *The asymmetrical brain* (pp. 511–532), Cambridge, MA: MIT Press.

Plomin, R., DeFries, J., McClearn, G.E. & Rutter, M. (1997). *Behavioral genetics* (3rd edn). New York: Freeman.

Rapaport, M.H., Clary, C., Fayyad, R. & Endicott, J. (2005). Quality-of-Life impairment in depressive and anxiety disorders. *American Journal of Psychiatry, 162(6)*, 1171–1178.

Robbins, S.B. & Kliewer, W.L. (2000). Advances in theory and research on subjective well-being. In R.W. Lent & S.D. Brown (eds), *Handbook of counseling psychology* (pp. 310–345). New York: John Wiley & Sons, Inc.

Roysamb, E., Harris, J.R., Magnus, P., Vitterso, J. & Tambs, K. (2002). Subjective well-being: Sex-specific effects of genetic and environmental factors. *Personality and Individual Differences, 32(2)*, 211–223.

Roysamb, E. & Strype, J. (2002). Optimism and pessimism: Underlying structure and dimensionality. *Journal of Social and Clinical Psychology, 21(1)*, 1–19.

Roysamb, E., Tambs, K., Reichborn Kjennerud, T., Neale, M.C. & Harris, J.R. (2003). Happiness and health: Environmental and genetic contributions to the relationship between subjective well-being, perceived health, and somatic illness. *Journal of Personality and Social Psychology, 85(6)*, 1136–1146.

Rush, A.J., Zimmerman, M., Wisniewski, S.R., Fava, M., Hollon, S.D., Warden, D., et al. (2005). Comorbid psychiatric disorders in depressed outpatients: Demographic and clinical features. *Journal of Affective Disorders, 87(1)*, 43–55.

Ryan, R.M. & Deci, E.L. (2000). On happiness and human potentials: A review of research on hedonic and eudaimonic well-being. *Annual Review of Psychology, 52*, 141–166.

Ryff, C.D., Keyes, C.L.M. & Hughes, D.L. (2003). Status inequalities, perceived discrimination, and eudaimonic well-being: Do the challenges of minority life hone purpose and growth? *Journal of Health and Social Behavior, 44(3)*, 275–291.

Ryff, C.D. & Singer, B. (1998). The contours of positive human health. *Psychological Inquiry, 9(1)*, 1–28.

Schimmack, U. (2003). Affect measurement in Experience Sampling research. *Journal of Happiness Studies, 4(1)*, 79–106.

Schmutte, P.S. & Ryff, C.D. (1997). Personality and well-being: Reexamining methods and meanings. *Journal of Personality and Social Psychology, 73(3)*, 549–559.

Schwarz, N. & Strack, F. (1999). Reports of subjective well-being: Judgmental processes and their methodological implications. In D. Kahneman, E. Diener & N. Schwarz (eds), *Well being: The foundations of hedonic psychology* (pp. 61–84). New York: Russell Sage Foundation.

Segerstrom, S.C., Castaneda, J.O. & Spencer, T.E. (2003). Optimism effects on cellular immunity: Testing the affective and persistence models. *Personality and Individual Differences, 35(7)*, 1615–1624.

Seligman, M.E.P. (2000). Positive psychology. In Gillham, J.E. (ed.), *The science of optimism and hope: Research essays in honor of Martin E. P. Seligman* (pp. 415–429). Philadelphia: Templeton Foundation Press.

Seligman, M.E.P. & Csikszentmihalyi, M. (2000). Positive psychology: An introduction. *American Psychologist, 55(1)*, 5–14.

Seligman, M.E.P., Park, N. & Peterson, C. (2004). The Values In Action (VIA) classification of character strengths. *Ricerche di Psicologia, 27(1)*, 63–78.

Seligman, M.E.P., Steen, T.A., Park, N. & Peterson, C. (2005). Positive psychology progress: Empirical validation of interventions. *American Psychologist, 60(5)*, 410–421.

Sheldon, K.M. & Lyubomirsky, S. (2004). Achieving sustainable new happiness: Prospects, practices, and prescriptions. In Joseph, S., Linley, P.A. (eds), *Positive psychology in practice* (pp. 127–145). New York: John Wiley & Sons, Inc.

Steel, P. & Ones, D.S. (2002). Personality and happiness: A national-level analysis. *Journal of Personality and Social Psychology, 83(3)*, 767–781.

Stone, A.A., Cox, D.S., Valdimarsdottir, H., Jandorf, L. et al. (1987). Evidence that secretory IgA antibody is associated with daily mood. *Journal of Personality and Social Psychology, 52(5)*, 988–993.

Stubbe, J.H., Posthuma, D., Boomsma, D.I. & De Geus, E.J.C. (2005). Heritability of life satisfaction in adults: a twin-family study. *Psychological Medicine, 35*, 1–8.

Suh, E., Diener, E. & Fujita, F. (1996). Events and subjective well-being: Only recent events matter. *Journal of Personality and Social Psychology, 70(5)*, 1091–1102.

Suh, E., Diener, E., Oishi, S. & Triandis, H.C. (1998). The shifting basis of life satisfaction judgments across cultures: Emotions versus norms. *Journal of Personality and Social Psychology, 74(2)*, 482–493.

Urry, H.L., Nitschke, J.B., Dolski, I., Jackson, D.C., Dalton, K.M., Mueller, C.J., et al. (2004). Making a life worth living: Neural correlates of well-being. *Psychological Science, 15(6)*, 367–372.

van Dierendonck, D. (2004). The construct validity of Ryff's Scales of Psychological Well-being and its extension with spiritual well-being. *Personality and Individual Differences, 36(3)*, 629–643.

Veenhoven, R. (1994). Is happiness a trait? Tests of the theory that a better society does not make people any happier. *Social Indicators Research, 32(2)*, 101–160.

Vitterso, J. (2001). Personality traits and subjective well-being: Emotional stability, not extraversion, is probably the important predictor. *Personality and Individual Differences, 31(6)*, 903–914.

Vitterso, J. (2003). Flow versus life satisfaction: A projective use of cartoons to illustrate the difference between the evaluation approach and the intrinsic motivation approach to subjective quality of life. *Journal of Happiness Studies, 4(2)*, 141–167.

Vitterso, J. (2004). Subjective well-being versus self-actualization: Using the flow-simplex to promote a conceptual clarification of subjective quality of life. *Social Indicators Research, 65(3)*, 299–331.

Watson, D. & Clark, L.A. (1984). Negative affectivity: The disposition to experience aversive emotional states. *Psychological Bulletin, 96(3)*, 465–490.

Watson, D. & Clark, L.A. (1992). On traits and temperament: General and specific factors of emotional experience and their relation to the five-factor model. *Journal of Personality, 60(2)*, 441–476.

Watson, D. & Clark, L.A. (1997). Measurement and mismeasurement of mood: Recurrent and emergent issues. *Journal of Personality Assessment, 68(2)*, 267–296.

Watson, D., Clark, L.A. & Tellegen, A. (1988). Development and validation of brief measures of positive and negative affect: The PANAS scales. *Journal of Personality and Social Psychology, 54(6)*, 1063–1070.

Watten, R.G., Vassend, O., Myhrer, T. & Syversen, J.L. (1997). Personality factors and somatic symptoms. *European Journal of Personality, 11(1)*, 57–68.

WHO. (1948). World Health Organization definition of health. http://www.who.int/about/definition/en/.

Widiger, T.A. & Clark, L.A. (2000). Toward DSM–V and the classification of psychopathology. *Psychological Bulletin, 126(6)*, 946–963.

Widiger, T.A. & Sankis, L.M. (2000). Adult psychopathology: Issues and controversies. *Annual Review of Psychology, 51*, 377–404.

Xie, H., McHugo, G.J., Helmstetter, B.S. & Drake, R.E. (2005). Three-year recovery outcomes for long-term patients with co-occurring schizophrenic and substance use disorders. *Schizophrenia Research, 75(2–3)*, 337–348.

PART II

Mediators of the Personality Health Relationship

CHAPTER 6

Mechanisms Relating Personality and Health

Deborah J. Wiebe and Katherine T. Fortenberry

University of Utah, USA

INTRODUCTION

For centuries, people have been intrigued by the possibility that personality can affect health. Although serious skeptics exist (Angell, 1985), the current literature offers compelling evidence that personality plays a causal role in the development and course of various health outcomes (Smith & Gallo, 2001). Friedman (2000) recently opined that 'Although news reporters are still surprised when they encounter a new finding indicating that associations really do exist between psychosocial factors and health and longevity, the serious research has long ago moved on to addressing the causal pathways underlying these associations' (p. 1090). The purpose of the present chapter is to describe these potential mechanisms. A good understanding of the complex linkages between personality and health is imperative to promote a steady accumulation of knowledge and to inform effective interventions. Toward this end, we initially describe the major models that have been developed to explain how personality may become linked to health. Second, we briefly review several personality constructs that have been the focus of serious examination to demonstrate and evaluate the utility of these models. Finally, we discuss current issues and future directions for understanding mechanisms linking personality and disease.

PATHWAYS LINKING PERSONALITY AND HEALTH

In this section, we discuss several models that have been developed to explain the processes through which stable characteristics of the individual may be associated with health (see also Cohen & Rodriguez, 1995; Contrada & Coups, 2002; Friedman, 2000). Two of these models—stress-moderation and health behavior—assume personality causes illness and detail plausible psychophysiological and biobehavioral links from personality to subsequent illness. The illness behavior and constitutional predisposition models articulate pathways through which personality may *appear* to be associated with illness in the absence of a causal relationship. These models raise methodological and conceptual issues that are important

Handbook of Personality and Health. Edited by Margarete E. Vollrath. © 2006 John Wiley & Sons, Ltd.

to consider when conducting or evaluating research. Although we provide a fair amount of detail regarding mediating processes within each model, these are highly simplified illustrations of the complex manner in which dynamic features of personality may contribute to health over a lifetime. For parsimony, the models are presented as unidirectional, although recurrent feedback processes are likely. The models are also discussed individually, but are neither mutually exclusive nor exhaustive explanations. Multiple models are commonly utilized to explain how a single personality variable is associated with health, several models may function simultaneously within a single individual as a function of the individual's profile across personality dimensions, and the processes identified across models may actually operate synergistically to affect health. These and other issues are discussed in a later section.

Stress-moderation Models

The most common explanation of links between personality and health involves stress-moderation (see Figure 6.1). In this model, it is assumed that stress can cause illness, and personality acts by making one more or less vulnerable to its deleterious effects (Cohen & Rodriguez, 1995; Vollrath, 2001; Wiebe & Smith, 1997). As a starting point, stress is believed to impair health by activating the sympathetic and neuroendocrine systems (i.e., the sympathetic-adrenomedullary and pituitary-adrenocortical axes), eliciting a cascade of responses across multiple physiological systems (Cohen et al., 2000; Kamarck & Lovallo, 2003). Growing evidence suggests that frequent, intense or prolonged experiences of stress-induced physiological arousal can contribute to the development or progression of illness, and our understanding of how this translates into the pathophysiology of specific stages and types of disease is becoming increasingly sophisticated (e.g., Lovallo & Gerin, 2003; Treiber et al., 2003). These systems also interface with and dysregulate the immune system, suppressing some immune responses but enhancing others (Robles, Glaser & Kiecolt-Glaser, 2005; Segerstrom & Miller, 2004). That is, in addition to the health-damaging aspects of stress-induced immunosuppression, stress can cause chronic inflammation which

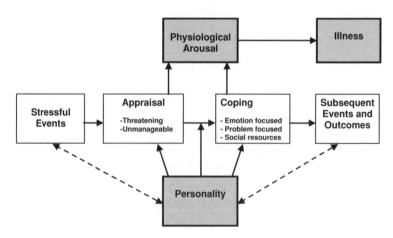

Figure 6.1 Transactional stress-moderation model

may contribute to a range of illnesses such as cardiovascular disease, diabetes, arthritis, and some cancers (Robles et al., 2005). Thus, stress-induced physiological arousal is likely to represent an important common pathway to disease.

To appreciate how personality may moderate stress-induced physiological arousal, it is useful to detail the ongoing stress and coping process. According to current models of stress, an objective event becomes stressful—and can elicit emotional and physiological arousal—to the extent that it is appraised by the individual as threatening and as taxing or exceeding one's coping resources (Lazarus & Folkman, 1984). Once threat is perceived, coping responses may influence arousal by altering the intensity, duration, or reoccurrence of the stressor. As shown in Figure 6.1, personality may moderate the effects of stress at several points (see also Contrada & Coups, 2003; Vollrath, 2001; Wiebe & Williams, 1992). First, there is ample evidence that personality alters the subjective appraisal of ongoing life experiences; neurotic individuals interpret neutral or ambiguous stimuli as threatening (Gallagher, 1990), while hardy individuals appraise stress as challenging and controllable (Wiebe, 1991). Second, personality may influence the availability, choice, or effectiveness of one's coping and social resources (Suls, David & Harvey, 1996). For example, neuroticism is routinely associated with more avoidance and emotion-focused coping, while conscientiousness is associated with positive reappraisal and more active problem-focused coping (Watson & Hubbard, 1996). Because specific coping behaviors are not uniformly adaptive or maladaptive across situations, it is important to note that personality traits can also influence the extent to which coping efforts match the adaptive demands of a given situation (e.g., Bolger & Zuckerman, 1995; Park, Armeli & Tennen, 2004).

This basic stress-moderation model is limited by its static view of personality. That is, personality traits are interpreted as creating stable *responses* to whatever random life events come one's way. This basic model misses the dynamic, reciprocally-determined transactions that occur between personality and one's social environment, and that are central to current social-cognitive and transactional models of personality (Buss, 1987; Cantor, 1990; Shiner & Caspi, 2003). As shown with the dashed lines in Figure 6.1, the more complex *transactional stress-moderation model* considers personality not only as influencing responses to stressful events, but as actively creating different types of life experiences. Thus, the interpersonal beliefs and behaviors of hostile individuals may generate interpersonal stress and minimize social support (Smith, 2003), while the careful planning and proactive coping of conscientious individuals may reduce stress and increase coping resources (Friedman et al., 1993). These processes may not only contribute to health, but are likely to reverberate back to confirm or stabilize personality (Shiner & Caspi, 2003), as when the hostile person's creation of interpersonal conflict confirms his or her antagonistic views of others. Such stress-engendering and stress-preventing personality processes are rarely studied in the context of health, but are likely to be quite important for understanding how personality can influence health across the life-span. Friedman (2000) has argued that personality has its real impact on health by considering these broad but consistent movements toward or away from healthy lives across the lifespan.

Health Behavior Models

In the health behavior model, personality is hypothesized to affect health by influencing one's engagement in health-enhancing or health-damaging behaviors (see top section of

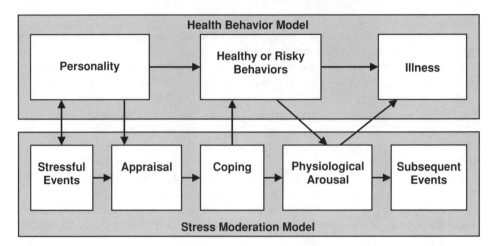

Figure 6.2   Health behavior model

Figure 6.2). For example, optimism is associated with better nutritional, exercise, and sexual behavior practices (Mulkana & Hailey, 2001; Zak-Place & Stern, 2004), while hostility predicts more smoking and alcohol use, avoidance of exercise, and poor diets (Siegler, Costa & Brummett, 2003; Smith, Glazer & Ruiz, 2004). Longitudinal studies reveal that personality can predict engagement in various health-related behaviors over a period of decades (Caspi et al., 1997; Roberts & Bogg, 2004), and there is evidence that health behaviors mediate associations between personality and health outcomes (Everson et al., 1997). As discussed below, a mediational role for health behavior makes one question the common practice of covarying behavioral risk factors when examining personality-health relationships.

Although there is considerable evidence that personality is associated with health behavior, our understanding of why these associations exist remains limited. Personality may shape one's health beliefs, which then set the stage for specific health behaviors. For example, neuroticism positively relates to perceived risk of HIV infection as a motivation for trial participation (Johnson, 2000), while low openness to experience predicts low perceived risk of HIV infection (Trobst et al., 2002). Personality may also create different motivational propensities for engaging in risky behaviors. Cooper, Agocha, and Sheldon (2000) demonstrated neuroticism and extraversion promote risky behaviors (i.e., alcohol and sexual practices) through different affect regulation needs; neurotic individuals appeared to engage in risky behaviors to cope with negative mood while extraverted individuals did so to enhance positive moods. Understanding these types of mediating processes will be necessary if personality-health behavior research is to influence successful behavior change interventions.

Health behavior pathways may also interface with other models of personality and health, such as the stress-moderation model (see bottom section of Figure 6.2). Health behaviors such as smoking and exercise may serve as coping strategies (e.g., some individuals cope by exercising while others do so by smoking; Ng & Jeffery, 2003; Wiebe & McCallum, 1986). Additionally, health behaviors may alter physiological reactions to stress. For example, chronic smoking increases adrenocortical and cardiovascular responses to laboratory stressors (al'Absi et al., 2003), and exercise reduces blood pressure reactivity (West, Brownley & Light, 1998). Thus, although rarely done, studying interactions between the health behavior and stress moderation models is likely to provide a more comprehensive understanding of personality-health relationships.

Illness Behavior Models

In contrast to the models discussed thus far, the illness behavior model details how personality may appear to be associated with health outcomes in the absence of an association with actual disease. The crux issue in this model is whether the measure of health is an unambiguous index of underlying disease (e.g., measured blood pressure, atherosclerosis, immune function, cardiac mortality), or whether it reflects illness behavior in the absence of disease. Illness behavior represents the actions people take when they think they are sick (e.g., report symptoms, visit a physician, take medication), and is reliably associated with actual health (Idler & Benyamini, 1997). However, this association is modest and is heavily influenced by complex psychological aspects of recognizing, interpreting and acting upon somatic sensations (Cioffi, 1991; Pennebaker, 1982; Watson & Pennebaker, 1989).

The mechanisms by which personality may influence illness behavior in the absence of underlying pathophysiology are displayed in the top part of Figure 6.3. All of us experience ongoing, fluctuating patterns of physical sensations. These sensations provide important cues to managing health and illness, particularly if one can accurately detect a symptom against the backdrop of constantly fluctuating sensations, label it as illness, and take appropriate action (e.g., myocardial infarction causes noticeable chest pain, you interpret it as a heart attack, and go to the emergency room). This symptom perception task is complex (Cioffi, 1991; Pennebaker, 1982), with plenty of room for people to err by missing important

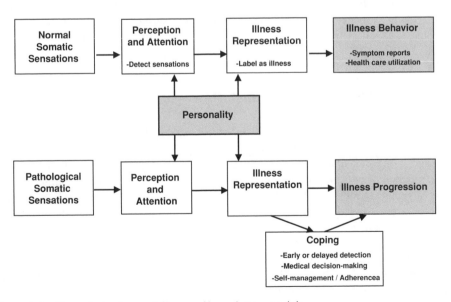

Figure 6.3 Illness behavior and illness self-regulation models

signs of illness or by over-responding to neutral ongoing physical sensations. Illness behavior models were developed to address the latter situation where dispositional aspects
of symptom perception and health/illness cognition play out to influence such outcomes
as increased symptom reports and health care utilization in the absence of clear pathology.
This has been a particular concern for research linking the broad personality dimension of
neuroticism to health.

This model raises important methodological concerns for personality-health research.
Although illness behaviors are clearly important, it is imperative to link personality to
unambiguous measures of physical health if we are to make lasting contributions beyond
the disciplinary bounds of personality and health psychology. Further, research designs and
the manner in which participants are recruited need to be carefully considered, as illness-
behavior can create selection biases by influencing who seeks medical care or receives
a diagnosis (e.g., Costa & McCrae, 1987). This is an obvious problem when personality
associations with health are explored by comparing cases of illness in a clinical sample
with community controls, but is likely to play out in more subtle ways across many research
designs and illness measures.

Although the illness behavior model provides a salient cautionary note, one must recognize that illness behavior *as a self-regulatory process* is crucial to ongoing illness management, and may strongly influence the progression of illness once a pathophysiological
process has begun (Cameron & Leventhal, 2003). The *illness self-regulation model* displayed in the bottom half of Figure 6.3 demonstrates how personality may influence illness
progression via the same illness behavior processes described above. In this case, however,
dispositional differences become reflected in how quickly actual illness is detected, the types
of illness representations one develops (e.g., commonsense beliefs about the cause, consequences, severity, and symptoms of one's illness), and resulting self-management decisions
and behaviors (e.g., treatment delays, adherence). To the extent that such models explain
personality differences in illness progression, personality-health research will benefit from
clearly distinguishing between illness behavior as an outcome and illness behavior as a
self-regulatory process. Again, careful attention to measuring unambiguous 'hard' health
outcomes, as well as linking personality and illness behavior to these outcomes, will be
useful.

Constitutional Predisposition or Biological Models

The constitutional predisposition model posits that statistical associations between personality and health occur because early biological responses—related to genetics, prenatal or
perinatal influences, and/or socialization effects on the nervous system—influence both
the expression of personality and vulnerability to illness. As displayed in Figure 6.4, this
model hypothesizes that relationships between personality and health may be noncausal
reflections of an underlying third variable. We do not discuss this model extensively as it
has not been studied systematically across personality variables, but believe it is important
to consider because health-relevant personality variables are partially heritable (Plomin &
Caspi, 1999). Furthermore, given the transactional personality processes described above
and the complex ways in which biological and environmental factors interact to influence
adult personality (Plomin & Caspi, 1999; Shiner & Caspi, 2003), these biological aspects
of personality may provide additional mediating pathways to health.

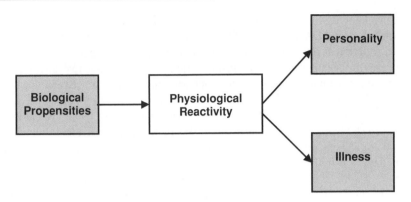

Figure 6.4 Constitutional predisposition model

SELECTED ILLUSTRATIONS OF SPECIFIC PERSONALITY-HEALTH ASSOCIATIONS

In this section, we briefly discuss several personality variables that have been extensively examined as predictors of health. Because a comprehensive review is beyond our scope, we focus on personality traits that have the most compelling evidence for prospectively predicting unambiguous signs of illness (e.g., mortality, documented heart disease, immune function). For each variable, we first review evidence of associations with health, and then discuss the mechanisms that have been examined to explain these associations.

Hostility, Type A, and Anger

Hostility can be defined as mistrust, cynicism, and negative beliefs and attributions concerning others (Smith, 2003). As the toxic component of multifaceted Type A behavior, hostility is among the most well-studied health-relevant personality variables. In Five Factor Model terminology, hostility is related to both high neuroticism (discussed below) and low agreeableness. Hostility and closely related constructs such as trait anger have been explicitly linked to coronary heart disease (CHD) at various stages of disease progression. Non-symptomatic individuals high in trait anger have a 50–75 % increased risk of developing CHD (Williams et al., 2000), and hostility is associated with early indications of atherosclerosis (Bleil et al., 2004; Harris et al., 2003). Following a cardiovascular event, hostility predicts a higher likelihood of recurrent myocardial infarction (Chaput et al., 2002) and cardiovascular-related death (Matthews, Gump, Harris, Haney & Barefoot, 2004). Hostility has also been shown to predict both CHD mortality and all-cause mortality in multiple prospective studies (Boyle et al., 2004; Everson et al., 1997; Matthews et al., 2004). Despite some null findings (e.g., Eng et al., 2003), reviews generally support the association of hostility with the development and progression of CHD (Gallo & Matthews, 2003; Kop, 1999; Smith, 2003).

Multiple explanations of the relationship between hostility and disease have been examined. In support of the transactional stress moderation model, data suggest that hostile individuals create more interpersonal conflict in their lives, and respond to conflict with more frequent and prolonged physiological reactivity. Hostile individuals report lower levels of social support (O'Neil & Emery, 2002) and more interpersonal conflict (Siegler et al., 2003) than individuals low in hostility. Daily monitoring studies suggest hostile individuals experience more negative interpersonal interactions and fewer positive interactions, and respond to interpersonal interactions with increased blood pressure (Brondolo, Rieppi & Erickson, 2003). Individuals high in hostility also show higher cardiovascular reactivity to laboratory stressors, particularly those with interpersonal features (Smith & Gallo, 2001). Hostility, therefore, appears to influence both the situations that individuals encounter, and their physiological reactions to these situations, creating a unique constellation of psychosocial vulnerability (Smith, 2003).

Processes described in the health behavior model are also important. Hostility measured in college predicts more smoking and alcohol use and less social support at midlife (Siegler et al., 2003), and cross-sectional studies indicate hostility is associated with a variety of poor health behaviors (Brisette & Cohen, 2002; Calhoun, Bosworth & Siegler, 2001; Kahler, Strong, Niaura & Brown, 2004). Everson et al. (1997) found that poor health behaviors mediate the relationship between hostility and subsequent CHD, although controlling for traditional behavioral risks does not generally eliminate the hostility-health relationship (Miller et al., 1996; Surtees et al., 2003). Health behavior pathways are, thus, likely to be only part of the causal process. The relationship of hostility to health behaviors may also exacerbate reactivity to stress as caffeine consumption increases cardiovascular reactivity in hostile individuals (B.D. Smith, Cranford & Green, 2001). Thus, examining the interactions among different explanatory models may provide a more complete understanding of the relationship between hostility and health.

The influence of hostility on illness behavior has received little empirical attention, although these processes have been explored in the context of Type A behavior. Type A individuals are less likely to detect symptoms of myocardial infarction, particularly when work is highly demanding (Matthews et al., 1983), and may be more likely to reject the sick role and return to work before recovering from illness (Alemagno et al., 1991). These associations appear to reflect the competitive and hard-driving facets of Type A, and are unlikely to play out in the context of hostility. The suspicion and mistrust of hostile individuals, however, may impair their likelihood of adhering to advice from physicians (Christensen, Wiebe & Lawton, 1997).

Neuroticism and Negative Affect

Neuroticism is a broad dimension of personality that represents the disposition to experience negative emotions (e.g., anxiety, depression). The hypothesis that neuroticism is damaging to one's health has a long and checkered history. Although a large literature appeared to support this hypothesis (Friedman & Booth-Kewley, 1987), methodological limitations led to important corrections in the field. Specifically, clear evidence that neuroticism is associated with subjective more than objective measures of illness, and the articulation of illness behavior models to explain this pattern, raised questions of whether neuroticism or the closely related negative-affectivity construct actively influence objective health (Costa & McCrae, 1987; Watson & Pennebaker, 1989).

The most recent wave of research, however, provides more compelling evidence that neuroticism or its negative emotional substrates predicts objective illness. Both quantitative and qualitative reviews conclude that negative emotions such as anxiety and depression prospectively predict 'hard' health endpoints, particularly in the context of CHD (e.g., Gallo & Matthews, 2003; Hemingway & Marmot, 1999; Kubzansky & Kawachi, 2000; Rutledge & Hogan, 2002; Suls & Bunde, 2005). These associations are found after controlling for traditional behavioral and biomedical risk factors. Furthermore, prospective studies following elderly community samples (Robinson, McBeth & MacFarlane, 2004; Wilson, DeLeon, Bienias, Evans & Bennett, 2004) reveal neuroticism-related constructs predict all-cause mortality, often in a dose-response fashion. There is also evidence of an association between the experience of negative emotions and subsequent illness progression in patients with HIV (Ickovics et al., 2001) and renal failure (Christensen et al., 2002).

It is important to note that these studies are not without critics and that inconsistent findings continue to be reported. It is also unclear whether diverse indicators of negative emotions are accurately interpreted as reflections of neuroticism, particularly as these indicators vary both in the specific emotion tapped and in the extent to which they represent current states, stable traits, or clinical conditions (e.g., anxiety disorders, major depression). It has been argued that these emotions are highly overlapping and recurrent across time, such that their shared variance reflects a latent dispositional variable that may be responsible for effects on health (Suls & Bunde, 2004; Watson & Clark, 1984). If so, consistent findings across such diverse measures are impressive, but more work is necessary to discern this possibility.

Stress moderation mechanisms are likely to be important for understanding these associations, as neuroticism has been linked to multiple steps in the stress and coping process (Contrada & Coups, 2003; Suls et al., 1996; Watson & Hubbard, 1996). Neuroticism is prospectively associated with higher exposure to stress and interpersonal conflict, even when self-report biases are experimentally controlled, suggesting neurotics create stressful lives for themselves (Bolger & Schilling, 1991; Bolger & Zuckerman, 1995; Kendler, Gardner & Prescott, 2003; Vollrath, 2000). Neurotic individuals appraise experienced stressors as more threatening and less manageable (Gallagher, 1990; Schneider, 2004), and display greater emotional reactivity when psychological stress is encountered (Bolger & Zuckerman, 1995; Mroczek & Almeida, 2004; Schneider, 2004). Neurotic individuals also report more frequent use of emotion-focused strategies such as avoidance and denial (Watson & Hubbard, 1996), and appear particularly adept at engaging in coping strategies that are ineffective or do not match the adaptive demands of a given stressor (Bolger & Zuckerman, 1995; Park et al., 2004).

These data clearly indicate that neuroticism associations with heightened *emotional-* reactivity to stress are mediated by stress-appraisal and coping processes. However, the interface between these *psychological* processes and the *physiological* pathways to illness remains understudied. Measures of trait neuroticism, as well as symptoms of anxiety and depression, have been linked to disruption of autonomic influences on the cardiovascular (e.g., Carney, Freedland, Rich & Jaffe, 1995; Kop, 1999) and immune systems (Herbert & Cohen, 1993; Kiecolt-Glaser, McGuire, Robles & Glaser, 2002), making stress-moderation a viable pathway to illness. Nevertheless, studies have generally not demonstrated that neuroticism effects on these more downstream links to illness actually reflect the stress-moderation processes described above. For example, two studies have demonstrated that both neuroticism and physiological reactivity to laboratory stress (as indexed by cortisol or immune changes) predict poorer subsequent immune response to vaccine. However, these effects occurred independently, with no evidence that stress-reactivity explained neuroticism associations with vaccine response (Marsland, Cohen, Rabin & Manuck, 2001; Phillips, Carroll, Burns & Drayson, 2005).

Health behavior models have also been considered. Although neuroticism has been associated with such risky behaviors as increased alcohol use, smoking, and physical inactivity (Booth-Kewley & Vickers, 1994; Caspi et al., 1997; Terracciano & Costa, 2004; Trobst et al., 2002), inconsistent findings abound. Vollrath and Torgersen (2002) argued inconsistencies may reflect inattention to multiple personality facets working simultaneously, and provided evidence that neuroticism is particularly damaging when combined with low conscientiousness. It is also possible that neuroticism effects on health behavior are more complex than these main-effect models imply, as neurotic individuals may engage in risky behaviors to cope with stress. Neurotic individuals are more likely to report using behaviors such as alcohol to cope with stress (Cooper et al., 2000), and display stronger associations between daily stress and alcohol consumption than low neurotic individuals (Carney et al., 2000). Thus, neuroticism may interact with the stress context to influence health behavior. Although neuroticism appears to influence health behaviors in definable contexts, its association with health outcomes typically remains when health behaviors are statistically controlled, indicating full mediation is unlikely.

Neuroticism clearly influences illness behavior and self-regulation processes (Cameron, 2003). Trait negative affectivity is associated with greater symptom complaints after exposure to a virus, even when objective disease is statistically controlled (Cohen et al., 1995). Such heightened symptom reports are unlikely to be simple reflections of inaccurate symptom-detection, because neurotic individuals appear equally accurate (e.g., Diefenbach, Leventhal, Leventhal & Patrick-Miller, 1996; Wiebe, Alderfer, Palmer, Lindsay & Jarrett, 1994) or even more accurate at detecting illness-related symptoms (Cameron, Leventhal & Love, 1998), although accuracy declines when neurotic individuals are placed in a context of threat (Van den Bergh et al., 2004). Individuals high in neuroticism do over-interpret the meaning of somatic sensations (i.e., misattribute benign sensations to illness or treatment; Cameron et al., 1998; Wiebe et al., 1994) and perceive threat in the face of symptoms and illness (Skinner, Hampson & Fife-Schaw, 2002). Such processes may explain why neurotic individuals display more illness detection behavior (Cameron et al., 1998), shorter delays in seeking help after documented illness (O'Carroll, Smith, Grubb, Fox & Masterton, 2001; Ristvedt & Trinkhaus, 2005), and in some cases better adherence (Skinner et al., 2002)—behaviors that presumably are beneficial to health.

These same processes, however, may impair health in other contexts. Wiebe et al. (1994) found trait anxiety predicted poorer blood glucose control among adolescents with diabetes, particularly when patients used symptoms to guide treatment decisions; the symptom misattributions of highly anxious participants presumably interfered with ongoing self-management in this situation. In a different vein, Ellington and Wiebe (1999) demonstrated that neurotic individuals may weaken their credibility during medical evaluations by providing more elaborate symptom descriptions and disclosing psychosocial information. Thus, neuroticism may be associated with symptom presentation styles that undermine their medical care. Taken together, it is clear that neuroticism is intimately linked to how people manage their health. Because these processes may play out in ways that are sometimes health-protective and other times health-damaging, illness behavior will continue to ambiguate neuroticism-health associations.

Optimism

Optimism is defined as a generalized and stable expectation that good things will happen (Scheier & Carver, 1985). This construct was developed out of Carver and Scheier's (1982; 1998) model of behavioral self-regulation, which posits that optimistic expectations are crucial to maintaining positive emotions and active goal pursuit in the face of adversity. Research suggests optimistic expectations are beneficial to health, particularly in the context of managing CHD. Individuals high versus low in optimism show less progression of coronary artery disease (Matthew, Raikkonen, Sutton-Tyrrell & Kuller, 2004; Todaro, Shen, Niaura, Spiro & Ward, 2003) and have lower risk of nonfatal myocardial infarction (Kybzansky, Sparrow & Vokonas, 2001). Positive expectations also predict reduced likelihood of a subsequent cardiac event over four years following coronary angioplasty (Helgeson, 2003), and fewer infection-related rehospitalizations and faster return to normal life activities following coronary artery bypass surgery (Scheier et al., 1999; Scheier et al., 2003). Prospective population-based studies have also found optimism to predict lower cardiovascular and all-cause mortality (Giltay, Geleijnse & Zitman, 2004; Kybzansky et al., 2001; but see Martin et al., 2002, for conflicting findings), relationships which remain after health behaviors are statistically controlled.

In other health contexts, particularly those involving immune functioning, the association of optimism with health is less straightforward (Segerstrom, 2005). Using a diverse sample of HIV-positive individuals, Ironson, Balbin and Stuetzle (2005) found that optimism predicted slower disease progression over two years. Milam, Richardson and Marks (2004), however, found a curvilinear relationship between optimism and immune parameters over 18 months, with moderate optimism predicting the best markers of immunity. Both studies controlled for baseline disease markers and demographic variables.

Careful attention to mechanisms of the stress-moderation model may clarify such inconsistencies. Segerstrom (2005) suggested that inconsistent associations between optimism and immune functioning may reflect unmeasured interactions with the stress context. That is, because optimism appears negatively related to cellular immunity when stressors are complex or uncontrollable, but positively related when stressors are easy to manage, inconsistencies may partially reflect the moderating stress context. If optimism promotes active engagement and coping when a stressor is uncontrollable, the optimistic individual may experience short-term physiological costs, while still having longer-term benefits (Nes, Segerstrom & Sephton, 2005). Optimism clearly predicts more problem-focused coping and less denial following bypass surgery (Scheier et al., 2003), coping efforts that may promote the sustained self-management behaviors demanded by chronic illness. De Ridder et al. (2000), however, found moderate levels of optimism predicted better coping among patients with multiple sclerosis and Parkinson's disease, illnesses that may be less amenable to active coping efforts. Although such data suggest optimism could be detrimental in the context of uncontrollable stress, optimists appear quite able to flexibly modify their coping beliefs and behaviors to match the situation at hand (Aspinwall & Richter, 1999; Aspinwall, Richter & Hoffman, 2001; Park et al., 2004).

Health behavior models may also be involved (Peterson & Bossio, 2001). There has been concern that optimism may function like denial, reducing perceptions of health risk and motivation to engage in health-promoting behaviors. Aspinwall and Brunhart (1996), however, found optimism actually predicts greater attention to risk information, and multiple studies support a positive relationship between optimism and positive health practices (e.g., Mulkana & Hailey, 2001; Yarcheski, Mahon & Yarcheski, 2004). Furthermore, optimistic chronically ill patients do not appear to have positively-biased perceptions of their health status; rather, positive expectancies appear to encourage better self-care over time (de Ridder, Fournier & Bensing, 2004). Taken together, optimism associations with health are likely to reflect a variety of complex processes that may work differently across the range of optimism scores and stress contexts.

PROGRESS AND PROBLEMS

This brief review reveals that personality has the potential to affect health in ways that are not easily attributable to illness behavior confounds, to personality change in response to disease, or to shared associations with a third variable. The mechanisms underlying these associations are beginning to be understood, although much work is needed to have a cohesive and comprehensive understanding of these relationships. In this section, we briefly discuss ongoing challenges in personality-health research, focusing on issues related to personality assessment, health outcomes, and tests of mechanisms. Space limitations prevent a thorough discussion, but a number of excellent and comprehensive reviews are available elsewhere (e.g., Contrada, Cather & O'Leary, 1999; Smith & Gallo, 2001; Smith & Ruiz, 2004).

Personality Assessment

Problems of construct validity continue to plague personality-health research, although the emergence of the five factor model as a comprehensive taxonomy of personality traits has brought structure to this issue. Some health-relevant personality constructs (e.g., hostility, optimism) represent blends of broad personality domains (Marshall et al., 1994). Such blends can create imprecision and inconsistent findings, but may also guide more complete understandings of how multiple personality domains work simultaneously to affect health. Studying additive and interactive effects across personality constructs adds complexity, but will likely improve our ability to detect and explain associations. In other cases, separate literatures have developed around narrow personality variables that may actually be different facets or measures of the same broad construct, as noted with neuroticism. Because it has been difficult to discern whether broad versus specific measures are most predictive of health outcomes (Suls & Bunde, 2005), future research will profit from simultaneously measuring broad domains and specific facets of personality.

Health Outcomes

Operational definitions of health and illness have enormous implications for interpreting personality-health associations. Given the interpretive ambiguities noted above, the use of self-assessed health to index underlying illness is unlikely to yield incremental knowledge gains. Different health outcomes also imply different causal mechanisms, as unique patho-physiological and biobehavioral processes contribute to the development and course of different diseases. Linking personality to different stages in the pathogenesis of disease, and attending to patterns of associations across stage and type of disease, may contribute to more complete and medically-plausible explanatory models (Scheier & Bridges, 1995; Smith & Gallo, 2001; Suls & Bunde, 2005). At the same time, one must recognize that personality may be associated with morbidity and mortality *across* diseases and with *all-cause* mortality (Scheier & Bridges, 1995). This creates the possibility that some pathogenic aspects of personality are not disease specific, or that personality works in conjunction with more 'upstream' determinants of health (e.g., socioeconomic status) to influence the expression of disease vulnerability (Kaplan, 1995; Schwartz et al., 2003). Careful consideration of both broad and specific mechanisms that might be functioning in the context of measured health outcomes will be important for continued progress.

Testing Mechanisms

Despite the existence of detailed models to explain personality associations with health, full models linking personality to mediating mechanisms to health outcomes across time are rarely tested. In the case of stress moderation, for example, sophisticated but quite separate literatures have evolved examining (a) the complex psychological workings of how a specific personality variable influences a mediating mechanism such as physiological reactivity to stress, and (b) the pathophysiological processes that represent plausible links between this mediator and the development of illness. The interface between these psychological processes and the physiological pathways to illness remains understudied (Friedman, 2000; Linden, Gerin & Davidson, 2003; Segerstrom & Miller, 2004; Wiebe & Smith, 1997).

It is also important to pay closer attention to testing specific conceptual models. For example, the stress-moderation model specifies a statistical interaction between personality and stress; that is, personality influences on stress appraisal and coping should matter more in the context of high versus low stress. Personality links to subsequent health, however, are often tested as main effects. Such tests are likely to miss or underestimate the stress-moderating aspects of personality, and may lead to confusing findings as was noted with optimism. Future research will benefit from careful attention to which features of the guiding conceptual model have and have not been tested.

The approach of testing personality-health associations while covarying traditional risk factors (e.g., behavioral risks, family history) is likely to obscure very important phenomena (Christenfeld, Sloan, Carroll & Greenland, 2004; Kaplan, 1995). If personality does not exert effects beyond traditional risks, one may inaccurately discount the impact of the personality variable. This is particularly problematic when the covariate is a plausible mediator, such as health behavior, because one is basically removing a presumed mechanism of action. In contrast, if personality associations with health are robust against behavioral risks, one may inaccurately discount health behavior as a contributing mechanism, ignoring the fact that health behaviors are often crudely assessed (e.g., self-reported answers to single questions), that covariate procedures are limited by measurement unreliability, and that it is almost certain that health behaviors only partially mediate the association. At a more complex level, personality may interact with other risk factors to exert synergistic effects on health (Schwartz et al., 2003). Light et al. (1999) found that cardiovascular reactivity to acute laboratory stress predicted rising blood pressure over subsequent years, but only among men with a family history of hypertension. Although not focused on personality, this study nicely illustrates how analytic choices can mask significant effects; if family history had been treated as a covariate, rather than as a moderator, this effect would likely have been missed.

These explanatory models have largely been considered separately, even though they are highly interrelated and are likely to interact. This was noted in the context of interactions between health behaviors and stress-induced physiological reactivity, but is likely to play out across all models. Studying multiple mechanisms simultaneously may enhance our explanatory models as some personality variables may push people toward unhealthy lives in multiple ways, while others create a more balanced system where risks through one mechanism are offset by health-promoting aspects of other mechanisms. A coordinated examination of mechanisms across the personality-health interface is required to construct a more coherent understanding of personality influences on health (c.f., Cohen & Rodriguez, 1995; Contrada et al., 1999; Friedman, 2000).

CONCLUSIONS

With compelling evidence that personality can contribute to the development and progression of health problems, it is time to *explain* rather than simply *describe* these associations. Detailed models have been developed to explain the cognitive, behavioral, social, and physiological processes through which personality may influence health. These models are highly complex and have not been fully tested. Future research will benefit from continuing the progression towards better specification of the personality predictors and health outcomes, and from carefully testing multiple mediating models simultaneously.

REFERENCES

Al'Absi, M., Wittmers, L.E., Erickson, J., Hatsukyami, D. & Crouse, B. (2003). Prospective examination of effects of smoking abstinence on cortisol and withdrawal symptoms as predictors of early smoking relapse. *Pharmacology, Biochemistry, and Behavior, 74*, 401–410.

Alemagno, S.A., Zyzanski, S.J., Stange, K.C., Kercher, K., Medalie, J.H. & Kahana, E. (1991). Health and illness behavior of Type A persons. *Journal of Occupational Medicine, 33*, 891–895.

Angell, M. (1985). Disease as a reflection of the psyche. *New England Journal of Medicine, 312*, 1570–1572.

Aspinwall, L.G. & Brunhart, S.M. (1996). Distinguishing optimism from denial: Optimistic beliefs predict attention to health threats. *Personality and Social Psychology Bulletin, 22*, 993–1003.

Aspinwall, L.G. & Richter, L. (1999). Optimism and self-mastery predict more rapid disengagement from unsolvable tasks in the presence of alternatives. *Motivation & Emotion, 23*, 221–245.

Aspinwall, L.G., Richter, L. & Hoffman, R.R. (2001). Understanding how optimism works: An examination of optimists' adaptive moderation of belief and behavior. In E.C. Edwards (ed.), *Optimism and pessimism: Implications for theory, research, and practice* (pp. 217–238). Washington, D.C.: American Psychological Association.

Bleil, M.E., McCaffery, J.M., Muldoon, M.F., Sutton-Tyrel, K. & Manuck, S.B. (2004). Anger-related personality traits and carotid artery atherosclerosis in untreated hypertensive men. *Psychosomatic Medicine, 66*, 633–639.

Booth-Kewley, S. & Vickers, R.R. (1994). Associations between major domains of personality and health behavior. *Journal of Personality, 62*, 281–298.

Bolger, N. & Schilling, E.A. (1991). Personality and the problems of everyday life: The role of neuroticism in exposure and reactivity to daily stressors. *Journal of Personality, 59*, 355–386.

Bolger, N. & Zuckerman, A. (1995). A framework for studying personality in the stress process. *Journal of Personality and Social Psychology*, *69(5)*, 890–902.

Boyle, S.H., Williams, R.B. & Mark, D.B. (2004). Hostility as a predictor of survival in patients with coronary artery disease. *Psychosomatic Medicine*, *66*, 629–632.

Brisette, I. & Cohen, S. (2002). The contribution of individual differences in hostility to the associations between daily interpersonal conflict, affect, and sleep. *Personality and Social Psychology Bulletin*, *28*, 1265–1274.

Brondolo, E., Rieppi, R. & Erickson, S.A. (2003). Hostility, interpersonal interactions, and ambulatory blood pressure. *Psychosomatic Medicine*, *65*, 1003–1011.

Buss, D.M. (1987). Selection, evocation, and manipulation. *Journal of Personality and Social Psychology*, *53*, 1214–1221.

Calhoun, P.S., Bosworth, H.B. & Siegler, I.C. (2001). The relationship between hostility and behavioral risk factors for poor health in women veterans. *Preventive Medicine: An International Journal Devoted to Practice & Theory*, *33*, 552–557.

Cameron, L.D. (2003). Anxiety, cognition, and responses to health threats. In L.D. Cameron & H. Leventhal (eds), *The self-regulation of health and illness behaviour* (pp. 157–183). London: Routledge.

Cameron, L.D. & Leventhal, H. (eds) (2003). *The self-regulation of health and illness behaviour*. London: Routledge.

Cameron, L.D., Leventhal, H. & Love, R.R. (1998). Trait anxiety, symptom perceptions, and illness-related responses among women with breast cancer in remission during a tamoxifen clinical trial. *Health Psychology*, *17*, 459–469.

Cantor, N. (1990). From thought to behavior: 'Having' and 'doing' in the study of personality and cognition. *American Psychologist*, *45*, 735–750.

Carney, M.A., Armeli, S., Tennen, H., Affleck, G. & O'Neil, T.P. (2000). Positive and negative daily events, perceived stress, and alcohol use: A diary study. *Journal of Consulting and Clinical Psychology*, *68*, 788–798.

Carney, R.M., Freedland, K.E., Rich, M.W. & Jaffe, A.S. (1995). Depression as a risk factor for cardiac events in established coronary heart disease: A review of possible mechanisms. *Annals of Behavioral Medicine*, *17*, 142–149.

Carver, C.S. & Scheier, M.F. (1982). Control theory: A useful conceptual framework for personality— social, clinical, and health psychology. *Psychological Bulletin*, *92*, 111–135.

Carver, C.S. & Scheier, M.F. (1998). *On the self-regulation of behavior*. New York: Cambridge University Press.

Caspi, A., Begg, D., Dickson, N., Harrington, H., Langley, J., Moffitt, T.E. & Silva, P.A. (1997). Personality differences predict health-risk behaviors in young adulthood: Evidence from a longitudinal study. *Journal of Personality and Social Psychology*, *73*, 1052–1063.

Chaput, L.A., Adams, S.H., Simon, J.A., Blumenthal, R.S., Vittinghoff, E. & Lin, F. (2002). Hostility predicts recurrent events among postmenopausal women with coronary heart disease. *American Journal of Epidemiology*, *156*, 1092–1099.

Christenfeld, N., Sloan, R.P., Carroll, D. & Greenland, S. (2004). Risk factors, confounding, and the illusion of statistical control. *Psychosomatic Medicine*, *66*, 868–875.

Christensen, A.J., Ehlers, S.L., Wiebe, J.S., Moran, P.J., Raichle, K., Ferneybough, K., et al. (2002). Patient personality and mortality: A 4-year prospective examination of chronic renal insufficiency. *Health Psychology*, *21*, 315–320.

Christensen, A.J., Wiebe, J.S. & Lawton, W.J. (1997). Cynical hostility, powerful other control expectancies, and patient adherence in hemodialysis. *Psychosomatic Medicine*, *59*, 307–312.

Cioffi, D. (1991). Beyond attentional strategies: A cognitive-perceptual model of somatic interpretation. *Psychological Bulletin*, *109*, 25–41.

Cohen, S., Doyle, W.J., Skoner, D.P., Fireman, P., Gwaltney, J.M., Jr. & Newsom, J.T. (1995). State and trait negative affect as predictors of objective and subjective symptoms of respiratory viral infections. *Journal of Personality and Social Psychology*, *68*, 159–169.

Cohen, S., Hamrick, N., Rodriguez, M.S., Feldman, P.J., Rabin, B.S. & Manuck, S.B. (2000). The stability of and intercorrelations among cardiovascular, immune, endocrine, and psychological reactivity. *Annals of Behavioral Medicine*, *22*, 171–179.

Cohen, S. & Rodriguez, M. (1995). Pathways linking affective disturbances and physical disorders. *Health Psychology*, *14*, 374–380.

Contrada, R.J. (1989). Type A behavior, personality hardiness, and cardiovascular response to stress. *Journal of Personality and Social Psychology*, *57*, 895–903.

Contrada, R.J., Cather, C. & O'Leary, A. (1999). Personality and health: Dispositions and processes in disease susceptibility and adaptation to illness. In L.A. Pervin & O.P. John (eds), *Handbook of personality: Theory and research* (pp. 576–604). New York: Guilford Press.

Contrada, R.J. & Coups, E.J. (2003). Personality and self-regulation in health and disease: Toward an integrative perspective. In L.D. Cameron & H. Leventhal (eds), *The self-regulation of health and illness behaviour* (pp. 66–94). London: Routledge.

Cooper, M.L., Agocha, V.S. & Sheldon, M.S. (2000). A motivational perspective on risky behaviors: The role of personality and affect regulatory processes. *Journal of Personality*, *68*, 1059–1088.

Costa, P.T. Jr. & McCrae, R.R. (1987). Neuroticism, somatic complaints, and disease: Is the bark worse than the bite? *Journal of Personality*, *55*, 299–316.

de Ridder, D., Fournier, M. & Bensing, J. (2004). Does optimism affect symptom report in chronic disease? What are its consequences for self-care behaviour and physical functioning? *Journal of Psychosomatic Research, 56*, 341–350.

de Ridder, D., Schreurs, K. & Bensing, J. (2000). The relative benefits of being optimistic: Optimism as a coping resource in multiple sclerosis and Parkinson's disease. *British Journal of Health Psychology*, *5*, 141–155.

Diefenbach, M.A., Leventhal, E.A., Leventhal, H. & Patrick-Miller, L. (1996). Negative affect relates to cross-sectional but not longitudinal symptom reporting: Data from elderly adults. *Health Psychology*, *15*, 282–289.

Ellington, L. & Wiebe, D.J. (1999). Neuroticism, symptom presentation, and medical decision making. *Health Psychology*, *18*, 634–643.

Eng., P.M., Fitzmaurice, G., Kubzansky, L.D., Rimm, E.B. & Kawachi, I. (2003). Anger expression and risk of stroke and coronary heart disease among male health professionals. *Psychosomatic Medicine*, *65*, 100–110.

Everson, S.A., Kauhanen, J., Kaplan, G., Goldberg, D., Julkunen, J., Tuomilehto, J. & Salonen, J.T. (1997). Hostility and increased risk of mortality and myocardial infarction: The mediating role of behavioral risk factors. *American Journal of Epidemiology*, *146*, 142–152.

Friedman, H.S. (2000). Long-term relations of personality and health: Dynamisms, mechanisms, tropisms. *Journal of Personality*, *68*, 1089–1107.

Friedman, H.S. & Booth-Kewley, S. (1987). The 'disease-prone personality': A meta-analytic view of the construct. *American Psychologist*, *42*, 539–555.

Friedman, H.S., Tucker, J.S., Tomlinson-Keasey, C., Schwartz, J.E., Wingard, D.L. & Criqui, M.H. (1993). Does childhood personality predict longerity? *Journal of Personality and Social Psychology*, *65*, 176–185.

Gallagher, D.J. (1990). Extraversion, neuroticism and appraisal of stressful academic events. *Personality and Individual Differences*, *11*, 1053–1057.

Gallo, L.C. & Matthews, K.A. (2003). Understanding the association between socioeconomic status and physical health: Do negative emotions play a role? *Psychological Bulletin*, *129*, 10–51.

Giltay, E.J., Geleijnse, J.M. & Zitman, F.G. (2004). Dispositional optimism and all-cause and cardiovascular mortality in a prospective cohort of elderly Dutch men and women. *Archives of General Psychiatry*, *61*, 1126–1135.

Harris, K.F., Matthew, K.A., Sutton-Tyrell, K. & Kuller, L.H. (2003). Associations between psychological traits and endothelial function in post-menopausal women. *Psychosomatic Medicine*, *65*, 402–409.

Helgeson, V.S. (2003). Cognitive adaptation, psychological adjustment, and disease progression among angioplasty patents: 4 years later. *Health Psychology*, *22*, 30–38.

Hemingway, H. & Marmot, M. (1999). Psychosocial factors in the aetiology and prognosis of coronary heart disease: systematic review of prospective cohort studies. *British Medical Journal*, *318*, 1460–1467.

Herbert, T.B. & Cohen, S. (1993). Stress and immunity: A meta-analytic review. *Psychosomatic Medicine*, *55*, 364–379.

Ickovics, J.R., Haven, C.T., Hamburger, M.E., Vlahov, D., Schoenbaum, E.E., Schuman, P., Boland, R.J. & Moore, J. (2001). Mortality, CD4 cell count decline, and depressive symptoms among HIV-seropositive women: Longitudinal analysis from the HIV epidemiology research study. *Journal of the American Medical Association, 285*, 1466–1474.

Idler, E.L. & Benyamini, Y. (1997). Self-rated health and mortality: A review of twenty-seven community studies. *Journal of Health and Social Behavior, 38*, 21–37.

Ironson, G., Balbin, E. & Stuetzle, R. (2005). Dispositional optimism and the mechanisms by which it predicts slower disease progression in HIV: Proactive behavior, avoidant coping, and depression. *International Journal of Behavioral Medicine, 12*, 86–97.

Kahler, C.W., Strong, D.R., Niaura, R. & Brown, R.A. (2004). Hostility in smokers with past major depressive disorder: Relation to smoking patterns, reasons for quitting, and cessation outcomes. *Nicotine & Tobacco Research, 6*, 809–818.

Kamarck, T.W. & Lovallo, W.R. (2003). Cardiovascular reactivity to psychological challenge: Conceptual and measurement considerations. *Psychosomatic Medicine, 65*, 9–21.

Kaplan, G.A. (1995). Where do shared pathways lead? Some reflections on a research agenda. *Psychosomatic Medicine, 57*, 208–212.

Kendler, K.S., Gardner, C.O. & Prescott, C.A. (2003). Personality and the experience of environmental adversity. *Psychological Medicine, 33*, 1193–1202.

Kiecolt-Glaser, J.K., McGuire, L., Robles, T.F. & Glaser, R. (2002). Psychoneuroimmunology: Psychological influences on immune function and health. *Journal of Consulting and Clinical Psychology, 70*, 537–547.

Kop, W.J. (1999). Chronic and acute psychological risk factors for clinical manifestations of coronary artery disease. *Psychosomatic Medicine, 1*, 476–487.

Kubzansky, L.D. & Kawachi, I. (2000). Going to the heart of the matter: Do negative emotions cause coronary heart disease? *Journal of Psychosomatic Research, 48*, 323–337.

Kubzansky, L.D., Sparrow, D. & Vokonas, P. (2001). Is the glass half empty or half full? A prospective study of optimism and coronary heart disease in the normative aging study. *Psychosomatic Medicine, 63*, 910–916.

Lazarus, R.W. & Folkman, S. (1984). *Stress, appraisal, and coping.* New York: Springer.

Light, K.C., Girdler, S.S., Sherwood, A., Bragdon, E.E., Brownley, K.A., West, S.G. & Hinderliter, A.L. (1999). High stress responsivity predicts later blood pressure only in combination with positive family history and high life stress. *Hypertension, 33*, 1458–1464.

Linden, W., Gerin, W. & Davidson, K. (2003). Cardiovascular reactivity: Status quo and a research agenda for the new millennium. *Psychosomatic Medicine, 65*, 5–8.

Lovallo, W.R. & Gerin, W. (2003). Psychophysiological reactivity: Mechanisms and pathways to cardiovascular disease. *Psychosomatic Medicine, 65*, 36–45.

Marshall, G.M., Wortman, C.B., Vickers, R.R., Kusulas, J.W. & Hervig, L.K. (1994). The five-factor model of personality as a framework for personality-health research. *Journal of Personality and Social Psychology, 67*, 278–286.

Marsland, A.L., Cohen, S., Rabin, B.S. & Manuck, S.B. (2001). Associations between stress, trait negative affect, acute immune reactivity, and antibody response to hepatitis B injection in healthy young adults. *Health Psychology, 20*, 4–11.

Martin, L.R., Friedman, H.S., Tucker, J.S., Tomlinson-Keasey, C. & Schwartz, J.E. (2002). A life course perspective on childhood cheerfulness and its relation to mortality risk. *Personality and Social Psychology Bulletin, 28*, 1155–1165.

Matthews, K.A., Gump, B.B., Harris, K.F., Haney, T.L. & Barefoot, J.C. (2004). Hostile behaviors predict cardiovascular mortality among men enrolled in the Multiple Risk Factor Intervention Trial. *Circulation, 109*, 66–70.

Matthews, K.A., Siegel, J.M., Kuller, L.H., Thompson, M. & Varat, M. (1983). Determinants of decisions to seek medical treatment by patients with acute myocardial infarction symptoms, *Journal of Personality and Social Psychology, 44*, 1144–1156.

Matthews, K.A., Raikkonen, K., Sutton-Tyrrell, K. & Kuller, L.H. (2004). Optimistic attitudes protect against progression of carotid atherosclerosis in healthy middle-aged women. *Psychosomatic Medicine, 66*, 640–644.

Milam, J.E., Richardson, J.L. & Marks, G. (2004). The roles of dispositional optimism and pessimism in HIV disease progression. *Psychology & Health, 19*, 167–181.

Miller, T.A., Smith, T.W., Turner, C.W., Guijarro, M.L. & Hallet, A.J. (1996). Meta-analytic review of research on hostility and physical health. *Psychological Bulletin, 119*, 322–348.

Mroczek, D.K. & Almeida, D.M. (2004). The effect of daily stress, personality, and age on daily negative affect. *Journal of Personality, 72*, 355–378.

Mulkana, S.S. & Hailey, B.J. (2001). The role of optimism in health-enhancing behavior. *American Journal of Health Behavior, 25*, 388–395.

Nes, L.S., Segerstrom, S.C. & Sephton, S.E. (2005). Engagement and arousal: Optimism's effects during a brief stressor. *Personality and Social Psychology Bulletin, 31*, 111–120.

Ng, D.M. & Jeffery, R.W. (2003). Relationships between perceived stress and health behaviors in a sample of working adults. *Health Psychology, 22*, 638–642.

O'Carroll, R.E., Smith, K.B., Grubb, N.R., Fox, K.A. & Masterton, G. (2001). Psychological factors associated with delay in attending hospital following a myocardial infarction. *Journal of Psychosomatic Research, 51*, 611–614.

O'Neil, J.N. & Emery, C.F. (2002). Psychosocial vulnerability, hostility, and family history of coronary heart disease among male and female college students. *International Journal of Behavioral Medicine, 9*, 17–36.

Park, C.L., Armeli, S. & Tennen, H. (2004). Appraisal-coping goodness of fit: A daily internet study. *Personality and Social Psychology Bulletin, 30*, 558–569.

Pennebaker, J.W. (1982). *The psychology of physical symptoms*. New York: Springer-Verlag.

Peterson, C. & Bossio, L.M. (2001). Optimism and physical well-being. In E.C. Chang (ed.), *Optimism and pessimism: Implications for theory, research, and practice* (pp. 127–145). Washington, DC: American Psychological Association.

Plomin, R. & Caspi, A. (1999). Behavioral genetics and personality. In L.A. Pervin & O.P. John (eds), *Handbook of personality: Theory and research* (2nd edn, pp. 251–276), New York: Guilford Press.

Phillips, A.C., Carroll, D., Burn, V.E. & Drayson, M. (2005). Neuroticism, cortisone reactivity, and antibody response to vaccination. *Psychophysiology, 42*, 232–238.

Ristvedt, S.L. & Trainkhaus, K.M. (2005). Psychological factors related to delay in consultation for cancer symptoms. *Psycho-Oncology, 14*, 339–350.

Roberts, B.W. & Bogg, T. (2004). A longitudinal study of the relationships between conscientiousness and the social-environmental factors and substance-use behaviors that influence health. *Journal of Personality, 72*, 325–353.

Robinson, K.L., McBeth, J. & MacFarlane, G.J. (2004). Psychological distress and premature mortality in the general population: a prospective study. *Annals of Epidemiology, 14*, 467–472.

Robles, T.F., Glaser, R. & Kiecolt-Glaser, J.K. (2005). Out of balance: A new look at chronic stress, depression, and immunity. *Current Direction in Psychological Science, 14*, 115.

Rutledge, T. & Hogan, B.E. (2002). A quantitative review of prospective evidence linking psychological factors with hypertension development. *Psychosomatic Medicine, 64*, 758–766.

Scheier, M.F. & Bridges, M.W. (1995). Person variables and health: Personality predispositions and acute psychological states as shared determinants for disease. *Psychosomatic Medicine, 57*, 255–268.

Scheier, M.F. & Carver, C.S. (1985). Optimism, coping, and health: Assessment and implications of generalized outcome expectancies. *Health Psychology, 4*, 219–247.

Scheier, M.F., Matthews, K.A., Owens, J.F., Schulz, R., Bridges, M.W., Magovern, G.J. & Carver, C.S. (1999). Optimism and rehospitalization after coronary artery bypass graft surgery. *Archives of Internal Medicine, 159*, 829–835.

Scheier, M.F., Matthews, K.A., Owens, J.F., Magovern, G.J., Lefebvre, R.C., Abbott, R.A. & Carver, C.S. (2003). Dispositional optimism and recovery from coronary artery bypass surgery: The beneficial effects of physical and psychological well-being. In P. Salovey & A.J. Rothman (eds), *Social Psychology of Health* (pp. 342–361). New York: Psychology Press.

Schneider, T.R. (2004). The role of neuroticism on psychological and physiological stress responses. *Journal of Experimental Social Psychology, 40*, 795–804.

Schwartz, A.R., Gerin, W., Davidson, K.W., Pickering, T.G., Brosschot, J.F., Thayer, J.F., Christenfeld, N. & Linden, W. (2003). Toward a causal model of cardiovascular responses to stress and the development of cardiovascular disease. *Psychosomatic Medicine, 65*, 22–35.

Segerstrom, S.C. (2005). Optimism and immunity: Do positive thoughts always lead to positive effects? *Brain, Behavior & Immunity, 19*, 195–200.

Segerstrom, S.C. & Miller, G.E. (2004). Psychological stress and the human immune system: A meta-analytic study of 30 years of inquiry. *Psychological Bulletin, 130*, 601–630.

Shiner, R. & Caspi, R. (2003). Personality differences in childhood and adolescence: Measurement, development, and consequences. *Journal of Child Psychology & Psychiatry, 44*, 2–32.

Siegler, I.C., Costa, P.T. & Brummett, B.H. (2003). Patterns of change in hostility from college to midlife in the UNC Alumni Heart Study predict high-risk status. *Psychosomatic Medicine, 65*, 738–745.

Skinner, T.C., Hampson, S.E. & Fife-Schaw, C. (2002). Personality, personal model beliefs, and self-care in adolescents and young adults with Type 1 diabetes. *Health Psychology, 21*, 61–70.

Smith, B.D., Cranford, D. & Green, L. (2001). Hostility and caffeine: Cardiovascular effects during stress and recovery. *Personality & Individual Differences, 30*, 1125–1137.

Smith, T.W. (2003). Hostility and health: Current status of a psychosomatic hypothesis. In P. Salovey & A.J. Rothman (eds), *Social psychology of health: Key readings* (pp. 325–341). New York: Psychology Press.

Smith, T.W. & Gallo, L.C. (2001). Personality traits as risk factors for physical illness. In A. Baum, T. Revenson & J. Singer (eds), *Handbook of health psychology* (pp. 139–172). Hillsdale, NJ: Lawrence Erlbaum.

Smith, T.W., Glazer, K. & Ruiz, J.M. (2004). Hostility, anger, aggressiveness, and coronary heart disease: An interpersonal perspective on personality, emotion, and health. *Journal of Personality, 72*, 1217–1270.

Suls, J. & Bunde, J. (2005). Anger, anxiety, and depression as risk factors for cardiovascular disease: The problems and implications of overlapping affective dispositions. *Psychological Bulletin, 131*, 260–300.

Suls, J., David, J.P. & Harvey, J.H. (1996). Personality and coping: Three generations of research. *Journal of Personlity, 64*, 711–735.

Surtees, P., Wainwright, N., Khaw, K., Luben, R., Brayne, C. & Day, N. (2003). Inflammatory dispositions: a population-based study of the association between hostility and peripheral leukocyte counts. *Personality & Individual Difference, 35*, 1271–1284.

Tennen, H. & Affleck, G. (1987). The costs and benefits of optimistic explanations and optimism. *Journal of Personality, 55*, 376–393.

Terracciano, A. & Costa, P.T., Jr. (2004). Smoking and the five-factor model of personality, *Addiction, 99*, 472–481.

Todaro, J.F., Shen, B.J., Niaura, R., Spiro, A. & Ward, K.D. (2003). Effect of negative emotions on frequency of coronary heart disease (the Normative Aging Study). *American Journal of Cardiology, 92*, 901–906.

Treiber, F.A., Karmarck, T., Schneiderman, N., Sheffield, D., Kapuku, G. & Taylor, T. (2003). Cardiovascular reactivity and development of preclinical and clinical disease states. *Psychosomatic Medicine, 65*, 46–62.

Trobst, K.K., Herbst, J.H., Masters, H.L. III & Costa, P.T. Jr. (2002). Personality pathways to unsafe sex: Personality, condom use and HIV risk behaviors. *Journal of Research in Personality, 36*, 117–133.

U.S. Department of Health and Human Services. (2000). Medical consequences of alcohol abuse. *Alcohol Research & Health, 24*, 27–31.

van den Bergh, O., Winters, W., Devriese, S., van Diest, I., Vos, G. & de Peuter, S. (2004). Accuracy of respiratory symptom perception in persons with high and low negative affectivity. *Psychology and Health, 19*, 213–222.

Vollrath, M. (2000). Personality and hassles among university students: A three-year longitudinal study. *European Journal of Personality, 14*, 199–215.

Vollrath, M. (2001). Personality and stress. *Scandinavian Journal of Psychology, 42*, 333–347.

Vollrath, M. & Torgersen, S. (2002). Who takes health risks? A probe into eight personality types. *Personality and Individual Differences, 32*, 1185–1197.

Watson, D. & Clark, L.A. (1984). Negative affectivity: The disposition to experience aversive emotional states. *Psychological Bulletin, 96*, 465–490.

Watson, D. & Hubbard, B. (1996). Adaptational style and dispositional structure: Coping in the context of the five-factor model. *Journal of Personality, 64*, 737–774.

Watson, D. & Pennebaker, J. (1989). Health complaints, stress, and distress: Exploring the central role of negative affectivity. *Psychological Review, 96*, 234–254.

West, S.G., Brownley, K.A. & Light, K.C. (1998). Postexercise vasodilation reduces diastolic blood pressure responses to stress. *Annals of Behavioral Medicine, 20*, 77–83.

Wiebe, D.J. (1991). Hardiness and stress-moderation: A test of proposed mechanisms. *Journal of Personality and Social Psychology, 60*, 89–99.

Wiebe, D.J., Alderfer, M.A., Palmer, S.C., Lindsay, R. & Jarrett, L. (1994). Behavioral self-regulation in adolescents with type 1 diabetes: Negative affectivity and blood glucose symptom perception. *Journal of Consulting and Clinical Psychology, 62*, 1204–1212.

Wiebe, D.J. & McCallum, D.M. (1986). Health practices and hardiness as mediators in the stress-illness relationship. *Health Psychology, 5*, 425–438.

Wiebe, D.J. & Smith, T.W. (1997). Personality and health: Progress and problems in psychosomatics. In R. Hogan, J. Johnson & S. Briggs (eds), *Handbook of personality psychology* (pp. 891–918). Academic Press: San Diego.

Wiebe, J.J. & Williams, P.G. (1992). Hardiness and health: A social psychophysiological perspective on stress and adaptation. *Journal of Social and Clinical Psychology, 11*, 238–262.

Williams, J.E., Paton, C.C., Siegler, I.C., Eigenbrodt, M.L., Nieto, F.J. & Tyroler, H.A. (2000). Anger proneness predicts coronary heart disease risk: Prospective analysis from the Atherosclerosis Risk in Communities (ARIC) study. *Circulation, 101*, 2034–2039.

Wilson, R.S., Mendes de Leon, C.F., Bienias, J.L. Evans, D.A. & Bennett, D.A. (2004). Personality and mortality in old age. *Journal of Gerontology, 59*, P110–P116.

Yarcheski, T.J., Mahon, N.E. & Yarcheski, A. (2004). Depression, optimism, and positive health practices in young adolescents. *Psychological Reports, 95*, 932–934.

Zak-Place, J. & Stern, M. (2004). Health belief factors and dispositional optimism as predictors of STD and HIV preventive behavior. *Journal of American College Health, 52*, 229–236.

CHAPTER 7

Personality and Illness Behavior

Paula G. Williams
University of Utah, USA

INTRODUCTION

The manner in which we assess and respond to perceived changes in health has important implications for health outcomes, subjective distress, and health care costs. The broad, multi-faceted construct involving the perception and reporting of physical sensations, actions made in response to perceived illness such as taking medications, staying home from work, seeking medical attention, and discussing physical problems with others, has been termed *illness behavior* (Mechanic, 1972). There are large individual differences in illness behavior. For example, the same physical sensation may be perceived or not, may receive different labels and attributions, may cause disability or not, and may lead to health care use or not depending on the individual.

Given the complexity of illness self-regulation, it is not surprising that individual differences in personality influence illness behavior. The purpose of this chapter is to present the representative literature on the relations between personality and illness behavior and to highlight directions for future research. Because the various aspects of illness behavior are only modestly related (e.g., Rief, Ihle & Pilger, 2003), the personality effects are considered separately by illness behavior component. First, the effects of personality on self-assessed health (i.e., symptom perception and reporting, global health assessments) are considered. Next, the relations between personality and functional disability (e.g., missing work, reducing social and recreational activities) are discussed. Relations between personality and self-care behaviors, including treatment adherence, are also reviewed. Finally, the manner in which personality factors affect use of health services is considered.

Personality Terminology

Comprehensive consideration of personality theory is beyond the scope of this chapter. Given its growing acceptance and general utility in both personality (Goldberg, 1993) and health (Marshall et al., 1994; Smith & Williams, 1992) research, the Five-Factor Model

Handbook of Personality and Health. Edited by Margarete E. Vollrath. © 2006 John Wiley & Sons, Ltd.

serves as the organizing framework for this chapter. The primary labels used are those that correspond to the domain labels of the NEO-PI-R (Costa & McCrae, 1992), a frequently utilized measure of the Five-Factor Model: neuroticism, extraversion, openness to experience, agreeableness, and conscientiousness. The use of these specific labels, however, does not imply dismissal of highly-related constructs. For each of the five factors terms, there have been other labels used in the literature for essentially the same construct. For example, the reader can assume that the use of term 'neuroticism' takes into consideration the large literature that includes trait anxiety, trait negative affectivity, and emotional stability. Similarly, the term 'surgency' has been used to describe extraversion traits, and the label 'constraint' (e.g., Tellegen, 1985) has been used for personality characteristics similar to conscientiousness.

Although the Five-Factor Model has its origins in the lexical tradition of personality research, there is growing consensus regarding the temperament and behavioral motivation underpinnings of adult personality constructs, especially neuroticism, extraversion, and conscientiousness. Because of the relevance to understanding personality-illness behavior relations, these concepts are outlined here. Briefly, neuroticism (or trait negative affectivity) is thought to reflect the Behavioral Inhibition System, which involves sensitivity to signals of punishment and non-reward, within Gray's (1982, 1987) model of behavioral motivation. Thus, anxiety is considered to be the manifestation of a highly-active behavioral inhibition system. In contrast, the Behavioral Activation System is associated with sensitivity to reward and removal of punishment and has been linked to individual differences in extraversion (or trait positive affect). Whereas neuroticism/negative affectivity and extraversion/positive affectivity are considered 'reactive' motivational traits, the temperament dimension termed 'effortful control' is related to the ability to engage executive control processes and 'over-ride' reactivity (e.g., Posner & Rothbart, 2000). The adult personality dimension of the Five-Factor Model most closely aligned to this temperament factor is conscientiousness. In addition to the direct effects of conscientiousness on important behavioral processes considered in this chapter, it may also be an important moderator of the effects of neuroticism and extraversion on a wide variety of mental and physical health outcomes, including illness behavior.

The agreeableness dimension of the Five-Factor Model reflects interpersonal tendencies toward social connectedness and cooperation on one end of the continuum and antagonism, skepticism of others' intentions, and competitiveness on the other end. Components of agreeableness have been associated with health, especially aspects related to cynical hostility, as discussed below. Openness to experience is a broad domain related to having an active imagination, an appreciation for aesthetics, and being attentive to inner feelings. Although correlated with education and intelligence, it is not considered to be equivalent to intelligence (Costa & McCrae, 1992). Of the five factors, openness to experience has received little attention in the personality and health literature and, where examined, there is little evidence of direct effects on either objective health or illness behavior.

Although the personality framework outlined above forms the primary focus of this review, where appropriate, personality factors that do not fall squarely within the Five-Factor Model framework are also considered. For example, optimism and pessimism are dispositional constructs that have been well-researched within the health domain. Individual differences in optimism-pessimism reflect generalized outcome expectancies—optimists generally expect positive outcomes (or the converse, pessimists generally expect negative outcomes)—and derives from models of behavioral self-regulation. Persistent questions about the construct optimism-pessimism and its measurement include (a) is it a bipolar construct or are they separate but related constructs? and, (b) to what extent is it distinct from Five-Factor Model traits? Research involving factor analysis of the Life Orientation Test (Scheier & Carver, 1985), the most prominently used measure of optimism-pessimism, suggests that they are distinct constructs and are separable from trait anxiety, a construct highly related to neuroticism (Kubzansky, Kubzansky & Maselko, 2004). However, because research has not consistently examined optimism and pessimism separately, it is not clear if findings in the literature are a function of optimism, pessimism, or both. Some research suggests that pessimism is significantly related to neuroticism and optimism is significantly related to extraversion (Marshall et al., 1992). Moreover, in some instances, when neuroticism is controlled the effects of optimism-pessimism on important outcomes are no longer significant (e.g., Smith, Pope, Rhodewalt & Poulton, 1989). Findings such as these led to revisions to the Life Orientation Test and evidence of the distinctiveness of optimism-pessimism using the new collection of items (Scheier, Carver & Bridges, 1994).

In this chapter, relevant optimism-pessimism research is cited separately from Five-Factor Model research. However, it is posited that general outcome expectancies may conceptually fit within the Five-Factor Model framework. Considering the Five-Factor Model conceptualization described above, it seems evident that an individual who is particularly oriented to signs of threat (neuroticism/behavioral inhibition system) may come to develop generally negative outcome expectancies (i.e., pessimism), whereas an individual who is particularly oriented to reward cues (extraversion/behavioral activation system) might come to generally expect positive outcomes (i.e., optimism). Put another way, pessimism might be characterized as either a component of neuroticism, or as a cognitive manifestation of neuroticism.

An additional dispositional construct that has been prominent in health research is the Type A behavior pattern. Much research has examined the hostility subcomponent of the Type A behavior pattern in relation to health. Although articulation of the Type A behavior pattern arose out of medical epidemiology research, as opposed to the personality tradition, the hostility aspect of this construct has been characterized in relation to the Five-Factor Model. Costa, McCrae and Dembroski (1989) present evidence that hostility is related to facets of neuroticism (especially the 'hostility' facet) and to low agreeableness. The majority of health-relevant research on the Type A behavior pattern and hostility has focused on psychophysiological mechanisms in relation to objective disease (especially cardiovascular disease), as opposed to relations to illness behavior. Nevertheless, in the relevant literature on the Type A behavior pattern, hostility and illness behavior is examined where possible.

Also worthy of consideration in examining personality factors and illness behavior is the construct alexithymia. Alexithymia is an individual difference factor characterized by difficulty identifying and expressing emotions. It is thought to reflect difficulty in the cognitive processing of emotion-relevant information and affect regulation (Taylor, Bagby & Parker, 1997). Alexithymia has been found to be related to high neuroticism, low extraversion, and low openness to experience (Luminet et al., 1999). Although unrelated to the broad domains of agreeableness and conscientiousness, Luminet et al. found that alexithymia was negatively related to the altruism facet of agreeableness and the competence facet of conscientiousness. These findings suggest that alexithymia may be a unique individual difference variable, characterized by a complex combination of Five-Factor Model traits. Relevant to the current chapter, alexithymia has been consistently linked to some aspects of illness behavior.

Personality and Self-assessed Health

Self-assessments of health are central to the management of illness. Judgments about the status of health and illness influence self-care decision-making, health care utilization, and communication with health care providers. Self-assessed health includes symptom perception and reporting, as well as global evaluations (i.e., 'poor' vs. 'excellent') of health. Although self-assessments of health and illness are a reflection of shifts in actual health status, a large body of research suggests that these assessments are not veridical; that is, they are imperfectly correlated with measures of objective health. Therefore, attention has turned to understanding the psychosocial factors that influence self-assessed health, including personality dimensions.

Of the Five-Factor Model traits, neuroticism has received the most attention with respect to self-assessed health. A large body of research has demonstrated significant relations between neuroticism and poorer self-assessed health (e.g., Brown & Moskowitz, 1997; Cohen et al., 1995; Costa & McCrae, 1987; Feldman, Cohen, Doyle, Skoner & Gwaltney, 1999; Larsen, 1992; Watson & Pennebaker, 1989; Williams, O'Brien & Colder, 2004; Williams & Wiebe, 2000). Findings regarding the strength of the relationship between neuroticism and self-assessed health, as well as the accuracy (i.e., relation to underlying objective illness) are variable in the literature, however (see Williams et al., 2002 for a more extensive review of this issue).

It has generally been assumed that individuals with high neuroticism report more symptoms, in part, because they are more sensitive to physical changes, as opposed to confabulating symptoms (i.e., malingering). In support of this notion, there is evidence to support the conclusion that neuroticism is related to specific symptoms consistent with underlying physical states (Cameron, Leventhal & Love, 1998; Cohen et al., 1995) (though see Diefenbach, Leventhal, Leventhal & Patrick-Miller, 1996 for evidence to the contrary). However, there is also evidence that high-N individuals are prone to misattribute unrelated symptoms to disease- or medication-specific processes (Cameron et al., 1998; Wiebe, Alderfer, Palmer, Lindsay & Jarrett, 1994). Several studies have found that neuroticism is related to symptom reports in the absence of objective signs of disease (Costa, 1987; Feldman et al., 1999; Shekelle, Vernon & Ostfeld, 1991). Rabin, Ward, Leventhal and Schmitz (2001) reported data suggesting that neuroticism is more strongly related to vague (i.e., subjective) vs. concrete (i.e., observable) symptoms, a finding that may help to reconcile the discrepancies in previous studies.

The mechanisms by which neuroticism is related to self-assessed health have not been fully explored. Important reviews on this relation by Watson and Pennebaker (1989) and Costa and McCrae (1987) issued caution to researchers that neuroticism/negative affectivity relations to self-reported illness may not reflect actual underlying illness, but may be more reflective of symptom perception and/or reporting tendencies. An unfortunate (and presumably unintended) result of these seminal papers was a movement toward simply treating neuroticism as a confound in health research (e.g., statistically controlling for the effects of neuroticism in research examining symptom reports as an outcome). However, research in the years since these reviews suggests that the relation between neuroticism and both self-assessed and objective health may be more complex than simply a tendency to be overly negative in reporting health status to others. For example, research has confirmed that neuroticism is related to both greater frequency of and reactivity to stressors

(Bolger & Shilling, 1991; Bolger & Zuckerman, 1995). Moreover, research has linked neuroticism to higher levels of cortisol (Miller et al., 1999), the stress hormone that reflects activation of the hypothalamic-pituitary-adrenal (HPA axis) branch of the stress response, as well as to decreased antibody response to vaccination (Marsland, Cohen, Ragin & Manuck, 2001). Additionally, higher neuroticism has been associated with mortality among end-stage renal patients (Christensen et al., 2002). Neuroticism is also related to some health behaviors that are potentially detrimental to health (e.g., substance use, Booth-Kewley & Vickers, 1994; Cooper, Agocha & Sheldon, 2000; sleep disturbance, Gray & Watson, 2002). Taken together, these findings suggest that neuroticism may indeed be related to objective health problems, at least under certain conditions. Thus, poorer self-assessed health among high-N individuals appears to be more than simply a reporting bias.

On the other hand, some evidence suggests that, in particular illness contexts, moderate neuroticism may be linked to better health outcomes. For example, neuroticism has been related to better glycemic control among individuals with type 2 diabetes (Lane et al., 2000) and moderate levels of neuroticism (compared to high and low neuroticism) have been associated with slower renal deterioration among individuals with type 1 diabetes (Brickman et al., 1996). Recently, Weiss and Costa (2005) presented evidence that neuroticism may be a protective factor in mortality rates among the elderly. Moreover, as discussed below, low neuroticism has been found to predict delay in seeking medical services following myocardial infarction (O'Carroll et al., 2001), suggesting that higher neuroticism may lead to better health outcomes in circumstances that require immediate medical attention.

Overall, a complex pattern has emerged regarding relations between neuroticism, self-assessed health, and objective health. Drawing upon the hypothesized behavioral motivation tendencies underlying neuroticism, it may be that the health-enhancing vs. health-detrimental effects of neuroticism depend on whether or not health concerns and physical symptoms are the target of threat or whether other non-health-related issues are most concerning at any given point in time. For example, when a high-neurotic individual is concerned and focused on an interpersonal stressor, they may neglect their health or possibly engage in unhealthy coping strategies. On the other hand, when diagnosed with an illness, symptoms may become the target of anxious apprehension and, in some circumstances this may lead to better illness self-regulation. It is likely, however, that at very high levels of neuroticism (especially in combination with other personality factors, such as low conscientiousness), positive illness self-regulation is unlikely to occur under any circumstance. Indeed, self-assessed health may be related to severe anxiety and dysfunction, as discussed below.

Other personality factors have been much less studied with respect to predicting self-assessed health. There is some limited evidence that extraversion is related to higher symptom reports, but only at high levels (Williams, O'Brien & Colder, 2004). Further research is needed to replicate these findings and elucidate the nature of this relationship; however, one hypothesis is that greater symptom reports may derive from relations between high extraversion and risky health behaviors, such as substance use (Cooper, Agocha & Sheldon, 2000).

Although conscientiousness has not been routinely examined in relation to self-assessed health, it has been linked to longevity (Friedman et al., 1993) and to greater beneficial health behavior and fewer risky health-related behaviors (Bogg & Roberts, 2004). These findings suggest that given proper scrutiny, conscientiousness may indeed be related to better perceived physical health.

Unfortunately, the other variables of the Five-Factor Model remain largely unexamined with respect to self-assessed health. However, several non-Five-Factor Model dispositional factors have been linked to self-reported health. For example, optimism has been associated with better general perceptions of health (Achat et al., 2000) and fewer physical symptoms (Scheier & Carver, 1985). Alexithymia is related to poorer self-assessed health (Lumley, Stettner & Wehmer, 1996), but does not appear to be related to the presence or severity of organic disease (Lumley, Tomakowsky & Torosian, 1997).

Heretofore, the review of self-assessed health has centered largely on symptom reports across the normal range. However, for some individuals, self-assessments of health become a source of preoccupation, emotional distress, and severe, sometimes chronic, disability. In our current diagnostic system, this is characterized as *hypochondriasis*. In non-clinical populations, less debilitating presentations of these characteristics have been termed *hypochondriacal tendencies* or *health anxiety*. The central feature of hypochondriasis is preoccupation with the belief that one has a serious disease, based on misinterpretation of bodily symptoms. This belief occurs in the absence of known organic pathology and persists despite appropriate medical evaluation and reassurance. Thus, hypochondriasis may be considered in the category of *abnormal illness behavior* (Pilowsky, 1997), which may also involve over-use of health services, unnecessary medical tests, missed work, and subjective distress.

Of the Five-Factor Model personality constructs, neuroticism has been the most consistently associated with health anxiety and hypochondriasis (McClure & Lilienfeld, 2001). Neuroticism is significantly associated with hypochondriacal concerns (Cox, Borger, Asmundson & Taylor, 2000; Ferguson, 2000) and individuals diagnosed with hypochondriasis report higher levels of neuroticism (Noyes et al., 1994). Although significant relations have also been found between hypochondriasis and extraversion and concientiousness, these relations drop to nonsignificant levels when the effects of neuroticism are controlled (Cox et al., 2000; Noyes et al., 2003). Thus, of the five factors, neuroticism shows the most robust relation to hypochondriacal tendencies. However, as highlighted throughout this chapter, there may be interactive effects between personality dimensions. In particular, conscientiousness may moderate the relation between neuroticism and the development of health anxiety and hypochondriasis. Moreover, because not all individuals high in neuroticism develop health anxiety, social learning processes may be important in understanding the mechanisms by which neuroticism is related to both self-assessed health, in general, and health anxiety and hypochondriasis in particular (see Williams, 2004 for more extensive discussion of this model).

Also in the category of abnormal illness behavior is somatization disorder. Somatization disorder is characterized by multiple unexplained physical symptoms of particular number and type, is chronic, is more common in females than males, and typically begins before age 30 (Noyes, 2001). Despite the distinction in diagnostic criteria, it is not uncommon for clinical research to consider hypochondriasis and somatization disorder as a single category. This strategy may derive from common features between the two categories including high symptom reporting and high rates of health care utilization. It is also clear that the term 'somatization' is used to describe high symptom reporters, and should be distinguished from the clinical syndrome of somatization disorder. Despite some common features, most recent research suggests that hypochondriasis and somatization disorder are distinguishable categories (Cloninger, Sigvardsson, von Knorring & Bohman,

1984; Kirmayer & Robbins, 1991) with different proposed etiological and maintaining factors. For example, recent research provides evidence for a familial connection between somatization disorder and antisocial personality disorder, suggesting that somatization disorder may be better classified as personality disorder (Frick, Kuper, Silverthorn & Cotter, 1995; Lilienfeld, Van Valkenburg, Larntz & Akiskal, 1986). Discerning the personality predictors of somatization disorder specifically (as distinct from hypochondriasis) in the current literature is difficult, given that the somatoform disorders are not often well-differentiated in clinical studies. Thus, examining personality correlates of these diagnostically distinct illness behavior psychopathologies remains an important endeavor for future research.

In summary, a substantial body of research has considered the relationship between personality and self-assessed health. Not surprisingly, the preponderance of this research has focused on neuroticism, with the nearly ubiquitous finding that individuals high in neuroticism report more physical symptoms and poorer overall health. With that relationship clearly established, recent research has begun to explore the mechanisms underlying this relationship more carefully. Relations between other personality dimensions and self-assessed health remain largely unexplored, as have interactive effects among the major personality dimensions on health perceptions.

Personality and Functional Disability

An additional aspect of illness behavior is the extent to which the individual is able to continue functioning in a variety of life domains, such as work/school, social, and recreational activities, in the face of either perceived or actual illness. Broadly speaking, this component of illness behavior may be termed *functional disability* (some have termed it *consequences of illness* [Rief, Ihle & Pilger, 2003] and others include it in the broader domain *quality of life*). Although conceptually separate from self-assessed health, perceived health clearly serves as the basis for the manifestation of subsequent functional impairment (Farmer & Ferraro, 1997). Although some measures include emotional responses to illness as a facet of functional disability, it has been hypothesized that behavioral withdrawal from important life activities is the mechanism by which poor self-assessed health is related to negative mood states, especially depression (Lewinsohn et al., 1996). Thus, understanding individual differences in functional disability is important not only in understanding behavioral responses to illness, but also in clarifying relations between personality and negative emotional outcomes.

Given the strong relation between neuroticism and poorer perceived health, one would hypothesize that neuroticism is also related to functional disability. There has been comparatively less research on neuroticism effects specific to this aspect of illness behavior, however. Nevertheless, there is both direct and indirect evidence that neuroticism is related to greater functional disability. Among healthy (i.e., non-chronically ill) young adults, neuroticism is related to several aspects of functional disability in relation to physical illness including sick days, poorer (perceived) work/school performance, and poorer ratings of the quality of social interactions (Williams & Hutchinson, 2003). Neuroticism is correlated with functional status in patients with rheumatoid arthritis (Radonov, Schwarz, Frost & Augustiny, 1997) and in older persons, in general (Kempen, Jelicic & Ormel, 1997). Neuroticism is also related to greater disability both prior to and six months after coronary artery bypass graft surgery (Duits et al., 2002) and poorer quality of life among individuals with HIV/AIDS (Penedo et al., 2003).

Neuroticism may also affect functional disability indirectly via relations to depression and anxiety. Substantial research suggests that depression is related to increased disability in the face of illness (e.g., coronary artery disease, Kopp, Falger, Appels & Szedmak, 1998) and that neuroticism is highly predictive of depression among ill individuals, placing them at risk for excess disability (e.g., Rovner & Casten, 2001). It is important to note, however, that much of this research is correlational. The relations between functional disability and depression are likely reciprocal.

Optimism/pessimism has also been the focus of research on individual differences in functional disability. Individuals higher in optimism have been found to have fewer sickness absence days from work following a major life event compared to those lower in optimism (Kivimaki et al., 2005), suggesting that optimism may buffer the effects of life stress on functional disability. Kivimaki and colleagues did not find effects for pessimism (measured as a separate construct). However, dispositional pessimism vs. optimism is related to greater pain and poorer functional status among individuals recovering from coronary artery bypass graft surgery (Mahler & Kulik, 2000). Additionally, dispositional pessimism (measured as a bipolar optimism-pessimism construct) has been found to be related to disruption of social and recreational activities following breast cancer surgery (Carver, Lehman & Antoni, 2003).

In summary, the strongest effects of personality on functional disability, broadly defined, have been found for neuroticism and, to a lesser extent, optimism/pessimism. Relations between other personality dimensions and adoption of the sick role have not been systematically examined. One issue in the study of this aspect of illness behavior may be that there has not been uniform agreement about what constitutes functional disability. Measures often include diverse outcomes including negative mood states, physical functioning, social and recreational activities, and missed work days which researchers may combine into a global 'quality of life' measure. Research using more refined measures of this illness behavior construct would facilitate better delineation of the effects of personality.

Personality, Self-care, and Treatment Adherence

An important aspect of illness behavior involves self-care activities in response to illness, including treatment adherence. In the case of acute illness, these activities may be of relatively short duration. In the case of chronic illness, however, self-care and treatment adherence may require long-term persistence in engaging in disease management activities. As with the other components of illness behavior, there are substantial individual differences in illness self-management, suggesting that personality may influence these activities.

Research has demonstrated relations between conscientiousness and longevity (Friedman et al., 1993). Subsequent findings regarding conscientiousness effects on health-related behaviors (Bogg & Roberts, 2004) suggest that this personality factor may influence self-care in response to illness and treatment adherence. To the extent that high conscientiousness represents the ability to overcome reactive tendencies in order to successfully meet goals, it is not surprising that it is frequently suggested as a personality factor that should influence adherence to medical treatment regimens. Indeed, conscientiousness has been found to be significantly related to adherence to medication regimen in renal dialysis patients (Christensen & Smith, 1995).

Despite the strong effects of neuroticism on other aspects of illness behavior, the role of neuroticism in treatment adherence has been relatively neglected. Although Christensen and Smith (1995) found a significant negative correlation between neuroticism and adherence, these effects were no longer significant when conscientiousness was considered. Both neuroticism and conscientiousness have been linked to renal deterioration in patients with type 1 diabetes (Brickman et al., 1996) and mortality among renal dialysis patients (Christensen et al., 2002). Brickman and colleagues found that individuals with moderate neuroticism and high conscientiousness evidenced slower deterioration compared to individuals with either high or low neuroticism. Neuroticism has also been reliably associated with better glycemic control (e.g., glycated hemoglobin) in patients with type 2 diabetes (Lane et al., 2000). Cameron et al. (1998) found that high trait anxiety was related to higher rates of breast self-examination in response to perceived risk-related symptoms among breast cancer patients. These findings suggest that a moderate amount of anxiety or arousal may be necessary to provide motivation to follow medical regimens across time. It is also apparent that examining interactive effects, particularly between neuroticism and conscientiousness, as well as curvilinear effects of personality constructs in predicting illness behavior is warranted, a point elaborated upon in the *Future Directions* section below.

The other constructs of the Five-Factor Model have been less consistently examined in the treatment adherence literature. Christensen and Smith (1995) did not find associations between openness to experience, extraversion, or agreeableness on various types of adherence among renal dialysis patients. However, Courneya and colleagues (2002) found that extraversion was an independent predictor of exercise adherence in cancer survivors, a finding that highlights the need to examine personality effects specific to different types of treatment regimen behaviors.

Whereas functional disability constitutes tendencies to adopt the sick role and disrupt activities in the face of illness, the other end of the illness behavior continuum—neglecting to take time from work to recover, etc.—is an often over-looked area of research on illness behavior. The effect of personality on this form of self-care has been virtually unstudied. One exception has been the examination of the Type A behavior pattern and sick role behavior. Consistent with theoretical prediction, individuals exhibiting aspects of the Type A behavior pattern have been found to be more likely to reject the sick role and return to work before full recovery (Alemagno et al., 1991).

It has also been hypothesized that the interpersonal style associated with the Type A behavior pattern might lead to poor adherence to medical regimen (e.g., Suls & Sanders, 1989); however, the empirical evidence for this relationship has not been consistently found (Wiebe & Christensen, 1996). A persistent issue in examining the Type A behavior pattern and illness behavior is that it is a multi-faceted construct and the various components of the Type A behavior pattern are not always examined. For example, cynical hostility is associated with poorer regimen adherence among renal dialysis patients (Christensen, Wiebe & Lawton, 1997).

Overall, the personality factor most clearly associated with self-care in response to illness, especially treatment adherence, is conscientiousness. Although there is some suggestion that neuroticism, at least at moderate levels, may be related to better self-care in the context of serious illness this must be further tested. It is important to note that self-care in response to illness may include highly diverse activities. For example, treatment adherence may require smoking cessation, dieting/weight loss, exercise, taking medication regularly, bed rest, etc., depending on the nature of the illness. It is likely that upon further scrutiny, other personality factors may prove to be relevant to some aspects of self-care.

Personality and Health Care Utilization

Another component of illness behavior involves both the decision-making process regarding health care use (i.e., seeking health services or not and the timeline for this process) and the manner in which health concerns are communicated to health care providers (i.e., provider-patient communication). Like other aspects of illness behavior, there are large individual differences in the use of health services, including rate of use (i.e., number of visits), as well as delay behavior—the lag time between detecting a symptom and seeking health care. There are also individual differences in the manner in which symptoms and health issues are described to health care providers, which has implications for treatment received. Theoretically, personality variables could affect each of the above-mentioned aspects of health care utilization. Although the personality effects on this particular component of illness behavior remain relatively understudied, there is evidence to suggest that personality may play an important role in both decision-making regarding health care use and in provider-patient communication.

As with most other aspects of illness behavior, neuroticism has been the most frequently examined personality characteristic in relation to the frequency of health care use. Findings regarding whether high-N individuals use more health services are mixed. Some studies have not found relations between neuroticism and health visits (e.g., Watson and Pennebaker, 1989). In some patient populations, neuroticism distinguishes patients who seek care from those that do not (e.g., fibromyalgia; Kersh et al., 2001); in other cases, treatment seeking is unrelated to neuroticism (e.g., headache; Rokicki & Holroyd, 1994). However, research has identified emotional disorders as robust predictors of frequency of health care use (Rief, Martin, Klaiberg & Brahler, 2005), suggesting that neuroticism may exert effects indirectly via links to psychopathology, especially depression, anxiety disorders, and hypochondriasis. Indeed, one mechanism by which neuroticism is related to frequency of health care use is via hypochondriacal tendencies (Williams & Hutchinson, 2003). Moreover, high-N individuals are more likely to utilize primary care services for mental health problems, and the combination of high neuroticism and emotional disorder predicts greater use of primary care services, in general (ten Have, Oldehinkel, Vollebergh & Ormel, 2005).

Although frequency of health care use, particularly in relation to over-use or misuse of health care services, is an important outcome in understanding personality effects on illness behavior, delay in seeking medical care is equally important. For some health issues, such as myocardial infarction or stroke, delay in seeking medical care has life-threatening implications. In examining psychological factors that affected delay (waiting over 4 hours) in seeking medical care after myocardial infarction, O'Carroll and colleagues (2001) found that lower scores on neuroticism differentiated those that delayed from those that did not. Similarly, Kenyon and colleagues (Kenyon, Ketterer, Gheorghiade & Goldstein, 1991) found that 'somatic and emotional awareness' was related to earlier treatment seeking for acute myocardial infarction, suggesting that a relative lack of such awareness among low-neurotic individuals may influence delay in seeking medical care. Neither of these studies of delay behavior, however, distinguished between delay in detecting the physical sensations and deciding they were ill, and delay between deciding they were ill and seeking treatment. Some research has suggested that whereas Type A characteristics predict the former, individuals who are more relaxed and easy-going (i.e., Type B) are more likely to delay in the later phase of treatment seeking (Matthews et al., 1983). These findings suggest that more comprehensive examination of the spectrum of personality factors, as well as differentiation of the stages of health care decision-making, may be important.

The manner in which individuals discuss their physical symptoms with health care providers is another important aspect of illness behavior. There is evidence to suggest that neuroticism also affects communication with health care providers. High-neurotic individuals have been found to provide more elaborate descriptions of symptoms and to disclose more psychosocial information as part of medical evaluations (Ellington & Wiebe, 1999). Relatedly, patients high in trait anxiety have been found to be more dependent on physicians to ask biomedical questions, and physicians have been found to provide more biomedical information to low-anxious patients (Graugaard, Eide & Finset, 2003). Such findings suggest that neuroticism not only affects communication patterns with health care providers, but that these patterns likely influence the medical care they receive and their satisfaction with medical care.

Overall, the literature examining patterns of health care use in relation to personality factors is rather small. Given the strong evidence that emotional disorders predict health care use, even when controlling for use specific to psychiatric services, it would seem that neuroticism is the personality factor most likely to affect treatment seeking. However, this supposition must be reconciled with findings that neuroticism does not predict health care use in some populations. As with the other aspects of illness behavior, examination of other relevant personality factors in relation to health care use appears warranted.

Future Directions

In considering the relations between the major personality dimensions and various aspects of illness behavior, several recurring themes emerged. First, neuroticism and related constructs have been the most widely studied in relation to illness behavior. This is perhaps not surprising given that anxiety is strongly linked to illness behavior. One exception is in the self-care domain of illness behavior, in which conscientiousness shows the strongest effects (at least in some treatment adherence contexts). In addition to revealing these broad patterns in personality-illness behavior relations, this selected review has also illustrated several gaps in the literature. Some suggestions for future research are highlighted below.

More Comprehensive Examination of Personality Factors

Of the prominent personality dimensions, neuroticism (and related personality constructs) remains the most researched with respect to relations with illness behavior. Most of the other personality dimensions remain relatively unexamined in the context of illness self-regulation. Future research on individual differences in illness behavior should, where possible, examine the spectrum of personality dimensions and the unique effects of each. That said, such research must be theoretically-driven with a priori predictions about which personality factors should be related to specific aspects of illness behavior and why. Thus, personality and illness behavior research should derive from our understanding of basic personality processes.

Examination of Interactive and Curvilinear Effects

The majority of the research on personality and illness behavior has focused on direct effects. Personality factors do not exist in isolation and may moderate each other. For example, research in the area of health risk behavior has demonstrated that the combination of low conscientiousness and either high neuroticism or high extraversion is associated with engaging in riskier health behaviors (Vollrath & Torgersen, 2002). This finding is consistent with the hypothesis that conscientiousness reflects underlying effortful control abilities and, thus, may moderate the effects of personality factors related to emotional reactivity. Future research on personality and the various components of illness behavior should explore the potential interactive effects of both neuroticism and extraversion with conscientiousness. To the extent that conscientiousness is related to attentional control and the ability to overcome emotional reactivity (e.g., responses to reward and punishment) to meet goals, one can hypothesize that it would influence attention and reaction to physical symptoms, functional disability, and treatment adherence.

Additionally, the effects of personality variables may differ depending on the level of the personality factor (i.e., curvilinear effects). For instance, some evidence suggests that moderate neuroticism may be related to better self-care than either high or low neuroticism. Moreover, low neuroticism may be related to treatment-seeking delay in the face of potentially serious illness. Thus, the assumption that lower neuroticism is uniformly related to better adjustment may be false. Curvilinear effects of extraversion on health-related cognition and behaviors have also been found. These types of findings need to be replicated and extended. Additionally, better theoretical explication of why varying levels of individual difference factors should be differentially related to illness behavior is needed.

Consideration of What is 'Optimal' Illness Behavior

Most research on the effects of personality on the various components of illness behavior makes the apparent assumption that more (i.e., greater health care use) is bad and less is better. Related to the issue of curvilinear effects outlined above, it may be that both low and high levels of illness behavior are problematic. One can hypothesize that under-detection of physical sensations, failing to engage in adequate self-care (which may include occasionally staying home from work or school), and under-use of health services may be equally if not more detrimental to health. Relevant to this chapter, there are likely personality factors that influence this hypothesized neglectful end of the illness behavior continuum. Additionally, the issue of accuracy particularly with respect to self-assessed health remains largely unstudied, as have the personality effects on accuracy.

Mechanisms for Personality-illness Behavior Relations

Some personality-illness behavior relations have been adequately documented and convincingly replicated (e.g., neuroticism is related to poorer self-assessed health). In these cases, one goal of future research should be to investigate potential mediating pathways. Longitudinal studies and innovative laboratory research are needed to better understand the mechanisms underlying relations between personality factors and illness behavior. For example, to the extent that cognitive processes are implicated in self-assessed health, these can be examined more directly via experimental information-processing paradigms (e.g., Williams, Wasserman & Lotto, 2003). Such paradigms also offer the opportunity to examine accuracy of health-relevant information processing. Research combining self-assessments of health with objective measures of health in predicting illness behavior over time will help inform our understanding of how personality factors influence illness self-regulation. Additionally, it has been well-documented that certain forms of psychopathology (e.g., depression, anxiety, hypochondriasis) are related to illness behavior. Because personality characteristics place individuals at risk for the development of psychopathology, this may be one mechanism by which personality is related to illness behavior. Thus, research examining personality-psychopathology relations appears to be quite relevant to the development of well-articulated models of illness behavior.

Moderators of Personality-illness Behavior Relations

Even in cases where there are demonstrated personality-illness behavior relations, the strength of the relations are typically not very high, suggesting that there are important moderators. For example, a potential moderator in the development of illness behavior involves social learning history (e.g., exposure to serious illness in a family member as a child or over-protectiveness in relation to illness by parents).

Other potential moderators of personality-illness behavior relations include gender, socioeconomic status, and ethnicity. All of these factors have been related to at least some aspects of illness behavior. Moreover, there are reliable gender differences in personality (e.g., women are higher in neuroticism compared to men) and psychopathology that may influence illness behavior (see Williams & Gunn, 2005). Testing the appropriate interactions between personality and theoretically-determined potential moderators will help elucidate the circumstances under which personality factors are and are not related to illness behavior outcomes.

REFERENCES

Achat, H., Kawachi, I. Spiro, A., DeMolles, D.A. & Sparrow, D. (2000). Optimism and depression as predictors of physical and mental health functioning: The Normative Aging Study. *Annals of Behavioral Medicine, 22*, 127–130.

Alemagno, S.A., Zyzanski, S.J., Stange, K.C., Kercher, K., Medalie, J.H. & Kahana, E. (1991). Health and illness behavior of Type A persons. *Journal of Occupational Health, 33*, 891–895.

Bogg, T. & Roberts, B.W. (2004). Conscientiousness and health-related behaviors: A meta-analysis of the leading behavioral contributors to mortality. *Psychological Bulletin, 130*, 887–919.

Bolger, N. & Schilling, E.A. (1991). Personality and the problems of everyday life: the role of neuroticism in exposure and reactivity to daily stressors. *Journal of Personality, 59*, 355–386.

Bolger, N. & Zuckerman, A. (1995). A framework for studying personality in the stress process. *Journal of Personality and Social Psychology, 69(5)*, 890–902.

Booth-Kewley, S. & Vickers, R.R. (1994). Associations between major domains of personality and health behavior. *Journal of Personality, 62*, 281–298.

Brickman, A.L., Yount, S.E., Blaney, N.T., Rothberg, S.T. & Kaplan De-Nour, A. (1996). Personality traits and long-term health status: The influence of neuroticism and conscientiousness on renal deterioration in Type-1 diabetes. *Psychosomatics, 37*, 459–468.

Brown, K.W. & Moskowitz, D.S. (1997). Does unhappiness make you sick? The role of affect and neuroticism in the experience of common physical symptoms. *Journal of Personality and Social Psychology, 72*, 907–917.

Cameron, L.D., Leventhal, H. & Love, R.R. (1998). Trait anxiety, symptom perceptions, and illness-related responses among women with breast cancer in remission during a tamoxifen clinical trial. *Health Psychology, 17*, 459–469.

Carver, C.S., Lehman, J.M. & Antoni, M.H. (2003). Dispositional pessimism predicts illness-related disruption of social and recreational activities among breast cancer patients. *Journal of Personality and Social Psychology, 84,* 813–821.

Christensen, A.J., Ehlers, S.L., Wiebe, J.S., Moran, P.J., Raichle, K. Ferneyhough, K. & Lawton, W.J. (2002). Patient personality and mortality: A 4-year prospective examination of chronic renal insufficiency. *Health Psychology, 21,* 315–320.

Christensen, A.J. & Smith, T.W. (1995). Personality and patient adherence: Correlates of the five-factor model in renal dialysis. *Journal of Behavioral Medicine, 18,* 305–313.

Christensen, A.J. Wiebe, J.S. & Lawton, W.J. (1997). Cynical hostility, powerful others control expectancies, and adherence in hemodialysis patients. *Psychosomatic Medicine, 59,* 307–312.

Cloninger, C.R., Sigvardsson, S., von Knorring, A. & Behman, M. (1984). An adoption study of somatoform disorders. *Archives of General Psychiatry, 44,* 573–588.

Cohen, S., Doyle, W.J., Skoner, D.P., Fireman, P., Gwaltney, J. & Newsom, J. (1995). State and trait negative affect as predictors of objective and subjective symptoms of respiratory viral infections. *Journal of Personality and Social Psychology, 68,* 159–169.

Cooper, M.L., Agocha, V.B. & Sheldon, M.S. (2000). A motivational perspective on risky behaviors: The role of personality and affect regulatory processes. *Journal of Personality, 68,* 1069–1088.

Courneya, K.S., Friedenreich, C.M., Sela, R.A., Quinney, H.A. & Rhodes, R.E. (2002). Correlates of adherence and contamination in a randomized controlled trial of exercise in cancer survivors: An application of the theory of planned behavior and the Five Factor Model of Personality. *Annals of Behavioral Medicine, 24,* 257–268.

Costa, P.T., Jr. (1987). Influence of the normal personality dimension of neuroticism on chest pain symptoms and coronary artery disease. *American Journal of Cardiology, 60,* 20J–26J.

Costa, P.T. & McCrae, R.R. (1987). Neuroticism, somatic complaints, and disease: Is the bark worse than the bite? *Journal of Personality, 55,* 299–331.

Costa, P.T. & McCrae, R.R. (1992). *Manual for the Revised NEO Personality Inventory (NEO PI-R) and NEO Five-Factor Inventory (NEO-FFI).* Odessa, FL: Psychological Assessment Resources.

Costa, P.T., McCrae, R.R. & Dembroski, T.M. (1989). Agreeableness versus antagonism: Explication of a potential risk factor for CHD. In A.W. Siegman & T.M. Dembroski (eds), *In search of coronary-prone behavior: Beyond Type A* (pp. 41–63). Hillsdale, NJ: Lawrence Erlbaum.

Cox, B.J., Borger, S.C., Asmundson, G.J.G. & Taylor, S. (2000). Dimensions of hypochondriasis and the five-factor model of personality. *Personality and Individual Differences, 29,* 99–108.

Diefenbach, M.A., Leventhal, E.A., Leventhal, H. & Patrick-Miller, L. (1996). Negative affect relates to cross-sectional but not longitudinal symptom reporting: Data from elderly adults. *Health Psychology, 15,* 282–288.

Duits, A.A., Duivenvoorden, H.J., Boeke, S., Mochtar, B., Passchier, J. & Erdman, R.A.M. (2002). Psychological and somatic factors in patients undergoing coronary artery bypass graft surgery: Towards building a psychological framework. *Psychology and Health, 17,* 159–171.

Ellington, L. & Wiebe, D.J. (1999). Neuroticism, symptom presentation, and medical decision making. *Health Psychology, 18,* 634–643.

Farmer, M.M. & Ferraro, K.F. (1997). Distress and perceived health: Mechanisms of health decline. *Journal of Health and Social Behavior, 38,* 298–311.

Feldman, P.J., Cohen, S., Doyle, W.J., Skoner, D.P. & Gwaltney, J.M. (1999). The impact of personality on the reporting of unfounded symptoms and illness. *Journal of Personality and Social Psychology, 77,* 370–378.

Ferguson, E. (2000). Hypochondriacal concerns and the five factor model of personality. *Journal of Personality, 68,* 705–724.

Frick, P.J., Kuper, K., Silverthorn, P. & Cotter, M. (1995). Antisocial behavior, somatization, and sensation-seeking behavior in mothers of clinic-referred children. *Journal of the American Academy of Child & Adolescent Psychiatry, 34,* 805–812.

Friedman, H.S., Tucker, J., Tomlinson-Keasey, C., Schwartz, J., Wingard, D. & Criqui, M.H. (1993). Does childhood personality predict longevity? *Journal of Personality and Social Psychology, 65,* 176–185.

Goldberg, L.R. (1993). The structure of phenotypic personality traits. *American Psychologist, 48,* 26–34.

Graugaard, P.K., Eide, H. & Finset, A. (2003). Interaction analysis of physician-patient communication: The influence of trait anxiety on communication and outcome. *Patient Education and Counseling*, 49, 149–156.

Gray, E.K. & Watson, D. (2002). General and specific traits of personality and their relation to sleep and academic performance. *Journal of Personality*, 70, 177–206.

Gray, J.A. (1982). *The neuropsychology of anxiety: An enquiry into the functions of the septohippocampal system*. New York: Oxford University Press.

Gray, J.A. (1987). *The psychology of fear and stress*. New York: Cambridge University Press.

Kempen, G.I.J.M., Jelicic, M. & Ormel, J. (1997). Personality, chronic medical morbidity, and health-related quality of life among older persons. *Health Psychology*, 16, 539–546.

Kenyon, L.W., Ketterer, M.W., Gheorghiade, M. & Goldstein, S. (1991). Psychological factors related to prehospital delay during acute myocardial infarction. *Circulation*, 84, 1969–1976.

Kersh, B.C., Bradley, L.A., Alarcon, G.S., Alberts, K.R., Sotolongo, A., Martin, M.Y., Aaron, L.A., Dewaal, D.F., Domino, M.L., Chaplin, W.F., Palardy, N.R., Cianfrini, L.R. & Triana-Alexander, M. (2001). Psychosocial and health status variables independently predict health care seeking in fibromyalgia. *Arthritis and Rheumatism*, 45, 362–371.

Kirmayer, L.J. & Robbins, J.M. (1991). Three forms of somatization in primary care: Prevalence, co-occurrence, and sociodemographic characteristics. *Journal of Nervous and Mental Disease*, 179, 647–655.

Kivimaki, M., Vahtera, J., Elovainio, M., Helenius, H., Singh-Manoux, A. & Pentti, J. (2005). Optimism and pessimism as predictors of change in health after death or onset of severe illness in family. *Health Psychology*, 24, 413–421.

Kopp, M.S., Falger, P.R.J., Appels, A. & Szedmak, S. (1998). Depressive symptomatology and vital exhaustion are differentially related to behavioral risk factors for coronary artery disease. *Psychosomatic Medicine*, 60, 752–758.

Kubzansky, L.D., Kubzansky, P.E. & Maselko, J. (2004). Optimism and pessimism in the context of health: Bipolar opposites or separable constructs? *Personality and Social Psychology Bulletin*, 30, 943–956.

Lane, J.D., McCaskill, C.C., Williams, P.G., Parekh, P.I., Feinglos, M.N. & Surwit, R.S. (2000). Personality correlates of glycemic control in type 2 diabetes. *Diabetes Care*, 23, 1321–1325.

Larsen, R.J. (1992). Neuroticism and selective encoding and recall of symptoms: Evidence from a combined concurrent-retrospective study. *Journal of Personality and Social Psychology*, 62, 480–488.

Lewinsohn, P.M., Seeley, J.R., Hibbard, J., Rohde, P. & Sack, W.H. (1996). Cross-sectional and prospective relationships between physical morbidity and depression in older adolescents. *Journal of the Academy of Child and Adolescent Psychiatry*, 35, 1120–1129.

Lilienfeld, S.O., Van Valkenburg, C., Larntz, K. & Akiskal, H.S. (1986). The relationship of histrionic personality disorder to antisocial personality and somatization disorders. *American Journal of Psychiatry*, 143, 718–722.

Luminet, O., Bagby, R.M., Wagner, H., Taylor, G.J. & Parker, J.D.A. (1999). Relation between alexithymia and the Five-Factor Model of personality: A facet-level analysis. *Journal of Personality Assessment*, 73, 345–358.

Lumley, M.A., Stettner, L. & Wehmer, F. (1996). How are alexithymia and physical illness linked? A review and critique of pathways. *Journal of Psychosomatic Research*, 41, 505–518.

Lumley, M.A., Tomakowsky, J. & Torosian, T. (1997). The relationship of alexithymia to subjective and biomedical measures of disease. *Psychosomatics*, 38, 497–502.

Mahler, H.I.M. & Kulik, J.A. (2000). Optimism, pessimism and recovery from coronary bypass surgery: Prediction of affect, pain and functional status. *Psychology, Health & Medicine*, 5, 347–358.

Marshall, G.N., Wortman, C.B., Kusulas, J.W., Hervig, L.K. & Vickers, R.R., Jr. (1992). Distinguishing optimism from pessimism: Relations to fundamental dimensions of mood and personality. *Journal of Personality and Social Psychology*, 62, 1067–1074.

Marshall, G.N., Wortman, C.B., Vickers, R.R., Kusulas, J.W. & Hervig, L.K. (1994). The five-factor model of personality as a framework for personality-health research. *Journal of Personality and Social Psychology*, 67, 278–286.

Marsland, A.L., Cohen, S., Rabin, B.S. & Manuck, S.B. (2001). Associations between stress, trait negative affect, acute immune reactivity, and antibody response to hepatitis B injection in healthy young adults. *Health Psychology, 20,* 4–11.

Matthews, K.A., Siegel, J.M., Kuller, L.H., Thompson, M. & Varat, M. (1983). Determinants of decisions to seek medical treatment by patients with acute myocardial infarction symptoms, *Journal of Personality and Social Psychology, 44,* 1144–1156.

McClure, E.B. & Lilienfeld, S.O. (2001). Personality traits and health anxiety. In G.J.G. Asmundson, S. Taylor & B.J. Cox (eds), *Health Anxiety: Clinical and research perspectives on hypochondriasis and related conditions* (pp. 65–91). New York: John Wiley & Sons, Inc.

Mechanic, D. (1972). Social psychological factors affecting the presentation of bodily complaints. *New England Journal of Medicine, 286,* 1132–1139.

Miller, G.E., Cohen, S., Rabin, B.S., Skoner, B.P. & Doyle, W.J. (1999). Personality and tonic cardiovascular, neuroendocrine, and immune parameters. *Brain, Behavior, and Immunity, 13,* 109–123.

Noyes, R., Jr. (2001). Hypochondriasis: Boundaries and comorbidities. In G.J.G. Asmundson, S. Taylor & B.J. Cox (eds), *Health Anxiety: Clinical and research perspectives on hypochondriasis and related conditions* (pp. 132–160). New York: John Wiley & Sons, Inc.

Noyes, R., Jr., Kathol, R.G., Fisher, M.M., Phillips, B.M., Suelzer, M.T. & Woodman, C.L. (1994). One-year follow-up of medical outpatients with hypochondriasis. *Psychosomatics, 35,* 533–545.

Noyes, R., Jr., Stuart, S., Langbehn, D.R., Happel, R.L., Longley, S.L., Muller, B.A. & Yagla, S.J. (2003). Test of an interpersonal model of hypochondriasis. *Psychosomatic Medicine, 65,* 292–300.

O'Carroll, R.E., Smith, K.B., Grubb, N.R., Fox, K.A. & Masterton, G. (2001). Psychological factors associated with delay in attending hospital following a myocardial infarction. *Journal of Psychosomatic Medicine, 51,* 611–614.

Penedo, F.J., Gonzalez, J.S., Dahn, J.R., Antoni, M., Malow, R., Costa, P. & Schneiderman, N. (2003). Personality, quality of life and HAART adherence among men and women living with HIV/AIDS. *Journal of Psychosomatic Research, 54,* 271–278.

Pilowsky, I. (1997). *Abnormal illness behavior.* Chichester: John Wiley & Sons, Ltd.

Posner, M.R. & Rothbart, M.K. (2000). Developing mechanisms of self-regulation. *Development and Psychopathology, 12,* 427–441.

Rabin, C., Ward, S., Leventhal, H. & Schmitz, M. (2001). Explaining retrospective reports of symptoms in patients undergoing chemotherapy: Anxiety, initial symptoms experience, and posttreatment symptoms. *Health Psychology, 20,* 91–98.

Radanov, B.P., Schwarz, H.A., Frost, S. & Augustiny, K.F. (1997). Relationship between self-rated functional status and psychosocial stress in patients suffering from rheumatoid arthritis. *Psychotherapy & Psychosomatics, 66,* 252–257.

Rief, W., Ihle, D. & Pilger, F. (2003). A new approach to assess illness behavior. *Journal of Psychosomatic Research, 54,* 405–414.

Rief, W., Martin, A., Klaiberg, A. & Brahler, E. (2005). Specific effects of depression, panic, and somatic symptoms on illness behavior. *Psychosomatic Medicine, 67,* 596–601.

Rokicki, L.A. & Holroyd, K.A. (1994). Factors influencing treatment-seeking behavior in problem headache sufferers. *Headache, 34,* 429–434.

Rovner, B.W. & Casten, R.J. (2001). Neuroticism predicts depression and disability in age-related macular degeneration. *Journal of the American Geriatrics Society, 49,* 1097–1100.

Scheier, M.F. & Carver, C.S. (1985). Optimism, coping, and health: Assessment and implications of generalized outcome expectancies. *Health Psychology, 4,* 219–247.

Scheier, M.F., Carver, C.S. & Bridges, M.W. (1994). Distinguishing optimism from neuroticism (and trait anxiety, mastery, and self-esteem): A reevaluation of the Life Orientation Test. *Journal of Personality and Social Psychology, 67,* 1063–1078.

Shekelle, R.B., Vernon, S.W. & Ostfeld, A.M. (1991). Personality and coronary heart disease. *Psychosomatic Medicine, 53,* 176–184.

Smith, T.W., Pope, M.K., Rhodewalt, F. & Poulton, J.L. (1989). Optimism, neuroticism, coping, and symptom reports: An alternative interpretation of the Life Orientation Test. *Journal of Personality and Social Psychology, 56,* 640–648.

Smith, T.W. & Williams, P.G. (1992). Personality and health: Advantages and limitations of the five-factor model. *Journal of Personality, 60,* 335–423.

Suls, J. & Sanders, G.S. (1989). Why do some behavioral styles place people at coronary risk? In A.W. Siegman & T.M. Dembroski (eds), *In search of coronary-prone behavior* (pp. 1–20). Hillsdale, NJ: Lawrence Erlbaum.

Taylor, G.J., Bagby, R.M. & Parker, J.D.A. (1997). *Disorders of affect regulation: Alexithymia in medical and psychiatric illness*. Cambridge: Cambridge University Press.

Tellegan, A. (1985). Structures of mood and personality and their relevance to assessing anxiety, with an emphasis on self-report. In A.H. Tuma & J.D. Maser (eds), *Anxiety and the anxiety disorders* (pp. 681–706). Hillsdale, NJ: Erlbaum.

ten Have, M., Oldehinkel, A., Vollebergh, W. & Ormel, J. (2005). Does neuroticism explain variations in care service use for mental health problems in the general population? Results from the Netherlands Mental Health Survey and Incidence Study (NEMESIS). *Social Psychiatry and Psychiatric Epidemiology*, *40*, 425–431.

Vollrath, M. & Torgersen, S. (2002). Who takes health risks? A probe into eight personality types. *Personality and Individual Differences*, *32*, 1185–1197.

Watson, D. & Pennebaker, J. (1989). Health complaints, stress, and distress: Exploring the central role of negative affectivity. *Psychological Review*, *96*, 234–254.

Weiss, A. & Costa, P.T., Jr. (2005). Domain and facet predictors of all-cause mortality among Medicare patients aged 65–100. *Psychosomatic Medicine*, *67*, 724–733.

Wiebe, D.J., Alderfer, M.A., Palmer, S.C., Lindsay, R. & Jarrett, L. (1994). Behavioral self-regulation in adolescents with type I diabetes: Negative affectivity and blood glucose symptom perception. *Journal of Clinical and Consulting Psychology*, *62*, 1204–1212.

Wiebe, J.S. & Christensen, A.J. (1996). Patient adherence in chronic illness: Personality and coping in context. *Journal of Personality*, *64*, 815–835.

Williams, P.G. (2004). The psychopathology of self-assessed health: A cognitive approach to health anxiety and hypochondriasis. *Cognitive Therapy & Research*, *28*, 629–644.

Williams, P.G., Colder, C.R., Lane, J.D., McCaskill, C.C., Feinglos, M.N. & Surwit, R.S. (2002). Examination of the neuroticism-symptom reporting relationship in individuals with type 2 diabetes. *Personality and Social Psychology Bulletin*, *28*, 1015–1025.

Williams, P.G. & Gunn, H.E. (2005). Gender, personality, and psychopathology. In M. Hersen, J.C. Thomas (Series eds) & J.C. Thomas, D.L. Segal (Vol. eds), *Comprehensive handbook of personality and psychopathology: Vol. 1 Personality and everyday functioning* (pp. 432–442). Hoboken, NJ: John Wiley & Sons, Inc.

Williams, P.G. & Hutchinson, J. (2003, March). *The role of hypochondriacal tendencies in the relation between neuroticism and health self-regulatory behavior*. Presented at the meeting of the Society of Behavioral Medicine, Salt Lake City, UT.

Williams, P.G., O'Brien, C.D. & Colder, C.R. (2004). The effects of neuroticism and extraversion on self-assessed health and health-relevant cognition. *Personality and Individual Differences*, *37*, 83–94.

Williams, P.G., Wasserman, M.S. & Lotto, A.J. (2003). Individual differences in self-assessed health: An information-processing investigation of health and illness cognition. *Health Psychology*, *22*, 3–11.

Williams, P.G. & Wiebe, D.J. (2000). Individual differences in self-assessed health: Gender, neuroticism, and physical symptom reports. *Personality and Individual Differences*, *28*, 823–835.

CHAPTER 8

Physiological Pathways from Personality to Health: The Cardiovascular and Immune Systems

Suzanne C. Segerstrom
University of Kentucky, USA
and
Timothy W. Smith
University of Utah, USA

INTRODUCTION

Among psychosocial factors, personality has the greatest potential to contribute to the diseases responsible for the most mortality in the Western world, including cancer, heart disease, and diabetes. Unlike the causes of death that predominated in earlier centuries, such as acute infectious disease, these disorders develop over long periods of time. For example, by the time cancer is clinically detectable, years or decades have passed from development of the first cancer cell (Friberg & Mattson, 1997); the process of gene mutation that led to that cell may have occurred over a period of decades before that. Formation of atherosclerotic plaques, likewise, takes place over a period of decades before those plaques lead to clinical consequences such as heart attack or stroke. Plaques are evident before 20 years of age and progress rapidly through the 20s and 30s (e.g., Strong et al., 1999), even though individuals do not display signs of coronary heart disease (CHD) or cerebrovascular disease until later adulthood. The time course of these diseases suggests that psychosocial factors that are consistently present over long periods will have the largest influence on disease progression. Of course, thoughts, emotions, or behaviors that are consistent over long periods of time are the very definition of personality.

In some cases, the pathway from personality (e.g., conscientiousness) to behavior (e.g., exercise) to disease (e.g., heart disease) appears obvious. In other cases, however, it is not as clear how personality gets from its home in the central nervous system to affect disease in the periphery. In this chapter, we will review evidence that personality is related to two organ systems, the cardiovascular and immune systems, that are potential physiological pathways from personality to health and disease.

THE CARDIOVASCULAR AND IMMUNE SYSTEMS

The Immune System

Immune Parameters

The immune system is an intricately regulated network of cells and organs whose functions, very broadly speaking, are to (1) discriminate between self and non-self and (2) to destroy that which is non-self. The following is a brief overview of the basic components of the immune system. For more detailed treatments, see standard immunology texts such as Janeway and colleagues (2004) or Parham (2005).

The immune system can be divided into two basic sections: natural or innate immunity and specific or acquired immunity. Natural immunity is primarily mediated by phagocytic (that is, eating) cells such as neutrophils and macrophages. These cells are attracted to sites of infection and injury, where they congregate, phagocytose any bacteria present, and begin to release chemical messengers known as cytokines. These cytokines cause local blood vessels to expand and become permeable, bringing more immune cells to the sites and allowing them to more easily exit the vessels. This result of this process is known as *inflammation*, the classic symptom profile of heat (*calor*), pain (*dolor*), redness (*rubor*), and swelling (*tumor*), caused by a local increase of both red and white blood cells and fluid and the products they secrete to kill invaders and fight infection.

Specific immunity is primarily mediated by lymphocytes, including the T and B cells. Each of these cell types has a specific role in fighting infection. Cytotoxic T cells recognize and attack intracellular invaders such as viruses. B cells produce antibodies, proteins that bind to extracellular invaders such as bacteria and parasites and promote their killing by phagocytic cells. Helper T cells produce cytokines that selectively activate either cytotoxic mechanisms (e.g., interleukin-2, interferon-γ) or antibody production (e.g., interleukin-5, interleukin-4). However, the label 'specific immunity' does not come from this specificity of function but from an even greater source of specificity: Each lymphocyte has a receptor 'lock' that is specific for a particular antigen 'key' produced by an invader. Therefore, any given lymphocyte will only recognize one target (e.g., one part of one bacterium) and no others.

Natural killer (NK) cells are the exception to the rule of specificity among lymphocytes. They can perform many of the same functions as cytotoxic T cells, but they are not restricted by the specificity of the T cell receptor. NK cells recognize problem cells not because of specific antigens but because the problem cells are failing to express normal proteins on their surfaces.

The status of the immune system can be assessed *in vitro* or *in vivo*. *In vitro*, cells can be counted to assess their number and proportions, or they can be stimulated to assess cytokine or antibody production. Antigen specificity among lymphocytes means that, when stimulated, each cell must be able to divide many times in order to produce enough clones of itself to combat that antigen. This ability is assessed in cell proliferation assays. Finally, the ability of NK cells to kill targets is assessed in the NK cell cytotoxicity (NKCC) assay.

Immune function *in vivo* can be assessed by examining end products of immune responses such as cytokines or antibody in peripheral blood or the degree of immune response in the skin in an allergy test or a delayed-type hypersensitivity (DTH) test, which measures the responsiveness of macrophages and T cells to antigen injected into the skin.

Links Between Nervous System and Immune System

Two discoveries played key roles in advancing psychoneuroimmunology, the study of the links among the mind, nervous system, and immune system. First, immunosuppression was classically conditioned (Ader & Cohen, 1975), and second, sympathetic innervation of immune organs was discovered (Felten, Overhage, Felten & Schmedtje, 1981). The number of identified pathways by which the nervous system and immune system communicate has since multiplied exponentially. Macrophages and lymphocytes receive messages from the sympathetic nervous system via functional alpha and beta adrenergic receptors (Sanders, Kasprowicz, Kohn & Swanson, 2001). Immune cells also have receptors for other neurotransmitters such as acetylcholine, serotonin, and dopamine; steroid hormones such as cortisol and sex hormones; opioids such as beta-endorphin; and myriad other substances either produced or regulated by the nervous system (Ader, Felten & Cohen, 2001). These anatomical links provide plausible pathways by which personality and other psychological factors can translate into immune function and thereby to health.

The Cardiovascular System

Cardiovascular Parameters and Links to the Nervous System

The primary function of the cardiovascular system is the regulation of blood flow in response to ever-changing demands across the body's wide range of tissues. Psychophysiological studies of cardiovascular mechanisms linking personality characteristics and health outcomes generally assess basic aspects of this system—changes in heart rate and blood pressure, as well as the determinants of these responses. Changes in heart rate can reflect direct neural input, as in the sympathetic excitation or parasympathetic inhibition of the heart. Heart rate also changes in response to neuroendocrine activity, such as the release of catecholamines into the blood stream. Short-term changes in blood pressure reflect changes in cardiac output and vascular resistance—the amount of blood forced through the system in a given period of time and the resistance against this flow, respectively. Longer-term changes in blood pressure are also influenced by changes in blood volume, which in turn is regulated by renal mechanisms.

Heart rate and blood pressure can be measured quite easily and accurately in psychophysiological studies, and with the addition of other techniques (e.g., impedance cardiography) determinants of these changes can also be assessed noninvasively (Sherwood, 1993). For example, parasympathetic influences on heart rate can be estimated through frequency analyses of heart rate variability. Heart rate rises and falls within cycles of respiration, and the degree of coupling between heart rate change and respiration (i.e., respiratory sinus arrhythmia) corresponds to the extent of parasympathetic input to the heart. Resting levels of respiratory sinus arrhythmia may reflect individual differences in parasympathetic activity (i.e., vagal tone), and changes in this parameter can indicate parasympathetic responses to environmental stimuli. In impedance cardiography, moment to moment changes in the electrical resistance in the thorax are monitored, which in turn correspond to beat by beat changes in the amount of blood present in the heart. This information is used to derive an index of stroke volume (SV)—the amount of blood ejected from the heart with each contraction. Cardiac output (CO) (i.e., volume of blood moved by the heart per minute) is estimated as CO = HR × SV. If mean arterial blood pressure (MAP) is also measured, an estimate of total peripheral resistance (TPR) can be derived (MAP = CO × TPR). When the ECG signal and the resistance signal from the impedance cardiograph are examined together, other valuable information can be obtained in the form of systolic time intervals. One of these intervals—pre-ejection period—provides an index of sympathetic excitation of the heart, and refers to the period of time elapsing between the beginning of the depolarization of the myocardium and the change in electrical resistance that indicates blood beginning to leave the heart. Under conditions of increased sympathetic excitation of the heart, this period is shorter, reflecting more rapid and forceful contraction of the myocardium. Hence, readily available technology permits estimates of changes in heart rate and blood pressure, and more complex but still non-invasive approaches permit measurement of the primary determinants of those cardiovascular responses.

Cardiovascular Reactivity

The concept of cardiovascular reactivity plays a central role in prevailing models of cardiovascular mechanisms linking personality and health (Manuck, 1994). It actually has two forms in this literature, although they are often not clearly distinguished (Smith & Gerin, 1998). In the first, cardiovascular reactivity is conceptualized as an individual difference, specifically as a characteristic pattern of cardiovascular responses to psychological stressors, challenges, or demands. This psychophysiological trait is seen as stable across time and situations, such that some individuals consistently respond to stressors with larger increases in heart rate and blood pressure, whereas other individuals consistently display intermediate or smaller responses. Hence, in this first general view cardiovascular reactivity is conceptualized as a continuously distributed trait. Further, this trait is seen as conferring risk of subsequent cardiovascular disease, including essential hypertension, atherosclerosis, and related conditions such as coronary heart disease and occlusive stroke.

In the simplest or main effect version of this model, this trait is seen as contributing directly to risk of cardiovascular disease. In a somewhat more complex version, cardiovascular reactivity is seen as a moderator of the effects of environmental stressors on cardiovascular disease. Risk is greatest for reactive individuals exposed to higher levels of stress. In another variation of this model, individuals are characterized not only in terms of the magnitude of their characteristic cardiovascular responses but also in terms of the rate with which these responses return to pre-stress, resting levels (Linden, Earle, Gerin & Christenfeld, 1997; Rutledge, Linden & Paul, 2000). In yet another variation, individuals are characterized in terms of the underlying determinants of their cardiovascular responses (Kamarck, Jennings, Pogue-Geile & Manuck, 1994). For example, some persons might be characterized by blood pressure responses that reflect mostly increases in cardiac output (i.e., cardiac reactors), whereas other persons might display increases in total peripheral resistance (i.e., vascular reactors). In assessing this individual difference and examining its association with health outcomes, many studies use a single stressor or challenging task. However, consistent with measurement models in the general study of individual differences, the measurement of responses to multiple stressful tasks results in a more stable (i.e., reliable) estimate of this trait and stronger associations with external criteria, such as ambulatory blood pressure (Kamarck et al., 1992; Kamarck, Debski & Manuck, 2000; Kamarck, Schwartz, Janicki, Shiffman & Raynor, 2003).

In the second general model, cardiovascular reactivity is described as a mediating mechanism rather than as an individual difference. That is, psychosocial risk factors (e.g., social support, trait anger, social dominance) are hypothesized to influence the frequency, magnitude, and/or duration of increases in blood pressure or heart rate in response to psychological stressors, and these effects on cardiovascular reactivity are seen as underlying the association between the psychosocial risk factor and subsequent cardiovascular health. In this view, cardiovascular reactivity does not necessarily reflect a physiological trait that is stable across time or situations. Rather, a stable psychosocial characteristic influences cardiovascular reactivity. Further, the nature of the psychosocial characteristic (e.g., trait anger vs. social dominance) may determine types of stressors where it is related to cardiovascular reactivity (e.g., harassment or frustration vs. challenges to status). In this conceptualization of cardiovascular reactivity, low levels of stability across time or types of stressors do not necessarily challenge the model. Rather than resembling a broad trait, stability or consistency for this conceptualization of cardiovascular reactivity is more similar to recent social-cognitive conceptualizations of personality characteristics (Mischel & Shoda, 1999) in which the consistency is reflected in stable profiles or patterns of responses across specific classes of situations (i.e., behavioral signatures).

Cardiovascular Reactivity and Cardiovascular Disease

Several models suggest that cardiovascular reactivity contributes to the development of cardiovascular disease. For example, more frequent, pronounced, and prolonged episodes of cardiovascular reactivity have been described as contributing to the development of essential hypertension (Obrist, 1981). In this view, heightened cardiovascular reactivity contributes to excessive cardiac output and the resulting over-perfusion of local tissues with oxygen. Over time, this excessive perfusion prompts increases in total peripheral resistance in a locally mediated autoregulatory response to over-perfusion. If sustained, this pattern leads to more permanent increases in total peripheral resistance, which in turn foster more permanent increases in blood pressure levels. Although not all of the related research is consistent, the results of several studies indicate that cardiovascular reactivity predicts increases in blood pressure levels over time, as well as the emergence of essential hypertension (Matthews, Salomon, Brady & Allen, 2003; Matthews et al., 2004; Ming et al., 2004).

Cardiovascular reactivity has also been described as contributing to atherosclerosis. In this view, cardiovascular reactivity contributes to microscopic injury to the arterial endothelium, thereby promoting deposition of lipids, inflammation, and other processes involved in the initiation and progression of atherosclerosis. Through this effect on atherosclerosis in the coronary and carotid arteries, cardiovascular reactivity can contribute to the risk of coronary heart disease and stroke, respectively. Cardiovascular reactivity could also contribute to later stages in the development of these conditions by contributing to the instability and rupture of advanced arterial plaques. By increasing myocardial demands for oxygen, episodes of cardiovascular reactivity could also contribute to myocardial ischemia, potentially increasing the likelihood of angina or cardiac arrhythmias. As in the case of the association of cardiovascular reactivity and essential hypertension, not all of the available evidence supports this view. However, several studies suggest that cardiovascular reactivity is associated with increased risk of atherosclerosis, stroke, coronary heart disease, and myocardial ischemia among patients with advanced coronary artery disease (Everson et al., 2001; Jennings et al., 2004; Treiberet et al., 2003; Waldstein et al., 2004).

The studies testing this general model have largely examined associations of heart rate and blood pressure responses to a single stressor as predictors of these endpoints. Few studies have tested other aspects of cardiovascular reactivity (e.g., recovery, determinants of HR and BP responses), although the association between heart rate variability as an indicator of parasympathetic responsiveness is promising in this regard (Gianaros et al., 2005). Similarly, few studies based on the individual difference model of cardiovascular reactivity have tested the predictive utility of aggregated indexes of the responses across a larger number of tasks and occasions, or the implicit interactive hypothesis in which this trait moderates the risk associated with exposure to environmental stressors. And few—if any—studies have tested the mediational hypothesis in which cardiovascular reactivity contributes to the association of personality traits or other psychosocial risk factors and the development of cardiovascular disease.

Inflammation: Where Immunological and Cardiovascular Health Meet

Much attention has recently been paid to the role of proinflammatory cytokines in a myriad of pathologies. Interleukin-6 (IL-6) has been linked to an especially broad range of disease states. IL-6 is produced in the latter stages of inflammation, primarily by macrophages. Its secretion can be also stimulated by acute stress or administration of epinephrine. IL-6 stimulates the production of cortisol by the adrenal gland and acute phase proteins, such as c-reactive protein, by the liver. It also has pronounced effects on B cell growth, bone cell maintenance, production of thyroid hormone, diuresis, and other diverse physiological functions. It has been implicated in the inflammatory processes that contribute to the pathophysiology of Alzheimer's disease (McGeer & McGeer, 2001; Papassotiropoulos, Hock & Nitsch, 2001), cancers such as multiple myeloma (Baraldi-Junkins, Beck & Rothstein, 2000), and osteoporosis (Ershler & Keller, 2000).

Inflammatory processes are also implicated in the formation of atherosclerosis, which in turn can lead to heart attack and stroke. Chronic inflammation in the arteries stimulates the incorporation of smooth muscle cells and low-density cholesterol into the inflamed vessel wall and formation of a fibrous cap, creating an atherosclerotic plaque (Ross, 1999). Both IL-6 and its downstream product, c-reactive protein, predict cardiovascular disease and mortality. For example, in the Women's Health Study, high levels of c-reactive protein quadrupled the risk of future cardiovascular events (Blake & Ridker, 2002). High levels of proinflammatory markers therefore represent not only lack of immune regulation but also risk for many other diseases, including cardiovascular disease.

PERSONALITY, PHYSIOLOGY, AND HEALTH: THREE MODELS

Theoretical models of the relationship of personality to physiology reflect different assumptions about the nature of personality. The first and most basic model arises from the assumption that personality has pervasive effects across time and situations. Under this model, extraversion, for example, will take the form of more assertive social behavior at home, at parties, and at work, and will be stable over long periods of time. In this *tonic influence* model, personality will influence tonic physiology and thereby provide the context for disease onset or progression over long periods of time.

The pervasiveness assumption of the tonic model has been questioned, however (e.g., Mischel, 1968). In its place, personality theorists have emphasized person-environment interactions and transactions. Person-environment interactions refer to patterns in which personality characteristics influence the individual's reactions to events in his or her environment (*reactivity*). Person-environment transactions refer to patterns in which personality influences the kinds of events that populate people's lives (*exposure*). That is, through their actions people influence the type, frequency, magnitude, and duration of stressful experiences they encounter. Personality traits can influence health through the combined effects of interaction and transaction. For example, people who are higher in neuroticism not only react to specific interpersonal conflicts with more negative affect but also experience more conflicts in their daily lives (Bolger & Schilling, 1991). With regard to physiology, this model has been particularly influential in understanding the effects of stressors. Both the frequency of exposure to stressors and intensity of the physiological response to those stressors have been proposed to increase the risk of disease via accumulating exposure to stress mediators such as cortisol (McEwen, 1998).

Finally, common cause models tend to focus on genetic or neurobiological explanations for the relationship between personality and physiology. For example, differences in sympathetic nervous system reactivity could lead both to behavioral differences in preference for stimulation and physiological differences in blood pressure reactivity (Eysenck, 1967).

PERSONALITY AND THE IMMUNE SYSTEM

All three models are represented in the empirical literature linking personality to various parameters of the immune system. This literature tends to focus on four dimensions of personality: hostility, sociability, optimism, and repression.

Hostility

Hostile individuals are suspicious and mistrustful of others, easily angered, and likely to behave in an unfriendly manner; as a consequence, they might be expected to have more extreme physiological reactions to interactions with others. Reactivity models generally support the idea that more hostile individuals have larger stress-related immune reactions, particularly in terms of NK cells. NK cells show a dramatic increase in the bloodstream (lymphocytosis) during acute stressors, possibly in preparation for wounding during fight or flight (Segerstrom & Miller, 2004). NK lymphocytosis was amplified in hostile, angry husbands during a problem discussion task for married couples compared with wives and nonhostile or nonangry husbands (Miller, Dopp, Myers, Felten & Fahey, 1999). Hostility also amplified NK lymphocytosis after public speaking in a predominantly male (69%) community sample and during a self-disclosure task in undergraduate men (Christensen et al., 1996; Mills, Dimsdale, Nelesen & Dillon, 1996). In another sample of undergraduate men, however, hostility only amplified NK lymphocytosis in a key-press task requiring low effort; in a mental arithmetic task requiring higher effort, less hostile men had a larger NK response (Peters, Godaert, Ballieux & Heijnen, 2003). In total, these studies suggest that hostility most consistently increases acute NK lymphocytosis among men engaging in interpersonal tasks; women and non-interpersonal tasks are less likely to show this effect. However, a fully crossed design (i.e., gender x task type) remains to be tested with regard to hostility and immune reactivity.

Hostility's relationship to cardiovascular disease (see below) has led to investigation of the relationship between this personality factor and tonic immune parameters that could contribute to the initiation and progression of cardiovascular disease, particularly proin-flammatory cytokines. In samples of young, healthy, nonsmoking men who were otherwise at low risk for cardiovascular disease, high levels of hostility were associated with higher production of the proinflammatory cytokine TNF-α by stimulated monocytes. TNF-α production was particularly elevated for men in the highest tertile of hostility (Suarez, Lewis & Kuhn, 2002). High levels of hostility were also associated with higher levels of serum IL-6, but only among men who had some depressive symptoms (Suarez, 2003). With regard to inflammatory processes, therefore, hostility does seem to increase cytokine parameters that are associated with cardiovascular disease risk. These risks appear to be particularly high for people with high versus low or moderate hostility and for those who also have high levels of negative affect (cf., the interaction between anger and hostility in married men for which hostility increased immune reactivity only among men who also became angry; Miller, Dopp, et al., 1999).

Elevated hostility and proinflammatory cytokines may also contribute to risk after the development of cardiovascular disease. In mostly (80 %) male patients with acute coronary syndrome (myocardial infarction or unstable angina), hostility was associated with higher numbers of monocytes in the circulation (Gidron, Armon, Gilutz & Huleihel, 2003). After migration into tissue, monocytes become macrophages and can contribute to further patho-physiology and progression of acute coronary events, and higher number of monocytes can contribute to poor prognosis after myocardial infarction. Hostility can therefore contribute to the proinflammatory mechanisms of cardiovascular disease development and progression from the earliest stage in healthy, young adults to later stages of disease. As in the acute reactivity literature, this newer avenue of investigation has focused on men, but cardiovascular disease is also a leading cause of death in women. In a large population-based sample, both men and women had higher lymphocyte counts with higher levels of hostility, but the relative risk of this immune difference for the development of cardiovascular disease for men and women was not tested (Surtees et al., 2003). The relationship of hostility to immune changes and especially proinflammatory mechanisms in women needs attention, especially because some of the reactivity literature suggests that the relationship between hostility and some immune parameters may not be the same for men and women (Miller, Dopp, et al., 1999).

Sociability

More sociable and less inhibited people appear to be more resistant to infectious and auto-immune diseases including the common cold, HIV, allergies, and asthma (Cohen, Doyle, Turner, Alper & Skoner, 2003; Cole, Kemeny & Taylor, 1997; Kagan, Snidman, Julia-Sellers & Johnson, 1991). They also show lower autonomic activity (Cole, Kemeny, Fahey,

Zack & Naliboff, 2003; Miller, Cohen, Rabin, Skoner & Doyle, 1999), which is consistent with a common cause model that posits that a lower central nervous system threshold for arousal leads to both greater behavioral inhibition and greater autonomic reactivity (Kagan & Snidman, 1991). Differences in autonomic activity could modify physiological systems, including the immune system, and result in differential disease risk.

In a large sample of healthy adults, extraversion was associated with lower arousal but also lower NK cytotoxicity, which would seem to imply greater, not lesser, risk for infectious disease (Miller, Cohen, et al., 1999). However, it is important to note that basal immune activity may not be representative of immune function after viral, bacterial, or even psychosocial challenge. A small sample of people bereaved of a close family member yielded two clusters of psychosocial, neuroendocrine, and immunological outcomes. In this study, decreased proliferative responses and NK cytotoxicity clustered with harm avoidance, a measure of behavioral inhibition (Gerra et al., 2003). Furthermore, in a series of studies with HIV seropositive gay men, social inhibition and rejection sensitivity associated with accelerated disease progression and poorer response to antiretroviral therapy, and autonomic reactivity mediated these effects (Cole et al., 1997, 2003).

Finally, sympathetic activity has also been associated with greater production of proinflammatory cytokines, and a report on chronic heart failure patients begins to establish an empirical link from personality to proinflammatory cytokines and heart disease risk (Denollet et al., 2003). Patients were divided into Type D or non-Type D patients (16/42 and 26/42, respectively). Type D reflects a high experience of negative affect (e.g., anxiety) combined with social inhibition (e.g., introversion), and was associated with higher TNF-alpha and soluble TNF-alpha receptors, which are thought to reflect longer-term TNF exposure. However, the two factors (negative affect and social inhibition) were not tested separately, and so the association with TNF-alpha may have been due to negative affect, social inhibition, or their combination.

Optimism

Some studies have found that people who are optimistic—that is, they have generally positive expectations for their futures—are more resistant to the progression of diseases that can be influenced by the immune system, particularly cancer and HIV. Optimistic individuals survived longer with mixed or head and neck cancers (albeit only the younger patients in the sample with mixed cancers), and optimistic individuals infected with HIV had slower disease progression as indexed by changes in CD4 (helper) T cell count and HIV viral load (Allison, Guichard, Fung & Gilain, 2003; Ironson et al., 2005; Milam, Richardson, Marks, Kemper & McCutchan, 2004; Schulz, Bookwala, Knapp, Scheier & Williamson, 1996). However, other studies have not found that optimism improved disease outcomes. A study of lung cancer found no benefit of optimism for disease survival, and optimism has also failed to predict HIV disease outcomes such as CD4 count, symptom onset, and survival (Reed, Kemeny, Taylor, Wang & Visscher, 1994; Reed, Kemeny, Taylor & Visscher, 1999; Schofield et al., 2004; Tomakowsky, Lumley, Markowitz & Frank, 2001). Consistent with these mixed clinical outcomes, the effects of optimism on the immune system *per se* are also mixed. In general, this literature has focused on a reactivity model for the relationship between optimism and immunity, in which optimism is generally hypothesized to be protective against immunosuppressive effects of stressors (Segerstrom & Miller, 2004).

In fact, under some circumstances, optimism appears to be protective against immunological consequences of stressors. In a laboratory study, optimism was associated with higher natural killer cytotoxicity (NKCC) after controllable loud noise stress, and in naturalistic studies, higher optimism was associated with higher T cell counts and DTH skin test responses when stressors were brief or uncomplicated (Cohen et al., 1999; Segerstrom, 2001, in press; Sieber et al., 1992). However, when circumstances were different, so were the effects of optimism. In laboratory studies in which control or mastery over the stressor were not possible, optimism was associated with lower NKCC and DTH (Segerstrom, Castaneda & Spencer, 2003; Sieber et al., 1992). In the naturalistic studies, optimism was associated with lower T cell counts and DTH when stressors were prolonged or complicated (Cohen et al., 1999; Segerstrom, 2001; in press). Although this interaction between optimism and stressor difficulty led some researchers to posit that optimism can confer a vulnerability to disappointment and distress when stressors are difficult, evidence does not support this hypothesis (Segerstrom, 2001; in press; Segerstrom et al., 2003). A more likely explanation is that more optimistic people exert themselves more to overcome difficult stressors and incur immune costs as a result.

These reactivity studies did not find main effects of optimism on immune function. However, one tonic influence study did find an immunological advantage to being optimistic. Among Black women co-infected with HIV and human papilloma virus (a pathogenic agent for cervical cancer), more optimistic women had higher NKCC and number of cytotoxic T cells (Byrnes et al., 1998). This finding was obtained with a different measure of optimism and pessimism (the Millon Behavioral Health Inventory) than the reactivity and disease outcome studies (the Life Orientation Test or its revision), so this difference may account for the discrepancy with other optimism-immunity findings. However, this study included a generally young, minority sample, so it is also consistent with the disease literature, in which younger age in cancer patients and more demographic diversity in HIV patients associate with positive findings for optimism, whereas older age and less demographic diversity associate with negative findings. In general, however, the reactivity studies suggest that there are both immunological costs and benefits to dispositional optimism, so that any advantage in immunologically mediated disease may depend on the context in which the optimist or pessimist is embedded.

Repression

Repression may be defined as the unconscious denial of negative affect and knowledge. Repression and related constructs such as lack of emotional expression, alexithymia (deficits in processing and understanding emotions), defensiveness (e.g., social desirability, absorption), and Type C personality (stoicism, perfectionism, over-agreeableness) have been hypothesized to increase the risk for poor health outcomes, especially cancer (Gross, 1989; Temoshok, 1997). Not surprisingly, given the broad range of operationalizations of repression, there are mixed results with regard to the relationship of repression to immune parameters.

Repression measured with the Millon Behavioral Health Scale was associated with higher antibody titers to latent virus. Because antibody to latent virus is stimulated by viral replication, higher titers may indicate a loss of control by the cellular immune system. Repression was also associated with failure of an emotional disclosure task to reduce latent virus antibody titers (Esterling, Antoni, Kumar & Schneiderman, 1990; Esterling, Antoni, Fletcher, Margulies & Schneiderman, 1994). Alexithymia also associated with lower lymphocyte counts in women with and without cervical intraepithelial neoplasia (Todarello et al., 1994, 1997). In other studies, the combination of high defensiveness and low anxiety, thought to represent repression, was associated with low monocyte and lymphocyte counts in both tonic and reactivity studies (Jamner, Schwartz & Leigh, 1988; Olff et al., 1995; Shea, Burton & Girgis, 1993).

However, various aspects of the broad construct of repression may have unique relationships to immunity. The combination of high defensiveness and *high* anxiety was associated with low monocyte counts, so that defensiveness was associated with fewer cells regardless of anxiety (Jamner et al., 1988). High defensiveness and high anxiety were independently associated with higher latent virus antibody titers in another study, but their interaction, and notably the high defensiveness-low anxiety combination, did not predict antibody titers (Esterling, Antoni, Kumar & Schneiderman, 1993). Finally, both extremely low and extremely high anxiety predicted fewer T cells and smaller DTH responses at the beginning of an exam period (Shea, Clover & Burton, 1991). Overall, defensiveness appears to be a more consistent predictor of immune parameters than anxiety, suggesting that repression may not always be successful and that trying to identify repressors via low anxiety may not be the best approach (Segerstrom, 2000).

The relationship of repression and related constructs to cancer, as well as the role of immune parameters in any such relationship, is controversial and hampered by heterogeneity in the repression construct, the diversity of diseases collected under the umbrella term 'cancer', and variability in the degree to which various elements of the immune system affect cancer progression. Methodological advances in all of these areas will be needed to establish each of these links (Segerstrom, 2000, 2003). In the case of repression, diverse relationships with immunity merely contribute to the lack of clarity in the broader personality-immune-disease literature.

PERSONALITY AND THE CARDIOVASCULAR SYSTEM

Hostility

Individual differences in anger, hostile attitudes and beliefs, and aggressive social behavior have been found to predict the development and course of cardiovascular disease, including essential hypertension, atherosclerosis, coronary heart disease and stroke (for reviews, see Rutledge & Hogan, 2002; Smith et al., 2004; Smith & MacKenzie, 2006; Suls & Bunde, 2005). A basic model guiding research in this area holds that these health consequences of hostility and related traits are mediated by cardiovascular reactivity (Williams, Barefoot & Shekelle, 1985). A substantial body of literature supports the view that individual differences in hostility and trait anger are associated with larger increases in heart rate and blood pressure during relevant interpersonal stress (Smith & Gallo, 2001). For example, in a laboratory study by Suarez and colleagues (1998), high and low hostility men underwent a challenging anagram task while the experimenter either behaved in a neutral manner or made harassing comments. Compared with non-hostile participants, those high in hostility displayed larger increases in blood pressure, heart rate and circulating neuroendocrine levels (i.e., cortisol, catecholamines) in response to harassment but not in the neutral condition. Several studies are consistent with this person by situation interaction in which differences between high and low hostility or trait anger groups in cardiovascular responses emerge in response to interpersonal stress (Miller et al., 1998; Smith, Cranford & Green, 2001). Other stressors found to evoke such differences between high and low hostility persons include the recall and discussion of past anger arousing events (Fredrickson, 2000), self-disclosure (Christensen & Smith, 1993), watching anger-inducing films (Fang & Myers, 2001), stressful marital interactions (Smith & Brown, 1991; Smith & Gallo, 1999) and discussions or debates about current events (Davis, Matthews & McGrath, 2000). Although some studies have failed to replicate this pattern (Kurylo & Gallant, 2000; Piferi & Lawler, 2000), the majority of studies provide consistent evidence of the expected association (Smith, Glazer, Ruiz & Gallo, 2004). Other recent conceptual models and related research suggest that these traits are also associated with slower physiological recovery after such stressors, perhaps contributing to adverse health consequences (Andersen, Linden & Habra, 2005; Brosschot & Thayer, 1998; Llabre, Spitzer, Siegel, Saab & Schneiderman, 2004).

Ambulatory studies indicate that hostility is also associated with higher levels of blood pressure during daily activities (Benotsch, Christensen & McKelvey, 1997; Guyll & Contrada, 1998; Polk, Kamarck & Shiffman, 2002; Raikkonen, Matthews, Flory & Owens, 1999). It is likely that these effects indicate that the greater reactivity associated with hostility in the laboratory is also observed in the natural environment. However, associations with ambulatory cardiovascular responses could also reflect greater exposure to stressors, as described in transactional models of hostility and health (Smith, 1992). Consistent with this interpretation, self-reported levels of interpersonal stress accounted for some of the association between hostility and ambulatory blood pressure in one such study (Benotsch et al., 1997), and in another, hostility was associated with both more exposure to negative interpersonal interactions and greater ambulatory blood pressure levels in response to such naturally occurring social stressors (Brondolo et al., 2003).

Sociability

Although there are some exceptions (e.g., Denollet, 2005), traditional conceptualizations of extraversion or sociability are not as widely studied as cardiovascular risk factors. However, social dominance is closely related to this dimension (McCrae & Costa, 1989; Trapnell & Wiggins, 1990). Dominance refers to the tendency to assert status, influence, and control during social interactions. Behavioral measures of this interaction style have been associated with increased risk of coronary heart disease and premature mortality (Houston, Babyak, Chesney, Black & Ragland, 1997; Houston, Chesney, Black, Cates & Hecker, 1992), as have self-reports (Siegman et al., 2000; Whiteman, Deary, Lee & Fowkes, 1997). These findings have an interesting parallel in non-human primate research in which socially dominant male macaques develop atherosclerosis more readily than submissive males when subjected to chronic social stress (Kaplan & Manuck, 1998). This association between individual differences in dominance and atherosclerosis is largely eliminated when the animals are maintained on a medication (i.e., propranolol) that blocks sympathetic excitation of the heart, suggesting that the interactive effects of social dominance and chronic stress on atherosclerosis may be due to the recurring activation of cardiovascular reactivity. In humans, the act of asserting dominance or control during social interactions evoked heightened cardiovascular reactivity (Smith, Allred, Morrison & Carlson, 1989; Smith, Ruiz & Uchino, 2000). Similar associations have been found when socially dominant behavior is measured rather than manipulated (Newton & Bane, 2001). Individual differences in dominance are also associated with greater cardiovascular reactivity, but this may be more true for men than women (Newton, Bane, Flores & Greenfield, 1999; Newton, Walters, Philhower & Wegel, 2005).

Optimism

Several different measures of individual differences in optimism/pessimism have been linked to the development and course of coronary heart disease and stroke (Scheier et al., 1989, 1999; for reviews, see Smith & MacKenzie, 2006; Smith & Ruiz, 2004). Optimism is associated with lower levels of ambulatory blood pressure (Raikkonen, Matthews, Flory, Owens & Gump, 1999), but few studies have examined its association with cardiovascular reactivity to controlled laboratory stressors. It is important to note that optimism could be related to both *greater* cardiovascular reactivity during stressful situations and *reduced* risk of cardiovascular disease. Optimists tend to persist in efforts to manage even difficult challenges, and effortful task engagement consistently evokes heightened CVR, which would seem to confer increased risk. However, if the optimist's efforts are successful in managing a stressor, they may face reduced exposure to that stressor over time. In this way, the short term effects of effortful coping on cardiovascular reactivity may be more than offset by reduced overall cardiovascular reactivity through the mechanism of reduced stress exposure.

Repression

Some evidence suggests that individual differences in defensiveness or the tendency to deny, minimize, or suppress anger and other negative emotions are associated with increased risk of essential hypertension (Perini, Muller & Buhler, 1991; Rutledge & Linden, 2000) and atherosclerosis (Jorgensen et al., 2001; Matthews, Owens, Kuller, Sutton-Tyrrell & Jansen-McWilliams, 1998). Among patients with established coronary heart disease, repressive coping is associated with greater susceptibility to myocardial ischemia during laboratory stress and daily activities (Helmers et al., 1995). When manipulated experimentally, the suppression of negative affect heightens cardiovascular reactivity and other aspects of autonomic reactivity (John & Gross, 2004). In a rare test of the mediating role of cardiovascular reactivity, Rutledge and Linden (2003) found that individual differences in defensiveness were associated with higher levels of ambulatory blood pressure over a three-year follow-up and that cardiovascular reactivity mediated this prospective effect of defensiveness.

CONCLUSION

All the pieces are in place, but where are the tests of mediated models? As reviewed above, there is ample literature linking personality traits to physiological parameters, either on a tonic basis or in interaction with stressful tasks or events. Further, there is considerable literature linking these physiological parameters with disease risk. For example, the levels of IL-6 found among hostile, depressed men are associated in epidemiological studies with increased risk of myocardial infarct in the next six years (Suarez, 2003), suggesting that IL-6 could mediate the relationship between hostility and cardiac events. Models suggesting that physiological parameters such as blood pressure reactivity or proinflammatory cytokines mediate any relationship between personality and health are not yet contradicted and remain plausible. However, in order to test such models, personality, the physiological mediator, and the health outcome must be assessed together. Further, convincing support for the model requires evidence that personality predicts both physiological parameters and health endpoints and, in turn, physiological parameters account for personality's relationship to health endpoints.

These mediated models have not been tested and in fact are rare in health psychology (e.g., studies have likewise not reported whether stressor-related changes in immunity mediate susceptibility to infectious disease; Segerstrom & Miller, 2004). This is an unfortunate situation, because such models are essential to our understanding of how cardiovascular and immune mechanisms play a role in the relationship between personality and health. Research on personality and health has goals beyond actuarial models; we are interested in more than simple statistical prediction of health outcomes. To understand *how* personality influences health and to translate this knowledge into interventions intended to manage and prevent disease, the next generation of research must include more complete tests of these mediational models.

REFERENCES

Ader, R. & Cohen, N. (1975). Behaviorally conditioned immunosuppression. *Psychosomatic Medicine*, *37*, 333–340.

Ader, R., Felten, D.L. & Cohen, N. (eds) (2001). *Psychoneuroimmunology* (3rd edn). San Diego, CA: Academic Press.

Allison, P.J., Guichard, C., Fung, K. & Gilain, L. (2003). Dispositional optimism predicts survival status 1 year after diagnosis in head and neck cancer patients. *Journal of Clinical Oncology*, *21*, 543–548.

Anderson, J.C., Linden, W. & Habra, M.E. (2005). The importance of examining blood pressure reactivity and recovery in anger provocation research. *International Journal of Psychophysiology*, *57(3)*, 159–163.

Baraldi-Junkins, C.A., Beck, A.C. & Rothstein, G. (2000). Hematopoiesis and cytokines: Relevance to cancer and aging. *Hemotology/Oncology Clinics of North America*, *14*, 45–61.

Benotsch, E.G., Christensen, A.J. & McKelvey, L. (1997). Hostility, social support and ambulatory cardiovascular activity. *Journal of Behavioral Medicine*, *20*, 163–176.

Blake, G.J. & Ridker, P.M. (2002). Inflammatory bio-markers and cardiovascular risk prediction. *Journal of Internal Medicine*, *252*, 283–294.

Bolger, N. & Schilling, E.A. (1991). Personality and the problems of everyday life: The role of neuroticism in exposure and reactivity to daily stressors. *Journal of Personality*, *59*, 355–386.

Brondolo, E., Rieppi, R., Erickson, S.A., Bagiella, E., Shapiro, P.A., McKinley, P., et al. (2003). Hostility, interpersonal interactions, and ambulatory blood pressure. *Psychosomatic Medicine*, *65*, 1003–1011.

Brosschot, J.F. & Thayer, J.F. (1998). Anger inhibition, cardiovascular recovery, and vagal function: A model of the link between hostility and cardiovascular disease. *Annals of Behavioral Medicine*, *20*, 326–332.

Byrnes, D.M., Antoni, M.H., Goodkin, K., Efantis-Potter, J., Asthana, D., Simon, T., Munajj, J., Ironson, G. & Fletcher, M.A. (1998). Stressful events, pessimism, natural killer cell cytotoxicity, and cytotoxic/suppressor T cells in HIV + Black women at risk for cervical cancer. *Psychosomatic Medicine, 60,* 714–722.

Christensen, A.J., Edwards, D.L., Wiebe, J.S., Benotsch, E.G., McKelvey, L., Andrews, M. & Lubaroff, D.M. (1996). Effect of verbal self-disclosure on natural killer cell activity: Moderating influence of cynical hostility. *Psychosomatic Medicine, 58,* 150–155.

Christensen, A.J. & Smith, T.W. (1993). Cynical hostility and cardiovascular reactivity during self-disclosure. *Psychosomatic Medicine, 55,* 193–202.

Cohen, F., Kearney, K.A., Zegans, L.S., Kemeny, M.E., Neuhaus, J.M. & Stites, D.P. (1999). Differential immune system changes with acute and persistent stress for optimists vs pessimists. *Brain, Behavior, and Immunity, 13,* 155–174.

Cohen, S., Doyle, W.J., Turner, R., Alper, C.M. & Skoner, D.P. (2003). Sociability and susceptibility to the common cold. *Psychological Science, 14,* 389–395.

Cole, S.W., Kemeny, M.E., Fahey, J.L., Zack, J.A. & Naliboff, B.D. (2003). Psychological risk factors for HIV pathogenesis: Mediation by the autonomic nervous system. *Biological Psychiatry, 54,* 1444–1456.

Cole, S.W., Kemeny, M.E. & Taylor, S.E. (1997). Social identity and physical health: Accelerated HIV progression in rejection-sensitive gay men. *Journal of Personality and Social Psychology, 72,* 320–335.

Davis, M.C., Matthews, K.A. & McGrath, C.E. (2000). Hostile attitudes predict elevated vascular resistance during interpersonal stress in men and women. *Psychosomatic Medicine, 62,* 17–25.

Denollet, J. (2005). Standard assessment of negative affectivity, social inhibition, and Type D personality. *Psychosomatic Medicine, 67,* 89–97.

Denollet, J., Conraads, V.M., Brutsaert, D.L., De Clerck, L.S., Stevens, W.J. & Vrints, C.J. (2003). Cytokines and immune activation in systolic heart failure: The role of Type D personality. *Brain, Behavior, and Immunity, 17,* 304–309.

Ershler, W.B. & Keller, E.T. (2000). Age-associated increased interleukin-6 gene expression, late-life diseases, and frailty. *Annual Review of Medicine, 51,* 245–270.

Esterling, B.A., Antoni, M.H., Fletcher, M.A., Margulies, S. & Schneiderman, N. (1994). Emotional disclosure through writing or speaking modulates latent Epstein-Barr virus antibody titers. *Journal of Consulting and Clinical Psychology, 62,* 130–140.

Esterling, B.A., Antoni, M.H., Kumar, M. & Schneiderman, N. (1990). Emotional repression, stress disclosure responses, and Epstein-Barr viral capsid antibody titers. *Psychosomatic Medicine, 52,* 397–410.

Esterling, B.A., Antoni, M.H., Kumar, M. & Schneiderman, N. (1993). Defensiveness, trait anxiety, and Epstein-Barr capsid antigen antibody titers in healthy college students. *Health Psychology, 12,* 132–139.

Everson, S.A., Lynch, J.W., Kaplan, G.A., Lakka, T.A., Sivenius, J. & Salonen, J.T. (2001). Stress-induced blood pressure reactivity and incident stroke in middle-aged men. *Stroke, 32(6),* 1263–1270.

Eysenck, H.J. (1967). *The biological basis of personality.* Springfield IL: Thomas.

Fang, C.Y. & Myers, H.F. (2001). The effects of racial stressors and hostility on cardiovascular reactivity in African American and Caucasian men. *Health Psychology, 20,* 64–70.

Felten, D.L., Overhage, J.M., Felten, S.Y. & Schmedtje, J.F. (1981). Noradrenergic sympathetic innervation of lymphoid tissue in the rabbit appendix: further evidence for a link between the nervous and immune systems. *Brain Research Bulletin, 7,* 595–612.

Fredrickson, B.L., Maynard, K.E., Helms, M.J., Haney, T.L., Siegler, I.C. & Barefoot, J.C. (2000). Hostility predicts magnitude and duration of blood pressure response to anger. *Journal of Behavioral Medicine, 23,* 229–243.

Friberg, S. & Mattson, S. (1997). On the growth rates of human malignant tumors: Implications for medical decision-making. *Journal of Surgical Oncology, 65,* 284–297.

Gerra, G., Monti, D., Panerai, A.E., Sacerdote, P., Anderlini, R., Avanzini, P., Zaimovic, A., Brambilla, F. & Franceschi, C. (2003). Long-term immune-endocrine effects of bereavement: relationships with anxiety levels and mood. *Psychiatry Research, 121,* 145–158.

Gianaros, P.J., Salomon, K., Zhou, F., Owens, J.F., Edmundowicz, D., Kuller, L.H., et al. (2005). A greater reduction in high-frequency heart rate variability to a psychological stressor is associated with subclinical coronary and aortic calcification in postmenopausal women. *Psychosomatic Medicine, 67(4)*, 553–560.

Gidron, Y., Armon, T., Gilutz, H. & Huleihel, M. (2003). Psychological factors correlate meaningfully with percent monocytes among acute coronary syndrome patients. *Brain, Behavior, and Immunity, 17*, 310–315.

Gross, J. (1989). Emotional expression in cancer onset and progression. *Social Science and Medicine, 28*, 1239–1248.

Guyll, M. & Contrada, R. (1998). Trait hostility and ambulatory cardiovascular activity: Responses to social interaction. *Health Psychology, 17*, 30–39.

Helmers, K.F., Krantz, D.S., Merz, C.N., Klein, J., Kop, W., et al. (1995). Defensive hostility: Relationship to multiple markers of cardiac ischemia in patients with coronary disease. *Health Psychology, 14*, 202–209.

Houston, B.K., Babyak, M.A., Chesney, M., Black, G. & Ragland, D. (1997). Social dominance and 22-year all cause mortality in men. *Psychosomatic Medicine, 59*, 5–12.

Houston, B.K., Chesney, M.A., Black, G.W., Cates, D.S. & Hecker, M.L. (1992). Behavioral clusters and coronary heart disease risk. *Psychosomatic Medicine, 54*, 447–461.

Ironson, G., Balbin, E., Stuetzle, R., Fletcher, M.A., O'Cleirigh, C., Laurenceau, J.P., Schneiderman, N. & Solomon, G. (2005). Dispositional optimism and the mechanisms by which it predicts slower disease progression in HIV: Proactive behavior, avoidant coping, and depression. *International Journal of Behavioral Medicine, 12*, 86–97.

Jamner, L.D., Schwartz, G.E. & Leigh, G. (1988). The relationship between repressive and defensive coping styles and monocyte, eosinophil, and serum glucose levels: Support for the opioid peptide hypothesis of repression. *Psychosomatic Medicine, 50*, 567–575.

Janeway, C.A., Travers, P., Walport, M. & Shlomchik, M.J. (2004). *Immunobiology* (6th edn) New York: Garland Publishing.

Jennings, J.R., Kamarck, T.W., Everson-Rose, S.A., Kaplan, G.A., Manuck, S.B. & Salonen, J.T. (2004). Exaggerated blood pressure responses during mental stress are prospectively related to enhanced carotid atherosclerosis in middle-aged Finnish men. *Circulation, 110(15)*, 2198–2203.

John, O.P. & Gross, J.J. (2004). Healthy and unhealthy emotion regulation: personality processes, individual differences, and life span development. *Journal of Personality, 72*, 1301–1333.

Jorgensen, R.S., Frankowski, J.J., Lantinga, L.J., Phadke, K., Sprafkin, R.P. & Abdul-Karim, K.W. (2001). Defensive hostility and coronary heart disease: a preliminary investigation of male veterans. *Psychosomatic Medicine, 63(3)*, 463–469.

Kagan, J. & Snidman, N. (1991). Temperamental factors in human development. *American Psychologist, 46*, 856–862.

Kagan, J., Snidman, N., Julia-Sellers, M. & Johnson, M.O. (1991). Temperament and allergic symptoms. *Psychosomatic Medicine, 53*, 332–340.

Kamarck, T.W., Debski, T.T. & Manuck, S.B. (2000). Enhancing the laboratory-to-life generalizability of cardiovascular reactivity using multiple occasions of measurement. *Psychophysiology, 37*, 533–542.

Kamarck, T.W., Jennings, J.R., Debski, T.T., Glickman-Weiss, E., Johnson, P. S., Eddy, M. J., et al. (1992). Reliable measures of behaviorally-evoked cardiovascular reactivity from a PC-based test battery: results from student and community samples. *Psychophysiology, 29*, 17–28.

Kamarck, T.W., Jennings, J.R., Pogue-Geile, M. & Manuck, S.B. (1994). A multidimensional measurement model for cardiovascular reactivity: stability and cross-validation in two adult samples. *Health Psychology, 13*, 471–478.

Kamarck, T.W., Schwartz, J.E., Janicki, D.L., Shiffman, S. & Raynor, D.A. (2003). Correspondence between laboratory and ambulatory measures of cardiovascular reactivity: a multilevel modeling approach. *Psychophysiology, 40*, 675–683.

Kaplan, J.R. & Manuck, S.B. (1998). Monkeys, aggression, and the pathobiology of atherosclerosis. *Aggressive Behavior, 24*, 323–334.

Kurylo, M. & Gallant, S. (2000). Hostility and cardiovascular reactivity in women during self-disclosure. *International Journal of Behavioral Medicine, 7*, 271–285.

Linden, W., Earle, T.L., Gerin, W. & Christenfeld, N. (1997). Physiological stress reactivity and recovery: conceptual siblings separated at birth? *Journal of Psychosomatic Research, 42(2)*, 117–135.

Llabre, M.M., Spitzer, S., Siegel, S., Saab, P.G. & Schneiderman, N. (2004). Applying latent growth curve modeling to the investigation of individual differences in cardiovascular recovery from stress. *Psychosomatic Medicine, 66,* 29–41.

Manuck, S.B. (1994). Cardiovascular reactivity in cardiovascular disease: 'Unto the breach'. *International Journal of Behavioral Medicine, 1,* 4–31.

Matthews, K.A., Katholi, C.R., McCreath, H., Whooley, M.A., Williams, D.R., Zhu, S., et al. (2004). Blood pressure reactivity to psychological stress predicts hypertension in the CARDIA study. *Circulation, 110,* 74–78.

Matthews, K.A., Salomon, K., Brady, S.S. & Allen, M.T. (2003). Cardiovascular reactivity to stress predicts future blood pressure in adolescence. *Psychosomatic Medicine, 65,* 410–415.

Matthews, K.A., Owens, J.F., Kuller, L.H., Sutton-Tyrrell, K. & Jansen-McWilliams, L. (1998). Are hostility and anxiety associated with carotid atherosclerosis in healthy postmenopausal women? *Psychosomatic Medicine, 60,* 633–638.

McCrae R.T. & Costa, P.T. (1989). The structure of interpersonal traits: Wiggins's circumplex and the five-factor model. *Journal of Personality and Social Psychology, 56,* 586–595.

McEwen, B.S. (1998). Protective and damaging effects of stress mediators. *New England Journal of Medicine, 338,* 171–179.

McGeer, P.L. & McGeer, E.G. (2001). Inflammation, autotoxicity, and Alzheimer disease. *Neurobiology of Aging, 22,* 799–809.

Milam, J.E., Richardson, J.L., Marks, G., Kemper, C.A. & McCutchan, A.J. (2004). The roles of dispositional optimism and pessimism in HIV disease progression. *Psychology and Health, 19,* 167–181.

Miller, G.E., Cohen, S., Rabin, B.S., Skoner, D.P. & Doyle, W.J. (1999). Personality and tonic cardiovascular, neuroendocrine, and immune function. *Brain, Behaviour and Immunity, 13,* 109–123.

Miller, G.E., Dopp, J.M., Myers, H.F., Felten, S.Y. & Fahey, J.L. (1999). Psychosocial predictors of natural killer cell mobilization during marital conflict. *Health Psychology, 18,* 262–271.

Miller, S.B., Dolgoy, L., Friese, M., Sita, A., Lavoie, K. & Campbell, T. (1998). Hostility, sodium consumption, and cardiovascular response to interpersonal stress. *Psychosomatic Medicine, 60,* 71–77.

Mills, P.J., Dimsdale, J.E., Nelesen, R.A. & Dillon, E. (1996). Psychologic characteristics associated with acute stressor-induced leukocyte subset redistribution. *Journal of Psychosomatic Research, 40,* 417–423.

Ming, E.E., Adler, G.K., Kessler, R.C., Fogg, L.F., Matthews, K.A., Herd, J.A., et al. (2004). Cardiovascular reactivity to work stress predicts subsequent onset of hypertension: the Air Traffic Controller Health Change Study. *Psychosomatic Medicine, 66(4),* 459–465.

Mischel, W. (1968). *Personality and assessment.* New York: John Wiley & Sons, Inc.

Mischel, W. & Shoda, Y. (1998). Reconciling processing dynamics and personality dispositions. *Annual Review of Psychology, 49,* 229–258.

Newton, T. L. & Bane, C.M. (2001). Cardiovascular correlates of behavioral dominance and hostility during dyadic interaction. *International Journal of Psychophysiology, 40,* 33–46.

Newton, T.L., Bane, C.M., Flores, A. & Greenfield, J. (1999). Dominance, gender, and cardiovascular reactivity during social interaction. *Psychophysiology, 36,* 245–252.

Newton, T.L., Walters, C.A., Philhower, C.L. & Wegel, R.A. (2005). Cardiovascular reactivity during dyadic social interaction: The roles of gender and dominance. *International Journal of Psychophysiology, 57,* 219–228.

Obrist, P.A. (1981). *Cardiovascular psychophysiology: A perspective.* New York: Plenum Press.

Olff, M., Brosschot, J.F., Godaert, G., Benschop, R.J., Ballieux, R.E., Heijnen, C.J., deSmet, M.B.M. & Ursin, H. (1995). Modulatory effects of defense and coping on stress-induced changes in endocrine and immune parameters. *International Journal of Behavioral Medicine, 2,* 85–103.

Papassotiropoulos, A., Hock, C. & Nitsch, R.M. (2001). Genetics of interleukin-6: Implications for Alzheimer's disease. *Neurobiology of Aging, 22,* 863–871.

Parham, P. (2004). *The immune system* (2nd edn). New York: Garland Publishing.

Perini, C., Muller, F.B. & Buhler, F.R. (1999). Suppressed aggression accelerates early development of essential hypertension. *Journal of Hypertension, 9,* 399–406.

Peters, M.L., Godaert, G.L.R., Ballieux, R.E. & Heijnen, C.J. (2003). Moderation of physiological stress responses by personality traits and daily hassles: Less flexibility of immune system responses. *Biological Psychology, 65,* 21–48.

Piferi, R.L. & Lawler, K.A. (2000). Hostility and the cardiovascular reactivity of women during interpersonal confrontation. *Women and Health, 30*, 111–129.

Polk, D.E., Kamarck, T.W. & Shiffman, S. (2002). Hostility explains some of the discrepancy between daytime ambulatory and clinic blood pressures. *Health Psychology, 21*, 202–206.

Raikkonen, K., Matthews, K.A., Flory, J. D. & Owens, J.F. (1999). Effects of hostility on ambulatory blood pressure and mood during daily living in healthy adults. *Health Psychology, 18*, 44–53.

Raikkonen, K., Matthews, K.A., Flory, J.D., Owens, J.F. & Gump, B. (1999). Effects of optimism, pessimism, and trait anxiety on ambulatory blood pressure and mood during everyday life. *Journal of Personality and Social Psychology, 76*, 104–113.

Reed, G.M., Kemeny, M.E., Taylor, S.E. & Visscher, B.R. (1999). Negative HIV-specific expectancies and AIDS-related bereavement as predictors of symptom onset in asymptomatic HIV-positive gay men. *Health Psychology, 18*, 354–363.

Reed, G.M., Kemeny, M.E., Taylor, S.E., Wang, H.Y.J. & Visscher, B.R. (1994). Realistic acceptance as a predictor of decreased survival time in gay men with AIDS. *Health Psychology, 13*, 299–307.

Ross, R. (1999). Atherosclerosis: An inflammatory disease. *New England Journal of Medicine, 340*, 115–126.

Rutledge, T. & Hogan, B.E. (2002). A quantitative review of prospective evidence linking psychological factors with hypertension development. *Psychosomatic Medicine, 64*, 758–766.

Rutledge, T. & Linden, W. (2000). Defensiveness status predicts 3-year incidence of hypertension. *Journal of Hypertension, 18(2)*, 153–159.

Rutledge, T. & Linden, W. (2003). Defensiveness and 3-year blood pressure levels among young adults: the mediating effect of stress-reactivity. *Annals of Behavioral Medicine, 25(1)*, 34–40.

Rutledge, T., Linden, W. & Paul, D. (2000). Cardiovascular recovery from acute laboratory stress: reliability and concurrent validity. *Psychosomatic Medicine, 62(5)*, 648–654.

Sanders, V.M., Kasprowicz, D.J., Kohm, A.P. & Swanson, M.A. (2001). Neurotransmitter receptors on lymphocytes and other lymphoid cells. In R. Ader, D. Felten & N. Cohen (eds), *Psychoneuroimmunology* (3rd edn) (pp. 161–196). San Diego, CA: Academic Press.

Scheier, M.F., Matthews, K.A., Owens, J., Magovern, G., Lefebure, R., Abbott, R. & Carver, C. (1989). Dispositional optimism and recovery from coronary artery bypass surgery: The beneficial effects of physical and psychological well-being. *Journal of Personality and Social Psychology, 57*, 1024–1040.

Scheier, M.F., Matthews, K.A., Owens, J.F., Schulz, R., Bridges, M.W., Magovern, G.J. & Carver, C.S. (1999). Optimism and rehospitalization after coronary artery bypass graft surgery. *Archives of Internal Medicine, 159*, 829–835.

Schofield, P., Ball, D., Smith, J.G., Borland, R., O'Brien, P., Davis, S., Olver, I., Ryan, G. & Joseph, D. (2004). Optimism and survival in lung cancer patients. *Cancer, 100*, 1276–1282.

Schulz, R., Bookwala, J., Knapp, J.E., Scheier, M. & Williamson, G.M. (1996). Pessimism, age, and cancer mortality. *Psychology and Aging, 11*, 304–309.

Segerstrom, S.C. (2000). Personality and the immune system: Models, methods, and mechanisms. *Annals of Behavioral Medicine, 22*, 181–090.

Segerstrom, S.C. (2001). Optimism, goal conflict, and stressor-related immune change. *Journal of Behavioral Medicine, 24*, 441–467.

Segerstrom, S.C. (2003). Individual differences, immunity, and cancer: Lessons from personality psychology. *Brain, Behavior, and Immunity, 17*, S92–S97.

Segerstrom, S.C. (in press). How does optimism suppress immunity? Evaluation of three affective pathways. *Health Psychology*.

Segerstrom, S.C., Castaneda, J.O. & Spencer, T.E. (2003). Optimism effects on cellular immunity: Testing the affective and persistence models. *Personality and Individual Differences, 35*, 1615–1624.

Segerstrom, S.C. & Miller, G.E. (2004). Psychological stress and the human immune system: A meta-analytic study of 30 years of inquiry. *Psychological Bulletin, 104*, 601–630.

Shea, J.D.C., Burton, R. & Girgis, A. (1993). Negative affect, absorption, and immunity. *Physiology and Behavior, 53*, 449–457.

Shea, J., Clover, K. & Burton, R. (1991). Relationships between measures of acute and chronic stress and cellular immunity. *Medical Science Research, 19*, 221–222.

Sherwood, A. (1993). Use of impedance cardiography in cardiovascular reactivity research. In J. Blascovich & E.S. Katkin (eds), *Cardiovascular reactivity to psychological stress & disease* (pp. 157–200). American Psychological Association: Washington, DC.

Sieber, W.J., Rodin, J., Larson, L., Ortega, S., Cummings, N., Levy, S., Whiteside, T. & Herberman, R. (1992). Modulation of human natural killer cell activity by exposure to uncontrollable stress. *Brain, Behavior, and Immunity, 6*, 141–156.

Siegman, A.W., Kubzansky, L.D., Kawachi, I., Boyle, S., Vokonas, P.S. & Sparrow, D. (2000). A prospective study of dominance and coronary heart disease in the normative aging study. *American Journal of Cardiology, 86*, 145–149.

Smith, B.D., Cranford, D. & Green, L. (2001). Hostility and caffeine: Cardiovascular effects during stress and recovery. *Personality and Individual Differences, 30*, 1125–1137.

Smith, T.W. (1992). Hostility and Health: Current status of a psychosomatic hypothesis. *Health Psychology, 11*, 139–150.

Smith, T.W., Allred, K.D., Morrison, C. & Carlson, S. (1989). Cardiovascular reactivity and interpersonal influence: Active coping in a social context. *Journal of Personality and Social Psychology, 56*, 209–218.

Smith, T.W. & Brown, P.W. (1991). Cynical hostility, attempts to exert social control, and cardiovascular reactivity in married couples. *Journal of Behavioral Medicine, 14*, 581–592.

Smith, T.W. & Gallo, L.C. (1999). Hostility and cardiovascular reactivity during marital interaction. *Psychosomatic Medicine, 61*, 436–445.

Smith, T.W. & Gallo, L.C. (2001). Personality traits as risk factors for physical illness. In A. Baum, T. Revenson & J. Singer (eds), *Handbook of Health Psychology* (pp. 139–172). Hillsdale, NJ: Lawrence Erlbaum.

Smith, T.W. & Gerin, W. (1998). The social psychology of cardiovascular response: Introduction to the special issue. *Annals of Behavioral Medicine, 20*, 243–246.

Smith, T.W., Glazer, K., Ruiz, J.M. & Gallo, L.C. (2004). Hostility, anger, aggressiveness and coronary heart disease: An interpersonal perspective on personality, emotion and health. *Journal of Personality, 72*, 1217–1270.

Smith, T.W. & MacKenzie, J. (2006). Personality and risk of physical illness. *Annual Review of Clinical Psychology*, in press.

Smith, T.W. & Ruiz, J.M. (2004). Personality theory and research in the study of health and behavior. In T. Boll (Series ed.), R. Frank, J. Wallander & A. Baum (Vol. eds), *Handbook of clinical health psychology: Vol. 1. Models and perspectives in health psychology* (pp. 143–199). Washington, DC: American Psychological Association.

Smith, T.W., Ruiz, J.M. & Uchino, B.N. (2000). Vigilance, active coping, and cardiovascular reactivity during social interaction in young men. *Health Psychology, 19*, 382–392.

Strong, J.P., Malcolm, G.T., McMahan, C.A., Tracy, R.E., Newman, W.P, Herderick, E.E. & Cornhill, J.F. (1999). Prevalence and extent of atherosclerosis in adolescents and young adults: Implications for prevention from the Pathobiological Determinants of Atherosclerosis in Youth Study. *JAMA, 281*, 727–735.

Suarez, E.C. (2003). Joint effect of hostility and severity of depressive symptoms on plasma interleukin-6 concentration. *Psychosomatic Medicine, 65*, 523–527.

Suarez, E.C., Lewis, J.G. & Kuhn, C. (2002). The relation of aggression, hostility, and anger to lipopolysaccharide-stimulated tumor necrosis factor (TNF)-α by blood monocytes from normal men. *Brain, Behavior, and Immunity, 16*, 675–684.

Suarez, E.C., Kuhn, C.M., Schanberg, S.M., Williams, R.B. & Zimmermann, E.A. (1998). Neuroendocrine, cardiovascular, and emotional responses of hostile men: The role of interpersonal challenge. *Psychosomatic Medicine, 60*, 78–88.

Suls, J. & Bunde, J. (2005). Anger, anxiety, and depression as risk factors for cardiovascular disease: the problems and implications of overlapping affective dispositions. *Psychological Bulletin, 131*, 260–300.

Surtees, P., Wainwright, N., Khaw, K.T., Luben, R., Brayne, C. & Day, N. (2003). Inflammatory dispositions: a population-based study of the association between hostility and peripheral leukocyte counts. *Personality and Individual Differences, 35*, 1271–1284.

Temoshok, L. (1987). Personality, coping style, emotion, and cancer: Towards an integrative model. *Cancer Survival, 6*, 545–567.

Todarello, O., Casamassima, A., Marinaccio, M., La Pesa, M.W., Caradonna, L., Valentino, L. & Marinaccio, L. (1994). Alexithymia, immunity, and cervical intraepithelial neoplasia: A pilot study. *Psychotherapy and Psychosomatics*, *61*, 199-204.

Todarello, O., Casamassima, A., Daniele, S., Marinaccio, M., Fanciullo, F., Valentino, L., Tedesco, N., Wiesel, S., Simone, G. & Marinaccio, L. (1997). Alexithymia, immunity, and cervical intraepithelial neoplasia: Replication. *Psychotherapy and Psychosomatics*, *66*, 208–213.

Tomakowsky, J., Lumley, M.A., Markowitz, N. & Frank, C. (2001). Optimistic explanatory style and dispositional optimism in HIV-infected men. *Journal of Psychosomatic Research*, *51*, 577–587.

Trapnell, P.D. & Wiggins, J.S. (1990). Extension of the Interpersonal Adjective Scales to include the big five dimensions of personality. *Journal of Personality and Social Psychology*, *59*, 781–790.

Treiber, F.A., Kamarck, T., Schneiderman, N., Sheffield, D., Kapuku, G. & Taylor, T. (2003). Cardiovascular reactivity and development of preclinical and clinical disease states. *Psychosomatic Medicine*, *65*, 46–62.

Waldstein, S.R., Siegel, E.L., Lefkowitz, D., Maier, K.J., Brown, J.R., Obuchowski, A.M., et al. (2004). Stress-induced blood pressure reactivity and silent cerebrovascular disease. *Stroke*, *35*, 1294–1298.

Whiteman, M.C., Deary, I.J., Lee, A.J. & Fowkes, F. G. R. (1997). Submissiveness and protection from coronary heart disease in the general population: Edinburgh Artery Study. *Lancet*, *350*, 541–545.

Williams, R.B., Jr., Barefoot, J.C. & Shekelle, R.B. (1985). The health consequences of hostility. In M.A. Chesney & R.H. Rosenman (eds), *Anger and hostility in cardiovascular and behavioral disorders* (pp. 173–185). New York: Hemisphere.

CHAPTER 9

Personality, Relationships, and Health: A Dynamic-transactional Perspective

Franz J. Neyer
University of Vechta, Germany
and
Judith Lehnart
Humboldt University Berlin, Germany

INTRODUCTION

Imagine two men, Peter and Paul, who both are about 45 years of age and are taking medical advice concerning their hypertension problems. Peter is an outgoing, sociable, and optimistic person. He is married and has two children. He works hard in a highly competitive environment, which brings him strife not only at the workplace but also in his family and private life. In contrast, Paul is single and has been unemployed for several years. He is introverted and always concerned with emotional ups and downs. He was left by his partner six months ago and is now looking hard for a new relationship. Concerning work, however, he has given up looking for a job, which makes him feel depressed and desperate. What kind of prediction can we make as personality and relationship psychologists regarding how Peter and Paul will handle their hypertension problems over the next few years? We know about the accumulating effects of both interpersonal and intrapersonal stress, but at the same time we are aware of the personality and relationship factors that may contribute to how people cope with health problems. Will Peter be more successful than Paul in controlling, or even overcoming, hypertension problems because of his personal and social life circumstances? Indeed, research has frequently provided evidence that being married, having family and friends, and being employed represent protective factors for health. However, these factors do not work on their own or independently of each other. For example, Peter may feel strongly attached toward his family simply because he is a social person, that is his social relationships are a function of his basic personality traits. In the future, however, the quality of these relationships may depend strongly on how he deals with interpersonal stress. Paul, on the other hand, may live alone because he generally feels insecure in social relationships.

Handbook of Personality and Health. Edited by Margarete E. Vollrath. © 2006 John Wiley & Sons, Ltd.

However, his well-being in the future depends on how successfully he will fulfil his needs for affiliation.

Research has shown strong associations between the amount and the quality of social relationships and health outcomes such as longevity, well-being, depression, and psychosocial stability. In contrast to a traditional perspective that has viewed relationships as a causal factor for physical and psychological health, we argue from a transactional point of view that dynamic transactions between personality and relationships may affect health outcomes. From this perspective, characteristics of the individual personality may lead to relationship outcomes that either promote or impair health, yet at the same time relationship experiences may induce personality change which in turn may have an impact on health. The concept of personality-relationship transaction describes how people induce changes in their social environment by virtue of their basic personality traits, and how social relationship experiences give rise to personality change. We argue that the processes and mechanisms of personality-relationship transaction unfold over longer periods of time, with strong implications for health psychology. The chapter gives an overview on the various kinds of personality-relationship transaction and discusses the multiple pathways in which these may influence health.

HOW CAN PERSONALITY AND RELATIONSHIPS AFFECT HEALTH?

It is a well-replicated finding that social support has a positive influence on the individual's health. Although the objective amount of social support does make a difference, it is the perceived social support that is even more important (Bost, Cox, Burchinal & Payne, 2002; Sarason, Sarason & Pierce, 1992). While the objective amount of support provided by relationship partners depends to a great extent on the characteristics of the relationship partner and the relationship itself, perceived support is a (stable) characteristic of the person who receives (or perceives) the support. Thus, the effect of social support as a relationship characteristic on health cannot be considered without taking the individual's personality into account (Sarason, Sarason & Gurung, 1997). Furthermore, it is very likely that other features of relationships, such as conflict, closeness, and satisfaction are also influenced by the individual's personality. We postulate that the perspective of personality-relationship transaction should move beyond the social support perspective and consider multiple facets of relationships and personality.

Relationships within one's personal network, such as with a romantic partner, children, family of origin, and peers, generate the social context of personality development. Therefore the characteristics of one's personality and social relationships cannot be viewed independently of each other. A social relationship is characterized by a stable pattern of interaction between at least two individuals, each bringing his or her life experiences and his or her basic dispositions to the relationship. The personality of each relationship partner is likely to affect different aspects of the relationship, which in turn have an effect on the individual personality. It is this kind of interaction, or *transaction*, which mirrors how individuals select relationship experiences, which in turn may initiate or foster change in personality characteristics. In the long run, we believe that continuous reciprocal transactions have strong impacts on health in its broadest sense, including well-being, life satisfaction, and longevity.

There are three general models that describe how the individual's personality, relationship experiences and health outcomes are interrelated.

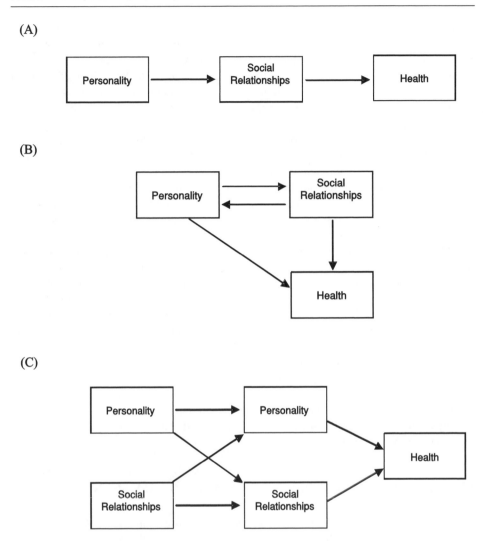

Figure 9.1 Models of personality-relationship transaction and effects on health: Mediational model (A), Interactional Model (B), and Dynamic-Transactional Model (C)

The first is the mediational model (Figure 9.1(a)). Mediation implies that there may be no direct influences of personality traits on health, but rather indirect influences negotiated by unique relationship experiences. For example, it has been frequently shown that individuals with low levels of emotional stability (i.e., neuroticism) report much lower levels of marital satisfaction, and experience more negative interaction patterns (e.g., Karney & Bradbury, 1995, 1997). If such relationship experiences induce interpersonal stress, the possible detrimental effects on health could be viewed as expressions of the underlying personality trait, that is, low emotional stability.

The second model assumes reciprocal interactions between personality and relationships, that is, personality and relationships are interrelated and produce both direct and indirect effects on health (see Figure 9.1(b)). This model is cross-sectional, and does not allow any inferences about the causal structure or the underlying mechanisms. For example, emotionally unstable individuals usually report broad and vague health complaints, which are frequently accompanied by troubled relationship experiences, but it is unclear whether individual dispositions lead to troubled relationships or whether the latter influence change in personality traits. Of course, the direction of effects can be modelled by mediation (or moderation) analyses, if these are warranted by theoretical considerations. However, both relationship and personality factors are always hopelessly confounded in cross-sectional designs (unless experimental methods are used).

Because personality and relationship factors are difficult to treat experimentally, a longitudinal perspective on personality-relationship transaction is very much required (Figure 9.1(c)). It is only possible by longitudinal observations such as cross-lagged panel designs to disentangle causes and effects, that is, to demonstrate how personality changes in response to relationship experiences, and how relationships change due to underlying personality traits (Asendorpf, 2002; Neyer, 2004). Besides methodological considerations, however, it should be kept in mind that transactions between personality and relationships unfold over longer time periods, sometimes even over years and decades. Only the observation of personality and relationship development over longer time periods covering at least two measurement points can reveal insights into the processes and mechanisms of personality-relationship transaction including its long-term effects on mental and physical health. The dynamic transactional design is complex, yet appropriate, because it incorporates several principles of personality and relationship development, which are explained in the following section.

Before we turn to the interrelations between personality and relationship experiences, we will briefly summarize what is currently known about personality and relationship development over the life course. A deeper understanding of the basic principles of personality and relationship development may help health psychologists to understand how, when, and why dynamic transactions between personality and relationships occur and how these may influence health outcomes.

PERSONALITY DEVELOPMENT ACROSS THE LIFE SPAN

Contemporary personality psychology is dominated by a trait approach, that is, personality is defined as the characteristic way in which a person thinks, feels, behaves, and relates to others. However, one should keep in mind that personality also contains characteristic adaptations such as personal goals, aspirations, social values, as well as features of the individual identity, which are reflected by the stories people tell about their lives (McAdams, 2001). Each of these different levels of personality serves to establish and maintain consistency in people's lives, and it comes as no surprise that personality development over the life course is characterized by stability *and* change.

Stability and change are not at all opposites. Viewed from a life-span perspective any argument in favour of either stability or change is misplaced. Both are two sides of the same coin and reflect basic features of individual and social development. Stability and change account for the fact that even though we change, we remain identical persons. This assumption has implications for health psychology and intervention purposes: It delineates the scope for changing health behaviour, yet at the same time acknowledges the relevance of stable personality traits as important bases of adaptive health behaviours. The two most important forms of stability and change are rank-order and mean-level stability (Asendorpf, 2004; Caspi, 1998; Caspi & Roberts, 1999).

The perspective of *mean-level stability and change* addresses the general or normative age-related trajectory of personality development (Roberts, Walton & Viechtbauer, 2006). Basic personality traits emerge from childhood temperament, and crystallize in adolescence and early adulthood (Caspi, 1998, 2000; Shiner, 1998). As various longitudinal studies have shown, personality in young adults generally changes toward maturity (e.g., Haan, Millsap & Hartka, 1986; Helson & Moane, 1987; Neyer & Lehnart, 2006), a stage where people may be ideally characterized by being happy, lacking neurotic and abnormal tendencies, and— of prime importance for the study of personality-relationship transaction—being able to maintain warm and compassionate relationships, especially with a romantic partner (Allport, 1961). From adolescence to middle adulthood personality traits related to extraversion, neuroticism, and openness decrease, whereas traits like conscientiousness and agreeableness increase (e.g., Srivastava, John, Gosling & Potter, 2003). Because these age-related trends tend to emerge in different cultures, McCrae et al. (1998, 2000) draw the provocative conclusion that this kind of personality change is due to intrinsic maturation and not at all contingent on environmental influences. Recent studies, however, have shown evidence that personality development in adulthood is influenced substantially by environmental factors such as relationship experiences (e.g., Neyer & Asendorpf, 2001; Robins et al., 2000, 2002).

The perspective of *rank-order stability and change*, in contrast, taps the relative standing of individuals on specific personality traits and relationship characteristics. Thus, high rank-order stability does not necessarily imply high mean-level stability. For example, although mean-level neuroticism may decline in early adulthood, individual differences may remain quite stable. More recently, Roberts and DelVecchio (2000) concluded from an extensive meta-analysis that the rank-order stability of the Big Five personality traits increases in a step-like function from childhood, adolescence, to young and middle adulthood but reaches its plateau not before the sixth decade of life. These findings show that personality development is not completed by age 30 and suggest substantial plasticity of personality across the adult lifespan.

In summary, rank-order and mean level stability and change can be described as a function of two principles of personality development (Roberts & Caspi, 2003): The *plasticity principle,* on the one hand, indicates that personality traits can be regarded as open to environmental influences at any time over the life course. From this perspective it is argued that personality is never set like plaster and does not stop changing at any age over the life course (Roberts, Helson & Klohnen, 2002; Roberts et al., 2006). The *maturity principle*, on the other hand, states that a person becomes more agreeable, conscientious, more socially dominant and less emotionally unstable as he or she grows older (McCrae et al., 1999, 2000; Roberts et al., 2006; Srivastava et al., 2003). Both principles also imply that people are able to cope with the various ups and downs in their lives by virtue of their basic personality traits. For example, we know from many studies that people do not change dramatically when confronted with major life events, but rather adapt even to extremely adverse life circumstances by mobilizing the most powerful resources: plasticity and maturity (Caspi & Moffitt, 1993).

In addition to the traditional view on mean-level and rank-order change, personality development can also be traced back to individual differences in intraindividual change, which is a central tenet of life-span developmental psychology (e.g., Baltes, 1997; Mroczek & Spiro, 2003, 2005). The concept of individual differences in change holds that people vary in the direction of change, the rate of change, and the time of change. For example, a mean-level decrease in neuroticism does not exclude the possibility that quite a sizeable minority may not follow this trend, and rather increase. Moreover, maturation does not necessarily mean that all individuals of a cohort change at the same time. Even though most people seem to mature between 20 and 30, some of them may decrease in neuroticism later or earlier than others depending on the relationship experiences that initiate personality change. Up to the present there exists (to the best of our knowledge) neither a meta-analytic study on individual differences in personality change nor a systematic review of the possible correlates of individual differences in personality change. We argue that individual differences in personality development are associated considerably with individual relationship experiences. More specifically, we expect that the consideration of such non-normative patterns of personality development will shed light on how individual and relationship development is interconnected with health outcomes.

Most recently, the maturational trends observed as mean-level change in personality traits have been interpreted in terms of the *social investment principle*, stating that investments in age-graded social roles are the driving forces for development (Roberts, Wood & Smith, 2005). Becoming a reliable partner, a nurturing parent, or a cooperative work mate reflect societal expectations, which 'come along with their own set of expectations and contingencies that promote a reward structure that calls for becoming more socially dominant, agreeable, conscientious and less neurotic' (p. 174). The *cumulative continuity* principle of personality development, on the other hand, accounts for the increasing rank-order stability of personality traits over the life course. Just as the continuity of personality gives rise to consistent life and relationship experiences, the accumulating effects of life and relationship experiences are assumed to consolidate one's personality (Roberts & DelVecchio, 2000). In general, however, the development of personality, relationships, and health may walk hand in hand, as is suggested by the *parallel continuity principle* (Branje, van Lieshout & van Aken, 2004). Parallel continuity is reflected by correlated change between conceptually independent factors without it being known how exactly these factors influenced each other over time, or whether a third variable might have concurrently influenced both constructs. In contrast, the predictions of the *corresponsive principle* are more precise: According to the *corresponsive principle*, life experiences accentuate those traits that lead to these experiences in the first place. This principle incorporates the selection and evocation effects of personality traits. Selection means that individuals choose their specific environments according to their personality. This means, for example, that individuals higher in conscientiousness may search actively for employment where a high amount of responsibility is necessary. The corresponsive principle predicts that over time those people become even more conscientious because of the environmental demands. Thus, experiences in specific environments and more specifically in relationships are dependent on the individual's personality and may accentuate individual differences in these traits (Roberts, Caspi & Moffitt, 2003; Roberts & Robins, 2004).

Why are these principles important for understanding the personality-relationship transaction and its associations with health? We argue that considering these principles helps to understand how and to what extent health status can be viewed as an expression of personality development across the life span. Consider again Peter and Paul with their hypertension problems. The current health status of both men can be viewed as an expression of the cumulative effects of consistent life and relationship experiences. This does not mean, however, that their health problems were inevitable and will persist during the next decades of their lives. Personality development is driven by multiple forces, most importantly by social relationships, which create the social context of our lives and sometimes initiate turning points on our developmental pathways.

SOCIAL RELATIONSHIPS ACROSS THE LIFE SPAN

Social or personal relationships are characterized by a stable interaction pattern between at least two persons (Asendorpf & Banse, 2000; Hinde, 1993). Thus, relationships characterize dyads, not individuals, and the quality of a relationship constitutes a function of the personality of both individuals and their interaction history. Social relationships are one of the most powerful sources of support throughout the life span, and the empirical evidence clearly shows that being involved in satisfying relationships is associated with enhanced emotional and physical health. It comes as no surprise that most people view social relationships as the most powerful ingredients of a good and satisfying life. Nevertheless, relationships can also be a source of intense anxiety, anger, and other negative emotions with health impairing consequences, and we argue that relationship effects on well-being and health are transformed through the way they are perceived by the individual personality.

Like personality development, the development of relationships is also characterized by stability *and* change. However, in relationship research these two developmental features have been studied less systematically than in personality trait research, which might be due to the greater heterogeneity in relationship research. In the following, we will discuss stability and change for different kinds of relationships. Generally, there are at least two different perspectives that have to be distinguished. Relationship development can be studied from a social network perspective, which means that all types of relationship a person has are studied simultaneously, typically in terms of structural features like network size, density, centrality, homogeneity, etc. The second perspective deals with specific types of relationships and their structure and quality. Partner relationships or relationships between parents and children are studied almost exclusively, without considering other relationships or relationships between different kinds of relationships. Whereas the latter perspective is frequently captured in psychological relationship research, the former perspective is genuinely sociological in that relations within groups such as families or non-kin groups are looked at in their entirety (e.g., Bott, 1957; Sprecher, Felmee, Orbruch & Willetts, 2002). However, in adopting this sociological approach, psychology has personalized the concept of social networks in considering various relationship types just from the perspective of one individual rather than of all group members. In other words, the psychological approach to social networks is one that considers the *knots* rather than the complete *net* of relationships (Asendorpf & van Aken, 1994; Asendorpf & Wilpers, 1998; Neyer, 1997; Neyer & Asendorpf, 2001; Neyer & Voigt, 2004). With this so-called *egocentered* or *personal network* approach, it is possible to scrutinize individual features of relationship status, for example, specific relationship qualities such as conflict or closeness across all members of one's social network or of members of a specific type of relationship such as parents, friends, colleagues, etc.

Stability and change of personal relationships pertains primarily to age-related changes in size of personal networks. It is well supported empirically that personal networks decrease in size when people reach old age, while at the same time individual differences in network size remain remarkably stable (Lang, 2000; Lang & Carstensen, 1998). In a longitudinal study with young adults we investigated social network development over a period of eight years at the point of emerging into young adulthood, that is, from about age 24 to age 32 (Neyer & Lehnart, 2006). The overall size of personal networks increased during the first four years of our study, and remained stable thereafter. More specifically, different types of relationship showed the expected change in this period of life: whereas the number of parents and siblings remained stable and the number of grandparents decreased, the number of children and colleagues increased. The number of friends and acquaintances increase in the emerging adulthood years, but tend to decrease when individuals reach young adulthood. This pattern reflects the orientation towards peers when young adults leave home. Later, when young adults tend to settle down and start having their own family, they become more selective as to whom they keep as friends in their social network. In line with this, the qualitative aspects of relationships such as contact frequency, conflict, importance, or emotional closeness also change. For example, the frequency of contact and the amount of conflict with other network partners generally decrease, possibly because young adults engage more heavily in relationships with partners and children (Neyer & Asendorpf, 2001; Neyer & Lehnart, 2006).

In addition to the social network perspective, there is also evidence that specific kinds of relationship undergo normative changes across the lifespan. For example, the relationships between siblings develop in a U-shaped fashion from adolescence to old age (Cicirelli, 1995). After leaving the family of origin, emotional closeness usually decreases until siblings reach their thirties and forties and are involved in raising children or in their careers. After the reproductive and generative ages—when their own children have left home and the siblings retire from working life—closeness increases again, and siblings may be rediscovered as close companions. Moreover, although the general developmental course of sibling relationships across adulthood takes on the form of a U-shaped curve, it is likely that those sibling dyads that feel closer and contact each other more frequently than others continue to do so over time. Exactly this pattern has been observed by the retrospective evaluations of twin relationships, revealing that despite age-related relationship change the dyadic differences between relationship qualities remained highly stable across adulthood (Neyer, 2002).

Because a relationship is basically the outcome of the interaction of two persons, it is likely that relationship characteristics are typically more malleable than individual personality traits. This unbalance of personality versus relationship stability has clear implications for the nature of the personality-relationship transaction. In general, it can be assumed that personality effects on later relationship development are more powerful and more frequent than the relationship effects of personality development. Thus the unbalance should be taken seriously by studying relationship effects on different levels of aggregation. For example, short-term relationships may have other effects than long-term relationships, and research has shown that long-term marital relationships maintained over many years may become stable and powerful social contexts, where both partners influence each other in specific individual traits, such as cognitive ability (Gruber-Baldini, Schaie & Willis, 1995). In the following, we discuss how such effects may come about, and how these may lead to health outcomes.

PERSONALITY-RELATIONSHIP TRANSACTIONS

The empirical study of the personality-relationship transaction is concerned with one basic question: How does personality influence the beginning, end, and the course of social relationships, and how does the beginning, end, and the development of relationships influence change in personality? Personal relationships can be regarded as being located at the interface between the person and the social environment (see Figure 9.2).

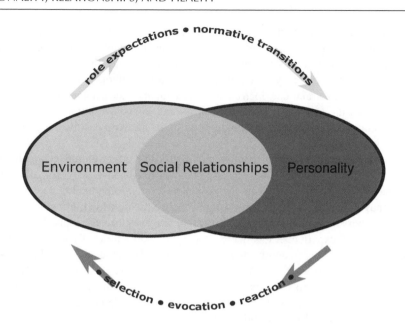

Figure 9.2 Social relationships are the interface between the individual personality and the environment

Relationships embody features of the person and the environment at the same time, and it is in this sense that they are part of one's personality *and* part of one's social environment. The dynamic-transactional perspective of individual development over the life span (Caspi, 1998, 2000; Caspi & Roberts, 1999; Magnusson, 1990; Sameroff, 1983) accounts for the interrelatedness of personality and social development in assuming that individuals generally develop over time through a dynamic, continuous, and reciprocal transaction with their environment, and there is good reason to believe that the environment is foremost social. People may become influenced or even socialized by relationship partners such as parents, siblings, children, friends, colleagues, and others, but at the same time they may also actively search, create, and change relationships in a way that suits them, which in turn gives feedback to their further development. Thus, the personality-relationship transaction is not just a special kind of transaction between the individual and his or her environment; it is the most central one.

We assume that personality effects on change in the environment unfold through the principles of selection, evocation, and reaction. Selection means that individuals actively select themselves into social environments and thus select relationships that suit their personality. Evocation, on the other hand, means that people evoke specific reactions from their environment because of their personality characteristics. Finally, reaction refers to the individual's perception of and reaction to the environment and more specifically their relationship partners according to their personality. Environmental effects on personality change come along with emerging new relationships that are typically constituted during normative life transitions. Consider again Peter and Paul who both have hypertension problems. Peter may continue his relationships at work and with his family in a consistent way in line with the unique interaction patterns that have emerged during the past years. It may be that the accumulating effects of stressful relationship experiences may intensify hypertension problems, yet at the same time it may happen that relationship problems become counterbalanced by the resilient parts of Peter's personality, resulting in more health promoting relationship patterns. Paul, in contrast, may have found a new partner. Although it is likely that he will mould this new partner relationship in accordance with his basic personality makeup, it may also happen that the new experiences of security and safety will improve his self-esteem and self-confidence thus creating a turning point in his life with positive long-term effects on well-being and health.

These possible pathways of personality and relationship co-development are all compatible with the principles of personality development outlined above, suggesting that individuals develop in an interplay between chance and necessity. In particular, the case of Peter and Paul may illustrate two basic facets of personality-relationship transaction. First, relationships and personality co-develop in a corresponding way, because individuals select and evoke relationship experiences that deepen their personality traits. Therefore, relationship experiences do not arise randomly, and in turn convey the cumulative stability of personality (Caspi & Bem, 1990; Caspi & Roberts, 2001; Fraley & Roberts, 2005; Lang et al., 2006; Neyer, 2004; Roberts & Caspi, 2003). Only a few longitudinal studies have addressed the associations of personality and relationship change in adolescence and early adulthood (Asendorpf & Wilpers, 1998; Asendorpf & van Aken, 2003; Branje, van Lieshout & van Aken, 2004; Neyer & Asendorpf, 2001; Robins, Caspi & Moffitt, 2002). Second, it is also possible that new relationships create a turning point in personality development, especially when they emerge in the context of life transitions. As Caspi and Moffitt (1993) have argued, such expectable and age-graded life transitions have the potential to 'catalyze' personality change, because they entail strong relationship experiences confronting the individual with new social tasks and behavior expectancies that represent a reward structure for personality maturation. Of course, normative life transitions can also contribute to individual differences or non-normative patterns of personality change, because not all individuals undergo a life transition at all, nor do all change in the same manner (Lang et al., 2006; Neyer, 2004; Roberts, Caspi & Moffitt, 2001, 2003; Roberts et al., 2006; Robins et al., 2002). For example, we found in our longitudinal study that the first partner relationship in young adulthood had a long-lasting effect on personality maturation (Neyer & Lehnart, 2006). Entering into a partner relationship for the first time induced a lasting decrease in neuroticism that obviously was not due to short-term boosts in life-satisfaction or well-being. This conclusion is supported additionally by our observations that separating from, or changing, a partner was not associated with personality change, with one exception: partner change went hand in hand with increase in extraversion. In sum, we therefore confidently repeat our previous conclusion that 'engaging in a serious partnership is a game you can only win' (Neyer & Asendopf, 2001: p. 1200). Still, this heartwarming conclusion pertains to a period early in adulthood, and does not exclude the possibility that partner change, divorce, or widowhood have different effects at different ages.

When the effects of normative or non-normative events on relationships, personality, or health are discussed, the timing of the event has also to be taken into account. Experiencing a normative transition or developmental task off time, e.g., earlier than most peers, may have detrimental effects whereas successfully completing the same developmental task on time has positive effects (Elder & Shanahan, 2006). Research has shown that an early transition to partnership and parenthood (in adolescence) has negative consequences on socioeconomic status, education, etc. Successfully accomplishing normative developmental tasks on time, e.g., during the transition from adolescence to adulthood, is also related to a person's health in terms of subjective well-being. Those who succeed in the tasks of achievement and affiliation are more likely to maintain a high level of well-being or to increase in well-being as compared to those who do not succeed (Schulenberg, Bryant & O'Malley, 2004).

In the following we will selectively review studies that have shown influences of personality traits and relationship experiences on health outcomes. It is our concern to discuss these studies in light of our conceptualization of the personality-relationship transaction in order to stimulate future theory and research on health to take the transactional perspective more seriously and to encourage researchers to conduct longitudinal studies that could empirically test the assumptions of the dynamic-transactional perspective. It is therefore important to realize that personality characteristics are malleable and far from being perfectly stable. Thus, like relationships and health outcomes, personality characteristics need to be assessed at multiple waves of data collection.

OVERALL EFFECTS ON MORTALITY

A central outcome variable in epidemiological health research is *mortality*, that is, whether and how long a person survives over a given time period. Mortality rates can easily be computed for a whole population or specific subgroups defined, for instance, by age or gender. Personality as well as relationship characteristics contribute to mortality and survival. One instructive example of relationship effects on mortality is the survival of the members of the so-called *Donner party,* a pioneer train on its way to California in 1846. Unfortunately, the train became trapped in the mountains when winter started early that year. Of the original 87 members, only 47 survived until a rescue party arrived in spring. Grayson (1990) found out that age, sex, and the 'degree of social connectedness' were important factors for survival. In particular, the likelihood to die was increased for men as compared to women. Furthermore, it was increased for both very young and very old people as compared to middle aged adults. Most interestingly, those who travelled in the company of many family members were more likely to survive. Thus, being embedded in a supportive family network reduces mortality risk even under extremely challenging life circumstances. This result shows that a structural aspect of relationships such as network size has an important effect on health for individuals. Generally speaking, people with larger social networks tend to be healthier and to live longer. For example, Shye, Mullooly, Freeborn & Pope (1995) discovered in a study with elderly people (65 years and above) that those who reported more informal social contact were more likely to be alive 15 years later. Large social network size was among the strongest predictors for survival.

The type of relationship that has been most intensively studied in relationship-health research is marriage. Marital status is often viewed as an indicator of social integration, suggesting that being married is beneficial for most people. Compared to unmarried people the mortality risk remains significantly lower for married people (e.g., Seeman, 2001). This effect is stronger in men than in women: the mortality risk of the unmarried is 50 % higher among women, whereas it is 250 % higher among men suggesting that men benefit more from marriage than women (Ross, Mirowsky & Goldsteen, 1990). Since the beginning of research on relationship effects on mortality, researchers have been wondering whether it is the mere presence of significant others or whether there are other underlying mechanisms involved in producing these mortality effects.

If having a spouse is a powerful predictor of mortality, does this also mean that losing a spouse has a detrimental effect on health and survival? A greater change in relationship is hard to imagine than the loss of a relationship partner either through rejection, separation, divorce, or death. Research on stressful life events has shown that the death of a spouse is considered to be one of the most stressful experiences (e.g., Holmes & Rahe, 1967). Findings from the Terman Life Cycle Study revealed that mortality risk is higher for those currently divorced, indicating that the stressful separation from a partner has negative effects on health. But even more interesting is the observation that compared to those who stay continuously married the mortality risk remains higher even for those who remarry after the divorce (Tucker, Friedman, Wingard & Schwartz, 1996; Tucker, Schwartz, Clark & Friedman, 1999). From the transactional perspective discussed above, the question arises whether there are individual characteristics that make it more likely for individuals to experience relationship changes such as divorce and remarriage. Tucker and colleagues (1996) reported that those participants of the Terman Study who were less conscientious in childhood or who experienced parental divorce were also more likely to divorce and remarry in their adult life. That is, individual characteristics make people prone to specific relationship experiences, which in turn affect longevity. But it is not only enduring characteristics that mould relationship experiences: being remarried was associated with a higher mortality risk only for those aged less than 70 years, whereas those aged 70 years and older did not have a higher mortality risk (Tucker et al., 1999). In contrast, no age-related relationship was found for being separated, divorced, or widowed. Thus, the detrimental effects of relationship loss may be long lasting, but after a while the buffering effect of a new relationship may overturn the adverse effects of the loss.

Martin and Friedman (2000) investigated whether childhood personality risk factors remain risk factors for mortality in adults. They found that conscientiousness, both in childhood as well as in adulthood, was related to a lower mortality risk. Although they expected neuroticism to be a predictor of a higher mortality risk, they found no relationship between neuroticism in adulthood and mortality risk. They argue that the trait of neuroticism may be too broad and characterize two subtypes, a healthy and an unhealthy neurotic. Another possible explanation for the heterogeneity of the neuroticism-health pattern is due to different relationship experiences. Those who find their 'safe haven' decrease in neuroticism due to their positive relationship experiences and stop engaging in unhealthy behaviour patterns.

In the following paragraphs, the relations between personality, relationship quality, and health are presented for different types of relationships: romantic relationships, family relationships, friendships, and working relationships.

ROMANTIC RELATIONSHIPS

As mentioned above, the relationship with a romantic partner is the most comprehensively studied type of relationship. In the following we will present results separately for marital relationships and romantic relationships in general, for the following reasons. Among studies of romantic relationships, the comparison between married and non-married couples was for a long time the dominating type of research. However, society changes and with this societal change, forms of partnership have changed and being married is no longer the single accepted form of partnership. Taking this societal change into account, researchers now focus on being in a stable, long-term partnership instead of focusing on the legal status when investigating the effects of romantic relationships on personality and health.

In our longitudinal study (Neyer & Lehnart, 2006) we found that those who were low in sociability and neuroticism regarded relationships in general as of less importance. Furthermore, the importance of relationships decreased in this group over the course of eight years. This result seems to indirectly support the selection hypothesis as well as the protection hypothesis. People may be predisposed to be less likely to engage in a romantic relationship because of their personality. But they also develop or change in response to their relationship experiences. In the case of unsociable, emotionally quite stable individuals, there seems to be a generalized indifference towards relationships, which expresses itself in remaining single. On the other hand, they cannot profit from positive relationship experiences in the same way as those who are engaged in a serious romantic relationship.

MARRIAGE

Does marriage make people healthier or do healthier people marry? This question refers to the two possible effects of marriage: a *protective effect* and a *selection effect*. One of the principles of person-environment transaction discussed above is selection. Who selects whom? It is part of most persons' common knowledge that *birds of a feather flock together* and *opposites attract*. Although these sayings seem to be contradictory, they are deeply rooted in our everyday experience. These rules refer to the principles of homogamy and heterogamy. Research has shown that similarity plays a more important role than dissimilarity (Lykken & Tellegen, 1993), especially for characteristics like intelligence or physical attractiveness. However, similarity in personality traits is only small in size. Although similarity may only be moderate, the relative amount of similarity remains stable (Caspi & Herbener, 1992) because spouses share the same environmental experiences.

Whether individuals marry is also dependent on their personality and it can be assumed that this is even more the case today because marriage is no longer the only socially legitimate way to cohabit as a couple. A recent twin study (Johnson, McGue, Krueger & Bouchard, 2004) has suggested that the correlation between marital status and personality is mediated by genetic influences. Married men and women score lower on the trait of alienation, which means that those individuals have less negative emotions and tend to have satisfying relationship experiences. The association between these personality attributes and better mental and physical health is highly plausible.

As discussed above, being married has positive effects on longevity and divorce has detrimental effects on health, especially for men. Personality aspects are associated with relationship stability and the likelihood of separation. Thus, personality structure can predict whether individuals are prone to specific relationship experiences, which in turn affect health. Neuroticism tends to be the strongest predictor of relationship stability and relationship satisfaction (Karney & Bradbury, 1995) in married couples. Moreover, personality not only predicts an individual's relationship experiences, it also influences a partner's relationship experiences, such as satisfaction and stability. In a study by Robins, Caspi and Moffitt (2000), both partners' personality traits predicted the individual's relationship satisfaction and the partners' relationship satisfaction independently of each other. Low negative emotionality in women, for example, could predict their partners' relationship satisfaction.

Having a spouse also enhances attachment and feelings of belonging, which are thought to influence well-being and mental health (House, Landis & Umberson, 1988) and may have an impact on health related behaviour. Married individuals are less likely to engage in risky activities and they smoke and drink less (Ross et al., 1990; Umberson, 1987). Additionally they might probably monitor each other for illness symptoms.

FAMILY AND KIN RELATIONSHIPS

Family and kin relationships play an important role in our lives as sources of instrumental and emotional support (e.g., Lang, 2000). Relationships with kin and with non-kin members of one's network are fundamentally distinct on at least three dimensions. First, kin relationships imply genetic relatedness. Second, kin relations are characterized by higher levels of emotional closeness and have a longer relationship history (Neyer & Lang, 2003), whereas non-kin relationships are characterized by the negotiation of equality and constitute a context of socialization at least since adolescence. Third, kin and non-kin relationships are distinct in terms of the likelihood of being ended deliberately, which is close to zero for family relationships but much higher for peer relations. From a transactional perspective, there is more to kin relations than just provision and receipt of social support. Our families are the place where primary socialization happens and where health related behaviors are learned. Despite changes in contact frequency with parents and siblings over the life course, feelings of emotional closeness toward family members remain relatively stable over time. Clearly, genetic kinship is one of the most powerful predictors of emotional closeness in relationships, and we are not aware of any other structural variable predicting relationship quality to such an extent (Neyer & Lang, 2003). Although kin relationships play such an important role, relationship research has only recently begun to explicitly address the psychological functions of different kinds of kin relationship such as grandparental or avuncular relationships, and future research is very much required pointing to the possible adaptive functions of the different subsystems of kinship.

FRIENDSHIP

Although the nature of friendships has concerned people at all times, our knowledge on this type of relationship is still very limited. In their recently published textbook on the psychology of interpersonal relationships, Ellen Berscheid and Pamela Regan (2005) subsume friend relationships under the category of neglected types of relationships. Research on friendship is fragmented and a consensus in the definition of friendship is still lacking. One aspect that distinguishes friend relationships from other types of relationships is that they are almost always voluntary. There is no social institution such as marriage for romantic relationships that defines the nature of the bond of friendship, nor is friendship determined by blood ties or place of residence. As Hays (1988) formulates, friendship is intended to facilitate social-emotional goals. Thus, friends can be an important source of social or emotional support, especially because of the voluntary character of friendship. Having a large network of friends and thus possible sources of social support is influenced by basic personality traits. Individuals who have higher values in extraversion, who are described as gregarious and warm and who like being in the centre of attention, tend to have larger friendship networks (Asendorpf & Wilpers, 1998).

WORKING RELATIONSHIPS

Work relationships are an even darker continent on the relationship map. Even though we spend most of our time with colleagues at work, we know nearly nothing about how these kinds of relationship affect well-being and health. One could easily imagine several possible relationships between relationships with co-workers or supervisors and health outcomes. Detrimental effects on well-being and even physical health are investigated in the context of mobbing. Mobbing refers to emotional abuse at the workplace and incorporates all means colleagues or superiors use to force someone out of the workplace through rumor, innuendo, intimidation, humiliation, discrediting, and isolation. These are negative relationship experiences in the context of work which have negative implications on health (e.g., Einarsen & Raknes, 1997), and one could speculate that these experiences in the long run may lead to personality change, e.g., an increase in negative affectivity. But being unemployed, on the other hand, is also a risk factor for developing health problems. Thus, in our society finding an occupation according to one's talents and interests is a central aspect of human development. Hence, starting an occupation is a central normative task in young adulthood. Mastering this task is associated with establishing relationships with colleagues. Roberts et al. (2003) investigated how new work experiences affected personality development. They found personality developed in such a way that those traits that lead individuals to choose a certain occupation became accentuated with the new experiences. According to the corresponsive principle these traits tend to become more pronounced, thus increasing person-environment fit. It can be assumed that a good fit between a person and his or her environment is related to positive affect and has beneficial effects on well-being.

THE DARK SIDE OF RELATIONSHIPS

So far, most of the evidence discussed emphasized the positive effect of relationships on health or well-being. But as everybody knows, relationships do not only have positive effects. Remember our two protagonists from the example given at the beginning of the chapter: Peter and Paul. Although we discussed that the extraverted, socially integrated Peter has a better prognosis for becoming healthy again, we only briefly mentioned the detrimental effects of his work and relationship environment as well as his personality structure for the improvement of his condition. Does his personality allow him to perceive and accept the support that his family can provide? How demanding are his colleagues? Does his boss accept that he has to reduce his work load? Will Peter be able to see himself as being unhealthy and a person in need?

Being aware of receiving support from relationship partners can have emotional costs. It could remind Peter of his illness, although he—being extraverted—prefers seeing himself as a strong, active, and independent person. This could reduce his self-esteem, which in turn could have negative effects on his immune system. Bolger, Zuckerman and Kessler (2000) tested the hypothesis that perceiving support has emotional costs for the individual. They found that if a person who is in a stressful life situation perceived receiving support but the partner did not report that he or she provided support, depression increased. However, in the situation they call invisible support, i.e. when a partner reports that he or she gave social support but the recipient did not report any perception of support, depression decreased over time.

CONCLUSION

The dynamic transactions between personality and social relationships can be summarized as follows: Interindividual differences in basic traits affect the environment through selective, evocative, and reactive transaction processes. We have argued that these processes become most profoundly sustained in the initiation, maintenance, and moulding of social relationships. On the contrary, during normative transitions and the acquisition of new social roles, new relationship experiences can affect and trigger personality change. Thus, personality and relationship development over the life span contribute to positive and negative health outcomes such as longevity, well-being, or differential susceptibility to diseases. The perspective of the personality-relationship transaction helps to understand the complex processes through which health is related to individuals' enduring characteristics and specific relationship experiences. In the end, we should keep in mind that relationships are among the most important things in people's lives. Zest in life comes more than anything from feeling love and giving love and affection. Meaningful relationships with others are an essential feature of what it means to be fully human.

REFERENCES

Aldwin, C.M. & Levenson, M.R. (1994). Aging and personality assessment. In M.P. Lawton & J.A. Teresi (eds), *Annual review of gerontology and geriatrics: Focus on assessment techniques* (pp. 182–209). New York: Springer.

Allport, G.W. (1961). *Pattern and growth in personality*. New York: Holt, Rinehart and Winston.

Asendorpf, J.B. (2002). The puzzle of personality types. *European Journal of Personality, 16*, 1–5.

Asendorpf, J.B. (2004). *Psychologie der Persönlichkeit (Personality Psychology)*. Berlin: Springer.

Asendorpf, J.B. & Banse, R. (2000). *Psychologie der Beziehung* [Psychology of relationships]. Berlin: Springer.

Asendorpf, J.B. & van Aken, M.A.G. (1994). Traits and relationships status: Stranger versus peer group inhibition and test intelligence. *Child Development, 65*, 1786–1798.

Asendorpf, J.B. & van Aken, M.A.G. (2003). Personality-relationship transactions in adolescence: Core versus surface personality characteristics. *Journal of Personality, 71*, 629–666.

Asendorpf, J.B. & Wilpers, S. (1998). Personality effects on social relationships. *Journal of Personality and Social Psychology, 74*, 1531–1544.

Baltes, P.B. (1997). On the incomplete architecture of human ontogeny: Selection, optimization, and compensation as foundation of developmental theory. *American Psychologist, 52*, 366–380.

Berscheid, E. & Regan, P. (2005). *The psychology of interpersonal relationships*. Upper Saddle River: Pearson.

Bolger, N., Zuckerman, A. & Kessler, R.C. (2000). Invisible support and adjustment to stress. *Journal of Personality and Social Psychology, 79*, 953–961.

Bost, K.K., Cox, M.J., Burchinal, M.R. & Payne, C. (2002). Structural and supportive changes in couples' family and friendship networks across the transition to parenthood. *Journal of Marriage and the Family, 64*, 517–531.

Bott, E. (1957). *Family and social network*. London, UK: Tavistock.

Branje, S.J.T., van Lieshout, C.F.M. & van Aken, M.A.G. (2004). Relations between Big Five personality characteristics and perceived support in adolescents' families. *Journal of Personality and Social Psychology, 86*, 615–628.

Caspi, A. (1998). Personality development across the life course. In W. Damon & N. Eisenberg (eds), *Handbook of child psychology* (pp. 311–388). Hoboken, NJ: John Wiley & Sons, Inc.

Caspi, A. (2000). The child is father of the man: Personality continuities from childhood to adulthood. *Journal of Personality and Social Psychology, 78*, 158–172.

Caspi, A. & Bem, D.J. (1990). Personality continuity and change across the life course. In L.A. Pervin (ed.), *Handbook of personality: Theory and research* (pp. 549–575). New York: Guilford Press.

Caspi, A. & Herbener, E.S. (1992). Shared experiences and the similarity of personalities: A longitudinal study of married couples. *Journal of Personality and Social Psychology, 62*, 281–291.

Caspi, A. & Moffitt, T.E. (1993). When do individual differences matter? A paradoxical theory of personality coherence. *Psychological Inquiry, 4*, 247–271.

Caspi, A. & Roberts, B.W. (1999). Personality continuity and change across the life course. In L.A. Pervin & O.P. John (eds), *Handbook of personality: Theory and research* (2nd edn) (pp. 300–326). New York: Guilford Press.

Caspi, A. & Roberts, B.W. (2001). Personality development across the life course: The argument for change and continuity. *Psychological Inquiry, 12*, 49–66.

Caspi, A. & Silva, P.A. (1995). Temperamental qualities at age three predict personality traits in young adulthood: Longitudinal evidence from a birth cohort. *Child Development, 66*, 486–498.

Cicirelli, V. (1995). *Sibling relationships across the life span*. New York: Plenum Publishing.

Costa Jr., P.T. & McCrae, R.R. (1994). Set like plaster? Evidence for the stability of adult personality. In T.F. Heatherton & J.L. Weinberger (eds), *Can personality change?* (pp. 21–40). Washington: American Psychological Association.

Einarsen, S. & Raknes, B.I. (1997). Harassment in the workplace and the victimization of men. *Violence and Victims, 12*, 247–263.

Elder, G.H. & Shanahan, M.J. (2006). The life course and human development. In W. Damon & R.M. Lerner (eds), *Handbook of child psychology*. Hoboken, NJ: John Wiley & Sons, Inc.

Fraley, R.C. & Roberts, B.W. (2005). Patterns of continuity: A dynamic model for conceptualizing the stability of individual differences in psychological constructs across the life course. *Psychological Review, 112*, 60–74.

Grayson, D.K. (1990). Donner party deaths: A demographic assessment. *Journal of Anthropological Research, 46*, 223–242.

Gruber-Baldini, A.L., Schaie, K.W. & Willis, S.L. (1995). Similarity in married couples: A longitudinal study of mental abilities and rigidity-flexibility. *Journal of Personality and Social Psychology, 69*, 191–203.

Haan, N., Millsap, R. & Hartka, E. (1986). As time goes by: Change and stability in personality over fifty years. *Psychology & Aging, 1*, 220–232.

Hays, R.B. (1988). Friendship. In S. Duck & D.F. Hay (eds), *Handbook of personal relationships: Theory, research and interventions* (pp. 391–408). Hoboken, NJ: John Wiley & Sons, Inc.

Helson, R. & Moane, G. (1987). Personality change in women from college to midlife. *Journal of Personality and Social Psychology, 53*, 176–186.

Hinde, R. (1993). Auf dem Weg zu einer Wissenschaft zwischenmenschlicher Beziehungen [On the way toward a science of social relationships]. In A. E. Auhagen & M. von Salisch (eds), *Zwischenmenschliche Beziehungen (Interpersonal Relationships)* (pp. 7–36). Göttingen: Hogrefe.

Holmes, T.H. & Rahe, R.H. (1967). The social readjustment rating scale. *Journal of Psychosomatic Research, 11*, 213–218.

House, J.S., Landis, K.R. & Umberson, D. (1988). Social relationships and health. *Science, 241*, 540–545.

Johnson, W., McGue, M., Krueger, R.F. & Bouchard, T.J., Jr. (2004). Marriage and personality: A genetic analysis. *Journal of Personality and Social Psychology, 86*, 285–294.

Karney, B.R. & Bradbury, T.N. (1995). The longitudinal course of marital quality and stability: A review of theory, methods, and research. *Psychological Bulletin, 118*, 3–34.

Karney, B.R. & Bradbury, T.N. (1997). Neuroticism, marital interaction, and the trajectory of marital satisfaction. *Journal of Personality and Social Psychology, 72*, 1075–1092.

Lang, F.R. (2000). Ending and continuity of social relationships: Maximizing intrinsic benefits within personal networks when feeling near to death. *Journal of Social and Personal Relationships, 17*, 155–182.

Lang, F.R. & Carstensen, L.L. (1998). Social relationships and adaptation in late life. In A. S. Bellak & M. Hersen (eds), *Comprehensive clinical psychology* (Vol. 7, pp. 55–72). Oxford: Pergamon Press.

Lang, F.R., Reschke, F. & Neyer, F.J. (2006). Social relationships, transitions, and personality development across the life span. In D.K. Mroczek & T.D. Little (eds), *Handbook of personality development* (pp. 445–466). Mahwah: Lawrence Erlbaum.

Lykken, D.T. & Tellegen, A. (1993). Is human mating adventitious or the result of lawful choice? A twin study of mate selection. *Journal of Personality and Social Psychology*, 65, 56–68.

Magnusson, D. (1990). Personality development from an interactional perspective. In L.A. Pervin (ed.), *Handbook of personality: Theory and research*. (pp. 193–222). New York: Guilford Press.

Martin, L.R. & Friedman, H.S. (2000). Comparing personality scales across time: An illustrative study of validity and consistency in life-span archival data. *Journal of Personality*, 68, 85–110.

McAdams, D.P. (2001). The psychology of life stories. *Review of General Psychology*, 5, 100–122.

McCrae, R.R., Costa, P.T.J., de Lima, M.P., Simoes, A., Ostendorf, F., Angleitner, A., Marusic, I., Bratko, D., Caprara, G.V., Barbaranelli, C., Chae, J.H. & Piedmont, R.L. (1999). Age differences in personality across the adult life span: Parallels in five cultures. *Developmental Psychology*, 35, 466–477.

McCrae, R.R., Costa, P.T.J., Ostendorf, F., Angleitner, A., Hrebickova, M., Avia, M.D., Sanz, J., Sanchez-Bernardoz, M.L., Kusdul, M.E., Woodfield, R., Saunders, P.R. & Smith P.B. (2000). Nature over nurture: Temperament, personality, and life span development. *Journal of Personality and Social Psychology*, 78, 173–186.

Mroczek, D.K. & Spiro, A. (2003). Modeling intraindividual change in personality traits: Findings from the Normative Aging Study. *Journals of Gerontology: Series B: Psychological Sciences and Social Sciences*, 58, 153–165.

Mroczek, D.K. & Spiro, A. (2005). Change in life satisfaction during adulthood: Findings from the Veterans Affairs Normative Aging Study. *Journal of Personality and Social Psychology*, 88, 189–202.

Neyer, F.J. (1997). Free recall or recognition in collecting egocentered networks: The role of survey techniques. *Journal of Social and Personal Relationships*, 14, 305–316.

Neyer, F.J. (2002). Twin relationships in old age: A developmental perspective. *Journal of Social and Personal Relationships*, 19, 155–177.

Neyer, F.J. (2003). Persönlichkeit und Partnerschaft [Personality and partnership]. In H. W. Bierhoff & I. Grau (eds), *Sozialpsychologie der Partnerschaft* [Social psychology of partnership] (pp. 165–189). Berlin: Springer.

Neyer, F.J. (2004). Dyadic fits and transactions in personality and relationships. In F.R. Lang & K.L. Fingerman (eds), *Growing together: Personal relationships across the lifespan* (pp. 290–316). Cambridge: Cambridge University Press.

Neyer, F.J. & Asendorpf, J.B. (2001). Personality-relationship transaction in young adulthood. *Journal of Personality and Social Psychology*, 81, 1190–1204.

Neyer, F.J. & Lang, F.R. (2003). Blood is thicker than water: Kinship orientation across adulthood. *Journal of Personality and Social Psychology*, 84, 310–321.

Neyer, F.J. & Lehnart, J. (2006). Relationships matter in personality development: Evidence from an 8-year longitudinal study across young adulthood. Manuscript submitted for publication.

Neyer, F.J. & Voigt, D. (2004). Personality and social network effects on romantic relationships: A dyadic approach. *European Journal of Personality*, 18, 279–299.

Roberts, B.W. & Caspi, A. (2003). The cumulative continuity model of personality development: Striking a balance between continuity and change in personality traits accross the life course. In U.M. Staudinger & U. Lindenberger (eds), *Understanding human development: Dialogues with lifespan psychology* (pp. 183–214). Dordrecht: Kluwer Academic Publishers.

Roberts, B.W., Caspi, A. & Moffitt, T.E. (2001). The kids are alright: Growth and stability in personality development from adolescence to adulthood. *Journal of Personality and Social Psychology*, 81, 670–683.

Roberts, B.W., Caspi, A. & Moffitt, T.E. (2003). Work experiences and personality development in young adulthood. *Journal of Personality and Social Psychology*, 84, 582–593.

Roberts, B.W. & DelVecchio, W.F. (2000). The rank-order consistency of personality traits from childhood to old age: A quantitative review of longitudinal studies. *Psychological Bulletin*, 126, 3–25.

Roberts, B.W., Helson, R. & Klohnen, E.C. (2002). Personality development and growth in women across 30 years: Three perspectives. *Journal of Personality*, 70, 79–102.

Roberts, B.W. & Robins, R.W. (2004). Person-environment fit and its implications for personality development: A longitudinal study. *Journal of Personality, 72,* 89–110.

Roberts, B.W., Walton, K.E. & Viechtbauer (2006). Patterns of mean-level change in personality traits across the life-course: A meta-analysis of longitudinal studies. *Psychological Bulletin, 132,* 1–25.

Roberts, B.W., Wood, D. & Smith, J.L. (2005). Evaluating Five Factor Theory and social investment perspectives on personality trait development. *Journal of Research in Personality, 39,* 166–184.

Robins, R.W., Caspi, A. & Moffitt, T.E. (2000). Two personalities, one relationship: Both partners' personality traits shape the quality of their relationship. *Journal of Personality and Social Psychology, 79,* 251–259.

Robins, R.W., Caspi, A. & Moffitt, T.E. (2002). It's not who you're with, it's who you are: Personality and relationship experiences across multiple relationships. *Journal of Personality, 70,* 925–964.

Ross, C.E., Mirowsky, J. & Goldsteen, K. (1990). The impact of the family on health: The decade in review. *Journal of Marriage and the Family, 52,* 1059–1078.

Sameroff, A.J. (1983). Models of development and developmental risk. In C.H. Zeanah (ed.), *Handbook of infant mental health* (pp. 3–13). New York: Guilford Press.

Sarason, B.R., Sarason, I.G. & Gurung, R.A.R. (1997). Close personal relationships and health outcomes: A key to the role of social support. In S. Duck (ed.), *Handbook of personal relationships: Theory, research and interventions* (2nd edn) (pp. 547–573). Hoboken, NJ: John Wiley & Sons, Inc.

Sarason, I.G., Sarason, B.R. & Pierce, G.R. (1992). The contexts of social support. In H.O. Veiel & U. Baumann (eds), *Meaning and measurement of social support* (pp. 143–154). New York: Hemisphere Publishing.

Schulenberg, J.E., Bryant, A.L. & O'Malley, P.M. (2004). Taking hold of some kind of life: How developmental tasks relate to trajectories of well-being during the transition to adulthood. *Development and Psychopathology, 16,* 1119–1140.

Seeman, T. (2001). How do others get under our skin? Social relationships and health. In C.D. Ryff & B.H. Singer (eds), *Emotion, Social Relationships, and Health* (pp. 189–210). Oxford: Oxford University Press.

Shiner, R.L. (1998). How shall we speak of children's personalities in middle childhood? A preliminary taxonomy. *Psychological Bulletin, 124,* 308–332.

Shye, D., Mullooly, J.P., Freeborn, D.K. & Pope, C.R. (1995). Gender differences in the relationship between social network support and mortality: a longitudinal study of an elderly cohort. *Social Science and Medicine, 41,* 935–947.

Sprecher, S., Felmlee, D., Orbuch, T.L. & Willetts, M.C. (2002). Social networks and change in personal relationships. In A.L. Vangelisti & H.T. Reis (eds), *Stability and change in relationships.* (pp. 257–284). Cambridge: Cambridge University Press.

Srivastava, S., John, O.P., Gosling, S.D. & Potter, J. (2003). Development of personality in early and middle adulthood: Set like plaster or persistent change? *Journal of Personality and Social Psychology, 84,* 1041–1053.

Tucker, J.S., Friedman, H.S., Wingard, D.L. & Schwartz, J.E. (1996). Marital history at midlife as a predictor of longevity: Alternative explanations to the protective effect of marriage. *Health Psychology, 15,* 94–101.

Tucker, J.S., Schwartz, J.E., Clark, K.M. & Friedman, H.S. (1999). Age-related changes in the associations of social network ties with mortality risk. *Psychology and Aging, 14,* 564–571.

Umberson, D. (1987). Family status and health behaviours: Social control as a dimension of social integration. *Journal of Health and Social Behaviour, 28,* 306–319.

CHAPTER 10

Personality Types, Personality Traits, and Risky Health Behavior

Svenn Torgersen and Margarete E. Vollrath
University of Oslo, Norway

INTRODUCTION

All fun is either prohibited or fattening. This German saying epitomizes the dilemmas surrounding many enjoyable but risky behaviors. Smoking, excessive consumption of alcohol, promiscuous sexual behavior, reckless driving, and unhealthy eating are major preventable risk factors for disease, disability, and death. These and other health compromising behaviors will be labeled risky health behaviors in the following. Like all behaviors, risky health behaviors are substantially influenced by personality. It is to the credit of two giants in personality psychology, Hans Jürgen Eysenck and Marvin Zuckerman, to have put this relationship onto the research agenda. Numerous other researchers have followed in their footsteps and contributed to a burgeoning literature.

However, their findings have not remained without contradictions. Although research in the Eysenck tradition has provided solid evidence that individuals high in Neuroticism, Extraversion, and Psychoticism are more prone to risky health behaviors, more recent studies do not always concur. This is particularly true for Neuroticism and Extraversion. The problem with Zuckerman's Sensation-seeking trait has been that the measure contains items tapping risky health behavior, whereby the outcome and the predictor partly overlap. The only major personality factor consistently predicting risky health behaviors is lack of Constraint or Non-conscientiousness, which strongly overlaps with the Impulsiveness component of both Eysenck's Psychoticism and Zuckerman's Sensation-seeking.

Risky health behaviors tend to cluster together. We all have among our acquaintances the model person leading a monastic life and the daredevil who burns the candle at both ends. Such individuals can be best understood not through an assembly of single traits but through configurations of characteristics that together lead to unique health consequences. These configurations are captured by the term personality types.

The aim of this chapter is to demonstrate the extent to which personality impacts on a broad range of health behaviors. We will sketch the body of research available on the link

---

Handbook of Personality and Health. Edited by Margarete E. Vollrath. © 2006 John Wiley & Sons, Ltd.

between major personality factors and risky health behaviors. Our focus, however, will be to show how the study of personality types complements and nuances this picture. The first part of this chapter gives background information on the most popular personality typologies to date, one of them proposed by Jack Block and Jeanne Block, the other by Avshalom Caspi and collaborators. In the second part of the chapter, we focus on empirical evidence relating major personality factors and personality types, including those from our own typology, to risky health behaviors.

Personality Types

Traits Versus Types

Disagreement between promoters of personality types and promoters of personality traits and dimensions has existed throughout the whole history of personality psychology. Those who like types put forward their heuristic value, their similarity to the way persons are described in everyday language, and the fact that combinations of traits or dimensions describe an individual with characteristics that are not revealed if only the single traits are studied. In contrast, the promoters of traits and dimensions maintain, first, that variance is lost if dimensions are collapsed into a dichotomy. Second, they hold that the same types are not uniformly observed in different samples when different assessment techniques are utilized.

There have been many attempts at a solution. For example, in the 2002 Special Issue of the *European Journal of Personality*, a number of authors devoted themselves to the problem of the validity of typological personality descriptions (Asendorpf, 2002; Barbaranelli, 2002; Boehm, Asendorpf & Avia, 2002; Costa, Herbst, McCrae, Samuels & Ozer, 2002; De Fruyt, Mervielde & Van Leeuwen, 2002; Schnabel, Asendorpf & Ostendorf, 2002). The authors addressed two questions: (1) whether the types or the interaction between dimensions explained more variance than the separate dimensions, and (2) whether the same types were replicated in different samples.

As expected, Costa and colleagues (2002) observed that if the Big Five personality dimensions were entered first into a regression analysis, the types (interaction terms) did not explain much more of the variance. But if the types were entered first, the Big Five explained a great deal more variance. This is hardly surprising; categorical types can seldom compete with continuous dimensions in taking care of variance. Yet, this fact has never bothered those who use diagnoses of mental disorders. The dimensions of psychic anxiety, somatic anxiety, phobic fears, shyness, and so on explain more variance than the categorical diagnoses of generalized anxiety, social anxiety, panic disorder, and others. Even so, any efforts to replace diagnoses with dimensions have always been in vain. The diagnoses of personality disorders are especially close to personality dimensions and can even be represented by personality dimension profiles (Saulsman & Page, 2004). Yet, nobody seriously believes that a substitution will take place in the foreseeable future. Diagnoses are simply a much better container of knowledge and much easier to communicate.

The historical split between personality psychology and clinical psychology may be responsible for much of the skepticism about types in personality psychology. However, not least because of the central position that personality disorders received in the third edition of the *Diagnostic and Statistical Manual of Mental Disorders* (DSM) (American

Psychiatric Association, 1980), clinical psychology and personality psychology have been approaching each other, as witnessed by recent issues of major journals in personality psychology.

Before addressing the second problem—whether the same types are consistently observed in different samples—we will draw a line back to the start of typological research in modern psychology.

Block and Block's Types

A natural point of departure is Jack Block and Jeanne Block's pivotal research. In the 1950s, they developed their concepts of Ego-Resilience and Ego-Control from psychoanalytic theory and Kurt Lewin's theory (J. Block, 1950; J.H. Block, 1951). Later, they used a tool for personality ratings by observers, the California Child Q-Set (CCQ) (J. Block, 1978) (first unpublished version 1961) to describe adolescents' personality in a longitudinal study reaching from adolescence to early adulthood (J. Block, 1971). A method of inverse factor analysis based on Q-sort was applied to identify clusters of individuals. Five clusters or types were discovered, three of which remained stable through adolescence and early adulthood: Ego-Resilients (well-adjusted and interpersonally effective), Unsettled Undercontrollers (highly impulsive and antisocial), and Vulnerable Overcontrollers (rigidly overcontrolled and maladapted). In addition they identified two types that not did not remain stable: Belated Adjusters (in adolescence: combined maladjusted characteristics of both Undercontrollers and Overcontrollers) having problems in adolescence, but not in adulthood, and Anomic Extraverts (in adolescence: gregarious, vigorous, cheerful, confident) first developing problems in early adulthood.

In addition, Block developed scales of Ego-resilience and Ego-control from the Minnesota Multiphasic Personality Inventory (MMPI) (J. Block, 1965), and finally constructed a new scale of Ego-resilience (ERI89), as a summing up of the experience over many years (Block and Kremen, 1996). However, much confusion has arisen because the typology of Ego-resilients, Undercontrollers, and Overcontrollers is not the same as the dimensions of Ego-resilience and Ego-control. Block originally developed both the types and the traits from the same Q-sort items (in addition to the MMPI and later new items). However, he classified individuals into types based on correlations with prototypes, while using the scores on the dimensions of Ego-resilience and Ego-control to validate the types. In fact, whereas the Resilients were expected to be high in Ego-resilience, they scored only average on the scale of Ego-control (J.H. Block & J. Block, 1980).

Robins, John, Caspi, Moffit and Stouthamer-Loeber (1996) set out to replicate this validation. They had parents rate their 12-year-old children using the same CCQ as Block and Block. The Q-sort techniques and inverse factor analysis yielded just the same types as Block and Block had found: a Resilient type (self-confident, independent, verbally fluent, and able to concentrate on tasks), an Overcontrolled type (shy, quiet, anxious, and dependable), and an Undercontrolled type (impulsive, stubborn, and physically active).

The relation of the types to the two dimensions Ego-resilience and Ego-control showed the pattern proposed by Block: children classified as Resilients scored high on Ego-resilience and average on Ego-control. Children classified as Undercontrollers scored low on Ego-resilience and toward the lower end of the Ego-control dimension. The Overcontrollers, in contrast, scored just as low on Ego-resilience as the Undercontrollers, but toward the higher end of the Ego-control dimension. Children that were either overcontrolled or un-dercontrolled from a dimensional point of view, and were at the same time high on the Ego-resilience dimension, were more or less absent, thus making it unnecessary to create two additional types, a Resilient Overcontrolled type and a Resilient Undercontrolled type. Robins et al. (1996) also found that Resilients had the highest IQs and the lowest preva-lence of psychopathology. Among Undercontrolleds, psychopathological problems were the most prevalent, as judged by teachers as well as parents, especially externalization problems only and externalization/internalization problems combined. In contrast, Overcontrolleds showed internalization problems the most often.

A longitudinal study following Icelandic children from the age of 7 used the same Q-sort technique for ratings of interview transcripts (Hart et al., 1997). These researchers found the same Resilient and Overcontrolled types as Block (1971) and Robins et al. (1996). Seven-year-old Resilients were attentive and able to concentrate, helpful, and cooperative. The Overcontrolled children kept their thoughts and feelings to themselves and yielded when in conflict with others. However, the (few) Undercontrolled children were different. They were vital, energetic, and lively, were unable to delay gratification, and had difficulty in maintaining prolonged focus on a single activity. They did not show the same extent of interpersonal maladaptation as did the Undercontrolleds in the study by Robins et al. (1996), that is, they were not as manipulative, stubborn, sensitive, irritated, and disobedi-ent. Some of the differences were probably because Robins et al. (1996) studied only boys. However, perhaps the most important reason for the difference is age; Robins et al. studied children aged 12–13 years, as opposed to 7-year-olds. In addition, it may be that children in Iceland are different from children in the United States (the study found few Undercon-trolled children in Iceland), and information about impulsivity was largely absent from the interview transcripts. However, by the time of the follow-up assessment in adolescence the Undercontrolleds in Iceland appeared to be more aggressive. The Overcontrolleds showed greater social withdrawal and lower self-esteem, whereas the Resilients had greater suc-cess in school, fewer concentration problems in the classroom, and higher levels of social cognitive development.

Caspi's Types

In the early 1970s, Phil A. Silva and collaborators initiated a study in Dunedin, a small town in New Zealand, the Dunedin Multidisciplinary Health and Development Study. This study has since had an immense effect on modern typology research (Silva, 1990). Having thoroughly assessed information on pregnancy and delivery, the researchers invited families of children born in a one-year period and living in the surrounding county to participate in the study: More than 1,000 children were studied every second year from age 3 to age 15 and thereafter at the ages of 18, 21, and 26 years. While initially the study had a somatic, medical leaning, it came to focus increasingly on the children's psychological, behavioral development. Ron McGee published a number of papers in this area early on (one of the first is by McGee, Silva and Williams (1984)). Later, Terrie Moffit became more and more involved in the study, and finally Avshalom Caspi (often publishing together with Moffitt) took over. One article from 1995 is authored by all the four central persons that have pro-moted the study at different times through the years (Caspi et al., 1995). The article described the development of factors based on the 1970s 'state of the art' ratings of temperament by psychologists. Although the examiners did not utilize well-tested psychometrical instruments, three factors emerged that showed moderate stability through childhood (Caspi et al., 1995). The first factor, Lack of Control, included items denoting emotional lability, restlessness, short attention span, and negativism. The second factor, Approach, described little caution around the examiner, quick adjustment to the new situation, extreme ease in social interactions, self-confidence, and self-reliance. The third factor, Sluggishness, included ratings of shyness, fearfulness, limited verbal communication, passivity, and flat affect. Caspi and colleagues then also applied cluster techniques to the temperament ratings, and five clusters were established. Undercontrolleds showed Lack of Control and were characterized by restlessness and concentration problems. They had somewhat elevated scores on the factor Approach. As compared to Undercontrolled children, Confidents were lower on Lack of Control. Inhibiteds differed from the Undercontrolleds in being more Sluggish and lower on Approach. However, they shared with Undercontrolleds the concentration problems. Reserveds were different from Inhibited children in being lower on the Lack of Control factor. They were especially much lower on concentration problems and somewhat less Sluggish. Finally, the large Well-adjusted group was average or low on all ratings and on all of the factors—in fact, they were also average on the adjustment traits! Hence, this group was large, making up around half of the sample.

Robins et al. (1996) incorporated the Dunedin typology into the Block typology by calling the Well-adjusteds Resilients, the Inhibited Overcontrollers, and the Undercontrolleds, yes simply, Undercontrollers. Subsequently, Costa and colleagues in their contribution to the Special Issue of the *European Journal of Personality* edited by Asendorpf et al. (2002), gallantly dubbed the typology the Asendorpf-Robins-Caspi (or ARC)-typology (Costa, Herbst, McCrae, Samuels & Ozer, 2002).

Several studies have examined the replicability of the three clusters in different populations, including children, adolescents, adults, and with various measures of the Big Five factors that were partly self-administered, partly administered by caretakers (Asendorpf, Borkenau, Ostendorf & van Aken, 2001; Barbaranelli, 2002; Boehm, Asendorpf & Avia, 2002; Costa, Herbst, McCrae, Samuels & Ozer, 2002; De Fruyt, Mervielde & Van Leeuwen, 2002; Rammstedt, Riemann, Angleitner & Borkenau, 2004; Robins, John, Caspi, Moffitt & Stouthamer Loeber, 1996; Schnabel, Asendorpf & Ostendorf, 2002). In most cases, the studies applied cluster analysis and presented z-scores in histograms and curves. The contributors and the editors of the Special Issue of the *European Journal of Personality* (Asendorpf, Caspi & Hofstee, 2002), in which a majority of the studies were published, concluded that the results were mixed. The only consistently verified cluster was the Resilient cluster.

We would like to interpret these results differently. We carried out a secondary analysis across these studies by systematizing the 25 reported three-cluster analyses. A z-score of 0.30 or higher on a personality dimension was taken as an indication that a type was characterized by the specific personality dimension. Across studies, we found that the Resilient cluster was consistently confirmed. However, the types the authors denoted as Overcontrollers, respectively Undercontrollers, in reality seemed to constitute not two, but three different types of clusters, as we shall see below.

Our secondary analysis showed that the Resilient cluster was characterized by low Neuroticism (100 % of the analyses), high Extraversion (84 %), high Conscientiousness (76 %), high Agreeableness (60 %), and high Openness (40 %). (Studies yielding negative results were subtracted; that is, if five studies yielded a z-score above .30 and one study yielded a z-score below −0.30, we concluded that four studies yielded a high z-score.)

The next most common cluster (found in 24 of the 25 analyses) was characterized by high Neuroticism (88 % of the analyses), high Introversion (76 %), low Openness (68 %), low Conscientiousness (46 %), and low Agreeableness (38 %). The individuals in this cluster were most often labeled Overcontrollers (54 %), but in some studies, they were also labeled Undercontrollers (21 %). In the rest of the studies, they did not receive any label. In reality, the cluster is clearly the opposite of the Resilient cluster, and it resembles Block's concept of 'Brittleness', as mentioned in Block and Kremen (1996), for example.

The third most common cluster (17 of 25) was most frequently named Undercontrollers (82 %). It was characterized by low Conscientiousness (88 %), high Extraversion (29 %), low Agreeableness (29 %), and high Neuroticism (12 %). It rightly deserves the label Undercontrollers.

Finally, eight additional clusters called Overcontrollers in 75 % of the cases were characterized by high Conscientiousness (100 %), high Introversion (63 %), high Neuroticism (38 %), low Openness (25 %), and high Agreeableness (13 %). This relatively rare cluster is really an Overcontrollers cluster according to the Block typology.

Thus, the frequently emerging cluster of non-resilient, brittle individuals, in Block's terms, seems to have confused the authors. There exists an axis from Resilience to Brittleness, with Undercontrollers and Overcontrollers on each side of the axis, as Figure 10.1 suggests.

If we turn back to Caspi and colleagues' typology (Caspi et al., 2003), we can examine the personality measurements they administered to their sample at 18 and 26 years. Looking at the personality profiles of the types on the Big Five, and not least the Multidimensional

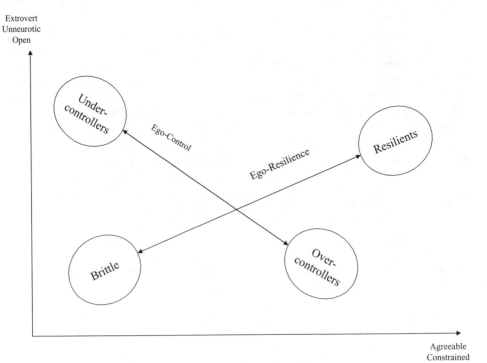

Figure 10.1 Block and Caspi's types in a personality dimensional space

Personality Questionnaire (Tellegen, 1982), we find that the type that Caspi and Silva (Caspi & Silva, 1995) called Undercontrolled is rather similar to the 'Brittle' type in our reanalysis of the empirical validation of the Block typology. The Inhibited type is most similar to the Overcontrollers, while the Well-adjusted, Reserved, and Confident types do not show a personality profile differing from that of the average participant at the ages of 18 and 26 (Caspi et al., 2003). If we adopt a liberal interpretation, the Well-adjusteds can be said to be most similar to the Resilients. The same is the case for the Confidents, while the Reserveds are something in between the Resilients and the Overcontrolleds. However, we should perhaps not expect so much more correspondence between a typology found in three-year-olds and their personality profile at the age of 18 and 26 years.

Torgersen's Types

Torgersen (1995) proposed eight types that were defined a priori based on a dichotomization of 'the Big Three', a personality paradigm of biologically rooted temperament or personality traits that precedes the Five-Factor model and competes with it (Clark & Watson, 1990, 1999; Eysenck, 1994; Eysenck & Eysenck, 1975; Gough, 1987; Tellegen, 1982). This personality paradigm comprises three broad dimensions of personality, labeled here Neuroticism vs. Emotional Stability, Extraversion vs. Introversion, and Constraint vs. Lack of Constraint. When high and low scores (above and below the median) on Neuroticism, Extraversion, and Constraint are combined, the following eight unique personality types result (see Table 10.1).

Torgersen examined the types' functioning with respect to mental disorders, including personality disorders, in various samples of twins and psychiatric patients and found marked differences. Spectators (introverted, emotionally stable, non-constrained) are detached from their own self, from other people, and from social norms. They are quiet, impassive, and tend to be loners. Insecures (introverted, neurotic, non-constrained) are self-conscious, dependent on dominating others, and poorly organized. Skeptics (introverted, emotionally stable, constrained) are effective and independent no-nonsense personalities. Brooders (introverted, neurotic, constrained) are shy and self-conscious, pedantic, often in doubt, and tend to ruminate about their own behavior and that of others. Hedonists (extraverted, emotionally stable, non-constrained) brim with self-confidence, crave intense experiences, and are neither persistent nor morally restrained. Impulsives (extraverted, emotionally unstable, non-constrained) are pleasure and attention-seeking, unpredictable, and chaotic individuals. Entrepreneurs (extraverted, emotionally stable, constrained) are socially skilled, energetic,

Table 10.1 Composition of Torgersen's Eight Personality Types

Type label	Extraversion	Neuroticism	Constraint
Spectator	Low	Low	Low
Insecure	Low	High	Low
Skeptic	Low	Low	High
Brooder	Low	High	High
Hedonist	High	Low	Low
Impulsive	High	High	Low
Entrepreneur	High	Low	High
Complicated	High	High	High

goal-oriented, perseverant, well-organized individuals with a talent for leadership. Complicateds (extraverted, neurotic, constrained) make up a contradictory configuration. Differing from Impulsives only in Constraint, and from Entrepreneurs in Neuroticism, their psychological functioning varies from domain to domain.

The extraverted, constrained, non-neurotic Entrepreneurs are similar to the Resilients in Block's and Caspi's typologies. The extraverted, non-constrained, neurotic Impulsives are similar to the Undercontrollers; the introverted, constrained, neurotic Brooders are like the Overcontrollers, whereas the introverted, non-constrained, neurotic Insecures resemble the Brittle type. As to the other Torgersen types, the introverted, constrained, non-neurotic Skeptics and the introverted, non-constrained, non-neurotic Spectators appear to resemble Caspi's Reserved type, while the extraverted, non-constrained, non-neurotic Hedonists are similar to Caspi's Confident type, and the extraverted, constrained, neurotic Complicateds constitute a type in between the Resilients and the Overcontrollers.

PERSONALITY AND RISKY HEALTH BEHAVIORS

In this part of the chapter, we will show how the study of personality types can elucidate some of the contradictions that emerge when single personality traits are used to predict risky health behaviors. Risky health behaviors are behaviors that increase morbidity and mortality in the short and longer term. There are many such behaviors, most of them characterized by providing short-term satisfaction while exposing a person to long-term health hazards. We will concentrate on those risk behaviors that show the greatest effects on morbidity and mortality (Belloc, 1973; Belloc & Breslow, 1972); these are heavy use of psychoactive substances (alcohol, illicit drugs, tobacco), risky driving, risky sexual behavior, unhealthy eating and overweight, and lack of regularity of health habits. These latter two risk behaviors have not been related to personality traits very often, so that corresponding research is harder to come by.

Many personality traits could be considered here. We chose to focus on traits from the domains of the Big Three mentioned above, as they constitute the building blocks of the personality typologies described earlier in the chapter. Our review of the literature was made easier by a recently published meta-analysis that integrated and evaluated the effects of the cluster of traits falling under the heading of Conscientiousness or Constraint (Bogg & Roberts, 2004). Regarding research on traits from the domains of Extraversion and Neuroticism, we included only studies from the normal population, because patients of mental health clinics or clients of intervention programs that aim at changing particular risky behaviors often suffer from comorbid mental disorders and tend to show elevated scores on Neuroticism.

Heavy Use, Abuse of or Dependency on Psychoactive Substances

Excessive Alcohol Use

According to the meta-analysis mentioned above, alcohol abuse, such as binge drinking, getting drunk, or alcohol dependence, is consistently related to traits of the lack of Constraint domain, with an average correlation coefficient of $r = 0.25$ (Bogg & Roberts, 2004). A relation has also been documented between excessive drinking and high Extraversion (Flory, Lynam, Milich, Leukefeld & Clayton, 2002; Kjærheim, Mykletun & Haldorsen, 1996; N.G. Martin & Boomsma, 1989; Martsh & Miller, 1997; McGregor, Murray & Barnes, 2003; Merenakk et al., 2003). However, a smaller number of studies found no relation between Extraversion and drinking (Cookson, 1994; McGue, Slutske & Iacono, 1999; Stein, Newcomb & Bentler, 1987). Most inconclusive were the findings regarding the relation of Neuroticism with excessive drinking or alcohol abuse (Almada et al., 1991; Cookson, 1994; Flory, Lynam, Milich, Leukefeld & Clayton, 2002; Grau & Ortet, 1999; Kjaerheim, Mykletun & Haldorsen, 1996; Vollrath, Knoch & Cassano, 1999; Wadsworth, Moss, Simpson & Smith, 2004).

Typological analyses from the Dunedin Study (Silva, 1990) showed that the neurotic, non-constrained Undercontrollers were dependent on alcohol most often (Caspi et al., 1997). Applying Torgersen's typology in 683 Swiss students, Vollrath and Torgersen (2002) showed that Hedonists were among the heaviest beer and wine drinkers, consuming the most drinks in one go and having been drunk most frequently. Impulsives followed in second place on the alcohol ranking. At the other end of the drinking spectrum, Skeptics and Brooders consumed and abused alcohol the least. A study of 612 Norwegian university students (mean age 22 years) showed exactly the same pattern (Vollrath & Torgersen, 2006). This suggests that Extraversion must be combined with lack of Constraint to increase the risk for alcohol abuse (both Hedonists and Impulsives are extraverted and non-constrained).

Drug Abuse

Again, the meta-analysis showed that traits from the lack of Constraint domain (Bogg & Roberts, 2004) are substantially related to the use of illicit drugs such as marijuana, LSD, cocaine, and heroin (average correlation $r = 0.28$). Regarding traits from the Extraversion domain, however, research reports have been conflicting, some showing higher drug consumption in Extraverts and some showing no such relationship (Booth-Kewley & Vickers, 1994; Flory, Lynam, Milich, Leukefeld & Clayton, 2002; Knyazev, 2004; McGue, Slutske & Iacono, 1999; Merenakk et al., 2003; Sigurdsson & Gudjonsson, 1996; Zuckerman & Kuhlman, 2000). With respect to traits from the Neuroticism domain, most studies found no associations with substance abuse (Booth-Kewley & Vickers, 1994; Flory, Lynam, Milich, Leukefeld & Clayton, 2002; Knyazev, 2004; McGue, Slutske & Iacono, 1999; Miller et al., 2004), and some studies even found negative associations (Kirkcaldy, Siefen, Surall & Bischoff, 2004; Zuckerman & Kuhlman, 2000).

Turning to typological analysis, Torgersen's types showed a picture that varied somewhat from that found for alcohol use. In Swiss students, Hedonists used marijuana the most often. However, Insecures took second place, and Impulsives ranked number three. At the other end of the spectrum, Brooders practically abstained from drugs, preceded by Entrepreneurs and Spectators. The findings for 612 Norwegian students were not much different (Vollrath & Torgersen, 2006). The most use of marijuana and other drugs occurred among Impulsives and Hedonists, followed by Insecures in third place. At the lower end of the spectrum ranged Skeptics, Brooders, and Entrepreneurs, which is identical to the ranking among Swiss students.

This finding suggests that it is not only the combination of Extraversion with lack of Constraint, as embodied by Hedonists and Impulsives, that increases the liability for drug use but also the combination of Neuroticism with lack of Constraint, as embodied by

Insecures. Conversely, a combination of Introversion with Constraint appeared to be protective (Skeptics). Moreover, high Constraint also protected types high in Neuroticism (Brooders) and high in Extraversion (Entrepreneurs).

Smoking

The average correlation between personality traits from the lack of Constraint domain and smoking is lower than that with alcohol and drug use ($r = 0.14$) but still significant (Bogg & Roberts, 2004). Regarding the associations of the Extraversion and Neuroticism domains with smoking, the findings are contradictory, as summarized by a review (Gilbert, 1995). Whereas some older studies showed positive associations between both Neuroticism and Extraversion and smoking (Arai, Hosokawa, Fukao, Izumi & Hisamichi, 1997; Forgays, Bonaiuto, Wrzesniewski & Forgays, 1993), findings from newer studies could rarely document a relation (Knyazev, 2004; Spielberger, Reheiser, Foreyt, Poston & Volding, 2004; Terracciano & Costa, 2004; Wadsworth, Moss, Simpson & Smith, 2004).

Our typological studies in Swiss students showed that Insecures smoked the most, followed by Impulsives and Hedonists. Skeptics were the least likely to smoke, followed by Brooders and Complicateds (Vollrath & Torgersen, 2002). Norwegian students were similar. Hedonists smoked the most, followed by Impulsives and Insecures. Skeptics in contrast, abstained from smoking, followed by Brooders and Entrepreneurs.

Looking across the three classes of psychoactive substances (see Table 10.2), we find that Impulsives and Hedonists took the most chances, whereas Skeptics and Brooders were very cautious. The typological results clearly suggest that the effects of Neuroticism and Extraversion are contingent on lack of Constraint. Types using the most psychoactive substances showed either a combination of high Extraversion with lack of Constraint (Hedonists), high Neuroticism with lack of Constraint (Insecures and Undercontrollers), or both (Impulsives). Types keeping away from psychoactive substances showed a combination of Introversion and high Constraint, irrespective of Neuroticism (Skeptics and Brooders).

Risky Sexual Behavior

Risky sexual behavior includes having multiple partners, having one-night-stands with previously unknown partners, and failure to use condoms with new or unknown sexual partners. Studies on the lack of Constraint domain show again a consistent, albeit small, average association ($r = 0.13$) (Bogg & Roberts, 2004). Two review studies taking into account traits from other domains as well concluded that the evidence for an influence of traits from the Extraversion and Neuroticism domains was absent (Hoyle, Fejfar & Miller, 2000) or at best mixed (Trobst, Herbst, Masters & Costa, 2002).

In the Dunedin study, Undercontrolleds practiced unsafe sex, defined as having many partners and seldom using condoms (Caspi et al., 1997). Our typological analysis showed that in Swiss students, Hedonists followed by Insecures and Entrepreneurs, engaged most often in risky sexual behaviors. Skeptics and Brooders were most cautious with regard to sex (Vollrath & Torgersen, 2002). In Norwegian students, Spectators together with Impulsives were the most daring with respect to number of sexual partners and unprotected sex, followed by Hedonists. Most cautious were Brooders, followed by Skeptics.

Table 10.2 Ranking of Torgersen's types with respect to health behaviors, happiness and adjustment

	Personality Types							
	Insecures	Spectators	Brooders	Skeptics	Impulsives	Hedonists	Complicateds	Entrepreneurs
Health behaviors								
No psychoactive substances	5	4	2	1	7	7	3	4
No risky sex	6	6	1	1	4	8	3	4
No reckless driving	3	3	6	3	7	8	1	2
Healthy eating	7	8	2	3	5	5	1	3
Low Body Mass Index	6	5	1	1	8	3	4	7
Regularity of health habits	5	5	4	1	7	7	3	2
Total health behaviors	6	5	3	1	7	7	2	4
Adjustment								
Positive affects	7	5	7	3	5	2	4	1
Low negative affects	5	3	5	1	5	3	5	1
Low stress	7	4	6	2	8	1	5	3
Functional coping	8	6	5	2	7	4	2	1
Social support	8	6	7	3	3	2	5	1
Few health complaints	5	4	5	1	5	1	5	1
Total adjustment	8	5	7	3	6	2	4	1

Note: 1 = best health behaviour; 8 = worst health behaviour

Across these studies (see Table 10.2), Hedonists took the most chances with respect to sex, followed by Insecures and Spectators in second place. Brooders and Skeptics, in contrast, kept away from risky sex. Again, we see a pattern where high Extraversion together with lack of Constraint constitutes a liability, whereas Introversion together with high Constraint provides protection. As before, Neuroticism together with lack of Constraint constitutes a risk factor as well.

Reckless or Unsafe Driving

Reckless driving comprises speeding, driving drunk, traffic law violations including driving without seatbelts, and at-fault involvement in traffic accidents. For traits from the lack of Constraint domain, an average correlation coefficient of $r = 0.25$ with reckless driving was found (Bogg & Roberts, 2004). The majority of studies also reports evidence for an association of Extraversion with reckless driving (J. Block & Kremen, 1996; Booth-Kewley & Vickers, 1994; Lajunen, 2001; Renner & Hahn, 1996; Vollrath, Knoch & Cassano, 1999), but null findings exist as well (Begg & Langley, 2004; Furnham & Saipe, 1993). With regard to Neuroticism, some researchers found higher Neuroticism among reckless drivers (Booth-Kewley & Vickers, 1994), others found no relation (Begg & Langley, 2004; Vollrath, Knoch & Cassano, 1999), or even lower Neuroticism (Furnham & Saipe, 1993). Finally, one large international study suggests a non-linear relationship between Neuroticism and fatalities (Lajunen, 2001), with higher risk for those either high or low in Neuroticism.

Turning to typological analyses, in the Dunedin study, neurotic, non-constrained Under-controllers engaged most often in dangerous driving (Caspi et al., 1997). Among Swiss students, Hedonists reported the most frequent drunk driving, followed by Insecures and Spectators. Complicateds reported drunk driving least frequently, followed by Skeptics and Entrepreneurs (Vollrath & Torgersen, 2002). In Norwegian students (Vollrath & Torgersen, 2006), Hedonists and Impulsives drove drunk most often, and Insecures and Spectators were the most cautious. Taking the two studies together, Hedonists, followed by Impulsives, were the most reckless drivers (see Table 10.2), whereas Complicateds, followed by Entrepreneurs, were the most prudent drivers.

In this case, different from the results shown before, the combination of Extraversion with lack of Constraint appears to increase exposure, whereas the combination of Extraversion with high Constraint (Complicateds, Entrepreneurs) is the most protective.

Unhealthy Eating and Overweight

Studies relating traits from the domains of Neuroticism, Extraversion, and Lack of Constraint with unhealthy eating are hard to come by. Bogg & Roberts' meta-analysis (2004) listed three studies showing that Lack of Constraint was related to poor attention to a healthy diet and eating more. Evidence regarding the effects of the Neuroticism and Extraversion domains on eating and weight is not clear-cut. Neuroticism negatively predicted eating junk food in one study (MacNicol, Murray & Austin, 2003) but was unrelated to healthy eating in another (Goldberg & Strycker, 2002). Traits from the Extraversion domain were unrelated to eating habits in both studies.

With respect to overweight, there is solid evidence for the influence of traits from the Lack of Constraint domain (Bogg & Roberts, 2004; Hampson, Goldberg, Vogt & Dubanoski,

2006). There is also evidence from prospective studies that traits from the Neuroticism domain predict the development of overweight (Hampson, Goldberg, Vogt & Dubanoski, 2006; Pulkki-Råback et al., 2005). However, one study found this to be true only for men (Hampson, Goldberg, Vogt & Dubanoski, 2006), another study only for women (Faith, Flint, Fairburn, Goodwin & Allison, 2001). We could not find studies demonstrating any effects of Extraversion on overweight.

Turning to the typological analyses, among the Swiss students, eating healthy food was the least important to Spectators, followed by Hedonists and Insecures. At the other end of the spectrum, eating healthy food was the most important to Brooders, Complicateds, and Skeptics (unpublished data). In a study of around 1,300 Norwegian adolescents aged 13–18 (unpublished data), eating junk food was the most popular among Hedonists, Impulsives, and Spectators, and the least common among Brooders, Skeptics, and Complicateds. Similarly, eating fresh fruit and vegetables was the least popular among Insecures, Spectators and Brooders, and the most popular among Complicateds, Entrepreneurs, and Hedonists. Traditional foods—meat, fish, cooked vegetables, and potatoes—were consumed the least often by Spectators, Impulsives, and Brooders and the most often by Complicateds, Entrepreneurs, and Skeptics. Taking the two studies together, Spectators and Insecures, combining Introversion with Lack of Constraint, showed the least healthy eating patterns, whereas Complicateds and Brooders (combining Neuroticism with Constraint) showed the healthiest dietary practices.

The picture for the Body Mass Index (BMI), a continuous measure used for weight classification, was slightly different. Among the Swiss students, Impulsives had the highest BMI followed by the Entrepreneurs, whereas Skeptics and Brooders were the thinnest (unpublished data). Here, it appears as if Introversion in combination with Constraint predicted staying slim, whereas Extraversion alone predicted higher weight.

Lack of Regularity of Health Habits

Findings from a large longitudinal study in Alameda County, California showed that regularity of health habits such as physical activity, eating, and sleeping has beneficial effects on morbidity and mortality. With respect to traits from the lack of Constraint domain, the mean association with exercise reported across 16 studies reached only $r = 0.05$ (Bogg & Roberts, 2004). Neuroticism appears to be related to less exercise (Courneya & Hellsten, 1998; Yeung & Hemsley, 1997); Extraversion appears to be related to exercising more often (Courneya & Hellsten, 1998; Yeung & Hemsley, 1997). We found only one study relating regularity of sleep with Neuroticism and Extraversion. The findings from that study were negative (Monk, Petrie, Hayes & Kupfer, 1994).

As an alternative to the literature on the Big Three, we consulted the literature on happiness. Happiness corresponds to a trait profile of high positive affects, low negative affects, coupled with a dose of Constraint (DeNeve & Cooper, 1998), which resembles the profile of the Entrepreneurs in Torgersen's typology. Studies examining different health habits showed that happy people showed higher sleep quality and quantity (Bardwell, Barry, Ancoli-Israel & Dimsdale, 1999) and that they were more active with respect to physical exercise (Lox, Burns, Treasure & Wasley, 1999; Watson, Clark & Carey, 1988).

In our typological analyses, we looked at regularity of sleep and mealtimes, as well as at regular physical activity. In the Norwegian study of adolescents aged 13–18, Insecures, Spectators, and Brooders engaged the least in exercise and outdoor activities, whereas

Entrepreneurs, Complicateds, and Skeptics were the most physically active. Insecures reported eating regular meals at home with the family least frequently, followed by Spectators and Hedonists. Skeptics reported the most regular family meals, followed by Entrepreneurs and Complicateds (unpublished data). Among the Swiss students, Impulsives and Insecures had regular meals least often (unpublished).

With respect to regular sleep, we looked at the normal duration of sleep, as well as at the variation of the sleep duration over several months in the Swiss students (unpublished). The data showed that Skeptics had the most regular sleeping patterns, followed by Insecures and Brooders. At the other end of the spectrum, Hedonists had the most irregular sleeping patterns, followed by Impulsives and Entrepreneurs.

If we take the Swiss and the two Norwegian studies together and consider the regularity of meals, sleep, and physical exercise, Impulsives and Hedonists together were at the bottom, followed by Insecures and Spectators in second place, displaying the least regular health habits. At the other end of the spectrum, Skeptics and Entrepreneurs had the most regular health habits, whereas Complicateds and Brooders held the middle ground. With respect to regularity, it appears that the combination of high Constraint with low Neuroticism is important. Conversely, those showing least regularity were high on Extraversion and low on Constraint.

Survival and Longevity

Individuals with personality types disposing to less risky and more health-promoting behaviors should be expected to live longer. Indeed, a number of studies have shown that individuals with different serious diseases are more likely to survive if they have higher scores on traits from the domain of Positive Affectivity (including Extraversion), that is, if they are happier and more optimistic, or if they resemble the Resilient type in Caspi's typology or the Entrepreneur type in Torgersen's typology. Longer survival has been documented in individuals high in Positive Affectivity with end-stage renal disease (Devins, Mann, Mandin & Leonard, 1990). The same association between Positive Affectivity and survival has been documented in women with recurrent breast cancer (Levy, Lee, Bagley & Lippman, 1988), patients with spinal cord injuries (Krause, Sternberg, Lottes & Maides, 1997), and patients with coronary heart disease (Kubzansky & Kawachi, 2000). Moreover, in several studies on the general population, it has been found that individuals with Positive Affectivity live longer (Danner, Snowdon & Friesen, 2001; Maruta, Colligan, Malinchoc & Offord, 2000; Ostir, Markides, Black & Goodwin, 2000; Palmore, 1969; Peterson, Seligman, Yurko, Martin & Friedman, 1998). Conversely, one important study that followed close to 1,000 children over a period of 65 years did not show that the most cheerful lived the longest (L.R. Martin et al., 2002). Rather, the most conscientious of these children had a remarkable increase in life expectancy (Friedman et al., 1995).

CONCLUSION

Our review of studies on health behaviors and personality shows that a high level of Constraint is generally related to engaging in less risky and more positive health behaviors. As for Neuroticism and Extraversion, the picture is far from clear. Neuroticism seems to be related to less exercise and more overweight. Extraversion may be related to risky sexual behavior, but otherwise, the findings are not conclusive.

Our typology based on these three trait domains appears to reveal a clearer picture of the relationship between personality and health behavior. As shown by the overview of health behaviors among the types in Table 10.2, the eight types vary with respect to the domains in which they adopt risky or protective health behaviors. For instance, Insecures shy away from reckless driving; however, their eating patterns are unhealthy, and they tend to smoke. In that way they are similar to Spectators. Even more dramatically, Brooders take no risks in the domain of sex and stay slim; however, they drive recklessly and are not very regular in their health habits. Hedonists stay slim and are average with respect to healthy eating, but they are reckless with respect to driving and sex, and they use psychoactive substances. The Entrepreneurs show regular health habits and careful driving, but they do not refrain absolutely from alcohol and risky sex, and they do not pay attention to their weight.

Across all health behaviors, Skeptics show a perfect pattern, followed by Complicateds in second and Brooders in third place. When looking at these three types, we understand why analyses of the influence of the single traits of Neuroticism and Extraversion on health behavior yield inconclusive results. While all three types have high Constraint in common, they are high, respectively low, on Neuroticism, and high, respectively low, on Extraversion. The same holds for those with the poorest health behavior, Impulsives, Hedonists, and Insecures. They are low on Constraint but vary on the other two personality domains. Those with average health behaviors, Entrepreneurs and Spectators, have only one thing in common, namely, that they are low on Neuroticism.

One often hears the argument that it is preferable to enjoy life to the fullest, even if this will cost some years of life expectancy. However, is it true that being happy and well adjusted and abstaining from risky health behavior are mutually exclusive? In Table 10.2 we summarize findings on the affectivity, stress experiences, health complaints, coping, and social support among our eight types, based on the sample of Swiss students mentioned above (Vollrath & Torgersen, 2000) and some additional analyses. The rankings show that the types that report the most happiness (low stress, high positive affect, little negative affect) and who are best at coping and mobilizing social support are the Entrepreneurs, closely followed by Hedonists and Skeptics. At the other end of the spectrum, Insecures, Brooders, and Impulsives report having difficult emotional and social lives and dysfunctional coping.

Partly, there is a discrepancy between the psychological adjustment and the health behavior of members of specific personality types. For instance, Entrepreneurs are extremely well functioning individuals, but their health behavior is average. Hedonists are very happy and well functioning, but their health behaviors are very poor. Brooders tend to be unhappy but show good health behaviors. On the other hand, Skeptics seem to be in a good position in all respects, in sharp contrast to Insecures and Impulsives, who prove that risky health behaviors are no guarantee for an exciting emotional life.

Life is not fair, and exemplary behavior is not always rewarded with a happy life. Some may say that being an Entrepreneur is the best of all possibilities, being neither a moralist nor a sinner, not being averse to all pleasures, and at the same time feeling lucky and being well-adjusted. These individuals are exactly those with the highest Happiness scores (Costa & McCrae, 1980; McCrae & Costa, 1991), and they show the longest life expectancy and highest recovery from somatic illness, as mentioned. They are the most resilient individuals, and as Block and Block (1980) and Robins and colleagues (1996) maintain, the real Resilient types score at the top of the Ego-resilience dimension (equal to Happiness, or Emotional

Stability, Extraversion, and Constraint), and at the same time, they are average on the Ego-control dimension. They do not turn away from temptations, but they can stop in time.

REFERENCES

Almada, S.J., Zonderman, A.B., Shekelle, R.B., Dyer, A.R., Daviglus, M.L., Costa, P.T., et al. (1991). Neuroticism and cynicism and risk of death in middle-aged men: The Western Electric study. *Psychosomatic Medicine, 53*, 165–175.

American Psychiatric Association (1980). *Diagnostic and statistical manual of mental disorders* (3rd edn). Washington, DC: American Psychiatric Association.

Arai, Y., Hosokawa, T., Fukao, A., Izumi, Y. & Hisamichi, S. (1997). Smoking behaviour and personality: A population-based study in Japan. *Addiction, 92(8)*, 1023–1033.

Asendorpf, J.B. (2002). Editorial: The puzzle of personality types. *European Journal of Personality, 16*, S1–S5.

Asendorpf, J.B., Borkenau, P., Ostendorf, F. & van Aken, M.A.G. (2001). Carving personality descriptions at its joints: Confirmation of three replicable personality prototypes for both children and adults. *European Journal of Personality, 15*, 169–198.

Asendorpf, J.B., Caspi, A. & Hofstee, W.K.B. (2002). The puzzle of personality types. *European Journal of Personality. Special Issue, 16 S1*.

Barbaranelli, C. (2002). Evaluating cluster analysis solutions: an application to the Italian NEO personality inventory. *European Journal of Personality, 16(S1)*, S43–S55.

Bardwell, W.A., Barry, C.C., Ancoli-Israel, S. & Dimsdale, J.E. (1999). Psychological correlates of sleep apnea. *Journal of Psychosomatic Research, 47*, 583–596.

Begg, D.J. & Langley, J.D. (2004). Identifying predictors of persistent non-alcohol or drug-related risky driving behaviours among a cohort of young adults. *Accident Analysis & Prevention, 36(6)*, 1067–1071.

Belloc, N.B. (1973). Relationship of health practices and mortality. *Preventive Medicine, 2(1)*, 67–81.

Belloc, N.B. & Breslow, L. (1972). Relationship of physical health status and health practices. *Preventive Medicine, 1*, 409–421.

Block, J. (1950). *An experimental investigation of the construct of ego-control*. Stanford University Press: Stanford, CA.

Block, J. (1965). *The challenge of response sets: Unconfounding meaning, acquiescence and social desirability in the MMPI*. New York: Appleton-Century-Croft.

Block, J. (1971). *Lives through time*. Berkeley, CA: Bancroft.

Block, J. (1978). *The Q-sort method in personality assessment and psychiatric research*. Palo Alto, CA: Consulting Psychologists' Press.

Block, J. & Block, J.H. (1980). The role of ego-control and ego-resilience in the organization of behavior. In W.A. Collins (ed.), *Minnesota Symposium on Child Psychology* (Vol. 13, pp. 39–101). Hillsdale, NJ: Lawrence Erlbaum.

Block, J. & Kremen, A.M. (1996). IQ and ego-resiliency: conceptual and empirical connections and separateness. *Journal of personality and social psychology, 70(2)*, 349–361.

Block, J.H. (1951). *An experimental study of topological representation of ego structure*. Stanford University Press: Stanford, CA.

Block, J.H. & Block, J. (1980). The role of ego-control and ego-resiliency in the organization of behavior. In W.A. Collins (ed.), *Minnesota Symposium on Child Psychology* (Vol. 13, pp. 39–101). Hillsdale, N.J.: Erlbaum.

Boehm, B., Asendorpf, J.B. & Avia, M.D. (2002). Replicable types and subtypes of personality: Spanish NEO-PI samples. *European Journal of Personality, 16(S1)*, S25–S41.

Bogg, T. & Roberts, B.W. (2004). Conscientiousness and health-related behaviours: A meta-analysis of the leading behavioral contributors to mortality. *Psychological Bulletin, 130(6)*, 887–919.

Booth-Kewley, S. & Vickers, R.R. (1994). Associations between major domains of personality and health behavior. *Journal of Personality, 62*, 281–298.

Caspi, A., Begg, D., Dickson, N., Harrington, H., Langley, J., Moffitt, T.E., et al. (1997). Personality differences predict health-risk behaviors in young adulthood: Evidence from a longitudinal study. *Journal of Personality and Social Psychology, 73(5)*, 1052–1063.

Caspi, A., Harrington, H.L., Milne, B., Amell, J.W., Theodore, R.F. & Moffitt, T.E. (2003). Children's behavioral styles at age 3 are linked to their adult personality traits at age 26. *Journal of Personality, 71(4)*, 495–514.

Caspi, A., Henry, B., McGee, R.O., Moffitt, T.E., Silva, P.A. et al. (1995). Temperamental origins of child and adolescent behavior problems: From age three to fifteen. *Child Development, 66(1)*, 55–68.

Caspi, A. & Silva, P.A. (1995). Temperamental qualities at age three predict personality traits in young adulthood: Longitudinal evidence from a birth cohort. *Child Development, 66*, 486–498.

Clark, L.A. & Watson, D. (1990). *The General Temperament Survey. Unpublished Manuscript.* Iowa City, IA: University of Iowa.

Clark, L.A. & Watson, D. (1999). Temperament: A new paradigm for trait psychology. In L.A. Pervin & O.P. John (eds), *Handbook of personality* (2nd edn, pp. 399–423). New York: Guilford Press.

Cookson, H. (1994). Personality variables associated with alcohol use in young offenders. *Personality and Individual Differences, 16(1)*, 179–182.

Costa, P.T., Herbst, J.H., McCrae, R.R., Samuels, J. & Ozer, D.J. (2002). The replicability and utility of three personality types. *European Journal of Personality, 16*, S73–S87.

Costa, P.T. & McCrae, R.R. (1980). Influence of extraversion and neuroticism on subjective well-being: happy and unhappy people. *Journal of Personal and Social Psychology, 38*, 668–678.

Courneya, K.S. & Hellsten, L.A.M. (1998). Personality correlates of exercise behavior, motives, barriers, and preferences: An application of the five-factor model. *Personality and Individual Differences, 24(5)*, 625–633.

Danner, D.D., Snowdon, D.A. & Friesen, W.V. (2001). Positive emotions in early life and longevity: Findings from the Nun Study. *Journal of Personality and Social Psychology, 80(5)*, 804–813.

De Fruyt, F., Mervielde, I. & Van Leeuwen, K. (2002). The consistency of personality type classification across samples and five-factor measures. *European Journal of Personality, 16(S1)*, S57–S72.

DeNeve, K.M. & Cooper, H. (1998). The happy personality: A meta-analysis of 137 personality traits and subjective well-being. *Psychological Bulletin, 124(2)*, 197–229.

Devins, G.M., Mann, J., Mandin, H.P. & Leonard, C. (1990). Psychosocial predictors of survival in end-stage renal disease. *Journal of Nervous and Mental Disease, 178*, 127–133.

Eysenck, H.J. (1994). The Big Five factors or Giant Three: criteria for a paradigm. In C.F. Halverson Jr., G.A. Kohnstamm & R.P. Martin (eds), *The developing structure of temperament and personality from infancy to adulthood* (pp. 37–51). Hillsdale, NJ: Lawrence Erlbaum.

Eysenck, H.J. & Eysenck, S.B.G. (1975). *Manual of the Eysenck Personality Questionnaire.* London: Hodder & Stoughton.

Faith, M.S., Flint, J., Fairburn, C., Goodwin, G.M. & Allison, D.B. (2001). Gender differences in the relationship between personality dimensions and relative body weight. *Obesity Research, 9(10)*, 647–650.

Flory, K., Lynam, D., Milich, R., Leukefeld, C. & Clayton, P. (2002). The relations among personality, symptoms of alcohol and marijuana abuse, and symptoms of comorbid psychopathology: Results from a community sample. *Experimental and Clinical Psychopharmacology, 10(4)*, 425–434.

Forgays, D.G., Bonaiuto, P., Wrzesniewski, K. & Forgays, D.K. (1993). Personality and cigarette smoking in Italy, Poland, and the United States. *International Journal of the Addictions, 28(5)*, 399–413.

Friedman, H.S., Tucker, J.S., Schwartz, J.E., Martin, L.R., Tomlinson-Keasey, C., Wingard, D.L., et al. (1995). Childhood conscientiousness and longevity: health behaviors and cause of death. *Journal of Personality and Social Psychology, 68*, 696–703.

Furnham, A. & Saipe, J. (1993). Personality correlates of convicted drivers. *Personality and Individual Differences, 14(2)*, 329–336.

Gilbert, D.G. (1995). *Smoking: Individual differences, psychopathology and emotions.* Washington, DC, USA: Taylor & Francis.

Goldberg, D. & Strycker, L.A. (2002). Personality traits and eating habits: the assessment of food preferences in a large community sample. *Personality and Individual Differences, 32*, 49–65.

Gough, H.G. (1987). *California Psychological Inventory (Administrator's guide)*. Palo Alto, CA: Consulting Psychologists Press.

Grau, E. & Ortet, G. (1999). Personality traits and alcohol consumption in a sample of non-alcoholic women. *Personality and Individual Differences, 27*, 1057–1066.

Hampson, S., Goldberg, L.R., Vogt, T.M. & Dubanoski, J.P. (2006). Forty years on: Teachers' assessments of children's personality traits predict self-reported health behaviors and outcomes at midlife. *Health Psychology, 25(1)*, 57–64.

Hoyle, R.H., Fejfar, M.C. & Miller, J. (2000). Personality and sexual risk taking: A quantitative review. *Journal of Personality, 68(6)*, 1203–1231.

Kirkcaldy, B.D., Siefen, G., Surall, D. & Bischoff, R.J. (2004). Predictors of drug and alcohol abuse among children and adolescents. *Personality and Individual Differences, 36(2)*, 247–265.

Kjærheim, K., Mykletun, R. & Haldorsen, T. (1996). Selection into the restaurant business based on personality characteristics and the risk of heavy drinking. *Personality and Individual Differences, 21(4)*, 625–629.

Knyazev, G.G. (2004). Behavioural activation as predictor of substance use: mediating and moderating role of attitudes and social relationships. *Drug and Alcohol Dependence, 75(3)*, 309–321.

Krause, J.S., Sternberg, M., Lottes, S. & Maides, J. (1997). Mortality after spinal cord injury: An 11-year prospective study. *Archives of Physical Medicine and Rehabilitation, 78*, 815–821.

Kubzansky, L.D. & Kawachi, I. (2000). Going to the heart of the matter: Do negative emotions cause coronary heart disease? *Journal of Psychosomatic Research, 48*, 323–337.

Lajunen, T. (2001). Personality and accident liability: are extraversion, neuroticism and psychoticism related to traffic and occupational fatalities? *Personality and Individual Differences, 31(8)*, 1365–1373.

Levy, S.M., Lee, J., Bagley, C. & Lippman, M. (1988). Survival hazard analysis in first recurrent breast cancer patients: Seven-year follow-up. *Psychosomatic Medicine, 50*, 520–528.

Lox, C.L., Burns, S.P., Treasure, D.C. & Wasley, D.A. (1999). Physical and psychological predictors of exercise dosage in healthy adults. *Medicine and Science in Sports and Exercise, 31*, 1060–1064.

MacNicol, S.A.M., Murray, S.M. & Austin, E.J. (2003). Relationships between personality, attitudes and dietary behaviour in a group of Scottish adolescents. *Personality and Individual Differences, 35*, 1753–1764.

Martin, L.R., Friedman, H.S., Tucker, J.S., Tomlinson-Keasey, C., Criqui, M.H. & Schwartz, J.E. (2002). A life course perspective on childhood cheerfulness and its relation to mortality risk. *Personality and Social Psychology Bulletin, 28*, 1155–1165.

Martin, N.G. & Boomsma, D.I. (1989). Willingness to drive when drunk and personality: A twin study. *Behavior Genetics, 19(1)*, 97–111.

Martsh, C.T. & Miller, W.R. (1997). Extraversion predicts heavy drinking in college students. *Personality and Individual Differences, 23(1)*, 153–155.

Maruta, T., Colligan, R.C., Malinchoc, M. & Offord, K.P. (2000). Optimists vs. pessimists: Survival rate among medical patients over a 30-year period. *Mayo Clinic Proceedings, 75*, 140–143.

McCrae, R.R. & Costa, P.T. (1991). Adding Liebe und Arbeit. The full Five Factor model and well-being. *Personality and Social Psychology Bulletin, 17*, 227–232.

McGee, R.O., Silva, P.A. & Williams, S.M. (1984). Behaviour problems in a population of seven-year-old children: Prevalence, stability, and types of disorder. A research report. *Journal of Child Psychology and Psychiatry, 25*, 251–259.

McGregor, D., Murray, R.P. & Barnes, G.E. (2003). Personality differences between users of wine, beer and spirits in a community sample: The Winnipeg Health and Drinking Survey. *Journal of Studies on Alcohol, 64(5)*, 634–640.

McGue, M., Slutske, W. & Iacono, W.G. (1999). Personality and substance users orders: II. Alcoholism versus in drug use disorders. *Journal of Consulting and Clinical Psychology, 67(3)*, 394–404.

Merenakk, L., Harro, M., Kiive, E., Laidra, K., Eensoo, D., Allik, J., et al. (2003). Association between substance use, personality traits, and platelet MAO activity in preadolescents and adolescents. *Addictive Behaviors, 28(8)*, 1507–1514.

Miller, J.D., Lynam, D., Zimmerman, R.S., Logan, T.K., Leukefeld, C. & Clayton, R. (2004). The utility of the Five Factor Model in understanding risky sexual behavior. *Personality and Individual Differences, 36(7)*, 1611–1626.

Monk, T.H., Petrie, S.R., Hayes, A.J. & Kupfer, D.J. (1994). Regularity of daily life in relation to personality, age, gender, sleep quality and circadian rhythms. *Journal of Sleep Research, 3*, 196–205.

Ostir, G.V., Markides, K.S., Black, S.A. & Goodwin, J.S. (2000). Emotional well-being predicts subsequent functional independence and survival. *Journal of the American Geriatrics Society, 48*, 473–478.

Palmore, E.B. (1969). Predicting longevity: A follow-up controlling for age. *Gerontologist, 9*, 247–250.

Peterson, C., Seligman, M.E.P., Yurko, K.H., Martin, L.R. & Friedman, H.S. (1998). Catastrophizing and untimely death. *Psychological Science, 9*, 127–130.

Pulkki-Råback, L., Elovainio, M., Kivimäki, M., Raitakari, O.T. & Keltikangas-Jarvinen, L. (2005). Temperament in childhood predicts body mass in adulthood: the Cardiovascular Risk in Young Finns Study. *Health Psychology, 24(3)*, 307–315.

Rammstedt, B., Riemann, R., Angleitner, A. & Borkenau, P. (2004). Resilients, Overcontrollers, and Undercontrollers: The replicability of the three personality prototypes across informants. *European Journal of Personality, 18(1)*, 1–14.

Renner, B. & Hahn, A. (1996). Stereotype Vorstellungen über eine gefährdete Person und unrealistisch optimistische Risikoeinschätzungen. *Zeitschrift für Gesundheitspsychologie, 6*, 220–240.

Robins, R.W., John, O.P., Caspi, A., Moffitt, T.E. & Stouthamer Loeber, M. (1996). Resilient, over-controlled, and undercontrolled boys: Three replicable personality types. *Journal of Personality and Social Psychology, 70(1)*, 157–171.

Saulsman, L.M. & Page, A.C. (2004). The five-factor model and personality disorders empirical literature: A meta-analytic review. *Clinical Psychology Review, 23*, 1055–1085.

Schnabel, K., Asendorpf, J.B. & Ostendorf, F. (2002). Replicable types and subtypes of personality: German NEO-PI-R versus NEO-FFI. *European Journal of Personality, 16(S1)*, S7–S24.

Sigurdsson, J.F. & Gudjonsson, G.H. (1996). Psychological characteristics of juvenile alcohol and drug users. *Journal of Adolescence, 19*, 121–126.

Silva, P.A. (1990). The Dunedin Multidisciplinary Health and Development Study: A 15 Year Longitudinal Study. *Paediatric and Perinatal Epidemiology, 4*, 76–107.

Spielberger, C.D., Reheiser, E.C., Foreyt, J.P., Poston, W.S.C. & Volding, D.C. (2004). Personality determinants of the use of tobacco products. *Personality and Individual Differences, 36(5)*, 1073–1082.

Stein, J.A., Newcomb, M.D. & Bentler, P.M. (1987). Personality and drug use: Reciprocal effects across four years. *Personality and Individual Differences, 8(3)*, 419–430.

Tellegen, A. (1982). *Brief manual for the Multidimensional Personality Questionnaire*. Minneapolis: University of Minnesota.

Terracciano, A. & Costa, P.T., Jr. (2004). Smoking and the Five-Factor Model of personality. *Addiction, 99*, 472–481.

Torgersen, S. (1995). *Personlighet og personlighetsforstyrrelser*. Oslo: Universitetsforlaget.

Trobst, K.K., Herbst, J.H., Masters, H.L.I. & Costa, P.T. (2002). Personality pathways to unsafe sex: personality, condom use, and HIV risk behaviors. *Journal of Research in Personality, 36*, 117–133.

Vollrath, M., Knoch, D. & Cassano, L. (1999). Personality, risky health behavior, and perceived susceptibility to health risks. *European Journal of Personality, 13*, 39–50.

Vollrath, M. & Torgersen, S. (2000). Personality types and coping. *Personality and Individual Differences, 29(2)*, 367–378.

Vollrath, M. & Torgersen, S. (2002). Who takes health risks? A probe into eight personality types. *Personality and Individual Differences, 32(7)*, 1185–1198.

Vollrath, M. & Torgersen, S. (2006). *Who is taking health risks? A typological study in Norwegian students*. Unpublished manuscript, Oslo, Norway.

Wadsworth, E.J.K., Moss, S.C., Simpson, S.A. & Smith, A.P. (2004). Factors associated with recreational drug use. *Journal of Psychopharmacology, 18(2)*, 238–248.

Watson, D., Clark, L.A. & Carey, G. (1988). Positive and negative affectivity and their relation to anxiety and depressive disorders. *Journal of Abnormal Psychology, 97*, 346–353.

Yeung, R.R. & Hemsley, D.R. (1997). Personality, exercise and psychological well-being: Static relationships in the community. *Personality and Individual Differences, 22(1)*, 47–53.

Zuckerman, M. & Kuhlman, D.M. (2000). Personality and risk-taking: Common biosocial factors. *Journal of Personality, 68(6)*, 999–1029.

CHAPTER 11

The Possibilities of Personality Psychology and Persons for the Study of Health

Suzanne C. Ouellette and David M. Frost
The City University of New York, USA

Given the amount of attention that will be given to narratives in this chapter, it seems right to begin with a couple of stories. Between the lines are our aims to reach audiences of both younger and older researchers, address both what the study of personality and health has been and what it might be, and say something useful about both the knowledge and practice of personality and health research.

SOME STORIES ABOUT THE STUDY OF PERSONALITY AND HEALTH

Wayne: A Psychology Student

Wayne has arrived at a critical point in graduate school training: he is ready to choose an area of research specialization. Wayne wants to understand more about what he has found in the literature and experienced in life about people's health. For example, while reading across a variety of research reports about the links between social inequities and poor health, he finds that both psychological factors and dimensions of social structure are considered, but usually in isolation of each other. He wants to know more about what really happens between the individual psyche of someone like a young, Black, poor, and underemployed man living in the South Bronx and the social forces with which he contends: How do these together reveal mechanisms that might explain this man's high risk for cardiovascular disease in later life? Wayne's personal experiences also matter. Reflecting on interactions with friends and family during his recent semester break, Wayne thinks most about his mother who has recently been diagnosed with ALS, Lou Gehrig's disease. Although his mother was as determined as ever to get her book to the publisher and as energetic as always

Handbook of Personality and Health. Edited by Margarete E. Vollrath. © 2006 John Wiley & Sons, Ltd.

in the kitchen getting food ready for whoever appeared, he knew his mother had changed. When she thought she was out of everyone's focus, she seemed more distracted and sadness came into her usually sparkling eyes. He heard his mother complain to a friend that she didn't want to be a person in a wheelchair. The student wishes he could understand more about how his mother has come to understand herself and her relationships, and how that might matter for her illness. He decides health psychology is what he will study.

In all that engages him, Wayne finds that there is something about the person, the whole person as she or he lives within a particular context that makes a critical difference for health. He thinks his specific research topic is likely to be the relationship between personality and health. Wayne's inclination is based on what he has read in basic personality research, from both classic sources and some recent overviews of new directions in the field. He has learned from both contributors who are no longer with us and still very active personality researchers. Henry Murray, Gordon Allport, Robert White, Abigail Stewart, Dan McAdams, Ruthellen Josselson, Todd Schultz, and others have provided research programs that emphasize the importance of understanding personality and people's lives, not just variables, in relation to the worlds in which they live. Wayne expects that the research on personality and health will involve a focus on full and complicated persons in context.

Yet early in his review of existing work on personality and health, he is disappointed. He searches long and hard within health psychology publications, all the while in wonder: 'Where is the person?' Just as Rae Carlson did in 1971 and again in 1984 in her review of basic studies of personality psychology, the student finds that in most of the work the person is absent and replaced by isolated variables. And like Billig did in 1994 for basic social psychology, Wayne discovers that the language investigators typically use in the description of participants, methods, and results depopulates and dehumanizes the research field. Missing are the studies of real persons living in complex interpersonal, social, cultural, historical, and political settings. Wayne is glad to feel in the company of Carlson and Billig but wishes he had more to show his research advisor from this search. He wonders why what he is finding in the body of research on health is so different from what he is finding more generally in the field of personality.

Renee: A Psychology Faculty Member

She has just delivered a talk at another university. Among the people Renee meets at the reception after the talk is a well-known philosopher. After some simple chatting, he tells her a chilling tale:

> I was in the clinic again. I was there for treatment of my third kind of cancer. I was quite anxious. A young woman approached me and she asked if I would be willing to fill out a questionnaire. I took a quick look at the first page. She wanted me to circle numbers next to sentences like: 'It is always better in life to plan ahead' and 'I am not the worrying type'. I was baffled. How can I think about myself this way in this place? What do these sentences mean about my cancer and me? The young woman explained that she was doing a research project in health psychology. Health psychology? Tell me, Professor, shouldn't psychologists be a little more sensitive than this? And how could such an experience be good for my health?

Renee, the psychology professor, offers the usual lines about how all of psychology is not clinical psychology and how research differs from intervention, recites the mantra about biopsychosocial approaches to health and illness, and gives some actual examples of how psychologists doing similar types of research have contributed to our understanding of health. The philosopher only shakes his head. Renee takes a deep breath to counteract that sinking feeling in her heart. She wishes she had more studies to describe; some that he might find more relevant to what he is struggling to understand about his life with cancer. Renee wishes that the young researcher he encountered in the clinic had also been more helpful to him in their encounter.

GOALS OF THE CURRENT CHAPTER

The intention of this chapter is to be of some use to Wayne and Renee. Our aim is to inspire more students and seasoned investigators to do a kind of personality research within the health arena that is about the lived experience of persons and what Robert White, a major figure in early personality psychology, called personality looked at 'the long way' (cf. Ouellette, 2005). For us, this kind of research requires more humanized practice and promises to contribute to health interventions in meaningful ways. We build on the concerns and questions raised in earlier reviews, such as the ideological dilemmas faced by personality and health researchers as they seek to identify both individual agency and the social structures associated with illness (Ouellette, 1999; Ouellette & DiPlacido, 2001). We seek to be responsive to increasingly frequent calls within health psychology for research that recognizes (a) change as definitive of both personality and physiological processes (Friedman, 2000), and (b) social and historical context in which personality is embedded in diverse yet specifiable ways (Murray et al., 2005).

We argue that modes of inquiry that involve narrative analysis and life study approaches—modes that have been relatively neglected within personality and health endeavors—have much to offer contemporary researchers. Health studies in which researchers have applied these approaches allow for an understanding of processes of self and identity; developmental change; the hearing of voices that have often been marginalized by researchers; personality as embedded within particular social structures, including ideology; and sites and means for effective health intervention.

We begin with a demonstration of the unequal distribution of the modes for doing personality research within current health psychology. Our point is not that the existing work lacks knowledge and is useless. This book and many other sources effectively argue its value. Our point is rather that health psychology and its almost exclusive emphasis on personality traits or simple personality characteristics has not taken full advantage of all the modes through which one can do personality research, of all that personality theorizing and methods have to offer it. Good news, however, seems to be on the way. We summarize recent reviews that propose new models for the study of personality and health; models that encourage the study of change across the life span, local and sociohistorical context, and lived experience.

The final section of the chapter has all to do with narratives and life studies. We review the ways in which such studies can provide answers to pressing personality and health concerns. The investigators of the studies we review are typically not health psychologists. Currently, medical sociologists and anthropologists are the major contributors to narrative studies of health. Nonetheless, health psychologists have much to contribute. The health studies are about psychological matters; the field of general personality psychology is increasingly about narrative and lives (cf. Singer, 2004); and the narrative and lives research on health now involves debates to which psychologists could usefully contribute. Under contention are issues such as individual health narratives that seem at odds with more public narratives, and the liberatory versus repressive consequences of stories people tell about their health and illness. Seeking to encourage new and seasoned investigators to actively engage in this kind of research, we pay special attention to the specific methodological strategies that investigators have employed and other issues of practice.

We also want to say at the outset that our concern is not simply with personality conceptualized as an independent variable that worsens or improves health conceptualized as a dependent variable. We find engaging theoretical frameworks and constructs that enable us to see that changes in health are as likely to influence changes in personality as changes in personality are likely to influence health outcomes. The closer one gets to observations of lived experience, the harder it is to make causal, linear, distinctions. Also, our emphasis here is less on prediction than it is on understanding the personality dimensions of experiences in life that include staying healthy, becoming sick, becoming sicker, and becoming healthier.

THE CURRENT STATE OF PERSONALITY AND HEALTH RESEARCH

Taking Another Look at the Distribution of Modes for Studying Personality in Health Research

In prior reviews of the research on links between personality and health (Ouellette, 1999; Ouellette & DiPlacido, 2001), the authors found that a restricted view of how personality might be conceptualized and studied was a key limitation in the field. They also noted the frequently cited problems such as inconsistent mediating and moderating effects; relationships between personality and psychological aspects of illness rather than disease; lack of prospective designs; failure to discriminate between the target personality characteristic and neuroticism; observations of isolated variables when prior research indicated the need for a multivariable and multilevel approach; claims for single direction causality from personality to health when reciprocal causation was as likely; and the lack of sufficiently inclusive and complex theoretical models. But they placed the restricted view of personality research at the top of their list of weaknesses. They concluded that health researchers could resolve many of their current concerns and dilemmas if they took better advantage of the theoretical and methodological tools now available to them within the enterprise of personality psychology, and the insights about the ideological and historical dimensions of their work provided by feminist (e.g., Stewart, 1994) and critical (e.g., Fox & Prilleltensky, 1997; Prilleltensky, 1997) psychology.

Using McAdams' (1996) tripartite scheme for organizing the many ways that personality psychologists do their work, Ouellette and DiPlacido (2001) found that the vast majority of the work on the relationship between personality and health was done with what McAdams calls Level 1 analysis; and his Levels 2 and 3 concepts, models, and methods were neglected. McAdams' Level 1 is the level of personality as traits or what McAdams calls the 'psychology of the stranger.' Working at Level 1, researchers assign scores to people on fixed and decontextualized characteristics (neuroticism, agreeableness, hostility, etc.) without regard to such things as the time or place in which people are observed, the other people they find themselves with, or their life stage. Level 2 involves the conceptualization of personality as what one does rather than what one has (cf. Cantor, 1990) or the 'personal concerns' level. McAdams places constructs such as Little's (1983) personal projects and Emmons' personal strivings (Emmons, 1986) on Level 2. On Level 3, McAdams puts personality conceptions that make personality a matter of self and identity, life stories, and persons' constructions of meaningful selves. The emphasis is upon those personality processes involved in meaning making (Bruner, 1990), narratives about the self through the life course (Cohler, 1991), and the dialogical self (Hermans, Rijks & Kempen, 1993).

The second and third levels allow the researcher to take seriously the structures in which personality resides. The best of the research on these levels shows that persons have concerns in particular settings (e.g., Ogilvie & Rose, 1995) and stories about self are told in historical and cultural space (Franz & Stewart, 1994). This broader view of personality in context enables one better to assess and seek to understand how it is that personality works similarly or differently across different groups to protect and enhance health. It also helps us to address the theoretical challenge of addressing both social structures and individual agency in health and illness matters. Take for example, the personality characteristic of hardiness. It is often approached through a Level 1 framework and conceived of as a trait. It was originally formulated, however, through existential and phenomenological theories as a dynamic characteristic of individuals that they constantly and responsibly create as embodied beings, with others, and with what is at hand in particular times and places. Clearer recognition of its Level 2 credentials would answer the call of personality and health researchers like Wiebe and Williams (1992) for the better specification of how one is to think about how hardiness operates in social settings. As early as 1982, Kobasa reported differences between occupational groups in how hardiness relates to the health of the members of those occupations; nonetheless, hardiness theory has yet to be elaborated sufficiently to explain these group differences. Recognizing its Level 3 dimensions, researchers would see that hardiness is about how the whole person seeks to understand self and the world and not just a single variable or the three variables of commitment, control, and challenge. So understood, the literature should include the idiographic, developmental, and historical work that the original theory required (cf. Allport, 1961; Carlson, 1984; Ouellette Kobasa, 1990).

Using the McAdams' (1996) tripartite scheme again as a lens, we find that a drastically unequal distribution of ways of working continues in the personality and health field, but also some reason for hope that the problems we cited in earlier work will be resolved. We began by looking at the simple numerical distribution of recent articles across McAdams' levels. Using the PSYCinfo database of work published in the ten years between 1995 and 2005, we operationalized McAdams' three distinct levels or ways of doing research into sets of search terms and sorted all of the articles into them, first sorting all of the personality articles generally at each level and then specifically sorting those dealing with personality and health.[1]

The vast majority of work captured by our searches, in general (18,939 articles) and on personality and health in particular (2,210 articles), falls within McAdams first level or trait way of working. The health work has essentially to do with the five factor model of personality, and in the arena of health with personality traits in their relationship to variables like stress and physical health, and with personality as coping constructs that

---

[1] For Level 1, we used 'personality and trait' or 'personality and trait and health' as search terms; for Level 2, 'personality and (motive or value or coping or striving or project or "life task")' or 'personality and (motive or value or coping or striving or project or "life task") and health' for Level 3. 'Personality and (life and [story or history] and [identity or self])' or 'personality and (life and [story or history] and [identity or self]) and health.' Also, finding that researchers looking at self and identity and health issues did not always use the personality word; we redid the Level 3 search on psychological sources with the search terms 'self and identity and health.' For all searches, we excluded articles having to do with mental rather than physical health.

buffer the effects of psychosocial variables on physical illness. Second in popularity is research on Level 2 in which personality is studied as what people do in the contexts of their lives through forms such as motives, values, coping, projects or life tasks (6,339 articles in the general personality literature and 1,081 on personality and health). Level 3 research, concerned with self, identity, and life stories, falls in a far more distant third place (204 articles in general and 27 on personality and health). Closely reviewing the articles within this last category, the one with which we are most concerned in this chapter, we found that it was actually only in eight that the researchers studied personality in ways that qualify for what McAdams calls a Level 3 way of working.

We used a very broad brush to present this picture of the current psychological literature on personality and health. Nonetheless, it is what a student like Wayne would find in his first pass through what he would think to be the relevant publications and background for his work.

We then did another search using the Social Science Citation Index database of work published in the ten years between 1995 and 2005 to ask: 'To what extent do researchers recognize that there are several ways of working as personality researchers?' We looked at how many articles cite either the 1996 McAdams' paper or a 1995 piece by him in which he also lays out his framework for how personality psychologists do what they do.

Of the 147 articles identified, 9 or 6% deal with personality and health concerns. Six are specific health investigations. In studies of eating disorders, Lindeman & Stark (1999, 2000) use an elaborated view of personality as about both personal strivings and identity expressions (specifically, the ways in which identity was expressed through food) to find a more nuanced view of food choice motives, and predict symptoms of disordered eating. Freund and Smith (1999), in a different research arena, worked with McAdams' ideas about personality psychology as that which reveals how an individual constructs his or her self. They show that old and very old persons (aged between 70 and 103 years) spontaneously define themselves as active and present-oriented, with an inward orientation, and with central themes that include health alongside life review and family. Those older individuals with more health-related constraints have a less multifaceted self-definition (i.e., they reported fewer and less rich self-defining domains). Stumpfer (1999) and Stumpfer and Gouws (1998) use McAdams' scheme to call for a fuller understanding of resilience in adults and a view of Antonovsky's sense of coherence (a key notion in many studies of health) as a construct that is not simply a trait and that involves a mixture of personality domains. Finally, Gallo and Smith (1998) stretch McAdams' Level 2 to include interpersonal personality processes and use the interpersonal circumplex model alongside the five-factor model to improve the construct validation of health-relevant personality characteristics. Although small in number, these studies all demonstrate the usefulness of a broad view of how personality psychologists can do their work and the complexity of the persons whom they seek to understand.

The three remaining articles are review pieces that build on McAdams' framework. They issue convincing calls by very productive researchers for a new kind of personality and health research. These reviews and proposals are just what we (and Wayne) are looking for.

New Models for the Study of Personality and Health

Tim Smith, a longtime and major contributor to the personality and health enterprise, argues that in order for the field to move forward, research models need to incorporate a life span perspective. Specifically, models must (a) increasingly incorporate longitudinal designs,

(b) strive toward conceptual clarity, and (c) place both personality and health in context (Smith & Spiro, 2002). Relying on concepts from McAdams' (1996) Levels 2 and 3, Smith and Spiro argue that a life span perspective allows for an understanding of the social, cultural, environmental, political, and life-stage contexts of personality. Like Ouellette and DiPlacido (2001) they also, in this article and in yet another review (Smith & Glazer, 2004), stress the importance of understanding *transactions* between persons and their environmental contexts for health promotion and reduction. Using interpersonal personality theory (Kiesler, 1996), they emphasize how individuals actively engage health-relevant aspects of their social environments, which in turn continually and reflexively shape their behavior as adaptive or maladaptive, health promoting or reducing. These personality-environment transactions occur repeatedly over time and form 'health-relevant trajectories' of development. They are usefully studied from a life span perspective alongside of time-variant health concerns such as disease progression and within-person biological changes.

Further, Smith and Spiro's (2002) framework illustrates the potential for variables like neighborhood characteristics, social class, and discrimination (both interpersonal and structural) in any understanding of persons and their health, especially when age and life-stage relevant concerns are taken seriously. The model for research they propose allows personality and health researchers to understand the changing relevance and importance of various contexts and personality variables in relation to health outcomes as people grow older and contend with different developmental concerns. Overall, their vision of the future of personality and health research takes seriously the notion that 'things change' in people's lives, and understanding when, why, and how they do makes researchers better able to both predict and prevent negative outcomes.

In yet another encouraging review that uses the framework provided by McAdams (1996), Karen Hooker (2002; Hooker & McAdams, 2003) goes beyond what she sees as his emphasis on personality structures and elaborates a set of personality processes related to those structures. Like Smith and his colleagues, she sees as key a lifespan perspective and presents her own developmental systems perspective and a concern with personality and aging. She proposes that McAdams' structures of traits, personal concerns, and life stories are best understood alongside of the processes of states, self-regulation, and self-narration, respectively. For example, according to Hooker, individuals' personal concerns (e.g., goals and possible selves) become more focused on health as these individuals enter mid-life. If, alongside these concerns, personality and health researchers better took into account how adults are engaging in self-regulatory processes such as self-efficacy and goal-directed behaviors, they could better predict the relationship between changes across the life span and health outcomes. In a study of individuals in later life, Cotrell and Hooker (2005) found evidence that Alzheimer's patients restructure their goals as they adjust to the constraints of their chronic illness. For Hooker, a focus on this kind of self-regulatory process in relation to health provides researchers not only with better predictive ability, but more insight into therapeutic interventions.

When she moves to an application of McAdams' Level 3, Hooker (2002; Hooker & McAdams, 2003) observes that aspects of individuals' life stories (e.g., structure, organization, coherence) have potential implications for health and well being. Indeed, Baerger and McAdams (1998) offer evidence for this. Hooker emphasizes that processes of self-narration (i.e., remembering, reminiscence, and story telling) influence individuals' life stories. For her, these processes and the life stories they produce are both personality and sociohistorical factors. Individuals' notions of self and identity as they appear in their life stories are likely to vary according to where an individual is located in terms of his or her culture and location in the life span. Although each person's life story is unique, as both McAdams and Hooker point out, life stories as units of analysis in personality research have a clear link to the discourses and other resources for the making of meaning that society provides (or in the case of some individuals, doesn't provide). Life stories and narrative processes thus represent important tools for putting personality and health and personality and health research in context.

In Smith and Hooker's turn to the importance of context and change and Hooker's to narrative, they are not lonely figures on the psychological scene. Good company for the engagement of the conceptual challenges they pose exists currently within the general field of personality psychology. For example, in his introduction to a recent special issue of the *Journal of Personality*, Jefferson Singer outlines a number of reasons why an increasing number of researchers 'place narrative identity at the center of personality' (Singer, 2004: p. 437). The narrative study of self and identity represents an extension of the humanistic approach to personality, pioneered in the personological work of Henry Murray (1938) and later represented in psychobiographical work (Schultz, 2005). Narrative strategies enable resurgence in the study of lives tradition (Barenbaum & Winter, 2003) when contributors from feminist psychology (Franz & Stewart, 1994) and other critical stances (Cohler, 1991) apply them.

Narrative researchers do not see important personality concepts like that of identity as reducible to variables or sets of variables like traits or motives. Instead, identity, as narratively constructed, represents a process of knowing, i.e., a person's attempt to make sense of his or her lived experience through the construction of a meaningful and coherent understanding of past, present, and potential future behavior and lived experiences. As noted above, for McAdams (1996) and Hooker (2002) this narrative representation of one's identity is a life story. Although researchers can investigate the motives that are served by particular narrations or life stories (Baumeister & Newman, 1994), they cannot reduce the conceptualization or assessment of narratives to motives.

Singer shows that an individual's narrative understanding of self includes autobiographical memories about goal pursuits, obstacles, and outcomes. But narrative study enables personality researchers to go beyond a study of simply *what* one's current concerns are to understanding how people incorporate those concerns into their own understanding of *who* they are; actively making meaning through their lived experiences.

The importance of lifespan and developmental approaches to personality are usefully incorporated into narrative identity research, particularly from a life story/life history approach. As Singer points out, individuals' narratives, and their abilities to construct narratives or make meaning, differ depending their current phase in the life span. Life span approaches, such as the life course approach to studying lives employed by Cohler and colleagues (Cohler & Hostetler, 1998; Cohler, Hostetler & Boxer, 1998), also help illuminate how cohort-specific life events (e.g., World War II; the AIDS crisis) exist as socio-historical and contextual factors that constitute forces that change and/or unify the meanings of lived experiences throughout and across individual lives. In this regard, personal narratives help individuals situate themselves 'meaningfully in their culture, providing unity to their past, present, and anticipated future' (Singer, 2004: p. 445). Thus narratives represent an important unit of analysis in personality research, helping us to understand whole persons, not variables, through their subjectively and reflexively lived experiences within the cultures and contexts of which they are inextricably part.

WHAT NARRATIVES AND THE STUDY OF LIVES CAN OFFER THE STUDY OF PERSONALITY AND HEALTH

The reviews by Smith and his colleagues and Hooker and recent trends in general personality psychology promise a great deal for future research on personality and health. In this section of the chapter, we present evidence to support their claims; and strategies for how to do at least some of the work they propose. We draw from the multidisciplinary and quickly growing field of narrative studies and the renewed emphasis on the life study tradition. Although narratives and life studies have been until very recently a rare tool for health psychologists, medical anthropologists (e.g., Kleinman, 1988) and medical sociologists (e.g., Charmaz, 1991) have usefully applied them for many years. In addition, health psychologists have begun to chart courses for programs of research in which narrative and discursive forms of analysis can be used to craft important answers to the questions psychologist researchers pose (Willig, 2000). Below, we present some of what we have learned about key personality and health issues and dilemmas (cf. Ouellette & DiPlacido, 2001). We will not review all of what is now a very large body of research; but select a few studies that well illustrate the value of narrative and life studies, and whose methodologies and interpretive strategies are effective models for future research.

With all of the following in mind—Rae Carlson's (1971, 1984) search for the person, Billig's (1994) call for a repopulated psychology, Wayne's desire to want to understand his mother as not just an ALS patient but a person with ALS, and Renee's yearning for a more sensitive and responsible way of doing personality and health, we begin with examples of how narrative and life studies have revealed the presence of the person amongst health and illness phenomena. We then turn to a consideration of how it is that through narrative and life studies, we can seriously address persons in context in health research, find ways of recognizing individual subjectivity and agency alongside the power of social structures, and craft a more ethical research practice.

Where is the Person in Health Research?

The Emerging Person in Studies of Dementia

In the late 1990s, a reviewer of research on dementia and Alzheimer's declared that people living with dementia had been absent from research reports for far too long. Understanding the challenges of keeping up with the rapid changes in personality that accompany the disease, she speculated that in their coping efforts, many health care providers, family members, and researchers had 'assumed that people with dementia experienced a steady erosion of personality and identity to the point at which no person remained' (Downs, 1997, p. 597). Downs called for more of a recently emerging body of work that revealed 'personhood.' This kind of work documented (a) the sense of self that persists for individuals with dementia, in spite of cognitive impairment, throughout the disease; (b) the importance of the rights of such persons around such issues as disclosure of diagnosis; and (c) the feasibility of obtaining the perspectives of persons with dementia about their illness, and the value of these for maximizing service provision.

Most of this new research has relied upon narrative and life study techniques. For example, Aggarwal et al. (2003) interviewed 27 people at various stages of dementia with open-ended

broad questions and an individualized approach. The researchers let respondents' preferences and their distinctive kind of cognitive impairment determine what specific visual and
other stimulus materials they used in the interview. They established that personality was
still very much at work in the personal and social values that their respondents retained
and reported. With regard to their perceptions of nursing home care, persons with dementia
expressed satisfaction with the physical environment of the home but dissatisfaction with
the lack of stimulations and lack of choice and independence. Researchers' films of day to
day events of respondents' lives confirmed their reports. With regard to their experiences of
dementia, all respondents described loss of independence, loss of memory, and communication difficulties. Researchers interpreted these reports not to be symptoms of the disease
process, but understandable reactions to their situation (e.g., the infrequency with which
they were given the opportunity to interrogate their experiences and make sense of what
was happening to their lives).

Finding Persons Who Are Often Neglected

Noting the insufficient attention to issues of race, ethnicity, class, and sexual orientation
in personality and health research, Ouellette and DiPlacido (2001) were forced to ask: To
whom does the link between personality and health apply and does it apply in the same
way to all? Importantly, in studies of lives, voices emerge of people too often relegated to
the margins.

For example, Aronson, Whitehead, and Baber (2003), as part of an evaluation of a program
they call 'Healthy Men in Healthy Families,' conducted extensive, in depth life histories
with 12 urban low-income African American men, aged 19 to 44. The four meetings with up
to two hours of interviewing for each established that intensive talking about the meanings
of individual experiences is not just for the educational and economic élite. The men show
the investigators how health problems are not to be isolated, but seen as embedded in their
lives that include many other problems, such as lack of jobs, financial strains, problems with
girlfriends, worries about their children, and drug use. Using Smith and Spiro's term, we
see complicated 'health-related trajectories' in the life histories of these men. From them,
the investigators learn why their intervention worked and why it didn't. They conclude that
only if the complexities of these lives are addressed and only if fit is established between
their lives and the interventions, will health interventions succeed.

The field of gay and lesbian health provides another example of health challenges that
are particular to certain groups in society, and the need to consider the lived experience of
individuals in those groups. Work on minority stress (Meyer, 1995, 2003) has focused on the
links between personality and mental health for diverse groups of lesbian, gay, and bisexual
individuals. Meyer's (2003) model of minority stress illustrates the potential moderating role
of personal identity characteristics in the relationship between proximal stressors distinctive
to lesbian, gay, and bisexual lives and negative health outcomes. This research points to the
importance of identity as a personality construct related to the health of lesbian, gay, and
bisexual people. Understudied, however, is the extent to which people actually *live* the social
categories that researchers often consider them as belonging to after they 'check the box'
next to any category label such as 'Black' or 'Latino'. McAdams' (1996) notion of identity
as a narratively constructed life story offers potential to address this absence. It will allow
researchers to look beyond whether or not people identify as both Black *and* Latino, and at

how someone's sense of him or herself as a *Black Latino* creates a unique identity category at the intersection of multiple cultures, socio-historical factors, and lived experiences in the form of critical, life-defining events. This presents the 'problem' of multiple social identities as a necessary complexity that should be embraced and understood in models of health and health behavior; and not factors that should be controlled for or partialed out in multiple regression models. An understanding of how *social* identities become *personal* is a necessary next step in personality and health research.

The Patient as Story Teller

In the 1980s when he was only in the early stages of mid-adulthood, the medical sociologist Arthur Frank suffered several serious health problems, including heart disease and testicular cancer (1995). He found that the theories and models of his discipline could not address all that he was experiencing. The knowledge of medical sociology fell far short as a representation of what he was living. At the same time, however, he could use what he had learned from the sociological study of modernity to understand the pull and responsibility he was feeling to create his own sense of meaning about what was happening to him. Sociology had taught him to appreciate the consequences for individuals of modernity's loss of traditional sources of meaning. Like all other social institutions, medicine and science no longer had their dominance, no longer provided all the answers. People with illness, like all people, are thrown back upon their own subjectivity and reflexivity.

In response to both sociology's gaps and insights, Frank wrote a memoir about his illness experiences and then a stunning little book (1995) in with he reflects on his own stories and the autobiographical reflections of other patients with other illnesses. This book is all about how the ill person narrates his or her own experiences. Frank reveals the many sorts of stories that people can tell and how those stories can change over time. In his book, given the conditions of modernity, Frank encourages the patient to take responsibility for 'what illness means in his or her life' (1995, p. 13). The story is a response to a 'moral imperative' to engage in 'perpetual self-reflection on the sort of person that one's story is shaping one into, entailing the requirement to re-shape that self-story if the wrong self is being shaped' (1995, p. 158). Frank makes the telling of stories by patients and then the listening to those stories by other patients, family and friends, health care providers *and health researchers* part of the ethics of care. He calls upon researchers seeking to understand phenomena of health and illness to leave room in their investigations for these stories and the people who tell them.

Yes, these illness stories certainly reveal persons in the midst of health and illness. For Frank, however, it is critical that these persons be seen in relationship to others. Stories in fact, for him, constitute relationships. They reveal community or interconnectedness with others and the dialogical nature of the self (Hermans, Rijks & Kempen, 1993). For Frank, as a person and as a researcher, one tells stories not just for oneself, but for others as well.

What Exactly is Context in Personality and Health Research?

Although we now often hear the recommendation to attend to context while we do health research (e.g., Smith & Spiro, 2002), it is not always so clear what is meant by 'context' and how exactly we are to observe it. In Frank's work on illness stories, context clearly has to do with specific other persons, the particular medical and scientific structures in which these persons find themselves, and general historical change. In his work and that of now many other social scientists of medicine, illness narratives and life stories become the vehicles through which context is revealed. Sometimes those contexts are very far removed from our usual field of vision. Goodman (2004), for example, used case-centered, comparative interviewing with 14 unaccompanied refugee male youths from the Sudan now resettled in the U.S. as the basis for her description of the contexts of violence in which they grew up and a recasting of our notions of resilience and coping. Leipert and Reuter (2005) studied women's stories to reveal the importance of geography for understanding health. Supplementing in-depth interactive interviews with other strategies such as observations of terrain and road conditions and collection of locally produced histories, investigators learned how the extreme northern climate affects health and how women individually and collectively develop resilience.

In other studies, particularly those that employ discourse analysis, aspects of context closer to home are revealed. Sabat and Harre (1992, 1994; Sabat, 1994), in their ground-breaking research on Alzheimer's disease that enabled the re-emergence of the person and the self of those living with the illness that we described earlier, showed how the discourses of those caregivers are an important part of the context. They used records of conversations with persons living with Alzheimer's disease, both in treatment centers and at their homes, interviews with caregivers, and interviews conducted by social workers with the Alzheimer's sufferer together with his or her caregiver. Applying discourse analysis, they revealed the experience of living with Alzheimer's and the consequences of the construction of that experience by those who are not the patient. Their interviews showed a higher level of cognitive functioning than had prior work, functioning that includes a subjective experience of self, what they call a *personal self*. But they also demonstrated compellingly the absence of a social self. The professional and family caregivers who should provide the audience for that social self are not there. Instead, these caregivers engage in the discourse that says dementia patients do not have selves. Because narratives are co-constructed by speaker and audience, the person with Alzheimer's loses a *social self* when he or she is not allowed to have one by those around him or her. The discourse of professionals and families is too often the discourse that lowers self-esteem and contributes to the general loss of personhood that researchers are now trying to challenge through greater attention to narratives and life stories.

In yet another area of what is now a very large literature within the social sciences of medicine on illness narratives and discourse, one finds a number of studies on gender as context. For example, through her reanalysis of the narratives of two men living with multiple sclerosis, Riessman (2003) discovered the many different versions of masculinity now in circulation in our society. Using a performative framework (Goffman, 1981), she observed Randy, one of the men, engage the several shifting masculine identities that define his social context. Randy tells her how in his positive response to his illness, he is the traditional masculine lone hero on the move. Randy also tells her: 'I've also become more comfortable . . . with my femininity'; and that in the past, his 'masculinity was threatened by homosexuality' but now he enjoys a 'more tangible sense of masculinity' (Riessman, 2003, pp. 11–12). Through his illness story, Randy tells Riessman about the new selves he is seeking to construct in the face of his illness *and* the complex views of gender that his society or context make available to him. In her revisiting of these men's narratives, Riessman appreciated the value of Bourdieu's ideas about social structure: It is through the explicit study of discourse or narrative that we can discover aspects of society like gender and class that are buried deep within people.

Finally, we want to close this section on narrative, lives, and context with an especially provocative and 'must read' piece for personality and health researchers. Mahoney (2005) shows how our research on stress, personality, and illness has created a particular kind of social discourse, indeed a context, with which individuals must now contend.

> The dominant discourse on the aetiology of stress locates the cause of stress within an individual's personality. Proponents of this discourse study hardiness, locus of control, coping and adaptation skills as well as stress-generating personality types . . . This emphasis on intrinsic stressors takes the focus away from stressors originating in the organization and value of work. Furthermore, with the accent on intrinsic stressors, employers and their managers can abrogate responsibility for creating stressors at the workplace. (p. 84)

Through his ethnographic approach to a medium sized ambulance service in the United Kingdom, examination of public records on this part of the British work force, and interviews and focus groups with a cross-section of ambulance personnel, he reveals the sources of stress to be instead with the restructuring of specific parts of the work (e.g., decreasing size of crews, greater tracking and surveillance of the personnel, longer shifts) connected with attempts to increase productivity and efficiency. An important part of his work was the serious consideration of the political and economic context in which he raised his research question about stress. As he seeks to have his findings make a difference for policy makers and those who control the workplace, and to encourage more humane work practices, Mahoney shows the inadequacy of the social discourses that our research has helped construct.

We are not suggesting here that personality researchers all need to become sociologists, political scientists, economists, or even social activists determined to take down the capitalist system that Mahoney so provocatively shows to be damaging to health. Instead, we are encouraging the use of narratives and life stories to broaden what we look at as researchers and include context in our investigations. As researchers like Spence (1987), Behar (1993), and Winter & Stewart (1995) show, when one looks very closely at a single life, one can come to see important dimensions of whole societies and cultures. And amongst what one sees, as Mahoney demonstrates, are social and cultural dimensions that our own research constitutes and maintains.

Looking at Both Person and Context in Health Research

Especially important for researchers intent on looking seriously at persons and context, the deeply psychological and the deeply sociological, is another set of recent studies. These consider discourses about health and illness that society makes available; and how it is that individuals actually experience them. What often emerges is how individuals contest and find those discourses to be insufficient and contradictory. According to Crossley (1999), in a very useful paper on how societal power works through cultural stories of illness, it is only by looking very closely at the specific practical and social context of each person's life that one can decide whether the illness story that he or she is telling is an oppressive story or a liberating story for that person. Willig (2002), in a very helpful review of the various ways that discourse analysis has been used in studies of health and illness, calls for more theorizing on the relationships between discourse, practice, subjectivity, and experience. In her proposed research agenda, she includes the study of individual history, motivation, and change and continuity. We describe two studies below that exemplify at least aspects of this agenda.

King et al. (2002) examined how a group of patients with renal disease were able to craft strategies of adaptation within their individual lives, while they simultaneously contended with moral judgments within society about what is and what is not appropriate adaptation. For these investigators, chronic illness is more than just a set of stressors that require specific coping tools. Very much like Mahoney (2005) in his discussion of stress in the workplace, they caution against simplistic calls for 'problem-focused coping' that fail to take into account the value assumptions about personal responsibility for health behind such calls. They conducted phenomenological interviews with 20 lower to middle class Caucasian men and women with a range of progression of renal dysfunction and other complications of diabetes. They collected stories of their experiences of adaptation. In the stories, patients expressed tensions between feeling resilient and victimized, stoic, and in despair. The dominant theme across all but one of the interviews, however, was that of stoic endurance. King et al. concluded that persons living with a chronic illness such as diabetic renal disease are forced to contend with a society that now values emotional self-expression and seeking of support, and not stoicism, as the appropriate responses to suffering. They call for more research to clarify how it is that persons with serious chronic illness can indeed satisfy their individual needs but also develop strategies of adaptation that will gain the approval of others around them.

In a recent study of gay men's narratives around HIV risk reduction practices conducted by M.J. Stirratt, Frost (2005) examined the role of intimacy-related motives for the practice of serosorting: a behavior that entails using HIV-status as a selection criterion for casual and romantic partners. Contextualizing serosorting in the lived experiences of both HIV-positive and HIV-negative gay men, he demonstrated the importance of a potential partner's HIV-status not only for the risk of viral transmission (as it has been traditionally conceptualized), but also for the formation and maintenance of long-term close relationships. Some HIV-positive men felt that they would not be able to communicate openly and disclose aspects of their inner selves with a negative partner due to dissimilarities in lived experiences. Others felt that having a positive partner would allow for a relationship that fostered sharing the burden of making health decisions and care taking.

Frost identified themes in the narratives that revealed men's negotiation of two conflicting sociohistorical, cultural ideologies. Through one that he called 'a healthy society ideology', men felt pulled toward decisions to select partners primarily on the basis of their HIV status. Through the other, 'an ideology of romance,' men expressed desires to find the right relationship partner regardless of HIV. The conflicting demands of these ideologies and values posed a dilemma for both HIV-positive and HIV-negative men who reported intimacy-related motives for serosorting. For most men, wanting to establish or maintain a close relationship meant 'finding the right person.' However, feeling the need to date only persons with the same HIV-status, the men severely restricted their dating pool and potential for finding the right person, for fear he might have the 'wrong' HIV-status. Thus promoting the health of one's self or others was often in contradiction to finding love and companionship, as it required making exceptions to partner selection strategies.

In order to understand how men actually negotiated this ideological dilemma, a more personological analysis based on aspects of these men's life histories was needed. As Frost demonstrated, these men's previous experiences in relationships, both seroconcordant and discordant, life expectancies, and the importance of intimacy relative to potential infection, all determined whether or not men would be willing to make exceptions to their serosorting behavior patterns. This type of analysis portrayed the men in Stirratt's study as actively engaged in their health-related decision making and behavior patterns. They are forced to contend with different ideologies and values in society but they are not passive subjects determined by dominant discourses. It allows for an understanding of how and why people make the choices they make regarding health behaviors. The analysis does more than point out the fact that there is a choice that needs to be made. Finding the person at the intersection of cultural and sociohistorical factors is an important concern for personality and health researchers employing narrative methodology.

Issues of Practice: How Do We Use What We Know about Personality and Health?

Given both the professional and popular attention now being given to narrative therapy and fields such as narrative medicine[2] in which stories are seen as means for healing of patients and their caregivers, it appears that there is much value in an application of what have been described here as research practices. And indeed, there are studies that document the effectiveness of narrative and life study strategies in health interventions. In the already cited study by Aronson et al. in their 'Healthy Men in Healthy Families' program, researchers learned how their interventions worked, how they didn't work, and how they might specifically be improved through their analyses of extensive life histories told by their participants.

In a more targeted intervention effort aimed at reducing smoking among adolescents, Johnson et al. (2003) used narrative inquiry to overcome the low participation and low success of existing youth smoking programs. Their review of the literature showed that very little is known about youths' experience of smoking. Even though studies in other areas demonstrated that smoking is very relevant to identity processes (i.e., we live in a social world that continues to tell us smoking is cool), we know little about how adolescents actually define themselves in relation to tobacco use. Johnson et al. also cited findings that smoking is a changing, dynamic process; not the deterministic and straightforward process that the early models of youth smoking portrayed. Deciding that their research needed to fill all these gaps by being 'grounded in the lives and experiences' of adolescents, Johnson et al. conducted in-depth interviews with 35 young men and women, 14 to 18 years of age, with a variety of smoking histories. Detailed and repeated readings of each transcript by the eight member multidisciplinary health research team revealed that adolescents accepted or rejected the social construction of smoking through their adaptation of seven different kinds of smoking identities: the confident, vulnerable, ardent, or accepting nonsmoker; and the in-control, confirmed, and contrite smoker. Researchers observed that although some of the youth made one identity dominant over the others, others held more than one and spoke of

---

[2] For readers interested in learning more about narrative medicine, the website maintained by the program at The College of Physicians and Surgeons at Columbia University is especially helpful (http://www.narrativemedicine.org/). The program offers an interdisciplinary approach to clinical medicine which emphasizes the importance of literature, autobiography, and other genres of the humanities for understanding persons and their lived experiences of health and illness. Students participate in narrative medicine rounds. They are taught to speak and write about patients in everyday language in order to improve their reflexive attention to their own role in shaping the patients' care, as well as best understand their patients' concerns and needs.

identities that are in transition. The adolescents did not engage in a simple internalization of the social constructions of smoking but relied upon their own personal experiences, were aware of the role of smoking in their lives, and had their own goals with regard to tobacco use.

Johnson et al.'s results made clear that there is not a simple binary smoker/nonsmoker identity and that change efforts need to address more than the popular idea of readiness to change. They concluded that if tobacco control interventions are to be effective, they must be responsive to and somehow incorporate knowledge about the multiple smoking identities that adolescents can enact. In fact, in their own work, by involving adolescents in a process that was meaningful to them—their telling of their own stories—they enabled them to envision alternatives to smoking and to create new stories about themselves that did not include smoking.

For a more extensive consideration of methods, we offer a third example of an evaluation and intervention project based in narrative and life study. Ouellette studied the intake process at the Gay Men's Health Crisis (GMHC); the first and largest community-based organization established in response to AIDS in New York City (Kobasa Ouellette, 1990; Ouellette, 1998). During the late 1990s, staff at GMHC were concerned about what they called the 'new clients,' i.e., clients who were more likely than earlier clients to be women, people worried about the current and future welfare of their children, people of color, and people struggling with the problems associated with poverty. A collaborative research team sought to determine clients' specific needs and expectations for the organization. The initial research questions were: (a) How does an increasingly diverse client population late in the second decade of AIDS, during a time of improved treatment options but declining financial support for community resources, perceive GMHC?; (b) What are they expecting from the organization?; (c) What does personality have to do with any of this? Specifically, how does personality matter for how clients make their way through an organization like GMHC?

To address these questions, our team conducted interviews with 35 prospective clients. Using phenomenological-existential strategies (cf. Smith, 1993), we sought to elicit how the client perceived, subjectively experienced, and understood GMHC; within the particular place and time in history of their telling of their stories. As we conducted the interviews, we were aware of certain realities and constraints operating within GMHC and the other social, political, and cultural structures with which the client was contending. Throughout the work, we attended as closely as we could to the individual person understood to be someone contending with powerful social structures. The team's interview strategy was explicitly designed to document and understand how context was having an influence on the narratives of both clients and interviewers. For example, when Ouellette interviewed an older Jamaican man, a first generation immigrant who associated his AIDS diagnosis with transmission through his sexual activity with other men and who spoke about the importance of his strong affiliation with a Pentecostal religious group, it mattered that she knew something about the extreme homophobia in Jamaica and within the particular religious community with which he was associated. What she knew and felt about these issues mattered for what the man was able and chose to say in the interview, and how it was later interpreted.

Interviewers took a particular stance in the interview setting. We were very engaged, and presented the interview context in a way that the client could take it in whatever direction he or she wanted. Interviewers sought to convey that we were curious about his or her particular situation and ready to learn something new. The authors of the current chapter see this approach to the doing of personality and health research as likely to have provoked responsiveness and provided help to that philosopher in Renee's story.

The data collected by the team included extensive notes taken during and immediately following the intake interviews, notes from a small number of follow-up interviews, field notes on various meetings including those with research team, GMHC staff members and volunteers; and general research journals that each team member kept. The data were analysed using the same phenomenological-existential stance (Smith, 1993) through which they were collected, using strategies of content, discursive analysis, and biographical analysis.

Through content analysis, we identified key themes, patterns, and relationships between issues. Trying to capture not only what was currently going on in clients' lives, but also where those lives seemed to be heading; we were concerned to identify the edges, the horizons, the possible futures in these lives (Widdershoven, 1993). Through discursive analysis, we attended to the local context of the interview and examined how it was co-constructed. Results of this were very helpful as we planned how we would deliver feedback to the intake staff. Also, discursive analysis was a way of identifying the many voices at work in the interview. Even though only the interviewer and interviewee were physically present in the room, there were many other characters cast in important roles in the narratives. Clients' mothers, fathers, lovers, and friends were all part of how the person was now coming to terms with AIDS and how he or she thought about the help they needed from a place like GMHC. The voices of health care providers, representatives of city and state bureaucracies were making a difference in plans the client could now make. Key to understanding the person and helping him or her select the right health services was the appreciation of all those voices; and their influences on such things as the client's emotional state and sense of possibility.

Because the key theoretical question was about the role of personality, the biographical or life study analysis was especially important. Very early on in the data collection, it was clear that personality mattered but not personality simply in the form of personality traits (McAdams', 1996 Level 1). Instead the narratives were comprised of current life projects and goals, concerns about identity, and health. They were filled with emotions and the interplay between emotions, motivations, and prospective clients' personal and social values. Participants were narrating the self that they were seeking to construct by coming to GMHC.

The interviewees included men and women, identified as gay and straight, were Latino/Hispanic, African/American, West Indian, and white, and were representative of the full client base of the Gay Men's Health Crisis. Each quickly shifted what was initially designed to be an intake interview into an opportunity to tell their life stories. They described their pasts before the AIDS diagnosis; their present lives in which AIDS is only one of the many challenges they contend with as members of marginalized groups; and the futures they seek to construct with help from structures like that of GMHC and the other organizations they consult. The narratives revealed the interplay or special kind of transactions between personalities and social systems. People's stories revealed what they wanted from GMHC but they also revealed themes of agency in their ideas and anticipations about the distinctive kind of involvement they might have with the organization. They included how they themselves might contribute to the organization. Several participants, when asked about what more they wanted to know about GMHC, asked how they could join not only as clients, but also as volunteers.

One client spoke very articulately about his struggles against stigmatizing identities that others within health systems were imposing on him (i.e., an AIDS patient who is also a former drug user and person of color). It was the threat that AIDS posed to his ideal self-image that seemed to provoke the greatest pain, indeed the pain that might lead him back to a history of excessive drug use. Others responsible for his health care may not see that pain while they are distracted by the stigmatized identities that they associate with him. GMHC emerges in his and many other prospective clients' depictions as a critical place for the construction of a new, less oppressed, and freer self. In this regard, the team's approach allowed the relationship between personality and health to be represented as reciprocal. Not only were the clients' agentic selves responsible for their seeking and active engagement in health services, but also the clients' sense of self and identity were transformed as a result of their involvement and experiences with GMHC.

Finally, in the spirit of the research interview as action and opportunity for change, these interviews were indeed interventions, interventions for both clients and interviewer. In doing these interviews, the team certainly and strongly appreciated that they were hearing stories that needed to be told and listened to. If GMHC was a place providing service to people with AIDS, then making room for these narratives was a key piece of the work. Something happened in that conversation that was healthful for the client. The example below illustrates such an instance:

> At the start of our interview, Mr. Ortiz seemed very reluctant to say anything. His body was all turned in on itself; he looked down at his shoes. In response to initial questions, he mumbled replies. But I pressed on, using that existential-phenomenological style that we had agreed upon in both meetings of the research team and clinical supervision. I was intent on remaining engaged in the process, intent on communicating the purpose of the interview, eager to have the client see the interview as joint work. I encouraged Mr. Ortiz to ask about unclear questions and to suggest alternative approaches to the interview to better meet the goals of registration for services and research that we shared. And then something clicked. Stories, self and identity, hardiness and sense of coherence filled the room (Ouellette, 1999).

CONCLUSION

Several personality psychologists responded in a special issue of the *Journal of Psychology* to the following question: 'What kinds of constructs—and at what levels and in what domains—must be proposed to account for a human life and/or predict what a person will do?' (Winter & Stewart, 1995: p. 711). In this chapter, we have sought to use observations of who and what persons are and might be as the basis for judging the adequacy of what our personality theories and methods enable us to say. Within the domain of personality and health research, we have found, with the help of investigators from psychology and other disciplines, that what is now available in personality psychology has not yet been taken full advantage of by personality and health researchers; and that persons reveal even more work for us to do. That work is to consist of a fuller characterization of personality—more theorizing and more development of methods; and a fuller and deeper use of what we know through engagement with the lives of others in health and illness. We hope that this chapter inspires personality and health researchers in these directions.

REFERENCES

Allport, G.W. (1961). *Pattern and growth in personality*. New York: Holt, Rinehart & Winston, Inc.

Aggarwal, N., Vass, A.A., Minardi, H.A., Ward, R., Garfield, C. & Cybyk, B. (2003). People with dementia and their relatives: Personal experiences of Alzheimer's and of the provision of care. *Journal of Psychiatric and Mental Health Nursing, 10*, 187–197.

Aronson, R.E., Whitehead, T.L. & Baber, W.L. (2003). Challenges to masculine transformation among urban low-income African American males. *American Journal of Public Health, 93*, 732–741.

Baerger, D.R. & McAdams, D.P. (1999). Life story coherence and its relation to psychological well-being. *Narrative Inquiry, 9*, 69–96.

Barenbaum, N.B. & Winter, D.G. (2003). Personality. In D.K. Freedheim (Vol. ed.), *Handbook of psychology, Volume I: History of Psychology* (pp. 177–203). Hoboken, NJ: John Wiley & Sons, Inc.

Baumeister, R.F. & Newman, L.D. (1994). How stories make sense of personal experiences: Motives that shape autobiographical narratives. *Personality and Social Psychology Bulletin, 20*, 676–690.

Behar, R. (1993). *Translated woman: Crossing the border with Esperanza's story*. Boston: Beacon Press.

Billig, M. (1994). Repopulating the depopulated pages of social psychology. *Theory & Psychology, 4*, 307–335.

Bruner, J.S. (1990). Culture and human development: A new look. *Human Development, 33*, 344–355.

Cantor, N. (1990). From thought to behavior: 'having' and 'doing' in the study of personality and cognition. *American Psychologist, 45*, 735–750.

Carlson, R. (1971). Where is the person in personality research? *Psychological Bulletin, 75*, 203–219.

Carlson, R. (1984). What's social about social psychology? Where's the person in personality research? *Journal of Personality and Social Psychology, 47*, 1304–1309.

Charmaz, K. (1991). *Good days, bad days: The self in chronic illness and time*. New Brunswick, NJ: Rutgers University Press.

Cohler, B.J. (1991). The life story and the study of resilience and response to adversity. *Journal of Narrative and Life History, 1*, 169–200.

Cohler, B.J. & Hostetler, A.J. (2002). Aging, intimate relationships, and life story among gay men. In R.S. Weiss & S.A. Bass (eds), *Challenges of the third age: Meaning and purpose in later life* (pp. 137–160). Oxford: Oxford University Press.

Cohler, B.J., Hostetler, A.J. & Boxer, A.M. (1998). Generativity, social context, and lived experience: Narratives of gay men in middle adulthood. In D.P. McAdams & E. de St. Aubin (eds), *Generativity and adult development: How and why we care for the next generation* (pp. 265–309). Washington, DC, US: American Psychological Association.

Cotrell, V. & Hooker, K. (2005). Possible selves of individuals with Alzheimer's disease, *Psychology and Aging, 20*, 285–294.

Crossley, M.L. (1999). Stories of illness and trauma survival: Liberation or repression? *Social Science and Medicine, 48*, 1685–1695.

Downs, M. (1997). The emergence of the person in dementia research. *Ageing and Society, 17*, 597–607.

Emmons, R.A. (1986). Personal strivings: An approach to personality and subjective well being. *Journal of Personality and Social Psychology, 51*, 1058–1068.

Frank, A. (1995). *The wounded storyteller: Body, illness and ethics*. Chicago: The University of Chicago Press.

Franz, C.E. & Stewart, A.J. (1994). *Women creating lives: Identities, resilience, and resistance*. Boulder, CO: Westview Press.

Friedman, H.S. (2000) Long-term relations of personality and health: Dynamisms, mechanisms, tropisms. *Journal of Personality, 68(6)*, 1089–1107.

Freund, A.M. & Smith, J. (1999). Content and function of the self-definition in old and very old age. *Journals of Gerontology: Psychological Sciences, 54B*, 55–67.

Frost, D.M. (2005). *Intimacy motivations for HIV-based partner selection processes among gay men*. Unpublished masters thesis. City University of New York, Graduate School and University Center. New York, NY.

Gallo, L.C. & Smith, T.W. (1998). Construct validation of health-relevant personality traits: Interpersonal circumplex and five-factor model analyses of the aggression questionnaire. *International Journal of Behavioral Medicine 5(2)*, 129–147.

Goffman, E. (1981). *Forms of talk*. Philadelphia: University of Pennsylvania.

Hermans, H.J.M., Rijks, T.I. & Kempen, H.J.G. (1993). Imaginal dialogues in the self: Theory and method. *Journal of Personality, 61*, 206–236.

Hooker, K. (2002). New directions for research in personality and aging: A comprehensive model for linking levels, structures, and processes. *Journal of Research in Personality, 36*, 318–334.

Hooker, K. & McAdams, D.P. (2003). Personality reconsidered: A new agenda for aging research. *Journal of Gerontology: Psychological Sciences, 58B*, 98–107.

Johnson, J.L., Lovato, C.Y., Maggi, S., Ratner, P.A., Shoveller, J., Baillie, L. & Kalaw, C. (2003). Smoking and adolescence: Narratives of identity. *Research in Nursing & Health, 26*, 387–397.

Kiesler, D.J. (1996). From communications to interpersonal theory: A personal odyssey. *Journal of Personality Assessment, 66*, 267–282.

King, N., Carroll, C. & Newton, P. (2002) You can't cure it so you have to endure it: The experience of adaptation to diabetic renal disease. *Qualitative Health Research, 12(3)*, 329–346.

Kleinman, A. (1988). *The illness narratives—Suffering, healing, and the human condition*. New York: Basic Books.

Kobasa, S. (1982). The hardy personality: Toward a social psychology of stress and health. In J. Suls & G. Sanders (eds), *Social Psychology of Health and Illness*. Hillsdale, NJ: Erlbaum.

Kobasa, S. & Ouellette, S.C. (1990). AIDS and voluntary associations: Perspectives on individual and social change. *Milbank Quarterly, 68(2)*, 280–294.

Lindeman, M. & Stark, K. (1999). Pleasure, pursuit of health, or negotiation of identity? Personality correlates of food choice motives among young and middle-aged women. *Appetite, 33(1)*, 141–161.

Lindeman, M. & Stark, K. (2000). Loss of pleasure, identity food choice reasons and eating pathology. *Appetite, 35*, 263–268.

Little, B.R. (1983). Personal projects: A rationale and method for investigation. *Environment & Behavior, 15*, 273–309.

Mahoney, K. (2005). Restructuring and the production of occupational stressors in a corporatised ambulance service. *Health Sociology Review, 14*, 84–96.

McAdams, D.P. (1996). Personality, modernity, and the storied self: A contemporary framework for studying persons. *Psychological Inquiry, 7*, 295–321.

McAdams, D.P. (1995). What do we know when we know a person? *Journal of Personality, 63*, 365–396.

Meyer, I.H. (1995). Minority stress and mental health in gay men. *Journal of Health and Social Behavior, 36*, 38–56.

Meyer, I.H. (2003). Prejudice, social stress, and mental health in lesbian, gay, and bisexual populations: Conceptual issues and research evidence. *Psychological Bulletin, 129(5)*, 674–697.

Murray, H.A. (1938). *Explorations in personality: A clinical and experimental study of fifty men of college age*. New York: Oxford University Press.

Murray, M., Evans, B., Willig, C., Sykes, C.M., Woodall, C. & Marks, D.F. (2005) *Health psychology: Theory, research, and practice* (2nd edn). Thousand Oaks, CA: Sage.

Ogilvie, D.M. & Rose, K.M. (1995). Self-with-other representations and taxonomy of motives: Two approaches to studying persons. *Journal of Personality, 63*, 643–679.

Ouellette, S.C. (1999). Self, social identity, and personality influences on health. In R.J. Contrada & R.D. Ashmore (eds) *Self, social identity, and physical health: Interdisciplinary explorations* (pp. 125–154). New York: Oxford University Press.

Ouellette, S.C. (2005). *Robert W. White and the study of lives and social justice in contemporary social and personality psychology*. New York: Unpublished manuscript.

Ouellette, S.C. & DiPlacido, J. (2001). Personality's role in the protection and enhancement of health: Where the research has been, where it is stuck, how it might move. In A. Baum, T.A. Revenson & J.E. Singer (eds), *Handbook of health psychology* (pp. 175–193). Mahwah, NJ: Erlbaum.

Ouellette, S.C. & Kobasa, S. (1990). Lessons from history: How to find the person in health psychology. In H.S. Friedman (ed.) *Personality and disease* (pp. 14–37). New York: John Wiley & Sons, Inc.

Prilleltensky, I. & Fox, D. (1997). *Critical psychology*. Thousand Oaks, CA: Sage.

Prilleltensky, I. (1997). Values, assumptions, and practices: Assessing the moral implications of psychological discourse and action. *American Psychologist, 52(5)*, 517–535.

Riessman, C.K. (2003). Performing identities in illness narrative: masculinity and multiple sclerosis. *Qualitative Research 3(1)*, 5–33.

Rosenwald, G. (2003). Task, process, and discomfort in the interpretation of life histories. In R. Josselson, A. Lieblich & D.P. McAdams (eds), *Up close and personal: The teaching and learning of narrative research* (pp. 135–150). Washington DC: American Psychological Association.

Sabat, S.R. (1994). Excess disability and malignant social psychology: A case study of Alzheimer's disease. *Journal of Community and Applied Social Psychology, 4*, 157–166.

Sabat, S.R. and Harré, R. (1992). The construction and deconstruction of self in Alzheimer's disease. *Ageing and Society, 12*, 443–461.

Sabat, S.R. and Harré, R. (1994). The Alzheimer's disease sufferer as a semiotic subject. *Philosophy, Psychiatry, and Psychology, 1*, 145–160.

Shultz, W.T. (2005). *Handbook of Psychobiography*. Oxford: Oxford University Press.

Singer, J.A. (2004). Narrative identity and meaning making across the adult lifespan: An introduction. *Journal of Personality, 72(3)*, 437–459.

Smith, J.K. (1993). Hermeneutics and qualitative inquiry. In D.J. Flinders & G.E. Mills (eds), *Concepts in qualitative research* (pp. 183–201). New York: Teachers College Press.

Smith, T.W. & Spiro, A., III. (2002). Personality, health, and aging: Prolegomenon for the next generation. *Journal of Research in Personality, 36*, 363–394.

Smith, T.W., Glazer, K. & Ruiz, J.M. (2004) Hostility, anger, aggressiveness, and coronary heart disease: An interpersonal perspective on personality, emotion, and health. *Journal of Personality, 72(6)*, 1217–1270.

Spence, D. (1987). Turning happenings into meanings: The central role of the self. In P. Young-Eisendrath & J.A. Ahll (eds), *The book of the self: Person, context, and process* (pp. 131–150). New York: New York University Press.

Stewart, A.J. (1994). The women's movement and women's lives: Linking individual development and social events. In A. Lieblich & R. Josselson (eds) *Exploring identity and gender* (pp. 230–250). Thousand Oaks, CA, US: Sage Publications.

Strumpfer, D.J.W. (1999). Psychosocial resilience in adults. *Studia Psychologica, 41(2)*, 89–104.

Strumpfer, D.J.W., Gouws, J.F. et al. (1998). Antonovsky's Sense of Coherence Scale related to negative and positive affectivity. *European Journal of Personality, 12(6)*, 457–480.

Widdershoven, G.A.M. (1993). The story of life: Hermeneutic perspectives on the relationship between narrative and life history. In R. Josselson & A. Lieblich (eds), *The Narrative Study of Lives*, Vol. 1, London: Sage, pp. 1–20.

Wiebe, D.J. & Williams, P.G. (1992). Hardiness and health: A social psychophysiological perspective on stress and adaptation. *Journal of Social and Clinical Psychology, 11*, 238–262.

Willig, C. (2000). A discourse-dynamic approach to the study of subjectivity in health psychology. *Theory & Psychology, 10*, 547–570.

Winter, D.G. & Barenbaum, N.B. (1999). History of modern personality theory and research. In L.A. Pervin & O.P. John (eds), *Handbook of personality: Theory and research* (2nd edn, pp. 3–27). New York: Guilford Press.

Winter, D.G. & Stewart, A.J. (1995). Commentary: Tending the garden of personality. *Journal of Personality, 63*, 711–727.

PART III

Targeting Personality:
Prevention and Intervention

CHAPTER 12

The Prevention and Treatment of Hostility

Redford B. Williams
Duke University Medical Centre, USA
and
Virginia P. Williams
Williams LifeSkills, Inc., USA

INTRODUCTION

It is most appropriate to have a chapter on the prevention and treatment of hostility in this *Handbook of Personality and Health*, for a variety of reasons. A large body of research has documented that hostility exerts an adverse influence on the development of a broad range of medical disorders, not only by itself but often acting in concert with other psychosocial risk factors. Further supporting the role of hostility in pathogenesis of major medical disorders is research showing that persons with high levels of hostility exhibit excessive responses to stress in several biological systems that regulate neuroendocrine, metabolic, cardiovascular, immune, and hemostatic functions. These findings make a strong case for the development of interventions to reduce levels of hostility, with the ultimate goal of reducing its impact on health. From the developmental perspective, it is becoming increasingly clear that both nature and nurture combine to influence the development of hostile personality traits and behaviors, beginning in early life. This research makes the case for the development of interventions that can prevent the development of hostility in the first place.

The good news is that research on behavioral and psychosocial interventions is showing that it is possible to reduce levels of hostility in persons with high levels and that such reductions are accompanied by improvements in biological accompaniments of hostility that are likely involved in mediating its impact on disease risk. Work is also now under way to develop training programs that can prevent the development of hostility in children and adolescents. While large scale, multicenter clinical trials will be required to document that these behavioral/psychosocial interventions reduce the incidence of disease and improve prognosis, the evidence now available makes a strong case for undertaking such trials.

Handbook of Personality and Health. Edited by Margarete E. Vollrath. © 2006 John Wiley & Sons, Ltd.

THE IMPACT OF HOSTILITY ON DISEASE RISK

Interest in hostility as a risk factor for medical disorders had its origins in the pioneering work of Friedman and Rosenman (1974) that showed a constellation of hostility, time urgency, and competitiveness, which they termed the Type A behavior pattern, predicted increased risk of coronary heart disease (CHD) in the Western Collaborative Group Study (Rosenman et al., 1975) When studies began to appear that failed to replicate the original Type A effects (e.g., Shekelle et al., 1985), however, several investigators turned their attention to an evaluation of the components of the global Type A behavior pattern. Beginning with the demonstration that high scores on a hostility scale (Ho) made up of 50 Minnesota Multiphasic Personality Inventory (MMPI) items (Cook & Medley, 1954) correlated with severity of angiographically documented coronary atherosclerosis (Williams, Haney, Lee, Blumenthal & Kong, 1980), there soon appeared several studies using archival MMPI data in samples of medical students (Barefoot et al., 1983) and Western Electric Study participants (Shekelle, Gale, Ostfeld & Paul, 1983) that found Ho scores to predict both CHD incidence and all cause mortality over extended follow-up periods.

Barefoot, Dodge, Peterson, Dahlstrom and Williams (1989) extended our understanding of the nature of hostility as it impacts risk of mortality by showing that it was only subsets of items reflecting a cynical mistrust of others, aggressive responding, and hostile affect (anger) that were accounting for the prediction of mortality in a sample of lawyers followed up 28 years after taking the MMPI in law school. In this study they also put what is being measured by the Ho scale in the context of contemporary, 'big five', personality theory by showing that Ho scale scores correlated positively with Neuroticism (N) and negatively with Agreeableness (A), but was uncorrelated with other personality domains assessed by the NEO-PI (Costa & McCrae, 1985).

In addition to predicting increased CHD and mortality in healthy populations, recent studies have also documented reduced survival among CHD patients with higher Ho scores (Boyle et al., 2004, 2005). A Finnish study (Vahtera, Kivimaki, Koskenvuo & Pentti, 1997) found that high hostility also predicted increased rates of work absences due to illness or injury.

Based on the extensive epidemiological evidence relating Ho scores to increased risk of CHD and all-cause mortality in multiple samples, a meta-analysis conducted in the mid-1990s concluded that the psychological trait of hostility is a risk factor for not only CHD but a broad range of life-threatening medical illnesses (Miller, Smith, Turner, Guijarro & Hallet, 1996). It has become increasingly clear, however, that hostility is not the only psychosocial characteristic that is 'coronary-prone' or health damaging in a broader sense.

Thus, *depression*, whether construed as a subsyndromal predisposition or a clinical disorder, has been shown to predispose to increased risk of CHD (Anda et al., 1993) or all-cause mortality (Barefoot & Schroll, 1997) in healthy people, as well as the risk of dying in post-myocardial infarction (MI) patients (Frasure-Smith, Lesperance & Talajic, 1994). Similarly, *social isolation* (or low social support) predicts increased risk of CHD and all-cause mortality (House, Landis & Umberson, 1988) as well as a poor prognosis in CHD patients (Williams et al., 1992). *Job stress*, whether defined as high strain (high demands/low control) or effort-reward imbalance, has also been shown to increase risk of CHD (Bosma, Peter, Siegrist & Marmot, 1998) in healthy people, though an impact on prognosis in CHD patients has not been confirmed (Hlatky et al., 1995). *Lower SES* also predisposes to increased risk of CHD and all-cause mortality in healthy people (Adler, Boyce, Chesney, Folkman & Syme, 1993) and a poorer prognosis in CHD patients (Williams et al., 1992).

It is now evident that hostility and these psychosocial risk factors do not occur in isolation from one another, but tend to cluster in the same individuals and groups. Thus, working women who report high job strain are characterized by increased levels of hostility, anger, depression, anxiety, and social isolation (Williams et al., 1997). And when psychosocial risk factors do co-occur, their impact on mortality is compounded (Kaplan, 1993). A specific example of this dynamic interaction among psychosocial risk factors comes from a recent study that found a larger impact of an intense episode of anger on risk of having a myocardial infarction in lower as compared to higher SES individuals (Mittelman, Maclure, Nachnani, Sherwood & Muller, 1997).

It is becoming increasingly evident that lower SES, rather than being simply one among a list of other psychosocial risk factors, may be, in fact, a 'master' risk factor that contributes to increased levels of the other risk factors. As noted above, both psychosocial risk factors and risky health behaviors are increased in lower SES groups (Barefoot et al., 1991; Matthews, Kelsey, Meilahn, Kyuller & Wing, 1989). And while health behaviors like smoking, alcohol consumption, obesity, and sedentary life style are all increased among lower SES individuals, these risky health behaviors account for no more than 12–13% of the predictive effect of lower SES on mortality in a nationally representative sample containing both men and women (Lantz et al., 1998). However, when a broader set of risk factors, including representatives from behavioral, biological, and psychosocial domains, are controlled for, the SES gradient in all-cause mortality becomes nonsignificant (Lynch, Kaplan, Cohen, Tuomilehto & Aalonen, 1996), suggesting that SES effects on health are mediated by factors in these three domains.

This epidemiological evidence leads us to conclude that hostility and other psychosocial risk factors do not occur in isolation from one another, but tend to cluster in the same individuals. Moreover, lower SES appears to be a driver of increased levels of the other psychosocial risk factors, likely acting through them, somehow, to increase risk of developing a wide range of diseases. Pathogenesis is something that happens at the level of cells and molecules. Psychosocial risk factors do not themselves act directly on cells and molecules, however. There must be mediators between the psychosocial domain and the cellular/molecular domain, and this leads us to consider the biobehavioral pathways that can link hostility and other psychosocial risk factors to pathogenesis.

BIOBEHAVIORAL PATHWAYS FROM HOSTILITY TO DISEASE

There is ample evidence that hostility, along with other psychosocial factors that cluster with it, is associated with biological and behavioral characteristics that are biologically plausible contributors to pathogenesis. Persons with high Ho scores show larger cardiovascular and neuroendocrine responses to anger-inducing laboratory tasks than their low Ho scoring counterparts (Smith & Allred, 1989; Suarez & Williams, 1989; Suarez, Kuhn, Schanberg, Williams & Zimmerman, 1998). Studies evaluating sympathetic nervous system (SNS) function in everyday life have also documented increased reactivity in high hostile persons (Suarez, Williams, Peoples, Kuhn & Schanberg, 1991) and persons with major depression (Veith et al., 1994).

There is also evidence that parasympathetic (PNS) function is reduced in both hostile and depressed persons. Laboratory research (Fukudo et al., 1992) has shown decreased PNS antagonism of SNS effects on myocardial function in high hostile subjects. Both hostility (Sloan et al., 1994) and depression (Carney et al., 1988) are associated with decreased PNS function during ambulatory ECG monitoring. Increased and dysregulated hypothalamic pituitary adrenocortical (HPA) axis function has long been a known accompaniment of depression (Holsboer, van Bardeleben, Gerken, Stallag & Muller, 1984). Persons with hostile personality have also been found to exhibit increased HPA activation, both in ambulatory (Pope & Smith, 1991) and laboratory (Suarez et al., 1998) conditions.

Hostility and other psychosocial risk factors have been found associated with other biological factors known to contribute to pathogenesis, including increased platelet activation (Markovitz, 1998), increased blood levels of inflammatory cytokines (Musselman et al., 2001; Rothermundt et al., 2001), and increased expression of the metabolic syndrome (Surwit et al., 2002; Niaura et al., 2000).

Psychosocial risk factors are also associated with increased behavioral/physical risk factor levels. Two large-scale studies, one prospective (Siegler, Peterson, Barefoot & Williams, 1992) and one cross-sectional (Scherwitz et al., 1992) and each involving over 5,000 subjects, found hostility to be associated with increased cigarette smoking, alcohol consumption, body mass index, 24-hour caloric intake, and cholesterol/HDL ratio. Hostility has also been found to predict increased incidence of hypertension (Barefoot, Dahlstrom & Williams, 1983). Increased smoking (Glassman et al., 1990) and alcohol consumption (Hartka et al., 1991) are also well-documented in depression. Persons with low social support are less likely to succeed in smoking cessation (Mermelstein, Cohen, Lichtenstein, Baer & Kamarck, 1986) or to adhere to a prescribed medical regimen (Williams et al., 1985).

All these behavioral and biological characteristics that cluster with hostility and other psychosocial risk factors are very plausible biological contributors to the pathogenesis of CHD and other major diseases, for example, via the promotion of endothelial injury along with other inflammatory, metabolic, and hemostatic changes known to promote atherogenesis (Kher & Marsh, 2004; Ross, 1993).

Before we consider how behavioral and psychosocial interventions might be used to reduce or prevent the impact of hostility and other psychosocial risk factors on the development and prognosis of CHD and other major illnesses, it is first in order to consider why and how these psychosocial and biobehavioral factors come to cluster in the same individuals and groups.

DEVELOPMENTAL ORIGINS OF HOSTILITY

In contrast to the progress just reviewed regarding the 'downstream' biological and behavioral mechanisms whereby hostility and other psychosocial risk factors contribute to pathogenesis, as Kaplan (1993) notes, relatively little attention has been given to the 'upstream' factors involved in the *development* of psychosocial (and, we would add, associated biobehavioral) risk factors. To explore this issue, we must take a developmental and neurobiological perspective.

Some time ago, a review of the extensive evidence linking a wide range of biological and behavioral characteristics to variations in brain serotonergic function led one of us to propose (Williams, 1994) the heuristic hypothesis that the clustering of health-damaging biobehavioral characteristics observed in hostile persons (and persons with the other psychosocial risk factors that tend to cluster with hostility) is mediated by decreased function of the neurotransmitter serotonin in the brain. Research showing that children in lower SES groups heard fewer positive communications from their parents from birth to three years of age (Hart & Risley, 1995), and research showing that, compared to mother-reared monkeys, rhesus monkeys who are reared in peer groups from birth to six months of age exhibit biobehavioral alterations that appear to be mediated by reduced brain serotonergic function (Higley, Suomi & Linnoila, 1992; Higley et al., 1993), have led to the expansion and extension of this hypothesis as follows: reduced brain serotonergic function resulting from the experience of relatively harsh and adverse circumstances in early childhood is one important factor contributing to the clustering of health-damaging psychosocial and biobehavioral characteristics in lower SES groups (Williams, 1998).

Given the potential importance of serotonergic mechanisms in mediating the clustering of psychosocial risk factors and biobehavioral mechanisms, it is important to consider recent molecular genetics research showing how polymorphisms of genes involved in regulating serotonin function can moderate the impact of environmental factors on these risk factors and mechanisms. Because of the key role played by the serotonin transporter in terminating, via reuptake, the action of serotonin released by presynaptic neurons, a functional insertion/deletion polymorphism of the serotonin transporter gene promoter (5HTTLPR; Lesch et al., 1996) has received much attention in this regard. Direct evidence that the transporter gene affects brain serotonin function comes from a recent study showing that 5HTTLPR genotypes are associated with levels of the major serotonin metabolite 5-hydroxyindoleacetic acid (5HIAA) in cerebrospinal fluid (Williams et al., 2003). The 5HTTLPR short allele makes about half as much transporter protein as the long allele and has been found to be associated with increased Neuroticism and decreased Agreeableness (Lesch et al., 1996)—the same personality profile that Barefoot et al. (1989) found associated with high Ho scores. The 5HTTLPR short allele has also been associated with increased risk of major depression in persons experiencing multiple stressful life events (Caspi et al., 2003). In contrast to the association between the short allele and increased psychosocial risk factor levels, the long allele has been associated with increased levels of cardiovascular reactivity to stress (Williams et al., 2001), which could account for the increased risk of myocardial infarction associated with the long allele in three studies (Arinami et al., 1999; Coto et al., 2003; Furmeron et al., 2002).

Of direct relevance to the role of serotonin-related genetic variants in moderating the impact of environmental adversity on the development of psychosocial risk factors is a recent study by Caspi et al. (2002) showing that men who were abused as children are more likely to be violent offenders if they carry the less active alleles of a promoter polymorphism of the gene that encodes for the major enzyme responsible for degrading serotonin, monoamine oxidase A (MAOA-uVNTR), than those with the more active alleles.

It is clear that much research remains to be done before we will be in a position to identify persons at risk for the development of health-damaging psychosocial risk factors and associated biobehavioral mechanisms, who might then be targeted for preventive measures. The evidence now available makes a strong case that this day will eventually arrive. In the meantime, it will be important to obtain DNA from participants in studies to evaluate behavioral/psychosocial interventions, so that it will be possible to determine whether persons with certain genetic variants are more likely to show a benefit from these interventions.

The foregoing review leads to these conclusions:

• Hostility, depression, social isolation, stress at work (high job strain, effort-reward imbalance), and lower SES have been shown in prospective epidemiological studies to increase risk of developing CHD as well as a broad range of other medical illnesses in healthy populations.

- In patients with clinical evidence of CHD, hostility, depression, social isolation, and lower SES have also been shown to confer a poorer prognosis.
- A wide range of potentially health-damaging behaviors and biological characteristics have been found in persons with psychosocial risk factors and are the likely mediators of the increased disease risk observed in such persons and groups.
- Reduced brain serotonergic function, known to be influenced by both genetic and environmental factors, is an attractive candidate to account for the clustering of biobehavioral and psychosocial risk factors in certain individuals and groups (i.e., lower SES).

The purpose of doing the research leading to these conclusions is, ultimately, to be able to use the knowledge gained to develop effective interventions to ameliorate the health-damaging effects of psychosocial risk factors and accompanying biobehavioral characteristics. Here also, there has been encouraging progress in recent years, especially with interventions aimed at improving prognosis in patients with disease already present.

BEHAVIORAL/PSYCHOSOCIAL INTERVENTIONS

Group-based behavioral interventions targeting psychosocial factors have already been shown to improve prognosis in both CHD (Blumenthal et al., 1997; Friedman, Thoresen & Gill, 1985) and cancer (Fawzy et al., 1993; Spiegel, Bloom, Kraemer & Gottheil, 1989). Based on these encouraging observations, albeit with small sample sizes, Williams and Chesney (1993) asserted that we already know enough about the impact of psychosocial factors on prognosis in established CHD to proceed with randomized clinical trials of behavioral interventions aimed at reducing the mortality associated with depression and social isolation in CHD patients. The National Heart, Lung, and Blood Institute has supported just such a trial—the ENRICHD study, the first large scale, multicenter randomized clinical trial of a psychosocial intervention in any major illness (Blumenthal et al., 1997).

Additional rigorously designed and implemented randomized clinical trials will be required, in larger samples, to establish the benefits of behavioral/psychosocial interventions in ameliorating the health-damaging effects of hostility and other psychosocial risk factors. The available evidence suggests the following key elements in the successful trials done this far:

- *Group settings* are more efficient than one-on-one approaches, enable patients to learn from one another, and serve as a powerful source of social support.
- Proven principles of *cognitive behavior therapy* and *behavior therapy*, along with social skills training enable patients to gain 'hands-on' practice in the use of skills they can use to handle the stressful situations and resulting negative emotions they need to face in the here and now.
- Treatment is limited to a fixed number of sessions, often no more than six to eight, during which each skill to be mastered is presented in a manualized, protocol-driven format that enables each patient to learn to practice and apply the skill to actual problems he/she is currently encountering at work, home or play.

Some years ago we (Williams & Williams, 1993) developed a behavioral intervention program incorporating these elements that was aimed at reducing the impact of hostility and anger on health. More recently, we have refined this program to develop the 'LifeSkills' program (Williams & Williams, 1997), a 12-hour workshop teaching ten skills that target not only hostility/anger but the other established psychosocial risk factors as well. Moreover, it aims to prevent stressful situations from occurring in the first place by providing training in skills that will enhance emotional competencies and the quality of interpersonal relationships. Rather than approaching people as broken and in need of fixing, the LifeSkills program takes a wellness focus based on the message that we can all benefit from learning and practicing skills that will improve our ability to cope and introduce a more positive focus into our life and relationships.

Before we describe the LifeSkills program in detail, we will present the evidence from secondary prevention trials in CHD patients showing that it reduces hostility and other psychosocial risk factors, as well as the accompanying biological mechanisms that lead to disease. As a first step, we developed a 30-item questionnaire in 5-point Likkert format with three questions measuring each of the ten skills taught in the LifeSkills workshop. Measurement was self-rated ability and confidence in using each of the ten skills (Hocking, Williams, Lane & Williams, 2003). The scale has good internal consistency (Cronbach's alpha = 0.85). On the 44 subjects tested, this questionnaire correlated with Spielberger's State Anxiety Scale (STAI) -0.54 (P = 0.0001; Spielberger's Trait Anxiety Scale (STAXI) -0.57 (P = 0.0001); Cook Medley Hostility Scale 0.30 (P = 0.05); Cohen's Perceived Stress Scale -0.53 (P = 0.0002 and Cohen's Social Support ISEL 0.75 (P = 0.0001)—indicating the persons who rate themselves as proficient in using the ten LifeSkills have reduced levels of the broad range of psychosocial risk factors.

There have been two small but carefully conducted randomized clinical trials that have evaluated some or all elements of the Williams LifeSkills Workshop as a means to reduce hostility and other psychosocial risk factors in CHD patients. In the first of these clinical trials, Gidron, Davidson and Bata (1999) found that, compared to patients randomized to usual care, high hostile post-MI patients receiving LifeSkills-based hostility reduction training showed reductions in both hostility and blood pressure that were maintained at follow-up two months after the end of the training. When followed up six months after the training, patients who received hostility reduction training experienced a 75 % reduction in days in hospital, with net savings of over C$ 4,000 per patient (Davidson, 1999).

In the second clinical trial, Bishop et al. (2005) conducted a randomized clinical trial of the Williams LifeSkills Workshop in a heterogenous group of post-CABG patients who had not been selected on the basis of any psychosocial risk factor. Compared to those randomized to a placebo condition (a one-hour lecture on stress), those randomized to the LifeSkills arm showed significant reductions in anger, depression, and perceived stress and increased satisfaction with social support and satisfaction with life at the end of training, with further improvements noted at three months follow-up. Those receiving LifeSkills training also showed reduced resting heart rate (HR) following training and at three months follow-up. Blood pressure reactivity to anger recall was also reduced both at the end of training and at follow-up. Heart rate reactivity to anger recall was not reduced at the end of training, but was reduced at follow-up, suggesting that patients had continued to use the skills they learned during the training, with an emerging impact on HR reactivity.

Larger trials with longer follow-up will be required to show that not only these psychosocial risk factors and biological mechanisms are reduced by LifeSkills training but also that mortality and recurrent cardiac events are reduced. Nevertheless, the results from these two trials provide encouraging proof of principle evidence that LifeSkills training has the strong potential to reduce hard endpoints when those larger trials are conducted. With this background in mind, we will now describe in some detail the LifeSkills program as delivered in face-to-face workshop format.

Each of the following ten skills is presented by the workshop facilitator in the same format:

- A description of the skill and the rationale for its use is presented.
- The facilitator illustrates use of the skill with a personal example.
- The use of the skill is modeled using an example from one of the participants.
- Participants practice use of the skill with their own examples.
- Participants follow homework assignments to use the skill in their own real life.
- At the next session, participants report on how their homework went.

Awareness of feelings. The first step in all anger management programs should be learning to be aware early on of angry feelings. This is a prerequisite for evaluation and subsequent skilled behavior. For hostile personalities, this is usually quite easy. Angry feelings are experienced by all human beings (Eckman, 1993). Effective anger control does not involve squashing all such feelings at the onset. Among individuals prone to hostility, some will try to solve the problem by never reacting, because they fear becoming out of control. Such unevaluated suppression is followed oftentimes by inappropriate expression later towards the wrong person at the wrong time for the wrong reason. On the other hand, some of those individuals who rarely acknowledge anger in the first place, but who have suppressed angry feelings could use increased recognition to make them pay closer attention to situational aggravations. What is called for in both profiles is early recognition, followed by evaluation to determine the best course of action, be it deflection or trying to get the situations that occasioned the angry feelings changed.

Suppressors may need to begin with an awareness of feelings that they can describe as generally negative or generally positive, without being able to label these feelings beyond that. Such suppressors can then progress over time to awareness of general feelings, like 'I feel upset.' Eventually, they may be able to admit anger, especially if they have been participating in a group and seen others, including the facilitator, reporting on having experienced anger themselves. Such recognition for suppressors is not only a prerequisite to practicing additional skills, but mentally healthful in and of itself. Using MRI brain imaging as well as psychoanalytic constructs, psychiatrist Richard Lane (Lane & Garfield, 2005) has related increasing attention and reflective awareness of feelings in oneself and others with greater brain activation and improved mental health.

In our experience, hostile personalities tend to interpret neutral situations as threatening. In addition, as their general mistrust of others makes them ever watchful, they find more situations that make them angry. Suppressors on the other hand interpret even negative situations as neutral. Both must be trained to separate out their interpretations—that is, their thoughts about this situation—from the objective facts they can see or hear.

Also important is for trainees to focus on one situation at a time: 'What happened just now that you can see and hear?'

Evaluation of thoughts and feelings. Once an individual has mastered awareness of feelings, objective observation, and sticking to one situation, he/she is ready to evaluate any situation that occasioned negative thoughts and/or feelings. One frequent misconception among the general public is that expression of negative feelings is always desirable. This conventional wisdom does not hold up when tested under tightly controlled laboratory conditions. Psychologists Bushman, Baumeister and Stack (1999) show that 'getting it out' not only won't help dissipate your anger, but will make you even angrier and more likely to lash out at the next person you encounter. Rather, each situation that engenders angry feelings needs to be evaluated carefully to determine the best course of action.

In our work, trainees are taught to ask four questions, once they are clear about the objective facts of a given situation and what their thoughts and feelings are. (1) 'Is the situation that occasioned my negative thoughts and feelings **Important** to me?' (2) 'When I focus only on the objective facts of this situation, are my thoughts and feelings **Appropriate**?' (3) 'Can I **Modify** this situation?' We counsel people to try all the new skills several times before assuming another person will not change their behavior, but the weather or a traffic jam on the other hand may not be modifiable. (4) 'When I consider the needs of myself and others, is taking action **WORTH IT**?' By repeating the sentence '**I AM WORTH IT!**' to themselves whenever they experience a stressful situation, participants remind themselves to ask these four questions. This encourages other people to get beyond their own perspectives and also operates as a safety control so that one thinks through the potential consequences of confronting an authority figure, before lashing out.

Any no answers, and the trainee stops asking the questions and switches attention to practicing *deflection* strategies to try to get over the negative thoughts and feelings. If four yeses, action is called for: *problem solving*, *assertion*, or *saying no* to a request.

Deflection. The skillful, emotionally mature person limits taking action to those situations that are important, objectively in need of change, where change is most likely possible, and worth it. By asking the evaluative questions, the first step has been taken towards calming back down. Self-talk can easily follow. 'Look I have decided this matter is unimportant. It's silly to allow myself to remain angry over something so petty!' If this doesn't work, trainees are taught thoughtstopping, distraction, one-minute relaxation techniques, and longer methods of meditation.

Problem solving. Sometimes situations that call for action involve unfortunate circumstances, rather than the behavior of another person. Perhaps one has insufficient funds to cover expenses; perhaps one's plane is delayed; perhaps the current marketing plan for the company is not leading to successful sales; perhaps junior is failing to do his homework, despite repeated requests to do so. The steps of problem solving are taught. Trainees are encouraged to get help from a group likely to have ideas about possible solutions, but that this exercise can be practiced alone if necessary. It's important that before a problem solving exercise is undertaken, the exact objective nature of the problem is stated precisely and the evaluative questions are asked. Not all problems are solvable and you don't want to sidetrack and discourage trainees by setting them up to focus their energies badly.

Assertion. This skill is quite helpful to both exploders and imploders. Carefully orchestrated steps of expression prevent both extremes, while enabling trainees to convey clearly exactly what explicit behaviors they want from the other person.

Saying no. Sometimes one is asked to do something and the reaction is to experience negative or some admixture of negative and positive thoughts and feelings. This calls for a slight variant on the four questions. (1) 'Is this matter important to me?' (2) 'Are my thoughts and feelings an appropriate reaction to what is being asked of me?' (3) 'Can I say no?' Most times one can. (4) 'When I consider the needs of myself and others—and the likely repercussions—is saying no worth it?' Perhaps the person asking is the supervisor and it's almost time for the annual review. Or maybe the needs of an elderly relative are greater. On the other hand, in situations both at work and home, maybe the trainee will likely experience significant overload if he/she agrees to whatever is being asked. If a trainee gets four yeses, he/she needs to learn how to say no in a way that sticks, but does not offend the person making the request. Trainees need to realize that they don't have to give an answer right away. Take the time needed to figure out their answers to the four questions. If their responses are both positive and negative, they are going to need to weigh their options carefully. If they do decide on a 'no', they want to keep their explanation simple. Justifying explanations can sidetrack everybody. Soon the topic for discussion is whether the justification is adequate. Trainees are taught always to include an explicit no.

Communication skills. In our experience and as suggested by the evidence presented earlier, hostile personalities are more likely than average to have problematic relationships. This provides a larger-than-average number of opportunities wherein hostility control is needed. Far more efficient would be to improve the relationship. Hence communication skills need to be an important feature of hostility prevention. We like to provide trainees with experiential exercises involving both speaking and listening.

Speaking up. Hostile individuals often need to change the way they address others. They are encouraged to make 'I' statements rather than 'You' statements. When dealing with a family member, it may be important to communicate feelings, though the person may want to tone them down. Reporting of feelings may not be appropriate in business or professional situations. Specificity is encouraged—no 'you always' or 'you never.' Also it's important to speak out of personal experience, rather than to come across as authoritarian. 'I feel cold!' is preferable to 'This room is too cold!'

Listening. In our experience, individuals high in hostility are usually not good listeners. They tend to interrupt the other person. Even if they manage not to do that, they are more likely than less hostile persons to be rehearsing their responding foray, once the original speaker has finished. While persons prone to hostility are unlikely ever to become superb listeners, they can improve. The first step is simply to keep quiet until the other person finishes. It's also important to use body language that conveys interest. The next step is to be able to repeat back what the other person has said, without further embellishment. All of this is of course much easier than listening with an open mind, though progress can be made here, too, if more slowly.

Empathy. Trainees are told if they can listen, they have taken an important step to being able to understand another person. They can build upon this foundation by learning to adopt the other person's perspective, albeit only temporarily. Hostile individuals usually have a long list of groups with whom they take umbrage. Self-righteous non-smokers who want to limit the rights of others. Or inconsiderate smokers who want to pollute additional lungs than just their own. People who drive too slowly. Or people who drive too fast. Religious zealots; or the sacrilegious. Political conservatives; or political liberals. Having to assume temporarily the identity of the disliked group can increase empathy. Assume a member of this group thinks he/she is a good person, trying to make the world a better place. How does he/she arrive at this conclusion? What is his/her perspective?

Initially, hostile personalities tend to see empathy as capitulation and are quite opposed to such an exercise. It must be emphasized that the choice between assertion or acceptance is a separate step. If one chooses assertion, having understood the other person will help in appreciating the ease or difficulty the other person may have in complying and suggest possible remarks reflecting that. Or one may choose acceptance, after seeing another's perspective. That in itself should reduce hostility.

If one can engage in this exercise, it may be possible to extend it to more intimate relationships. Here the goal is to understand an annoying behavior, from the perspective of the person behaving that way. Chances are differences will remain, but some of the rancor may be gone. In our experience, this latter exercise needs to be repeated over and over.

Emphasize the positive. Learning and then practicing all of the skills we have just discussed involves a lot of hard work. In our experience, it's important to tie these behavioral changes to the larger goals and objectives in the trainee's life. In training Type A individuals to become less hostile, time-oriented, and career-focused, Meyer Friedman used the exercise of having people compose their own obituary. We have asked (Williams & Williams, 1997) trainees to pretend a meteor heading for Earth will destroy everything in a day. How does the person want to spend that day? This exercise can be done pretending one has to go to work or can have a free day to fill. 'Are you living a life right now that aligns with how you want to be living your life?'

Hostility Prevention and Training on a Broader Scale

Any hostility prevention and training program needs to be efficacious, as tested in randomized controlled clinical trials. Unfortunately, such trials, while necessary, are expensive and usually conducted under ideal conditions. Rolling out such studies on a society-wide basis is not always practical for a number of reasons. Nevertheless, in order to demonstrate that an intervention is *effective* in the real world, it will be necessary to develop delivery systems to be rolled out on a large scale.

In most mental and physical health clinics, personnel have many demands on their time. In addition, patients may not have an easy time showing up for face-to-face training. This is especially true when training is conducted in groups that meet at a set time each session. Our experience is that the effectiveness of such groups is greatly increased if membership is closed. Participants eventually become much more comfortable than at first revisiting failures in hostility control. Unfortunately, goals of accessibility and closed membership can be at odds with each other. Trainees learn as much from the other participants, their successes and failures, as they learn from a skilled facilitator. In fact, the more skilled the facilitator, the more that role recedes in participants' awareness and the more obvious become the roles of the other participants.

With the goal of increasing accessibility, we have developed an online training program as well as a videotape with accompanying 100-page workbook. The videotape is Network TV-quality and 70 minutes long. In the United States, we have reasoned that a commercial product is most easily adopted and implemented, though other forms of distribution may work better elsewhere.

We have evaluated 196 participants screening positive for elevated psychosocial distress on hostility, anxiety, depression, social isolation, or perceived stress in a randomized clinical trial evaluating the LifeSkills Video (Kirby, Williams, Hocking, Lane & Williams, under review). They were randomized to either a control group or one of the three intervention groups: face-to-face workshop only; videotape with accompanying workbook only; or workshop, plus videotape with accompanying workbook. All participants were evaluated at baseline, 10 days after training/wait-period, as well as two and six months later. At the 10-day assessment those receiving LifeSkills training using either delivery format, including Video Only, showed improvements, relative to controls, in perceived stress and anxiety. When treatment groups were combined, analysis revealed that they showed significant improvement over controls in state and trait anxiety, and perceived stress, as well as near significant improvements in depression and burnout. Over long-term follow-up, treatment groups maintained these gains while controls slowly improved to reach similar levels to treated groups by six months post-training. The LifeSkills intervention appears to lead to an immediate reduction in psychosocial distress, regardless of format. While controls eventually do reach similar levels of psychosocial wellbeing as treated groups, the return to normal psychosocial wellbeing is greatly accelerated by treatment.

In another outreach program, aimed at the *primary prevention of hostility in adolescents*, we have partnered with the Georgia Prevention Institute at the Medical College of Georgia to modify the adult version of LifeSkills training for students in public high schools to be a 12-session program imbedded in a standard school health curriculum. After making initial modifications to create a 100-page teacher's manual and a student workbook, we presented the LifeSkills program to a high school class. We found that high school students are reluctant to practice in front of their peers reliving stressful situations they wished they could have handled better, but they are quite willing to role play situations typical to students like themselves. In this first round, 38 high school students (13 females; mean age 16.9 years) were randomly assigned by classroom to either LifeSkills training (n = 20) or wait list control (CTL, n = 18) groups. Psychosocial risk factors were assessed prior to group assignment and at completion of the intervention using the LifeSkills Questionnaire described earlier. Adjusting for baseline differences, the LifeSkills group improved in psychosocial risk by +5.0±2.0 (on a scale ranging from 0 to 30) compared to –0.93±2.1 in the CTL group (p = 0.05) from pre- to post-test (Barnes, Williams & Williams, 2004).

The second round of school-based LifeSkills training, which incorporated what we had learned in the first round, was conducted by a regular high school teacher and focused on the biomarker, blood pressure, as well as measures of anger. Thirty-six adolescents (mean age 16±1.5 years), approximately 50 % males were randomized to LifeSkills (n = 16) or CTL (n = 20) groups. Anger reductions were significantly larger in those randomized to LifeSkills training. Resting (seated) systolic BP (SBP) measurements were obtained pre- and post-test in the classroom setting on three consecutive school days using Dinamap 1846SX BP monitor at pre- and 10 weeks post-intervention. Changes in estimated least squared means from pre-test to post-test were statistically different between the LifeSkills (−2.3 mmHg) and CTL (+2.7 mmHg) groups for resting SBP (p < 0.03) (Barnes, Williams & Williams, 2005a, 2005b).

SUMMARY AND CONCLUSIONS

An extensive evidence base documents the adverse impact of hostility and other psychosocial risk factors on health, in both healthy and clinical groups. Laboratory research has demonstrated the presence of several biological and behavioral characteristics in persons with hostility and other psychosocial risk factors that are likely accounting for their impact on disease risk. Adverse early environments contribute to the development of hostility and psychosocial risk factors, particularly in persons predisposed on the basis of variation in certain candidate genes—most evidence now is for serotonin-related genes, but ongoing research will surely identify susceptibility genes in other biological systems. Intervention research makes a good case for the potential of behavioral/psychosocial interventions to prevent or ameliorate the health-damaging effects of hostility and other psychosocial risk factors, but further, larger scale clinical trials will be required to document the effectiveness of such interventions. We have described in some detail the LifeSkills program we have developed for reducing hostility and other psychosocial risk factors and reviewed evidence showing its efficacy in randomized clinical trials.

ACKNOWLEDGEMENTS

Preparation of this paper was supported by National Heart, Lung, and Blood Institute grants P01HL36587, R44HL67584 and R41HL072644; National Institute of Mental Health grants K05MH79482 and R44MH58498; National Institute on Aging grant R01AG19605; Clinical Research Unit grant M01RR30, and the Duke University Behavioral Medicine Research Center.

AUTHORS' DISCLOSURE

The authors are founders and major stockholders of Williams LifeSkills, Inc., a company whose mission is to develop, test, and market behavioral interventions to reduce stress and anger.

Portions of this chapter are adapted from previous publications by the first author (Williams, 2000; 2002).

REFERENCES

Adler, N.E., Boyce, T., Chesney, M.A., Folkman, S. & Syme, S.L. (1993). Socioeconomic inequalities in health: No easy solution. *Journal of the American Medical Association*, *269*, 3140–3145.

Anda, R., Williamson, D., Jones, D., Macera, C., Eaker, E., Glassman, A. & Marks, J. (1993). Depressed affect, hopelessness, and the risk of ischemic heart disease in a cohort of U.S. adults. *Epidemiology*, *4*, 285–294.

Arinami, T., Ohtsuki, T., Yamakawa-Kobayashi, K., Amemiya, H., Fujiwara, H., Kawata, K., Ishiguro, H. & Hamaguchi, H. (1999). A synergistic effect of serotonin transporter gene polymorphism and smoking in association with CHD. *Thrombosis and Haemostasis*, *81*, 853–856.

Barefoot, J.C., Dahlstrom, W.G. & Williams, R.B. (1983). Hostility, CHD incidence, and total mortality: A 25-year follow-up study of 255 physicians. *Psychosomatic Medicine*, *45*, 59–63.

Barefoot, J.C., Dodge, K.A., Peterson, B.L., Dahlstrom, W.G. & Williams, R.B. (1989). The Cook-Medley hostility scale: Item content and ability to predict survival. *Psychosomatic Medicine*, *51*, 46–57.

Barefoot, J.C., Peterson, B.L., Dahlstrom, W.G., Siegler, I.C., Anderson, N.B. & Williams, Jr., R.B. (1991). Hostility patterns and health implications: Correlates of Cook-Medley Hostility scale scores in a national survey. *Health Psychology*, *10*, 18–24.

Barefoot, J.C. & Schroll, M. (1996). Symptoms of depression, acute myocardial infarction and total mortality in a community sample. *Circulation*, *93*, 1976–1980.

Barnes, V.A., Williams, V.P. & Williams, R.B. (2004). Impact of LifeSkills on 'Positive' psychosocial risk factor profile. Society of Behavioral Medicine, Baltimore, MD., 27 March 2004.

Barnes, V.A., Williams, V.P. & Williams, R.B. (2005a) Impact of Williams LifeSkills Training on blood pressure in adolescents. Society of Behavioral Medicine, Boston, 15 April 2005.

Barnes, V.A., Williams, V.P. & Williams, R.B. (2005b). Effects of Williams LifeSkills Training on anger reduction in African American adolescents. Poster session at the annual meeting of the American Psychosomatic Society, Vancouver, Canada, 3 March 2005.

Bishop, G.D., Kaur, D.J., Tan, V.L.M., Chua, Y.L., Liew, S.M. & Mak, K.H. (2005). Effect of a psychosocial skills training workshop on psychophysiological and psychosocial risk in patients undergoing coronary artery bypass grafting. *American Heart Journal, 150,* 602–609.

Blumenthal, J.A., O'Connor, C., Hinderliter, A., Fath, K., Hegde, S.B., Miller, G., Puma, J., Sessions, W., Sheps, D., Zakhary, B. & Williams, R.B. (1987). Psychosocial factors and coronary disease. A National Multicenter Clinical Trial (ENRICHD) with a North Carolina focus. *North Carolina Medical Journal, 58,* 802–808.

Blumenthal, J.A., Jiang, W., Babyak, M., Krantz, D.S., Frid, D.J., Coleman, R.E., Waugh, R., Hanson, M., Appelbaum, M., O'Connor, C. & Morris, J.J. (1997). Stress management and exercise training in cardiac patients with myocardial ischemia. *Archives of Internal Medicine, 157,* 2213–2223.

Bosma, H., Peter, R., Siegrist, J. & Marmot, M. (1998). Two alternative job stress models and the risk of coronary heart disease. *American Journal of Public Health, 88,* 68–74.

Boyle, S.H., Williams, R.B., Mark, D.B., Brummett, B.H., Siegler, I.C. & Barefoot, J.C. (2005). Hostility, age, and mortality in a sample of cardiac patients. *American Journal of Cardiology, 96,* 64–66.

Boyle, S.H., Williams, R.B., Mark, D.B., Brummett, B.H., Siegler, I.C., Helms, M.J. & Barefoot, J.C. (2004). Hostility as a predictor of survival in patients with coronary artery disease. *Psychosomatic Medicine, 66,* 629–632.

Bushman, B.J., Baumeister, R.F. & Stack, A.D. (1999). Catharsis, aggression, and persuasive influence: Self-fulfilling or self-defeating prophecies? *Journal of Personality and Social Psychology, 76,* 367–376.

Carney, R.M., Rich, M., teVelde, A., Saini, J., Clark, K. & Freedland, K.E. (1988). The relationship between heart rate, heart rate variability and depression in patients with coronary artery disease. *Journal of Psychosomatic Research, 32,* 159–164.

Caspi, A., Sugden, K., Morritt, T.E., Taylor, A., Craig, I.W., Harrington, H., McClay, J., Mill, J., Martin, J., Braithwaite, A. & Poulton, R. (2003). Influence of life stress on depression: moderation by a polymorphism in the 5-HTT gene. *Science, 301,* 386–389.

Caspi, A., McClay, J., Moffitt, T.E., Mill, J., Martin, J., Craig, I.W., Taylor, A. & Poulton, R. (2002). Role of genotype in the cycle of violence in maltreated children. *Science, 297,* 851–854.

Cook, W. & Medley, D. (1954). Proposed hostility and pharisaic virtue scales for the MMPI. *Journal of Applied Psychology, 38,* 414–418.

Costa, P.T. & McCrea, R.R. (1985). *The NEO Personality Inventory Manual.* Odessa, FL: Psychological Assessment Resources.

Coto, E., Reguero, J.R., Alvarez, V., Morales, B., Batalla, A., Gonzalez, P., Martin, M., Garcia-Castro, M., Iglesias Cubero, G. & Cortina, A. (2003). 5-Hydroxytryptamine 5-HT2A receptor and 5-hydroxytryptamine transporter polymorphisms in acute myocardial infarction. *Clinical Science (Lond). 104,* 241–245.

Davidson, K. (1999). Cost offset of an anger management intervention for CVD patients. Paper presented at annual meeting, Society of Behavioral Medicine, Nashville, TN, March.

Ekman, P. (1993). Facial expession and emotion. *American Psychologist, 48,* 384–392.

Fawzy, F.I, Fawzy, N.W., Hyun, C.S., Elashoff, R., Guthrie, D., Fahey, J.L. & Morton D.L. (1993). Malignant melanoma: Effects of an early structured psychiatric intervention, coping, and affective state on recurrence and survival 6 years later. *Archives of General Psychiatry, 50,* 681–689.

Frasure-Smith, N., Lesperance, F. & Talajic, M. (1994). Post-myocardial infarction depression and 18-month prognosis. *Circulation, 90,* I614.

Friedman M. & Rosenman R. (1974). *Type A behavior and your heart.* New York: Knopf.

Friedman, M., Thoresen, C.E. & Gill, J.J. (1986). Alteration of type A behavior and its effect on cardiac recurrences in post myocardial infarction patients: Summary results of the Recurrent Coronary Prevention Project. *American Heart Journal, 112,* 653–665.

Fukudo, S., Lane, J.D., Anderson, N.B., Kuhn, C.M., Schanberg, S.M., McCown, N., Muranaka, M., Suzuki, J. & Williams, R.B. (1992). Accentuated vagal antagonism of beta adrenergic effects on ventricular repolarization: differential responses between Type A and Type B men. *Circulation, 85,* 2045–2053.

Fumeron, F., Betoulle, D., Nicaud, V., Evans, A., Kee, F., Ruidavets, J.B., Arveiler, D., Luc, G. & Cambien, F. (2002) Serotonin transporter gene polymorphism and myocardial infarction: Etude Cas-Temoins de l'Infarctus du Myocarde (ECTIM). *Circulation, 105,* 2943–2945.

Gidron, Y., Davidson, K. & Bata, I. (1999). The short-term effects of a hostility-reduction intervention in CHD patients. *Health Psychology. 18*, 416–420.

Glassman, A.H., Helzer, J.E., Covey, L.S., Cottler, L.B., Stetner, F., Tipp, J.E. & Johnson, J. (1990). Smoking, smoking cessation, and major depression. *Journal of the American Medical Association, 264*, 1546–1549.

Hart, T. & Risley, T.R. (1995). *Meaningful differences in the everyday experience of young American children.* Baltimore, MD: Paul H. Brookes.

Hartka, E., Johnstone, B., Leino, E.V., Motoyoshi, M., Temple, M.T. & Fillmore, K.M. (1991). A meta-analysis of depressive symptomatology and alcohol consumption over time. *British Journal of Addiction, 86*, 1283–1298.

Higley, J.D., Suomi, S.J. & Linnoila, M. (1992). A longitudinal assessment of CSF monoamine metabolites and plasma cortisol concentrations in young rhesus monkeys. *Biological Psychiatry, 32*, 127–145.

Higley, J.D., Thompson, W.W., Champoux, M., Goldman, D., Hasert, M.F. & Kraemer, G.W. (1993). Paternal and maternal genetic and environmental contributions to cerebrospinal fluid monoamine metabolites in Rhesus monkeys *(Macaca mulatta). Archives of General Psychiatry, 50*, 615–623.

Hlatky, M.A., Lam, L.C., Lee, K.L., Clapp-Channing, N.E., Williams, R.B., Pryor, D.B., Califf, R.M. & Mark, D.B. (1995). Job strain and the prevalence and outcome of coronary artery disease. *Circulation, 92*: 327–333.

Hocking, M.C., Williams, V.P., Lane, J.D. & Williams, R.B. (2003) Development of a new LifeSkills scale to measure a 'positive' psychosocial risk factor profile. Poster session presented at the annual meeting of the Society for Behavioral Medicine, Salt Lake City, UT.

Holsboer, F., van Bardeleben, U., Gerken, A., Stallag, K. & Muller, O.A. (1984). Blunted corti-cotrophin and normal response to human corticotrophin-releasing factor in depression. *New England Journal of Medicine, 311*, 1127.

House, J.S., Landis, K.R. & Umberson, D. (1988). Social relationships and health. *Science, 241*, 540–545.

Kaplan, G.A. (1993). Where do shared pathways lead? Some reflections on a research agenda. *Psychosomatic Medicine, 57*, 208–212.

Kher, N. & Marsh, J.D. (2004). Pathobiology of atherosclerosis—a brief review. *Seminars in Thrombosis and Hemostasis, 30*, 665–672.

Kirby, E.D., Williams, V.P., Hocking, M.C., Lane, J.D. & Williams, R.B. (under review) Psychosocial benefits of three formats of a standardized behavioral stress management program.

Lane, R.D. & Garfield, D.A.S. (2005). Becoming aware of feelings: Integration of cognitive developmental, neuroscientific, and psychoanalytic perspectives. *Neuro-Psychoanalysis, 7*, 1–23.

Lantz, P.M., House, J.S., Lepkowski, J.M., Williams, D.R., Mero, R.P. & Chen, J. (1998). Socioeconomic factors, health behaviors, and mortality: Results from a nationally representative prospective study of US adults. *Journal of the American Medical Association, 279*, 1703–1708.

Lesch, K.P., Bengel, D., Heils, A., Sabol, S.Z., Greenberg, B.D., Petri, S., Benjamin, J., Muller, C.R., Hamer, D.H. & Murphy, D.L. (1996). Association of anxiety-related traits with a polymorphism in the serotonin transporter gene regulatory region. *Science, 274*, 1527–1531.

Lynch, J.W., Kaplan, G.A., Cohen, R.D., Tuomilehto, J. & Aalonen, J.T. (1996). Do cardiovascular risk factors explain the relation between socioeconomic status, risk of all-cause mortality, cardiovascular mortality and acute myocardial infarction? *American Journal of Epidemiology, 144*, 934–942.

Markovitz, J.H. (1998). Hostility is associated with increased platelet activation in coronary heart disease. *Psychosomatic Medicine, 60*, 586–591.

Matthews, K.A., Kelsey, S.F., Meilahn, E.N., Kuller, L.H. & Wing, R.R. (1989). Educational attainment and behavioral and biologic risk factors for coronary heart disease in middle-aged women. *American Journal of Epidemiology, 129*, 1132–1144.

Mermelstein, R., Cohen, S., Lichtenstein, E., Baer, J.S. & Kamarck, T. (1986). Social support and smoking cessation and maintenance. *Journal of Consulting and Clinical Psychology, 54*, 447–453

Miller, T.Q., Smith, T.W., Turner, C.W., Guijarro, M.L. & Hallet, A.J. (1996). A meta-analytic review of research on hostility and physical health. *Psychological Bulletin, 119*, 322–348.

Mittelman, M.A., Maclure, M., Nachnani, M., Sherwood, J.B. & Muller, J.E. (1997). Educational attainment, anger, and the risk of triggering myocardial infarction onset. *Archives of Internal Medicine, 157,* 769–775.

Musselman, D.L., Miller, A.H., Porter, M.R., Manatunga, A., Gao, F., Penna, S., Pearce, B.D., Landry, J., Glover, S., McDaniel, J.S. & Nemerof, C.B. (2001). Higher than normal plasma interleukin-6 concentrations in cancer patients with depression. *American Journal of Psychiatry, 158,* 1252–1257.

Niaura, R., Banks, S.M., Ward, K.D., Stoney, C.M., Spiro, A., Aldwin, C.M., Landsberg, L. & Seiss, S.T. (2000). Hostility and the metabolic syndrome in older males: the normative aging study. *Psychosomatic Medicine, 62,* 7–16.

Pope, M.K. & Smith, T.W. (1991). Cortisol excretion in high and low cynically hostile men. *Psychosomatic Medicine, 53,* 386–392.

Rosenman, R.H., Brand, J.R., Jenkins, D., Friedman, M.H., Straus, R. & Wurm, M. (1975) Coronary heart disease in the Western Collaborative Group Study: final follow-up experience of $8\frac{1}{2}$ years. *Journal of the American Medical Association, 233,* 872–877.

Ross, R. (1993). The pathogenesis of atherosclerosis: a perspective for the 1990s. *Nature, 362,* 801–805.

Rothermundt, M., Arolt, V., Peters, M., Gutbrodt, H., Fenker, J., Kersting, A. & Kirchner, H. (2001). Inflammatory markers in major depression and melancholia. *Journal of Affective Disorders, 63,* 93–102.

Scherwitz, K.W., Perkins, L.L., Chesney, M.A., Hughes, G.H., Sidney, S. & Manolio, T.A. (1992). Hostility and health behaviors in young adults: the CARDIA study. Coronary Artery Risk Development in Young Adults Study. *American Journal of Epidemiology, 136,* 136–145.

Shekelle, R.B., Gale, M., Ostfeld, A.M. & Paul, O. (1983). Hostility, risk of coronary disease, and mortality. *Psychosomatic Medicine, 45,* 219–228.

Shekelle, R.B., Hulley, S., Neaton, J.D., Billings, J.H., Borhani, N.O., Gerace, T.A., Jacobs, D.R., Lasser, N.L., Mittlemark, M.B. & Stamler, J. (1985). The MRFIT behavioral pattern study: II. Type A behavior and the incidence of coronary heart disease. *American Journal of Epidemiology, 122,* 559–570.

Siegler, I.C., Peterson, B.L., Barefoot, J.C. & Williams, R.B. (1992). Hostility during late adolescence predicts coronary risk factors at midlife. *American Journal of Epidemiology, 136,* 146–154.

Sloan, R.P., Shapiro, P.A., Bigger. J.T. Jr., Bagiella, E., Steinman, R.C. & Gorman, J.M. (1994). Cardiovascular autonomic control and hostility in healthy subjects. *American Journal of Cardiology, 74,* 298–300.

Smith, T.W. & Allred, K.D. (1989). Blood pressure reactivity during social interaction in high and low cynical hostile men. *Journal of Behavioral Medicine, 11,* 135–143.

Spiegel, D., Bloom, J.R., Kraemer, H.C. & Gottheil, E. (1989). Effect of psychosocial treatment on survival of patients with metastatic breast cancer. *Lancet, 2,* 888–890.

Suarez, E.C., Kuhn, C.M., Schanberg, S.M., Williams, R.B. & Zimmermann, E.A. (1998). Neuroendocrine, cardiovascular, and emotional responses of hostile men: The role of interpersonal challenge. *Psychosomatic Medicine, 60,* 78–88.

Suarez, E.C. & Williams, R.B. (1989). Situational determinants of cardiovascular and emotional reactivity in high and low hostile men. *Psychosomatic Medicine, 51,* 404–418.

Suarez, E.C., Williams, R.B., Peoples, M.C., Kuhn, C.M. & Schanberg, S.M. (1991). Hostility-related differences in urinary excretion rates of catecholamines. Paper presented at the Annual Meeting of the Society for Psychophysiological Research, Chicago, IL.

Surwit, R.S., Williams, R.B., Siegler, I.C., Lane, J.D., Helms, M., Applegate, K.L., Sucker, N., Feinglos, M.N., McCaskill, C.M. & Barefoot, J.C. (2002). Hostility, race, and glucose metabolism in nondiabetic individuals. *Diabetes Care, 25,* 835–839.

Vahtera, J., Kivimaki, M., Koskenvuo, M. & Pentti, J. (1997). Hostility and registered sickness absences: A prospective study of municipal employees. *Psychological Medicine, 27,* 693–701.

Veith, R.C., Lewis, N., Linares, O.A., Barnes, R.F., Raskind, M.A., Villacres, E.C., Murburg, M.M., Ashleigh, E.A., Castillo, S., Peskind, E.R., Pascualy, M. & Halter, J.B. (1994). Sympathetic nervous system activity in major depression: Basal and desipramine-induced alterations in plasma norepinephrine kinetics. *Archives of General Psychiatry, 51,* 411–422.

Williams, C.A., Beresford, S.A., James, S.A., LaCroix, A.Z., Strogatz, D.S., Wagner, E.H., Kleinbaum, D.G., Cutchin, L.M. & Ibrahim, M.A. (1985). The Edgecombe County High Blood Pressure Control Program, III: Social support, social stressors, and treatment dropout. *American Journal of Public Health*, 75, 483–486.

Williams, R.B. (1994). Neurobiology, cellular and molecular biology, and psychosomatic medicine. *Psychosomatic Medicine*, 56, 308–315.

Williams, R.B. (1998). Lower socioeconomic status and increased mortality. Early childhood roots and the potential for successful interventions. *Journal of the American Medical Association*, 279, 1745–1746.

Williams, R.B. (2000) Hostility (and other psychosocial risk factors): Effects on health and the potential for successful behavioral approaches to prevention and treatment. In Baum, A., Revenson, T.R. & Singer, J.E. (eds), *Handbook of psychology and health* (pp. 661–668). Hillsdale, NJ: Lawrence Erlbaum Associates.

Williams, R.B. (2002). Hostility, psychosocial risk factors, changes in brain serotonergic function, and heart disease. In Stansfeld, S. & Marmot, M. (eds), *Stress and heart disease* (pp. 86–100), London: BMJ Books.

Williams, R.B., Barefoot, J.C., Blumenthal, J.A., Helms, M.J., Luecken, L., Pieper, C.F., Siegler, I.C. & Suarez, E.C. (1997). Psychosocial correlates of job strain in a sample of working women. *Archives of General Psychiatry*, 54, 543–548.

Williams, R.B., Barefoot, J.C., Califf, R.M., Haney, T.L., Saunders, W.B., Pryor, D.B., Hlatky, M.A., Siegler, I.C. & Mark, D.B. (1992). Prognostic importance of social and economic resources among medically treated patients with angiographically documented coronary artery disease. *Journal of the American Medical Association*, 267, 520–524.

Williams, R.B. & Chesney, M.A. (1993). Psychosocial factors and prognosis in established coronary artery disease. The need for research on interventions. *Journal of the American Medical Association*, 270, 1860–1861.

Williams, R.B., Haney, T.L., Lee, K.L., Blumenthal, J.A. & Kong, Y. (1980). Type A behavior, hostility, and coronary atherosclerosis. *Psychosomatic Medicine*, 42, 539–549.

Williams, R.B., Marchuk, D.A., Gadde, K.M., Barefoot, J.C., Grichnik, K., Helms, M.J., Kuhn, C.M., Lewis, J.G., Schanberg, S.M., Stafford-Smith, M., Suarez, E.C., Clary, G.L., Svenson, I.K. & Siegler, I.C. (2001). Central nervous system serotonin function and cardiovascular responses to stress. *Psychosomatic Medicine,*, 63, 300–305.

Williams, R.B., Marchuk, D.A., Gadde, K.M., Barefoot, J.C., Grichnik, K., Helms, M.J., Kuhn, C.M., Lewis, J.G., Schanberg, S.M., Stafford-Smith, M., Suarez, E.C., Clary, G.L., Svenson, I.K. & Siegler, I.C. (2003). Serotonin-related gene polymorphisms and central nervous system serotonin function. *Neuropsychopharmacology*, 28, 533–541.

Williams, R.B. & Williams, V.P. (1993) *Anger Kills: Seventeen strategies for controlling the hostility that can harm your health*. New York: Times Books, Trade paperback edition published by Harper-Collins, Spring, 1994.

Williams, V.P. & Williams, R.B. (1997) *Lifeskills: 8 simple ways to build stronger relationships, communicate more clearly, and improve your health*. New York: Times Books/Random House.

CHAPTER 13

Expressive Writing, Psychological Processes, and Personality

Amanda C. Jones and James W. Pennebaker

The University of Texas, USA

Psychologists have long known psychological factors affect physical health (see Davison & Pennebaker, 1996 for review). Yet in all of the ways that psychologists study health, very few interventions that improve health have been developed. Most research has instead focused on who becomes ill and who reports feelings of poor health. For example, in personality research a common goal is to link personality traits to physical manifestations of potential illnesses. The most common strategy for examining this link has been correlational. A great weakness of correlational research is that it does not provide real or potential benefit for people prone to health problems.

Through questions of who becomes ill and why some people may be more prone to illness, the field of psychosomatics is closely allied with personality and individual differences. From the first investigations by Helen Flanders Dunbar (1935), psychosomatic investigators have argued that socialized or inherited dispositions are correlated with specific illnesses. Angry or hostile people have been found to be at elevated risk for heart disease (e.g., Alexander, 1950; Niaura et al., 2002). People who repress thoughts and memories have been hypothesized to suffer from cancer at higher rates than normal (Temoshok, 1987). Children who are highly inhibited may be more likely to develop respiratory problems, including asthma and upper respiratory infections (e.g., Kagan, 1992).

Knowing what individual differences correlate with what illness is one thing, preventing or reducing the impact of illness is another. When we know more about how some personalities are linked to which illness, can we be proactive and minimize that risk or improve health? Beyond highly specific behavioral interventions, two psychological strategies of improving health have been studied and found effective. One is general relaxation, which includes meditation, yoga, biofeedback, hypnosis, and the relaxation response (e.g., Eppley, Abrams & Shear, 1989; Linden & Chambers, 1994; Van Rood, Bogaards, Goulmy & Van Houselingen, 1993). The second includes various types of cognitive-oriented therapies. These therapies attempt to change the ways people think about their problems or themselves. Cognitive-oriented therapies include insight-oriented talk therapies such as psychoanalysis

Handbook of Personality and Health. Edited by Margarete E. Vollrath. © 2006 John Wiley & Sons, Ltd.

and client-centered therapy as well as more focused behavioral and cognitive therapies (e.g., Mumford, Schlesinger & Glass, 1983; Smith, Glass & Miller, 1980).

What do these two broad approaches to therapy have in common? Generally, the client in either type of therapy acknowledges the existence of a problem. In cognitive and talk therapies, words are often the major therapeutic tool. People are encouraged to openly discuss their problem(s) with another person (the therapist). This often includes a process of labeling of the problem, discussion of its causes, and discussion of how it impacts the person's life (Rogers, 1951; Rush, Khatami & Beck, 1975).

In all therapies, disclosure may be a powerful therapeutic agent. Psychologists have long pointed to the relationship between disclosure and mental and physical health (Jourard, 1958; Jourard & Lasakow, 1958). The act of disclosure alone—apart from the therapist—may be at the root of much of the healing process that takes place in therapy. Is disclosure beneficial without the presence and assistance of the therapist? Over the last few decades, several laboratories have begun to answer this question by examining simple, verbal self-disclosure through expressive writing. In the expressive writing paradigm, a person typically writes about emotional, traumatic experiences. The person does not talk with another person, disclose information to another person, or receive feedback. Yet health benefits arise and participants report that the writing experience was valuable and meaningful in their lives.

Although participants have indicated they appreciate the expressive writing experience, many questions about benefiting from expressive writing remain. For example, who benefits most from expressive writing? Why do some individuals benefit more than others? Can a further understanding of who benefits from expressive writing help elucidate the mechanisms by which expressive writing works? In this chapter, we begin to address these and other questions about the interaction of personality with expressive writing.

The chapter is divided into three major sections. The first part reviews the basic expressive writing paradigm, recent findings, and concerns about the paradigm. The second section describes proposed explanations for why expressive writing has health benefits. The final section focuses on the links of personality and individual differences that have been found to moderate the expressive writing effects.

AN INTRODUCTION TO EXPRESSIVE WRITING

The first expressive writing study was published two decades ago (Pennebaker & Beall, 1986). Across several early studies, when people were randomly assigned to write about emotional upheavals, they showed improved physical health relative to controls who had written about superficial topics. Ten years later, approximately 20 studies had been published. In recent years, the number of expressive writing studies has grown dramatically. Well over 150 have now been published in English language journals.

Since the first study there have been several permutations of the basic expressive writing paradigm. Multiple studies have examined the effectiveness of expressive writing in improving the health of individuals with AIDS, diabetes, cancer, and other physical health problems. A wide variety of time schedules and writing instructions have been used across an even wider range of participant populations. As more studies are conducted, we are beginning to get a sense of some of the boundary conditions of writing.

It is beyond the scope of this chapter to provide anything more than a taste of the growing literature. The current section will build a basis for following sections by placing personality and individual differences' role in expressive writing into perspective. After a brief summary of the basic expressive writing paradigm, procedural variations that affect outcome will be described. Next, the health benefits of expressive writing will be reviewed. Finally, criticisms of and concerns about expressive writing will be addressed.

The Basic Expressive Writing Paradigm

The standard laboratory writing technique has involved randomly assigning participants to one of two or more groups. All writing groups are asked to write about assigned topics for 10 to 30 minutes per day, for one to five consecutive days. Writing is generally done in a laboratory, and no feedback is given. Participants assigned to the control conditions are typically asked to write about superficial topics (e.g., how they use their time). The standard instructions for participants assigned to the experimental group are a variation on the following:

> For the next three days, I would like for you to write about your very deepest thoughts and feelings about the most traumatic experience of your entire life. In your writing, I'd like you to really let go and explore your very deepest emotions and thoughts. You might tie this trauma to your childhood, or your relationships with others, including parents, lovers, friends, or relatives. You may also link this event to your past, your present, or your future, or to who you have been, who you would like to be, or who you are now. You may write about the same general issues or experiences on all days of writing or on different topics each day. Not everyone has had a single trauma but all of us have had major conflicts or stressors—and you can write about these as well. All of your writing will be completely confidential. Don't worry about spelling, sentence structure, or grammar. The only rule is that once you begin writing, continue to do so until your time is up.

After individuals write about their experiences, they are asked to place their essays into an anonymous-looking box and are promised that their writing will not be linked to their names. Unlike talk therapies and even everyday discussions, the expressive writing paradigm does not offer feedback to the participant. In a study comparing the effects of having students either write on paper that would be handed in to the experimenter or on a magic pad (wherein the writing disappears when the person lifts the plastic writing cover), no autonomic or selfreport differences were found (Czajka, 1987). It appears that the fundamental element of the expressive writing paradigm may lie somewhere in the act of writing.

The simple expressive writing paradigm has a clear impact on participants' physical and mental health as well as on their behaviors. Individuals—from young children to the elderly, from honor students to maximum security prisoners—disclose a broad range and depth of human experiences. Lost loves, sexual and physical abuse incidents, and tragic deaths and failures are common themes in expressive writing samples. When individuals are given the opportunity to disclose deeply personal aspects of their lives, even in the laboratory, they readily do so. Based on participants' subjective experiences, the expressive writing has a significant impact on them. A large number of participants report crying or being deeply upset by the experience, yet the overwhelming majority report that the writing experience was valuable and meaningful in their lives (for reviews see Lepore & Smyth, 2002; Pennebaker, 1997).

Procedural Differences that Affect Expressive Writing

Writing about emotional experiences clearly has an impact on participants. It also influences measures of physical and mental health. In recent years, several investigators have attempted to define the boundary conditions of the effect. This section summarizes some recent findings that show how variations in the expressive writing paradigm may produce varying outcomes (see also recent summary by Pennebaker & Chung, in press).

Topic

The original expressive writing studies asked people to write about traumatic experiences. Later studies extended the scope of writing topics to general emotional events or specific experiences shared by other participants (e.g., diagnosis of cancer, living with HIV, coming to college).

Across variations, the majority of studies have found that expressive writing is beneficial. However, as the number of studies experimenting with focused writing topics has increased, some studies have found that the topic of writing may selectively influence outcome. Virtually all studies find expressive writing has positive effects on physical health, but only certain assigned topics appear related to improvement on other specific outcomes. For example, beginning college students who wrote about the emotional experience of beginning college showed improvements in both health and grades. Beginning college students who wrote about a general emotional trauma showed improvements only in health (see Pennebaker, 1995; Pennebaker & Keough, 1999).

It is important to note, however, that participants write about a broad range of experiences even in studies with assigned, focused topics. For example, participants with breast cancer, lung cancer, or HIV have been asked to write about living with their particular disease (e.g., de Moor, Sterner & Hall, 2002; Mann, 2001; Petrie, Fontanilla, Thomas, Booth & Pennebaker, 2004; Stanton & Danoff-Burg, 2002). Although participants with one of these diseases share the disease as a common trauma, when they write about living with the disease, their topics vary. Each participant writes about individual experiences. Experiences—whether traumatic, benign, or joyous—and how the experiences are processed and described vary across individuals. Experience, and thus writing and selection of writing topics, is influenced by individual differences (e.g., cognitive awareness of emotions) and personality (e.g., neuroticism, tendency to be emotionally upset) when participants take part in expressive writing.

Several variations on the expressive writing paradigm have been tested, but none have been found consistently superior to the original paradigm which encouraged participants to choose their writing topic. It may be important for participants to select their own topic or to individualize their topic by explaining how the focus (e.g., being diagnosed with cancer) interacts with other parts of their lives. A strict writing assignment may be undesirable because narrow, specific writing may lead participants to focus on their writing itself— on the mechanics, or on staying focused on the assigned topic. It may be impossible for participants to process, explore, and disclose the role of their emotions in a trauma if the topic is too strictly defined. As researchers and outsiders who assign writing topics, we might assume the diagnosis of a life-threatening disease is the most important issue for a person to write about. However, the experience of a trauma may bring other issues to the forefront. The diagnosis may be secondary to a recent failure, an abusive partner, or some other trauma that may have occurred years earlier. Encouraging participants to select their own topics or assigning a broad topic allows participants the freedom to write about their most emotionally important experiences.

Consequently, we recommend that writing researchers and practitioners provide sufficiently open instructions to allow people to deal with whatever important topics they want to write about. The more the topic or writing assignment is constrained, the less successful it usually is in affecting health.

Timing

Studies have varied the timing of all the parts of expressive writing paradigm—including the length of each session, the time between sessions, the number of writing sessions, and the timing of the outcome measures. This section discusses what, if any, impact each temporal variation has on the health benefits of expressive writing.

Time after trauma. Is it better to write immediately after a traumatic experience or is it preferable to wait several weeks or months before setting pen to paper? The only direct experiment involved having new college students write about the experience of coming to college—either within the first two weeks of classes or up to three months after starting (Pennebaker, Colder & Sharp, 1990). Although this experience wouldn't be classified as a true traumatic experience, there were no differences in benefit as a function of emotional writing time.

More recent studies examining the impact of emotional expression immediately after a trauma paint a more disturbing picture. Various studies that have tested the effectiveness of post-trauma debriefing as is common in programs such as Critical Incident Stress Debriefing have generally found it to be ineffective and, in some cases, harmful (McNally, Bryant & Ehlers, 2003). A study with women who had recently given birth discovered that deeply emotional talks in the day after the birth actually increased the chance of post-partum depression compared with no such talks (Small, Lumley, Donohue, Potter & Waldenstrom, 2000). An emerging consensus is developing to suggest that in the first few days or weeks after a trauma, it is best to let people choose their own ways of coping rather than encouraging the expression of emotion. In the months after, however, if people feel as though they are thinking about a trauma too much and/or they don't have others in whom to confide, expressive writing may be appropriate.

Length of each session. Single writing sessions have ranged from 10 minutes to 45 minutes in length. No studies have directly compared the effectiveness of the various writing periods nor have any meta-analyses reported any differences. At this point, then, there is no clear evidence for any kind of dose-response relationship between the length of writing sessions and any outcome variables.

Time between sessions. In some studies, writing sessions occur once per day for three to five consecutive days. In others, the writing sessions all take place within a single day, once every other day, or even weekly for up to four weeks. In Joshua Smyth's (1998) meta-analysis, he found a trend suggesting that the more days over which the experiment takes place (i.e., the more time there is between sessions), the stronger the impact on outcomes. Two subsequent studies (Pennebaker & Chung, in press; Sheese, Brown & Graziano, 2004) that manipulated time between writing sessions failed to support the meta-analytical findings.

Particularly intriguing is the recent study by Pennebaker and Chung (in press) where students were randomly assigned to write three times for 15 minutes each either once a day, once an hour, or three times in an hour. Immediately after the last writing as well as at the one-month follow-up, the three groups did not differ on most of the major outcome measures. Indeed, the group that wrote three times in a little over an hour reported the study to be more personal and slightly more beneficial than the other experimental groups.

Number of sessions. Studies have used anywhere from one to seven sessions. No studies—including the Smyth meta-analysis have found clear evidence for a relationship between number of writing sessions and long-term benefit of writing.

Time until impact or measurement of outcome. Expressive writing outcomes have been measured up to about six months after the writing sessions are completed. Some psychological and physical health changes may be immediately apparent but fleeting. Other effects may take days, weeks, months, or even years to emerge as significant changes on the various health measures employed. The timing of improvements may also vary as a function of the subject population and outcomes measured. For example, in an expressive writing study in which participants suffered from either asthma or rheumatoid arthritis (RA), asthmatics who had taken part in the experimental condition showed health benefits as early as two weeks after writing. However, the health profile of RA participants in the experimental writing condition did not differ from the health profiles of participants in the control condition until four months after writing (Smyth, Stone, Hurewitz & Kaell, 1999).

Conclusions about timing. Although multiple variations have been used, there is not yet conclusive evidence indicating an ideal timing between writing sessions. The lack of convergent evidence may be due to the wide variety of factors (e.g., population, trauma, writing topic, outcomes measured) that vary across studies. The data may be further complicated if different people show benefits at different rates. For example, do some people benefit sooner than others? Just as some personalities are more susceptible to trauma, are some more susceptible to benefit?

Similarly, because studies examine a wide range of health outcomes, it is impossible to prescribe an ideal, standard time for follow-up. Determining the appropriate time to measure the outcome variable requires knowing the general time-course of proposed underlying mechanisms. Measurement could be further improved by considering whether an individual is prone to be readily influenced by participation. And, as with any measure, utilizing multiple convergent measures, which may reveal the same health benefits on varying time courses, will aid in validating specific measurements of health outcomes.

Health Benefits of Expressive Writing

Researchers have used a variety of physical and mental health measures to evaluate the effects of expressive writing. Early studies focused on physician visits to student health centers and self-reports of moods and symptoms as outcome measures (e.g., Pennebaker & Beall, 1986). Recently, studies have also included a variety of biological markers such as t-helper cell growth, CD4 counts, liver enzymes, and antibody response to Epstein-Barr virus and hepatitis B vaccinations (see Pennebaker, 1997; Pennebaker & Graybeal, 2001; Smyth, 1998 for reviews). Thus, expressive writing has demonstrated health benefits across a wide range of measures. This section will focus on the health benefits of expressive writing, including the types of benefits incurred and how they are measured.

Physiological Arousal

During the first writing session, cortisol levels of participants in a disclosure condition tend to be more elevated than cortisol levels of participants in control conditions (Sloan & Marx,

2004). Cortisol elevation is a physiological marker of stress and arousal. In the first writing session, participants writing about traumas experienced greater physiological arousal than participants in the control condition. In later writing sessions, participants' physiological arousal was similar across disclosure and control groups, indicating the initial physiological arousal was not long-term. Moreover, high initial elevation in cortisol in the first writing session predicted improved psychological (but not physical) health one month after the last writing session. It is possible that confronting a traumatic experience led to reactions like the ones aimed for in exposure-based therapy (e.g., Foa & Rothbaum, 1988). Initially, participants who confront trauma are distressed by the confrontation and show elevated cortisol levels. By writing about the trauma in multiple writing sessions, the participants expose themselves to their memory of the experience many times. Repeated exposure may desensitize the participant to the trauma so that memory of the trauma no longer causes physiological arousal.

Autonomic Nervous System

Activity of the autonomic nervous system is influenced during participation in the expressive writing paradigm. The degree to which the system is activated varies by the degree to which the participant discloses. Individuals who disclose their thoughts and emotions to a particularly high degree show significantly lower skin conductance levels when they write about trauma during trauma disclosures than individuals who disclose similarly but write about superficial topics. Following writing, individuals who write about trauma show significant decreases in systolic blood pressure and heart rate to levels below baseline; individuals who write about superficial topics do not (Pennebaker, Hughes & O'Heeron, 1987).

In short, when individuals talk or write about deeply personal topics, their immediate biological responses are similar to the responses seen among people participating in relaxation exercises or relaxation therapy. McGuire, Greenberg and Gevirtz (2005) have shown that these effects can become long-term in participants with elevated blood pressure. A month after writing, people who participated in the emotional disclosure condition exhibited lower systolic and diastolic blood pressure (DBP) than before writing. Four months after writing, DBP remained lower than baseline levels.

Behavioral Changes

Behavioral changes have also been found. Students who write about emotional topics evidence improvements in grades in the months following the study (e.g., Lumley & Provenzano, 2003). Senior professionals who have been laid off from their jobs get new jobs more quickly after writing (Spera, Buhrfeind & Pennebaker, 1994). Interestingly, relatively few reliable changes emerge using self-reports of health-related behaviors. That is, in the weeks after writing, experimental participants do not report exercising more or smoking less (e.g., Smyth, 1998). The one exception is that the study with laid off professionals found that writing reduced self-reported alcohol intake (Spera et al., 1994). A question that remains is whether these behavioral changes (e.g., improved grades, employment) in turn lead to health benefits through, for example, decreased daily stress.

Self-reports

Research using self-reports suggests that writing about upsetting experiences produces an initial elevation in negative moods (e.g., Smyth, 1998)—much like going to a sad or upsetting movie. However, over time, the sadness and distress give way. In the long run expressive writing leads to improvements in the mood and well-being of participants in disclosure conditions, compared to controls (Smyth, 1998).

It should be emphasized that most meta-analyses suggest that the writing paradigm produces stronger effects for more objective measures than for self-reports of mental or physical health. A recent meta-analysis by Frisina, Borod and Lepore (2004) found that the effect sizes for expressive writing averaged about 0.21 for physical health problems and only about 0.07 for self-report measures of mental health. This general pattern was also reported by Smyth (1998).

Conclusions on Health Benefits

It is well-known that health is a product of the interaction of many variables. In practice, however, it may be easy for researchers and practitioners to lose sight of these complex interactions. The three types of health benefits described above, plus self-reported perceptions of health and well-being, cannot be fully understood if examined separately—just as physical health cannot be fully understood without examining its interaction with psychological health.

WHY AND HOW DOES EXPRESSIVE WRITING WORK? THE SEARCH FOR MECHANISMS

At first glance, expressive writing sounds simple and straightforward. Participants write about their traumatic experiences; they then feel better and their health improves. However, there is no simple explanation for the effectiveness of expressive writing. First, expressive writing draws from and is affected by many factors. For example, health benefits, expressive writing content, and time until benefit vary across participants. Benefit may also vary by individual differences, such as personality traits, cognitive style, and baseline emotional tendencies. Second, the process of deriving physical benefit is complex. Any causal explanation can be dissected at multiple levels of analysis—from social processes to changes in chemical processes in the brain. Furthermore, an event that takes weeks or even months to unfold will necessarily have multiple determinants that can inhibit or facilitate the process over time. Therefore, a single mechanism explaining how expressive writing benefits participants will not be found. Yet many explanations have been put forth, and many have been shown partially correct.

This section broadly summarizes three overarching explanations for the expressive writing-health relationship: inhibition theory, cognitive processing theory, and affective processing theory. The first expressive writing projects were guided by a general theory of inhibition (Pennebaker, 1989; Pennebaker & Beall, 1986). Today, the inhibition theory and cognitive processing theory are probably the most commonly proposed mechanisms for explaining how expressive writing works. The theories are derived from the idea that writing provides some sort of relief from stress or other difficulties associated with not disclosing and that it helps make sense of a chaotic emotional experience. The third theory, affective processing, may be less common, but addresses the important issue of baseline emotional tendencies. All three theories tie directly to personality and individual differences that may influence the effectiveness of expressive writing.

Inhibition Theory

When people actively inhibit thoughts, feelings, or behaviors, they experience an internal conflict that becomes a stressor. To inhibit, people must consciously restrain, hold back, or in some way exert effort not to think or talk about their experiences and emotions. For example, someone may avoid feelings of relief that his ill, elderly grandmother passed away.

The process of inhibition requires physiological work and resembles the processes Sapolsky (2004) and Selye (1978) describe as part of the experience of stress. It exacerbates a number of adverse biological processes (e.g., increased cortisol production, immune suppression). Physiological work has been hypothesized to be a long-term stressor which may cause or exacerbate psychosomatic processes leading to illness or ineffective functioning (Janoff-Bulman, 1992; Pennebaker et al., 1987; Petrie, Booth & Pennebaker, 1998).

People who suppress thoughts or feelings may actually end up dwelling on them at greater length—inhibition provokes a rebound effect (Wegner, 1994). By suppressing their thoughts or feelings, people do not work through them. Thoughts or events that are not assimilated are more likely to surface, becoming intrusive and invasive.

The tendency for people's thoughts to be drawn to the thoughts they are suppressing, which they have not worked through or assimilated, is in line with the Zeigarnick effect— the tendency for people to remember interrupted and unfinished tasks better than tasks they have completed (Karniol & Ross, 1996). Through inhibition, people keep themselves from finishing the task of dealing with their stressful thoughts. When the thoughts become intrusive, many people find themselves spending excessive amounts of time with the intrusive thoughts. Ruminating on a stressful event reinforces negative affect (Nolen-Hoeksema & Morrow, 1991).

The inhibition theory of how and why expressive writing works suggests that expressive writing makes people think through the emotions and thoughts they have been avoiding, effectively removing the stress associated with the work of active inhibition (Pennebaker & Beall, 1986). In support of this theory, research suggests individuals who are not inclined to talk regularly about their emotions may benefit more than individuals who are more inclined to talk about their emotions and experiences.

Following the logic of inhibition as a stressor, it was assumed that if people were encouraged to talk or write about a previously inhibited event, health improvements would be seen. The act of writing about an emotional topic would allow individuals to organize and assimilate the event, bypassing the need for further inhibition (Pennebaker, 1989). Despite the helpfulness of the theory in generating interesting and testable hypotheses, the supporting evidence has been decidedly mixed.

Several correlational studies hinted that such processes may be at work (e.g., Cole, Kemeny, Taylor & Vissher, 1996; Cole, Kemeny, Taylor, Vissher & Fahey, 1996; Gross & Levenson, 1997; Major & Gramzow, 1999). Note that these ideas are consistent with Wegner's (1994) work on thought suppression and ironic processing. That is, by attempting to control ongoing thoughts, individuals are ultimately monitoring more information at higher rates which could help to explain the apparent physiological work of inhibition.

Several studies attempted to evaluate the degree to which people wrote about secret versus more public traumas and previously disclosed versus not previously disclosed events. In no case did these factors differentially predict improvements in health (e.g., Greenberg & Stone, 1992; Pennebaker, Kiecolt-Glaser & Glaser, 1988). Similarly, individuals are not able to report (or even understand) questions that ask them the degree to which they are actively inhibiting or holding back their thoughts, emotions, or behaviors (Pennebaker et al., 1988). At this point, then, the inhibition hypothesis would have to be considered as unproven and still not adequately tested.

Cognitive Processing of Emotional Upheavals

Cognitive processing of trauma has been proposed as a complementary mechanism to further explain the beneficial effects of expressive writing (e.g., Greenberg, Wortman & Stone, 1996; Pennebaker et al., 1990). Expressive writing may improve health for at least two reasons rooted in cognitive processing of emotional experience. Expressive writing serves as a means of habituation, diminishing arousal and affective reactions to thoughts of the trauma through repeated exposure to thoughts of the trauma during writing sessions (e.g., Mendolia & Kleck, 1993; Pennebaker, 1989; Sloan, Marx & Epstein, 2005). Expressive writing may also help a participant to make sense of and reframe the trauma. Through the course of expressive writing, participants may be able to change their appraisal of trauma, coming to view it as more benign and controllable, and less overwhelming (Brewin, 1996; Greenberg et al., 1996).

Personality and other individual differences shape cognitive styles. Consequently, some people may readily habituate to a negative experience such that they either do not need expressive writing, or benefit from expressive writing very quickly. For others, the structured process of expressive writing is necessary to facilitate thinking through and cognitively frame their experiences, to make sense of the experiences.

A large number of labs have been working with the assumption that processes like these occur—that writing about a traumatic experience helps the participant to organize or assimilate the complex features of traumatic experience. Part of the complexity of the experience is processing the emotions—which involves emotional experiences and requires cognitive work. In the first expressive writing study, people who wrote about only the facts of a trauma, excluding emotional experience, did not show improvements in health (Pennebaker & Beall, 1986). In a more recent study, students were randomly assigned to either express a traumatic experience using bodily movement, or to express an experience using movement and then write about it, or to exercise in a prescribed manner for three days, 10 minutes per day (Krantz & Pennebaker, 1995). Whereas the two movement expression groups reported that they felt happier and mentally healthier in the months after the study, only the movement plus write group evidenced significant improvements in physical health and grade point average. Emotional expression alone is not sufficient. Health gains appear to require cognitive, linguistic processing, integrating the experiential aspects of a trauma with the facts of the trauma.

Smyth, Stone, Hurewitz and Kaell (1999) have followed such thinking further assuming that writing pushes a participant to organize an upsetting experience. As an indirect test, the authors had participants either write about a trauma in an organized or fragmented way. Only writing in an organized way was associated with health and mood improvements.

Williams-Avery (1998) reported similar effects such that writing instructions that stressed organization provided better outcomes than instructions that did not. Several labs are now finding support for the idea that constructing an organized narrative over the course of writing helps the individuals to integrate the experience. At this point, there is a fair amount of evidence supporting various aspects of the cognitive-affective assimilation theory of why and how expressive writing works, but many details remain to be examined.

Affective Processing of Emotional Upheavals

Individual differences in emotional tendencies and affective processing styles may interfere with or facilitate coping with emotional upheaval. For example, after two people have had an especially upsetting verbal argument, one may have difficulty thinking about the trauma, never processing it fully, never recognizing the emotions involved. The other person may find his or her thoughts constantly returning to the trauma. Expressive writing may improve health for reasons rooted in affective processing and individual differences in emotional tendencies. The act of confronting the trauma by writing about it may push the person to confront and think through emotions, breaking the loop of avoidance and of rumination so he or she can overcome the emotional trauma.

Affective and cognitive processing clearly work together. From the time of Breuer and Freud (1895/1966), most therapists have explicitly or tacitly believed that the activation of emotion is necessary for therapeutic change. Most current talk therapies require the cognitive processes of recognizing and labeling, and then discussing emotions. Consistent with the experiential approach to psychotherapeutic change, emotional acknowledgement ultimately fosters important cognitive changes (Ullrich & Lutgendorf, 2002). In indirect support of this theory, research suggests that individuals who have a deficit in describing feelings to others, or poor emotional verbalization skills, are less likely to disclose their experiences and less able to cognitively process their emotional experiences, and less likely to incur health benefits from expressive writing (see Lumley, 2004 for review).

Conclusions

Just as health is a product of the interaction of many variables, the effectiveness of expressive writing is a product of the interaction of many mechanisms. While this is likely disappointing to many research psychologists, it is familiar to practicing therapists. Overcoming traumatic experiences is not a simple process. Many variations of therapy exist, implying what the research on expressive writing has found: there are multiple mechanisms driving benefit from expressive writing.

INDIVIDUAL DIFFERENCES AND PERSONALITY AS MODERATORS OF EXPRESSIVE WRITING

Despite the complexity of measurement issues, expressive writing has consistently been shown to benefit a wide variety of individuals, from senior professionals with advanced degrees to maximum security prisoners with sixth-grade educations (Richards et al., 2000;

Spera et al., 1994). Although people in general benefit from expressive writing, each expressive writing study yields a great deal of variability in responding. Some individuals benefit more than others. What characterizes the individuals who benefit most from expressive writing? What characterizes the individuals who do not benefit?

These questions are difficult to answer because most expressive writing studies focus on group effects rather than on individual or personality differences. Focusing just on group effects hinders understanding other important theoretical and practical issues—individual difference and personality factors that cause variability in benefit from expressive writing.

From a practical, applied perspective, knowledge of the factors that impact the effectiveness of expressive writing could reveal who benefits from disclosure, which could lead to more reliable prescriptions for the use of expressive writing, in addition to more accurate predictions of outcomes. From a theoretical perspective, the study of individual differences might reveal why some participants benefit and others do not, which could lead to the refinement and advancement of theory.

The goal of this section is to review the existing evidence for individual difference and personality factors that have been found predictive of benefit from expressive writing. The evidence is relatively scant, and sometimes contradictory. However, the factors that are revealed can be organized into three major categories: inhibition, cognitive processing and assimilation of a trauma, and affective processing and baseline emotional tendencies. Although these categories overlap, they are still useful constructs for considering who benefits from expressive writing. Because of these factors' intimate relationship with proposed mechanisms for how expressive writing works, consideration of these predictive factors may also serve to elucidate the mechanisms.

Inhibition-related Individual Difference Factors

In support of the inhibition theory, research suggests that individuals who do not naturally tend to talk about their emotions may benefit more than individuals who tend to discuss their emotions openly.

Measuring Inhibition

Before research can address whether people who are more inhibited benefit more from expressive writing, inhibition must be measured. In some studies, researchers have attempted to assess inhibition directly. For example, in some early studies researchers asked participants to rate the degree to which they tend to hold back from telling others about what they wrote in their expressive writing sessions (e.g., Pennebaker & Beall, 1986; Pennebaker et al., 1988).

Pennebaker and colleagues (1988) found that participants who wrote about traumas were significantly more likely to have written about a previously undisclosed topic. Consistent with the theory that relief from the work of inhibition leads to health benefits, the researchers predicted that participants who wrote about a trauma they reported to have previously avoided discussing would benefit most. Their findings were mixed. In the short term, high disclosure participants experienced a greater decline in systolic and diastolic blood pressure than low disclosure participants. After writing, people who wrote about previously undisclosed topics, or 'high disclosers,' also had improved mitogen concentrations relative to low disclosers, indicating an improvement in immune function. However, none of the differences were enduring.

These differing results, added to the complexity of accurately answering the question 'Have you been inhibiting discussion of this topic?' have led researchers to move on to more indirect measures of participants' inhibition. Researchers are now examining a broad array of individual difference and personality factors that may affect how likely a person is to refrain from discussing traumatic events.

Alexithymia

Alexithymia has gained a fair bit of research attention as a potential moderator or predictor of benefit from expressive writing. Alexithymia, a term coined in the early 1970s, literally translates to 'lacking words for feelings' (Lumley, 2004). The expressive writing paradigm expressly requires using words to work through traumatic experiences and related feelings. Alexithymic people have difficulty identifying, describing, differentiating, and discussing their emotions, particularly negative emotions. Alexithymic patients are likely to have difficulty engaging in and benefiting from traditional talk therapies. The evidence with regard to whether alexithymia predicts benefit or lack of benefit from expressive writing is mixed, but also patterned.

Multiple studies of clinical populations have found alexithymia (measured by the Toronto Alexithymia Scale, or TAS) predictive of a lack of benefit, or a worsening, of condition after expressive writing (e.g., CPP patients, Norman et al., 2004; migraine sufferers, Kraft et al., 2003; see Lumley 2004 for review). Why might alexithymic people be less likely to benefit from expressive writing? They may have trouble identifying stressors to write about, or they may focus on external rather than psychological processes in their writing, not processing their own emotions and thoughts related to the stressor.

In contrast, studies of psychologically healthy populations have found high scores on one of the three subscales of the TAS to be predictive of the opposite—a greater degree of benefit from expressive writing (e.g., Paez, Velasco & Gonzalez, 1999; Solano, Donati & Pecci, 2003). This subscale measures difficulties describing feelings (DDF). DDF is sometimes described as related to inhibited emotional expression and consistent with ambivalence over emotional expression (Lumley, 2004). Participants who have difficulty describing their emotions show a greater degree of benefit from expressive writing than particpants who have little difficulty describing emotions. It is possible that expressive writing provides people who have difficulty describing how they feel with the extra push they need to think and work through their emotions.

Motivation to Keep it in

Internally motivating factors, such as introversion and embarrassment over one's own experiences, may inhibit a person from thinking about and talking about emotional experiences. Active concealment of personal information that is perceived as negative or distressing is called 'self-concealment' (Larson & Chastain, 1990). Although they did not experiment with self-concealment in the context of expressive writing, Larson and Chastain (1990) did find self-concealment is distinct from self-disclosure—not simply the opposite. Furthermore, tendencies to self-conceal were significantly correlated with self-report measures of anxiety, depression, and bodily symptoms. In their study, self-concealment accounted for a significant amount of variance in physical and psychological symptoms even after controlling for occurrence of trauma, trauma distress, disclosure of the trauma, social support, social network, and self-disclosure.

Reluctance and Ambivalence about Disclosure

Ambivalence towards emotional expression is seen as an important mediator in the link between emotional styles and psychological and physical well-being (King & Emmons, 1990). Although ambivalence's relationship to other factors appeared very complex in this study, it was positively correlated with several indices of psychological distress.

In a randomized trial seeking to identify individual difference moderators of the effects of written disclosure among women with chronic pelvic pain (CPP), greater baseline ambivalence about disclosure was a predictor of benefit from expressive writing (Norman, Lumley, Dooley & Diamond, 2004). Again, at follow-up two months after writing, baseline ambivalence predicted improved positive affect and reduced daily and physical disability among women in the disclosure group. Again, ambivalence at baseline was unrelated to change in positive affect or disability among women in the other condition (who had written about a positive event). Despite this study and Lumley's (2004) discussion of ambivalence over emotional expression, few studies have examined ambivalence as a predictor of benefit from expressive writing. Ambivalence about emotional expression, does, however, appear to be the reverse of being motivated to express emotions and valuing emotional expression.

The Individual-environment Combination

The social environment is external to the individual and thus not an individual difference or personality factor. However, people choose their environments—either directly or indirectly through other life choices. People's social environments can be viewed as external representations of their past, individual difference, personality, and choices.

Furthermore, individual differences and personality factors may have strong social connotation, or stigmas, associated with them. Members of stigmatized groups (e.g., HIV-positive individuals, gays, lesbians, prisoners convicted of sex crimes) may be discouraged from disclosing their emotional experiences in their daily lives. In a study of a psychiatric prison population in which prisoners varied in the degree to which they were stigmatized, prisoners who were most stigmatized incurred the greatest benefit from expressive writing (Richards et al., 2000).

Sex Differences

There has been a great deal of interest in knowing if sex differences exist in the potential benefits of expressive writing. Smyth's (1998) meta-analysis revealed that men tend to benefit more from the expressive writing. Several studies have explored this—usually with college students—and have not replicated the meta-analytic results. For example, a study of 48 male and 46 female college students recorded the students' heart rates during expressive writing and examined their expressive writing samples for linguistic content, finding no differences in either (Epstein, Sloan & Marx 2005). Additionally, psychological and physical health, measured a month after expressive writing, showed no sex-related differences. In a large study of 546 college students (306 women), Sheese and colleagues (2004) examined self-reported health and expression in e-mail. There were no apparent differences between men and women. At this point, there is simply no compelling information to suggest sex differences.

Inhibition-related Factors: Conclusions

All things considered, many aspects of behavioral and emotional inhibition are unhealthy. However, there is only suggestive evidence indicating people who actively avoid talking and thinking through emotional experiences benefit more from expressive writing. Research with different groups, like people with alexithymia, suggests that how much people benefit from expressive writing may vary by how they are inhibited and by the cause of their inhibition.

Cognitive Tendencies and Benefit from Expressive Writing

Research suggests that individuals who cognitively process the emotions they experience in conjunction with trauma do not suffer as much from the trauma. Researchers have long suggested that thinking through the emotions associated with a traumatic event may help people to organize their thoughts and memories (Meichenbaum, 1977), assimilate the experience (Horowitz, 1976), and give the experience meaning (Silver & Wortman, 1980). Expressive writing researchers have looked at many different ways people process and view emotional experiences.

Putting a Positive Spin on it: Optimists vs. Pessimists

There are a number of theoretical and practical reasons to assume that some strategies for approaching emotional upheavals are better than others. With the growth of the field of Positive Psychology, several researchers have reported on the benefits of having a positive or optimistic approach to life (Carver & Scheier, 2002; Diener, Lucas & Oishi, 2002; Seligman, 2000). Particularly persuasive have been a series of correlational studies on benefit finding. People who are able to find benefits to negative experiences generally report less negative affect, milder distress, fewer disruptive thoughts, and greater meaningfulness in life. People who engage in benefit-finding fare better on objective physical and mental health outcomes (e.g. children's developmental test scores, recurrence of heart attacks) even after controlling for a host of possible confounding factors (for a review, see Affleck & Tennen, 1996). Being able to see things in a positive light, then, might be a critical component to successful adjustment.

In a study examining adjustment to college, Cameron and Nicholls (1998) had participants previously classified as dispositional optimists or pessimists participate in one of three writing conditions: a self-regulation condition (writing about thoughts and feelings towards coming to college, then formulating coping strategies), a disclosure condition (writing about thoughts and feelings only), or a control task (writing about trivial topics). Generally, participants in the disclosure task had higher GPA scores at follow-up. However, only the participants in the self-regulation task experienced less negative affect and better adjustment to college, as compared to the control participants. Optimists visited their doctors less in the following month if they had participated in either the self-regulation condition or the disclosure condition. Pessimists visited their doctors less in the following month only if they have participated in the self-regulation condition. With the added encouragement of formulating coping strategies, pessimists may be able to reap the same health benefits from writing about their thoughts and feelings as optimists naturally might do.

Benefiting from Trauma

When confronting traumatic experiences, is it best to ask people to simply write about them or to write about the positive sides of the experiences? Several studies have addressed this question. Particularly interesting has been a series of studies by Laura King and her colleagues. When asked to write about intensely positive experiences (IPE) or control topics, participants who wrote about IPEs reported significantly better mood, and fewer illness-related health center visits than did participants who wrote about trivial topics (Burton & King, 2004). In another study, students were asked to write about traumas in the standard way (King & Miner, 2000). In the benefit-finding condition, participants were encouraged to focus on the benefits that have come from the trauma. Finally, in the mixed condition, participants were first asked to write about the trauma, and then to switch to the perceived benefits arising from the trauma experience. Counter to predictions, the trauma–only and benefits–only participants evidenced health improvements whereas the mixed group did not. It could be that writing about the perceived benefits is enough to organize thoughts and feelings about a trauma, and to cope effectively. However, as evidenced from the mixed condition, if people are unable to integrate their perceived benefits into their trauma story in their own way, writing may be ineffective.

Deriving Meaning from Traumas

Some people naturally tend to derive meaning from traumatic experiences so that they can, in effect, learn and gain from these experiences. People derive meaning from traumatic experiences when they change the situational meaning (by changing their appraisal of the traumatic experiences) or the global meaning (by adjusting their world views, coping styles, or even personality) of the experience to reduce the discrepancy between the two. Reduction of discrepancy helps the experience fit into a 'bigger picture', or make more sense. However, in Park and Blumberg's (2002) studies of whether facilitating or encouraging people's cognitive processing of difficult experiences leads to changes in the experiences' situational meaning, global meaning, or both, evidence was mixed as to the value of writing to help derive meaning.

Story-making Abilities

One aspect of expressive writing that is suggested as a mechanism for benefit is making sense of an experience. By making sense of an experience, participants are able to organize the experience in their minds, perhaps making their thoughts about it less chaotic and overwhelming. This implies that structured writing would be more beneficial than entirely unstructured writing, and that the ability to put together and tell an organized, structured story might enhance benefit from expressive writing. In a study that explored story-making ability as an individual difference, researchers found no evidence that a person who writes a good story in one domain (e.g., about a photograph) writes well in another domain (e.g., about a life experience) (Graybeal et al., 2002). This study also failed to find any evidence to suggest that good story writing is related to benefiting from expressive writing. However, participants who wrote well about emotional topics tended to score highly on measures of agreeableness and emotional intelligence. Thus the ability to tell a good narrative varies by content, but also appears to be related to personality and individual differences. Whether people who write a good story are most likely to benefit from expressive writing is still in question.

Cognition-related Factors: Conclusions

How people think influences how they process trauma; some people have tendencies to think through their emotional experiences in ways that help them cope. Some participants may be more likely to benefit from expressive writing, and some may not need expressive writing because they naturally tend to think through emotional experiences. Furthermore, studies show that encouraging certain participants to use certain cognitive strategies increases their benefit from expressive writing (e.g., Cameron & Nicholls, 1998).

Affective Tendencies and Benefit from Expressive Writing

Individual differences in baseline affective tendencies may also affect the degree to which a person benefits from expressive writing. Research suggests that people who are experiencing negative emotions but are able to address and disclose the negative emotions may benefit most.

Negative Affect

In the same randomized trial that found ambivalence about emotional expression to be a predictor of benefit from expressive writing, greater baseline negative affect was a predictor of benefit from expressive writing (Norman et al., 2004). In this study of women with CPP, women in the disclosure group wrote about their physical pain. These women were compared with a group who wrote about positive events. This differs from traditional expressive writing studies in that there was no traditional control group writing about an emotionally neutral topic (e.g., time management).

At follow-up, two months after writing, baseline negative affect was one of the predictors of improved positive affect and reduced daily and physical disability among women in the disclosure group; negative affect at baseline was unrelated to change in positive affect or disability among the other women. Other studies measuring negative affect have not found the factor predictive of benefit from expressive writing (e.g., Pennebaker & Beall, 1986; Pennebaker et al., 1990).

Hostility as Interference

There are other motivators for avoiding disclosing personal information. For example, for individuals who are very hostile, feelings of anger and hostility may interfere with both the expression of emotions and the processing and assimilation of traumatic events. Even if they do not inhibit expression of their thoughts and emotions, people with high levels of hostility have been found to have benefited more from writing than people low in hostility (Christensen & Smith, 1993; Christensen et al., 1996).

Affect-related Factors: Conclusions

Individual differences in baseline affective states shape both how people react to events and how likely they are to benefit from expressive writing. At times, affect may interfere with processing and experiencing emotions. For example, when a person is high in hostility, expressive writing may give that person the push needed to face and process emotions.

SUMMARY AND CONCLUSIONS

The purpose of this chapter has been to review the expressive writing paradigm, the psychological processes that may enable people to benefit from expressive writing, and the current knowledge of how personality and individual difference variables influence expressive writing's effects. Expressive writing has been used and researched with increasing interest since the 1980s. We are learning a great deal about the parameters that impact expressive writing, from how long after a trauma to write, to how focused a topic should be. In addition, many theories have been proposed and tested to explain how and why expressive writing works. Ironically, most of the proposed theories have been found to work—at least to some degree. Less research has addressed the personality and individual difference factors that may impact whether people benefit from expressive writing. There are few clear answers to questions of which personalities are most likely to benefit, perhaps because of the overwhelming complexity of the expressive writing phenomenon.

That being said, there are some patterns that reveal who might benefit most from expressive writing, and some reasons for why they might benefit. This chapter has outlined three theories to explain why and how expressive writing may work: inhibition theory, cognitive processing theory, and affective processing theory. It is useful to consider the individual difference variables that influence benefit in three parallel categories: inhibition, cognitive style, and affective style or baseline emotional tendencies.

A logical extension of this pattern is to suggest that different people benefit from expressive writing through different mechanisms, for different reasons. For example, individuals who experience a trauma and then try to avoid thoughts about the trauma may benefit from expressive writing because it frees them from the physiological work of inhibition by encouraging them to think through the trauma and associated emotions. Others who experience a similar trauma may tend to be very hostile, and hostility may interfere with the processing of the emotional trauma. They too may benefit from expressive writing because it pushes them to think through and deal with the trauma.

Ultimately, we simply lack adequate knowledge of the roles that individual differences play in the expressive writing paradigm. Most writing studies have only modest effect sizes (d = 0.07 to 0.50) and rely on extremely variable real world outcome measures, such as physician visits or biological measures (cf., Pennebaker & Chung, in press). Under these conditions, it would be rare to find a reliable individual difference moderator. Future research must include much larger samples with a broad array of individual differences. Indeed, we would urge researchers to look past the traditional self-reports. Given that expressive writing appears to work on real world behaviors better than with self-reports, it would follow that the most effective moderators may be beyond participants' knowledge or awareness. An exciting world of research possibilities lies ahead of us.

REFERENCES

Affleck, G. & Tennen, H. (1996). Construing benefits from adversity: Adaptational significance and dispositional underpinnings. *Journal of Personality*, *64*, 899–922.

Alexander, F. (1950). *Psychosomatic Medicine*. New York: Norton.

Breuer, J. & Freud, S. (1966). *Studies on Hysteria*. New York: Avon. (Original work published 1895.)

Brewin, C.R. (1996). Theoretical foundations of cognitive-behavioral therapy for anxiety and depression. In J.T. Spence, J.M. Darley & D.J. Foss (eds), *Annual review of psychology* (Vol. 47, pp. 33–57). Palo Alto, CA: Annual Reviews.

Burton, C.M. & King, L.A. (2004). The health benefits of writing about intensely positive experiences. *Journal of Research in Personality*, *38*, 150–163.

Cameron, L.D. & Nicholls, G. (1998). Expression of stressful experiences through writing: Effects of self-regulation manipulation for pessimists and optimists. *Health Psychology*, *17*, 84–92.

Carver, C.S. & Scheier, M.F. (2002). Optimism. In C.R. Snyder & S.J. Lopez (eds), *Handbook of positive psychology*. Oxford: Oxford University Press.

Christensen, A.J. & Smith, T.W. (1993). Cynical hostility and cardiovascular reactivity during self-disclosure. *Psychosomatic Medicine*, *55*, 193–202.

Christensen, A.J., Edwards, D.L. & Wiebe, J.S. (1996). Effects of verbal self-disclosure on natural killer cell activity: Moderating influence of cynical hostility. *Psychosomatic Medicine*, *58*, 150–155.

Cole, S.W., Kemeny, M.E., Taylor, S.E. & Visscher, B.R. (1996). Elevated physical health risk among gay men who conceal their homosexual identity. *Health Psychology*, *15*, 243–251.

Cole, S.W., Kemeny, M.E., Taylor, S.E., Visscher, B.R. & Fahey, J.L. (1996). Accelerated course of human immunodeficiency virus infection in gay men who conceal their homosexual identity. *Psychosomatic Medicine*, *58*, 219–231.

Czajka, J.A. (1987). Behavioral inhibition and short term physiological responses. Unpublished master's thesis, Southern Methodist University, Dallas, TX.

Davison, K.P. & Pennebaker, J.W. (1996). Emotions, thoughts, and healing: After Dafter. *Advances*, *12*, 19–23.

de Moor, C., Sterner, J. & Hall, M. (2002). A pilot study of the effects of expressive writing on psychological and behavioral adjustment in patients enrolled in a Phase II trial of vaccine therapy for metastatic renal cell carcinoma. *Health Psychology*, *21*, 615–619.

Diener, E., Lucas, R.E. & Oishi, S. (2002). Looking up and down: Weighting good and bad information in life satisfaction judgments. *Personality and Social Psychology Bulletin*, *28*, 437–445.

Dunbar, H.F. (1935). *Emotions and bodily changes. A survey of literature on psychosomatic interrelationships, 1910–1933*. Oxford: Columbia University Press.

Eppley, K.R., Abrams, A.I. & Shear, J. (1989). Differential effects of relaxation techniques on trait anxiety. *Journal of Clinical Psychology*, *45*, 957–974.

Epstein, E.M., Sloan, D.M. & Marx, B.P. (2005). Getting to the heart of the matter: Written disclosure, gender, and heart rate. *Psychosomatic Medicine*, *67*, 413–419.

Foa, E.B. & Rothbaum, B.O. (1998). *Treating the trauma of rape: Cognitive behavioral therapy for PTSD.* New York: Guilford Press.

Frisina, G.F., Borod, J.C. & Lepore, S.J. (2004). A meta-analysis of the effects of written emotional disclosure on the health outcomes of clinical populations. *The Journal of Nervous and Mental Disease, 192,* 629–634.

Graybeal, A., Sexton, J.D. & Pennebaker, J.W. (2002). The role of story-making in disclosure writing: The psychometrics of narrative. *Psychology and Health, 17,* 571–581.

Greenberg, M.A. & Stone, A.A. (1992). Emotional disclosure about traumas and its relation to health: Effects of previous disclosure and trauma severity. *Journal of Personality and Social Psychology, 63,* 75–84.

Greenberg, M.A., Wortman, C.B. & Stone, A.A. (1996). Emotional expression and physical health: Revising traumatic memories or fostering self-regulation? *Social Psychology, 71,* 588–602.

Gross, J.J. & Levenson, R.W. (1997). Hiding feelings: The acute effects of inhibiting negative and positive emotion. *Journal of Abnormal Psychology, 106,* 95–103.

Horowitz, M.J. (1976). *Stress response syndromes.* New York: Jacob Aronson.

Janoff-Bulman, R. (1992). *Shattered assumptions: Towards a new psychology of trauma.* New York: Free Press.

Jourard, S.M. & Lasakow, P. (1958). Some factors in self-disclosure. *Journal of Abnormal and Social Psychology, 56,* 91–98.

Jourard, S.M. (1958). A study of self-disclosure. *Scientific American, 198,* 77–82.

Kagan, J. (1992). Temperamental contributions to emotion and social behavior. In M.S. Clark (ed.), *Emotion and social behavior* (pp. 99–118). Thousand Oaks, CA, US: Sage Publications, Inc.

Karniol, R. & Ross, M. (1996). The motivational impact of temporal focus: Thinking about the future and the past. In J.T. Spence, J.M. Darley & D.J. Foss (eds), *Annual review of psychology* (Vol. 47, pp. 593–620). Palo Alto, CA: Annual Reviews.

King, L.A. & Miner, K.N. (2000). Writing about the perceived benefits of traumatic events: Implications for physical health. *Personality and Social Psychology Bulletin, 26,* 220–230.

King, L.A. & Emmons, R.A. (1990). Conflict over emotional expression: Psychological and physical correlates. *Journal of Personality and Social Psychology, 58,* 864–877.

Kraft, C., Lumley, M., D'Souza, P., Roberson, T., Stanislawski, B. & Ramos, M. (2003). Emotional disclosure and relation training for migraine headaches: Moderating effects of alexithymia and self-efficacy. Abstract published in *Psychosomatic Medicine, 65,* A13.

Krantz, A. & Pennebaker, J.W. (1995). Bodily versus written expression of traumatic experience. Dallas, Texas: Southern Methodist University, unpublished manuscript.

Larson, D.G. & Chastain, R.L. (1990). Self-concealment: Conceptualization, measurement, and health implications. *Journal of Social and Clinical Psychology, 9,* 439–455.

Lepore, S.J. & Smyth, J.M. (2002). *The writing cure: How expressive writing promotes health and emotional well-being.* Washington, DC, US: American Psychological Association.

Linden, W. & Chambers, L. (1994). Clinical effectiveness of non-drug treatment for hypertension: A meta-analysis. *Annals of Behavioral Medicine, 16,* 35–45.

Lumley, M.A. & Provenzano, K.M. (2003). Stress management through written emotional disclosure improves academic performance among college students with physical symptoms. *Journal of Educational Psychology, 95,* 641–649.

Lumley, M.A. (2004). Alexithymia, emotional disclosure, and health: A program of research. *Journal of Personality, 72,* 1271–1300.

Major, B. & Gramzow, R. (1999). Abortion as stigma: Cognitive and emotional implications of concealment. *Journal of Personality and Social Psychology, 77,* 735–745.

Mann, T. (2001). Effects of future writing and optimism on health behaviors in HIV-infected women. *Annals of Behavioral Medicine, 23,* 26–33.

McGuire, K.M.B., Greenberg, M.A. & Gevirtz, R. (2005). Autonomic effects of expressive writing in individuals with elevated blood pressure. *Journal of Health Psychology, 10,* 197–209.

McNally, R.J., Bryant, R.A. & Ehlers, A. (2003). Does early psychological intervention promote recovery from posttraumatic stress? *Psychological Science in the Public Interest, 4,* 45–79.

Meichenbaum, D. (1977). *Cognitive-behavior modification: An integrative approach.* New York: Plenum Press.

Mendolia, M. & Kleck, R.E. (1993). Effects of talking about a stressful event on arousal: Does what we talk about make a difference? *Journal of Personality and Social Psychology*, *64*, 283–292.

Mumford, E., Schlesinger, H.J. & Glass, G.V. (1981). Reducing medical costs through mental health treatment: Research problems and recommendations. In A. Broskowski, E. Marks & S.H. Budman (eds), *Linking health and mental health* (pp. 257–273). Beverly Hills, CA: Sage.

Niaura, R.S., Todaro, J.F., Stroud, L., Spiro III, A., Ward, K.D. & Weiss, S. (2002). Hostility, the metabolic syndrome, and incident coronary heart disease. *Health Psychology*, *21*, 588–593.

Nolen-Hoeksema, S. & Morrow, J. (1991). A prospective study of depression and posttraumatic stress symptoms after a natural disaster: The 1989 Loma Prieta Earthquake. *Personality and Social Psychology*, *61*, 115–121.

Norman, S.A., Lumley, M.A., Dooley, J.A. & Diamond, M.P. (2004). For whom does it work? Moderators of the effects of written emotional disclosure in women with chronic pelvic pain. *Psychosomatic Medicine*, *66*, 174–183.

Páez, D., Valesco, C. & González, J.L. (1999). Expressive writing and the role of alexithymia as a dispositional deficit in self-disclosure and psychological health, *Journal of Personality and Social Psychology*, *77*, 630–641.

Park, C.L. & Blumberg, C.J. (2002). Disclosing trauma through writing: Testing the meaning-making hypothesis. *Cognitive Therapy and Research*, *26*, 597–616.

Pennebaker, J.W. (1989). Confession, inhibition and disease. In L. Berkowitz (ed.), *Advances in experimental social psychology* (Vol. 22, pp. 211–244). San Diego, CA: Academic Press.

Pennebaker, J.W. (1995). Emotion, disclosure, and health: An overview. In: *Emotion, disclosure & health*. Washington, DC, US: American Psychological Association, pp. 3–10.

Pennebaker, J.W. (1997). Writing about emotional experiences as a therapeutic process. *Psychological Science*, *8*, 526–537.

Pennebaker, J.W. & Beall, S.K. (1986). Confronting a traumatic event: Toward an understanding of inhibition and disease. *Journal of Abnormal Psychology*, *95*, 274–281.

Pennebaker, J.W. & Chung, C.K. (in press). Expressive writing, emotional upheavals, and health. In H. Friedman and R. Silver (eds), *Handbook of health psychology*. New York: Oxford University Press.

Pennebaker, J.W., Colder, M. & Sharp, L.-K. (1990). Accelerating the coping process. *Social Psychology*, *58*, 528–537.

Pennebaker, J.W. & Graybeal, A. (2001). Patterns of natural language use: Disclosure, personality, and social integration. *Current Directions in Psychological Science*, *10*, 90–93.

Pennebaker, J.W., Hughes, C.F., O'Heeron, R.C. (1987). The psychophysiology of confession: Linking inhibitory and psychosomatic processes. *Journal of Personality and Social Psychology*, *52*, 781–793.

Pennebaker, J.W. & Keough, K.A. (1999). Revealing, organizing, and reorganizing the self in response to stress and emotion. In R. Ashmore & L. Jussim (eds), *Self and Social Identity: Vol. II* (pp. 101–121). New York: Oxford University Press.

Pennebaker, J.W., Kiecolt-Glaser, J. & Glaser, R. (1988). Disclosure of traumas and immune function: Health implications for psychotherapy. *Journal of Consulting and Clinical Psychology*, *56*, 239–245.

Petrie, K.P., Booth, R.J. & Pennebaker, J.W. (1998). The immunological effects of thought suppression. *Journal of Personality and Social Psychology*, *75*, 1264–1272.

Petrie, K.P., Fontanilla, I., Thomas, M.G., Booth, R.J. & Pennebaker, J.W. (2004). Effect of written emotional expression on immune function in patients with human immunodeficiency virus infection: A randomized trial. *Psychosomatic Medicine*, *66*, 272–275.

Richards, J.M., Beal, W.E., Seagal, J. & Pennebaker, J.W. (2000). The effects of disclosure of traumatic events on illness behavior among psychiatric prison inmates. *Journal of Abnormal Psychology*, *109*, 156–160.

Rogers, C.R. (1951). *Client-centered therapy*. Oxford: Houghton Mifflin.

Rush, A.J., Khatami, M. & Beck, A.T. (1975). Cognitive and behavior therapy in chronic depression. *Behavior Therapy*, *6*, 398–404.

Sapolsky, R.M. (2004). *Why zebras don't get ulcers*. New York: Henry Hold and Company.

Seligman, M.E.P. (2000). Positive psychology. In J.E. Gillham (ed.), *Science of optimism and hope: Research essays in honor of Martin E.P. Seligman*. Philadelphia: Templeton Foundation Press.

Selye, H. (1978). *The stress of life.* Oxford: McGraw Hill.

Sheese, B.E., Brown, E.L. & Graziano, W.G. (2004). Emotional expression in cyberspace: Searching for moderators of the Pennebaker disclosure effect via e-mail. *Health Psychology, 23,* 457–464.

Silver, R.L. & Wortman, C.B. (1980). Coping with undesirable life events. In J. Garber & M.E.P. Seligman (eds), *Human helplessness: Theory and applications* (pp. 279–375). New York: Academic Press.

Sloan, D.M. & Marx, B.P. (2004). Taking pen to hand: Evaluating theories underlying the written disclosure paradigm. *Clinical Psychology: Science and Practice, 11,* 121–137.

Sloan, D.M., Marx, B.P. & Epstein, E.M. (2005). Further examination of the exposure model underlying the efficacy of written emotional disclosure. *Journal of Consulting and Clinical Psychology, 73,* 549–554.

Small, R., Lumley, J., Donohue, L., Potter, A. & Waldenstrom, U. (2000). Randomised controlled trial of midwife led debriefing to reduce maternal depression after childbirth. *British Medical Journal, 321,* 1043–1047.

Smith, M.L., Glass, G.V. & Miller, R.L. (1980). *The benefits of psychotherapy.* Baltimore: Johns Hopkins University Press.

Smyth, J.M. (1998). Written emotional expression: Effect sizes, outcome types, and moderating variables. *Journal of Consulting and Clinical Psychology, 66,* 174–184.

Smyth, J.M., Stone, A.A., Hurewitz, A. & Kaell, A. (1999). Effects of writing about stressful experiences on symptom reduction in patients with asthma or rheumatoid arthritis: A randomized trial. *Journal of the American Medical Association, 281,* 1304–1309.

Solano, L., Donati, V. & Pecci, F. (2003). Postoperative course after papilloma resection: Effects of written disclosure of the experience in subjects with different alexithymia levels. *Psychosomatic Medicine, 65,* 477–484.

Spera, S.P., Buhrfeind, E.D. & Pennebaker, J.W. (1994). Expressive writing and coping with job loss. *Academy of Management Journal, 37,* 722–733.

Stanton, A.L. & Danoff-Burg, S. (2002). Emotional expression, expressive writing, and cancer. In Lepore, S.J. & Smyth, J.M. (eds), *The writing cure: How expressive writing promotes health and emotional well-being* (pp. 31–51). Washington, DC, US: American Psychological Association.

Temoshok, L. (1987). Personality, coping style, emotion and cancer: Towards an integrative model. *Cancer Surveys, 6,* 545–567.

Ullrich, P.M. & Lutgendorf, S.K. (2002). Journaling about stressful events: Effects of cognitive processing and emotional expression. *Annals of Behavioral Medicine, 161,* 356–364.

Van Rood, Y.R., Bogaards, M., Goulmy, E. & Van Houwelingen, H.C. (1993). The effects of stress and relaxation on the in vitro immune response in man: A meta-analysis. *Journal of Behavioral Medicine, 16,* 163–181.

Wegner, D.M. (1994). Ironic processes of mental control. *Psychological Review, 101,* 34–52.

Williams-Avery, R. (1998, March). Cognitive processing: Linking disclosure, inhibition and health. Paper presented at the meeting of the Society of Behavioral Medicine, New Orleans.

CHAPTER 14

Media, Sensation Seeking, and Prevention

Lewis Donohew
University of Kentucky, USA

INTRODUCTION

This chapter describes a theoretical perspective on information exposure and processing which holds that, beyond verbal content, message characteristics such as intensity, movement, or novelty interact with biologically-based personality characteristics of the audiences to play a major role in attracting and holding attention. The central focus is on media messages, individual differences in how they are attended, and implications for media-based interventions designed to reach individuals most likely to engage in risk-taking behaviors such as drug abuse or risky sex.

The predictive and explanatory model on which this research draws (Donohew, Bardo & Zimmerman, 2004; Donohew, Lorch & Palmgreen, 1998; Donohew, Palmgreen & Duncan, 1980), has guided a 20-year program of study on persuasive communication, the biologically-based personality trait of sensation seeking or novelty seeking, and prevention of risky health behaviors, funded by the National Institute on Drug Abuse and other agencies of the U.S. National Institutes of Health.[1] Some of this perspective also has been incorporated into programs of the Partnership for a Drug-free America (Delaney, 2003) and the National Youth Anti-drug Media Campaign of the Office of National Drug Control Policy (ONDCP).

In this chapter, we will describe sensation seeking, including some of its biological connections, its relationship to risky health behaviors, implications for exposure to messages, and the checkered history of media-based health interventions. We will also discuss the nature of message sensation value and describe a theory of information exposure—which draws on some of the central tenets of sensation seeking—and an applied model for health

[1] The research reported in this chapter was supported by Grants DA03462, DA05312, DA06892, DA04887, DA06892-08, and DA12490 from the National Institute on Drug Abuse (Lewis Donohew, PI); Grant AA10747 from the National Institute on Alcohol Abuse and Alcoholism (Lewis Donohew, PI), Grants DA05312 and DA12964 from the National Institute on Drug Abuse (Mike Bardo, PI), Grant AA013927 from the National Institute on Alcohol Abuse and Alcoholism (Rick Zimmerman, PI), Grants MH 061187 and MH63705 from the National Institute on Mental Health (Rick Zimmerman, PI), and Grant DA12371from the National Institute on Drug Abuse (Philip Palmgreen, PI).

Handbook of Personality and Health. Edited by Margarete E. Vollrath. © 2006 John Wiley & Sons, Ltd.

campaigns grounded in the theory. Finally, we will describe a number of studies which have offered strong support for the model.

SENSATION SEEKING

Sensation seeking is described by Zuckerman (1994) as a trait defined by 'the seeking of varied, novel, complex, and intense sensations and experiences, and the willingness to take physical, social, legal, and financial risks for the sake of such experience' (p. 27). He reports that high sensation seekers are receptive to stimuli that are intense, novel and arousing, whereas those producing lower arousal may be considered 'boring' and cause them to seek alternative sources of stimulation.

Zuckerman (1979, 1988) has consistently found four dimensions to sensation seeking:

1. *Thrill and adventure seeking*: A desire to seek sensation through physically risky activities that provide unusual situations and novel experiences (e.g., parachuting and scuba diving).
2. *Experience seeking*: A desire to seek sensation through a nonconforming lifestyle, travel, music, art, drugs, and unconventional friends.
3. *Disinhibition*: A desire to seek sensation through social stimulation, parties, social drinking, and a variety of sex partners.
4. *Boredom susceptibility*: An aversion to boredom produced by unchanging conditions or persons and a great restlessness when things are the same for any period of time.

High sensation seekers are far more likely to engage in risky behaviors, such as drug and alcohol use, unprotected sex, or sex with multiple partners, for example (e.g., Donohew, Helm, Lawrence & Shatzer, 1990; Donohew, Lorch & Palmgreen, 1991; Palmgreen, Lorch, Donohew, Harrington, Dsilva & Helm, 1995; Zimmerman et al., in press; Zuckerman, 1979, 1994). On the other hand, low sensation seekers tend to engage in safer practices, prefer stimuli that are familiar and less complex and reject those that are highly intense.

The author and associates (Bardo, Donohew & Harrington, 1998) have observed previously that:

> Numerous historical anecdotes are available to underscore the human attraction to novelty. Indeed, discovery of the 'new world' may not have been possible had it not been for the innate human attraction to novelty. In the middle of the nineteenth century, Charles Darwin recognized that 'it is human nature to value any novelty, however slight, in one's own possession.' (p. 33)

BIOLOGICAL BASIS

When individuals are processing messages they may be largely unaware of the sources of stimulation because some of the mechanisms guiding the attention process lie deep within the brain. These mechanisms, which operate below an individual's level of conscious awareness, remain something of a mystery, but brain imaging studies involving instrumentation such as functional magnetic resonance imaging (fMRI) are mapping this process. Colleagues of the research team conducting much of the research reported here, are currently among those conducting such research.

In reviewing the neurobiology of novelty seeking, Bardo, Donohew, and Harrington (1996) have proposed:

> In sum, there is considerable evidence to indicate that novelty seeking behavior, similar to drug seeking behavior, involves activation of the mesolimbic DA [dopamine reward] system. This conclusion does not preclude an important role for other neural systems in novelty seeking. Indeed, response to novelty has also been shown to be dependent on nondopaminergic systems, including opioid . . . and GABAergic systems. Further, various other brain structures are also thought to play a role in novelty seeking behavior . . . (p. 29)

Elsewhere, members of the research group (Donohew et al., 2004) added:

> There is little doubt that the mesolimbic DA reward pathway has evolved in mammals as a critical neural substrate underlying the motivation to seek out and consume primary reinforcers, such as food, water, and sexual encounters. In addition, the mesolimbic DA system seems to play a vital role in SS [sensation seeking] or novelty seeking behavior. (p. 228)

Zuckerman and associates (1979, 1983, 1988, 1993, 1994) have connected sensation seeking with the mesolimbic dopamine pathway in work which found that the trait is associated with levels of monoamine oxidase (MAO-B), the brain-specific enzyme which breaks down dopamine and other neurotransmitters, and with the male hormone testosterone. Sensation seeking also has been found to be related to the D1 and D2 dopamine receptor genes (Bardo, Bowling, Robinet, Rowlett, Lacy & Mattingly, 1993; Bardo & Hammer, 1991; Bardo, Neisewander & Pierce, 1989). Others have found a connection with the D3DR gene (e.g., see Lerman, Patterson & Shields, 2003, for a review of some of this research). A number of others have connected it with the D4 dopamine receptor gene (Benjamin et al., 1996; Cloninger, Adolfson & Svrakic, 1996; Ebstein et al., 1996).

Bardo and colleagues (1996) suggest that the mesolimbic dopamine reward pathway presumably has evolved because it subserves behaviors that are vital to survival, and particularly because it is posited to be responsible for producing reinforcement (Glickman & Schiff, 1967; Vaccarino, Schiff & Glickman, 1989). Still others have shown the mesolimbic dopamine reward pathway to be a critical link in drug reward (e.g., Koob, Le & Creese, 1987; Wise, 1989).

MESSAGES AS NOVEL STIMULI

According to Zuckerman (1979, 1990, 1994), sensation seeking and sensation avoidance may represent fundamental survival behaviors for adaptation to a dangerous environment, with novel stimuli alerting the system for fight or flight and serving as either sources of reward or threats to survival. Absence of these novel stimuli means safety, and the system can turn to other activities (Bardo et al., 1998).

These stimuli may appear in the form of messages, which are more likely to be attended to by high sensation seekers if they possess one or more of the unsafe characteristics signaling a need for an alertness response (Donohew, Palmgreen & Lorch, 1994). On the other hand, messages not containing these characteristics may be perceived to be safe and left unattended. Both the verbal content and the formal features of these messages may offer stimulation that alerts the system (Donohew, Sypher & Higgins, 1988). Media messages must compete with other content, such as news stories or broadcast programming and commercials. They must also compete with the receiver's environment, including other persons. In order to inform and motivate, they must be capable of immediately attracting the attention of an intended audience and holding it for the rest of the message, even though the message may be intense and even complex (Palmgreen et al., 1995). Thus, designing such messages is not an easy process. Although humans have evolved far beyond other creatures in their cognitive abilities, they appear to be still somewhat primitive in what attracts and holds attention.

In order to reach high sensation seekers (Donohew, Palmgreen, Zimmerman, Harrington & Lane, 2003; Hoyle, Stephenson, Palmgreen, Lorch & Donohew, 2002; Zuckerman, 1979), who may be the prime target audiences in prevention campaigns, the messages ordinarily should possess high sensation value and elicit strong sensory, affective, and arousal responses.

Characteristics of messages possessing high sensation value were first identified in focus groups shown hundreds of messages (Lorch, et al., 1994) and later these characteristics were drawn upon to design messages used in experiments. High sensation value messages have been described as those exhibiting higher levels of the following attributes: (a) novel, creative, or unusual; (b) complex; (c) intense, emotionally powerful or physically arousing; (d) graphic or explicit; (e) somewhat ambiguous; (f) unconventional; (g) fast-paced; or (h) suspenseful. Low sensation value messages are those exhibiting lower levels of these attributes. Support for the effectiveness of this approach has been found in a number of subsequent studies (Palmgreen, et al., 1995). The characteristics identified in the research reported above are similar to characteristics Berlyne (1971) called arousal potential.

According to Lorch et al. (1994, p. 395), message sensation value 'should be an important factor in attracting and holding the attention of individuals with varying degrees of need for sensation.' Zuckerman (1988) states that high sensation seekers 'might be characterized by strong attention reactions and the capacity to readily shift attention to a novel stimulus' (p. 180). He (Zuckerman, 1994) adds that:

> Their preferences in art, media, and humor reflect a liking for stimuli that arouse strong emotions, demand a suspension of reality and an acceptance of ambiguity or absurdity, or that vicariously involve spectators in activities that they find particularly rewarding in life, such as sex. Low sensation seekers prefer a predictable, understandable, rational, and unemotional world where there are few surprises and where everything is clear. (p. 224)

MEDIA APPROACHES TO PREVENTION

The media, offering possible access to millions of people, have held out great promise to persons seeking to persuade others on a large scale. In this group, many of those seeking to bring about health behavior change have sought to incorporate the media as a carrier of interventions. Among the sources of encouragement for use of media in persuasive efforts were the successes with the German people of propaganda campaigns directed by Hitler's deputy Joseph Goebbels before and during World War II. The campaigns were intensely studied by American social and behavioral scientists—psychologists, political scientists, sociologists, anthropologists, and others—generating a body of research which eventually gave birth to the current discipline of communication (DeFleur & Ball-Rokeach, 1975).

Despite these studies, however, most media campaigns aimed at bringing about socially-sanctioned results have failed. In much of the history of such campaigns, efforts to employ the media in prevention efforts have largely produced sparse results (Flay & Sobel, 1983; Rogers & Storey, 1987).

Failure to produce greater effects may be in part because developers of mass media health campaigns and other health interventions have tended to assume implicitly a rational model of information exposure and decision-making. This perspective assumes that individuals confronted with situations involving threats to their health and well-being would weigh possible choices and outcomes described for them carefully and choose behaviors rationally. There is much evidence to refute this assumption, and we have noted that such programs show 'a discouraging lack of success' (Donohew & Zimmerman, 1996; Zimmerman & Donohew, 1996; Zimmerman et al., in press). We also have proposed, based on research to date, that sensation seeking is a component of a decision-making process that may or may not be 'rational.' We (Donohew, Palmgreen, Lorch, Zimmerman & Harrington, 2002) observed that

> ... Human beings are not the consistently aware, thoughtful creatures we often assume them to be, at least not until we can engage them in some way and lure or jolt them into a higher level of awareness ... Many individuals may be more likely to choose to be in situations or to engage in behaviors that are novel, reduce boredom, lead to disinhibition, or are thrilling or adventuresome ... (and) are less likely to act in ways that might be predicted by rational models of health-related behavior. (p. 119)

Support for an approach which connects risk-taking personality, health behaviors, and the design of interventions has been suggested by Caspi and associates (Caspi et al., 1997), who have been conducting a longitudinal study of a wide range of behavioral characteristics of children and young adults in New Zealand. The study began with boys and girls when they were three years old and is continuing with the same persons, who are now well into their twenties. Its authors noted that if investigators know the personality characteristics of a target audience, it may be possible to tailor campaigns to the characteristic motivations, attitudes, and feelings of the audience. They added that:

> ... Knowledge of the psychological characteristics that motivate you to engage in health-risk behaviors may thus help public health officials choose more effective campaigns that would motivate risk takers to minimize harm. (p. 1061)

A similar suggestion is offered by Lerman (2003):

> ... Improved knowledge about the mediating role of sensation seeking ... can inform the development of broad-based approaches that target the informational and behavioral needs of these high-risk subgroups of adolescents. (p. 164)

Efforts toward development of a more advanced science of persuasive communication in the drug abuse prevention process eventually have borne fruit, and new approaches have yielded powerful new theoretic and methodological bases. A former director of the National Institute on Drug Abuse (Leschner, 2002) observed that:

> Based on rigorous research paradigms . . . and despite daunting methodological and logistical problems, some successful research models in substance abuse campaigns emerged. These studies, in turn, have served as models for considerable research today. (p. ix)

One of the most successful models is the information exposure-SENTAR model, in which sensation seeking is central to both risk-taking and exposure to information (Donohew, et al., 2003).

Our program of research in communication was begun two decades earlier and evidence for the observations reported here comes from a wide variety of research projects (cited throughout this chapter) involving media and school-based campaigns aimed at risky sexual behaviors and abuse of drugs and alcohol.[2] In describing this research, we (Donohew, et al., 2003) stated

> . . . A central assumption . . . is that in order for health messages to be seriously attended, they must be capable of attracting and holding attention long enough for persuasive content . . . to be processed. This requires that they provide enough stimulation to generate a level of attention many implicitly assume is present all the time . . . we posit . . . a somewhat more primal human than is implicitly assumed in some of the theories of human behavior. (p. 119)

Related research has been conducted in neuropsychology (see, for example, the work of Bardo and associates, cited here).

A THEORY OF INFORMATION EXPOSURE

The original theoretic model leading to the theory reported below was developed (Donohew, et al., 1980) in the tradition of 'use-inspired basic research' described as Pasteur's quadrant (Stokes, 1997). Such research begins with a real-life problem, then carries out basic research leading to a theory which explains causal relations involved in the situation. The activation theory of information exposure emerged from a process of determining why messages about fundamental political issues vital to the welfare of a democratic society were not well-attended, whereas those on more trivial topics achieved large readership in newspapers and more viewers on television. The early model drew upon a somewhat more cognitively-based conception of novelty seeking which was later revised so that an individual's level of need for novelty and sensation became a critical component.

The current theory of information exposure (Donohew, Lorch & Palmgreen, 1998) offers propositions about information exposure behaviors, with particular attention to activation needs. The model posits that messages with high sensation value—those with the ability to elicit sensory, affective, and arousal responses (Everett & Palmgreen, 1995; Palmgreen & Donohew, 2003)—are required for attracting and holding the attention of high sensation seekers. As revised, the deductive nomological theory assumes that need for stimulation

---

[2] In studies as far back as the 1970s, a positive correlation has been found between sensation seeking and alcohol and other drug use (Carrol & Zuckerman, 1977; Segal, 1976). Donohew and others in their early studies of junior and senior high school students (Donohew, 1988; Donohew, et al., 1990), found that high sensation seekers were twice as likely as low sensation seekers to report use of beer and liquor during the past thirty days and up to seven times as likely to report use of other drugs. Donohew, Zimmerman, and others found that high sensation seeking adolescents are considerably more likely to initiate sex at an early age, have multiple sexual partners, not use condoms, and have sex following substance use (Donohew, Zimmerman, et al., 2000).

is a function of the catecholamine system (Zuckerman, 1994), and reflects involvement of needs for novelty and sensation. It has three principal tenets:

1. A central assumption (as in sensation seeking) that
   (a) human beings have individual levels of need for stimulation at which they are most comfortable, and that
   (b) attention is a function primarily of an individual's level of need for stimulation and the level of stimulation provided by a stimulus source (which can be cognitive or affective in nature);
2. The deduced proposition that if individuals do not achieve or maintain this state upon exposure to a message—the arousal response the message generates is too high or too low—it is very likely that they will turn away and seek another source of stimulation which helps them achieve the desired state;
3. The deduced proposition that if activation remains within some acceptable range, individuals are most likely to continue exposure to the information.

The theory does not seek to define the way messages are cognitively processed nor to specify the nature of persuasive strategies for attitude and behavior change. It has guided an extensive series of experiments and field studies and has been drawn upon to design an applied procedure for use of mass media in improving the effectiveness of public health campaigns—particularly prevention campaigns—called SENTAR, for sensation seeking targeting (Palmgreen & Donohew, 2003). Its basic principles are to (a) use SS as a targeting variable (with high sensation seekers as primary targets), (b) do formative research (e.g., use focus groups involving members of the target audience), and (c) place the messages in high sensation value programming or other high sensation value settings, as indicated by surveying the target audience.

What was important from a prevention perspective was that high sensation seekers have distinct and consistent preferences for particular kinds of messages based on their needs for the novel, the unusual, and the intense. In other words, the same need for novelty and sensation associated with risky health behaviors could be employed to attract and hold attention to messages persuading individuals not to engage in these behaviors.

Describing the body of work growing out of their studies, the authors (Donohew et al., 2003) state:

> The result of these studies is a coherent and parsimonious theoretical framework . . . that guides intervention strategies from inception to delivery and meshes well with a number of other theoretical approaches to prevention. It has proven effective in drug abuse prevention campaigns and also has potential for the prevention of unprotected sex, drinking, smoking, and a variety of other risk-related behaviors that the individual has the option to engage in or avoid. (p. 167)

PSAs AS MESSAGES

Messages offered in prevention campaigns ordinarily are designed in the form of public service announcements on television and radio, and sometimes as advertisements in the print media. They may be based on extensive formative research with focus groups or other types of reaction groups usually made up of representatives of the target group for the campaign to determine if they are likely to be capable of: (1) immediately attracting the attention of target audience members; and (2) motivating them to attend to the remainder of the message. In many instances, they reach out to the target groups—in prevention campaigns it might be those considered most at risk for the substance or behavior being attacked—to motivate participation in other phases of prevention programs. In others, such as some of those to be reported in this chapter, they may stand alone, serving as the intervention itself. These messages become the primary manipulations in the experimental designs.

EXAMPLE OF A HIGH SENSATION VALUE PUBLIC SERVICE ANNOUNCEMENT

As an illustration of a public service announcement used in a prevention project, it was decided to base a message on an actual event reported in an out-of-town newspaper. The incident, which was believed by focus groups to be realistic and to support the intervention with an audience of high sensation seekers, involved a young African-American male. While scenes of an amusement park and other entertainment flashed on the screen, the public service announcement was narrated by an off-camera voice. The young man related that one night, after getting high on marijuana with his friends, he took part in a game of Russian roulette. As the scene changed to a close-up of the narrator, he was shown lifting a revolver and pointing it at his head. There was a muffled sound of a shot and his voice added: 'And I lost.' As the next scene came up, moving back to show him sitting in a wheelchair, only moving one arm, and with a prescription bottle, he added: 'I only tried drugs once. Now I'm on them for life.' The script was written by the research staff and produced by an award-winning producer. In televised showings (paid for at commercial rates) as part of a campaign on largely prime time shows, it was found through surveys to be effective with high sensation seekers. Descriptions of some of the actual studies are presented below.

COMMUNICATION STUDIES

The investigators carried out a number of laboratory and field experiments in the process of developing the mass media-based approach to prevention. Early steps involved determining characteristics of messages that would attract and hold the attention of high sensation seekers and those that would attract and hold the attention of low sensation seekers, then determine if messages employing these characteristics elicited sensory, affective, and arousal responses. In the formative research on message characteristics, a large number of public service announcements and advertisements—which are frequently used to reach and motivate at-risk audiences—were shown to persons chosen from a randomly generated list of registered voters and from students. Focus groups of participants divided into high sensation seeker and low sensation seeker focus groups were asked to say what they liked and disliked about the messages. Anti-drug messages high or low in the selected characteristics were then designed using these characteristics and in a series of laboratory experiments run to determine if the messages elicited differential responses from high sensation seekers, low sensation seekers, and a control group on intent to call a hotline, it was found that the messages discriminated across groups as expected (Donohew, et al., 1991)

A follow-up laboratory study (Lorch et al., 1994) designed to avoid demand characteristics of TV presentations gave participants a chance to watch the television programs including

PSAs, or to turn them off and read or simply sit. It was at this point it was learned that, although high sensation seekers tended to watch only high sensation value content, low sensation seekers watched not only low sensation value content, but also much of the high sensation value content as well. This pointed to a parsimonious campaign strategy in which messages designed for high sensation seekers, the primary target audience, would reach low sensation seekers, the secondary target audience, as well. In other words, campaigns designed with high sensation value content would reach the principal target audience of greater risk-taking high sensation seekers without losing a possible reinforcement effect on the lower risk-taking high sensation seekers.

Other studies included a field study involving an actual high sensation value television campaign (Palmgreen, et al., 1995), in which data were collected from pre- and post-campaign surveys, and from individuals calling a hotline listed on the program. Three-fourths of callers were high sensation seekers, one-third of whom reported having used drugs in the past 30 days. An extensive study of peer influence, sensation seeking, and drug and alcohol use was also carried out (Donohew et al., 1999) involving a cohort of adolescents roughly divided by sex and measured at three points in time on drug and alcohol use. At the start of the study each of the adolescents named three peers in their cohort who had the most influence on them. Structural equation modeling analyses showed direct effects of SS of peers on subsequent use of both marijuana and alcohol.

TWO CITIES STUDIES: A MAJOR FIELD TEST

All these served as preliminary studies to large-scale field studies which have offered strong evidence of ability to bring about behavior change (on drug use in two studies, and on increased sexual abstinence or prevention of risky sexual behaviors by adolescents in another). The first of these was a study in two cities—Lexington and Knoxville—matched on a number of demographic characteristics employing a controlled interrupted time series design (Palmgreen et al., 2001). In this study, personal interviews, each lasting approximately one hour, were conducted with samples of 100 adolescents in each community during each of 32 months, for a total sample of 6,400. In Lexington, drug use was showing a sharp rise during the first eight months in the half of the sample with the higher sensation seeking scores, then a four-month television campaign was conducted and use dropped sharply, while continuing to rise in Knoxville in the high sensation seekers half of the sample where no campaign was conducted. At the 20-month mark, drug use was starting to rise again in Lexington and a second campaign was conducted, this time in both Lexington and Knoxville, followed by sharp drops in use continuing to the end of the study eight months later. In all, the campaigns lowered marijuana use among high sensation seekers by about one-fourth. All changes in slopes for the time series regression models were statistically significant. In each of the two cities, low sensation seekers showed little use and only slight variation as they maintained positions at the bottom of the chart.

Reflecting on the findings, the authors observed:

> These findings do not indicate that all antidrug public service announcements will produce behavior change or that public service announcements alone should be the only avenue to prevention. However, with carefully targeted campaigns that achieve high level of reach and frequency, and with messages designed specifically for the target audience on the basis of social scientific theory and formative research, we believe that public service announcements can play an important role in future drug abuse prevention efforts. (p. 295)

TWO CITIES STUDIES: THE NATIONAL YOUTH ANTI-DRUG MEDIA CAMPAIGN

The most recent of the drug abuse prevention studies (Palmgreen, Lorch, Hoyle, Stephenson & Donohew, in press) did not involve messages designed by the project team, but as part of the National Youth Anti-drug Media Campaign of the Office of National Drug Control Policy (ONDCP). The campaign was part of the largest public health communication effort in history, with a total of $ 180 million invested and media matches—donated time or space—bringing the total to approximately twice that much.

The other part of the campaign was aimed at parents. The entire project drew upon both scientists and contractors for advice or interpretation but the campaign offered was one that, after four years, was described by the Office of National Drug Control Policy director as ineffective.[3] The director called for more 'hard-hitting' messages, and the resulting ads, or public service announcements, met criteria designed to appeal to high sensation seekers.

The two-city tracking project—again, Lexington and Knoxville—which involved the same data collection and analysis procedures as the earlier two-cities design, had up to this point reflected essentially what was being shown in other studies of the national campaign, that the media intervention was having little effect. When the new messages meeting criteria for reaching high sensation seekers were introduced, effects were almost immediate and the final six months of the campaign showed dramatic results.

The time-series lines on attitudes, beliefs, and use, which had tilted slightly upward for 42 months, turned significantly downward during the final six months. A number of post-tests also indicated it was the nature of the messages employed during this period which was principally responsible for the various positive effects.

ADOLESCENTS AND RISKY SEX

In another study of adolescents—in this instance involving a cohort of over 2,000 ninth grade students who were followed to the end of 12th grade—we sought to determine if the approach guided by the theoretic model of information exposure would apply to risky sexual behavior (Zimmerman, et al., in press). Here, a second, potentially related, individual difference variable—impulsive decision-making—was added. Interventions decided upon were a combination of media (radio) and a classroom program (Reducing the Risk) which had already proved to be effective (Kirby, Barth, Leland & Fetro, 1991). It was believed that an individual who was both a high sensation seeker and an impulsive decision maker would be most at risk, and one who was a low sensation seeker and a rational decision maker (the other end of the impulsive-decision making scale), would be least likely to engage in risky behaviors. The latter would be most likely to either avoid situations putting them at risk or plan ahead for any encounters (e.g., by having a condom available).

In a preliminary study, it was noted that of nine risk-taking behaviors measured, such as 'ever had sex,' 'have a condom', and 'had unwanted sex while drunk', for example, eight

---

[3] This point had been earlier urged by Philip Palmgreen and others as members of the behavioral science expert panel advising the board on the project (personal conversation).

were found to be related to both sensation seeking and impulsive decision-making (Donohew, Zimmerman, Cupp, Novak, Colon & Abell, 2000).

The three-year longitudinal study was conducted in Louisville and Cleveland. Here, an effort was made to build on the success of the Reducing the Risk program, but to add elements which would increase the sensation value and inhibit impulsive decision making to reach the prime target audiences. Radio public service announcements were to follow guidelines for high sensation value messages whose criteria were described earlier. Classroom activities intended to increase the sensation value of the interventions included use of peer facilitators, HIV positive speakers, videos and music, and student production of videos.

In this study, three groups were compared: those receiving our newly-developed classroom intervention, those receiving the standard Reducing the Risk curriculum, and a comparison group, which received the regular—and limited—school instruction on HIV and health. The three groups in one city also received radio public service announcements and the three groups in the other city did not. A number of comparisons were made to determine comparability of intervention groups.

The principal finding was that intervention participants were less than half as likely as those in the comparison group to have initiated sexual activity. However, in this first effort at adapting high sensation value to a classroom format, there were no significant differences between the modified Reducing the Risk intervention (ours), and the standard Reducing the Risk intervention. Some of the activities—including HIV positive speakers—turned out well, but others, such as use of peer facilitators, videos and music, and student production of videos, did not turn out to be as popular as focus groups had expected.

Another HIV prevention study involving a media intervention only was recently carried out by Zimmerman, Palmgreen, and colleagues. The experimental study replicated the time series design and locations of the two cities studies. Despite facing the limitations posed in preparing effective prevention messages to be viewed not only by the target audience, but also by the general public, the approach was successful with the principal target audience. A detailed report of the findings was in preparation at the time this was written.

ADOLESCENTS AND SMOKING

Another dimension of risky adolescent behavior and prevention explored using the information exposure model was an adolescent smoking study carried out by Helme and others (in press) among students in Colorado. Although conducted in classroom settings, it was a simulated television campaign in which programming was delivered on the screens of laptop computers. Participants were 1,272 middle-school students aged 12–14 stratified by level of sensation seeking and exposed to high sensation value and low sensation value anti-smoking public service announcements. Significant main effects predicted from the propositions of the underlying theory were found among high sensation seekers on attitudes and behavioral intentions, but no differences in effects were found between those high sensation seekers exposed to high sensation value messages and those exposed to low sensation value messages. Further analysis based on perceived effectiveness of the messages—all of them borrowed from other anti-smoking campaigns and none of them produced specifically to meet sensation value criteria as used in previous studies—led to a possible conclusion that *all* the messages used in the study were high in sensation value.

OTHER STUDIES

Many social and biological forces combine to generate risky behaviors in a substantial number of young people, as indicated in some of the research reported here. Sensation seeking has been used as a surrogate for these forces. Its relationship to risk taking is further validated by its relationship to what are considered risk and protective factors.

Effects of sensation seeking are present across environments, risky or safe. White and African-American high sensation seeking students in an inner-city urban high school were substantially more likely than low sensation seeking students to have become sexually active, had unwanted sex under pressure or when drunk, and used alcohol and marijuana (Donohew et al., 2000).

The author and colleagues (Hoyle, Stephenson, Palmgreen, Lorch & Donohew, 2002) have found sensation seeking to be positively related to every risk factor measured (e.g., deviance, perceived peer use of marijuana, and perceived family use of marijuana), and negatively related to every protective factor measured (e.g., an absence of depression, quality of home life, religiosity, and perceived sanctions against marijuana use). High sensation seekers also tend to choose peers similar to themselves, helping strengthen their tendencies to take part in risky activities (Donohew et al., 1999). Sensation seeking is a trait which remains throughout an individual's life, although it is not as strong in later life.

Although no single stratagem for messages has emerged, one alternative to pointing out harmful effects has been stimulus substitution, in which high sensation seekers (and low sensation seekers) are directed to alternative activities capable of fulfilling needs for sensation and novelty. Although high sensation seekers are found to change activities more often than LSS in a continuing need for new experiences, some of the activities for which high sensation seekers show preferences (Donohew, et al., 1994; Goma-i-Freixanet, 2004) include: (1) Thrilling and risky activities, such as hang gliding, parachuting, bungee jumping, kayaking, and skiing, (2) body-contact sports, (3) outdoor activities, such as mountain and rock climbing, hiking, and cave exploration, (4) aesthetic and intellectual activities, such as museums, live theater, and concerts, (5) computer and video games.

CONCLUSIONS

The studies described in this chapter have shown rather conclusively that media interventions using procedures designed to meet higher needs for novelty and sensation can attract the attention of high sensation seekers likely to engage in health-risk behaviors, enhance their information processing, and motivate attitude and behavior change.

Predictions of whether individuals will seek or avoid prevention messages rely to a substantial degree on how well the sensation value—or arousal potential—of the message content matches the sensation seeking level of the individual. In all but one of multiple studies, and possibly even in that one, across a number of behaviors—risky sex, drug use, and smoking—this expectation has been supported.

The theory of information exposure on which the predictions are based does not specify if it is the verbal content or formal features of the messages—those characteristics beyond the words—which cause them to attract and hold attention. It merely states that attention will be based on whether or not their sensation value matches the sensation needs of the individual who is processing them, whether high sensation seekers or low sensation seekers.

The studies reported in this chapter provide affirmation for the covering laws from which the propositions are derived, offering both support for the propositions and an approach to prevention programs involving the mass media which can have a significant effect in bringing about behavior change.

REFERENCES

Bardo, M., Bowling, S.L., Robinet, P.M., Rowlett, J.K., Lacy, J.K. & Mattingly, M. (1993). Role of dopamine D_1 and D_2 receptors in novelty-maintained place preference. *Experimental Clinical Pharmacology*, *1*, 101–109.

Bardo, M., Donohew, L. & Harrington, N.G. (1996). Psychobiology of novelty-seeking and drug-seeking behavior. *Brain and Behavior*, *77*, 23–43.

Bardo, M. & Hammer, R.P., Jr. (1991). Autoradiographic localization of dopamine D_1 and D_2 receptors in rat nucleus accumbens: Resistence to differential rearing conditions. *Neuroscience*, *45*, 281–290.

Bardo, M.T. & Mueller, C.W. (1991). Sensation seeking and drug abuse prevention from a biological perspective. In L. Donohew, H.E. Sypher & W.J. Bukoski (eds), *Persuasive communication and drug abuse prevention* (pp. 209–226). Hillsdale, NJ: Lawrence Erlbaum.

Bardo, M.T., Nieswander, J.L. & Pierce, R.C. (1989). Novelty-induced place preference behavior in rats: Effects of opiate and dopaminergic drugs. *Pharmacology, Biochemistry & Behavior*, *32*, 683–689.

Benjamin, J., Li, L., Patterson, C., Greenberg, B., Murphy, D. & Hamer, D. (1996). Population and familial association between the D4 dopamine receptor gene and measures of novelty seeking. *Nature Genetics*, *12*, 81–84.

Berlyne, D. (1971). *Aesthetics and psychobiology*. New York: Appleton-Century-Crofts.

Carrol, E.N. & Zuckerman, M. (1977). Psychopathology and sensation seeking in 'downers,' 'speeders,' and 'trippers': A study of the relationship between personality and drug choice. *The International Journal of the Addictions*, *12(4)*, 591–601.

Caspi, A., Harrington, H., Moffitt, T.E., Begg, D., Dickson, N., Langley, J. & Silva, P.A. (1997). Personality differences predict health-risk behaviors in young adulthood: Evidence from a longitudinal study. *Journal of Personality and Social Psychology*, *73*, 1052–103.

Cloninger, C.R., Adolfson, R. & Svrakic, N.M. (1996). Mapping genes for human personality. *Nature Genetics*, *13*, 3, 4.

DeFleur, M.L. & Ball-Rokeach, S. (1975). *Theories of mass communication*, 3rd edn. New York: David McKay Co.

Delaney, B. (2003). Adolescent risk behavior research and media-based health messages. In D. Romer (ed.), *Reducing adolescent risk*. Thousand Oaks: Sage.

Donohew, L., Bardo, M. & Zimmerman, R.S. (2004). Personality and risky behavior: Communication and prevention. In R. Stelmack (ed.), *On the psychobiology of personality: Essays in honor of Marvin Zuckerman* (pp. 223–245). London: Elsevier.

Donohew, L., Hoyle, R., Clayton, R., Skinner, W., Colon, S. & Rice, R. (1999). Sensation seeking and drug use by adolescents and their friends: Models for marijuana and alcohol. *Journal of Studies on Alcohol*, *60*, 622–631.

Donohew, L., Helm, D., Lawrence, P. & Shatzer, M. (1990). Sensation seeking, marijuana use, and responses to drug abuse prevention messages. In R. Watson (ed.), *Drug and alcohol abuse prevention* (pp. 73–93). Camden, NJ: Humana Press.

Donohew, L., Lorch, E.P. & Palmgreen, P. (1991). Sensation seeking and targeting of televised anti-drug PSAs. In L. Donohew, H.E. Sypher & W.J. Bukoski (eds), *Persuasive communication and drug abuse prevention* (pp. 208–226). Hillsdale, NJ: Lawrence Erlbaum.

Donohew, L., Lorch, E.P., Palmgreen, P. (1998). Applications of a theoretic model of information exposure to health interventions. *Human Communication Research*, *24(3)*, 454–468.

Donohew, L., Palmgreen, P. & Duncan, J. (1980). An activation model of information exposure. *Communication Monographs*, *47*, 295–303.

Donohew, L., Palmgreen, P. & Lorch, E.P. (1994). Attention, sensation seeking, and health communication campaigns. *American Behavioral Scientist*, *38*, 310–332.

Donohew, L., Palmgreen, P., Lorch, E.P., Rogus, M., Helm, D. & Grant, N. (1989). *Targeting of televised anti-drug PSAs*. Paper presented at the annual meeting of the International Communication Association, San Francisco.

Donohew, L., Palmgreen, P., Lorch, E.P., Zimmerman, R. & Harrington, N. (2003). Attention persuasive communications and prevention. In William Crano and M. Burgoon (eds), *Mass media and drug prevention: Classic and contemporary theories and research* (pp. 119–143). Mahwah, NJ: Lawrence Erlbaum Associates.

Donohew, L., Palmgreen, P., Zimmerman, R., Harrington, N. & Lane, D. (2003). Health risk takers and prevention. In D. Romer (ed.), *Reducing adolescent risk*. Thousand Oaks: Sage.

Donohew, L., Sypher, H.E. & Higgins, E.T. (eds) (1988). *Communication, social cognition, and affect*. Hillsdale, NJ: Lawrence Erlbaum Associates.

Donohew, L., Zimmerman, R., Cupp, P., Novak, S., Colon, S. & Abell, R. (2000). Sensation seeking, impulsive decision-making, and risky sex: implications for risk-taking and design of interventions. *Personality and Individual Differences*, *28*, 1079–1091.

Ebstein, R., Novick, O., Umansky, R., Priel, B., Osher, Y., Blaine, D., Bennett, E., Nemanov, L., Katz, M. & Belmaker, R. (1996). Dopamine D4 receptor (D4DR) exon III polymorphism associated with the human personality trait of novelty seeking. *Nature Genetics*, *12*, 78–80.

Everett, M.W. & Palmgreen, P. (1995). Influences of sensation seeking, message sensation value, and program context on effectiveness of anticocaine public service announcements. *Health Communications*, *7(3)*, 225–248.

Flay, B. & Sobel, J.L. (1983). The role of mass media in preventing adolescent substance abuse. In T.J. Glynn, C.G. Leukefeld and J.P. Lundford (eds), Preventing adolescent drug abuse: Intervention strategies (pp. 5–35). Rockville, MD: National Institute on Drug Abuse.

Glickman, S.E. & Schiff, B.B. (1967). A biological theory of reinforcement. *Psychology Review*, *74*, 81–109.

Goma-i-Freixanet, M. (2004). Sensation seeking and participation in physical risk sports. In R.M. Stelmack (ed.), *On the psychobiology of personality* (pp. 185–201). London: Elsevier.

Helme, D., Donohew, L., Baier, M. & Littleman, L. A classroom adjusted simulation of a television campaign on adolescent smoking: testing an activation model of information exposure. *Journal of Health Communication*, *12* (in press).

Hoyle, R., Stephenson, M., Palmgreen, P., Lorch, E. & Donohew, L. (2002). Reliability and validity of a brief measure of sensation seeking. *Personality and Individual Differences*, *32*, 401–414.

Kirby, D., Barth, R., Leland, N. & Fetro, J.V. (1991). Reducing the risk: Impact of a new curriculum on sexual risk-taking. *Family Planning Perspectives*, *23*, 253–263.

Koob, G.F., Le, H.T. & Creese, I. (1987). The D1 dopamine receptor antagonist SCH 23390 increases cocaine self-administration in the rat. *Neuroscience Letters*, *79*, 315–320.

Lerman, C., Patterson, F. & Shields, A. (2003). Genetic basis of substance use and dependence: Implications for prevention in high-risk youth. In Daniel Romer (ed.), *Reducing Adolescent Risk* (pp. 149–164). Thousand Oaks: Sage.

Leshner, A. (2002). Foreword. In W. Crano & M. Burgoon (eds), *Mass media and drug prevention: Classic and contemporary theories and research* (p. ix). Mahwah, NJ: Lawrence Erlbaum Associates.

Lorch, E.P., Palmgreen, P., Donohew, L., Helm, D., Baer, S.A. & Dsilva, M.U. (1994). Program context, sensation seeking, and attention to televised anti-drug public service announcements. *Human Communication Research*, *20(3)*, 390–412.

Palmgreen, P. & Donohew, L. (2003). Effective mass media strategies for drug abuse prevention campaigns. In W.J. Bukoski and Z. Sloboda (eds) *Handbook of drug abuse theory, science and practice*. New York: Plenum.

Palmgreen, P., Donohew, L., Lorch, E., Hoyle, R. & Stephenson, M. (2001). Television campaigns and adolescent marijuana use: Tests of sensation seeking targeting. *American Journal of Public Health*, *91*, 292–296.

Palmgreen, P., Donohew, L., Lorch, E., Rogus, M., Helm, D. & Grant, N. (1991). Sensation seeking, message sensation value, and drug use as mediators of PSA effectiveness. *Health Communication*, *3*, 217–234.

Palmgreen, P., Lorch, E.P., Donohew, L., Harrington, N.G., Dsilva, M. & Helm, D. (1995). Reaching at-risk populations in a mass media drug abuse prevention campaign: Sensation seeking as a targeting variable. *Drugs and Society, 8*, 29–45.

Palmgreen, P., Lorch, E.P., Hoyle, R., Stephenson, M. & Donohew, L. (in press). The ONDCP campaign in two cities: a time series study. *American Journal of Public Health.*

Rogers, E.M. & Storey, J.D. (1987). Communication campaigns. In C.R. Berger and S.H. Chaffee (eds), *Handbook of communication science* (pp. 817–846). Newbury Park, CA: Sage.

Segal, B. (1976). Personality factors related to drug and alcohol use. In D.J. Lettieri (ed.), *Predicting adolescent drug abuse: A review of issues, methods, and correlates* (Publication Ms. ADM 77-299). Washington, D.C.: Department of Health, Education, and Welfare.

Stokes, D.E. (1997). *Pasteur's quadrant: Basic science and technological innovation.* Washington: Brookings Institution Press.

Vaccarino, F.J., Schiff, B.B. & Glickman, S.E. (1989). Biological view of reinforcement. In S.B. Klein and R.R. Mowrer (eds), *Contemporary Learning Theories* (pp. 111–142). Hillsdale, NJ: Lawrence Erlbaum.

Zimmerman, R. & Donohew, L. (1996, November). *Sensation seeking, impulsive decision-making, and adolescent sexual behaviors.* Paper presented at the American Public Health Association, New York.

Zimmerman, R.S., Donohew, L., Sionean, C., Cupp, P., Feist-Price, S. & Helme, D. (in press). Effects of a school-based, theory-driven HIV and pregnancy prevention curriculum.

Zuckerman, M. (1979). *Sensation seeking: Beyond the optimal level of arousal.* Hillsdale, NJ: Lawrence Erlbaum.

Zuckerman, M. (ed.) (1983). *Biological bases of sensation seeking, impulsivity, and anxiety.* Hillsdale, NJ: Lawrence Erlbaum.

Zuckerman, M. (1988). Behavior and biology: research on sensation seeking and reactions to the media. In L. Donohew, H.E. Sypher & E.T. Higgins (eds), *Communication, social cognition, and affect* (pp. 173–194). Hillsdale, NJ: Lawrence Erlbaum.

Zuckerman, M. (1991). *The psychobiology of personality.* New York: Cambridge University Press.

Zuckerman, M. (1993). Impulsive unsocialized sensation seeking: The biological foundations of a basic dimension of personality. In J. Bates & T. Wachs (eds), *Temperament: Individual differences at the interface of biology and behavior* (pp. 219–225). Washington, D.C.: American Psychological Association.

Zuckerman, M. (1994). *Behavioral expressions and biosocial bases of sensation seeking.* Cambridge, UK: Cambridge University Press.

CHAPTER 15

The Promotion of Optimism and Health

Derek R. Freres and Jane E. Gillham

University of Pennsylvania, USA

INTRODUCTION

Numerous studies suggest a close connection among optimism, depression, and physical health. Depression and pessimism appear to exacerbate some health problems (e.g., Buchanan, 1995; National Institutes of Health 2000) and may predict the onset of future health problems (e.g., Ferketick, Schwartzbaum, Frid & Moeschberger, 2000; Peterson, Seligman & Vaillant, 1988). Such findings raise the possibility that physical health may be improved through interventions, like cognitive-behavioral therapy, that reduce depression or boost optimism (Barber & DeRubeis, 2001; Hollon & Shelton, 2001; Seligman et al., 1988).

This chapter explores the relationship of optimism to depression and physical health and the pathways between optimism and health that may be affected by cognitive-behavioral interventions. We describe techniques and skills from two such interventions, the Penn Resiliency Program (Gillham, Jaycox, Reivich, Seligman & Silver, 1990) and the APEX program (Gillham et al., 1991), that we and our colleagues have been evaluating over the past several years. We review research assessing the effects of these interventions on optimism and depression and briefly discuss research on intervention effects related to physical health outcomes, which is in its early stages.

OPTIMISM, DEPRESSION, AND HEALTH

Optimism

Several different but overlapping constructs related to optimism have been discussed in the psychology literature. 'Optimism' and 'pessimism' are most commonly used to refer to the tendencies to adopt positive or negative expectations about the future (e.g., Scheier & Carver, 1993). This use of 'optimism' best captures our intuitive or day-to-day notion of optimism. The terms optimism and pessimism are sometimes used to describe other types of interpretive styles. For example, according to the Reformulated Learned Helplessness

Theory (Abramson, Seligman & Teasdale, 1978), a pessimistic explanatory style is the tendency to attribute negative events to internal, stable, and global factors and to attribute positive events to external, unstable, and specific factors. An optimistic explanatory style is characterized by the opposite pattern of explanations. To use a health related example, an individual with an optimistic explanatory style might attribute headaches and fatigue to a long day at work or to the initial symptoms of a minor illness (an unstable and specific cause). In contrast, an individual with a pessimistic explanatory style might conclude she has inoperable cancer or another serious and life-threatening illness (a stable and global cause). These different explanations produce different expectancies, which in turn, lead to different behaviors and emotions. The individual with the optimistic explanatory style experiences the symptoms as a temporary set-back and expects to feel better soon. She may try to get some extra rest, but will soon be back to her regular schedule. The individual with the pessimistic style experiences the symptoms as a sign of impending catastrophe. She may worry excessively, feel anxious and depressed, and, as a result, experience tremendous difficulty resuming her normal activities.

Hope Theory, which is closely related to optimism, emphasizes the role of an individual's goals and the perception that he can produce the pathways to these goals and sustain movement along those pathways (Snyder, 2000). Thus, Hope Theory highlights the relationship between goal setting, expectations, and self-efficacy (Bandura, 1982, 1997). Individuals who have goals, who are able to identify multiple routes to those goals, and who feel confident about their problem-solving abilities will experience higher levels of hope. Several other theories related to optimism have emphasized personal control or agency. For example, the original Learned Helplessness Theory posits that helpless expectations develop when people expect negative events to befall them and believe they will be powerless to influence or escape these events (Seligman, 1972). Thus, a sense of control or power may be one route to optimistic expectations. However, optimism may also arise when individuals believe that, issues of control aside, things will work out for the best (Carver & Scheier, 2002; Scheier & Carver, 1993). Religious faith is often a source of this kind of optimism (Eckstein, 2000).

Taken together these different theoretical perspectives suggest a broad view of optimism, which we adopt in this chapter. Optimism is a cognitive construct that includes beliefs about one's experiences and the future. Optimistic individuals have positive expectations about the future that derive, in part, from their optimistic interpretations and explanations for events in their lives, their sense of meaning or purpose, their goals, and their perceived capacity to realize these goals.

Optimism and Depression

These facets of optimism are closely connected to unipolar depression and are often implicated in cognitive models of depression (e.g., Beck, 1967; Ellis, 1962; Seligman, 1991). Depression is frequently characterized by hopelessness and pessimistic interpretive styles (Abramson, Metalsky & Alloy, 1989; Beck, 1967; Beck, 1976; Seligman, 1991), a sense that life has no meaning or purpose (Beck, 1967), and negative evaluations of one's abilities or competence (Beck, 1967; Beck, 1976).

Optimistic interpretive styles may protect individuals from developing depression (Abramson et al., 2000; Hankin & Abela, 2005; Nolen-Hoeksema, Girgus & Seligman, 1992). In support of this, a recent prospective longitudinal study found that 17 % of college students with pessimistic explanatory styles developed major depression during a two and one half year follow-up period. In contrast, only 1 % of students with optimistic interpretive styles developed depression during this time (Abramson et al., 2000). Among those students who had previously suffered from depression, those with optimistic interpretive styles were less likely to experience a recurrence than those with pessimistic interpretive styles (Abramson et al., 2000).

Optimism is related to a variety of outcomes in addition to depression. For example, optimistic explanatory style has been linked to academic achievement, job success, athletic performance, and marital satisfaction (Buchanan & Seligman, 1995). Dispositional optimism (or the tendency to have generalized positive expectations about the future) is associated with many of these same outcomes (Scheier, Carver & Bridges, 2001).

Optimism and Physical Health

There is considerable evidence that optimism is related to physical health. Although much of this research is cross-sectional, several prospective studies suggest that optimism predicts at least some future health outcomes. For example, dispositional optimism has been found to predict better physical recovery following coronary artery bypass surgery (Scheier et al., 1989; Scheier et al., 2003). Similarly, in a study of males who had experienced a heart attack, optimistic explanatory style predicted survival over an eight year follow-up period (Buchanan, 1995). A study of cardiovascular risk factors in women found that optimists had less carotid disease progression over a three year follow-up period than did pessimists (Matthews, Raikkonen, Sutton-Tyrrell & Kuller, 2005). Optimism also has been found to predict slower disease progression in men and women diagnosed with HIV (Ironson et al., 2005). In a 35 year longitudinal study of male Harvard graduates, explanatory style in early adulthood predicted overall health in middle age (Peterson et al., 1988). In a recent study that followed a large group of 65–85 year olds, dispositional optimism predicted survival over a nine year follow-up period (Giltay, Geleijnse, Zitman, Hoekstra & Schouten, 2004).

Optimism also may predict lower levels of pain, better psychological well-being and quality of life in the face of serious health problems (Garofalo, 2000; Scheier et al., 2001). For example, among patients with digestive tract cancers, optimists reported less pain and gave more positive ratings to a number of life domains than did pessimists (Allison, Guichard & Gilain, 2000). Similarly, dispositional pessimism predicted higher rates of emotional distress following surgery for breast cancer (Carver et al., 1993).

Peterson and Bossio described several pathways and mechanisms that may link optimism to physical health outcomes (Peterson, 2000; Peterson & Bossio, 1991). For example, optimism may reduce the risk of illness, reduce the severity of illness, speed recovery, and/or reduce the likelihood of relapse (Peterson, 2000). Although it is possible that optimism affects health directly, more likely it affects health by influencing other outcomes and behaviors that, in turn, affect physical health. Optimism may reduce or prevent depression and this change in depression may directly affect immune functioning (Peterson, 2000). Optimism may affect behaviors related to health outcomes. For example, it may increase engagement in active problem-solving (Aspinwall & Brunhart, 2000; Aspinwall & Taylor, 1997; Ironson et al., 2005). Optimism about one's ability to control health may lead to exercise, healthy dietary practices, or other preventive measures (Peterson, 2000; Peterson and de Avila, 1995) and may encourage individuals to seek out information about the best treatment or management strategies for an existing health risk or disorder (Aspinwall & Brunhart, 2000; Hornung et al., 1995). Optimism about the competence of medical providers or effectiveness of medical treatments may increase compliance with prescribed treatment, thereby facilitating recovery. Social pathways may also exist. Although the direction of the relationship is unclear, optimism is linked to extroversion and increased social support. This is important since social isolation predicts poor health while social support predicts improved psychological and physical well-being (Miyazaki et al., 2005; Peterson, 2000).

Optimism and Accuracy

So far, we have outlined pathways between optimism and positive health outcomes. A critical issue in optimism research includes whether optimism or optimistic biases have harmful effects. On the one hand, several research studies suggest that optimistic biases are common, adaptive and positively related to emotional well-being (Taylor & Brown, 1988). Many, perhaps most individuals, exhibit self-enhancement biases and make overly optimistic predictions about their futures (Taylor & Brown, 1988). Individuals with depressive symptoms may be more accurate in their judgments (Alloy & Abramson, 1979; Taylor & Brown, 1988; but see Ackermann & DeRubeis, 1991).

On the other hand, most cognitive-behavioral theories posit that accuracy is generally beneficial. Cognitive behavioral models link depression to unrealistically negative views of the self, the world, and the future that are maintained through a variety of information processing biases (Beck, 1976). Unrealistic optimism, which in its extreme form may be seen in mania, is equally maladaptive, as it can lead to a variety of problems that result from poor judgment and increased risk taking (Beck, 1976). Cognitive-behavioral therapists often describe a therapeutic goal of helping clients generate more accurate interpretations of the events they experience (e.g., Hollon & DeRubeis, 2004).

Some research suggests that extreme optimism and optimistic biases can have deleterious effects. Very high levels of optimism have been linked to lower academic achievement (Satterfield, Monahan & Seligman, 1997), for example. Unrealistic optimism may adversely impact physical health outcomes as well. People frequently underestimate their risk for a variety of health-related problems, particularly those that are common or viewed as controllable (Weinstein, 1984; Weinstein & Klein, 2002). Several studies suggest that heightened risk perception is positively related to engagement in preventive health practices. For example, a study of individuals living in the Northeastern United States (where Lyme Disease is most common) found that those with higher risk perception were more likely to get vaccinated (Brewer, Weinstein, Cuite & Herrington, 2004). Similarly, a study of homeowners in an area at high risk for radon indicated that increased risk perception predicted participation in radon testing (Weinstein & Lyon, 1999). Findings from these and other studies suggest that an optimistic bias may undermine physical health by discouraging individuals from seeking treatment or engaging in preventive practices. Accordingly, several health promotion interventions strive to promote increased (and accurate) perceptions of risk (e.g., Weinstein, 1983; Weinstein, Grubb & Vautier, 1986; Weinstein, Lyon, Sandman & Cuite, 1998).

In part, these different views regarding the benefits versus costs of optimism may result from the different methodologies, samples, and questions posed across studies. Research on the benefits of dispositional optimism and optimistic explanatory style typically examines individual differences in these variables without assessing the accuracy of predictions or explanations. Research on unrealistic optimism, in contrast, typically examines optimism at the group, not individual, level. Unrealistic optimism is demonstrated when, on average, group members expect better than average outcomes. Rarely is the discrepancy between optimism and accuracy evaluated at the individual level. Such research is quite difficult since researchers rarely know the objective probability of specific outcomes for specific individuals.

Our own view, which derives from the cognitive-behavioral therapy perspective, is that accuracy is important and adaptive. For depressed individuals and individuals at risk for depression, accuracy most often involves moving towards optimism. However, cognitive-behavioral interventions also help individuals to appreciate real risk, and to recognize when goals are unlikely to materialize and when it may be most adaptive to engage efforts and resources in another direction.

We believe that optimism and realism are often compatible. As Schneider (2001) points out, in many of the situations people encounter there is not one exact or knowable truth. In others, where an objective truth exists, it is rare for people to have access to all of the information necessary to make a completely accurate assessment (Schneider, 2001). We usually don't have complete knowledge about the causes of events in our lives or the likelihood with which future events may occur. When knowledge is imprecise, there are a range of views we can reasonably hold. From a signal detection perspective, erring on the side of optimism, rather than pessimism, may be adaptive in many situations because it will help to ensure that we persevere when circumstances are in fact controllable and changeable (Baumeister, 1988; Scheider, 2001). However, this does not imply that unrealistic optimism is adaptive. Schneider also draws a useful distinction between meaning and knowledge. Knowledge is ultimately about objective facts while the meaning of life circumstances or events is often subjectively determined. For example, adversities can be viewed as hassles or as challenges from which one can learn. There is no correct or objective view, although one is clearly more 'optimistic' and is likely to be more adaptive over the long run (Schneider, 2001).

PROMOTING OPTIMISM (AND ACCURACY)

Cognitive-behavioral therapy (CBT) for depression promotes optimism (and accuracy) through a variety of methods. A major goal of CBT includes teaching clients to challenge pessimistic beliefs by considering alternative interpretations and examining evidence for and against these different interpretations. CBT usually includes training in a variety of skills that increase effective problem-solving and coping, such as assertiveness and relaxation (Beck, Rush, Shaw & Emery, 1979). A positive feedback loop likely exists between optimism and problem-solving as increased problem-solving enhances self-efficacy and optimistic expectations which, in turn, increase engagement in problem-solving. CBT is an efficacious treatment for depression in adults (Hollon & DeRubeis, 2004; Hollon & Shelton, 2001) and shows promise as a treatment for depression in children and adolescents (Compton et al., 2004; Rohde, Lewinsohn, Clarke, Hops & Seeley, 2005). Recent research suggests that intervention programs that teach cognitive-behavioral skills may also prevent depressive symptoms and depressive disorders (for reviews, see Dozois & Dobson, 2004; Gillham, Shatté & Freres, 2000; Merry, McDowell, Hetrick, Bir & Muller, 2004). One of the mechanisms through which CBT appears to affect depression is through increasing optimism (Barber & DeRubeis, 2001; Gillham, Reivich, Jaycox & Seligman, 1995; Seligman et al., 1988; Seligman et al., 1999).

The Penn Resiliency and APEX Programs

For the past decade, our research team has been developing and evaluating cognitive-behavioral interventions designed to promote resilience and prevent depression. This work has focused largely on two interventions, the Penn Resiliency Program (PRP: Gillham et al., 1990), which is designed for early adolescents (ages 10–14), and the APEX Program (Gillham et al., 1991), which is designed for late adolescents and young adults (ages 17–22). Both programs are group interventions that can be delivered in school, primary care, or other community settings. Both programs are based on cognitive-behavioral therapy for depression (Beck et al., 1979; Ellis, 1962). Thus, although designed for different age groups, there is considerable overlap in the concepts and skills covered in these programs. These skills fit neatly within the broad view of optimism as they enhance positive expectations and interpretations of events, encourage goal-setting, and increase self-efficacy by providing a variety of tools that can be used for solving and coping with obstacles and set-backs that participants may encounter.

The PRP and APEX programs include two major components. The cognitive component targets the maladaptive cognitive styles and information processing biases that are correlated with depression and anxiety (e.g., Abramson et al., 1978; Beck, 1976; Ellis, 1962). By altering these patterns of thought early in life, the PRP and APEX aim to prevent symptoms of depression and anxiety. As many of these same maladaptive patterns are associated with negative health outcomes, their improvement may yield healthier adolescents who become healthier adults. A second intervention component addresses interpersonal relationships, problem solving, and coping skills. Depressed or pessimistic adolescents frequently experience interpersonal difficulties, often making incorrect attributions about the source of another's behavior (Quiggle, Garber, Panak & Dodge, 1992). Many depressed and pessimistic adolescents display passive response styles (Abela, Vanderbilt & Rochon, 2004; Chaplin & Cole, 2005; Nolen-Hoeksema, 1991; Spence, Sheffield & Donovan, 2002), while others exhibit aggressiveness and other interpersonal difficulties (Angold & Costello, 1993; Gotlib, Lewinsohn & Seeley, 1995). The PRP and APEX programs confront these issues by teaching assertive, rather than aggressive or passive, styles of interaction. A variety of other behavioral skills are covered in these programs. For example, participants are encouraged to approach decision making and large projects through a serious of concrete steps and to take a step back and relax when they feel really overwhelmed. By learning—through these skills—to solve problems and manage stress effectively, participants are better able to remain optimistic when faced with day-to-day challenges.

The PRP is usually delivered in twelve 90-minute group lessons. The APEX program is delivered in eight two-hour group lessons. Both programs include a scripted leader's manual, a set of in-lesson materials, and a homework workbook designed to re-enforce skills taught during in-person lessons. The PRP leaders across evaluations have included the program's developers, graduate students, guidance counselors, middle and high school teachers, psychologists, and social workers. Leader training typically consists of an approximately 30 hour course delivered by the program developers. In the current version of the PRP and APEX training, prospective leaders learn about the cognitive model and how to apply the key PRP concepts and skills to their own lives. Then, trainers walk through the delivery of each lesson by example and coach prospective leaders as they practice intervention delivery. In most studies, leaders have also received supervision from the program developers at least every other week during intervention delivery. Not surprising, the most robust effects of the PRP have been found when the program developers themselves lead the program (Gillham et al., 1995; Gillham, Reivich, et al. in press; Jaycox, Reivich, Gillham & Seligman, 1994). However, the PRP has also demonstrated effectiveness with leaders who have little or no prior education in the cognitive model (Gillham, Hamilton, Freres, Patton & Gallop, 2006; Gillham et al., in preparation; Yu & Seligman, 2002). To date, the APEX Program has only been evaluated in two studies. In both studies, cognitive-behavioral therapists and clinical psychology graduate students served as group leaders (Seligman, Schulman & Tryon, in preparation; Seligman et al., 1999).

The Penn Resiliency Program Skills

A description of the PRP will help to further articulate the ways in which these programs intervene with depression and optimism (see also Freres, Gillham, Reivich & Shatté, 2002) and how, through these outcomes, they may affect physical health. Our description focuses on the PRP since this is the intervention that we have researched most extensively. APEX covers most of the PRP concepts and skills, although activities and discussions are modified to be appropriate for older adolescents and young adults. In addition, APEX includes more extensive coverage than the PRP of complex skills from cognitive-behavioral therapy, such as examining underlying beliefs (Brown & Beck, 2002; Persons, Davidson & Thompkins, 2001) and recognizing and evaluating dysfunctional attitudes such as 'should' statements (Brown & Beck, 2002; Burns, 1980; Ellis, 1962).

Cognitive restructuring, or evaluating and altering beliefs in accordance with evidence, comprises the first PRP component. The program builds the background for this skill by employing Ellis's ABC Model (Ellis, 1962) as a means of introducing participants to the idea that cognitions may affect behavior. The ABC model states that Activating Events or Adversities (A) lead to Beliefs (B) that in turn result in emotional and/or behavioral Consequences (C). Through the use of scripted skits, participants are taught that often we conclude that Adversities (A) lead directly to Consequences (C); but, there is actually an additional intervening step that concerns the attributions we make regarding these adversities (B) and it is usually this step, more than the adversity itself, which determines consequences. The skits depict fictional characters producing negative attributions regarding a plausible adversity. Participants are asked how these characters might feel as a result of their beliefs. For example, in one skit 'Sam' receives a really bad haircut and concludes that he cannot possibly attend school until his hair grows back because everyone will laugh at him.

Three panel cartoons (one panel for each step in the ABC model) are used to further illustrate the intervening role of beliefs in determining emotions and behaviors. In some cartoons participants are given an adversity and a consequence and asked to fill in an intervening belief that might lead to that particular consequence. In other cartoons, participants are given an adversity and a belief and asked to determine which consequences might result from that belief. Eventually, participants apply this framework to their own lives, filling in blank cartoons that inquire about their own adversities, beliefs, and consequences.

After establishing the link between beliefs and consequences, the program illustrates pessimistic and optimistic thinking styles. As in lesson one, skits are used to demonstrate different explanatory styles and, importantly, the types of outcomes that are likely to result from employing each style. In one skit, a character 'Greg' is turned down when he asks someone to dance at a school event. Following this adversity, he makes pessimistic explanations and concludes 'I'm a loser' and 'No one likes me,' which leads to pessimistic expectations like 'No one will ever dance with me'. Consequently, Greg becomes passive, sits on the sidelines, and does not ask anyone else to dance, thus fulfilling his negative expectations. Greg is contrasted with another character 'Kim' who is also turned down when she asks someone to dance. Kim makes more optimistic explanations and predictions following this adversity, however, and concludes that the person she asked did not want to dance, but that other people might. This interpretation enables Kim to ask others to dance and eventually leads Kim to find a dance partner. Throughout the remainder of the program participants are taught that the goal is to produce more accurate explanations and predictions regarding negative events, not solely to generate beliefs that are more optimistic. Often our pessimistic attributions are not accurate and can be replaced by more realistic attributions, which happen to be much more optimistic. The illustration of more and less adaptive patterns of thought through the use of the Kim and Greg skits segues into a discussion of restructuring thoughts. As before, participants read skits in which characters make inaccurate and maladaptive causal attributions. But this time the participants re-write the skits, such that the adversities remain the same, but the attributions characters make about them are more realistic and more optimistic.

Once participants have learned to evaluate and re-write the causal attribution of fictitious characters, the program turns to intrapersonal cognitive restructuring. Participants are taught to generate alternative beliefs, to evaluate their beliefs against evidence, and to choose the belief that is most accurate based on the available evidence. The issue is approached by contrasting two detectives who are trying to solve the same crime. The bad detective attempts to solve the crime by choosing the first suspect that pops into his mind. The good detective, in contrast, generates a list of possible suspects and looks for evidence that supports or refutes the culpability of any particular suspect. We suggest to participants that the qualities good detectives possess in solving a crime are an analogy to and model for intrapersonal cognitive restructuring. Participants initially practice examining alternatives and evidence through an activity called the file game. We provide a 'file' on a fictitious adolescent that includes automatic thoughts about negative events (the first thought that pops into the fictitious person's head) and a variety of evidence, some of which supports and some of which refutes these automatic thoughts. We task participants with looking through and weighing this evidence to find out which automatic thoughts are true and which are false. It is through the general rubric of acting like a detective against their own and other people's thoughts that participants learn to reject inaccurate pessimistic cognitive styles and generate more optimistic alternatives.

Another cognitive restructuring skill, decatastrophizing, may affect health outcomes by explicitly targeting negative thoughts about the future. In the PRP we term this skill 'putting it in perspective'. Adolescents who are at risk for depression often expect negative events to yield dire consequences. For example, the adolescent who fails a test may conclude that this failure will prevent her from being accepted to a good college and will therefore have permanent adverse effects on her future career path. In this section of the program, participants are encouraged to consider the possibility that their catastrophic thoughts might not be the most likely outcome of a given situation. Instead, these thoughts probably actually constitute the very worst and most unlikely scenario. Participants are asked to put these negative expectations in perspective by generating the worst, best, and most likely possible outcomes for a given situation and to come up with plans for minimizing the possibility of the worst, maximizing the possibility of the best, and coping with the most likely. In the program we acknowledge that sometimes the most likely outcome will be the worst outcome. For example, if an adolescent witnesses his parents fighting repeatedly and concludes that they will divorce, this may be at once his worst and the most likely outcome. In these circumstances we encourage the use of cognitive-restructuring to re-evaluate the implications of an event. For example, even though an adolescent continues to perceive divorce as a negative outcome, he may also recognize that there are potential positive effects. In this example, after divorce, both his parents may fight less and may ultimately be happier.

By this point in the curriculum, most students have learned to apply cognitive-restructuring techniques methodically through worksheets and discussion. Many life experiences, however, will require online disputation of negative beliefs. In the PRP, online disputation is taught through an activity called the 'hot seat,' in which participants are asked to refute thoughts provided by the leader in front of the group. Each participant takes a turn and is given an adversity and a thought, such as 'I fail a test. I think to myself, "I'm so stupid. I'll never do anything right"'. The participant must refute the thought by providing contradictory evidence (e.g., 'I receive As and Bs in all my other classes so I must not be stupid'), generating alternatives (e.g., 'I didn't study the material enough'), or by Putting it in Perspective (e.g., 'Well, it's just an F on one test. If I work really hard and ask the teacher for some help, I can maximize the possibility that I'll pass the class, which really is the most likely outcome'). After practicing the hot seat with hypothetical events, students begin to apply the rapid fire disputation to negative beliefs in their own lives. We continue rapid fire disputation practice throughout the remainder of the program.

The second component of the program includes behavioral techniques, such as assertiveness, negotiation, overcoming procrastination, building social skills, decision making, and problem solving. Adolescents with pessimistic thinking styles frequently experience difficulty navigating social situations because they may generate unrealistic negative interpretations for others' behavior and these may lead to a passive response. For example, an adolescent with a pessimistic thinking bias who fails to receive an invitation to a friend's party on the same day others do may immediately assume that this friend 'Really does not like me' or that 'I'm a loser' without appropriately considering and evaluating alternatives (e.g. the invitation was lost in mail, was sent on a different day, or will be delivered by the friend in person). Because these initial pessimistic thoughts include stable causes, the situation is perceived as unchangeable and their holder reacts with avoidance or passive acceptance. We actively discourage this style through the teaching and practice of an assertiveness technique, which is especially helpful for navigating social stressors. Assertiveness also helps individuals to gather evidence, facilitating a more accurate interpretation of events.

We begin assertiveness training by using skits to contrast three different fictional characters, one of whom interacts aggressively, one passively, and one assertively. Emphasis is placed on the outcomes of these three different interaction styles, with assertiveness producing the best outcome even though it might not be exactly what the character wanted. Participants are encouraged to follow a four-step approach to assertiveness, which includes describing the problem in objective terms, describing their own feelings, requesting a specific change from the other person, and, finally, indicating how this change will improve their feelings. Participants practice applying this skill to their own problems through in-class activities and homework assignments. We use the same general rubric for teaching negotiation. We also provide some training in social skills, as interpersonal relationships often prove problematic for depressed and pessimistic adolescents (Gotlib et al., 1995).

Procrastination is a problem for many adolescents, especially those with pessimistic biases in their thinking styles. Rather than avoiding and prolonging large projects, we encourage participants to view these as a set of smaller projects, each of which can be ap-proached as a unique unit. Participants practice this division process by playing against each other in teams. The winner is chosen by evaluating which team broke a project into the most reasonable parts. Participants are then encouraged to apply this technique to projects in their own lives. At each step adolescents are encouraged to articulate their cognitions (e.g., 'I'll never be able to do that') and then to evaluate and dispute them using cognitive restructuring techniques. They are also encouraged to build in rewards (taking a break, listening to mu-sic, talking with a friend) after completing some of the steps. This combination of breaking projects up, celebrating small successes along the way, and disputing inaccurate cognitions helps to decrease feelings of helplessness and increase positive expectancies regarding the future. Training in overcoming procrastination may also decrease the stress invoked when adolescents approach large projects.

The PRP also teaches decision making and problem solving skills that can increase optimism by providing participants with concrete methods to solve problems and reduce the effects of stressors in their lives. Decision making is introduced through a plausible fictional example in which a character witnesses a classmate cheating on a test and needs to decide what actions, if any, to take. We ask participants to list the different responses they might consider and to identify the pros and cons of each response. For example, telling the teacher might have positive aspects because it is just—the cheater will get in trouble—but negative aspects because the cheating student might not like the person who told on him. In choosing what to do, participants are encouraged to evaluate the pros and cons they generated, placing particular weight on the pros and cons that are extremely important to them.

Near the end of the program, we teach a 5-step approach to problem-solving that in-corporates cognitive restructuring, decision making and many of the previous skills. This approach is based, in part, on Dodge and Crick's social information processing framework (1990). The first step in this skill is to stop and think about what happened and to consider alternatives and evidence to ensure an accurate understanding of the problem situation. The second step involves considering one's goals. The third step is to problem-solve creatively by generating a list of possible solutions to the problem. We emphasize assertiveness and talking to someone as strategies that may prove helpful in many situations. The fourth step involves applying the decision making techniques to decide among the generated solutions. Finally, participants enact the solution and evaluate the outcome. We emphasize that of-ten our initial attempts to solve a problem may not succeed. In these cases, it may prove beneficial to make sure we are evaluating the problem accurately and, if so, to consider implementing other solutions.

The PRP also teaches other behavioral techniques that can be helpful for managing strong negative emotions and for coping with uncontrollable stressors. For example, participants are taught a variety of relaxation techniques including deep breathing, muscle relaxation, and the use of imagery.

EVALUATIONS OF THE PRP AND APEX PROGRAMS

Initial School-based Evaluation of the PRP

The initial evaluation of the PRP was conducted with 143 10–13 year olds identified as at-risk for depression based on elevated levels of depressive symptoms and parental conflict (Gillham et al., 1995; Jaycox et al., 1994). This study was conducted with two neighboring school districts using a matched controlled design. The program developers lead after-school groups for the 69 participants in the intervention condition. Participants were administered a battery of questionnaires before and after the intervention, and at follow-up assessments 6, 12, 18, 24, 30, and 36 months after the intervention ended. Findings indicated that the PRP improved explanatory style, relative to controls, through the three year follow-up assessment. The PRP prevented depressive symptoms and reports of moderate to high levels of symptoms through the two-year follow-up (Gillham & Reivich, 1999; Gillham et al., 1995). Effects appeared to be substantial as the PRP participants were about a third as likely as controls to report moderate to severe symptoms at the 18 month follow-up and only half as likely as controls to report these levels of symptoms at the two year follow-up (Gillham et al., 1995). Though findings from this study were promising, they must be interpreted with caution since the study did not use a randomized design.

Randomized Controlled Evaluations of the PRP

In the past 10 years, at least 10 additional published or in press evaluations of the PRP have been conducted and we recently completed a large evaluation of the PRP with approximately 700 children (Gillham et al., in preparation). All of these studies used randomized controlled designs and measured depressive symptoms. Several studies examined the PRP's effects on cognitive styles, including explanatory style, or anxiety symptoms (e.g., Cardemil, Reivich & Seligman, 2002; Chaplin et al., 2006; Gillham, Reivich, et al., in press; Gillham et al., in preparation), and one study examined the PRP's effects on depression, anxiety and adjustment disorders (Gillham, Hamilton et al., 2006). The existing studies have evaluated the PRP with different racial and ethnic groups, in different countries, and with leaders who ranged from the program developers to school teachers with little or no prior training in the cognitive model.

Taken together, findings suggest that the PRP makes explanatory styles more optimistic and reduces and prevents symptoms of depression and anxiety. In addition, the PRP's effects may be long lasting, enduring through two or more years of follow-up (e.g., Gillham et al., in preparation). It is important to note, however, that a few studies have failed to replicate the PRP's effects on depressive symptoms (e.g., Cardemil et al., 2002, Study 2; Roberts, Kane, Thompson, Bishop & Hart, 2003; Roberts, Kane, Bishop, Matthews & Thompson, 2004) and some studies have failed to find effects of the PRP with sub-groups of participants (e.g., Gillham et al., in preparation; Gillham, Hamilton et al., 2006). We briefly summarize the results for studies conducted by our research group in this chapter. In all of these studies, participants were randomly assigned to the PRP or control condition and completed standardized measures of symptoms prior to the intervention, immediately after the intervention, and during a follow-up phase that typically lasted for six months or more after the intervention ended. In all outcome analyses, the PRP's effects were evaluated controlling for baseline levels of symptoms.

School-based Evaluations of the PRP

The PRP has been evaluated in school-based settings among different ethnic, racial and socio-economic groups, including low-income Latinos (Cardemil et al., 2002, study 1), low-income African Americans (Cardemil et al., 2002, study 2), and Asians in China (Yu & Seligman, 2002), as well as with predominantly Caucasian samples (e.g., Gillham, Reivich, et al., in press).

Cardemil and colleagues adapted the PRP for use in schools serving predominantly low income Latino and African American urban communities (Cardemil, Reivich, Gillham, Jaycox & Seligman, 1997). This inner city version of the PRP was evaluated in two schools, one serving a predominantly Latino community and one serving a predominantly African American community. In the first school, the PRP was examined with a sample of 49 5th and 6th graders. The intervention was delivered by graduate students trained by the program developers. Findings indicated that the PRP reduced depressive symptoms at all three (post, three and six month) follow-up assessments. The PRP participants reported significantly less hopelessness than controls at the three and six month assessments. No significant effects were found for explanatory style. In the second school, the PRP was evaluated with 106 5th and 6th graders. The PRP groups were led by graduate students and one of the program developers. Findings indicated that the PRP did not significantly affect depressive symptoms, hopelessness, or explanatory style among this low-income African-American sample. Average levels of depressive symptoms decreased dramatically in both the PRP and control conditions, however, perhaps diminishing the ability to detect an intervention effect.

Yu adapted and evaluated the PRP with 202 4th–6th grade children in Beijing, China, who were identified as at risk for depression based on elevated levels of depressive symptoms and perceptions of family conflict (2002). The major adaptations to the PRP involved altering the assertiveness module for cultural appropriateness and removing some portions of the social problem solving and decision making components to allow for intervention delivery in 10 sessions. School teachers trained by the program's reviser led the intervention groups. Findings indicated that the PRP reduced depressive symptoms and improved explanatory styles across the six month follow-up period.

In the largest evaluation of the PRP to date, our research group tested the program against a usual care control and an alternate intervention designed to control for non-specific (non-cognitive behavioral) intervention ingredients (Gillham et al., in preparation). Approximately 700 11–14 year olds were randomly assigned among these three conditions. Intervention groups were led by school teachers, counselors, and graduate students in psychology and education who were trained by the program developers. The alternate intervention was designed to mirror the PRP in as many ways as possible. Adolescents met in groups for the same length of time, leaders attended a similar amount of training, and participants discussed many of the same topics as those in the PRP, but without the cognitive behavioral ingredients. Although still preliminary, findings indicated that in two schools, the PRP reduced depressive symptoms relative to control and relative to the alternate intervention through 30 months of follow-up. In the third school, no significant intervention effects were found (Gillham et al., in preparation). Intervention effects on explanatory style and hopelessness have not yet been evaluated.

Evaluation of the PRP in a Primary Care Setting

In addition to the school-based studies, we have also examined the effects of the PRP in a managed care setting (Gillham, Hamilton et al., 2006). Participants were recruited from mailings sent to managed care plan members and postings in pediatrician offices. Two hundred and seventy-one 11 and 12 year olds with elevated but sub-clinical levels of depressive symptoms were randomly assigned to the PRP or usual care conditions. Psychologists and a social worker trained by one of the program's developers led the intervention groups. Outcome measures included self-report measures of explanatory style and depressive symptoms as well as diagnoses of depression, anxiety and adjustment disorders obtained from the HMO's computerized database. Results indicated that the PRP significantly improved explanatory style for positive events relative to control. Intervention effects on explanatory style for negative events and depressive symptoms were moderated by sex. The PRP significantly improved these outcomes in girls but not boys. The intervention effect on psychological disorders was moderated by initial symptom level. The PRP significantly prevented these diagnoses among participants with high levels of depressive symptoms at baseline, but not among participants with low levels of baseline symptoms. As a part of this study we also collected data on medical utilization, which we are currently analysing.

Improving the PRP's Effectiveness

Recent work in our research group has focused on boosting the PRP's effectiveness overall and among subgroups of participants. To this end, we have been working to develop and evaluate a parent component, booster sessions, and a girls' version of the PRP that more effectively targets gender-related risk factors that may be especially important among girls during the transition to adolescence.

Gender Disparities in School-based Evaluations

A re-analysis of the two year follow-up data from the initial PRP evaluation suggested that over the long term, the program worked better for boys than for girls (Reivich, 1996). While gender disparities in depression prevention program effects are not uncommon (for reviews of depression prevention research see Gillham et al., 2000; Merry et al., 2004), little research has examined potential explanations or corrections for these differences. Chaplin et al. suggest that conducting all girls prevention groups as opposed to co-ed groups may lead to stronger preventive effects in girls by providing a more comfortable atmosphere for girls to share personal information and by eliminating a bias toward male conversation domination in classrooms that is often present in co-ed settings (2006). Our research group tested this possibility in a small pilot study. Two hundred and eight public school students took part in the study. Boys were randomly assigned to control and co-ed intervention conditions. Girls were randomly assigned to control, co-ed intervention, and all-girl intervention conditions. School teachers, graduate students and research assistants trained by the program's developers led the prevention groups. Pre to post findings indicated that the PRP reduced depressive symptoms relative to control for both girls and boys. Among girls, all girls PRP was effective across more outcomes than co-ed PRP. No significant difference was found between all girls and co-ed PRP on depressive symptoms (both interventions reduced depressive symptoms relative to control). However, all girls PRP was linked to greater reductions in hopelessness and higher attendance than co-ed PRP (Chaplin et al., in press). We are currently exploring ways to more powerfully prevent depression in girls. To that end, we have begun to pilot a new intervention, the Girls in Transition Program, which incorporates the PRP skills but also includes intervention components specifically designed to target body image concerns and media and cultural messages that may affect girls negatively during the transition to adolescence (Gillham, Chaplin, Reivich & Hamilton, in press).

Adding a Parent Component and Booster Sessions

Our research group developed booster lessons and a parent component in an attempt to strengthen and extend the duration of PRP's effects. In the booster sessions, participants review past material and apply it to their current problems. In the parent program, parents are taught cognitive-behavioral skills with the intention that they will use these skills in their own lives and model them for their adolescents. Although we do not directly assess this, parent programs may prove particularly helpful in improving adolescent health because many adolescent health behaviors (e.g., food consumption and doctor's visits) are largely under parental control.

A pilot study of the parent component to the PRP yielded promising findings (Gillham, Reivich et al., in press). Forty-four public school adolescents with higher levels of depressive and anxiety symptoms were randomly assigned along with their parents to intervention and control conditions. Adolescents in the intervention condition attended adolescent PRP. Their parents were invited to attend the PRP for parents (PRP-P). The PRP-P includes eight 90-minute lessons and is similar in content to the PRP-CA, but at an adult level (for a more detailed description see Gillham, Reivich, et al., in press). Intervention groups were led by the program developers and other members of the research team. Results indicated that adolescents in the intervention condition reported significantly fewer symptoms of anxiety and depression across the follow-up period relative to controls. These effects were significant at six and twelve month assessments, but not at post. Further, 30 % of controls compared to only 5 % of intervention participants reported high (clinically relevant) levels of anxiety at some point across the follow-up period. A large scale evaluation of the PRP parent and booster components is currently underway.

APEX Program Evaluations

The initial evaluation of the APEX program was conducted with 231 first-year college students identified as at risk for depression based on scoring within the most pessimistic quartile on a measure of explanatory style (Buchanan, Gardenswartz & Seligman, 1999; Seligman et al., 1999). Group leaders were clinicians and doctoral students with substantial training in cognitive therapy. Findings indicated that the APEX program reduced symptoms of anxiety and depression across the three year follow-up period. Intervention participants also reported significantly more optimistic explanatory styles and less hopelessness than controls across the follow-up period. An evaluation of a revised version of the APEX program, which includes a web-based booster component, is underway. Findings at the six month follow-up indicate that the enhanced APEX program significantly improved explanatory style and reduced symptoms of depression and anxiety relative to control (Seligman et al., in preparation). A longer follow-up is in progress.

Effects of the PRP and APEX on Physical Health

Only recently has our research group begun to examine the potential effects of the PRP and APEX on physical health outcomes. In one of these studies, participants in the initial APEX evaluation were invited to take part in a health extension study (Buchanan et al., 1999). One hundred and twenty-three students agreed to participate. A variety of health measures were collected including subjective assessments of physical symptoms, global health, health visits, health behaviors, and objective records of medical visits from a university student health service. APEX participants reported fewer physical health symptoms and made fewer illness-related doctor visits than controls. Intervention participants also made significantly more wellness visits to student health relative to controls based on the subjective measure (Buchanan et al., 1999).

In the evaluation of the PRP in a primary care setting (Gillham, Hamilton et al., 2006), we also collected data on physical health symptoms and medical utilization. At baseline, somatic complaints were significantly correlated with depressive symptoms and explanatory style. Children with elevated depressive symptoms and pessimistic explanatory styles reported more physical health complaints. We are in the process of analysing these data to determine if the PRP intervention affects physical health outcomes.

DISCUSSION

A large body of research suggests that physical health relates to optimism and depression. As some of this research indicates, it is even possible that promoting optimism may help to produce improved health. The road to better physical health, like many causal chains (e.g., Rosenberg, 1968), is likely one filled with a series of intervening pathways that includes many symmetric and asymmetric relationships. One variable affects another, some of these variables affect each other, and the desired end—a healthy person—can probably and perhaps only be realized by employing several of these complex pathways together. Although depression and optimism have been extensively researched, their potential linkages to physical health have received relatively little investigation, particularly among adolescent populations. We know that associations exist between depression and physical health and optimism and physical health, but few studies have examined and articulated the causal pathways that produce these associations.

Optimism is perhaps most reasonably conceptualized as an indirect causal factor, exerting its influence on physical health through other variables. It constitutes an approach to the world that influences many facets of persons' interactions with that world. In this view, improving optimism can affect many other outcomes and some of these outcomes will in turn feed back, producing more optimism. On a broad level, the person who believes he can live longer and that many of the factors influencing life span are under his control, will engage in more health-related behaviors to effect a longer life. By intervening at this more distal level, at the level of optimism, strong influences on physical health can be produced by affecting a myriad of factors that in turn influence other more proximal factors, eventually realizing their effects on physical health. Improving optimism through cognitive behavioral techniques may prove one way to produce a healthier approach to the world, potentially preventing illness.

In several studies, the PRP and APEX have increased optimism and reduced and prevented depression. Considering the association among depression, optimism, and physical health, these findings suggest that the PRP and APEX may also promote physical health. Our research group has only recently begun to investigate this possibility. While examining whether these programs improve physical health constitutes an important goal, it is equally essential to examine how these effects might occur. For example, these programs might affect physical health through cognitive restructuring, increasing the tendency to produce optimistic and accurate causal explanations for life events. Increases in these more adaptive attributions may, in turn, affect many other variables. As an example, believing that health is controllable may lead to more health-promoting behaviors such as scheduling and attending well visits, tooth brushing, exercise, and healthy eating. Alternatively or concurrently, adaptive cognitions combined with other skills, such as decision making, problem solving, and assertiveness, may increase one's ability to manage negative events, decreasing overall stress. This decrease may, in turn, diminish the biological concomitants of stress thereby improving health. As evidenced by the studies described in this chapter, the PRP and APEX also affect psychological health. Decreasing and preventing depression by itself may also lead to a reduction in stress and improved health-seeking behaviors. Many other potential pathways from the PRP and APEX to physical health can be hypothesized. However, despite our hypothesizing we know little about how these processes actually function. Only by developing an understanding of how optimism affects physical health through future research can we maximize the effects and efficiency of prevention interventions on physical health outcomes.

ACKNOWLEDGMENTS

The authors are grateful to the children, parents, and students who have participated in research on the Penn Resiliency and APEX programs. The research on the Penn Resiliency Project described in this chapter was funded by the National Institute of Mental Health (MH52270) and the Kaiser Foundation Research Institute (KFRI#20-161-9728). Research on the Girls in Transition Program is funded by a Swarthmore College faculty research support grant. Research on the APEX program is funded by the National Institute of Mental Health (MH63430).

REFERENCES

Abela, J.R.Z., Vanderbilt, E. & Rochon, A. (2004). A test of the integration of response styles and social support theories of depression in third and seventh grade children. *Journal of Social and Clinical Psychology, 23*, 653–674.

Abramson, L.Y., Alloy, L.B., Hankin, B.L., Clements, C.M., Zhu, L., Hogan, M.E. & Whitehouse, W.G. (2000). Optimistic cognitive styles and invulnerability to depression. In J.E. Gillham (ed.), *The science of optimism and hope: Research essays in honor of Martin E. P. Seligman* (pp. 75–98). Radnor, PA: Templeton Foundation Press.

Abramson, L.Y., Metalsky, G.I. & Alloy, L.B. (1989). Hopelessness depression: A theory based subtype of depression. *Psychological Review, 96*, 358–372.

Abramson, L.Y., Seligman, M.E.P. & Teasdale, J.E. (1978). Learned helplessness in humans: Critique and reformulation. *Journal of Abnormal Psychology, 87*, 49–74.

Ackermann, R. & DeRubeis, R.J. (1991). Is depressive realism real? *Clinical Psychology Review, 11*, 565–584.

Allison, P.J., Guichard, C. & Gilain, L. (2000). A prospective investigation of dispositional optimism as a predictor of health-related quality of life in head and neck cancer patients. *Quality of Life Research, 9*, 951–960.

Alloy, L.B. & Abramson, L.Y. (1979). Judgment of contingency in depressed and nondepressed students: Sadder but wise? *Journal of Experimental Psychology: General, 108*, 441–485.

Angold, A. & Costello, E.J. (1993). Depressive comorbidity in children and adolescents: Empirical, theoretical, and methodological issues. *American Journal of Psychiatry, 150*, 1779–1791.

Aspinwall, L.G. & Brunhart, S.M. (2000). What I do know won't hurt me: Optimism, attention to negative information, coping, and health. In J.E. Gillham (ed.), *The science of optimism and hope: Research essays in honor of Martin E.P. Seligman* (pp. 163–200). Radnor, PA: Templeton Foundation Press.

Aspinwall, L.G. & Taylor, S.E. (1997). A stitch in time: Self-regulation and proactive coping. *Psychological Bulletin, 121*, 417–436.

Bandura, A. (1982). Self-efficacy mechanism in human agency. *American Psychologist, 37*, 122–147.

Bandura, A. (1997). *Self efficacy: The exercise of control.* New York: Freeman.

Barber, J.P. & DeRubeis, R.J. (2001). Change in compensatory skills in cognitive therapy for depression. *Journal of Psychotherapy Practice & Research, 10*, 8–13.

Baumeister, R.F. (1988). The optimal margin of illusion. *Journal of Social and Clinical Psychology, 8*, 176–189.

Beck, A.T. (1967). *Depression: Clinical, experimental, and theoretical aspects.* New York: Harper & Row.

Beck, A.T. (1976). *Cognitive therapy and the emotional disorders.* New York: International Universities Press.

Beck, A.T., Rush, A.J., Shaw, B.F. & Emery, G. (1979). *Cognitive therapy of depression: A treatment manual.* New York: Guilford Press.

Brewer, N.T., Weinstein, N.D., Cuite, C.L. & Herrington, J.E. (2004). Risk perceptions and their relation to risk behavior. *Annals of Behavioral Medicine, 27*, 125–130.

Brown, G.P. & Beck, A.T. (2002). Dysfunctional attitudes, perfectionism, and models of vulnerability to depression. In G. Flett & P. Hewitt (eds), *Perfectionism: Theory, research, and treatment* (pp. 231–251). Washington, DC: American Psychological Association.

Buchanan, G.M. (1995). Explanatory style and coronary heart disease. In G.M. Buchanan & M.E.P. Seligman (eds), *Explanatory style* (pp. 225–232). Hillsdale, NJ: Lawrence Erlbaum Associates.

Buchanan, G.M., Gardenswartz, C.A. & Seligman, M.E.P. (1999). Physical health following a cognitive-behavioral intervention. *Prevention and Treatment, 2*, online journal.

Buchanan, G.M. & Seligman, M.E.P. (1995). *Explanatory style.* Hillsdale, NJ: Lawrence Erlbaum Associates.

Burns, D.D. (1980). *Feeling good: The new mood therapy.* New York, NY: Avon Books.

Cardemil, E.V., Reivich, K.J., Gillham, J.E., Jaycox, L. & Seligman, M.E.P. (1997). *Penn Resiliency Program for inner-city students.* Unpublished manuscript: University of Pennsylvania.

Cardemil, E.V., Reivich, K.J. & Seligman, M.E.P. (2002). The prevention of depressive symptoms in low-income minority middle school students. *Prevention & Treatment, 5,* online journal.

Carver, C.S., Pozo, C., Harris, S.D., Noriega, V., Scheier, M.F., Robinson, D.S., Ketcham, A.S., Moffat, F.L. & Clark, K.C. (1993). How coping mediates the effect of optimism on distress: A study of women with early stage breast cancer. *Journal of Personality and Social Psychology, 65,* 375–390.

Carver, C.S. & Scheier, M.F. (2002). The hopeful optimist. *Psychological Inquiry, 13,* 288–290.

Chaplin, T.M. & Cole, P.M. (2005). The role of emotion regulation in the development of psychopathology. In B.L. Hankin & J.R.Z. Abela (eds), *Development of psychopathology: A vulnerability-stress perspective* (pp. 49–74). Thousand Oaks, CA: Sage

Chaplin, T.M., Gillham, J.E., Reivich, K., Elkon, A.G.L., Samuels, B., Freres, D.R., Winder, B. & Seligman, M.E.P. (2006). Depression prevention for early adolescent girls: A pilot study of all-girls versus co-ed groups. *Journal of Early Adolescence, 26(1),* 110–126.

Compton, S.N., March, J.S., Brent, D., Albano, A.M., Weersing, V.R. & Curry, J. (2004). Cognitive-behavioral psychotherapy for anxiety and depressive disorders in children and adolescents: An evidence-based medicine review. *Journal of the American Academy of Child & Adolescent Psychiatry, 43,* 930–959.

Dodge, K.A. & Crick, N.R. (1990). Social information-processing bases of aggressive behavior in children. *Personality & Social Psychology Bulletin, 16,* 8–22.

Dozois, D.J.A. & Dobson, K.S. (eds) (2004). *The prevention of anxiety and depression: Theory, research and practice* (pp. 185–204). Washington, DC: American Psychological Association.

Eckstein, Y. (2000). The role of faith in shaping optimism. In J.E. Gillham (ed.), *The science of optimism and hope: Research essays in honor of Martin E. P. Seligman* (pp. 341–345). Radnor, PA: Templeton Foundation Press.

Ellis, A. (1962). *Reason and emotion in psychotherapy.* New York: Lyle Stuart.

Ferketick, A., Schwartzbaum, J.A., Frid, D.J. & Moeschberger, M.L. (2000). Depression as an antecedent to heart disease among women and men in the NHANES I study. National Health and Nutrition Examination Survey. *Archives of Internal Medicine, 160,* 1261–1268.

Freres, D.R., Gillham, J.E., Reivich, K. & Shatté, A.J. (2002). Preventing depressive symptoms in middle school students: The Penn Resiliency Program. *International Journal of Emergency Mental Health, 4,* 31–40.

Garofalo, J.P. (2000). Perceived optimism and chronic pain. In R. Gatchel and J. Weisberg (eds), *Personality characteristics of patients with pain* (pp. 203–217). Washington, DC: American Psychological Association.

Gillham, J.E., Chaplin, T.M., Reivich, K.J. & Hamilton, J. (submitted). Preventing depression in early adolescent girls: The Penn Resiliency and Girls in Transition Programs. Chapter submitted for publication in LeCroy, C. & Mann, J. *Handbook of prevention and intervention programs for adolescent girls.*

Gillham, J.E., Hamilton, J., Freres, D.R., Patton, K. & Gallop, R. (2006). Preventing depression among early adolescents in the primary care setting. A randomized controlled study of the Penn Resiliency Program. *Journal of Abnormal Child Psychology.* Published online.

Gillham, J.E., Jaycox, L.H., Reivich, K.J., Hollon, S.D., Freeman, A., DeRubeis, R.J. & Seligman, M.E.P. (1991). *The APEX Project: Manual for group leaders.* Unpublished manuscript, University of Pennsylvania.

Gillham, J.E., Jaycox, L.H., Reivich, K.J., Seligman, M.E.P. & Silver, T. (1990). *The Penn Optimism Program.* Unpublished manual, University of Pennsylvania.

Gillham, J.E. & Reivich, K.J. (1999). Prevention of depressive symptoms in school children: A research update. *Psychological Science, 10,* 461–462.

Gillham, J.E., Reivich, K.J., Freres, D.R., Chaplin, T.M., Shatté, A.J., Samuels, B., Elkin, A.G.L., Litzinger, S., Lascher, M., Gallop, R. & Seligman, M.E.P. (in preparation). School-based prevention of depressive symptoms: Effectiveness and specificity of the Penn Resiliency Program.

Gillham, J.E., Reivich, K.J., Freres, D.R., Lascher, M., Litzinger, S., Shatté, A., et al., (in press). School-based prevention of depression and anxiety symptoms in early adolescence: A pilot of a parent intervention component. *School Psychology Quarterly.*

Gillham, J.E., Reivich, K.J., Jaycox, L.H. & Seligman, M.E.P. (1995). Preventing depressive symptoms in schoolchildren: Two year follow-up. *Psychological Science, 6,* 343–351.

Gillham, J.E., Shatté, A.J. & Freres, D.R. (2000). Depression prevention: A review of cognitive-behavioral and family interventions. *Applied & Preventive Psychology, 9*, 63–88.

Giltay, E.J., Geleijnse, J.M., Zitman, F.G., Hoekstra, T. & Schouten, E.G. (2004). Dispositional optimism and all-cause and cardiovascular mortality in a prospective cohort of elderly Dutch men and women. *Archives of General Psychiatry, 61*, 1126–1135.

Gotlib, I.H., Lewinsohn, P.M. & Seeley, J.R. (1995). Symptoms versus a diagnosis of depression: Differences in psychosocial functioning. *Journal of Consulting and Clinical Psychology, 63*, 90–100.

Hankin, B.L. & Abela, J.R.Z. (2005). Depression from childhood through adolescence and adulthood: A developmental vulnerability and stress perspective. In B.L. Hankin & J.R.Z. Abela (eds), *Development of psychopathology: A vulnerability-stress perspective.* Thousand Oaks, CA: Sage Publications.

Hollon, S.D. & DeRubeis, R.J. (2004). Effectiveness of treatment for depression. In R.L. Leahy (ed.), *Contemporary cognitive therapy: Theory, research, and practice* (pp. 45–61). New York: Guilford Press.

Hollon, S.D. & Shelton, R.C. (2001). Treatment guidelines for major depressive disorder. *Behavior Therapy, 32*, 235–258.

Hornung, R., Vollrath, M., Hättlich, A., Helminger, A., Filipp, S. & Ferring, D. (1995). Cognitive illness representations. In B. Boothe, R. Hirsig, A. Helminger, B. Meier & R. Vokart (eds), *Perception-evaluation-interpretation.* Swiss monographs in psychology, *3*, 154–159. Ashland, OH: Hogrefe & Huber Publishers.

Ironson, G., Balbin, E., Stuetzle, R., Fletcher, M.A., O'Cleirigh, C., Laurenceau, J.P., Scheiderman, N. & Solomon, G. (2005). Dispositional optimism and the mechanisms by which it predicts slower disease progression in HIV: Proactive behavior, avoidance coping, and depression. *International Journal of Behavioral Medicine, 12*, 86–97.

Jaycox, L.H., Reivich, K.J., Gillham, J. & Seligman, M.E.P. (1994). Prevention of depressive symptoms in school children. *Behaviour Research & Therapy, 32(8)*, 801–816.

Matthews, K.A., Raikkonen, K., Sutton-Tyrrell, K. & Kuller, L.H. (2005). Optimistic attitudes protect against progression of carotid atherosclerosis in healthy middle-aged women. *Psychosomatic Medicine, 66*, 640–644.

Merry, S., McDowell, H., Hetrick, S., Bir, J. & Muller, N. (2004). Psychological and/or educational interventions for the prevention of depression in children and adolescents. *The Cochrane Library, 2*, online journal.

Miyazaki, T., Ishikawa, T., Nakata, A., Sakurai, T., Miki, A., Fujita, O., Kobayashi, F., Haratani, T., Iimori, H., Sakami, S., Fujioka, Y. & Kawamura, N. (2005). Association between perceived social support and Th1 dominance. *Biological Psychiatry, 1*, 30–37.

National Institutes of Health (NIH) (2000). Depression and Diabetes: A fact sheet that is available at http://www.nimh.nih.gov/publicat/depdiabetes.cfm

Nolen-Hoeksema, S. (1991). Responses to depression and their effects on the duration of depressive episodes. *Journal of Abnormal Psychology, 100*, 569–582.

Nolen-Hoeksema, S., Girgus, J.S. & Seligman, M.E.P. (1992). Predictors and consequences of childhood depressive symptoms: A 5-year longitudinal study. *Journal of Abnormal Psychology, 101*, 405–422.

Persons, J.B., Davidson, J. & Thompkins, M.A. (2001). Schema change methods. In J.B. Persons, J. Davidson & M.A. Thompkins (eds), *Essential components of cognitive-behavior therapy for depression* (pp. 171–203). Washington, DC: American Psychological Association.

Peterson, C. (2000). Optimistic explanatory style and health. In J.E. Gillham (ed.), *The science of optimism and hope: Research essays in honor of Martin E.P. Seligman* (pp. 145–161). Radnor, PA: Templeton Foundation Press.

Peterson, C. & Bossio, L.M. (1991). *Health and optimism.* New York: Free Press.

Peterson, C. & de Avila, M.E. (1995). Optimistic explanatory style and the perception of health problems. *Journal of Clinical Psychology, 51*, 128–132.

Peterson, C., Seligman, M.E.P. & Vaillant, G.E. (1988). Pessimistic explanatory style is a risk factor for physical illness: A thirty-five-year longitudinal study. *Journal of Personality and Social Psychology, 55*, 23–27.

Quiggle, N.L., Garber, J., Panak, W.F. & Dodge, K.A. (1992). Social information processing in aggressive and depressed children. *Child Development, 63*, 1305–1320.

Reivich, K.J. (1996). *The prevention of depressive symptoms in adolescents.* Unpublished doctoral dissertation, University of Pennsylvania, Philadelphia.

Roberts, C., Kane, R., Bishop, B., Matthews, H. & Thompson, H. (2004). The prevention of depressive symptoms in rural children: A follow-up study. *International Journal of Mental Health Promotion, 6,* 4–16.

Roberts, C., Kane, R., Thomson, H., Bishop, B. & Hart, B. (2003). The prevention of depressive symptoms in rural school children: A randomized controlled trial. *Journal of Consulting and Clinical Psychology, 71,* 622–628.

Rohde, P., Lewinsohn, P.M., Clarke, G.N., Hops, H. & Seeley, J.R. (2005). The Adolescent Coping with Depression Course: A cognitive-behavioral approach to the treatment of adolescent depression. In E.D. Hibbs & P.S. Jensen (eds), *Psychosocial treatments for child and adolescent disorders: Empirically based strategies for clinical practice* (2nd edn) (pp. 218–237). Washington, DC: American Psychological Association.

Rosenberg, M. (1968). *The logic of survey analysis.* New York: Basic Books.

Satterfield, J.M., Monahan, J. & Seligman, M.E.P. (1997). Law school performance predicted by explanatory style. *Behavioral Sciences & the Law, 15,* 95–105.

Scheier, M.F. & Carver, C.S. (1993). On the power of positive thinking: The benefits of being optimistic. *Current Directions in Psychological Science, 2,* 26–30.

Scheier, M.F., Carver, C.S. & Bridges, M.S. (2001). Optimism, pessimism, and psychological well-being. In E. Chang (ed.) *Optimism & pessimism: Implications for theory, research, and practice* (pp. 189–216). Washington, DC: American Psychological Association.

Scheier, M.F., Matthews, K.A., Owens, J., Magovern, G.J., Sr., Lefebvre, R.C., Abbott, R.A. et al. (1989). Dispositional optimism and recovery from coronary artery bypass surgery: The beneficial effects on physical and psychological well-being. *Journal of Personality and Social Psychology, 57,* 1024–1040.

Scheier, M.F., Matthews, K.A., Owens, J.F., Magovern, G.J., Lefebvre, R.C., Abbott, R.A. & Carver, C.S. (2003). Dispositional optimism and recovery from coronary artery bypass surgery: The beneficial effects on physical and psychological well-being. In P. Salovey & A. Rothman (eds), *Social psychology of health. Key readings in social psychology* (pp. 342–361). New York, NY: Psychology Press.

Schneider, S.L. (2001). In search of realistic optimism. *American Psychologist, 56,* 250–263.

Seligman, M.E.P. (1972). Learned helplessness. *Annual Review of Medicine, 23,* 407–412.

Seligman, M.E.P. (1991). *Learned Optimism.* New York: Knopf.

Seligman, M.E.P., Castellon, C., Cacciola, J., Schulman, P., Luborsky, L., Ollove, M. & Downing, R. (1988). Explanatory style change during cognitive therapy for unipolar depression. *Journal of Abnormal Psychology, 97,* 13–18.

Seligman, M.E.P., Schulman, P., DeRubeis, R.J. & Hollon, S.D. (1999). The prevention of depression and anxiety. *Prevention and Treatment, 2,* online journal.

Seligman, M.E.P., Schulman, P. & Tryon, A.M. (in preparation). Group prevention of depression and anxiety symptoms.

Snyder, C.R. (2000). Hypothesis: There is hope. In C.R. Snyder (ed.), *Handbook of hope: Theory, measures, and applications* (pp. 3–21). San Diego, CA: Academic Press.

Spence, S.H., Sheffield, J. & Donovan, C. (2002). Problem-solving orientation and attributional style: Moderators of the impact of negative life events on the development of depressive symptoms in adolescence? *Journal of Clinical Child & Adolescent Psychology, 31,* 219–222.

Taylor, S.E. & Brown, J.D. (1988). Illusion and well-being: A social psychological perspective on mental health. *Psychological Bulletin, 103,* 193–210.

Weinstein, N.D. (1983). Reducing unrealistic optimism and illness susceptibility. *Health Psychology, 2,* 11–20.

Weinstein, N.D. (1984). Why it won't happen to me: Perceptions of risk factors and susceptibility. *Health Psychology, 3,* 431–457.

Weinstein, N.D., Grubb & Vautier (1986). Increasing automobile seat belt use: An intervention emphasizing risk susceptibility. *Journal of Applied Psychology, 71,* 285–290.

Weinstein, N.D. & Klein, W.M. (2002). Resistance of personal risk perceptions to debiasing interventions. In T. Gilovich, D. Griffin & D. Kahneman (eds), *Heuristics and biases: The psychology of intuitive judgment* (pp. 313–323). New York: Cambridge University Press.

Weinstein, N.D. & Lyon, J.E. (1999). Mindset, optimistic bias about personal risk and health-protective behaviour. *British Journal of Health Psychology, 4*, 289–300.

Weinstein, N.D., Lyon, J.E., Sandman, P.M. & Cuite, C.L. (1998). Experimental evidence for stages of health behavior change: The precaution adoption process model applied to home radon testing. *Health Psychology, 17*, 445–453.

Yu, D.L. & Seligman, M.E.P. (2002). Preventing depressive symptoms in Chinese Children. *Prevention and Treatment, 5*, online journal.

Index

5HTTLPR genotypes 263
ABC Model 321
ABI *see* ankle-brachial index
abnormal illness behaviour, concepts 162–3
acceptance coping style, cancer survival 43–7
accident-prone personality 2, 52–67
achievement-driven behaviour 17
   see also Type A behaviour
active/problem-focused coping 43–7, 317–18
Activity Level 5, 51–2, 59–67
additive effect, temperamental traits 63–4
ADHD *see* Attention-Deficit/Hyperactivity
   Disorder
adolescents
   see also children
   cognitive behavioural intervention 7, 270,
      320–30
   depression 7, 315, 320–30
   media messages 308–10
   PRP 7, 315, 320–30
   risky health behaviours 1, 51–67, 249–50,
      308–10
   risky sex 308–10
   smoking 249–50, 309–10
   unintentional injuries 1, 51–67
adversities, ABC Model 321–4
affective processing theory, expressive writing
   7, 284–5, 287–95
affiliative stress 81
age risk factors, CHD 15
Aggarwal, N. 243–4
aggression
   see also anger
   concepts 16–17, 52–3, 59–60
Agreeableness
   concepts 5, 16, 22, 76–83, 89–90, 95, 124–7,
      143–4, 158–69, 219–30, 260–1
   life-span development 199
   studies 22
   well-being 5, 124–7
AIDS 250–2, 278
   see also HIV
alcohol consumption 3, 25–7, 37, 117, 140–1,
   146, 215, 222–30, 283, 300, 304

expressive writing 283
risky health behaviour 222–3, 261–2, 300,
   304
studies 222–3, 283, 304
alexithymia 40, 159, 162, 184–5, 289–90
   see also suppressed anger
alienation 207
allergies 182–3
Alzheimer's disease 180, 243–4, 246
ambulance services 247
anger 13, 16–29, 40, 88–9, 97–8, 143–4, 260–71
   see also Hostility
   awareness of feelings 266–71
   components 16–17, 88, 260–1, 266–71
   concepts 16–29, 88–9, 97–8, 143–4, 260–71
   evaluation of thoughts/feelings 266–71
   expression of negative feelings 266–7
   'I AM WORTH IT' questions 267–8
   LifeSkills program 264–71
   management programmes 265–71
   measurement 17–18
   state anger 18, 22
   STAXI 18, 20–5, 88–9, 265
   suppressed anger 21, 40, 43–7, 266–71
   trait anger 18, 22, 88–9, 143–4, 185–6, 265
anger-control measures, concepts 18, 89, 98
anger-in measures, concepts 18, 20–2, 89, 98
anger-out measures, concepts 18–21, 89, 98
angina pectoris
   see also cardiovascular disease
   concepts 14–15, 16–18, 20–5, 29
   diagnosis 15, 16
   inwardly-focused neurotic hostility 16–18
   studies 20–5, 29
angry reactions, trait anger 18, 22, 88–9, 185–6,
   265
angry temperament, trait anger 18, 22, 88–9,
   185–6, 265
ankle-brachial index (ABI) 15, 16
antagonism, expressed emotions 98–9
anti-emotionality 40–2, 45
antisocial personality disorder 163
   see also symptom reporting
anxious coping style, cancer survival 43–7